# MASTERPLOTS II

## SHORT STORY SERIES
### REVISED EDITION

# MASTERPLOTS II

## SHORT STORY SERIES
### REVISED EDITION

## Volume 8
Two–Z
Indexes

*Editor, Revised Edition*
**CHARLES MAY**
*California State University, Long Beach*

*Editor, First Edition*
**FRANK N. MAGILL**

SALEM PRESS
Pasadena, California     Hackensack, New Jersey

*Editor in Chief:* Dawn P. Dawson

| | |
|---|---|
| *Editorial Director:* Christina J. Moose | *Assistant Editor:* Andrea E. Miller |
| *Project Editor:* R. Kent Rasmussen | *Research Supervisor:* Jeffry Jensen |
| *Production Editor:* Cynthia Beres | *Acquisitions Editor:* Mark Rehn |
| *Copy Editor:* Rowena Wildin | *Layout:* Eddie Murillo |

Some of the essays in this work originally appeared in *Masterplots II, Short Story Series*, edited by Frank N. Magill (Pasadena, Calif.: Salem Press, Inc., 1986), and in *Masterplots II, Short Story Series Supplement*, edited by Frank N. Magill and Charles E. May (Pasadena, Calif.: Salem Press, Inc., 1996).

∞ The paper used in these volumes conforms to the American National Standard for Permanence of Paper for Printed Library Materials, Z39.48-1992 (R1997).

**Library of Congress Cataloging-in-Publication Data**

Masterplots II : Short story series / editor Charles May. — Rev. ed.
    p.  cm.
    Includes bibliographical references and index.
    ISBN 1-58765-140-8 (set : alk. paper) — ISBN 1-58765-148-3 (vol. 8 : alk. paper) —
    1. Fiction—19th century—Stories, plots, etc. 2. Fiction—19th century—History and criticism. 3. Fiction—20th century—Stories, plots, etc. 4. Fiction—20th century—History and criticism. 5. Short story. I. Title: Masterplots 2. II. Title: Masterplots two. III. May, Charles E. (Charles Edward), 1941-
PN3326 .M27 2004
809.3'1—dc22

                2003018256

First Printing

PRINTED IN THE UNITED STATES OF AMERICA

# TABLE OF CONTENTS

TABLE OF CONTENTS

# MASTERPLOTS II

## SHORT STORY SERIES
### REVISED EDITION

# THE TWO BOTTLES OF RELISH

*Author:* Lord Dunsany (Edward John Moreton Drax Plunkett, 1878-1957)
*Type of plot:* Horror
*Time of plot:* The 1930's
*Locale:* Southern England
*First published:* 1932

> *Principal characters:*
> SMETHERS, the narrator, a traveling salesperson
> LINLEY, a gentleman of leisure and an amateur detective
> STEEGER, a clever and unscrupulous murderer
> INSPECTOR ULTON, a Scotland Yard detective

*The Story*

An affable, but not very bright, traveling salesperson named Smethers begins sharing a London flat with an Oxford-educated gentleman named Linley, who displays extraordinary mental gifts. (Their relationship is similar to that between Arthur Conan Doyle's Sherlock Holmes and Doctor Watson.) One day Smethers calls his friend's attention to a newspaper account of a murder case that has the police baffled and challenges Linley to solve it.

A man named Steeger is suspected of murdering a pretty blond companion named Nancy Elth in order to get his hands on the money she had brought to their cottage in the south of England. The local police have kept the place surrounded but have been unable to find a trace of the young woman's body and cannot arrest Steeger without a corpse. Steeger claims that the woman has left the country, but he has a large amount of cash that he cannot account for.

Because Linley is constitutionally lazy, he sends Smethers to study the crime scene and talk to everyone in the neighborhood. Smethers reports back that there appears to be no way in which Steeger could have buried the body on the premises or spirited it away undetected. The most curious fact is that Steeger obtained his landlord's permission to chop down a stand of ten larch trees and cut them into two-foot logs, but he has never used the wood for any purpose. Smethers reports that two bottles of Numnumo—the brand of relish that he himself peddles as a traveling salesperson—were found when the police searched the premises. Linley continues to question Smethers for the smallest details he can remember from his investigations.

Smethers reports that the local constable is suspicious of Steeger because he is a vegetarian, and vegetarians are unknown in that isolated county. Linley takes special interest in the two bottles of relish because Smethers, who knows the product better than anyone else, assures him that it can be used only with meats and savories. He has Smethers telephone to inquire whether Steeger bought the bottles of Numnumo at the same time or on separate occasions. Smethers ascertains that they were bought separately, with an interval of about six days between purchases.

After considering all the information at his disposal, Linley calls in a Scotland Yard inspector and explains the whole method of the crime in the privacy of his bedroom. Smethers, who only overhears snatches of their conversation, does not pass along all the details, but leaves them to the reader's imagination. It becomes horribly obvious that Steeger cut up the body and ate it, using the two bottles of relish to help him overcome his natural revulsion to cannibalism. Smethers relates that he overheard Linley tell the inspector that Steeger went through the trouble of chopping down the trees and cutting them into logs, "Solely in order to get an appetite."

*Themes and Meanings*

"The Two Bottles of Relish" is an example of the "perfect crime" story. The message in all such stories is invariably the same: "Crime does not pay." To highlight and dramatize the message, the author contrives a nearly perfect crime and makes it appear that the perpetrator is going to get away with it. Then at the last moment the criminal's nemesis, the detective, manages to come up with the answer to the problem, proving that even the most carefully contrived scheme by the most brilliant mind will fail because a nearly universal law governs matters of morality, dictating that good deeds are rewarded and wicked deeds are punished.

Readers enjoy perfect-crime stories such as "The Two Bottles of Relish" because they permit them to indulge their own fantasies about violence and antisocial behavior while receiving the assurance at the end that they live in an orderly society in which they can count on their personal security being protected. The popular *Columbo* films on television, starring Peter Falk, were all based on the supposition that has been expressed in various ways in such comfortable homilies as "Crime does not pay," "Murder will out," and "There is no such thing as a perfect crime." In William Shakespeare's classic murder drama *Macbeth* (1606), his hero repeatedly reflects on the impossibility of getting away with murder. For example:

> It will have blood, they say; blood will have blood.
> Stones have been known to move and trees to speak;
> Augures and understood relations have
> By maggot-pies and choughs and rooks brought forth
> The secretest man of blood.

In *Civilization and Its Discontents* (1930), Sigmund Freud, the founder of modern psychoanalysis, stated that modern civilization is a thin veneer and that all human beings harbor aggressive instincts that they conceal under clean linen and proper manners in order to maintain the illusion of peace, order, and respectability. Perfect-crime stories provide a sort of safety valve by giving readers a taste of blood while simultaneously assuring them that civilization is intact because it is protected by the authorities as well as by such master amateur sleuths as Sherlock Holmes, Lord Dunsany's

Linley, Agatha Christie's Miss Marple and Hercule Poirot, and a host of other fictional detectives.

## Style and Technique

The technique used in "The Two Bottles of Relish" resembles that of Arthur Conan Doyle in his famous Sherlock Holmes stories. Both Doyle and Dunsany were indebted to the American genius Edgar Allan Poe, who is credited with being the father of the detective story with two 1840's "tales of ratiocination": "The Murders in the Rue Morgue" and "The Purloined Letter." J. Brander Matthews, a distinguished literary critic, wrote that the history of the detective story began with the publication of "The Murders in the Rue Morgue." Branders called the story "a masterpiece of its kind, which even its author was unable to surpass; and Poe, unlike most other originators, rang the bell the very first time."

Poe invented many of the conventions of the detective story that are still in use today. He had the wisdom to tell his tales of ratiocination from the point of view of a minor character, so that it was unnecessary for him to disclose any of his hero C. Auguste Dupin's thought processes until the surprising climax of the story. Just as Dupin had his anonymous biographer and Holmes had his friend Dr. Watson, so Linley is provided with the good-natured, loyal, but slow-witted Smethers to chronicle his genius. The narrative style of Dunsany's story is conversational, deliberately amateurish, and full of slang, because Smethers has less education than Poe's or Doyle's narrators and belongs to a lower social class.

All three heroes are "amateur detectives." Poe established the useful convention that the amateur detective had to be intellectually superior to the bungling police and also indifferent to fame. Because Dupin, Holmes, and Linley are useful to the police, they are given easy access to police assistance. The ineffectual police, who usually get the credit, are so grateful that they are happy to give the amateur detectives an aegis, a cloak of authority that enables them to question witnesses, poke around crime scenes, and generally act as official detectives themselves. Without this aegis, the amateur detective would be severely handicapped, especially when investigating a murder, and stories of their exploits would be less interesting or less credible.

"The Two Bottles of Relish" is a variation of the so-called "locked room mystery," which was invented by Poe in "The Murders in the Rue Morgue" and used innumerable times by Doyle. In a locked room mystery, the central problem is how the criminal entered or exited or managed to get incriminating evidence off the premises under seemingly impossible circumstances. In "The Two Bottles of Relish," the central problem is how the murderer could dispose of the corpse under tight police surveillance.

Although Dunsany borrows from both Doyle and Poe in his nine "little tales of Smethers," as he called them, he contributes two innovations. The first is his method of dangling the most important clue right under the reader's nose. Poe and Doyle often withheld important information from the reader; Dunsany presents the vital clues on a silver platter, thereby giving readers a sporting chance to arrive at the solution by themselves. It is noteworthy that Dunsany actually used the most important clue, the two bottles of relish, as the title of his story.

His solution to the crime seems almost a parody of Poe and Doyle, who never thought of anything as weird as having a murderer eat his victim in order to dispose of the corpus delicti. The macabre humor in "The Two Bottles of Relish," another important innovation, is so characteristic of Dunsany's fiction that it might be called a Dunsany trademark. Many writers have copied him over the years. Some of the classic films of director Alfred Hitchcock display a similar playful attitude toward murder that suggests that both the writer and the viewer share a secret "relish" for the details of gory crimes.

*Bill Delaney*

# TWO BROTHERS

*Author:* Brian Evenson (1966-        )
*Type of plot:* Grotesque
*Time of plot:* The 1990's
*Locale:* Utah
*First published:* 1997

> *Principal characters:*
> DADDY NORTON, a self-appointed prophet
> MAMA, his wife
> THERON, their older son
> AUREL, their younger son

*The Story*

Daddy Norton, a self-appointed prophet and religious fanatic, has fallen in the front hall of the house and broken his leg. Professing that he has foreseen this event in a vision, he refuses medical attention and gathers his sons Theron and Aurel and his wife to attend him. He commands his wife to read to him from the book of the Holy Word, in which he has recorded the revelations he has received from God. As the hours pass, Theron begins to get hungry and asks Mama for breakfast. Following Daddy Norton's instructions, Mama refuses and threatens him when he tries to get past her to the kitchen. Eventually Theron gets up and brings back some bread and a bottle of whiskey for him and his brother Aurel.

Waking in the middle of the night, Aurel discovers his father attempting to saw off his leg with a butcher knife, which gets snagged in the bone and falls to the floor. When Daddy Norton asks him to retrieve the knife, Aurel hesitates and then wakes up Theron. With his eyes closed, Aurel listens while Theron repeatedly stabs their father with the butcher knife. Sometime in the night, Mama has died. Theron moves his mother's body beside Daddy Norton, wipes her hands in the blood, and places the knife in her hands.

On the day of their parents' funeral, the brothers remain in the house alone. Taking off the clothes given to them for the funeral by a rival preacher, the boys sit naked in the hallway of the house in which their parents died. They are visited by one of their parents' creditors, a woman, who runs away when she is confronted by the naked brothers. Becoming sexually aroused by the encounter with the strange woman, Theron rapes his brother Aurel.

As Aurel becomes increasingly lethargic and unresponsive, eventually slipping into a catatonic state, Theron begins to explore the house. Wandering into the many rooms and halls, Theron cannot bring himself to enter the chamber that was Daddy Norton's private sanctuary. The supplies in the kitchen having finally run out, the boys put on shorts and venture out of the house in search of food. They find a dog chained to a tree outside a house. Theron shoots the dog in the head with an air rifle that he finds in an upstairs room back home. The pellets from the gun do little damage, however, so Theron has to shoot the dog repeatedly in order to kill it. In its death struggles, the dog bites Theron on the foot. Limping on his wounded foot, Theron is forced to carry the dog on his shoulders while dragging Aurel along the road behind him.

Theron's foot becomes infected and infested with maggots. While he lies on the floor of the hall, Aurel recovers and begins to explore the house himself. He enters Daddy Norton's room and finds the Holy Word, a collection of his father's divine revelations and prophecies. While Aurel becomes obsessed with Daddy Norton's books, Theron dies from the neglected wound. Slowly starving to death, Aurel finally lies down in the hall, holding the putrid corpse of his brother.

*Themes and Meanings*

In "Two Brothers," Brian Evenson portrays the devastating effects of religious fanaticism in the life of one family. Daddy Norton's self-appointed status as a prophet and visionary has catastrophic consequences on all the members of his family. By refusing to allow his family to call for an ambulance when he falls and suffers a compound fracture to his leg, he condemns himself to suffer an excruciating death. Claiming that he has foreseen this event and learned God's intentions, Daddy Norton assembles his family around him and uses the opportunity of his accident to effect a moral and religious lesson. He asks his wife to bring him the book of the Holy Word, the volume in which he has recorded his prophecies and inspired words.

As the brief scenes leading up to his death poignantly reveal, Daddy Norton's religious fanaticism dominates every aspect of his family's lives. The exhortation to live not by bread but by the word of God lies at the heart of Daddy Norton's refusal to allow his wife to prepare a meal for his two sons as the day drags on. Theron's hunger is seen as a sign of moral weakness and evokes threats and condemnation from Mama. Consumed by religiosity, Daddy Norton and his wife view their children as sinners rather than as children. It is noteworthy that the author never reveals the ages of Theron or Aurel. Evenson portrays a world in which the age of the two boys, their situation as children, is irrelevant. They are only sinners, the victims of a pernicious objectification.

Daddy Norton's religious practice suggests a connection with the Mormon tradition of prophecy. Beginning with Joseph Smith and Brigham Young, the Church of Jesus Christ of Latter-day Saints has viewed its church leadership as the modern heirs of the prophetic tradition familiar in the Hebrew scriptures. The pronouncements of Smith, Young, and their successors have acquired the status of revealed texts. Collected in *The Doctrine and Covenants* and continuing in messages issued by the First Presidency of the Church, these writings form the foundation of Mormon belief and practice. Daddy Norton sees himself as a prophet in a similar fashion, anointed by God as a prophet to speak the divine word.

Evenson's story eerily parallels the story of Esau and Jacob in chapter 27 of Genesis. Like Esau, the older son of Isaac, Theron is primarily concerned with practical issues such as going to the kitchen for bread to feed himself and his brother, exploring the house in search of supplies after the death of Daddy Norton, and going outside the house in search of food when starvation threatens. From the beginning, he rejects his father's religiosity and focuses on the material needs of his brother and himself. Aurel, like Jacob, is the heir of his parents' religious faith. His sensitivity is badly shaken by the scene of conflict between his parents and Theron. Even as he slips further and further into physical paralysis, his focus remains on spiritual concerns. He takes special interest in his brother's description of Daddy Norton's room. While his brother lies dying from an untreated dog bite, Aurel seeks out his father's prophetic writings and reads them over and over. In the end, he reaffirms the spiritual legacy of his upbringing and lays himself down to die beside his brother. Like Esau and Jacob, the two brothers of Evenson's story are the heirs of a religious patriarch. However, unlike Isaac's blessing of prosperity on his sons, Daddy Norton's legacy holds the promise only of madness and self-destruction.

*Style and Technique*

Evenson combines horrific and grotesque elements against an almost surreal background to achieve the overwhelming effects of this story of madness and destruction. The story opens with Daddy Norton's devastating injury and the open wound's progressive stages of infection and decay. The scene of Daddy Norton's attempt to amputate the injured portion of his leg with a butcher knife is followed by an act of patricide. Theron slaughters and mutilates his father with the butcher knife while his brother crouches nearby on the floor with his eyes closed. The actual cause of Mama's death is never revealed; Theron simply tells his brother that she too had died as he arranges the scene of the crime in order to shift the blame for his father's death onto his mother.

The episode in which Theron shoots the dog continues this pattern of horror. Evenson describes in excruciating detail the effects of each pellet fired from the air gun, the dog's pitiable attempts to escape, and his prolonged death throes. The ending scenes of the story mirror the carnage of the opening as Theron's foot begins to fester and rot. Evenson recounts Aurel's attempts to scrape away the maggots that have infested the wound. The story ends with Aurel's discovery of his brother's rotted corpse in the hallway, his attempt to embrace it, and the disintegration of the flesh itself when he touches it.

The accumulation of grotesque details is overpowering, filling the reader with nightmare images that bring into sharp relief the effects of religious fanaticism on this family. Evenson's interweaving of flashes of surrealism with this pattern of horror heightens the impact of the tragedy. The scene of the two boys, stripped naked and sitting alone in the house of death, and their confrontation with the woman who comes to collect the rent touches upon the absurd. Theron's rape of his brother Aurel is presented in the most understated terms. As Theron explores the house, the reader is drawn into his madness as rooms, hallways, and levels begin to proliferate in a impossible manner. Aurel's own madness is underscored by his confusion of the dead dog's eyes with the visionary eyes of his father. Looking through this oracle, Aurel re-creates the prophetic vision of his father, where his brother Theron can see only nothingness.

*Tony Rafalowski*

# THE TWO DROVERS

*Author:* Sir Walter Scott (1771-1832)
*Type of plot:* Historical
*Time of plot:* The 1790's
*Locale:* The border country between Scotland and England
*First published:* 1827

> *Principal characters:*
> ROBIN OIG M'COMBICH, a highland drover
> HARRY WAKEFIELD, an English drover
> JANET OF TOMAHOURICH, Robin's aunt, a seer
> HUGH MORRISON, a lowland farmer

*The Story*

Because the story describes an earlier time—about thirty years before the date of its telling—and tells of a way of life unfamiliar to many readers, the narrator begins by describing the occupation of the drovers, men who herded highland cattle from the fairs in Scotland down across the border to markets in England. The two drovers of the story, Robin Oig M'Combich, a Scottish highlander, and Harry Wakefield, an English lowlander, are classic representatives of their cultures. Robin embodies the fierce spirit of the Highlands: he takes pride in his skill as a drover, his highland heritage, and his name, taken from the most famous of the highland outlaws, Rob Roy, his grandfather's friend. Harry Wakefield takes pride in his work and his prowess as a fighter.

After the Doune Fair, as Robin prepares to set off to the south, his aunt, Janet of Tomahourich, delays him so that she can perform the deasil, a traditional ceremony to protect the herd and the drover from harm. She cuts short her performance and warns Robin of danger, urging him to delay his journey. With the second sight of the highland seer, she sees English blood on his dirk, the dagger that the highlander carries for protection. Less a believer in highland superstition than his aunt, Robin tries to ignore her plea, but she insists that he leave his dirk behind. Finally, he agrees to entrust it to another drover, Hugh Morrison, who plans to follow Robin to the English markets.

Although they have traveled together for three years, Robin and Harry understand little of each other's culture. Harry cannot master Robin's unfamiliar tongue, and beyond their cattle and their occupation they have little about which to talk. Their personal friendship is deep, if unspoken, however, for they have shared many journeys, and on several occasions they have saved each other from danger.

On the fateful journey in the story, however, their personal friendship cannot overcome the cultural differences between them. Their falling out begins after they cross the English border and separate temporarily to seek pasturage for their herds. Harry negotiates for his pasture with a bailiff, the agent for a landowner. Unaware of Harry's agreement, Robin secures permission for the same field from the landowner himself.

The misunderstanding between the landlord and his bailiff becomes a quarrel between Harry and Robin. Bitterly Harry takes his herd to a poorer pasture, feeling that he has been mistreated and tricked by his Scottish friend.

That evening, Robin tries to patch up the quarrel, but Harry, urged on by his countrymen in the local inn, refuses to concede without a fight. He challenges Robin to settle their differences with his fists. When Robin declines to take on the much-larger Harry at his own game, Harry calls him a coward, taunts him, and knocks him to the ground. Robin reaches under his plaid for his dirk, the natural weapon of the highlander, before he remembers that he has given it to Morrison. Harboring the humiliation of Harry's punches and the taunts of the Englishmen in the inn, Robin sets out to find Morrison and retrieve the weapon.

Two hours later, after walking six miles each way, he returns to the inn and confronts Wakefield. By this time, Harry has forgotten his injuries, and he offers his hand to his friend, but Robin pulls the knife and fatally stabs Harry through the heart. He has recovered his honor and shown that a highlander knows how to fight. Then he turns himself over to the law.

At the trial in Carlisle, the English judge recognizes that Robin's act was not an act of cowardice but one prompted by a different code of honor. Had Robin responded to Harry's taunts by pulling his dagger and stabbing his friend on the spot, the judge could have understood his crime as a highlander's natural response to provocation. In that case, the charge would have been manslaughter. However, the two-hour delay while Robin went off to secure his dirk changed manslaughter into premeditated murder in the judge's mind. In such a case the judge is compelled to demand the death penalty.

The judge's distinctions are beyond Robin's comprehension. He considers his death the natural conclusion to his destiny. "I give a life for the life I took," he says as the tragic story ends, "and what can I do more?"

*Themes and Meanings*

Sir Walter Scott's best work nearly always treats Scotland's emergence to nationhood in the eighteenth century, following its union with England in 1707. The contact and struggles between the two allied nations shaped the Scottish identity, as Scotland changed its clannish past for its part in Great Britain. In the cross-cultural contact among the migratory drovers, Scott found a metaphor for the larger assimilation of Scotland into Britain and for the tumult brought on by this process of cultural transition. The friendship of the highland Scot and the English yeoman, like the alliance between the two nations, is a recent and fragile one.

Robin's contact with English culture on his journeys across the border has diminished his belief in some Scottish superstitions. He seems to be humoring his aunt, for example, when he responds to her prophetic vision of doom by turning his dirk over to Morrison for safekeeping. For him "second sight" has become Scottish superstition. However, he is still profoundly Scottish in his attitudes. His belief in honor to the point of death and his final act of giving his life for the life he has taken embody the traditional code of the Highlands. Similarly, Harry Wakefield is not so chauvinistically English as his countrymen in the inn. His love of boxing and his bumptious eagerness to settle their differences with a brawl represents the traditional attitude of the English yeoman, but his willingness to settle for a face-saving charade rather than a real fight marks a departure from traditional attitudes. Their occupation has begun the process of cultural assimilation, but neither Robin nor Harry understands the other's culture well enough to prevent the misunderstanding that leads to their deaths. Their friendship falls victim to the traditional distrust between highland Scots and lowland English produced over centuries by cultural isolation and national prejudice.

Scott adds a historical perspective to this cultural theme. By placing the story about thirty years before the time of its telling, Scott implies that his audience, given the advantages of the later historical point of view, will see some differences that the actors in the story fail to see. Like the English judge, they will recognize that Robin did not act out of cowardice. Unlike the judge, however, later readers may also understand Robin's unrelenting vengeance as an expression of his culture rather than as premeditation. Human beings are always limited by the perspective of their time and place. As well as showing the power of culture to mold human actions, "The Two Drovers" also suggests that men can see this determining force of culture only with the benefit of historical distance. The thirty-year gap between the story and its telling gives the reader the benefit of this distance.

*Style and Technique*

Scott embodies the historical and cultural differences he describes in differences of language. Robin speaks the language of the Highlands, a dialect frequently requiring parenthetical translation even for readers of Scott's time. Harry's language is that of an uneducated farmer from the north of England, and it contrasts with the more literate and literary prose of the judge of the English court where Robin is tried.

The gaps of understanding between cultures that lead to Harry's murder, Robin's execution, and the failure of understanding on the part of the judge lie at the heart of the pattern of tragic inevitability that gives this story its force. None of the actors can be said to be acting only out of individual character or to be revealing personal flaws. Each articulates the limitations of his culture. Scott sets the tone of tragic inevitability with the prophecy of Janet of Tomahourich, who prophesies her nephew's doom. As the story moves forward, her prophecy becomes increasingly probable until the final meeting of Robin and Harry brings the inevitable conclusion. In his longer novels, Scott usually found means for comic resolution to the problem of cultural assimilation: The hero could learn how to live between two cultures, between his traditional Scottish identity and his growing British allegiance. However, in this short story, Scott presents the confrontation in stark and tragic terms. Only the distance of history, that later view shared by Scott and his readers, can provide the larger perspective necessary to understand the destruction caused by cultural prejudice and historically determined shortsightedness.

*Paul B. Davis*

# THE TWO ELENAS

*Author:* Carlos Fuentes (1928-　　)
*Type of plot:* Domestic realism
*Time of plot:* The 1960's
*Locale:* Mexico City
*First published:* "Las dos Elenas," 1964 (English translation, 1973)

> *Principal characters:*
> VICTOR, the narrator-protagonist, an architect in Mexico City
> ELENA, his wife
> DONA ELENA, Elena's mother
> DON JOSE, Elena's father

*The Story*

Dona Elena's complaint regarding the conduct of her daughter, Elena, the previous Sunday (she defended the idea that a woman can live with two men) causes Victor, an architect, to recall the night that he and Elena, his wife, saw the film *Jules and Jim* (1962). That night over dinner, as he recalls, they discussed the film and Elena arrived at certain conclusions—for example, that misogyny is the condition of love, that one day Victor would want another man to share their lives, and that she wanted an outfit like the one worn by Jeanne Moreau in the film. As he pondered the likelihood of the second proposition, he watched Elena among their men friends, imagining how each of them would supplement what he himself might be incapable of offering her. Later, they walked home through cobblestone streets ("a meeting ground for their common inclinations toward assimilation") and made love to the music of Brother Lateef.

At Sunday dinner with her parents, Elena and her father begin to argue about blacks when Dona Elena saves the day by changing the subject to her own activities during the past week. While she speaks, Victor observes her gestures and appearance, especially her caressing fingers, slim wrist, full arms, and taut breasts. After dinner, Don Jose excuses himself to reminisce over some old boleros. In another room, Elena falls asleep on her husband's lap while he and his mother-in-law carry on a conversation about Veracruz, which is in fact a description of the fundamental difference between the two Elenas: their origins and, consequently, their attitudes.

The following morning, Victor prepares to leave for work, and Elena outlines her schedule for that day, which includes a film, a class, some appointments, readings, and other activities, and mentions some plans for later on that week. On the way to work, Victor attempts to sort out that barrage of information, wondering if perhaps a vacation might not bring their lives closer together again. Suddenly, he finds himself steering his car not in the direction of his work, but toward Lomas, the house of Elena's parents, where his other Elena awaits him.

*Themes and Meanings*

The cultural schizophrenia brought about by the Spanish conquest of the New World is the theme underlying the events of "The Two Elenas." The protagonist, Victor, is simultaneously attracted to two women who are completely different types. His wife is a composite of all that is foreign: She sees French and American motion pictures, drives a British car, glorifies the American black, studies French and reads French poetry, and listens to American jazz. In another sense, her ideas and behavior are foreign, that is, strange or uncharacteristic within the context of her upbringing. Victor admires her so-called naturalness, but the trait he describes has less to do with nature than with an adolescent sort of rebellion against all established norms of conduct. She denies rules, not to replace them with others, but to open a door, suggesting a fascination with the innovative. Her motives are dubious, however, because she merely challenges, regardless of the standard in question. For example, Elena continually strives to subvert the middle-class values of her parents by shocking their bourgeois morality, while at the same time, to her liberal-minded friends she dismisses the possibility of unfaithfulness because it has become as much a rule as communion every Friday used to be. Her refusal to conform may account for her modern, vivacious attitude, but it is also a sign of immaturity, or incomplete development.

The consequent limitations on her ability to understand are like a blindness that she has in common with her father; both are asleep, but whereas her dreams belong to other places, his belong to other times. Through nostalgia he sustains the myth of a victorious postrevolutionary society of opportunity, indifferent to what lies beyond the nation's borders and ignorant of the country's reality for the majority. His static vision prevents him from engaging in conversation at any other level than that of clichés, for even the most minor variation or concession would threaten his entire ideological structure. Don Jose's adverse physical reaction to any such disturbing notions demonstrates a fundamental inability to adapt to change. What Victor refers to in the text as "assimilation" is the resolution of the old and the new: His father-in-law's intolerance of the new is one type of failure to assimilate, and Elena's reactionism is another.

Dona Elena lives in the present, yet she remains mindful of her past. Her reality is rooted in Mexico City (especially the Lomas area, a wealthy suburb) of the 1960's, amid her family. She willingly and conscientiously fulfills the duties and obligations that go with her social position. Nevertheless, her origins in Veracruz, a region synonymous with nature and life, determine her real character. Certain physical features such as her black, wakeful eyes, transparent skin that exposes her veins, taut breasts, caressing fingers, and full arms are the visible evidence of strong bonds with the authentic, intrinsically Mexican existence of the Gulf region. Dona Elena is a mature woman capable of understanding and reconciliation (be it of contrary points of view, present and past, or different lifestyles). She is indeed the center of her family, for she supplies the deficiencies, makes up for shortcomings, and resolves potentially volatile situations.

As it is surprising to learn that it is Victor rather than Elena who is involved in a *ménage à trois*, so also it is interesting to note that it is not Elena but Victor who is undergoing an identity crisis. To the extent that he can be defined by who he is not (his opposite or complement), Victor has two nearly antithetical identities. Because both women have a complementary function in his life (compared to the supplementary role played by the other men in Elena's circle), they would seem to be of equal significance in that definition of being. However, in spite of his conscious desire to find completion in his wife, when Victor "liberates" himself and "ascends" to his other Elena, he seems to find his true complement.

## Style and Technique

Carles Fuentes is a master storyteller, for he has a remarkable ability to create suspense, surprise, and interest as he leads the reader from beginning to end of his tales. Often filmlike in technique, Fuentes's stories abound in direct discourse and visual images. Particularly effective uses of the script mode, for example, are the opening monologue, which draws the reader into the story; the intercalated speech of Elena and Dona Elena among the thoughts of Victor, foreshadowing other parallels between them; the fragments of conversation and the alternating voices, which vary the pace of the text; and the use of highly character-specific comments, which reinforce, animate, and instantly re-create a given character. Moreover, the numerous visual descriptions seem to function like the lens of a camera, complementing the audio and focusing on significant details that lend to the accomplished creation of character, or perhaps contribute to advancing the plot or developing the theme.

Fuentes's well-known proclivity toward rhetorical ornamentation surfaces only briefly in "The Two Elenas." One passage illustrating this tendency is the scene that describes lovemaking in terms of saxophone music and seems to function only as a tenuous link between the night in bed and the conversation at the dinner table. Many readers will find such passages unnecessary, a distraction from the story's authentic dialogue, credible characters, and captivating plot, but others will revel in Fuentes's baroque stylization.

*Krista Ratkowski Carmona*

# TWO GALLANTS

*Author:* James Joyce (1882-1941)
*Type of plot:* Parody
*Time of plot:* About 1900-1907
*Locale:* Dublin
*First published:* 1914

> *Principal characters:*
> LENEHAN, a parasite and "leech"
> CORLEY, a bully and seducer
> A SLAVEY, a domestic who is preyed on by Corley

*The Story*

"Two Gallants" sets up a series of expectations that are violated and reversed at the end of the story. First, the title suggests a world of gallantry, romance, and perhaps a doubling of lovers similar to a Shakespearean comedy. This expectation is reinforced by the narrator's description of the place and mood:

> The streets, shuttered for the repose of Sunday, swarmed with a gaily coloured crowd. Like illumined pearls the lamps shone from the summits of their tall poles on the living texture below which, changing shape and hue unceasingly, sent up into the warm grey evening air an unchanging, unceasing murmur.

There is even a moon shining above them. Also, the conversation of the two main characters, Lenehan and Corley, suggests a romantic involvement. Lenehan calls Corley a "gay Lothario" and wonders if Corley can succeed or "bring it off" with the girl whom he has recently met. However, there are some discordant notes that undercut the romantic mood. Corley has accepted gifts of cigarettes and cigars from the girl rather than giving gifts to her. Lenehan speaks of the romantic code of giving gifts such as flowers and chocolates as a "mug's game." Both Corley and Lenehan despise the conventional love game because they do not profit from it. The fictional rules of romantic love do not seem to apply here.

Also, the characters do not seem right for a romantic tale. Corley is described as "squat and ruddy" with a "large, globular and oily" head. Furthermore, his behavior and conversation show him to be rude and a braggart. He brags about his conquests of women and at being in the know at police headquarters. He is the son of a police officer and a "conqueror," which seems inappropriate for a lover or a patriotic Irishman. In contrast, Lenehan is a hanger-on and a "leech." His main role seems to be as an audience for Corley's bragging tales. If Corley talks only about himself, then Lenehan has no self: His pleasures, and his life, are vicarious. The characters, then, seem to be in the wrong story. They should be in a satiric comedy or a realistic story about Irish life.

The most important violation of the romantic story is, perhaps, the break in the narrative structure. The reader has been led to expect a romantic quest narrative; Corley is sent off to see if he can succeed with the girl, however, and the story then concentrates on the sycophant Lenehan. Why does James Joyce choose such an unusual plot pattern? One reason is that Corley's success or failure must be suspended until the end of the story. One cannot see the process, only the result. Another reason may be that in Lenehan one sees what the real life of a "gallant" is. First, his "gaiety" vanishes when he is alone and can no longer play his accustomed role. He finds "trivial all that was meant to charm him." All he can do is wander aimlessly, controlled by the rhythm of the harp, a conventional symbol for Ireland. He eats a frugal meal and worries about the price of a plate of peas. His imagination is not stirred by anything around him, including the harp, except for the thought of Corley's adventure. However, this lack makes him even more aware of his own "poverty of purse and spirit." He then imagines alternatives, a job, a home, a wife; all these would be pleasant alternatives to his aimless life on the streets. Once more, however, the vision is undercut. "He might yet be able to settle down in some snug corner and live happily if he could only come across some good simpleminded girl with a little of the ready." This "snug" life would not be a change in his leeching but a final confirmation of it. He can aim no higher than to feed on a simpleminded girl for the rest of his life.

The narrative reaches a climax when Lenehan spots the couple and anxiously follows to see if Corley has succeeded. "Well? . . . Did it come off? Can't you tell us? Did you try her?" The answer is provided by the small gold coin in Corley's palm. The reader knows by this point that romantic love is not Corley's aim, but the reader, perhaps, then assumes that he is looking for a sexual encounter. However, it is finally evident that he does not want sex, let alone love. What he wants and triumphantly shows Lenehan is the money he has extracted from the girl; finding a "simpleminded girl with a bit of the ready" to live on is the goal of the Dublin "gallants."

## Themes and Meanings

The most important theme in "Two Gallants"—and it is the great theme of *Dubliners* (1914), the collection of which it is a part—is the way love is turned into, or perverted into, a commodity. The "gallants" do not want love but a girl who will give them money or even support them. Corley does not even want sex from his "slavey," but the coin that she gives to him. He is, therefore, seen as a Judas who has sold out love, instead of Christ, for a coin, and he has a most willing "disciple" in Lenehan.

Another important theme is the enslavement of the Dubliners and, by extension, the Irish. First, there is a harp in the story, which is a traditional symbol for Ireland. The harp is controlled by a "master" and subject to "strangers." This, at first, may suggest the domination of Ireland by a foreign power, such as England. However, the point that Joyce wishes to make, above all, is that the Irish have enslaved themselves. The Irish "slavey" willingly pays the coin of tribute to the "conqueror," Corley, while his anxious collaborator, Lenehan, looks on. Corley is the "base betrayer" of his own country, and Lenehan the informer; these are familiar themes in Irish history.

*Style and Technique*

Joyce uses a number of styles in "Two Gallants." There is, first, the formal and evocative style of the third-person narrator that is used to set up romantic expectations. Describing the lamps of a Dublin street as "illumined pearls" is a good example of this style. In contrast, these expectations are violated by the clichés of Lenehan: "That takes the biscuit!" Almost every sentence of Lenehan's conversation contains a cliché. More important, however, is the low and crude style of Corley. His many references to women as "fine tarts" are examples of this style. His advice to Lenehan on how a gallant should behave shows the reader what they are really like: "There's nothing to touch a good slavey," he affirms, "Take my tip on it."

There are two significant symbols in "Two Gallants." The first is the reference to the harp. The harpist is weary, and "His harp too, heedless that her covering had fallen about her knees, seemed weary alike of the eyes of strangers and of her master's hand." The harp, which is given female characteristics, is unable to transcend her condition. This symbol contrasts to one of the great symbols of Ireland, Cathleen ni Houlihan, who is transformed from an old servant to a grand and beautiful lady when revolution breaks out. However, there is no revolt in Joyce's story; the harp remains sunken in weariness and oppression.

The most important technique in the story is the use of a Joycean epiphany. An epiphany is a "showing forth," a revelation of what a character or his or her situation is. This epiphany can be made by the character or the reader. In "Two Gallants" the characters are totally unaware of their true situation. It is the reader who, in a negative epiphany, recognizes the "coin" in the hands of Corley as a sign of the true nature of these Dublin gallants.

*James Sullivan*

# TWO KINDS

*Author:* Amy Tan (1952-    )
*Type of plot:* Vignette
*Time of plot:* The late 1980's
*Locale:* San Francisco
*First published:* 1989

> *Principal characters:*
> JING-MEI "JUNE" WOO, the narrator and protagonist
> SUYUAN WOO, her mother

## The Story

A young Chinese American woman, Jing-Mei "June" Woo, recalls, after her mother's death, her mother's sadness at having left her twin baby girls in China in 1949. June has used her mother's regret as a weapon in a battle of wills focusing on what her mother wants her to be and what she wants. June wins, leaving her mother, Suyuan, stunned when she says she wishes she were dead like the twins. Although this scene characterizes the common struggle for power between mother and daughter, the story also illustrates the cultural division between an Asian immigrant and her Asian American daughter. These cultural clashes resonate throughout the short story, as does the discordant sound of June's piano playing.

Wanting her daughter to be an American prodigy, Suyuan Woo epitomizes the mother living through her child. With the American ideal that you can be anything you want, she prepares and coaches June into becoming a Chinese Shirley Temple. June believes in her mother's dreams for her and admits she was filled with a sense that she would soon become perfect.

She and her mother, who cleans houses for extra money, begin searching through the latest American magazines, such as *Good Housekeeping* and *Reader's Digest*, for stories of child prodigies. Every evening her mother tests her relentlessly for intellectual prowess, such as knowing all the world capitals and multiplying large numbers in her head. June grows resentful as she sees the disappointment on her mother's face as she fails to measure up to her expectations.

Discovering a powerful side of herself, June resolves not to become something she is not simply to please her mother. One evening while watching *The Ed Sullivan Show* on television, her mother sees a young Chinese girl play the piano with great skill. Much to June's chagrin, her mother strikes up a deal with a retired piano teacher, Mr. Chong, who agrees to give June piano lessons in exchange for weekly housecleanings. June soon discovers that Old Mr. Chong is deaf, like the great composer Ludwig von Beethoven.

Ultimately, June must appear in a talent show to display her great talent. Her mother invites all of her friends from the Joy Luck Club, a group of four Chinese women who meet regularly to play mah-jongg, a parlor game, and socialize. Knowing she is not prepared but somehow thinking that the prodigy in her actually exists, June plays to her surprised and somewhat embarrassed parents. Only her deaf teacher applauds with enthusiasm as she completes a piece from Robert Schumann called "Pleading Child."

June feels that after her dismal performance, her mother's dream for her will end. A few days later while she watches television, her mother reminds her that it is time to practice. It is the final showdown between mother and daughter. June tells her mother she will never be a genius or the daughter that her mother wants her to be. Her mother explains that there are only two kinds of daughters: those who are obedient and the ones who follow their own minds. Although her mother thinks she was won by identifying which kind of daughter can live in her house, the daughter, feeling her own power, strikes the final blow by shouting that she wishes she were dead. Suyuan, because she had to leave her young twins for dead on a roadside, while fleeing war-torn China, is profoundly affected by June's outburst. Painfully, June looks back on this as an unresolved conflict that has followed her into adulthood. She believes that this was the moment that her mother gave up hope for her only daughter's success, and that she internalized this self-defeating attitude. A few years before her death, her mother offers her the piano for her thirtieth birthday. June accepts, seeing this as a peace offering, a shiny trophy that she has finally won back.

*Themes and Meanings*

In her essay "Mother Tongue," Amy Tan identifies the reader she envisions for her novel *The Joy Luck Club* (1986) as her own mother, because these were stories about mothers. Appearing in the novel as a chapter about the major protagonist of the entire novel, "Two Kinds" represents the central theme of the voracious love between mother and daughter and the arduous journey that one already has taken and the other will take both for herself and for her mother. It is a journey of self-discovery made through painful yet joyful connections. Just as June puts her mother's things in order for her father, she does the same for herself by gathering up her past childhood struggles with her mother, turning them over and examining them, then carefully putting them into order.

In the novel, June retraces her mother's and her three aunties' journeys from China to the United States. Initiated by Suyuan Woo's death at the start of the novel, this long pilgrimage is interwoven with the past and present lives of four Chinese mothers and their four American daughters. June's mother, as originator of the Joy Luck Club, holds a special place at the mah-jongg table, which must be assumed by her daughter. To complicate June's life further, her mother's twin daughters, whom she left in China forty years earlier, have been found alive and well. Now the familial connection between China and the United States is made even stronger by June's desire to know her half sisters and, by doing so, to understand both her mother and herself.

The theme of two seemingly opposite sides of a person is symbolized in the two musical pieces by Schumann: "Pleading Child," the one she plays at her first and last piano recital, and its companion piece, "Perfectly Contented." At the conclusion, June realizes that they were two halves of the same song, and that by playing both she becomes whole.

Although the self-realization completes this rich vignette, it is not without pain and loss. For June to come to this conclusion, she has had to lose her mother and revisit, through memory, the terrible moment of final conflict, betrayal, and guilt: "For after our struggle at the piano, she never mentioned my playing again. . . . The lid to the piano was closed, shutting out the dust, my misery, and her dreams." In the process of reexamining the duality of a daughter's existence—obedience versus willfulness—June reconciles and finally resolves her guilt and disappointment in herself and embraces both the memory of her mother and the strong woman she has become.

*Style and Technique*

Tan describes herself as a lover of language, not a scholar of English. Therefore, it is her translation into English of what she calls her mother's internal language that is at the heart of this story. Drawing the reader into the story, the narrator directs the reader through a world in which readers experience the power of a rich, colorful language. For example, when Mother Woo characterizes Auntie Lindo's daughter, an accomplished chess player at a young age, as "best tricky," the reader knows not only what it means but also how it sounds. This brand of English, often called fractured or broken, becomes a vernacular that captures the tone and color of the experience of growing up in a bilingual environment.

Further illustrating the conflict between Chinese mother and American-born daughter, the spoken language of the two creates a verbal duel. For example, when June demands that her mother look at who she really is, saying "I'm not a genius!" her mother responds with, "Who ask you be genius?" The mother's question, although incomplete grammatically, projects her confusion over being unable to understand her daughter's anger or ungratefulness.

The language also characterizes the rich, layered texture of a household built on two languages and two cultures, which often are combined to form, for example, a Chinese Shirley Temple. As her mother offers her the piano, the tense shift in her words is purposeful: "You could been genius if you want to." Even though it starts in the past, the sentence ends in the present, indicating to June and to the reader that it is not too late for June to find her genius. Ultimately, it is Tan's command of the "Englishes" that transforms the short story into one that captures not only her mother's voice but also other mothers' voices that have been silenced or, at best, standardized into an "imperfect" English that does not convey their essence, their internal language.

*Cynthia S. Becerra*

# TWO LITTLE SOLDIERS

*Author:* Guy de Maupassant (1850-1893)
*Type of plot:* Realism
*Time of plot:* The mid-1800's
*Locale:* The French countryside near the town of Courbevoie
*First published:* "Petit Soldat," 1885 (English translation, 1903)

> *Principal characters:*
> Luc le Ganidec, a soldier
> Jean Kerderen, also a soldier
> A young maid, who attracts the attention of both soldiers

## The Story

Luc and Jean are two soldiers who habitually spend their free time on Sundays away from the barracks, out in the countryside. Their day off has taken on the character of a ritual. Every Sunday, they bring food for breakfast to the same spot in the woods and lie back to enjoy the food, wine, and sights of an area that reminds them of home.

Eventually, their ritual comes to include a bit of innocent ogling of a young village girl who brings her cow out to pasture every week at the same time. One Sunday, however, the girl speaks to them on her way to the pasture, and when she returns later, she shares the cow's milk with them and leaves them with a promise to meet the following Sunday.

The next weekend, Jean suggests that they bring something for her. They settle on candy as an appropriate present, but when the girl arrives, both are too shy to tell her that they have brought something. Finally, Luc tells the girl of the treat, and Jean, who always carries the provisions, give the bonbons to her.

As the weeks pass, the girl becomes the topic of conversation for these soldiers as they spend time at the barracks, and the three become fast friends. The girl begins to share their Sunday breakfast meal and appears to devote equal attention to the two recruits.

Then, in an uncharacteristic move, Luc seeks leave on a Tuesday, and again the following Thursday. He borrows money from Jean on that day but offers no explanation for his behavior. Jean lends the money.

The following Sunday, when the girl appears with the cow, she immediately rushes up to Luc and they embrace ardently. Jean is hurt because he is left out and does not understand why the girl has suddenly turned all of her attention to Luc. Luc and the girl go off to care for the cow and disappear into the woods for a long time. Jean is stupefied. When they return, the lovers kiss again, and the girl offers Jean a kind "Good evening" before going away.

Neither soldier speaks of the incident, but as they return to their barracks they stop momentarily on the bridge over the Seine. Jean leans over toward the water, farther than he should in Luc's judgment, then suddenly tumbles into the torrent. Luc can do nothing; he watches in anguish as his good friend drowns.

## Themes and Meanings

A first-time reader of this story, or of many other Guy de Maupassant stories, may be surprised by the ending because it is difficult to imagine such catastrophic consequences in the lives of characters as simple as these soldiers. For precisely this reason, though, Maupassant is able to have significant impact on readers: The universal aspects of the tale stand out sharply beneath the surface simplicity. In "Two Little Soldiers," the tragedy of the traditional "love triangle" is brought into sharp focus, and the readers' sympathies are immediately and directly engaged by these young men whose lives are forever altered by the arrival of a woman whom they both admire.

The central issue that Maupassant treats is the conflict between friendship and love. In its simplest terms, the "moral" of this story is that a person and his best friend cannot love the same person. That notion, however, takes on poignant overtones in Maupassant's skillful handling of the story of these two soldiers.

It is clear from the outset that the two recruits share a special relationship. Thrown together in a system that traditionally offers little freedom and little dignity for individuals, the soldiers have found in each other a much-needed comrade whose shared interests and similar background make military life bearable. The opening scenes show the genuine bond that exists between them: They survive the week in order to spend their Sundays together. What these men share is a kind of male bonding that often occurs in soldiers, a special friendship that the military hierarchy relies on to ensure that men will fight bravely to save their comrades in war.

Suddenly, another emotion enters the lives of both recruits, one that challenges the strength of that bonding. Both are smitten by the young girl who befriends them. In their quiet way, they vie for her attention, although neither seems aware that the other is in love. To win the girl, however, one of them must "betray" the bond of friendship; it is impossible that one should become the girl's lover and still maintain the same relationship with his fellow soldier that existed before the girl came into their lives. Thus, Luc must resort to deception to ensure that he will win the girl's favor: He seeks leave without explaining his motives to Jean and takes advantage of his comrade (by borrowing money) to further his own suit. It is small wonder that Jean is hurt and bewildered when Luc and the girl make him aware of their special relationship.

The fact that the reader does not see any difference between Luc's and Jean's initial reactions and behavior toward the girl only heightens the tragedy. It becomes apparent that Jean feels the same about the girl as Luc does. Perhaps his friendship for Luc has kept him from pursuing the girl himself; perhaps shyness has prevented him from making public his feelings. In any case, when he sees that Luc and the girl are in love, he feels betrayed, and his decision to commit suicide is a logical consequence of his realization that he will have neither friend nor lover. Thus, the happiness that Luc and the girl experience is achieved at great cost.

*Style and Technique*

"Two Little Soldiers" relies heavily on setting and point of view for its effectiveness. The pastoral surroundings in which the majority of the action takes place suggest serenity and appear to promise happiness. Maupassant is careful not to reveal too much of barracks life; only its regimentation intrudes on the story, adding to the sense of release the two soldiers feel when they escape to the countryside each weekend. The idyllic setting is no escape from the harsh realities of the world, however, as the reader discovers when Jean is cast aside by the two people who mean the most to him.

Perhaps the most significant technique that allows Maupassant to make his tragedy hit home with readers is his manipulation of the point of view. Though the action of the story appears to be continuous, "Two Little Soldiers" can actually be viewed as a series of dramatic scenes, and the point of view shifts as scenes change. For much of the story, Maupassant adopts what appears to be the voice of an omniscient narrator. He tells the reader what both soldiers think and do, giving each equal attention. Because he appears to be providing simple and straightforward information, it is easy to pass over the fact that he says almost nothing about what the young girl feels or thinks in these first encounters.

Then, at key points, Maupassant adopts a more limited view: When Luc decides to go on leave, and when the two soldiers travel to the countryside for the last time, he restricts himself to the viewpoint of one character, Jean. The reader sees only the confusion that wells up in this young man as his friend and the girl go off without him. When the two soldiers begin their trek back to the barracks, the scene is viewed through Luc's eyes: The reader is denied knowledge of Jean's feelings, and hence is given no explanation of his motivation for committing suicide.

This technique may lead to charges of poor writing; certainly Maupassant does not follow the tenet of many proponents of the school of realism that point of view should be consistent throughout a story, novel, or poem. Nevertheless, the author's conscious decision to move selectively between characters is directly responsible for the aura that he wished to create in this tragedy of the common man.

*Laurence W. Mazzeno*

# TWO LOVELY BEASTS

*Author:* Liam O'Flaherty (1896-1984)
*Type of plot:* Social realism
*Time of plot:* 1938
*Locale:* The western part of Ireland
*First published:* 1946

> *Principal characters:*
> COLM DERRANE, the protagonist, a modest peasant farmer
> MRS. DERRANE, his wife
> KATE HIGGINS, a widow and neighbor
> ANDY GORUM, the village elder

*The Story*

The rather pastoral title of this story suggests that it might deal with animals and nature, two subjects common to Liam O'Flaherty's writing. As the reader quickly discovers, however, the "two lovely beasts" are of only minor importance, for the true concerns of this story revolve around their human masters.

The story opens with the misfortunes of Kate Higgins, a widow whose cow has calved and then died. She brings her tale of woe to the kitchen of the Derranes, a neighboring family whose own cow has just given birth to a calf. Kate, in wild hysterics, begs Colm Derrane to buy her calf, so that she might purchase another cow. "I must have a cow for the children," she tells Colm. "The doctor said they must have plenty of milk. . . . They are ailing, the poor creatures."

Because "traditional law" allows only one cow for each family, Colm refuses her at once. Grazing land is scarce—there is only enough grass on each household plot to support one cow. By the same token, the milk is shared with those in the community who have been struck by misfortune—people such as Kate Higgins. As Mrs. Derrane, Colm's wife, tells Kate, "We couldn't leave neighbours without milk in order to fill a calf's belly."

Eventually, Colm agrees to allow his cow to feed her calf until she can find a buyer. She rejoices at this news, but soon she begins to tempt him again with the idea of owning two calves. "You'll be the richest man in the village," she whispers into his ear. "You'll be talked about and envied from one end of the parish to the other." Colm refuses her again, but with far less conviction than before.

The seed of temptation has been planted, and it comes into full blossom the following morning when Kate comes to him with the news that she can find no buyer. "Unless you buy him," she tells Colm, "I'll have to give him to the butcher at Kilmacalla." He refuses her one last time but is unable to sleep at night because of the idea of owning two calves. The idea, O'Flaherty writes, "gave him both pleasure and pain. The pleasure was like that derived from the anticipation of venery. The pain came from his conscience."

Despite the objections of his wife, the following day Colm buys Kate Higgins's calf. There is an immediate uproar in the community. Andy Gorum, the village elder, remonstrates with Colm about his decision, but Colm is adamant: He will keep the two calves, no matter what laws he is breaking. In the end, Gorum says that he has little choice but to have the rest of the community ostracize the Derranes. He predicts a dark fate for Colm and his family. Even Kate Higgins, who is unable to buy a cow, turns against Colm.

Instead of giving in, however, Colm becomes harder, more determined "to rise in the world." Every drop of milk from his cow goes to the mouths of his "two lovely beasts"—even at the expense of feeding his own children. The family, living on a diet of potatoes and salt, soon begins to starve. When his wife confronts him and threatens to beat him to his senses, Colm in turn gives her a savage beating.

Suddenly and inexplicably, she no longer sees Colm as an obsessed fool, but as someone who is trying to better their family. She and the children, despite a few setbacks, stand firmly behind him. They and their cows survive the next two winters, and slowly the villagers begin to turn away from the counsel of Gorum—whom they see as a jealous old fool—and come to get the advice of Colm. In the meantime, Kate Higgins has gone completely insane and has been taken away to a lunatic asylum.

In the final scene of the story, Colm has decided to start a shop in his cottage. He knows that the start of the "Emergency," as World War II is known in Ireland, will bring about a great demand for all sorts of foodstuffs. Though this means even more prolonged hardship for his family, they accept his decision. It is a successful decision because, before long, "there was full and plenty in the house. The little girls had ribbons to their hair and dai-dais to amuse their leisure. His wife got a velvet dress and a hat with feathers. There was bacon for breakfast."

Ironically, his great wealth alienates him once again from the community. However, this isolation does not trouble him, for he is planning to open a shop in the town. As Colm is leaving his farm—having sold his two lovely beasts—Andy Gorum and his neighbors jeer him. Colm, however, is "completely unaware of their jeers. His pale blue eyes stared fixedly straight ahead, cold and resolute and ruthless."

*Themes and Meanings*

There are several themes running through this story, the most important being the nature of human greed. In the first part of the narrative, there is an almost direct parallel with the biblical story of Adam and Eve, especially in the manner in which Colm is tempted from his Garden of Eden by the idea of owning that which he is not allowed to possess. Instead of an apple, Colm's obsession revolves around the two beasts.

His banishment from Eden is far more spiritual than physical, however, because, instead of leaving behind a garden of plenty, he is forced to give up a frame of mind that allows him satisfaction with all that he possesses. After he purchases the two beasts, though, nothing is good enough for him. He wants more and more and more— the vicious upward spiral of greed.

The fact that Andy Gorum ostracizes Colm and his family to the point that they decide to leave the community is trivial, because Colm has already made his decision to leave (spiritually, at least) by owning the two calves. Though Gorum prophesies that the Derranes will have their downfall, this does not happen in the latter half of the story. Indeed, Colm thrives to an extent that the community has never before seen. He becomes a hero.

By making Colm successful, O'Flaherty departs from the tale of Adam and Eve. No God of wrath, as Gorum would like to see, has made Colm tremble in fear for his transgression of the "traditional laws." No lightning bolts have come from the heavens; no diseases have killed his calves; no deaths have taken place in his family. Nothing unfortunate has happened to Colm.

In the end, however, greed has taken its toll on Colm. Whereas once he was hardworking yet amenable, he is now cold and calculating, obsessed with the idea of "rising in the world." To O'Flaherty, this is Colm's true fall from Eden—the notion that he will never escape his own greed, but that it will imprison him forever, continuously taunting and beckoning, so that in the end, he will have nothing but a restless and ruthless mind, unable to appreciate what he has, always wanting more.

*Style and Technique*

Though O'Flaherty wrote this story in English, it almost reads like a translation from his native Gaelic. The style is simple and straightforward, using few metaphors or other literary devices, and the brief paragraphs serve mainly as connecting points between the long portions of dialogue.

In fact, it is the dialogue that is the true strength of this story, for it is full of Irish phrases and sayings ("God between us and all harm!" or "God spare your health, Colm") that are both true-to-life and lively. This is a technique that O'Flaherty adopts again and again in his writing: simple (almost childish) prose that is strongly counterpointed by lively Irish peasant dialogue. Without the dialogue, this story (and many of his other works) would fall flat, for its theme is so universal and its prose so anonymous that it might have taken place anywhere. With the dialogue, however, the setting could be nowhere other than the west of Ireland.

*Michael Verdon*

# TYPHOON

*Author:* Joseph Conrad (Jósef Teodor Konrad Nałęcz Korzeniowski, 1857-1924)
*Type of plot:* Adventure
*Time of plot:* The 1890's
*Locale:* The China Seas
*First published:* 1902

> *Principal characters:*
> CAPTAIN TOM MACWHIRR, the master of the steamer *Nan-Shan*
> YOUNG JUKES, the chief mate
> SOLOMON ROUT, the chief engineer
> THE SECOND MATE
> THE BOATSWAIN
> THE STEWARD
> TWO HUNDRED CHINESE COOLIES, who are returning to their
> homes after several years of working in the tropics

*The Story*

The protagonist of Joseph Conrad's narrative of a typhoon in the China Seas is Captain Tom MacWhirr. Recommended by the builders of the *Nan-Shan* to Sigg and Sons, who want a competent and dependable master for their vessel, MacWhirr is gruff, empirical, without imagination. Although his reputation as a mariner is impeccable, his manner does not inspire confidence; yet, when he is first shown around the *Nan-Shan* by the builders, he immediately notes that its locks are poorly made.

Young Mr. Jukes, MacWhirr's first mate, full of himself, curious about others, always rushing off to meet trouble before it comes, is satiric concerning MacWhirr's limitations, especially his literal-mindedness, his inability to communicate with others in ordinary terms, and his taciturnity. For his part, MacWhirr is amazed at Jukes's capacity for small talk and his use of metaphorical language, for MacWhirr himself notes only the facts by which he lives. However, he is astute enough to respect in others the ability to perform their tasks ably. Having just enough imagination to carry him through each day, tranquilly certain of his competence—although it has never been fully tested—MacWhirr communicates the essential details of his voyages to his wife and children in monthly letters that they read perfunctorily. These same letters are furtively and eagerly read by the steward, who, somehow, appreciates the truths that they distill.

A minor contretemps between Jukes and the captain occurs early in the narrative when, Jukes believes, MacWhirr fails to understand the implications of the *Nan-Shan*'s transfer from its original British to a Siamese registry. MacWhirr reads Jukes's displeasure at the change as a literal comment on the size and shape of the Siamese flag. He checks its dimensions, colors, and insignia in his naval guide and then tells Jukes that it is correct in every way. Jukes, nevertheless, continues to feel resentment against MacWhirr and the flag's Siamese elephant on a blue ground, lamenting the loss of the red, white, and blue of the Union Jack, symbol of security and order. Another minor disagreement concerns MacWhirr's and Jukes's differing opinions over the boatswain: Jukes dislikes the man for his lack of initiative and for a good nature that he thinks amounts almost to imbecility; MacWhirr respects him as a first-rate seaman who performs his tasks without grumbling.

The other members of the *Nan-Shan* crew are Solomon Rout, the chief engineer, who writes colorful and entertaining accounts of his voyages to his wife and aged mother; the second mate, who finds that he cannot function during the typhoon and is later dismissed for his failure of nerve; and the steward. MacWhirr and his crew are responsible for two hundred Chinese passengers, who, with their belongings and the silver dollars they have saved during the years that they have worked in the tropics, are returning home.

As MacWhirr and Jukes notice the rapidly falling barometer that portends the typhoon ahead, they react characteristically to the "fact" of the coming storm. Jukes is amazed at, yet respectful of, MacWhirr's decision to meet the weather head-on rather than to sail behind or around it. MacWhirr consults the textbooks; he then concludes that one Captain Wilson's account of a "storm strategy" cannot be credited because Wilson could not testify to the activities of a storm he had not experienced. "Let it come, then," says MacWhirr with "dignified indignation."

The gale arrives, in ever-increasing ferocity, attacking the *Nan-Shan*, the crew, and the passengers "like a personal enemy." At one point, as the storm nears its apex, the boatswain makes his way to the bridge to tell MacWhirr of the chaos that the pounding waves have caused in the hold where the coolies are billeted. The storm has buffeted those below with the same vehemence it has hit those above the decks: to the brink of dissolution. The Chinese and their unsecured silver dollars have been hurled against the stairs and the bulkheads by the savage waves. MacWhirr tells Jukes to see to the confusion below and to return to the bridge as soon as he can, for it may be necessary for him to assume command of the ship. Afraid, Jukes makes his way belowdecks. During the lull, as the *Nan-Shan* finds the eye of the storm, he and the boatswain rig lifelines and secure the hold. It is, however, only when he hears MacWhirr's voice through the speaking tube, with which the captain communicates with Solomon Rout and the engine room, that Jukes musters sufficient initiative to obey MacWhirr's order and to secure the hold.

The turning point of the story occurs when MacWhirr, uncertain of the outcome of his decision to confront the storm, finds his matches in their accustomed place. "I shouldn't like to lose her," he says of the *Nan-Shan* as he gives in, momentarily, to the unaccustomed sensation of mental fatigue. Jukes, once he has settled the Chinese workmen, returns to the bridge and there experiences such self-confidence as to make him equal to the challenge of the storm—once the ship sails out of its eye—and to any future challenges as well.

Once the storm is over, the ship, grayed by salt and devastated by wind, sails into port with life restored, as much as possible, to normal order. The second mate, who had frozen on deck, is put off the ship. MacWhirr, the reader learns, has solved the problem of the Chinese and their money by dividing the silver dollars equally among them. The three dollars left over he has given to the three most seriously injured men.

The tale does not dramatize the second half of the storm. It concludes instead with an epilogue of sorts, during which the principal characters detail in written form their impressions of the typhoon.

### Themes and Meanings

"Typhoon" is remarkable primarily for the immediacy with which the storm, in its elemental and objective fury, is dramatized. It is experience so intensely and forcefully narrated that its reality is felt as it is read. The tale is adventure so brilliantly accommodated by language that one becomes oblivious of the very words that communicate the experience.

The story is, furthermore, a perfect combination of the literal and the symbolic. As he confronts the storm, MacWhirr sees beyond the vault of the sky, past the stars into a vast and lonely cosmos beyond. He defines humanity's protest against nature as he finds in himself the determination to confront and conquer the facts of creation. The several references to the loneliness of command, to the privileges and burdens of authority, suggest, in addition, a simple but provocative allegory: A human being confronts the self through a task provided by the subconscious as a means of determining the capacity to be. The ship can be seen, in an equally viable reading, as a microcosm, MacWhirr as a god-figure on whom all depends, and his shortcomings as an index of the limitations of a godhead who has lost or never had control of his creation. Solomon Rout, in the bowels of the ship, can then be read as that aspect of the psyche on which the intelligence depends for power and drive. Jukes, who discovers his place within the human community, as Everyman, who, in doing his work under the eye and encouragement of the god figure, succeeds in discovering his courage and verifying his humanity; the boatswain as one who does not fail in matters of trust; and the second mate as one who fails in responsibility and succumbs, as a result, to fear and terror.

### Style and Technique

The means by which the adventure of MacWhirr and the *Nan-Shan* is narrated is the chief challenge of Conrad's tale. The principal characters are themselves all storytellers of different sorts. MacWhirr writes his dutiful letters to a wife who fears and dreads them, as she does his return to her and their children. Only the steward has some notion of the purity of the events they describe. When he reads MacWhirr's account of the storm, he is so reluctant to tear himself away from the letter that he is almost caught. Solomon Rout, in the habit of sending his wife and aged mother long and picturesque accounts of his travels, is curiously unable to lend romance to the events he has experienced. His wife is disappointed by the letters' paucity of description.

Solomon, the reader infers, has perhaps learned somewhat more from the adventure than the others, for the typhoon has brought forth in him a desire to be reunited with his family, as well as making him aware of his mortality. Jukes's account, written to his friend in the western ocean trade, somewhat more animated than is usually the case in his correspondence, concludes that MacWhirr has gotten the *Nan-Shan* out of a difficult predicament and that he reconciled the claims of the Chinese workers fairly creditably "for such a stupid man."

The overall narrator of the tale, who is privy to the correspondence of MacWhirr, Rout, and Jukes, for his part recounts the adventure in a tone of astonished and incredulous surprise. His is a tone compounded as much of a satiric and ironic awareness of MacWhirr's limitations as of a grudging acceptance of the man's determination to survive and an appreciation of his ability to provide fair play, not only for the coolies but also for the second mate. It is the tone of tolerant yet bemused irony that transforms the narrative into a remarkable comedy, a form unusual within Conrad's oeuvre.

The comedy of "Typhoon" depends chiefly on the reader's awareness that neither MacWhirr nor Jukes changes as a result of his experience. Perhaps Solomon Rout changes, but if he does, it is left ambiguous so as not to intrude on the happy ending. Young Jukes, as does MacWhirr, passes the test of self, but he remains unaware that without MacWhirr he might have failed. This awareness, that the characters remain largely unchanged, comments, furthermore, on an absurd cosmos beyond the stars that allows for surprises of all kinds, even to the promise of hope in humanity.

Jukes and MacWhirr can ultimately be seen as comic foils for such characters of deep introspection as Jim of *Lord Jim* (1900) and Razumov of *Under Western Eyes* (1910), characters whose failure propels them into an ethical universe and defines the form of the novels in which they appear. If Marlow's willed descent into the self transforms the setting that he observes in *Heart of Darkness* (1902) into meaningful symbolism, then MacWhirr and Jukes's inability to fathom the depths of the self explains the straightforward and objective description of the storm, as well as the narrator's incredulousness. MacWhirr, Jukes, and Rout perform their comic parts admirably and make "Typhoon" equal to the best of Conrad's novels.

*A. A. DeVitis*

# THE UGLIEST HOUSE IN THE WORLD

*Author:* Peter Ho Davies (1966-    )
*Type of plot:* Domestic realism
*Time of plot:* The 1990's
*Locale:* A small village in Wales
*First published:* 1995

> *Principal characters:*
> DR. WILLIAMS, the narrator
> HIS FATHER
> GARETH WATKINS, the dead six-year-old
> KATE WATKINS, Gareth's mother

*The Story*

"The Ugliest House in the World" is told from the perspective of a first-person narrator named Dr. Williams. The narrative is in the present tense, but much of the text consists of flashbacks and background material that provide context for the present-tense action.

The narrator, a young doctor in London working to pay back his student loans, describes his work environment in a geriatric ward and some of the slang vocabulary used by him and his colleagues. Although a native of London, he is of Welsh descent and, therefore, considered a Welshman by his English colleagues and teased for it at every opportunity. The teasing is done with generally good nature and accepted in kind.

The narrator does have one connection to Wales. His father, who has been laid off after thirty-five years with the same company in London, has returned to his childhood home, a small village in Wales, where he has spent his entire severance on a small cottage on a stream where he fished in his boyhood. The narrator, concerned about arson-prone Welsh nationalists who are resentful of outsiders and feeling that his father has wasted his severance, is unhappy about the move. However, he does make regular visits to check up on his father. He brings groceries when he visits and offers repeatedly to whitewash the house, having gone so far as to buy paint, but his father always refuses his offer. Although the previous owners had renovated the interior of the cottage, the grounds and fences around are in disrepair.

The father's neighbors are Arwyn Watkins; Kate, his daughter who returned home from England alone and pregnant at the age of sixteen; and Gareth, her six-year-old child. Gareth has become close to the narrator's father, and they often play football in his front yard. The old man has promised to take Gareth fishing in the stream behind the house. The narrator and Kate are surreptitious lovers, meeting in a falling-down stone hovel located in the field between the two properties.

The present-tense action of the story begins with the narrator informing his colleagues that he is going to Wales for the weekend to attend a funeral. A couple of days earlier, Gareth had arrived at the father's cottage at the appointed time for the promised fishing expedition and, finding the cottage empty, amused himself by swinging on the front gate of the stone fence. His weight caused the gatepost, a solid piece of slate, to fall over, crushing the child beneath it and killing him.

At the funeral, two local men confront the narrator and his father, claiming that if the property had been maintained Gareth would not have been killed. They tell the narrator that he and his father are not welcome at the burial and to take his father back to England. The narrator and his father return to the cottage, and the son tells the father that he is taking him back to England the next morning. The old man goes down to the stream behind the cottage and tries to catch a fish with his hands.

After the burial, Kate comes down to the stream and apologizes for the scene at the funeral. She tells the narrator that the accident was not anybody's fault—it was everybody's fault. She, the narrator, and his father build a dam in the stream to try to catch a fish barehanded, the way the old man did as a boy. The old man falls to his knees in the water, sobbing, and Kate comforts him.

The next morning, when the narrator and his father go out to the car to leave for England, Welsh nationalist slogans have been written across the front of the house with red paint. The narrator gets some white paint from the shed and quickly paints over the walls of the cottage while his father waits in the car.

### Themes and Meanings

The overriding theme of "The Ugliest House in the World" is responsibility—how it is met and how it is shirked. Before the action of the story begins, the narrator defines "ash cash"—a slang term used by the narrator and his colleagues for a special payment by the hospital to physicians for signing a cremation order. The hospital administration prefers cremation to burial because the impossibility of exhumation, in the case of questions about the cause of death, protects the hospital from any embarrassing discoveries. The special payment is, according to the narrator, for taking "responsibility." Although "ash cash" is not mentioned again and is not an element in the action of the story, this early and specific reference to it informs everything that follows.

There is also the issue of the father's severance pay. After thirty-five years of work for the same company and just before being eligible to collect his pension, he is laid off with a single cash payment. Like the hospital paying its "ash cash," the father's employer buys its way out of its responsibility. In another case of shirked responsibility, the father of the dead child abandoned the pregnant mother at the age of sixteen. Finally, the local men at the funeral confront the narrator and his father about their responsibility in Gareth's death.

Both the hospital and the father's employer are able to deflect responsibility with monetary payments, and neither the narrator nor any of the characters openly question the propriety of these policies. However, it is not just the impersonality of the organizations that allows their callousness to be accepted. The absent father of the dead child is mentioned only in passing and dismissed by Kate as a "wanker," but there is no examination of his failure to perform his paternal duties, even though he is an individual and directly responsible for his actions.

However, the narrator and his father are confronted at the funeral and taken to task for their perceived culpability in the death of the child. The difference is that they are there and are accessible. Although the gatepost had not been maintained for years before the narrator's father purchased the cottage and was probably a hazard for some time, the former owners are not blamed. Furthermore, the precarious stone hovel between the two properties is equally dangerous and could just as easily have been the site of a fatal accident—but it was not. The accident happened when and where it did, and the narrator and his father were available to be blamed.

A secondary theme in the story has to do with nationalism, specifically Welsh nationalism, and the sense of belonging. The narrator's father returns to Wales because he feels that he belongs there. It is where he grew up and where his ancestors are buried. However, to the local Welshmen, he has been away and lost his status as a Welshman. In their minds, he does not belong. This makes it easier to blame him for the death of the child. Again, blame has as much to do with who is available and blamable as it does with actual responsibility. When Kate tells the narrator that it is nobody's fault because it is everybody's fault, the pool of potential culprits is expanded infinitely. Now, blame can be assigned to whomever is handy and useful for the purpose.

## Style and Technique

In this story, as in most of his others, Davies treats thematic concerns with a delicate hand. Subtle hints of thematic concerns are embedded in descriptions of relationships, personal history, and habitual traits of the characters and then revisited as minor elements of the action of the narrative. For instance, the first portion of this story consists of a description of the social environment and professional slang of the geriatric ward in which the narrator works. None of this information is important to the narrative or mentioned again, but it foreshadows certain thematic elements (culpability and nationalism) and establishes a perspective from which to interpret them.

Structurally, the story is deconstructed into several separate parts—some in present tense, some in past—each with a heading drawn from some textual reference within the section. The parts are not in chronological order and, as the narrative shifts tense between them, give an impressionistic quality to the whole. For example, although it is made clear in the first pages that the reason for the narrator's visit is to attend the funeral and Gareth is introduced in the next few sections, it is not until the narrator and his father are seated in the chapel, more than halfway through the story, that it becomes apparent that it is Gareth who is dead.

Davies avoids heavily metaphorical language and imagery, using straightforward and inventive adjectival description to establish place and character.

*Darryl Erlandson*

# THE UGLIEST PILGRIM

*Author:* Doris Betts (1932-    )
*Type of plot:* Psychological
*Time of plot:* 1969
*Locale:* A bus traveling from Spruce Pine, North Carolina, to Tulsa, Oklahoma
*First published:* 1973

> *Principal characters:*
> VIOLET KARL, the narrator
> GRADY "FLICK" FLIGGINS, a black soldier
> MONTY HARRELL, a white paratrooper
> AN ELDERLY WHITE WOMAN
> MR. WEATHERMAN, a bus driver

*The Story*

Violet Karl is making a pilgrimage to Tulsa, Oklahoma, to have her disfigured face healed by a prominent television evangelist. Her injury resulted from a childhood accident when she accompanied her father to chop wood, and the head of the ax came off the handle, striking her in the face.

Throughout her journey, Violet keeps a journal about the things that she sees and the people whom she meets. With each settlement through which she passes, she praises the Lord for leading her one step closer to her salvation and cure. To these comments Violet adds her impressions of her fellow passengers and recounts how they pass the time during their journey from Spruce Pine, North Carolina, to her fabled Tulsa.

On the bus, Violet makes the acquaintance of three fellow passengers: an older white woman; a black soldier, Grady "Flick" Fliggins; and a white paratrooper, Monty Harrell. Each acquaintance adds to Violet's growing need for acceptance. Each shows Violet that everyone is on some sort of quest.

When she first boards the bus, Violet's only companions are the older white woman and the black soldier. She takes a seat beside the older woman, strikes up a conversation, and soon learns that the woman is on her way to visit her son in Nashville, where he works in a cellophane plant. The woman adds that she may make a permanent move to her son's home.

After the older woman goes to sleep, Violet strikes up a conversation with Grady Fliggins and begins playing a game of draw poker. Grady seems not to care that Violet's face is deformed. While they are in a snack bar during a rest stop in Kingsport, Tennessee, Violet and Flick meet a white paratrooper, Monty Harrell, who joins them on the bus and becomes the third player in the card game.

During the trip, Violet and the two young men discuss her reason for going to Tulsa. Monty seems to be most opposed to Violet's intended meeting with the television preacher. Monty freely voices his suspicion that the preacher is a "fake," but Violet will not be sidetracked.

In Nashville, the older woman leaves the bus, but not before warning Violet about her companions and men in general. She cautions Violet to be on her guard because people will recognize her weaknesses and take advantage of them. As she gets off the bus, she chats with their driver, Mr. Weatherman, about Violet, but he is replaced by another driver who shows no personal interest in his passengers.

As the journey continues, the three passengers become a closer knit group with each community through which they pass. They decide to spend the night in Memphis before resuming their journey. While she is asleep in her room, Violet has what she thinks is a dream in which Flick and Monty come into her room. From the discussion Flick and Monty have, the reader realizes that this is not a dream but, in fact, a rape. The most telling comment comes when Flick admits that looks have nothing to do with sexual pleasure; therefore, he has no feelings, one way or the other, about Violet's appearance.

When the bus trip resumes, Violet finds herself being drawn more closely to Monty. Because no one is meeting her in Tulsa, she has her ticket changed so that she can accompany Monty and Flick to Fort Smith, with Monty making up the difference in the cost. When the bus reaches Fort Smith, Monty promises Violet that he will be there waiting when she returns from Tulsa. Flick makes no such promise but merely says good-bye. Monty runs beside the bus promising that he will meet Violet on her return and asking her to promise that she will return.

Violet eventually reaches Tulsa and finds the preacher's headquarters. To her dismay, the preacher is on a publicity tour, so she must deal with one of his assistants. To every question that Violet poses concerning her disfigurement, the assistant gives a canned response about her true need being spiritual. She leaves uncured and dissatisfied.

On her bus ride back, Violet refuses to look at her face. When she reaches the Fort Smith bus station, Violet hears Monty calling her name. As she turns toward the voice, she sees her reflection in a large mirror over the jukebox. She realizes that she is still ugly and tries to flee. Monty, however, will not let her escape. As the story ends, Violet, no longer thinking about her face, realizes that Monty is about to catch up to her.

*Themes and Meanings*

Through the trials of Violet Karl, Doris Betts continues a theme that pervades her work, most of which is concerned with people trying to find themselves within the lives in which they have been placed. Most often, this search comes in the form of an individual in search of love. Although her themes transcend geographical confines, Betts uses the isolation of the rural South to provide little obvious escape for her characters. However, these characters' acquired psychological independence intensifies the need of all persons to strive to conquer their fears and low self-images.

Life is a quest or a pilgrimage. By selecting this motif for the thematic center and title for her story, Betts makes the seemingly least obvious heroine the stand-in for her readers who themselves, no doubt, attempted to find meaning in their lives.

Violet Karl seeks deliverance from the physical aberration that has made her an outcast through her deep belief that the evangelist in Tulsa will be her deliverer. When she arrives in Tulsa, she finds that her deliverer is not to be found and that his assistant regales her with prepared and standard abstract responses that do not address her needs.

When Violet returns to Fort Smith and finds Monty waiting for her as he had promised, she begins to push her deformity aside and realizes that she possesses something that may indeed be attractive. Her realization that Monty is not as bothered by her injured face as she is leads Violet to take the first step toward self-realization that is central to Betts's fiction. At this point, the reader understands that, although the evangelical assistant made his comments out of habit, the problem that Violet faced did, indeed, lie more within her spirit than on her face.

## Style and Technique

Betts's short stories are vivid examples of moments in individual lives isolated in time. Utilizing a "slice-of-life" approach allows Betts clearly to depict the epiphanic moments of realization that most humans experience at one time or another. Thus, through her brief trip in search of rejuvenation, Violet Karl becomes an "everyperson."

Violet Karl's journey is an internal journey, one that will be completed only after she accepts herself and ceases to worry whether others accept her. Betts demonstrates, through Violet's isolation because of her injured face, that psychological pains are as real as physical pains. In both cases, however, the pains can be overcome with time and proper treatment. Monty's lack of revulsion at Violet's injury goes a long way toward demonstrating that others can accept her, helping her to accept herself as she is.

The surface simplicity of the structure of "The Ugliest Pilgrim" in fact provides the work's deeper complexity. In this work, Betts allows her story's form to match its thematic function. Violet's problem seems to be simple. If she can get to Tulsa, her problem will be solved. Below Violet's surface, however, the reader finds a more debilitating problem, lack of self-esteem. The reader also finds that beneath a simple narrative form is a universal theme that is complex in both cause and resolution.

*Thomas B. Frazier*

# UNCLE

*Author:* R. K. Narayan (1906-2001)
*Type of plot:* Psychological
*Time of plot:* The twentieth century
*Locale:* South India
*First published:* 1970

> *Principal characters:*
> BOY, the protagonist, grown up when he tells the story
> UNCLE, the narrator's uncle
> AUNT, the narrator's aunt
> SURESH, a boy in the narrator's class
> THE TAILOR
> JAYRAJ, a frame maker

*The Story*

The narrator and protagonist, occupying and owning the house in which he was reared, recalls the stages by which he comes on some crushing knowledge, how he lives with it and finally realizes his present gain. Seated in the easy chair once occupied by his uncle, he reminisces in the silent, solitary setting, ideal and natural for a reverie, on how the man and woman he called his uncle and aunt used to dote on him as though he were their own child. Memories of simple joys such as are universal in happy homes crowd his mind—how Uncle used to push his snuffbox out of his reach when the narrator was a toddler, how delighted he was when the little fellow tumbled, and how his aunt would carry him off and set him to the entertainment of water-splashing and then attempt with loving determination to feed him. He sees their lives revolve around himself not only when he was small, but also through all of his remembered days, when even under the pressure of silent agony he maintains their sweet relationship.

When the youngster starts going to school, his uncle and aunt pay meticulous attention to every detail of his daily routine. The reader, regaled with lively descriptions of the early morning scrub, the prayers and recitations, the organization of the school satchel with a pointy pencil and all, is left in no doubt whatsoever that the boy (the narrator) is happy and content in the tender, loving care of his uncle and aunt. They take absurd parental pride in all of his childish antics; his pretense at saying holy verse, for example, is seen as a sign that he will one day be renowned as a saint.

The first shadow of a doubt about Uncle falls on the unsuspecting little boy's mind when Suresh, a classmate in the first grade, asks him his father's name, what he does for a living, and whether they are rich. This battery of questions, which would have seemed natural and which would have posed no problem to any other boy, bewilders him. When asked about his father, all he can say is that he calls him Uncle. He does not know what work his uncle does, for Uncle is home all day, either meditating or eating. To the question of riches perhaps he responds adequately; he does not know, but "they make plenty of sweets at home." (At this the reader is imperceptibly led to wonder about the child's use of the third person, an intuitive distancing of himself even from those closest to him in the whole world.) When he asks Uncle where his office is and whether he is rich, his aunt drags him off to eat some goodies and cautions him about asking things Uncle does not like to talk about.

Some days later, the same classmate informs the boy that his uncle came from another country—which sounds like a good thing. He also says, however, that Uncle "impersonated"—which sounds ominous even though neither boy knows what the word means. Eager as he is to find out, he cannot broach the subject when he gets home, and instead entertains Uncle with an imagined account of his physical prowess.

One day when he is being measured for a shirt to be expressly made for a picture-taking at school (a matter of monumental importance on which much thought and energy are expended), the boy gathers some more information about his uncle. The tailor, very respectful toward Uncle, expresses his family's gratitude by recounting how Uncle revived him when he was left for dead, and how he helped him go over mountain passes although Uncle had a baby in his arms. Uncle, however, tells him not to bring up the past.

Whenever Aunt wants to go out, she sends the boy to get a carriage from the street corner, where he hears the men talk among themselves, making disparaging remarks about Uncle, calling him "that Rangoon man."

The day the class photograph arrives amid much excitement, the boy and Uncle go on foot to Jayraj the frame maker, who, to the boy's astonishment, addresses Uncle as "Doctor." Mystified, the boy makes a timid and predictably futile attempt at asking Uncle for a clarification. As Jayraj is full of his own importance, full of talk and jokes, and has other customers to attend to, he cannot finish their work till the evening. With Jayraj's promise to give him food from a restaurant across the street and to bring him home, the boy, with a sense of adventure, begs his uncle to let him stay on at the shop.

Following Uncle's departure, Jayraj starts talking with a bald man about Uncle, speaking in undertones and casting sidelong glances at the boy, who grows more and more uncomfortable and hungry. From half-heard whispered phrases, the boy gathers that Jayraj addressed his uncle as "doctor" only for effect, for he is no doctor, but an impersonator of one. The real doctor—the boy's father—was a rich and successful doctor in Rangoon, where he had ten doctors employed under him. Uncle was then only a syringe washer. When the Japanese bombed Rangoon, the doctor and his wife, with their fifteen-day-old baby and the syringe washer (Uncle), trekked back to India over the mountains. Apparently, Uncle pushed the doctor over a cliff to his death and impersonated him in India, thereby acquiring his gold, jewels, and a bank account in Madras. He kept the doctor's wife a prisoner, and then, having given her a lethal injection, wound up his crimes with her speedy cremation. The baby, he reared.

After recounting all these shocking matters, Jayraj digs out an unclaimed photograph from his storage room, and, shoving it at him, asks the boy if he wants it. The boy knows by now that the stranger in European clothes is his father, the doctor. Hungry, confused, and terrified, though, he runs home without the photograph. He runs the entire unfamiliar way of looming shadows to the comforting arms of his uncle, the murderer and swindler of his parents.

When the boy confides the whole story to his aunt, she simply asks him to forget it. He suppresses questions even when he grows up. At college, he ignores unfavorable remarks about his uncle, but once tries to strangle a classmate for gossiping about him. When Uncle dies, he leaves everything to the boy, the narrator. In going through his uncle's things, he finds that the only connection to Burma is a lacquered box.

*Themes and Meanings*

Many of R. K. Narayan's novels and short stories paint vivid pictures of the imaginary South Indian village of Malgudi and the small world of little boys. The descriptive realism of the setting and the psychological realism of the characters convincingly unfold human predicaments and the choices that people make. Narayan's protagonists are confronted by circumstances that they either accept and learn to live with or take on as a challenge and endeavor to change. Such situations, naturally, reveal character, and, quite often, also an attitude toward life. "Uncle" is a story that conforms to this endearing pattern of universal relevance.

In this story, the boy, a mild and passive character, lives with a painful situation for many years before life, not he himself, brings about the final resolution—his uncle's death and his own substantial inheritance from his uncle of the money that was most probably his by right anyway. As the boy is only a first-grader when the crisis occurs, and as the crisis is of a magnitude that bears comparison with Hamlet's dilemma, the boy's response seems wholly credible. A scared and hungry little boy is likely to run home to a villain, even if that villain has killed his parents, if the villain is the only father he knows, and the world to him is a hostile place.

What is intriguing is that even as a grown-up with a college education, the protagonist does not confront Uncle or take him to court. A rare outburst of passion in him, a violent attempt at vindication, is not directed at Uncle. Rather, ironically, it is meant to defend Uncle's good name. Though too big to sit comfortably in Uncle's chair, and though he sees himself as "the monarch of all he surveys," the protagonist is hardly a formidable character. His reasons for not pursuing justice and truth are deliberately left unexplored, for the springs of action and inaction lie deep and hidden in the complex human psyche. His general passivity and lack of tenacity are convincing, for even as a boy he does not persist in getting answers to things about which he is curious. For example, he wants to know how a Hindu goddess in a picture can stand on a lotus without crushing it. When his aunt tells him not to ask such questions, he lets the matter rest without any protest whatsoever. Questions about Uncle's work and evil past are similarly put to rest. His character as portrayed by Narayan is consistent and credible.

Besides writing and reading an engrossing and satisfying story, the writer, as well as the reader, needs to discover a deeper significance in terms of human values. In this story, the dilemma of the protagonist creates interest. The choice he makes reveals not only his character but also his values, even the values of his culture. Nonviolence, tolerance, acceptance, loyalty, and patience bring a sweet harmony to life, and even a substantial reward. The opposite choice might well have brought bitterness and disaster.

## Style and Technique

The hallmarks of Narayan's style are lucidity and humor, both of which are readily apparent in this story. The leisurely pace of a reverie suits the quiet personality of the protagonist, whereas the liveliness of phrase and observation lifts insipid details of everyday routines into sheer delight.

He delineates characters and their relationships obliquely; he does not state them directly, but presents situations from which they can be perceived. Vivid descriptions of the child's world—how he prays with Uncle, how he eats with him, or plays while Uncle naps on his bench—delightful in themselves, move the story along, for they show the close bond that is later threatened by the revelation of villainy. The enchantingly described market, which initially stands for the outside world that the boy is eager to discover, loses its allure, coming to represent a hostile world from which he flies to the safe sanctuary of the arms of Uncle—ironically, the person responsible for his agony.

His own feelings are more real to the boy than the moral judgments of other people. Narayan shows this superbly by employing the technique of juxtaposition, using contrasts to highlight an idea. Every time the boy learns something negative about Uncle, a scene follows that shows that Uncle is his world. Uncle's crimes are not real to the boy, for he has experienced only his love. To the boy, the only thing embarrassing about Uncle is his enormous girth. All the consistent testimony against Uncle cannot, therefore, indict him in the protagonist's mind. The final, tangible evidence of Uncle's mysterious and questionable past—a Burmese laquered box—is in like manner dismissed as negligible. Uncle and Aunt's given names are never mentioned. People, places, and events in the story are seen not as they might appear to an objective observer, but as they appear to the protagonist. Everything has import within the psychological realism of the narrative.

*Sita Kapadia*

# UNCLE WIGGILY IN CONNECTICUT

*Author:* J. D. Salinger (1919-    )
*Type of plot:* Satire
*Time of plot:* The 1950's
*Locale:* Suburban Connecticut
*First published:* 1948

> *Principal characters:*
> ELOISE, a suburban upper-middle-class wife
> MARY JANE, her close friend and former college roommate
> RAMONA, Eloise's child, who is about ten years old

*The Story*

Mary Jane, the secretary to a New York executive named Mr. Weyinburg, has most of the day off as a result of her employer's illness but has promised to drop his mail off and take some dictation every afternoon for the duration of his illness. At three o'clock (two hours late for the lunch that her hostess had prepared), she stops to see her friend Eloise at her home in suburban Connecticut. Later she plans to drive on to Larchmont, New York, with Mr. Weyinburg's mail. Eloise, in her camel-hair coat, greets her in front of the house.

Eloise is comfortably well-off, with an attractive house, a husband who commutes to New York, a young daughter named Ramona, and a black maid named Grace. Mary Jane is single but about the same age as Eloise, who has been married for about ten years.

The two women gossip as they drink highballs in Eloise's living room. Much of the talk becomes nostalgic as the two women continue to drink. Mary Jane carelessly spills her drink while Eloise's conversation becomes more outspoken and her expressions more vulgar, referring to Grace as "sitting on her big black butt" in the kitchen.

Ramona appears. In the stilted conversation that ensues between Ramona and Mary Jane, it is obvious that Ramona is not taken in by Mary Jane's feigned enthusiasm ("Oh, what a pretty dress!"). Mary Jane questions Ramona about her imaginary companion, Jimmy Jimmereeno. Significantly, Jimmy is an orphan and has "no freckles."

The two women continue drinking, and by a quarter to five Eloise is lying on the floor recalling a long-dead lover, a GI named Walt. Walt's sense of humor, his tenderness to Eloise, and his manner of speaking are all remembered fondly by Eloise. Lew, Eloise's husband, is compared unfavorably to Walt in many respects as Eloise is questioned by Mary Jane. Eloise tearfully recalls Walt's death in an accident with a Japanese camp stove. Ramona reappears and is instructed to get her supper from the maid and go to bed.

Eloise reveals several rather unpleasant aspects of her character when she refuses to allow Grace's husband to spend the night with his wife, even though the weather is bad and driving hazardous. By now it is after seven o'clock, and Eloise lies to her husband, who is waiting to be picked up at the train station, claiming that she cannot find the keys to Mary Jane's car, which is blocking the driveway.

Next, Eloise looks in on Ramona and, finding that she is sleeping on one side of her bed, wakes her for an explanation. She learns of a new imaginary playmate, Mickey Mickeranno. She drags her passively resistant daughter to the middle of the bed and orders her to shut her eyes.

Finally, both mother and daughter are in tears as Eloise presses Ramona's glasses against her cheek saying "Poor Uncle Wiggily," which repeats Walt's phrase from many years before when Eloise had twisted her ankle outside the army PX.

Eloise finally returns to the living room, where Mary Jane has passed out. She wakens her and tearfully tries to invoke her sympathy in a desperate plea, "I was a nice girl . . . wasn't I?"

*Themes and Meanings*

The perennial themes of J. D. Salinger's stories are present in "Uncle Wiggily in Connecticut." His satire often deals with upper-middle-class alienation amid the complacency of the Eisenhower era. "Uncle Wiggily in Connecticut" is a story in this vein. The author characterizes Eloise and Mary Jane as modern, cynical suburbanites who are not always morally scrupulous and have never been meticulously honest. Eloise has been expelled from the university for an incident with a soldier in her residence hall. Mary Jane's marriage to an aviator cadet is marred by his imprisonment for two months after stabbing a member of the Military Police. It is assumed that Mary Jane will have to lie to explain her failure to reach her employer's house in Larchmont after her drunken afternoon with Eloise. Eloise seems unashamed and undisturbed when she lies to her husband about Mary Jane's car keys. She also seems to be offhand and casual in the extreme in performing her duties as a mother. The very fact that Ramona needs an imaginary friend who has "no mommy and no daddy" relates directly to her feelings toward her parents.

It is clear from the way that Eloise refers to Lew, her husband, that she has by now lost all respect for him and prefers to escape through alcohol rather than come to terms with her situation soberly.

Eloise and Mary Jane in their reminiscences seek an earlier manifestation of their lives, before they made the mistakes that now haunt them. Candidly, they seek their lost innocence.

Like the old wise rabbit with glasses, Uncle Wiggily of the nursery stories, everyone here seems to seek some solution to the puzzles of modern society. Lew seeks some sort of agreeable relationship with his wife, who detests him; Ramona seeks love and is constantly disappointed; even Grace, the maid, seeks faith through a popularized version of biblical history.

The concern and interest in the lives of others represented by Eloise's dead former lover, Walt, when he shows concern for her injured ankle ("poor Uncle Wiggily"), is totally lacking in the sterile relationships of the contemporary characters. "[D]on't tell your husband anything" Eloise warns Mary Jane. "You can tell them stuff. But never honestly." When Ramona goes to bed, she places her glasses carefully on the bedside table "folded neatly," stems down. After Eloise picks up the glasses she places them back on the night table "lenses down." Ramona's lenses allow her to see the domestic situation only too clearly; Eloise would much rather the lenses faced down rather than up. At this point she feels guilty about her relationship with her child but cannot see any easy release from her dilemma. She seeks to avoid the pitiless gaze of Ramona, whose glasses (counter-myopic lenses) tend to enlarge the child's eyes and create an impression of intense concentration.

The two women seem unpoised and rather crude, their conversation containing no cultural allusions save those of popular film fare and an obscure American romantic novelist. As with most of the other stories in this collection, Salinger's contempt for the elders is balanced by his admiration for the perceptive "wise child" mature beyond her years. Ramona has become an Uncle Wiggily to her rather adolescent parents, both lost in dreams of their youth. Mary Jane and Eloise in name and character relate back to the youngsters of the original tale, guided and advised by the wise, bespectacled Uncle Wiggily.

*Style and Technique*

Salinger created his reputation in the 1950's by counterpointing the whimsical with the mystical. The author's tone is critical of his characters and could even be said, at times, to be sarcastic. Mary Jane, "with little or no wherewithal for being left alone in a room," is seen to be of limited intelligence. Eloise is, perhaps, more intelligent but insensitive in her dealing with her maid and relates tasteless gossip endlessly to Mary Jane. Mary Jane at one point comes "back into drinking position"; Eloise "lunged . . . to her feet."

Salinger's satire on the college-girl speech of Eloise and Mary Jane is evident in the initial paragraph ("everything had been absolutely perfect . . . that she had remembered the way exactly"). The author's contempt for these drunken women is conveyed almost totally by the dialogue and the manner in which he describes the characters. As in some other Salinger stories, the author assumes a certain sophistication on the part of the reader regarding suburban life and even this particular section of the New York suburbs. Salinger refers glibly to the Merritt Parkway (even Mary Jane calls it "Merrick") in southwestern Connecticut, Larchmont (another fashionable commuter town in Westchester), and stores such as Lord and Taylor, which caters to an upper-middle-class clientele. Artifacts such as the camel-hair coat, the convertible car, and the elaborate luncheon menu all indicate a certain social and economic status presumably familiar to the reader. Thus, Salinger wastes little time on the setting and concentrates his focus on the appearance and speech of the three central characters. He treats Eloise and Mary Jane with a certain deliberate malice and the child Ramona with compassion.

The unhappiness and duplicity of both Mary Jane and Eloise become more evident as the plot develops, and the author cleverly intensifies not only the vulgarity but also the open hostility in the speeches of the two women. Their speech becomes slurred and their swearing more frequent: "I don't wanna go out there. The whole damn place smells of orange juice." Eloise's attitude toward her husband and her feelings of guilt toward her child are finally revealed unmistakably in her telephone conversation with Lew (to whom she gives short shrift) and her tearful breakdown in Ramona's bedroom, followed by the final anxious question to Mary Jane that concludes the narrative.

*F. A. Couch, Jr.*

# UNDER A GLASS BELL

*Author:* Anaïs Nin (1903-1977)
*Type of plot:* Psychological
*Time of plot:* The 1920's and 1930's
*Locale:* A mansion in France
*First published:* 1941

> *Principal characters:*
> JEANNE, a wealthy young woman
> JEAN, Jeanne's brother and also the narrator
> PAUL, Jeanne's other brother

*The Story*

In "Under a Glass Bell," Anaïs Nin describes the lifestyle of Jeanne and her two brothers, Jean and Paul. The narrator, presumably Jean, first describes the family residence, a well-appointed French mansion where many generations have lived. The furnishings, while beautiful, are so fragile that the butlers are careful not to touch anything. The rooms are lighted by glass chandeliers that the narrator refers to as "blue icicle bushes." Giving off an indirect light, these "icicle bushes" cast an aura that makes everything in the house appear to exist "under a glass bell"—the kind of glass bell often used to preserve bouquets of flowers.

Next, the narrator records a long monologue in which Jeanne, her face seeming to be "stemless," tells of her relationship with her brothers and her mother. Speaking for her brothers as well as for herself, Jeanne insists that their relationships to one another are more important than their relationships to their spouses or their children, that all three scorn the demands of the real world in which their bodies age, and that the three need to live heroic lives, a present-day impossibility. That seeds of this unusual relationship were clearly planted by the mother becomes evident when Jeanne calls her mother the "true" queen of France, who retreated from daily existence by taking drugs and by having hallucinatory talks with Napoleon Bonaparte.

Then the narrator tells the story of Jeanne's aborted affair with Prince Mahreb, a Georgian prince. Jeanne cannot respond to the prince because she believes that he is too ordinary. When the narrator sends her an exquisitely romantic Persian print, Jeanne, assuming that the print has come from the prince, renews the affair. Each day, for four days, the narrator sends Jeanne another Persian print, each one more romantic than the first. However, by the fifth day, Jeanne discovers that the prince has no imagination, and her face hangs down once more like a "stemless plant."

The remainder of the story is framed by two incidents with Paul. Jeanne, finding Paul asleep in the garden, kisses his shadow. Returning to the house, she enters the room of mirrors. Jeanne is disturbed by the fact that the multiple images show that her silk dress is eaten away and that her brooch has lost its stones. Trying to peer into the truth of her soul, she sees instead the actress in herself, not her true self.

Frightened by her experience with the mirrors, she runs back to the garden where Paul is still sleeping. The narrator intimates that at this point Jeanne reaches a crossroads. She can smash the glass bell that separates her and her brothers from the rest of the world or she can elect to remain in her comfortable womblike existence. Predictably, Jeanne's choice is the latter, and once more she kisses Paul's shadow. When Paul awakens, Jeanne tells him fearfully that she has seen the image of her body as it lies in the tomb. At that precise moment, Jeanne's guitar string breaks and she presumably dies.

## Themes and Meanings

When Nin could not get her stories published, she printed them herself on a treadle press. Nevertheless, Nin considered the thirteen stories collected in *Under a Glass Bell, and Other Stories* (1944) to represent her best work. Each piece presents characters who are isolated from normal human existence by some kind of protective enclosure. The isolation is presented as alluringly peaceful on one hand and terrifyingly devoid of life on the other.

Although two other stories in the collection, "Hejda" and "Birth," are more frequently anthologized, "Under a Glass Bell" presents Nin's protective enclosure motif most clearly. Jeanne and her two brothers are symbolically imprisoned in their family mansion where giant chandeliers or "icicle bushes" cast a blue film over the furnishings that Nin compares to a "glass bell."

However, the isolation is more psychological than physical. It is the three siblings' feelings of superiority that isolate them from other human beings. They see themselves as more sensitive, more creative, and more appreciative of creativity than other people. As a result, they cannot love their spouses, their children, and certainly not Jeanne's Georgian prince. Turning to one another for affection and inspiration, they develop a psychological romantic triangle, the most obvious attachment being that of Jean for Jeanne when Jean courts his sister by anonymously sending her the series of romantic prints.

Jeanne, having received some insight into the nature of her existence while she is in the room of mirrors, returns to the garden where she has the opportunity to free herself from the "glass bell" that encases her life. Choosing safety, she once more kisses Paul's shadow and dies, her death being implied by the snapping of her guitar string.

Nin suggests, then, that life cannot be lived in a vacuum, no matter how attractive the inside or sordid the outside.

## Style and Technique

Nin, whose first published work was entitled *D. H. Lawrence: An Unprofessional Study* (1932), was clearly influenced by Lawrence's work. Although her characters lack Lawrence's complexity and her plots lack his excitement, she shares his interest in exploring the interior lives of men and women, especially women. Nin said that her aim was to strip through the facades that human beings present to the world in order to get to the hidden self. Having practiced psychotherapy under the supervision of Otto Rank, Nin clearly had the tools for such an investigation. The room of mirrors in which images reflect images becomes a metaphor for Jeanne's attempt to discover the secrets of her soul.

Perhaps the most distinctive characteristics of Nin's style are the visual images and verbal beauties that give a poetic quality to her prose. For example, such phrases as "minuet lightness of step," "gardens cottoned the sound," Jeanne's "stemless" face, "little silver hooks clutching emptiness," and the "glass bushes" convey the dreamlike quality of life as it is lived under the glass bell.

*Sandra Hanby Harris*

# UNDER THE BANYAN TREE

*Author:* R. K. Narayan (1906-2001)
*Type of plot:* Sketch
*Time of plot:* The 1940's
*Locale:* Somal, a remote village in southern India
*First published:* 1947

> *Principal characters:*
> NAMBI, a traditional storyteller
> THE VILLAGERS

*The Story*

"Under the Banyan Tree," the title story in R. K. Narayan's collection *Under the Banyan Tree, and Other Stories* (1985), appeared originally in his earlier volume, *An Astrologer's Day, and Other Stories* (1947). It is the story of an old-fashioned story-teller named Nambi, in whom Narayan has created a character of mythic dimensions. The story radiates its author's deep love for tradition as he, using the omniscient point of view, nostalgically evokes the Old World charm of oral storytelling by showcasing Nambi.

The story begins in a remote village in southern India where people live "in a kind of perpetual enchantment," unmindful of their dismal surroundings. The "enchanter" is Nambi, the storyteller whose tales work like magic to transmute the drab existence of the villagers. The story focuses on Nambi, an old man of indeterminate age. Though illiterate, he is gifted with a fertile imagination. He can weave a story in his head with great ease, at least one every month, and then he narrates the story to an eager audience in an open space in moonlight.

The narrator further reveals Nambi's simple, tranquil, and austere lifestyle. Nambi lives in the front portion of a little temple dedicated to the goddess Shakti, at the end of the village. A man with no material possessions, he spends most of his day in the shade of the Banyan tree in front of the temple. On Friday evenings, he serves as the temple priest and leads the villagers in the worship of the goddess.

The narrator recounts in detail the rituals and the method of Nambi's storytelling. On the night Nambi is to tell a story, he lights a small lamp and keeps it at the trunk of the banyan tree to send a signal to the villagers. At moonrise, men, women, and children rush to the temple and gather under the banyan tree, while Nambi sits inside the temple, before the goddess, lost in deep meditation. When he comes out ablaze with inspiration, he takes his seat on the stone platform in front of the temple and begins the story with a question and a dramatic gesture to capture the attention of the audience.

Building each story on an epic scale, he takes several days to finish it. He narrates continuously for three hours each night, luxuriating in every detail of the setting, the characters, and the episodes. His vivid imagination makes everything come alive for the audience. With a dramatic modulation of his voice, he even sings the songs appropriate to the occasion. At the end of the story, he and the entire audience go into the temple to offer their thanks to the goddess.

This goes on for years. Nambi makes the villagers laugh; he makes them cry. Transported on the wings of his imagination, they forget the harsh realities of life and live in the enchanted world created by him.

The turning point in the story comes when Nambi experiences a gradual but steady deterioration in his narrative powers. One evening, for example, he begins the story and goes on for an hour or so, but then he begins to falter and stumble. He prays to the goddess, but he cannot remember the story. The villagers wait patiently for his story to continue, but he just sits there staring at the ground. One by one, the villagers slip away. When the same thing happens a few more times, people stop taking notice of the lit lamp at the trunk of the banyan tree.

After some time, Nambi goes to the village one morning and makes a personal appeal to the people to come to the temple because he has a great story to tell. At night a large crowd shows up under the banyan tree in great curiosity. When Nambi comes out of the temple, he tells them humbly that his storytelling was a gift from the goddess and that she has taken the gift away. He then adds that these are his "last words on this earth" and that this is his "greatest story." Speaking these words, he silently goes back into the temple and spends the rest of his life in "one great consummate silence."

### Themes and Meanings

Because "Under the Banyan Tree" celebrates the life and art of an illiterate storyteller, its underlying theme is the concept of art as divine inspiration. Nambi's character embodies and exemplifies this concept. He represents the maker or magician who dreams up fantastic tales. Because he never learned how to read and write, he believes that his talent to weave enchanting stories in his imagination and then deliver them eloquently to his audience is a gift from the goddess. Being a staunch and self-effacing devotee, he regards himself as only a medium through which the goddess speaks. His isolation in the sanctum, his deep meditation, and his dreamlike inspiration before the commencement of each story all seem to support this interpretation. When he comes out of the temple in a trancelike state, he looks like an old wizard, with his forehead resplendent with ash, vermilion, and the white heat of imagination.

Narayan's recurrent use of a number of images and symbols in the story further supports this interpretation. For example, Nambi attributes his creative powers to the goddess Shakti. The word *shakti* literally means power or energy. The goddess Shakti, as consort of the god Siva, represents the creative energy of the universe in Hindu art and mythology. Further, every time Nambi tells a story, he lights a small lamp and keeps it at the trunk of the banyan tree. A lamp, which illuminates, projects, and transfigures ordinary objects, is an established symbol of romantic imagination. Also, Nambi tells stories only during moonlight. In Indian mythology, moonlight is regarded as the counterpart on Earth of *amrita*, the heavenly drink of the gods. Finally,

Nambi's deep meditation in the dark sanctum symbolizes his plunge into the deep reservoirs of his collective unconscious to bring out material for his narratives.

Narayan seems to subscribe to the view that because the art of narration or any other artistic creativity is a divine gift, the artist should use it for the pleasure as well as moral and spiritual exaltation of all humankind. That Nambi uses his narrative gift for the entertainment and moral uplift of the villagers is clearly seen in the impact his stories have on them. As the story points out, "the village folk considered Nambi a sort of miracle, quoted his words of wisdom, and lived on the whole in an exalted plane of their own, though their life in all other respects was hard and drab." Overall, the story reinforces the theme that all creative art is generated by an inexplicable force, not through a person's learning a craft or receiving academic training.

*Style and Technique*

In keeping with the chronological movement of the story's plot, Narayan uses a simple and straightforward narrative style, without his habitual use of intermittent irony. The only ironic twist comes at the story's end when Nambi's greatest story turns out to be his vow of absolute silence for the rest of his life. Because the story is steeped in Hindu ethos and sensibility, it contains several references to Indian epics, history, myth, and legend.

Narayan's choice of the omniscient author-narrator vantage is controlled by the demands of plot and character. Because Narayan admires the timeless beauty of the traditional art of oral storytelling, as is clearly evident from the tales in his *Gods, Demons, and Others* (1964), his use of an omniscient narrator is necessary to show Nambi in an admirable rather than an ironic light. Consequently, he maintains an enthusiastic, exalted, and sympathetic tone through most of the narration.

Narayan has created the story's setting like a picture in perspective. He provides the physical as well as the spiritual background against which the narrative action takes place. In the opening paragraph, with a few deft strokes of the pen, he paints a dreary picture of the village, with its narrow, twisted lanes, sprawling cottages, unclean sources of water, poor sanitary conditions, and puddles of stagnant water in every house drain, breeding all kinds of diseases. However, the story transcends this physical setting to reveal the true spirit of the village people, who lead a life of pristine innocence, uncorrupted by the influence of urban civilization. The village community consists of simple, caring, and open-hearted people who admire and support the storyteller.

As the story unfolds, the physical setting recedes into the background, and the focus shifts to the spiritual setting, which serves the development of character, theme, and action. The secluded temple, situated at the edge of the forest, and the sprawling banyan tree in the front of the temple provide the most natural and serene environment for Nambi's contemplation and creativeness. Serving as the fountainhead of Nambi's divine inspiration, this setting becomes the focal point of the story.

*Chaman L. Sahni*

# UNDER THE LION'S PAW

*Author:* Hamlin Garland (1860-1940)
*Type of plot:* Regional, realism
*Time of plot:* The late 1800's
*Locale:* Cedar County, in a midwestern state (probably Wisconsin)
*First published:* 1891

> *Principal characters:*
> TIM HASKINS, a displaced farmer
> STEPHEN COUNCIL, a good-hearted farmer
> JIM BUTLER, a land speculator

*The Story*

Tim Haskins, with wife and children, have been driven from their farm by bad luck and a scourge of grasshoppers. On their way to an undetermined destination, they reach Stephen Council's farm and ask to rest there before continuing their journey. Council and his wife not only give them food and a place to rest but also, after hearing Haskins's story, persuade him to consider settling on a nearby vacated farm.

The farm is owned by Jim Butler, who acquired it along with several other farms through legal but ethically questionable mortgage foreclosures. Council, apparently unaware of Butler's methods of land speculation, assumes Butler is an honorable businessperson who will give Haskins a good deal. He introduces them, and they soon agree that Haskins can rent the place. Because it is quite dilapidated, Butler sets the rent and the selling price quite low, commensurate with the farm's poor condition (and to some extent clearly within Haskins's ability to pay). Though Haskins can barely afford to make such a commitment, he agrees to rent for three years with an option to either renew the lease or buy the farm at the end of the three-year period.

For three years, Haskins, with his wife and children, works the farm. Council and some of the other farmers in the area lend him tools and seed, and with backbreaking toil, the Haskins family brings about a metamorphosis in the place. They make all kinds of improvements: new fencing, a garden, a pigpen, a new well, and kitchen renovations. Along with the physical improvements, Haskins also manages to produce a fine crop of wheat. Things are going so well that he believes he can afford to purchase the farm.

Butler comes to see Haskins at the farm and is impressed and pleased with the many improvements. When Haskins says he thinks he can afford to buy the farm, Butler tells him that the purchase price is now twice the amount he cited when Haskins first rented the property. He justifies the huge increase by pointing to the improvements.

Haskins is stunned. He argues that the price increase is unreasonable because all the improvements were made at his expense, in terms of both money and labor. However, Butler is unmoved because he knows that if Haskins will not purchase or rent the property, someone else will. Either way, he will profit handily.

Haskins is enraged by the unfairness and injustice of the predicament and grabs up a pitchfork with the intention of killing Butler. He declares that no one else will be robbed by the unscrupulous thief and liar. However, before he can commit the act, he catches sight of his baby daughter toddling across the yard and realizes what he stands to lose in killing Butler. Resigned, he agrees to buy the farm and orders Butler off his land, threatening to kill him if he ever sets foot on it again.

### Themes and Meanings

Hamlin Garland's early works, such as "Under the Lion's Paw," deal with the unromantic life of harried generations on the farms and in the towns of America's prairie states. Believing, as he stated in his theory of "veritism," that a writer must write of "what is" with an eye toward "what is to be," he wrote about the hard life in the midwestern states of Wisconsin, Iowa, and North and South Dakota, which he called the Middle Border. He aimed to show what real farm life was like as opposed to the idealized portrayals prevalent at the time in nineteenth century literature. He used commonplace themes with everyday incidents and ordinary people in an attempt to discredit the notion that literary heroes and heroines must be people with unusual qualities.

Garland's short stories deal with everyday life, from birth through youth, adulthood, courtship, marriage, and death, and with the tragic and the humorous. Very often his tendency to propagandize would get the better of him, but in "Under the Lion's Paw," his social protest against the practices of the land speculators is subtle and masterfully handled. His main character, Tim Haskins, is an ordinary man who believes in fairness and honesty and the rewards of hard work. He seems to assume that everyone else is pretty much the same as he. When he has to deal with Jim Butler, though, he learns that there are unscrupulous men who will and do take advantage of men like him and profit from their unethical practices. This revelation does not so much defeat him as it demoralizes him and makes him wonder briefly whether his efforts to do the right thing have any merit.

Garland grew up knowing the same kind of farm life that he portrays in his stories of the Middle Border. He found little in that life that was poetic or idyllic. The farmer he knew was a man with hands like claws scratching out a poor living on a farm that belonged to someone else, and his wife was a drudge ceaselessly performing never-ending chores from dawn to dusk. He shows this life in "Under the Lion's Paw." The Haskins family asks nothing more than the chance to work at a life that will provide a reasonable living. When their work is used against them, when Butler turns their hard-won farm improvements into a windfall for himself at their expense, it indicts the economic system prevalent in the United States in the years following the Civil War. Decency and righteousness are shown to be outmatched in the face of avarice and legal loopholes. Garland subtly but forcefully condemns the oppressive tactics of the land speculators without mounting the reformer's soapbox.

### Style and Technique

"Under the Lion's Paw" is a realistic story with characteristics of Garland's veritism. He defines "veritism" as a form of realism that uses true-to-life detail with an impressionist's subjectivity. True-to-life detail is immediately apparent in the somber opening paragraphs as Garland describes the end of a farmer's (Council's) workday. Local color elements, such as the dialogue, help sustain the realism: Council, dressed in a ragged greatcoat against the cold weather, is plowing his field with four horses and calls out to them: "Come round there, boys!—Round agin! . . . *Stiddy*, Kate—stiddy! None o' y'r tantrums, Kittie." Garland captures the regional speech rhythms and words in the fashion of the true local colorist.

In his narration and description, he uses traditional figures of speech—simile, metaphor, personification, alliteration, and others—to fine effect: "squalls of snow," "dripping, desolate clouds," "tenacious as tar," "holding at bay the growl of the impotent, cheated wind," the children had a "sort of spasmodic cheerfulness, as insects in winter revive when laid on the hearth."

In addition to realism, there are elements of naturalism and impressionism in "Under the Lion's Paw." Naturalism is suggested in the fact that Haskins is a victim of circumstances not of his making but of happenstance: the failure of his first farm because of the grasshoppers, the good luck of happening on the Councils and receiving the benefit of their kindness, and the misadventure of meeting and dealing with Jim Butler. All the events of the story, except Haskins's decision not to commit violence against Butler, have occurred because of circumstances outside his control.

Impressionistic elements are not as widely apparent. Garland became acquainted with some American followers of the French Impressionism movement when he was living in Boston from 1885 to 1893, and he became a proponent of the movement. The objectives of Impressionism intrigued him, and he began incorporating certain impressionistic techniques in his work. Though other of his writings show this influence more than does "Under the Lion's Paw," at least one passage in the story demonstrates his leaning toward impressionism: When Garland describes a flock of geese flying overhead, he says they "sprawled sidewise down the wind." The word "sprawl," an odd choice when describing bird flight, conveys Garland's personal reaction, or impression, of the image.

The power of the story is in Haskins's hapless situation. Shown as a husband and father determined to make a decent life for himself and his family, he is clearly willing to make a Herculean effort. When, paradoxically, his efforts become the key reason he could lose all for which he has worked, the reader understands how devastated, hopeless, and betrayed he feels and why he is ready to resort to violence. His basic goodness, however, is recovered at the sight of his child, as he remembers what is important, what he has worked for. Resigned to the injustice and yet determined to keep hoping for a better life, Haskins is a character most readers can relate to, empathize with, and understand. Unlike other literary portrayals of farm life in the United States during the nineteenth century, "Under the Lion's Paw" is one of the most powerful indictments against the cruelties of nature and of human nature.

*Jane Lee Ball*

# UNDER THE ROSE

*Author:* Thomas Pynchon (1937-    )
*Type of plot:* Parody
*Time of plot:* September, 1898
*Locale:* In and around Alexandria and Cairo, Egypt
*First published:* 1961

> *Principal characters:*
> PORPENTINE, a British secret agent
> ROBIN GOODFELLOW, his partner
> LEPSIUS, a foreign spy
> HUGH BONGO-SHAFTSBURY, his partner
> MOLDWOERP, their chief
> VICTORIA WREN, a young Englishwoman

*The Story*

"Under the Rose" centers on the activities of Porpentine, a British spy in Egypt during the Fashoda crisis of 1898, when the British forces of General Kitchener encountered a French expeditionary troop in the contested area of the Sudan. The "Situation," as it is referred to in the story, portends an international crisis that could lead to war in Europe, but the real focus of "Under the Rose" is on a small company of secret agents hoping either to promote or to prevent the final catastrophe.

Porpentine and his partner, Robin Goodfellow, are committed to preventing the "balloon" from "going up," their phrase for the outbreak of an international catastrophe. They are opposed in their efforts by a group of agents, presumably German, who are equally committed to the eventual outbreak of war. The foreign agents are led by an old veteran spy named Moldwoerp and include his subordinate Lepsius and one other agent unfamiliar to the British. Porpentine soon deduces, though, that the other agent is actually one Hugh Bongo-Shaftsbury, supposedly an amateur British archaeologist.

Bongo-Shaftsbury has attached himself to the family of Sir Alastair Wren, who are on tour. In turn, Goodfellow has formed an attachment to Sir Alastair's oldest daughter, Victoria. The entire company of tourists and spies embarks on the train for Cairo, and en route Goodfellow is nearly killed by an Arab hired by Lepsius. Bongo-Shaftsbury also manages to frighten Victoria's young sister, Margaret, when he shows her an electrical throw switch stitched into his arm.

In Cairo, Porpentine observes Goodfellow and Victoria in bed together, although Goodfellow is apparently impotent. Despite this interlude, the British agents get to work. They believe that the foreign spies are planning to assassinate Lord Cromer, the British consul-general, hoping that the incident will precipitate the general crisis into all-out war. To try to force the diplomat to take precautions, the two stage several mock assassination attempts, but Cromer seems to take no notice of them.

Finally, Porpentine and Goodfellow follow the consul-general to an opera house where *Manon Lescaut* (1893) is being performed. There, the two find Moldwoerp and Lepsius arrayed and Bongo-Shaftsbury in the audience with a gun. Porpentine is tempted to shoot Lord Cromer and resolve the situation once and for all, but when confronted by Moldwoerp, he fires "perhaps at Bongo-Shaftsbury, perhaps at Lord Cromer. He could not see and would never be sure which one he had intended as target."

Shoving aside Moldwoerp, whom he tells to "go away and die," Porpentine rejoins Goodfellow. Despite Goodfellow's misgivings, the two pick up Victoria and pursue the foreign agents into the desert, near the Great Sphinx of Gizeh. Porpentine, though, finds himself weaponless and outnumbered and is killed by Bongo-Shaftsbury for having insulted his chief. In the final paragraph of the story, the reader finds Goodfellow years later at Sarajevo, futilely hoping to prevent the rumored assassination of the Archduke Francis Ferdinand that will finally precipitate World War I.

*Themes and Meanings*

In this story, Thomas Pynchon introduces modernist concerns into historical settings, as he also does·in his novels *V.* (1963) and *Gravity's Rainbow* (1973). Porpentine and Goodfellow already seem quaint and out of place in a world that is readying itself for the massive holocausts of the twentieth century. The two operate by "The Rules," the unspoken code of Victorian propriety that governs even international espionage. Even as they seek to prevent an Armageddon, their efforts are comical and the results are temporary at best—the story closes on the outbreak of World War I.

Hints of the new society that plays by different rules are seen in some of the other characters. Victoria, for example, is quite unlike her regal namesake in consenting to go to bed with Goodfellow. Porpentine is especially contemptuous of Bongo-Shaftsbury for frightening Victoria's sister on the train, telling him, "One doesn't frighten a child," but Bongo-Shaftsbury, too, represents a new order. The throw switch in his arm marks him as part human, part machine, one who does not play by the old rules of espionage or even by the old rules of human behavior.

To be machinelike is to strive for a nonhuman purity. That wish drives Moldwoerp and his agents and even begins to affect Porpentine himself. Aiming his gun at Lord Cromer, Porpentine realizes that an assassination would end not only Porpentine's immediate worries but also any reason to worry about Europe itself again. Although Porpentine does falter at this thought, he does still break The Rules by insulting Moldwoerp. For that insult, Porpentine pays the ultimate price.

Underlying the characters and actions in this story is the theme of paranoia that runs through all of Pynchon's works. Defined in *Gravity's Rainbow* as the belief that everything is ultimately connected and leading to some sinister purpose, paranoia manifests itself in "Under the Rose" both generally and individually. The foreboding of international catastrophe runs through the whole story. Characters seem to have the firm conviction that if the Fashoda crisis does not result in war, then something else will later on, a feeling that is borne out by the story's ending. For Porpentine himself, the international crisis itself seems to be only a symptom of something even larger. Riding toward his final confrontation with Moldwoerp's agents, Porpentine has the suspicion that the foreign spies are really working for something nonhuman, the statistical law of averages that reduces all numbers to zero, all human action to nothing. With Porpentine dead and Goodfellow impotently trying to prevent World War I, the story concludes with the triumph of the inhuman forces that have governed this new century.

### Style and Technique

Pynchon's story is not as stylistically interesting as its later reworking as chapter 3 of *V,* in which the story is fragmented into eight different segments told from eight different points of view. "Under the Rose," though, is a polished work of fiction with a number of interesting aspects. Pynchon's story is told straightforwardly by a third-person narrator, who is limited mostly to Porpentine's point of view. As a result, the reader shares Porpentine's thoughts while also regarding his actions from a distance. This narrative technique, traditional enough in modern literature, gives the story its combination of philosophical rumination and slapstick comedy. Even while Porpentine is trying to make sense out of his assignment and the actions of his partner and his enemies, he is engaged in buffoon-like behavior. He bursts into song in public, takes pratfalls, and engages in comic-opera fake assassination attempts. This combination of metaphysical musings and low comedy is typical of Pynchon's fiction, although Porpentine's surroundings mark the author's first use of a historical and foreign setting (whose details he lifted from a copy of Karl Baedecker's 1899 tourist guide to Egypt).

Also typical of Pynchon's early fiction is his subtle use of allusion. As in most of Pynchon's short stories, there are veiled references to T. S. Eliot's *The Waste Land* (1922). For example, the story opens on a dry, dusty square in Alexandria with Porpentine wishing for rain. When rain comes, though, it is only in squalls and showers, not the steady, nourishing rain that is needed to make deserts bloom. The most obvious references in the story are Giacomo Puccini's opera *Manon Lescaut*: Porpentine tends to burst into arias from the opera and it is *Manon Lescaut* that Lord Cromer is viewing during the assassination attempt. The opera itself is a story of foolish and doomed love that reflects both Goodfellow's affair with Victoria and Porpentine's foolish and romantic nature. At one point, realizing his impending failure, Porpentine compares himself to an inept singer in the Puccini opera.

Although Pynchon himself, in an introduction to his collected short stories, has denigrated "Under the Rose" as an "apprentice effort," the story has an important place among the author's works. It marks the beginning of Pynchon's mature style, which would root itself in *V.* and fully blossom in *Gravity's Rainbow*. In the story, characters are more fully realized than in his earlier fiction, although Pynchon's particular style of comedy is truer and more amusing than in those stories. Perhaps the most interesting aspect of the story is Pynchon's command of physical detail. Working only from secondhand sources such as Baedecker, Pynchon is able to sketch in a physical environment and suggest a world and worldview that go with it. If not as fully accomplished as his later novels, "Under the Rose" marks a very good beginning.

*Donald F. Larsson*

# THE UNKNOWN MASTERPIECE

*Author:* Honoré de Balzac (1799-1850)
*Type of plot:* Psychological
*Time of plot:* 1612
*Locale:* Paris
*First published:* "Le Chef-d'œuvre inconnu," 1831 (English translation, 1885)

> *Principal characters:*
> MASTER FRENHOFER, an old painter
> FRANCOIS PORBUS, a former painter to the king of France
> NICHOLAS POUSSIN, a young painter
> GILLETTE, Poussin's mistress

*The Story*

In "The Unknown Masterpiece," Honoré de Balzac describes two meetings of three artists, the old painter Master Frenhofer, the prominent master Francois Porbus, and the young man Nicholas Poussin. As the story begins, Poussin is hesitating before Porbus's door. When Frenhofer appears and is admitted, Poussin follows him into the only painter's studio he has ever seen. Here he is struck by the first important piece of art in the story, Porbus's painting of the Virgin Mary. To Poussin's surprise, Master Frenhofer criticizes the painting for lacking life. When Poussin objects, the older artists challenge him to prove his right to be in the studio by producing a sketch. To illustrate his own emphasis on life and movement, Frenhofer then applies his own touches of color to Porbus's Virgin Mary, making the figure live as he had insisted he could.

Invited to Frenhofer's home, Poussin sees a second fine painting, the *Adam* of Frenhofer's own master, Mabuse. However, to Frenhofer, this painting, too, lacks some spark of life. As the painters talk, Poussin observes the esteem in which Frenhofer is held, his own lofty standards for art, his wealth, and his knowledge. Poussin is impressed by Frenhofer's description of the painting that he hopes will be his masterpiece, a portrait of a courtesan, Catherine Lescault. Frenhofer, who has devoted ten years to this painting without completing it to his satisfaction, muses that perhaps he simply lacks the right model. At any rate, he refuses to allow anyone to see the painting.

Returning to his garret, Poussin embraces his devoted mistress Gillette, to whom love is all-important, so important that she resents his concentrating on the canvas rather than on her when she poses for him. Hesitantly, Poussin proposes that Gillette pose for Frenhofer. Only when Poussin seems to renounce art for love does she consent, but she warns him that the experiment may result in the end of their love. Perhaps he no longer loves her, she thinks; perhaps, she thinks, he is not worthy of her love.

The second meeting of the three artists takes place three months later. Depressed over his inability to perfect his painting, Frenhofer again thinks of finding a model.

When, however, Poussin offers Gillette in return for allowing Porbus and him to view the painting, Frenhofer refuses, as if their seeing his Catherine Lescault would profane her. However, when Gillette, still doubtful, arrives, Frenhofer agrees. At last admitted to his studio, Poussin and Porbus look in vain for the masterpiece. The canvas that Frenhofer shows them is merely a mass of paint, with no discernible image, except for the tip of a foot, which has escaped the layering of colors. To Frenhofer, the figure is there, brought to life by the paint that conceals it. When Poussin blurts out the truth—that there is nothing on the canvas—Frenhofer falls into despair, but soon his dream recaptures him, and once again he sees his Catherine Lescault. At that moment, Poussin remembers his Gillette, discarded and crying. She rebukes him and says that she hates him. Shown to the door by Frenhofer, the painters are chilled by his farewell. That night he burns his pictures and dies.

## Themes and Meanings

Balzac's concern in "The Unknown Masterpiece" is the problem of reconciling the various opposing forces in life, a problem that is particularly difficult for the artist. The problem is illustrated appropriately in the very pattern of the short story.

The story is divided into two chapters, one entitled "Gillette," the second, "Catherine Lescault." Gillette is the actual mistress of Poussin: She is a devoted young woman who considers love more important than art and feels somehow diminished whenever Poussin uses her as a model. At those times, she senses, he draws away from her and into some visionary world in which she is merely an object. Catherine Lescault, on the other hand, is the vision of Frenhofer, a vision so real that he will not show his painting of her to others, as if such an action would profane their love.

When the other painters see Frenhofer's canvas, they realize that the true painting exists only in Frenhofer's mind. Gillette's prophecy comes true when all three painters are so obsessed with their art that they completely forget her. At the end of the story, she tells Poussin that, although she loves him, she hates him for turning her over to Frenhofer, thus proving that love is far less important than art. In a sense, Poussin loves his art as completely as Frenhofer does. A Catherine Lescault will always win any artist from the Gillettes of this world.

However, if the artists are alike in their devotion to art, they differ in their approach. Having learned his master Mabuse's secret, Frenhofer insists that he can paint the essence, the spirit of his subject. He insists that painters such as Porbus, who cannot decide between the precision of lines and the emotional splash of color, can never truly bring their subjects to life. When the younger painters at last see Frenhofer's masterpiece-in-progress, they realize that in his ten years of seeking essence, of applying layer on layer of color in order to attain the abstraction, he has retreated totally into his own dream. The implication of Balzac's story, then, is that the true artist must combine life and love with art, objectivity with subjectivity, mechanical copying of life with vision of the unknown and unseen essence of life. For all of his genius, Frenhofer has dedicated his life to creating a masterpiece that will always remain unknown.

*Style and Technique*

In a short story that is about art, it is appropriate that Balzac pictures reality as artists would perceive it. For example, young Poussin first sees Frenhofer in the light peculiar to dawn and thinks of his figure in terms of Rembrandt. In Porbus's studio, he again notes the light, as it touches objects in the clutter. Returning to Gillette, he thinks of her love in terms of light, her smile as a sun that shines in darkness. Finally, looking at Frenhofer's "masterpiece," they think that the studio light may be hiding the form that Frenhofer insists lives on his canvas, and they peer at the chaos of color in search of some form before they perceive that all that remains of reality in Frenhofer's painting is the foot of Catherine Lescault.

A consistent metaphor in the story is that of the mistress. Gillette, the living mistress, is justifiably jealous of Poussin's art, whose claim on him is made clear in the first sentences of the story, when he waits at Porbus's door like a lover attending a new mistress. Clearly, when Gillette models for him, he thinks about his vision, not his model, and she senses his infidelity. When he wishes her to model for Frenhofer, she sees this activity as a kind of prostitution, and Poussin admits that the idea makes him feel dirty.

To Frenhofer, all living mistresses are unfaithful eventually, but his ideal—ironically, a courtesan—will always be faithful to him. However, he senses the existence of some imperfection in his painting, which causes him to consider using a live model and finally accepting Gillette. Like Poussin, who is ashamed of having offered Gillette, Frenhofer believes that to show his canvas to other painters would be a kind of prostitution. To him, she is a wife, yet a virgin; in the painting, she is naked and must be clothed before she can be seen. Jealously, he accuses the younger painters of wishing to steal her; even after his brief suspicion that he has created nothing, he turns them away and covers the canvas where he believes Catherine exists. Finally, the metaphor of the mistress is suggested in the last lines, for, once having destroyed his painting, his beloved, Frenhofer can no longer live. Unlike Poussin, who can survive without Gillette's love, but like the most romantic of lovers, Frenhofer must die without his love, even though she is only an artistic illusion.

*Rosemary M. Canfield Reisman*

# UNMAILED, UNWRITTEN LETTERS

*Author:* Joyce Carol Oates (1938-    )
*Type of plot:* Epistolary
*Time of plot:* 1969
*Locale:* Detroit
*First published:* 1969

> *Principal characters:*
> AN UNNAMED WOMAN, the narrator
> GREG, her husband, a Detroit politician
> MR. KATZ, a visiting professor from Boston University who is
>     having an affair with the narrator
> MRS. KATZ, his wife, in Boston
> MARSHA KATZ, their precocious ten-year-old daughter, in Boston

*The Story*

Unmailed letters exist in the everyday world, in some sort of objective reality, yet unwritten letters exist only in the mind. The title of the story is strategic; it forces the reader into the uncomfortable role of voyeur. As the reader looks over the shoulder of the writer of these "letters," the reader is actually looking into her mind, reading her fears and desires. Because of this, the action of the story is not sequential but psychological.

In the first letter, addressed to her parents, the narrator discusses a change of doctors and dentists. The banality of this first paragraph ("everything is lovely here and I hope the same with you") acts as a foil to the remainder of the letter. That is, the first paragraph is recognizable as a letter, perhaps "unmailed," but the second paragraph is truly "unwritten" thoughts directed at the narrator's parents. The change is obvious both in the subject matter ("your courage, so late in life, to take on space") and in diction ("I think of you and I think of protoplasm being drawn off into space"). Such is the tension between writing and thought that the reader must continually bear in mind.

The second letter addresses Marsha Katz, who, it seems, has been sending odd gifts anonymously to the narrator. The narrator and Marsha's father are having an affair; the precocious daughter is trying to incite guilt feelings in the narrator. At times the narrator tries to "read" the little girl's meanings, to interpret her stories; one story deals with a dead white kitten, representing (the narrator thinks) the victimized daughter herself.

She "writes" to Greg, her husband, next. The letter is an attempt to remember their first meeting, but its more submerged meanings deal with her inability to carry children to term and with her infidelity—her feelings of inadequacy and guilt. She refers to Marsha's father, her lover, as "X." She cannot bear to write (think) his name before her faithful husband.

Next she addresses her "darling," Marsha's father. She recounts a dream of his death, "mashed into a highway." His face is so badly disfigured that it is unrecognizable. In the same way that she converts him into a nonentity in the previous letter, an "X," so here she psychologically removes his face. She also dreams of suicide; the two deaths become equivalent in her dreamworld.

As the story proceeds, the narrator reveals the details of her marriage and of her affair. Greg has been a sincere, but at times ineffectual, politician in Detroit during the racial turmoil of the late 1960's. Ridden with guilt, the narrator writes to Greg of her infidelity with Katz; falling in love a second time, she says, is "terrifying, bitter, violent." However, she does nothing to become fulfilled in this new love; her letters are unmailed, unwritten. Writing to Mrs. Katz in Boston, to Mother and Father in the Southwest, to an undefined Editor, the narrator demonstrates her paralysis, her claustrophobia, her inability to confront overtly the forces that have shaped, and continue to shape, her emotional life.

In the last long letter, these frustrations culminate. It is addressed to Greg and appears to be a straightforward confession. Although it begins "I want to tell you everything," the second paragraph reflects the same tortured mind: "I seem to want to tell you something else." Marsha Katz has just attempted suicide. Mr. Katz, who must return to Boston immediately to be with Marsha and his wife, has called the narrator, asking her to accompany him to the airport. He is shaken by his daughter's desperation; she is angry that the daughter has apparently conquered the mistress. In this emotional chaos, the two lovers sneak off to a deserted stairway in the airport to make love. He leaves. She has difficulty finding her "husband's car"; feeling literally and figuratively soiled, she checks into the airport motel to bathe and to write the preceding confession. The conclusion of the story is formed by the first words of a letter addressed to "My darling." She may be writing to Greg (if the confession means something), or she may be writing to Katz (if it does not).

*Themes and Meanings*

Because the action of the story occurs primarily within the consciousness of one character, Joyce Carol Oates has necessarily limited her control over meaning. One must remember to distinguish what Oates means from what her character means.

This writer of unmailed, unwritten letters is trapped in a tortuous world of uncertainties. She looks to Mother, Father, husband, and lover for a sense of security; her parents are literally and figuratively distant, her husband is good but ineffectual, her lover is appealing but weak. At one point, in a letter addressed to "The Editor," she asks the startling question, "Why are white men so weak, so feeble?" Rephrased, it might be, "Why cannot the men in my life make me a strong woman?" The question comes from the vantage point of a deep-seated neurosis, from the neurotic position of being a well-educated, middle-class woman in the United States who regresses into an infantile dependency.

The nature and consequences of this neurosis manifest themselves in the very form of the story. Because Oates allows her subject to reveal herself through a series of unuttered utterances, the story remains open-ended, unresolved. The reader remains trapped in the claustrophobic confines of an unproductive mind. The form of the story is in itself meaningful. The narrator exists within the cycle of modern lovings and leavings. Her life is directionless, pathetic. She is forced to make love in transit—on a staircase in an airport.

Appropriately, the collection of stories in which this story is included is entitled *The Wheel of Love, and Other Stories* (1970); as this story ends, the wheel is about to take another turn. Oates may be questioning whether the identity of this last "darling" makes a difference at all to her troubled letter unwriter.

### Style and Technique

Stories told by means of a series of letters (called epistolary narratives) were rather common in the eighteenth century; in the twentieth century, however, such a form of storytelling is rare. For this and other reasons, Oates's story is considered experimental.

Oates takes a somewhat obsolete form of narration and radically modernizes it. Because these letters have no specified destination (and therefore no respondents), one's attention is not, as it conventionally would be, on an interchange of two or more points of view, but rather on the workings of a single psyche. One's attention is paradoxically not on communication but on an inability to communicate (hence, "unmailed" and "unwritten").

The style of the work follows from the epistolary noncommunication. That is, it becomes an interior monologue that admits a broad range of styles. Whatever such a person (a white, middle-class, well-educated woman of the 1960's) could think is, in this story, stylistically appropriate. Oates's style is therefore a not very distant cousin of the stream-of-consciousness technique.

At times the prose sounds like letter-writing ("I don't know how to begin this letter except to tell you"), at times like metaphysical speculation ("that delicate hint of death"); at times, it is reminiscent ("we met about this time years ago"); at times, the prose exists in a sexually vivid present tense ("he kisses my knees, my thighs, my stomach"). In short, the story contains an ever-changing style that reflects the nuances of the panic-stricken woman who is the story's center and its circumference.

*Mark Sandona*

# UNPERFORMED EXPERIMENTS HAVE NO RESULTS

*Author:* Janette Turner Hospital (1942-    )
*Type of plot:* Psychological
*Time of plot:* The 1980's
*Locale:* Ontario, Canada, and Queensland, Australia
*First published:* 1992

> *Principal characters:*
> PHILIPPA, the narrator, an Australian writer living in Canada
> BRIAN, her longtime friend, a scientist

*The Story*

"Unperformed Experiments Have No Results" is made up of several seemingly unrelated events, the sequence of which the narrator no longer knows. The events include Philippa's sitting on her dock observing a man rowing a canoe upstream, her memory of climbing a waterfall in Queensland with her friend Brian during their last year in high school, a dream in which she sees the body of Brian on a submerged suspension bridge at the end of her dock, and her discovery that Brian is ill and has disappeared. A fifth "event" is Philippa's reading historical accounts of French Jesuits who came to Ontario in the seventeenth century.

Much of the story is taken up by Philippa's experience on a summer afternoon when, while sitting on her dock, she sees a man paddling upriver in a birch-bark canoe against a strong current. She describes in great detail the man, "all manic energy and obstinacy," fighting the stream with almost supernatural strength. Thinking she recognizes something about the man's physical gestures, she is astonished when he looks up and she thinks it is her friend Brian. Although she knows it cannot be Brian, who is in either Japan or Australia, she is mesmerized by the man until he paddles out of sight. Later at a dinner party with her husband, she hears about a birch-bark canoe having washed up on shore. When someone says the authorities are searching for the body of the man, Philippa says she hopes they do not find him.

In a second section of the story, Philippa remembers her senior year in high school when she and her friend Brian climbed a waterfall in their native Queensland, Australia. When they reached the top, they talked about their "unmapped future." Brian said that he hoped to go to Japan after university to do research in physics and told Philippa that she would probably end up in Africa or Canada.

In the third section, Philippa dreams she is at the end of her dock when she notices that Wolfe Island across the way has been transformed into a rain forest in Queensland. She then sees a submerged suspension bridge between her dock and Wolfe Island, with Brian, his eyes open but unseeing, lying beneath the water, looking like Ophelia from William Shakespeare's *Hamlet, Prince of Denmark* (c. 1600-1601). She asks, "Alas then, are you drowned?" He answers "Drowned, drowned."

When Philippa logs on to her e-mail to tell Brian about the dream, she sees an undated message from him, saying he is going away and that he thinks it is a pity that they cannot go back to when they were young together. She then quotes a letter she received from her mother telling her that Brian has some nervous system disorder and that after refusing treatment has flown to Tokyo. She sends daily e-mail messages to Brian, trying to goad him into responding, but she gets no answer.

The story ends with Philippa watching for news about the discovery of the missing man, relieved that no body is found. She reads the accounts of the seventeenth century Jesuit missionaries, checks her e-mail every day, sends out messages, and tries to formulate theories to account for the parallel nature of the events.

### Themes and Meanings

Typical of Janette Turner Hospital's stories, "Unperformed Experiments Have No Results" is a story in which a personal experience of considerable emotional significance is controlled by the central character's attempt to understand the philosophical significance of the event. In this story, the philosophical issue of time and accident is announced in the first two paragraphs when Philippa says she is no longer certain of chronology and finds herself obsessed with the neatness of patterns of chance and the random conjunction of events. However, she says the closer she tries to focus her memory about the sequence of the events that seem so randomly conjoined, the hazier things become. She theorizes that this is the result of the scientific notion that a person cannot engage in an act of observation without changing the thing observed.

The man she sees paddling the canoe and who she thinks is her friend Brian is an emblem of her perception of him—persistent, determined, adventurous, and battling against all odds—all qualities that she feels she does not possess. Brian is a risk taker and a man of some passion, thus appearing in her dream as Ophelia. Philippa, however, like Hamlet, can only look on and is never able to take the same kinds of risky plunges that Brian does. Although there is no indication of any romantic relationship between Philippa and Brian, they do seem complementary soul mates: he the scientist, but passionate and adventurous, and she the artist, but cool and repressed.

The theme of decisions avoided and roads not taken is paralleled by the theme of time in the story. When Brian says in his message to her, "Pity we can't go backwards," she considers writing to Brian's mother telling her that Brian is not lost but has simply lost track of time. She thinks that given the rules of relativity, she and Brian could unclimb the waterfall and go back through the looking glass to watch the future before it became the present. However, Philippa is much too logical to believe in such fantasies; she is simply recalling Brian's own chiding her that artsy types like her do not know the basic facts about relativity.

When Philippa hears about the birch-bark canoe being washed up without the man, she fantasizes a conversation with Brian in which he scolds her for living in a vague world of her mind, making things up and believing they are real. When she tries to argue with him in her fantasy that she verifies things the same way he does, checking around to determine whether the story about the man in the birch-bark canoe is a figment of her mind or an actual event, he says he is not even going to respond to that. Philippa imagines Brian telling her the trick is to approach old problems from a new angle every time because half the battle is how one frames the question. "Unperformed experiments have no results," he says. Although Philippa agrees with this statement, she is more reluctant than Brian to take experimental chances. Brian's being lost (like the man in the canoe) may suggest the danger of taking chances and fighting against the current, but Philippa's timid reluctance leaves her becalmed and safe but somehow unfulfilled.

*Style and Technique*

The style of "Unperformed Experiments Have No Results" reflects the mind of the first-person narrator, Philippa: It is meditative, ruminative, and discursive. From the very beginning of the story, her primary concern is a detached, philosophical interest in the curious way that events come together to suggest some significance. "Spooked by coincidence," she has the typical writer's need to create a pattern; not content with meaningless accident, she finds the neatness of coincidence thought provoking. When she does not find a meaningful connection between events, she imagines or creates one. Because of this obsession, she can never be quite sure what the man in the canoe has to do with Brian or what the seventeenth century Jesuit missionaries she reads about have to do with the man in the canoe. However, writerlike, she persists in exploring these connections, reading about the survival against all odds of the priests and connecting that to the survival against all odds of the man in the canoe. If he is not found, if he survives, then in an imaginative way, Brian survives also. Whenever she wants to question herself, to challenge herself in her beliefs and opinions, she always summons up Brian, who knows very well that she lives more in her creative imagination than she does in the real world.

"Unperformed Experiments Have No Results" is thus a kind of philosophic set piece in which observations, readings, and emotional experiences all become grist for the writer's mill. The narrator who has assembled all these seemingly unrelated bits of experience cannot be sure whether the events actually happened in real time and space or in her mind because what happens in her reading and in her dreams and fantasies has the same reality as what happens in real life. The style of the story reflects this uncertainty.

*Charles E. May*

# AN UNSOUND SLEEP

*Author:* Nhât Tiên (1936-    )
*Type of plot:* Political, domestic realism
*Time of plot:* The early 1960's
*Locale:* Towns in South Vietnam
*First published:* 1969?

*Principal characters:*
OLD PHAN, an old man
MISS PHAN, his daughter
SU, his daughter's boyfriend and later husband

## The Story

"An Unsound Sleep" takes place in Vietnam during the Vietnam War. The main concern of the story is how people's lives are changed by political censorship and war. The story traces the Phan family's downfall after a daughter and her husband participate in Buddhist demonstrations. Nhât Tiên skillfully incorporates descriptions of the local lifestyle and historical facts in his fiction.

The story begins in early afternoon in what is typically a boisterous, poor part of town. Old Phan is watching beggars and finishing off some dry shrimp and alcohol. He gets up to leave for the marketplace, then spots a rather cheap eating place. Again drinking alcohol and eating dry shrimps, he hears someone yelling about a fire at Lo-Gom hamlet. After expressing surprise, he finishes up his food and drink and heads for a park. He hears news of revolution in his state of half-sobriety. Afterward Old Phan heads for home.

After a day's work as a porter for numerous storehouses in the marketplace Cholon, Old Phan usually sits on his doorstep enjoying a drink and peanuts. However, since the Buddhist demonstration, his daughter has been coming home from her greengrocer job later and later. Old Phan is very annoyed by the fact that dinner has been left to grow cold lately because his daughter, Miss Phan, is always late. He grows very impatient with her increasing lack of punctuality, when she used to get home before 7:00 P.M.

When Miss Phan finally comes home, Old Phan furiously reprimands her and accuses her of sneaking off with some man to some city corner for a love tryst. He warns her not to bring scandal and shame to the family. Miss Phan reassures him that she has not done and will never do such things, and that if she finds a lover, she will introduce him properly so no shame would be brought on the family.

Miss Phan tells her father why she is often late and shows him a stack of leaflets. Old Phan scolds her for going to pagodas and taking part in the Buddhist demonstrations. He fears his daughter's illegal activities will place them in great danger from the government. She reassures him that she will be fine, dismissing his fears about censorship.

A few days later, Miss Phan brings home Su, a man she met at the demonstrations, to meet her father. Su is arrested two weeks later for being active in the Buddhist demonstrations, and Miss Phan also disappears. Old Phan visits Su in prison and worries about his daughter. After he is released from prison, Su marries Miss Phan.

Su loses his job working in a garage in Saigon, and the now-pregnant Miss Phan and her father become worried about their livelihood. The couple has to leave the city, and Su looks for a job elsewhere while Old Phan stays behind. One day he receives a letter from his daughter and has it read to him because he is illiterate. The letter says Su lost his promised garage job but has found another one at a bus parking lot even though his wages are poor.

Physically weakened, Old Phan staggers in his porter job. A few days later, he is thrown out of his house because he can no longer afford his rent. He sells what few valuables he has to pay the landlord. Haggard and weak, Old Phan leaves Lo-Gom hamlet for Saigon and picks pockets to survive. He sleeps in corners and on park benches with newspapers for a blanket. The only things of value that Old Phan carries with him are his daughter's letters and her wedding photo wrapped in newspaper.

*Themes and Meanings*

The dominant subject matter is war and government oppression. Though not clearly stated by Nhât, the setting is various towns in South Vietnam during the earlier part of the war and during the presidency of Ngo Dinh Diem (1955-1963). "An Unsound Sleep" creates a story around the Buddhist demonstrations that actually took place in South Vietnam during 1963. One of the primary reasons that the Buddhist demonstrations were severely suppressed was because the members of the Diem family (which was similar to the Kennedy family in the United States in terms of fame and fortune) were Roman Catholics who fervently disapproved of the monks' suicides. Catholics were a minority in Vietnam during that time, amounting to no more than 10 percent of the population. However, they predominated in government positions because Diem was Catholic. The Buddists' resettlement resulted from Diem's severe discrimination against them.

Miss Phan and Su are portrayed as taking part in the Buddhist demonstrations. Although Nhât does not identify the demonstrations, they are most likely the May, 1963, demonstrations against Diem. The demonstrators are fired on by police. Miss Phan and Su are arrested and imprisoned along with thousands of high school and grade school students who are involved in protests against the Diem government. Although Diem is never mentioned by name in the story, readers familiar with the history of the Vietnam War will recognize what regime was ruling South Vietnam and remember how oppressive it was. Readers may also remember that at least seven Buddhist monks set themselves on fire to protest the repression, but Diem dismissed these suicides as publicity stunts and promptly arrested fourteen hundred monks.

The author illustrates that Diem government as no better than the communists, who ruled North Vietnam at the same time, by the fact that his characters are promptly jailed and stripped of their livelihoods when they show discontentment with the government. Almost as if they had been subject to communist reeducation, Miss Phan and Su lose their jobs and have to leave the city to find jobs in other areas of the country.

The loss of jobs is also a dominant motif in "An Unsound Sleep." The first scene in the story is of beggars doing what they do to survive—begging. Economic downfall and financial difficulty are recurrent motifs throughout the narrative, although the story never addresses the cause. This economic motif is an allusion to the fact that the Vietnamese people were discontented with their government and viewed the Diem government as corrupt. Living under the Diem regime was really no better than living under the communist regime, especially for Buddhists. As a result, the communists of North Vietnam had many Buddhist sympathizers. Miss Phan and Su are not explicitly depicted as communist sympathizers; however, they talk about revolution and are imprisoned for distributing leaflets and participating in the Buddhist demonstrations.

*Style and Technique*

Even in translation, Nhât's concise but ample prose style is still evident. He conveys the local flavor through vivid and vibrant descriptions of urban life in war-torn towns and cities of Vietnam during the early 1960's. The author favors descriptions of everyday, banal sights and activities, such as beggars eating filthy rice and Old Pham's penchant for rice alcohol with dry shrimps, not to mention his dwindling monetary flow because of that penchant. These details are banal and mundane; however, because they are part of the fabric of Vietnamese life and unfamiliar to Western readers, they may seem exotic. These details are one of the salient features that produce the overall effect of the local and ethnic milieu of "An Unsound Sleep."

As demonstrated by his portrayal of the lowest class of people in war-torn Vietnam, the author's sympathies lie with the common person. His choice of subject is a literary convention or technique used to deliver a larger message that the poor and unrepresented are being trampled on by the government, the well-to-do, and the privileged.

Old Pham and his daughter are character types that represent their socioeconomic class and the proletariat. The old man and his daughter are not unique and important as individuals but as representatives, as stand-ins, for the masses. The author uses these character types in order to convey his critical view of the political suppression of the Buddhist demonstrations. The reader can see that Nhât is much more sympathetic with the politics of North Vietnam than with the supposedly democratic South Vietnam.

Nhât uses a basic literary convention of a simple family, socioeconomic class, political struggle, and locality to create a profile sketch of the overall sentiment and popular discontentment of the time in a country fighting a civil war.

*Hanh Nguyen*

# UP AMONG THE EAGLES

*Author:* Luisa Valenzuela (1938-    )
*Type of plot:* Magical Realism, mythological
*Time of plot:* The 1980's
*Locale:* A remote village in Mexico
*First published:* "Donde viven las águilas," 1983 (English translation, 1988)

> *Principal character:*
> THE NARRATOR, an unnamed city woman

*The Story*

"Up Among the Eagles" is told in the first person through the consciousness of a woman who journeys through a primitive indigenous world and discovers a magical dimension. The interaction with mythical characters and a series of rituals lead her to a metaphysical awakening and metamorphosis.

At the beginning, the narrator refers to the events that led her to live in a high place in the mountains, up among the eagles. She lives there because one day, after she had climbed up a path, she realized that the cliffs on the way down were too dangerous and prevented her return to the city below. In her new surroundings, she got to know hunger and misery and had to trade her material possessions for food. She kept her Polaroid camera because the villagers had no use for it.

The protagonist describes her difficult life in the village. The inhabitants seem like strange creatures to her. They use a meaningless language, full of silences and with no references to the past or the future, and they live in the immediate present, with no notion of time, verb tenses, or conjugations. In this static and quiet place, time endures and keeps the local people looking the same until they die—then their corpses are taken to a secret city and mummified.

Secretly, the woman appreciates being subject to the passage of time because it makes her feel alive. Because there are no mirrors, she takes photographs of herself so she can see her evolution as she ages. The fate of her existence after the film runs out worries her. One day, when the villagers keep dancing in the marketplace to a mournful sound and seem not to see her, the fearful protagonist decides to take the last remaining picture.

In the darkness, a sudden light and the sound of death make the protagonist trip the shutter of the camera. She sees that the photo does not contain an image of her, only a blurry vision of a stone wall. As if summoned by the light and the sound, she runs desperately to the city of the dead because she wants to leave all the images of her face to the mummies. At the end, she hopes to go down freely, with the last photo in which she sees herself as a stone.

*Themes and Meanings*

In this story, as in many of her other works, Luisa Valenzuela expresses her interest in women's relationship to language, myths, rituals, and nature. Searching is a basic theme in Valenzuela's writings. The protagonist in "Up Among the Eagles" is the narrator herself. Unnamed—reflecting her universality and lack of connections to anyone—she undertakes a symbolic journey out of the abyss of a valley and up to the peaks where the eagles dwell. She travels back in time through a natural world that she does not understand well until the end, when, in a brilliantly lit scene—signifying inner enlightenment and self-awareness at the moment of a literal or symbolic death—she is finally empowered to see and understand the mythical world around her.

The narrator, a city woman, arrives in the archaic country town wearing shoes and carrying a watch and a camera, among other things—all items of the modern world. Her relationship to nature may lead to an analysis of the meaning of civilization and barbarism. Representing modern society, she associates time with progress. She is unable to comprehend the functioning of a language that is only insinuated and not verbalized and thinks of the native culture and villagers as strange because they are different.

Although the protagonist is focused on external reality and the preservation of her physical self, the villagers concentrate on the inner reality and the creation of mental images that they materialize into fantastic visions—making magical thinking visible. She refuses to be like them and live in subjective contemplation. Protective of her rationality and existence, she avoids participating in religious ceremonies and ritual slow dances that emphasize a common identity and remind her of death. Because she equates immobility, sameness, and eternity with death, she struggles for movement, self-realization, and change. She verifies the concrete passage of time by capturing herself and the fleeting moments in the tangible and visible form of the photographs.

Whenever the principal character begins to feel lost, isolated, suffocated, and invisible in this mysterious and timeless environment, she needs to reaffirm her ideas about time and death. In the successive and linear arrangement of the snapshots—in reality a series of fragmented and multiplied images of herself—she is able to observe the marks of aging on her face but not the mystery of her inner world. The perception of the chronological movement of time by means of the photographs makes her feel alive and more secure. The protagonist dreads running into the mummies in the city of the dead; however, she freezes or "mummifies" herself as a reproduced image in each picture—if this is discovered by the villagers, she may be scorned or revered as a goddess for materializing herself in such a way.

The revelation of the blankness in the last photo provides the climax of the story and signals the end of the narrator's control of images in space and time. The blankness visualizes nonexistence, signifies an absence and silence, and suggests the disappearance or death of corporeal life. In her voyage through the world of nature and before her disintegration, the protagonist had acquired the color of the clay of the landscape. At the end of the story, in the final phase of her quest, she undergoes a utopian transformation into a new reality; she sees herself as a stone rolling down freely and with audacity to her origins—meaning that she has attained the features and the essence of nature, represented by the mountain and the rocks, in the magical yet real world in which time is cyclical and rebirth is possible.

*Style and Technique*

"Up Among the Eagles," like other stories in Valenzuela's book of the same title, depicts the land, language, and mythical culture of rural Mexico in a pictorial way. The classical voyage of adventures and trials provides a thematic and structural framework for the narrative. This tale of self-discovery and transformation is told informally to an audience by a narrator who is trying to make believable what seems to be unbelievable. Interior monologue, dialogues, impersonal discourse with a distancing effect, and numerous rhetorical questions are included in the narration to create a sense of supposition, doubt, and ambiguity with different possibilities of interpretation.

Valenzuela believes that reality and truth are fictional constructs of the mind and linguistic inventions, and as such, they are not always what they seem to be. In this story, she strives to uncover another dimension of reality and a different way of thinking. She dramatizes an existential search for something not defined—perhaps for another truth or another face of reality—with challenging complexity and surrealistic style. The author shrouds the landscape in semidarkness and creates a surrealistic atmosphere through the insurmountable distance that must be overcome between the world up on the mountains and the world down below in the valley. The phantasmagoric effect is achieved by the merging worlds of the living and the dead. The focus on myth and magic, the interplay of fantasy and reality, the theme of the quest, and the role of language in fiction connects this story with Magical Realism and the literary movement known as the Latin American Boom.

The narrator, obsessed with death and fearful of the unknown, undergoes a sense of disintegration of the self. She takes photos of herself in search of self-recognition—likewise, the whole village creates a city of the dead as a mirror city of itself in a game of doubles, space, and time. In a climactic scene, at the end of the story, she becomes disembodied and her former self vanishes in the last picture. However—as in the case of her identity, which is deconstructed and constructed again as it transforms itself into a new reality—in a cyclical and mythical world, there is always hope of a future existence and voice created from nothingness and evolving into a narrative—as the literary telling of this story exemplifies.

*Ludmila Kapschutschenko-Schmitt*

# UP THE BARE STAIRS

*Author:* Seán O'Faoláin (John Francis Whelan, 1900-1991)
*Type of plot:* Social realism
*Time of plot:* The early 1900's and 1930's
*Locale:* County Cork and the city of Cork, Ireland
*First published:* 1948

> *Principal characters:*
> SIR FRANCIS JAMES NUGENT, the protagonist, an eminent civil
> servant
> BROTHER ANGELO, a monk, Nugent's teacher
> THE NARRATOR, Nugent's traveling companion

## The Story

"Up the Bare Stairs" opens on a train traveling through Ireland. The first-person, anonymous narrator describes his traveling companion as a big man, about sixty years old, "dressed so conventionally that he might be a judge, a diplomat, a shopwalker, a shipowner, or an old-time Shakespearean actor." The narrator notices the man's initials, F. J. N., on a hat case and reads in the paper that a Francis James Nugent has been made a baronet for his military service. The ensuing conversation and the fact that the boy went to the same school, West Abbey, leads to Nugent's recollections.

This section, the main action in the story, is narrated by Nugent, as the narrator assumes the role of listener. At West Abbey, Frankie (Nugent) was very fond of one of his teachers, Brother Angelo. Nugent describes Angelo as handsome and full of life, a man who enjoyed solving quadratic equations as much as he liked playing games with the boys. With the perspective of a sixty-year-old man looking back on his childhood, Nugent says that they were "too fond of him. . . . He knew it . . . and it made him put too much of himself into everything we did . . . perhaps he wasn't the best kind of teacher; perhaps he was too good. . . . With him it wasn't a job, it was his life, it was his joy and his pleasure."

Angelo frequently divided the class into teams representing two political factions, the Molly Maguires and the All for Irelanders. Frankie and Angelo both supported John Redmond of the Molly Maguires. One afternoon, Frankie caused his team to lose. Angelo laughed it off—and kept Frankie two hours after class, knowing that Frankie would be in trouble when he got home. Frankie's politically passionate father, a poor tailor, struggling to send Frankie to school, awakens Frankie's sick mother, a seamstress, with a roar: "A nice disgrace! Kept in because you didn't know your Euclid!" His fury increases when he learns that Frankie let down the Redmond side. The scene ends with the entire family in tears and Frankie promising to work harder.

The next day, Angelo asks Frankie to do the same problem, which he completes perfectly and insolently. Frankie continues to answer questions correctly and rudely, goading Angelo into striking him. Frankie never forgives Angelo, and their personal war continues until Frankie graduates. From then on, Frankie studied every night until midnight. When he sat for the civil service exam, he placed first throughout the British Isles in three out of five subjects. This experience in school caused him to despise and pity his parents.

Here the anonymous traveler begins narrating again, and the purpose for Nugent's trip to Cork is revealed: his mother's funeral. "I meant to bury her in London. But I couldn't do it. Silly, wasn't it?" The story ends with the narrator's description of Nugent with his "poor relations" as they leave the station.

*Themes and Meanings*

The main theme of "Up the Bare Stairs" is the relationship between individuality and (to use a neutral term) "background"—perhaps a more loaded and revealing term might be "culture." The relationship is dealt with problematically, as a tension, not schematically, as a matter to be resolved or explained away. Within a narrow framework, Seán O'Faoláin provides a dynamic series of contrasts: past and present, youth and age, personal and public history, poverty and reward, home and exile, self and community or institution, appearance and reality. These opposites confirm the tension and its continuing active presence in the protagonist's life.

A sense of the protagonist's context is important for an appreciation of the significance of Nugent's rising above it. It has become commonplace to describe the political life of Ireland at the beginning of the twentieth century as stagnant and degraded. (A celebrated representation of this state of affairs is James Joyce's "Ivy Day in the Committee Room.") As "Up the Bare Stairs" makes plain, however, there was much vivid political activity at the local, as distinct from the national, level. This activity is characterized in the story by a passionate, if unthinking, adherence to a given faction. Nugent's father's slavish loyalty to Redmond is presented as an inevitable counterpart to the slavery of tailoring.

It is in reaction against such subjection that Nugent immerses himself in his schoolwork. The moment of confrontation between Nugent and his parents leads to supplanting one form of coherence (the Redmondite) with a more authentic, self-generated one ("the work"). The result of that dedication is to give him the appearance of an Englishman. The "War Services" for which Nugent receives his knighthood have nothing to do with the Irish armed struggle for independence from the British Crown, a struggle whose linguistic repercussions, at least, leave him "indifferent."

Despite Nugent's scholastic brilliance, his extraordinary (perhaps even slightly incredible) success in the public realm, and his strenuous efforts to repudiate the oppressions of the past, he still remains deeply involved with his formative influences. He may have gained autonomy of action, as his war with Angelo suggests, but it remains moot as to whether he has achieved autonomy of spirit. His comprehension of and fidelity to the traditions of his people is impressively enacted in the scene of reunion with which the story closes, as well as in the reason for that scene, the decision to bury his mother in her native soil.

Rejection of the dependent relationships of his youth, both the one with his parents and the one with Angelo, is a valuable declaration of personal independence. However, to reject the anonymous traditions that animate the powerful authority articulated by parents and teacher proves to be a more difficult task, or at least a task that Nugent has not thoroughly analyzed. However, perhaps because his rebellion is a subjective one, a substitution of self-respect for pitiable dependence, the protagonist has not felt the need to explore the more general influence of communal traditions. Thus, the story's conclusion may denote reconciliation and acquiescence as well as constraint and enclosure. Nugent, despite appearances, has remained "unmistakably a Corkonian."

It is not merely the end of "Up the Bare Stairs" that bears witness to the continuing presence of the past in the present. There are numerous subtle instances of this relationship during the course of the story. A case in point is the marked contrast between how little Nugent divulges of his present elevated position or of the career that led to it and the seemingly total recall he possesses of his days at West Abbey. Another representation of the emotional force and unexpected vitality of Nugent's memories is the fact that once he embarks on his recollections, the anonymous narrator becomes merely an auditor, a pretext for the past.

The narrator, despite his temporary obliteration and the reader's ignorance of him, is a crucial feature of the story's coherence. In a number of ways he embodies the unmediated present. It may be inferred that he came of age in the new independent Ireland of which Sir Francis knows nothing. The narrator's encounter with the great man, and his unwitting initiation of Nugent's revelations, illustrate the availability of the present to the past and its unpredictable involvement with it. At the end of the story, the narrator does not turn his back on the scene into which his traveling companion steps.

However, the present exists in the story passively. The two narrators' companionship and the ostensibly uneventful nature of the journey facilitate a temporary suspension of the present. The past rushes in with increasing emotional vehemence to fill the apparent vacuum. Although the story's structure of conflict has rich cultural and conceptual repercussions, because its origin is located in "the heart" (as the epigraph, the opening two lines of William Butler Yeats's poem, "The Pity of Love," has it), it can only be lived and relived, not alleviated or dispelled.

*Style and Technique*

Like many Irish short stories of its generation, "Up the Bare Stairs" relies on the reproduction of a voice for its principal stylistic effect. Mimicry of the voice gives the material immediacy and dramatic impetus. Its use also evokes the age-old Gaelic tradition of storytelling, redolent of hearthside yarning at close of day. "Up the Bare Stairs" is not necessarily structured in terms of an updated version of the traditional scenario. Given the story's complex sense of personal and cultural legacies, however, it is not inappropriate that hints of such complexity are to be found in the story's organization.

Use of the voice also influences the story's pace and development. From a bland, innocuous, casual-sounding opening (like everything else about him, the narrator's voice is not particularly distinctive), the story builds in intensity. The gradual development, punctuated initially by revelations concerning Nugent's real identity, gains markedly in momentum and vividness once Nugent takes over as narrator. Indeed, the anonymous narrator's mistaken assumption that his traveling companion is an actor seems in retrospect a revealing error because Nugent displays a decided flair for the dramatic—and for self-dramatization. His story is not merely a chronicle of unhappiness and how it was overcome; it is a reenactment of the experience of that unhappiness. Nugent's excoriation of pity—so necessary if the story is to rise above sentimentality—occurs with a sense of shock and completeness appropriate to a dramatic climax.

"Up the Bare Stairs" also cleverly uses the story-within-a-story device. This device emphasizes the story's dual character, its interaction between different times and temperaments. In addition, however, although Nugent's narrative is the heart of the story, it does not overwhelm its surrounding framework. The story's technique articulates in its own right an overall sense of continuity and compatibility as well as a sense of distance and division. Nugent embodies the latter sense, although the anonymous narrator bears witness to the former. The elaborately conceived, but fluently presented, structure of "Up the Bare Stairs" unobtrusively and efficiently underpins the story's graphic comprehension of how complex and far-reaching simple, early lessons can be.

*George O'Brien*

# UPON THE SWEEPING FLOOD

*Author:* Joyce Carol Oates (1938-    )
*Type of plot:* Naturalistic
*Time of plot:* Probably the early 1960's
*Locale:* Eden County, in an unspecified state
*First published:* 1963

> *Principal characters:*
> WALTER STUART, a thirty-nine-year-old man who is on his way
>     home after his father's funeral
> THE GIRL, who is about eighteen
> THE BOY, her brother, who is about thirteen

*The Story*

In Eden County, a sheriff's deputy stops Walter Stuart, warns him about a hurricane that is developing, and continues on down the road. Stuart is in a hurry to get home to his wife and two daughters, having spent a week at his father's farm, making arrangements for his father's funeral. Stuart is a district vice president of a gypsum mining plant, a thirty-nine-year-old man who has achieved, quite naturally, success in both finance and love.

A girl of about eighteen and a boy of about thirteen jump into the road by their farmhouse and try to stop another car going back to town. It passes them, and Stuart offers to give them a ride to safety. The car gets mired in mud, however, and the boy sees that his frightened horse has gotten loose. Although the girl frantically protests and slaps at her brother, Stuart tries to help the boy round up the horse, but it gets away. Unable to flee the storm, they take refuge in the kitchen of the farmhouse, pushing furniture up against the door. The girl and the boy scream at each other and at Stuart, inexplicably angry at each other. When the water seeps up through the floorboards, they climb into the attic.

When the windows downstairs explode, Stuart makes a hole in the roof with an ax, and they climb out onto the roof and hold on as the wind and the rain assail them. Then the house collapses, and they float free on the roof. They cling to it, huddled together in the dark, terrified. The boy has "gone loony."

The dawn reveals a small hill and some trees, and they wade toward it. Stuart stirs up some snakes. In a frenzy, he and the boy try to kill them. For no reason, Stuart suddenly starts hitting the boy with a stick. Then he confronts the girl, who prepares to defend herself with a board. As Stuart lunges at her, she points toward a rescue boat. Wading out to meet it, Stuart cries, "Save me! Save me!"

*Themes and Meanings*

Stuart thinks of himself as normal and gentle. However, interacting with the violent, unfeeling, and crude boy and girl, he finds himself taking on their characteristics. The hurricane and the flood provoke this process, as it aggravates the worst qualities in the girl and her "loony" brother. Joyce Carol Oates shows how something in human nature produces, needs, and thrives on violence, personal and vicarious. Morality and convention, according to Oates, cannot control this urge and may contribute to it. Stuart's altruism saves them, but he wants to force them to be grateful. The violent intrusions of chance can significantly aggravate a person's innate inclinations toward violence.

During the course of the story, Stuart is put through a profoundly wrenching experience. He goes from asking the deputy, "Do you need help?" to begging the rescue boat, "Save me!" He goes from declaring, "I know what I'm doing!" to doing something totally uncontrollable. Because the deputy assumes that Stuart is better off than "these folks coming along here" and that he would not care what the hurricane does to them, Stuart believes that he must act on the social obligation to "see if anybody needs help."

Stuart is isolated from his own people in this remote region of swampland. As "the slashing of rain against" his face excites him and he feels "a strange compulsion" to "laugh madly," he breaks out of his normal life. The engine of his car and the wind "roared together." In the farmhouse, he is isolated even from the other people who live in the swampland: In the attic, on the flood-surrounded roof, and finally on the hill, his isolation intensifies, allowing the free expression of his most primitive instincts.

The horse that runs amok at the beginning of the story is an expression of the violence of the storm as a pure force and of the irrational, erratic behavior of the strange boy and girl. These insane elements contrast with Stuart early in the story. The pair represents the mindless, valueless forces in nature that work on people who try to live within some rigid, civilized context. When Stuart goes for the ax, the boy thinks that he might hit him: Stuart's sense of "helplessness, at the folly of his being here, for an instant almost made him strike the boy with the ax." The girl senses his impulse and attacks Stuart.

The Good Samaritan of the beginning of the story is so transformed by psychological and natural disruptions that he is moved to kill the boy and the girl for whom he has risked his life (and neglected his own family) to save. As the horse is an expression of the violence of wind and rain, the writhing snakes are a manifestation of the flood stage of the hurricane. Beating the snakes with a stick is the trigger that releases irrational violence in Stuart, and he strikes the boy. The raw vitality of suppressed desires, impulses, urges, and instincts suddenly explodes. The girl is so impressed by the change in him that she does not defend her brother this time; she falls back on brute survival, preparing to defend herself. Thus, Stuart's instinctive altruism is converted, by a climate of natural and human violence, into hatred and homicide. In her depiction of motiveless violence, Oates suggests that much ordinary human behavior apparently is as motiveless as that of the panicked horse and the snakes.

Stuart can no longer believe that "his mind was a clear, sane circle of quiet . . . inside the chaos of the storm." He believes that he has "blundered" into "the wrong life," and that "his former life" was incomplete. He knows that he has "lost what he was just the day before," that he has "turned now into a different person, a stranger even to himself." The wind "tolled" the death knell of his former self. The howling outside becomes internalized in "the howling inside his mind." It is from external forces that he has now internalized that he begs the rescue team to "save" him.

## Style and Technique

It is difficult, and perhaps unproductive, to discuss Oates's stories as literary constructs. If "Upon the Sweeping Flood" has form, it is so submerged in "experience" as to defy analysis. If there is control, it is not aesthetic control, but the control of gathered forces in a hurricane. The lack of shape and focus makes this story linger in the reader's consciousness as if it were an actual event one wants to forget. Would greater attention to style, technique, and structure dilute the intensity of her vision and the terror conveyed by her themes?

Oates very seldom uses either the first-person or the third-person central-intelligence point of view; omniscience seems most suited to her vision of life. In this story, the elements are filtered through the perceptions of Walter Stuart, except when Oates alludes to the manner in which he will remember this incident years later, and except for the tale-telling tone in the first line: "Not long ago in Eden County, in the remote marsh and swamplands to the south, a man named Walter Stuart was stopped in the rain." With stark authorial authority, that omniscient tone is sustained throughout. The author seems to have written in a frenzied burst of energy, the heat of which one feels simultaneously with a cold objectivity, as she violently renders her own involvement in the miserable predicament of her characters. Narrative drive, character depiction, the author's vision—in this as in many of Oates's stories—seem to rush on the reader like the wind, the rain, and the panicked horse, to startle like the snakes, animated by an omnipotent God, expressed by an inspired omniscient author in a shotgun style.

The reader's sense that Oates is not aesthetically in control of her style contributes to the nightmare quality of her depiction of characters; landscapes; wind, rain, and flood; eerie darkness and light; horses and snakes; the erratic blows of the ax and the sticks; descriptions of the house and of the characters (enhanced by their dialogue)—a bizarre atmosphere of calamity, in which the characters, too, are out of control. It is a wonder that her style distracts no more than it does. Would a more refined style dissipate the wayward energy of all the elements in the story? The raw materials of her story and the seriousness of the theme are more commanding than her style. Even so, the power of her writing can be overwhelming; the reader feels the author's compulsion to hack a path, as Stuart hacks a hole in the roof with an ax, through a dense thicket to reach the site of a disaster.

*David Madden*

# THE UPTURNED FACE

*Author:* Stephen Crane (1871-1900)
*Type of plot:* Sketch
*Time of plot:* The late 1800's
*Locale:* A battlefield in an unspecified war
*First published:* 1900

> *Principal characters:*
> TIMOTHY LEAN, a lieutenant
> AN ADJUTANT
> BILL, a dead man
> TWO PRIVATES

### The Story

As two soldiers contemplate the body of a dead comrade, lying on the battlefield at their feet, its face turned toward the sky, the adjutant asks Lieutenant Timothy Lean, "What will we do now?" Lean decides that the body must be buried and calls two enlisted men to dig a grave. Meanwhile, the adjutant and Lean decide that the clothes of the dead man must be searched, and the task falls to Lean. Hesitant to touch the corpse, he shakily completes the chore. As the grave is being dug and the search is being performed, enemy bullets fly overhead. Finally, the two enlisted men finish their hastily dug and shallow grave. The adjutant and Lean stand almost unsure of what to do next. They decide it would be proper if they put their fallen comrade into the grave themselves rather than order the enlisted men to do it. They are careful to avoid touching the body itself as they position the corpse in the grave.

Lean remembers part of a burial service and begins it. The adjutant lamely adds a word or two that he recalls. After Lean abruptly orders the two privates to begin filling in the grave, rifle fire from sharpshooters hits one of them in the arm. Both men are sent back to their lines, so Lean, almost feverishly, fills in the grave himself. Finally, all that is left of their fallen companion is his chalk-blue upturned face. Fighting off his sense of horror, Lean takes a shovelful of dirt and swings it toward the grave. The dirt makes a plopping sound as it lands, and the story ends.

### Themes and Meanings

Beginning with Stephen Crane's most famous work, *The Red Badge of Courage* (1895), but continuing through his other works, the horror of encountering death is a constant theme. Often, rather than confront death directly, Crane's characters do their best to avoid it. They walk around dead men lying on battlefields, avoid wounded, or express loathing about touching the dead or the dying. However, in this brief tale, written less than a year before his own death, Crane forces his characters, and readers, to face death squarely. In this story there is no way to avoid the issue, just as there is no way for Lean or the adjutant to avoid it on the battlefield. The story begins with two men struggling to decide what to do. At first neither man seems exactly certain, as both grapple with emotions barely under control. At moments each man lashes out at the two enlisted men, but one senses that their anger is not really directed at the hapless privates. Rather, Lean and the adjutant wrestle with both the reality of death and its meaninglessness.

Each man resists touching the body, but ultimately they must put the corpse into the ground. It is interesting to note that although Lean could order the privates to do the job, he instead decides that he and the adjutant should put the body in the grave. Even though it is not entirely clear whether their motivations are due to their rank, or their relationship to the fallen man, the symbolic aspect of confronting the unpleasant "face" of death cannot be ignored. Lean will not simply walk away, leaving someone else to confront the terror of death for him. What makes the issue even more immediate is the imminent possibility of any of their own deaths. Bullets continue to fly around them as they complete the funeral service.

The image of the upturned face of the dead man is prominent not only at the beginning of the story, but also in several later instances. As the privates initially prepare to fill in the grave one of them hesitates, unsure where to throw the first shovelful of dirt. For some reason Lean is horrified at the thought of the dirt falling on the upturned face. As the private throws the dirt on the corpse's feet instead, Lean feels "as if tons had been swiftly lifted from off his forehead." Momentarily, when the private is wounded and Lean must continue the task himself, he fills the entire grave except for the "chalk-blue" face. Lean seems to struggle with his feelings and even snaps an angry remark at his superior, the adjutant. However, ultimately the tension releases all in a moment as the shovel swings back, then forward, and the dirt covers the face. In the end, the reality of death cannot be avoided, neither walked around nor walked away from. The face of death must be stared into and addressed.

*Style and Technique*

Crane's writing is often appreciated for its brevity, spareness, and attention to realistic detail. In "The Upturned Face" the reader may note all these elements. The story is one of Crane's final, and finest, efforts. What is particularly notable about "The Upturned Face" is the vivid nature of the scene created in just fifteen hundred words. For example, the reader senses that bullets are whizzing by as a continual threat, but Crane only once mentions that they "snap" overhead, bullets are "spitting" overhead, and, at the opening, that bullets are cracking near their ears. The crisp effectiveness of these concise images forces the reader not only to perceive a tangible danger, but also to consider the importance of anything that requires enduring such a risk. Why is this so important to Lean and the adjutant?

Crane depicts death realistically, often describing wounds in bloody detail, or the odd positioning of a dead person's limbs, perhaps emphasizing a certain revulsion to death, perhaps reflecting the realistically alien nature of the state. In this story, however, Lean's and the adjutant's sense of horror is expressed through the spare, yet focused image of the "chalk-blue" upturned face of their comrade. The reality is made into something alien and horrible not by its unnaturalness, but by its terrible immediacy.

The tension between the lieutenant and the adjutant, as well as the tension of each toward the dead man, skillfully builds from their initial debate over what to do. The first line describes the adjutant as "troubled and excited," and it is another example of Crane's art. At first these seem like antithetical states, yet soon we discover that the body of a fallen friend, coupled with the need to bury him as bullets fly close by, makes Crane's opening remark an excellent summation. From this initial tension, caused by the conflict between the need to act quickly and the inability to quite face the situation, Crane leads the two men through a series of almost meaningless rituals that serve both to delay the outcome and to heighten the anxiety caused by the delay. The adjutant lets out a strange laugh that shows his mounting tension as they are faced with the reality of actually burying the body. However, first they must set it in the grave. This brings new levels of disgust to Lean and the adjutant, and they are "particular that their fingers should not feel the corpse."

In an almost comedic moment they decide that some words should be read over the body, but neither can remember the service. This further delay, coupled with the sense of futility at the few meager words finally said, causes Lean to erupt against the innocent privates as he "tigerishly" commands them to throw in the dirt.

Then, the tension that has been building to this point is momentarily released as the first dirt falls on "Bill's" feet rather than his face. Lean thinks "How satisfactory!" However, the respite is brief, for the private is wounded and Lean must finish filling in the grave himself.

Lean and the adjutant have ordered a grave to be dug, searched the body, dragged it to the grave, arranged it inside, read a snatch of scripture, and then, finally, run out of options. Crane propels the reader not only toward the inevitable point of burial, but also to a release of the stresses building in Lean throughout the narrative. Finally, they are released in a shovelful of dirt that covers the upturned face of their friend and ends the story. The unadorned "plop" of the dirt as it falls adds to the realism of the portrayal, while at the same time suggesting death's finality.

*George T. Novotny*

# THE USE OF FORCE

*Author:* William Carlos Williams (1883-1963)
*Type of plot:* Psychological
*Time of plot:* The early twentieth century
*Locale:* The United States
*First published:* 1938

> *Principal characters:*
> A DOCTOR, the unnamed narrator
> MATHILDA OLSON, a little girl who is his patient
> MRS. OLSON, her mother
> MR. OLSON, her father

*The Story*

The doctor who narrates "The Use of Force" knows that the Olsons, a working-class couple, must fear that their young daughter is quite ill if they are willing to pay the three-dollar fee for his visit. Mathilda Olson is an unusually attractive child who clearly has a high fever, and the doctor sets out in his best professional manner to discover the cause. The unspoken possibility on his mind and on her parents' is that she might have diphtheria, several cases having been reported at the school the child attends.

The story is based on the simple premise that the doctor must examine Mathilda's throat and get a throat culture for her own protection and for the protection of others around her. It promises to be an easy enough task. A simple throat examination, however, becomes instead a battle between doctor and child, and William Carlos Williams traces the first-person narrator's shifting attitude toward the child and the task as the doctor moves well beyond reasoned professionalism to delight in the use of force.

The doctor first tries kindness: "Awe, come on, I coaxed, just open your mouth wide and let me take a look." In a single catlike movement, the child claws at his eyes and sends his glasses flying. Next, he tries firmness: "Look here, I said to the child, we're going to look at your throat. You're old enough to understand what I'm saying. Will you open it by yourself or shall we have to open it for you?" The child refuses, and the battle is on. The doctor has fallen in love with the spirited child by this point and sees her as magnificent in her terror of him. With the father's help, he manages to get a tongue depressor into Mathilda's mouth, but she splinters it with her teeth. The doctor sees that it would be best to stop and come back later, but he is beyond reason, and in his fury he asks for a makeshift tongue depressor that she cannot destroy: a spoon. In spite of Mathilda's bleeding mouth and hysterical shrieks, he persists and finally manages to reveal the secret that she has been hiding for three days: Her tonsils are covered with the membrane that indicates diphtheria.

*Themes and Meanings*

As Williams's title indicates, the narrative is a study of the use of force and of its effects on the individual who uses it. As the story progresses, the doctor degenerates from a reasonable professional concerned with his patient's welfare to an irrational being who takes pleasure in the pure muscular release of forcing the child to submit. The doctor remains well aware of the reasonableness of his ultimate goal—the girl's throat must be examined—but even as he persists in pursuing that goal he knows that he is no longer concerned with what is best for the child: "The worst of it was that I too had got beyond reason. I could have torn the child apart in my own fury and enjoyed it. It was a pleasure to attack her. My face was burning with it." His sense of logic tells him that it is a social necessity to protect the child and others against her idiocy in refusing the examination. Even as he acknowledges the truth in this line of reasoning, however, he knows that it has little if anything to do with the motivation behind his ruthless determination to force the child to do as he wishes: "A blind fury, a feeling of adult shame, bred of a longing for muscular release are the operatives. One goes on to the end."

With a "final unreasoning assault," the doctor overpowers the child. Then it is the child's turn to react in a blind fury, her turn to attack. She tries unsuccessfully to escape from her father's arms and fly at the doctor, "tears of defeat" blinding her. She knows that she has lost a battle, yet her anger is quite justified, considering the assault that she has just endured, as is her earlier fear of the doctor who has come to see if she has a disease that could kill her. It is as though the sore throat did not exist as long as it was her secret and hers alone. The fact that Williams chose for the story a patient who is not only a child but also a truly ill child at that emphasizes all the more the violence of the doctor's actions. Child is pitted against adult, illness against health, ignorance against experience. Reason would dictate that undue force should not have been necessary, but reason ceases to be the controlling factor once the battle begins.

The parents stand by, anxious but helpless as the struggle takes place, their spiritlessness in contrast to the child's spirit, their unwillingness to hurt their daughter in contrast to the doctor's use of force. They do not interfere even when Mathilda is cut, bleeding, and hysterical because of their trust in what the doctor represents. They do not question the doctor's aggressive methods, let alone try to stop him, because of the infallibility and ultimate good that doctors represent in their minds: health as opposed to illness, life as opposed to death.

*Style and Technique*

Point of view is critical in this story about force. The external facts of the story are fairly simple: The doctor does what is necessary to diagnose a potentially fatal disease. The fact that the story is told from the doctor's point of view, however, makes it possible to see the changes that take place in his mind as he progresses from cool professional to animalistic assailant. He could have justified on the basis of logic alone his persistence in forcing the examination. What he cannot justify even to himself is his motivation for doing so. Still, the doctor is calm and controlled in telling the story.

He exposes for analysis his mental state just as he exposes for examination the little girl's throat.

There are clear sexual undertones to the act of violence that the doctor directs against the child. That element could have been avoided completely had the patient been a little boy. As it is, the doctor acknowledges early the physical attractiveness of the child and the fact that he loves her for her spirit. The doctor's aggression toward Mathilda takes on characteristics of a rape as his anger builds up at her resistance and finally results in violence. The examination becomes an assault on her mouth cavity with the phallic tongue depressor, which she renders useless, and then with the spoon.

As her fear of the doctor increases, Mathilda's breathing becomes more rapid. The doctor's face burns with the pleasure he feels in attacking her. Mathilda resists as she would resist an actual sexual assault, and she bleeds as a result of his probes into her mouth. The story and the assault reach their climax when the doctor achieves a sense of physical release by forcing Mathilda's mouth open and revealing the hidden membrane. Ironically, her parents let the assault take place and actually aid in it because they fear their child's death more than they fear any other form of assault on her. Mathilda herself, however, is left with a sense of violation and defeat.

*Donna B. Haisty*

# THE USED-BOY RAISERS

*Author:* Grace Paley (1922-     )
*Type of plot:* Psychological
*Time of plot:* The 1950's
*Locale:* Greenwich Village in New York City
*First published:* 1959

> *Principal characters:*
> FAITH DARWIN, a wife and the mother of two boys
> LIVID, her first husband
> PALLID, her current husband

*The Story*

Faith is preparing breakfast for both her husband and her former husband, who is back from a British colony in Africa and has slept on an aluminum cot in the living room as an overnight guest. As they talk over breakfast, it is difficult to tell the men apart. Faith privately assigns them names that make them seem like twins, so that although she calls one "Livid" and the other "Pallid," they are otherwise indistinguishable. Faith derives these names from the way the men respond to the eggs that she prepares for them. One rejects the eggs in a livid way, the other in a pallid way, but both sigh in unison because they are disappointed in breakfast, and both are eager for a drink. Faith does not keep liquor in the house, however, and pointedly brings out her God Bless Our Home embroidery, which she seems to see as a protective talisman against Livid's presence. The complaints about the eggs introduce a bickering note that continues throughout breakfast.

The two men share no sense of rivalry or jealousy; they are such a convivial pair that Faith seems to be the outsider. Livid has casually ceded the children to Faith's new husband as if they are a used car he no longer wishes to maintain. Neither man takes full responsibility for the children. After establishing the shallow ties that the two rather feckless men have to the boys, the story drifts into an unsettling discussion of yet another of Faith's old lovers, a man named Clifford, who is soon to marry. While Livid and Pallid dwell on the charms of Clifford's new girlfriend, Faith's silence suggests that she has unresolved issues with Clifford.

The two children, Richard and Tonto, wake up and are delighted to find their father and breakfast. Livid expresses concern about their education and becomes enraged when Pallid raises the issue of Catholic parochial schooling. Both Livid and Pallid are lapsed Catholics, and the conversation turns to religious and political topics concerning Jews, Catholics, and the state of Israel. Faith surprises the men by speaking out against Zionism and on her identity as a Diaspora Jew, an identity that she feels she can affirm in the bohemian mix of Greenwich Village as readily as in Israel itself. For Faith, Judaism is not a nationalist identity but an exacting moral and spiritual condition. The two men are astonished, because Faith is usually more silent and subservient; as she puts it, she only lives out her destiny, "which is to be laughingly the servant of man." This clever phrase has a double edge to it, suggesting a certain mockery as well as good nature, which is why she keeps this particular remark to herself. Her two husbands continue the religious conversation and point out that Faith has abandoned her faith by marrying out of it, but she responds that she has forgotten nothing of her past, and that Judaism is a religion that does not take up space but continues in time. Taken aback by her comments, the men let go of the discussion and relax in her cozy kitchen. Faith extends the olive branch by apologizing about the eggs but, eager to see them go, reminds them of their work responsibilities.

As the men prepare to leave for their appointments, Faith happily plans a day that excludes them, involving morning housekeeping, playtime and the park with her children, and finally, as a reward for having endured beans all week, a rib roast with little onions, dumplings, and pink applesauce. She tells the two boys to hug their father. The older one runs to Livid, the younger to Pallid. Both men kiss Faith good-bye, but Pallid's kiss is the more erotic. She sends her two boyish men off into the outside world, wishing them well but with little interest in their concerns, preferring to find fulfillment in her home and children.

*Themes and Meanings*

This story invites the reader to share Faith Darwin's perspective. She lives apart from the men in her life, emotionally, religiously, and politically. Her children are more central to her daily life, and she devotes much time and energy to caring for them. This is a woman's world, one that the men in this story take for granted and perhaps do not fully appreciate or understand. Similarly, when Grace Paley first started to write, she worried that no one would be interested in reading about women at home with their children. Faith seems at first to exist in the margins of Paley's story, keeping her opinions, which are far more astute and mordant than the men suspect, to herself.

By the end of the story, readers realize that the seemingly marginal Faith has her own purposes, which are just as important as those of the men in her life. This image of marginality applies not only to Faith's identity as a woman but also to her identity as a Jew. As is characteristic of Paley's writing, this story mixes the personal and the political. Faith celebrates herself not only as a wife and mother but also as a Diaspora Jew, described as "a remnant in the basement of world affairs" or "a splinter in the toe of civilization," images of marginality that contain a subversive moral integrity; the final image of the Diaspora Jew is that of "a victim to aggravate the conscience."

"The Used-Boy Raisers" introduces Paley's most durable character, Faith Darwin, who figures in many of her other stories. Her name, like the sardonic nicknames of her two husbands, invites interpretation. Her first name, Faith, suggests her Judaism. Unlike the men, who are associated with fixed geographical spaces, Faith affirms Judaism as a religion of seasons and days, and a religion that prevails in the home and through the offices of the mother. It is significant that this story takes place on a Saturday, the Jewish Sabbath, which Faith will observe through the celebratory meal that she is planning. During her conversation with Livid and Pallid, she admits that she lost God a long time ago, but she still has faith, that is, her own identity as a Jewish woman. Her last name, Darwin, suggests her capacity to adapt and survive in changing or challenging circumstances.

*Style and Technique*

Paley's style is compressed and economical, even by the standards of the short-story form. Sardonic and clever, there is also something slightly exotic about her voice, which Paley attributes to Yiddish and Russian influences. Her characters come to life through her use of odd, quirky turns of phrase. In "The Used-Boy Raisers," for example, Faith describes Livid's problems with the Roman Catholic church as his "own little dish of lava," a phrase that in an original but biting way puts him in his place.

On the surface, "The Used-Boy Raisers" is short and virtually plotless. Employing considerable dialogue, the narrative seems to be nothing but aimless and unstructured table talk. Paley circles around her themes and meanings, approaching them indirectly, under the guise of inconsequence. She is, however, pitting Faith against her two husbands as she introduces a series of topics—eggs, her old flame, the children, Israel, her plans for the day. The narrative is artfully structured so that by the end of the story, Faith's character and values have been firmly established, and important distinctions have been made between herself and the two men. Although her conversation seems to flow in a guileless, conversational way, at times Paley retreats inside Faith's mind to secure Faith's perspective as the guiding point of view in the story. Faith's sudden speech about the Diaspora Jews takes the reader in a surprising new direction. This is characteristic of Paley's stories, which often take disarming twists and turns. The conclusion imagines Faith as a woman living in a world apart from that of her husbands, underlining the series of distinctions Paley has made between her female protagonist and the two similar men.

*Margaret Boe Birns*

# THE VALIANT WOMAN

*Author:* J. F. Powers (1917-1999)
*Type of plot:* Psychological
*Time of plot:* The 1940's
*Locale:* American Midwest
*First published:* 1947

*Principal characters:*
> FATHER JOHN FIRMAN, an aging Roman Catholic priest
> FATHER FRANK NULTY, another priest and his friend
> MRS. STONER, his housekeeper

*The Story*

Father Firman celebrates his fifty-ninth birthday by inviting his old friend, Father Nulty, to dinner in the rectory. Their association goes back to their seminary days, and their conversation would turn to sentimental memories if it got the chance. The occasion, however, is thoroughly dominated by the aggressive housekeeper, Mrs. Stoner, who simply does not know her place. Mrs. Stoner has assumed the role of the priest's wife, although the relationship is innocent of any explicit sexual complications, and she has forcefully extended her authority over his life and society and opinions. She gossips about the bishop—who is not the man that his predecessor was—who cut poor housekeeper Ellen Kennedy out of Father Doolin's will, who ignored the dinner she cooked for him on his last visit, and who is coming again for confirmations this year. Clearly, there is a society of priests' housekeepers with their own gossip and social ranking, as is evidenced when she comments about the new Mrs. Allers at Holy Cross, as if she herself were the pastor there. She scolds Father Firman when he strikes a match on his chair to light the candle on his birthday cake. To him, the candle looks suspiciously like a blessed one taken from church.

The two priests have a moment to themselves when Mrs. Stoner returns to the kitchen. Father Nulty is very much aware of Father Firman's aggravation. He points out that another priest of their acquaintance, Fish Frawley, got rid of his snooping housekeeper with a clever stratagem. He told her the false story that his "nephews" (a long-standing euphemism for the children of supposedly celibate priests) were visiting him, an item that promptly appeared in the paper. Not only did Frawley dismiss her, but he even made a sermon out of the event. Then he hired a Filipino housekeeper; the implication is clear that Asiatic women will be more deferential to male authority.

In laughing about how Fish Frawley painted all the dormitory toilet seats on a New Year's morning while they were in seminary, the two priests show they wish to return to a time of male bonding, when all women were in the background. When a mosquito lands on Father Nulty's wrist, he swats it and flicks it away, telling his friend that only the female bites.

Mrs. Stoner returns to the study with Father Firman's socks and mechanically reviews all the prominent converts in the news. When this subject is exhausted, she prods the others with disconnected bits of information. Do they know that Henry Ford is making steering wheels out of soybeans? Father Nulty has had enough and gets up to leave. "I thought he'd never go," Mrs. Stoner exclaims. Now that the housekeeper and Father Firman are alone, she promptly sets up the card table for their nightly game of honeymoon bridge. Mrs. Stoner is highly competitive, playing for blood, a need Father Firman recognizes by not trying too hard to win.

As Mrs. Stoner slaps down her cards in triumph, Father Firman daydreams about getting rid of her. What has he done to make God put this burden on him? In charity, he tries to enumerate her good points, but he comes up with nothing except that she is obsessively clean and thrifty. She has run his life, turned away his friends, and intruded into the affairs of the parish. Although pitiable for having lost her husband after only a year of marriage, she settled in with him and never made a further attempt to remarry. Years ago she moved into the guest room because the screen was broken in the housekeeper's room, and she never moved back. The truth of her assumed position suddenly strikes him, and long after everyone else has seen it—she considers herself his wife. He is shocked and panicked by the realization.

In desperation, he looks up the regulations governing priests and their housekeepers. Clerics can reside only with women about whom there can be no suspicion, either because of a natural bond, such as that of a mother or sister, or because of advanced age. Mrs. Stoner, however, is younger than he is. Is there some loophole in the contract that would allow him to send her packing? He recognizes, however, that she meets the spirit if not the letter of the law, and that he cannot afford to pension her off. There appears to be no way out.

A mosquito bites him in the back. He slaps at it, and it takes refuge in the beard of Saint Joseph on the bookcase. He swats it again with a folded magazine, and the statue falls to the floor and breaks. Having heard the noise, Mrs. Stoner comes to his door. He tells her that he has only been chasing a mosquito.

"Shame on you, Father. She needs the blood for her eggs," Mrs. Stoner says as the priest once more lunges for the tormenting insect.

*Themes and Meanings*

The Catholic priesthood was a favorite subject of J. F. Powers. In "The Valiant Woman," he gives a sly and witty account of an ongoing struggle between a priest and his housekeeper. This small and ironic comedy is quite successfully set off against larger and darker issues involving human needs and limitations, and the theology that guides the characters.

Quite against his inclinations, Father Firman, a celibate priest, has "married" Mrs. Stoner by passively allowing her to assume the role of his domestic partner. Unlike the suggestion buried in his name, he has been anything but firm and has steadily dwindled into the role of a husband. Without asking for these responsibilities he has allowed them to overtake him, and he can no longer in good conscience back away. He cannot divorce her, just as his religion forbids divorce. In his fantasy, a Filipino house-keeper would give him the life of freedom he craves—not sexual freedom, but free-dom from responsibility in his personal life. The priest is thrust into the commitment his theology teaches, and which he has no doubt preached to others.

Although the reader need not accept any particular religious view to appreciate its argument, the story is deeply rooted in its Catholic theology. None of the three charac-ters has an unusual spiritual gift. With her garrulous and trivial nature, Mrs. Stoner is indeed a millstone around the neck of the priest. Father Firman, although conscien-tious in his duties, seeks only a comfortable and trouble-free life, an ideal that Father Nulty urges on him. The author thus creates limited human beings who are confused and frustrated by their needs and fantasies. On the surface, their religion is only a so-cial framework into which they have fallen. However, the demands of that religion make Father Firman stand larger than he ever could on his own. Husbands, as well as priests, take vows before God. Father Firman finally begins to realize that his respon-sibility is not simply defined by the vows he took as a priest. In becoming a "hus-band," he is bound by the spirit as well as the letter of the law.

*Style and Technique*

The story is rich in detail and human observation, and it cannot be summarized by an account of its symbolic meanings. However, those meanings are important to un-derstand as part of the author's wit. The symbolic use of the mosquito is clever and economical. In the course of the story, Father Firman learns two things about the mos-quito. When Father Nulty tells him that only females bite, he conveys a cynicism with which Father Firman is ready to agree. They both wish to escape from the domination of females. There is another symbolic application as well: The mosquito is a part of nature, a creation of God, yet it is a persistent tormentor that humans never quite man-age to eliminate. It nags and gives pain and comes back again and again, representing as well as anything the inevitable frustrations of the human condition. Accepting such frustrations, and perhaps much more, is one's lot in life.

At the end of the story, when Father Firman attacks the mosquito on the statue of Saint Joseph, the symbolism extends to more explicit religious parallels. Joseph, the husband of Mary, was also ambiguously involved in a marriage in a way that he did not seek. Mrs. Stoner's declaration that the mosquito needs blood for her eggs seals the argument. The female mosquito not only torments its victim, but must do so, be-cause of its nature and inner need.

*Bruce Olsen*

# THE VALLEY OF SIN

*Author:* Lee K. Abbott (1947-    )
*Type of plot:* Fable
*Time of plot:* The 1970's to 1980's
*Locale:* Deming, New Mexico
*First published:* 1985

> *Principal characters:*
> DILLON RIPLEY, a prosperous banker and golf addict
> JIMMIE RIPLEY, his wife
> ALLIE MARTIN, a golf pro
> TOMMY STEWARD, a caddy
> DR. TIPPIT, the pastor of St. Luke's Presbyterian church
> WATTS GUNN,
> PHINIZY SPALDING, and
> POOT TAYLOR, Dillon's golf companions

*The Story*

At a country club in Deming, New Mexico, Dillon Ripley practices his golf swing with the help of the resident pro, Allie Martin. There is little question that Dillon Ripley approaches the game as a sacred experience and not merely as an entertaining sport. On weekends he is accompanied by his wife, Jimmie, as he tries to instill in her his own reverence for the game. Golf, he tells her, is bliss and bane, like love itself. Ripley so reveres the game that he uses archaic terms such as "mashie," "niblick," and "spoon" to describe various kinds of golf clubs. Having delved into the ancient history of golf, he is familiar with its lore and minutiae.

In his daily life, Ripley is a prosperous vice president of the Farmers and Merchants Bank (loan department), and he repeatedly tells his favorite golfing partners—Watts Gunn, Phinizy Spalding, and Poot Taylor—that he intends to take his wife and four children to Scotland to play at the Old Course at St. Andrews—the home of the Royal and Ancient Golf Club. His love and enthusiasm for the sport is so profound that he once declared, on the fourteenth hole, that he had discovered "what best tested the kind we are . . . the hazards of unmown fescue and bent grass, or a sand wedge misplaced from a bunker known as the Valley of Sin." In short, what separates humans from beasts and makes them most human is how successfully they emerge from their struggles in the Valley of Sin—literally and metaphorically.

It is at the fourteenth hole on a beautiful May afternoon, however, that Dillon Ripley faces the most traumatic vision of his life when his caddy, Tommy Steward, spots a Volvo speeding toward them. In it are Ripley's golf pro, Allie Martin, and his wife, Jimmie Ripley—both naked. Dillon's golf partners recognize—as does Ripley—that a corrupting agent has entered their lovely Eden and destroyed it utterly. When Ripley sees his naked wife, he immediately collapses with a heart attack.

The second part of the story takes up months after Ripley's heart attack. He seems to be on the mend, though his physician, Dr. Weems, has warned him that he is not yet ready to play golf. The Deming Golf Club has lost its Edenic glow, now that Ripley's friends realize that human beings are no more noble or charmed than "thinking worm or sentient mud." Most people accepted the view of Dr. Tippit, the Presbyterian minister, that the world is "a fallen orb." Although Ripley has seemingly accepted the terrible loss of his beloved, strange events and signs began to appear at selected places on the golf course, especially on the fourteenth hole—Deming's own Valley of Sin.

Three weeks after Ripley puts his house up for sale, apocalyptic messages begin to appear in different parts of the golf course, written in tiny script with messages such as "We are a breed in need of fasting and praying. . . . The world is almost rotten. . . . *Porpozec ciebie nie prosze dorzanin*" (a quotation from a John Cheever short story). Ripley's friends interpret these hermetic statements according to their own lights and obsessions. Garland Steeples, the high school guidance counselor, views them—especially "the downward arc of time"—as foreboding signs of an imminent communist takeover.

It is Tommy Steward who first confronts the vision of horror near midnight on an early summer night. As he and Eve Spalding are making out near the fourteenth hole—the Valley of Sin morally—he beholds "the thing, wretched as a savage," leaping in front of him. It is dressed in skins, and as dirty as an orphan in a French movie, with one fist shaking overhead and the other holding a golf club heavy with sod like a cudgel. There are terrifying roars everywhere, and Tommy cannot believe the thing's blind pink eyes and its teeth as wet as a dog's. He feels as if he is staring at the hindmost of human nature.

Poot Taylor and Watts Gunn patrol the country club for a month, but the night that they cease their rounds, something begins digging pits and new notes appear: "We are blind . . . and nothing can be done about it."

In August, Dillon Ripley sells his house and moves twenty miles south into the desert, where the only sport is hunting. There is no golf course in this barren place where the winds blow constantly, as if they come from a land whose lord is dark and always angry.

*Themes and Meanings*

Lee K. Abbott's unique story is about the fall of a local hero in a corrupt world. Dillon Ripley embodies the high moral standards of the Deming Country Club; indeed, his old-fashioned passion and reverence for golf as an ancient rite of passage make him a modern hero. He sees himself in an idealized form as "slender and tanned and strong as iron, a hero wise and blessed as those from Homer himself." Once he is betrayed by Allie Martin, his friend and guide, and his beloved wife, Jimmie, he enters the fallen world that literally and metaphorically breaks his heart. More important, the corruption of the Edenic country club takes place at the fourteenth hole—Ripley's Valley of Sin—where Allie and Jimmie appear in adulterous embrace, scandalizing the entire community. Their sin desecrates a hallowed place, a location that hitherto symbolized the highest spiritual ideals of both Ripley and his faithful entourage. His three golfing companions—Watts, Phinizy, and Poot—function as a Greek chorus commenting on the consequences of that terrible fall into reality. Abbott describes Ripley as a general and attributes to him many of the characteristics of a Homeric hero; however, his heroism is not demonstrated in his golf game. Rather, it consists in his ability to mythologize the game of golf and reconnect it with its ancient origins. His use of archaic terms such as "passion and weal," "enchantments," and "bliss and bane," and the ways that he applies them to golf, revivify and reestablish ancient energies to the game by which Ripley lives his life. Once Ripley's spiritual fall takes place—and Ripley is mythically connected to that particular location—the place itself begins to show signs of its own imminent collapse. It begins to take on the look of a wasteland, and messages of its corruption begin to appear at the place of sacrilege, the fourteenth hole. Tommy Steward, "fuzzy-minded on red-dirt marijuana," believes that he sees the physical manifestation of evil appear as a demoniac figure at the very place that he is necking with a girl, who is named, aptly, Eve.

*Style and Technique*

The major method that Abbott uses throughout this brilliantly rendered story is what T. S. Eliot called the "Mythical Method." This narrative is about the fall of a local hero in Deming, New Mexico, but it is also an old story about the fall of an ancient local leader's fall from a condition of familial love and community into one of fragmented corruption. Most of the names of the characters, once their archaic origins are uncovered, are associated with ancient Scottish and Celtic families, locations, and clan wars. Dillon—a name that means "a spoiler, or corrupting agent"—emerges as a kind of Celtic chieftain whose spiritual health determines the health of his community. Allie Martin becomes the mythic wise guide betrayer—the one who abducts the leader's wife—very much the way that Sir Lancelot took away King Arthur's wife, Guinevere. The result is the same: the end of the communal Round Table and the destruction of Camelot.

What establishes the connection between these two worlds and stories is the archaic language—the language of those heroic Arthurian tales—which Ripley uses to define his spiritual value system. It is the language that Abbott uses that keeps those ancient ideals alive and functioning in the fallen world of the twentieth century. Oddly enough, the name Ripley means "a stripe of land or clearing," which is exactly what a golf course is. Abbott also gently satirizes the modern version of this "old story" by holding it up for comparison to the ancient one, though he is not satirizing those venerable values that golf (and other sports) embody. The Valley of Sin is also the notorious fourteenth hole on one of the courses where the British Open is played each year.

*Patrick Meanor*

# THE VANE SISTERS

*Author:* Vladimir Nabokov (1899-1977)
*Type of plot:* Fantasy
*Time of plot:* The early 1950's
*Locale:* New England and New York City
*First published:* 1959

> *Principal characters:*
> THE NARRATOR, a French literature professor
> CYNTHIA VANE, a recently deceased artist
> SYBIL VANE, her sister, a student who committed suicide four
> years earlier
> D., Sybil's lover, a former college instructor

*The Story*

The unnamed narrator, a French professor at a New England women's college, runs into D., whom he has not seen for several years, and hears about the recent death of Cynthia Vane. Four years earlier, the narrator knew D. and Cynthia in the small town where he still teaches literature. He is surprised to find D., a former instructor at his school, revisiting the site of unpleasant memories. D.'s shame is an extramarital affair that he had conducted with Cynthia's younger sister, Sybil, who was one of the narrator's students.

Cynthia once summoned the narrator to Boston and begged him to make D. end his relationship with her sister and to have D. kicked out of the college if he refused to comply. When the narrator met with D., the latter told him that he had already decided to end the relationship; he was about to quit his teaching job and join his father's firm in Albany, New York. The next day, Sybil seemed normal when she took her examination in the narrator's French literature class. Later, however, when the narrator read her essay, he found it full "of a kind of desperate conscientiousness, with underscores, transposes, unnecessary footnotes, as if she were intent on rounding up things in the most respectable manner possible." At its end it contained what appeared to be a suicide note:

> *Cette examain est finie ainsi que ma vie. Adieu, jeunes filles!* Please, *Monsieur le Professeur,* contact *ma soeur* and tell her that Death was not better than D minus, but definitely better than Life minus D.

Immediately after reading this note the narrator phoned Cynthia, who told him that Sybil was already dead, then rushed to see her. As Cynthia read Sybil's note, the narrator pointed out its grammatical mistakes. Amused by her sister's use of an exclamation mark, Cynthia was strangely pleased by its trivialities. She then took the narrator to Sybil's room to show him two empty pill bottles and the bed from which her body was removed.

After Cynthia moved to New York a few months later, the narrator began seeing her regularly while visiting the city to do research in the public library. He disliked almost everything about her and wondered at the tastes of her three lovers, but he admired her paintings.

Fearing that Sybil's spirit was displeased at the conspiracy to end her romance, Cynthia began sending mementos—such as a photograph of Sybil's tomb—to D. She wanted to placate her dead sister because of her own belief in the spirit world. Cynthia felt herself especially susceptible to the recently dead. Although the highly rational narrator sneered at her fondness for spiritualism, he describes two of her séances at which the spirits of Oscar Wilde, Leo Tolstoy, and others appeared. He preferred these silly events to Cynthia's awful house parties, at which she was always the youngest woman present. After an argument over his snobbery, they stopped seeing each other.

Despite his skepticism, the narrator senses Cynthia's presence after her death when strange physical manifestations in his bedroom make him suspect her of staging a cheap poltergeist show.

## Themes and Meanings

Stylistic techniques are never sharply separated from the themes in Vladimir Nabokov's work. "The Vane Sisters" is an excellent example of his interest in the playfulness of fiction for its own sake and his joy in the potential for deceitfulness in art. His main thematic and stylistic device here is the use of an unreliable narrator. The events of the story of the Vane sisters and D. probably occurred much as the professor says they do, but his interpretations of characters and events are not always fully accurate. In this regard, he resembles Charles Kinbote, in Nabokov's *Pale Fire* (1962), who ostensibly is explaining a poem by John Shade but is actually writing about himself.

Nabokov presents his protagonist ironically because the narrator thinks he is far more capable of understanding than he truly is. At one point, he considers himself "in a state of raw awareness that seemed to transform the whole of my being into one big eyeball rolling in the world's socket." He feels that he must ridicule others to elevate himself. Thus he emphasizes how Sybil's face was scarred by a skin disease and was heavily made up and how Cynthia's skin had a "coarse texture" masked ineptly by cosmetics applied even more slovenly than her sister's. He glories in calling attention to Cynthia's body odor and to the fading looks of her female friends. At Cynthia's parties, even though everyone is connected with the arts, "there was no inspired talk," so he amuses himself by poking "a little Latin fun at some of her guests." He will not accompany Cynthia to séances conducted by professional mediums because he "knew too much about that from other sources." He does not need to experience something firsthand to be able to dismiss it.

The narrator will not consort with two of Cynthia's friends until he is satisfied "that they possessed considerable wit and culture." How he determines this sophistication is not explained; the reader must simply take his word for it. Cynthia rightly accuses him of being "a prig and a snob" and of seeing only "the gestures and disguises of people."

Nabokov grants the sisters a measure of revenge by having them control the story that the professor thinks he alone is telling. The narrator, who once peruses the first letters of the lines of William Shakespeare's sonnets to discover what words they might form, is the victim of an elaborate literary joke. Later, the narrator vaguely recalls a message from the dead concealed in the final paragraph of some novel or short story. His own final paragraph in this story is itself an acrostic in which the first letters of its words spell out "Icicles by cynthia meter from me sybil":

> I could isolate, consciously, little. Everything seemed blurred, yellow-clouded, yielding nothing tangible. Her inept acrostics, maudlin evasions, theopathies—every recollection formed ripples of mysterious meaning. Everything seemed yellowly blurred, illusive, lost.

The dead sisters thus select the very words and images used by the pompous narrator, who has laughed at the powers of the dead. Nabokov himself explains that the sisters use the acrostic "to assert their mysterious participation in the story" in his preface to the story in the collection *Tyrants Destroyed, and Other Stories* (1975).

Cynthia, whom the narrator describes as "a painter of glass-bright minutiae," does this by causing the professor to describe icicles and other prismatic images throughout the story. On a walk near a place where D. once lived, the narrator admires "a family of brilliant icicles drip-dripping from the eaves of a frame house." He tries to spot the shadows of the falling drops, but they prove as elusive as ghosts because he lacks the proper angle of vision: "I did not chance to be watching the right icicle when the right drop fell. There was a rhythm, an alternation in the dripping that I found as teasing as a coin trick." The trick played by the Vane sisters mocks his lack of perception into the true nature of what he encounters. When he arrives at D.'s former home, he finally sees what he wants: "the dot of an exclamation mark leaving its ordinary position to glide down very fast." Sybil is also present later on his walk: "The lean ghost, the elongated umbra cast by a parking meter upon some damp snow, had a strange ruddy tinge."

The pun on parking meter and the meter of language is typical of Nabokov. He enjoys playing games with his readers, whom he expects to pay attention to every detail, such as the description of the exclamation mark in Sybil's suicide note and Cynthia's delight in her sister's punctuation. This incident, like others in the story, also questions the randomness of events. Do things happen by chance or design? Nabokov and Cynthia, controlling artists, endorse the latter.

### Style and Technique

Nabokov also involves his reader through literary and historical allusions. It is no accident that Oscar Wilde appears at one of Cynthia's séances: In Wilde's *The Portrait of Dorian Gray* (1891) "Sybil Vane" is a character who commits suicide for the love of a man named "D." In classical mythology, a sibyl is a prophetess who intercedes with the gods on behalf of human supplicants, just as Sybil intercedes in the professor's narrative.

The essence of Nabokov's playfulness can be seen in his allusions to Samuel Taylor Coleridge's *Kubla Khan* (1816), which the poet labeled a fragment that he dreamed until interrupted by a neighbor from Porlock. Cynthia is friends with "an eccentric librarian called Porlock" who examines old books looking for misprints—the quintessential close reader. Three days after Porlock's death, Cynthia comes across Coleridge's poem and interprets it as a message from Porlock himself. "The Vane Sisters," like *Kubla Khan*, is incomplete until the imaginative reader recognizes the sisters' part in an elaborate trick. The intermingling of life, death, love, art, and the imagination is too airy a conceit for Nabokov's literal-minded narrator.

*Michael Adams*

# VANKA

*Author:* Anton Chekhov (1860-1904)
*Type of plot:* Social realism
*Time of plot:* The late nineteenth century
*Locale:* Moscow
*First published:* 1886 (English translation, 1915)

> *Principal characters:*
> IVAN "VANKA" ZHUKOV, a nine-year-old boy apprenticed to a
> shoemaker
> KONSTANTIN MAKARICH, his easygoing, bibulous "Grandad"

## The Story

Ivan Zhukov, known by the diminutive "Vanka," is an unhappy orphan who has been apprenticed for three months to the shoemaker Alyakhin in Moscow. On Christmas Eve, while his master and mistress and the senior apprentices are all at church, Vanka sits down to write a pleading letter to "Grandad" Konstantin Makarich in the nearby village where Vanka lived before being sent to the city. Vanka's mother, Pelageya, had been in service at a country estate, where his life had been idyllic as he roamed freely with Grandad, "one-eyed Yegor," and other servants. After his mother's death three months earlier, Vanka had first been dispatched to the back kitchen with Grandad and from there to the shoemaker. His homesickness and misery emerge heartbreakingly as he writes his letter.

As Vanka writes, he muses on his grandfather. The old man—about sixty-five—is night watchman on the estate. Vanka imagines him at his usual diversions: hanging around the kitchen, dozing, and joking with the cook and the kitchen maids before going out to walk all night around the premises shaking his rattle. Vanka knows that Grandad's dogs Kashtanka and Eel will be with him. Kashtanka is too old for mischief, but the wily Eel—long, black, and weasel-like—is sly and treacherous, snapping at unsuspecting feet or stealing chickens. For these depredations, Eel is beaten severely, but his behavior is unchanged.

Vanka's most cherished memory is of going with Grandad to chop down a fir tree for the master's Christmas. The old man would preface the felling with a chuckle, a few moments with his pipe, and a pinch of snuff. When a hare bounded by, he would shout his outrage at the "stub-tailed devil."

Vanka's letter reveals how his child's world on the estate, warmed by the love of his mother and the affection of Miss Olga Ignatyevna from the big house, has been replaced by a nightmare of exhaustion and loneliness. He recalls being beaten because he fell asleep while rocking the master's baby. Whenever the older apprentices have forced him to steal cucumbers and he has been caught, he has received more beatings. His rations are meager. He gets bread in the morning, gruel at noon, and bread again in the evening. He enjoys no tea or cabbage and must sleep in the hallway, where the crying baby keeps him awake.

His song of suffering completed, the young servant turns his letter into a plea for salvation, begging his Grandad to take him away. He vows to pray for Grandad, to do the steward's job of cleaning boots, to replace Fedya as the shepherd-boy, and to protect Grandad. Moscow is a big town, Vanka laments, with many fine houses and horses, but no sheep. Its customs are unfamiliar. He cannot sing in church, and when he goes in the butcher's shop no one even knows where the game was shot. Vanka is lost in an alien land.

The letter ends with Vanka's final cry for Grandad to take him home to the village with the familiar animals and servants. He folds the letter, puts it in an envelope, and writes on it "GRANDAD," adding on reflection "KONSTANTIN MAKARICH IN THE VILLAGE." An hour after he runs to the letter box, he is asleep, "lulled by rosy hopes." He dreams of a stove, with Grandad sitting on its ledge reading his letter to the kitchen help. As the grandfather reads, the sly Eel paces back and forth in the kitchen, wagging his tail and watching for his chance.

*Themes and Meanings*

Many stories dramatize a young person's loss of innocence, but few embody the theme in the misery of a child so young as Vanka. Only the waifs in Charles Dickens's novels come readily to mind. Vanka's plight is especially bewildering and painful for him because of the earlier good years with his mother and grandfather and others on the estate who petted him. As Vanka sits alone on Christmas Eve, watching for his tormentors to return and struggling to find words that will move his Grandad to action, he is a picture of forlornness.

Although this story has only four pages, it creates with swift characterizations a scene that goes far beyond a lonely boy's composing of a letter that will surely never reach its addressee. A whole social world opens up in "Vanka," with its rigid class system, its family life, and its cruel indifference to poor children. Much can be read into the narrative's silence about Vanka's father. Vanka describes himself as an orphan, but the story says nothing about his father's fate. Did he die by farm accident? By typhus? The unnamed father remains hidden, just one among the thousands who died early and left no trace behind except in their progeny.

Vanka's touching love for his grandfather, as well as his fond memory of bringing home a Christmas tree, suggests a kindly Grandad. Why then did the old man let the child be sent to such a cruel master? The most generous answer would be that a child with no prospects should learn a trade as soon as possible, and that a difficult apprenticeship is better than no preparation for a world that takes no interest in either its winners or its losers. From this perspective, "Vanka" is an example of the critical tradition known as literary naturalism, with its victims tossed about by forces beyond their control. The hope that buoys up Vanka as he thrusts his letter in the letter box and dreams of Grandad reading it to the servants are merely the typical hoaxes of a creation pervaded by irony.

The slight glimpse given of the Zhivarev family who own the estate comes in the person of Miss Olga Ignatyevna, Vanka's personal favorite. Miss Olga treats Vanka with sweets and would "amuse herself by teaching him to read, write and count to a hundred, and even to dance the quadrille." The word "amuse" reveals Miss Olga as one who regards Vanka as equivalent to a trained monkey whom she would exploit for her private entertainment. Her relationship to Vanka suggests what is called a synecdoche, a term for a situation in which the part stands for the whole: In this case Miss Olga's patronizing treatment of a child is the part that stands for the whole Russian class system. "Vanka" is thus a fitting document for a literary criticism that stresses a social conscience.

*Style and Technique*

The economy of Anton Chekhov's style is a model for writers. The first paragraph identifies Vanka and establishes his plight in just ten quick lines. Grandad leaps to life in two sentences that fix his appearance and his habits. However, Chekhov's genius for minute observation shows up perhaps most wonderfully in his characterization of the dogs. Kashtanka is old and resigned to a dog's life, but the clever Eel is a treacherous thief animated by "the most Jesuitical spite and malice." Eel is such a romantic, satanic figure of life in the servants' quarters that Chekhov concludes the story with Eel pacing the floor, wagging his tail within Vanka's dream.

The brief descriptive passages achieve genuine poetry. The desperate Vanka, struggling with his "rusty nib" and his "crumpled sheet of paper," imagines the village on Christmas Eve: The air is still, "transparent" and "fresh" on a dark night; above the village with its white roofs, the sky is sprinkled with stars and the Milky Way stands out as clearly "as if newly scrubbed for the holiday and polished with snow." When Vanka visits the forest with Grandad to get a Christmas tree, the young fir trees coated with frost stand "motionless, waiting to see which one of them was to die."

The pathos of this story is so sharp that its depiction of childhood loneliness does not fade over time.

*Frank Day*

# THE VELDT

*Author:* Ray Bradbury (1920-    )
*Type of plot:* Science fiction
*Time of plot:* The early twenty-first century
*Locale:* An American town
*First published:* 1951

> *Principal characters:*
> GEORGE HADLEY, a middle-class American
> LYDIA, his wife
> WENDY and
> PETER, their children
> DAVID MCCLEAN, a psychologist and a friend of the Hadleys

*The Story*

George and Lydia Hadley are the proud owners of a "Happylife Home which had cost them thirty thousand dollars installed, this house which clothed and fed and rocked them to sleep and played and sang and was good to them." This is the dream home of the story's futuristic world, and its most elaborate feature is a nursery, which can reproduce any scene in complete aural, visual, or olfactory detail in response to the occupants' thought waves. The Hadleys' children, Wendy and Peter, have used the nursery to conjure up such fantasies as Oz, Wonderland, or Doctor Doolittle, but lately the children have used it to re-create an African veldt. The Hadleys, investigating the nursery, are frightened by the image of charging lions.

Indeed, the incident so unnerves them that Lydia suggests locking the nursery for a few days even though she knows that the children almost live for the nursery. She begs George to turn off all the labor-saving devices in the house so that they can have a vacation and do things for themselves. At dinner, George thinks of how the children have become obsessed with the African veldt, with its hot sun, vultures, and feeding lions. The nursery shows that thoughts of death have become prominent in his children's minds. Returning to the nursery, he orders it to remove the veldt and bring forth an image that he thinks is more healthy for his children, but the room does not respond. The nursery's apparatus will not alter the veldt either because of a malfunction caused by excessive use or because someone, possibly Peter, has tampered with the machinery.

When the children arrive home from a carnival, George questions them about the nursery, but the children deny all knowledge of the veldt. Going to the nursery again, the Hadleys find a different scene in it, which must have been put in by Wendy. However, George finds an old wallet of his on the nursery floor, with tooth marks, the odor of a lion, and blood on it. Later, the Hadleys hear the sounds of human screams and lion roars coming from the nursery. They know that the children have defied orders and are once again in their playroom. When George suggests to his children that the family give up the house's mechanical aids, including the nursery, for a time, Wendy and Peter are decidedly against it. Peter apparently sees no other purpose in life than watching and hearing sophisticated electronic entertainments. He ominously tells his parents that they should forget about closing the nursery.

Worried about the growing secrecy and disobedience of the children, George and Lydia invite their friend David McClean, a psychologist, to examine the use that the children make of the nursery. As George and David enter the nursery, they see lions eating something in the distance. This carnage and the entire veldt disturbs David. He explains that the nursery can be used as a psychological aid, with the images left on the walls serving as an index of a child's mind. According to David, the veldt image reflects the children's hostility toward their parents. They resent their parents' author-ity, preferring instead the ever responsive nursery. The psychologist strongly urges them to leave their Happylife Home and start a new life elsewhere. As they leave the room, David finds a scarf of Lydia's with bloodstains on it.

George finally turns off the nursery and the rest of the house. The children throw an elaborate temper tantrum in which Peter implores the now disconnected machinery not to let his father kill the house. The children beg for one minute more of nursery viewing, to which Lydia adds her support until George relents. The children are al-lowed one minute while George and Lydia await David McClean's arrival so that they can fly to a new life in Iowa. The Hadleys are preparing for departure when they hear Wendy and Peter calling to them. They run into the nursery, but all they find is the fa-miliar veldt scene with the lions looking at them. Suddenly the door is slammed and locked, and the Hadleys hear Peter shouting to the house. Then the lions start moving toward them "and suddenly they realized why those other screams had sounded famil-iar." When David McClean arrives at the house, he finds only the children in the nurs-ery watching lions feeding on something in the distance.

*Themes and Meanings*

On the most obvious level, "The Veldt" is a gruesome fable about the destructive consequences of sparing the rod and spoiling the child. However, it is also a satire on the modern consumer society from a traditional, humanistic viewpoint in the style of several other Ray Bradbury works, such as *Fahrenheit 451* (1953) and *The Martian Chronicles* (1950). In all these stories, technology, backed up by commercialism and a utilitarian philosophy, tries to remove the inconveniences, difficulties, and chal-lenges of being human and, in its efforts to improve the human material condition, im-poverishes its spiritual condition.

Technology's offering in this story is the Happylife Home, which mechanically performs almost every human function, including that of the imagination. The nurs-ery reproduces images of the children's thoughts, in effect becoming their imagina-tion. This relieves the children of the necessity of developing their imagination by contact with the outside world, so that, despite their high intelligence, the children never grow up; significantly, Wendy and Peter have the same names as the hero and heroine of *Peter Pan* (1904). Without the chance to mature, the children sink to the level of beasts, demonstrated when Peter says that all he wants to do is see, hear, and smell. Thus, they identify not with characters in traditional children's literature, such as "Aladdin's Lamp" or *The Wizard of Oz*, but with the predatory lions of the veldt.

The elder Hadleys also participate in this dehumanizing process. They have allowed the nursery to usurp their role as parents while becoming the childish dependents of their house. As David McClean tells them, they have built their life around creature comforts. They, too, have refused to grow up, to accept their duties as parents. Their avoidance of responsibility reduces them to the level of prey to lions. Unlike their children, they know what a more active life is like, and their present inactivity becomes constraining. They try to escape to a simpler life in Iowa, but they give in to the children once too often and are destroyed by the house.

The house itself becomes a living presence in the story; it is designed to provide services that should have been left to humans. When it makes the lions real, something it was not designed to do, the Happylife Home becomes almost godlike. Peter, in fact, regards it as a god. The killing of the elder Hadleys is the house's way of survival. Ironically, the technological marvel that was to provide a safe and carefree environment for the Hadleys creates instead the violent world of the veldt.

*Style and Technique*

Bradbury's style is marked by lyricism and a profusion of metaphors. In "The Veldt," these create an illusion of reality that brilliantly mirrors the deceptions that the characters in the story undergo. His description of the electronically produced African veldt contains such exact sensory details that it almost seems to be real, and indeed it is by the story's end. Moreover, his description of the veldt also conveys an atmosphere of menace and hostility mirroring the psychological state of the Hadley family. In a similar fashion, Bradbury employs active verbs and personifications, describing the workings of the house's mechanical devices in a way that suggests the living, human quality that the house is acquiring. When the devices are turned off, the house is a "mechanical cemetery," reinforcing the idea that the house is a living thing.

Characteristically, Bradbury's poetic style transports the reader out of the everyday world and into a fantasy world, often reminiscent of the unchecked imagination of childhood. The world of "The Veldt" is one in which childhood fantasies are made concrete. Hence, the story has an air of unreality about it as if it were simply a child's daydream of a world in which children have the power and competence given to adults and adults have the helplessness of children.

This dreamlike quality is counterbalanced by the use of clichés and advertising language, which levels a satiric thrust against modern society. Phrases such as "nothing's too good for our children" and "every home should have one" direct attention to the permissiveness, commercialism, and worship of material comforts that dominate American life. These serve to anchor the bizarre events of the story in an objective framework and give the child's daydream an adult moral.

*Anthony J. Bernardo, Jr.*

# VENUS, CUPID, FOLLY, AND TIME

*Author:* Peter Taylor (1917-1994)
*Type of plot:* Satire
*Time of plot:* The early 1930's
*Locale:* Chatham, a fictional city on the northwestern edge of the American South
*First published:* 1958

> *Principal characters:*
> MR. ALFRED DORSET, an eccentric elderly bachelor
> MISS LOUISA DORSET, his equally eccentric spinster sister
> NED MERIWETHER, the fourteen-year-old son of an upper-
>     middle-class family
> EMILY MERIWETHER, his thirteen-year-old sister
> TOM BASCOMB, the paperboy and an uninvited guest

*The Story*

To the conventional "establishment" community of Chatham's West Vesey Place, the Dorsets are definitely peculiar. They are seen shopping in public places wearing bedroom slippers or with the cuffs of a nightdress hanging down beneath daytime clothing. Mr. Dorset washes his own car, not in the driveway or in the garage but in the street of West Vesey Place. Miss Dorset not only appears on her front terrace at midday in her bathrobe but also has been seen (through the tiny glass panels surrounding the front door) doing her housecleaning in the nude. Their home was once a mansion, but to reduce their taxes, they ripped off the third floor, tore down the south wing, and disconnected some of the plumbing—not bothering to conceal the resulting scars. Nevertheless, they are the last two of a Chatham "first family," and in a community that prizes family above fortune, their social standing is not to be questioned.

The Dorsets were orphaned while still in their teens; afterward, they not only refused any opportunity to marry but also deliberately cut themselves off from wealthy relatives who had moved away from the town. They subsist in an odd fashion: Mr. Dorset grows figs, plentiful but juiceless, and Miss Dorset makes paper flowers, plentiful but artless, which they sell to those members of the community whom they count as their peers. Their single social gesture is an annual dancing party for the pubescent children of suitable families, and the parties have become a predebutante ritual, which all the children must undergo but which give some of them nightmares.

Arrangements for the parties are as strange as the Dorsets. Alfred goes around the neighborhood in his old car, collecting the juvenile guests; no adults have been inside the house for twenty years. Alfred and Louisa are always garbed in the latest fashion of tuxedo or ball gown, none of them ever worn twice. The house is festooned with paper flowers (perhaps to be sold later), with reproductions of somewhat lubricious artworks such as Auguste Rodin's *The Kiss* and Il Bronzino's *Venus, Cupid, Folly, and*

*Time*, with lighting designed to emphasize the artworks. The Dorsets are inclined to notice and to nudge each other when they see the children paying particular attention to the prints and statues. The high point of the parties is a tour of the house, during which the Dorsets talk about their past social triumphs and display ancestral evening wear that they keep in glass cases. The only dancing is done by Alfred and Louisa, to Victrola music, while the children watch. When not dancing, they keep up a running dialogue about being wellborn, being young together, believing that "love can make us all young forever."

There comes a year when Ned and Emily Meriwether are of a proper age to be invited, and the Dorsets arrange a party to end all parties. It starts as a small, adolescent practical joke, merely a plan to smuggle in Tom Bascomb as an extra guest. (Tom does not live in West Vesey Place and is not wellborn; he delivers the morning paper and once saw Miss Louisa doing her nude housecleaning one day when he came to collect.) However, the joke has repercussions that last for the rest of their lives.

Tom takes Ned's place in Mr. Dorset's old car; Ned walks to the Dorset house and slips in with a group of guests. As the tour of the house progresses, Tom and Emily put on a great show of affection; he kisses her ears and the tip of her nose, and they embrace and pose among the flowers in front of the Rodin replica. Mr. Dorset and Miss Louisa are delighted by the show, which proves to them that love can "make us all young forever." However, Ned's reaction is something he has not foreseen: He cannot bear the sight of his sister cuddling with Tom. Finally, he cries out in pain: "Don't you know? . . . They're brother and sister!" The other children, taking this to be the punch line for the joke, laugh aloud.

However, the Dorsets do not turn on the incestuous pair. They turn on Ned, whom they thought to be Tom, saying that they knew all along that he did not belong among the wellborn. Ned flees up the front stairs, pursued by Mr. Dorset, down the back stairs, where he confronts Miss Dorset, up the front stairs again—until he is finally cornered and locked in one of the dismantled bathrooms. Tom, claiming to be Ned, offers to call the police and calls the Meriwether parents instead. Then he slips out the back door.

The aftermath of the joke is much more sad than comic. The hapless Dorsets, unwilling to believe that they cannot tell the wellborn from the paperboy, believe that the Meriwether parents as well as all the children are being mischievous. At last convinced of their error, they simply withdraw to their rooms and leave the bewildered parents to close the house and see the children home.

Ned and Emily are sent off to boarding schools; they never regain their childhood intimacy, and later they become indifferent or even antagonistic to each other. Chatham's children are free forever from Dorset dancing parties.

### Themes and Meanings

On the landing of the stairway to the Dorsets' ballroom is a small color print of Il Bronzino's *Venus, Cupid, Folly, and Time,* torn out of a book and tacked to the wall. Its presence gains significance because of the story's title. The original is a Mannerist work depicting allegorical figures listed in the title: Venus and Cupid engaged in sly flirtation with each other, a desiccated shape of Time prophesying the end of Folly. It does very well as an illustration of Alfred and Louisa, with their faintly incestuous devotion to each other and their staunch refusal to acknowledge the passing of time. It is this unhealthy and unproductive relationship that poses a threat to the children of Chatham—not the Dorsets' simpleminded snobbery. The dancing parties seem designed to encourage others to follow their pattern, and perhaps the children's joke was born of a not-wholly-realized sense of the danger. Perhaps, also, that accounts ultimately for the breach between Ned and Emily.

Some readers see the story as an allegory of the decay of southern gentility, a Faulknerian theme, but that social significance seems too heavy for the tone of this narrative. There is obvious social criticism in the mockery of Vesey Place manners, but the mockery contains more amusement than disgust. The narrator is still in and of the society he describes; he sees past the facade and acknowledges changes in the new generation, but he has not rejected either Chatham or its old-fashioned values. He seems more concerned with individual people than with the social scene as a whole—somewhat sorry for the Dorsets though glad that the children are free of them, forever puzzled and a bit unhappy about consequences for the Meriwethers.

### Style and Technique

The point of view is the most important device in this story, combining schoolboy experience with mature understanding. The unnamed narrator speaks in the first person; he is a child of West Vesey Place, somewhat older than Ned Meriwether, and has served his turn at the dancing parties but was not present at the last one. He does not tell the story in chronological order but mingles memories, his own and others', with reports of the fiasco from several sources. He speaks often of "we" and "us," so that he seems to be a composite voice of the community, at least for his generation. He also tells the story in retrospect, many years after the event.

The last pages include information and impressions gleaned from Ned's wife at some time after World War II. By this means the reader knows the unhappy aftereffect for the Meriwethers of their impractical joke. Reasons for the family breach are not clear—the children were too young to analyze their own thoughts and feelings—but Ned's wife is sure that it started that night at the Dorsets'. She comes from outside Chatham; she lives in it but is not part of it, and her view helps the narrator shape his reactions.

The narrator is a born storyteller. His voice is conversational, his attention sometimes digressive, his insight keen. He understands Chatham, its pretensions and its social values—Bascomb, Meriwether, and Dorset. Peter Taylor has used similar narrators in other stories, and one hears much of the author's voice in the voice of the fictional storyteller.

*Rosamond Putzel*

# VERONA
## A Young Woman Speaks

*Author:* Harold Brodkey (1930-1996)
*Type of plot:* Impressionistic, coming of age
*Time of plot:* Winter, the 1950's
*Locale:* Verona, Italy
*First published:* 1977

> *Principal characters:*
> A YOUNG AMERICAN WOMAN, the narrator
> MOMMA, her young, adventurous, and doting mother
> DADDY, her charming, generous, and indulgent father

*The Story*

"Verona" takes place in the Italian city of Verona and depicts the narrator's memories of a time in her childhood when her mother and father took her there as part of a European tour. Although the narrator recalls the period as one of happiness, she also describes this happiness as including components of cruelty and crime. As she describes the various incidents from her brief time in Verona, her evocations of exquisite happiness are invariably accompanied by details that suggest its opposite. For instance, the young girl is overwhelmed by her parents' massive shopping sprees and a succession of strange cities and hotel rooms, and her sense of excitement shades into pain and anxiety. Similarly, although the narrator recalls it was her father who set the tone of endless magical abundance and happiness, she adds a disturbing element to her memories with a subsequent description of this holiday spree as a manipulative game that her father was playing for his own mysterious purposes.

All through their travels, she remembers that her innocent and youthful beauty as a child made her the object of much affection. This seems to be particularly the case in Verona when she is taken to a piazza to feed the pigeons. Her father gives her newspaper cones filled with grain, causing dozens of pigeons to light on her arms and head and to feed from her hand. However, as the birds continue to sit on her arms and shoulders and feed on the grain she is giving them, her enjoyment begins to attenuate. She suddenly senses that her mother, jealous of her father's beneficence, is a powerful and even dangerous force to be reckoned with. Furthermore, as her father continues to pour grain on her hands, head, and shoulders to attract the birds, she feels something that oscillates between joy and nausea, and her laughter heightens into hysteria. At this point, she seems to lose complete touch with her ordinary self and feels she has been transformed by her own laughter into a brilliant, fantastic angel or bird-child. Later, she cannot stop remembering the pigeons or the special attention her father gave her, attention that she worries he does not visit on her mother.

The family dines and boards the night train from Verona, but in the middle of the night, her mother wakes her to look out the window at the moonlit landscape of extraordinary mountains, which, unlike the messy pigeons in the piazza, seem to be clean, cool, and otherworldly. Later, when her father wakes and looks at the mountains, the little girl finds she is jealous when her mother uses honeyed language to regain her father's affection and interest. After her father falls back asleep, and mother and daughter continue to look at the almost unbearably beautiful mountains together, the girl concludes that her mother is, mysteriously, the winner of an unarticulated competition or contest being played under the surface of the little family's life together. She bonds with her mother and regards her as the one to whom she will give her ultimate loyalty because she feels they both share the vulnerability that comes with loving men, whose affection she feels one can never completely secure. The narrator concludes her story by once again describing this complicated, intense, and troubling period as a time of happiness.

## Themes and Meanings

One of the major themes in this story is that of the emerging consciousness of a young child. The overwrought and almost exhausting flood of sensations and emotions, collecting around but also subtly contradicting the idea of happiness, eventually reveals a psychological portrait of the narrator and of her childhood. The narrative's series of episodes demonstrates how a child begins to lose her innocence and develops an awareness of complexity within her own consciousness and in the characters of her two parents. The little girl begins to discern differences in her parents and in her relationship with them, and in retrospect, she begins to see that the magical happiness of that time was a mysterious and complicated condition that involved suffering as well as joy. That she is actually speaking about this is in itself a sign that she is articulating impressions and sensations only tentatively felt at the time, but that, with maturity, she can identify and name.

As she begins to sort through her overwhelming sensations, she struggles to get to the heart of the family drama that is being played out underneath the surface. Describing herself and her mother as two moons who bask in the reflected light of her charismatic father, the little girl is also haunted by her jealousy of her mother, as well as her mother's jealousy of her. In the end, however, this conflict is resolved in her mother's favor. The emphasis on her mother as the "winner" suggests a contest on the part of the parents to gain the affection of the child, turning her into a pawn or victim even as she is also the beloved. It also suggests that her mother has, if not altogether consciously, regained her own center of power by the end of the story, winning not only her daughter but also her husband back after seeming to lose them when they pair off during the fevered feeding of the pigeons in the piazza.

As a result of the complicated dynamics inside this family, the theme of "happiness" becomes increasingly unstable and ironic. At the outset of the story, the narrator promises a depiction of happiness that includes cruelty and criminality, a promise fulfilled by the narrator's series of epiphanic moments in which pleasure is inevitably mixed with pain, and in which her mother and father themselves display powers and possibilities that are not altogether innocent or virtuous.

Another theme in this story is the human capacity for mystical experience or transformation within an unlikely consciousness or context—such as that of a little girl feeding pigeons. During the time she is feeding the pigeons, the little girl's experience becomes virtually hallucinatory; at one point she feels she has metamorphosed into an angel or fantastic bird-child. Similarly, her experience of watching the nighttime mountains with her mother also has a mystical, consciousness-transforming aspect. In this story, ordinary incidents have the capacity to extend the boundaries of normal consciousness and to introduce exquisite, intense spiritual experiences whose import nevertheless is indeterminate and unstable. This adds to the complexities of the narrator's inner life, which, ultimately, is the central subject of this story.

*Style and Technique*

This story is structured as a retrospective monologue, in which an older narrative voice looks back on an earlier self. This structure creates two perspectives that compete with each other: One is an older, more disillusioned perspective, which insinuates itself subtly into the stream of impressions and sensations that emanate from the more childlike consciousness of the younger self. The narrator will remind us strategically that what she is describing is what she as a little girl experienced "then," with the inference that the narrator has revised and rethought her situation with the passing years and is now ready to speak with both the voice of herself as a child and as an older, wiser adult who is summoning up a childhood plethora of sensations and feelings.

It is this flood of sensations and feelings that constitutes the major portion of this narrative, creating a dense mass of impressions that become so overwhelming that the narrative quickly moves from ordinary realism into a kind of lyric poetry, or into a stream-of-consciousness narrative that suggests an altered state. The overall impression is of a consciousness that is immensely alive to the all-abundant sensations and impressions around and within her.

However, although the normal flow of time seems to mystically give way to an intense accumulation of insights and emotions, the narrative also incessantly and subtly exposes family divisions and problems lurking below the surface. Harold Brodkey uses two specific incidents to reveal the troublesome family dynamic in which the little girl finds herself enmeshed. The first of these is the overheated, earthy experience of feeding the pigeons with her father; the second is the otherworldly experience of watching the mountains with her mother. In each case, Brodkey explores the exquisite aesthetic and sensual pleasure the girl feels, but qualified by the introduction of words that dissent from this premise. At the very outset of the story, Brodkey introduces the idea of crime and cruelty; later on, he insinuates words such as awful, nausea, vomit, illness, and spit. That these are interwoven with moments of joy effectively suggests the struggle within the narrative consciousness to come to terms with the darker side of her experience.

*Margaret Boe Birns*

# THE VERTICAL LADDER

*Author:* William Sansom (1912-1976)
*Type of plot:* Psychological
*Time of plot:* Around World War II
*Locale:* An abandoned gasworks in urban England
*First published:* 1947

> *Principal characters:*
> FLEGG, the protagonist, a young man
> OTHER YOUNG PEOPLE, two boys and two girls

*The Story*

A young man named Flegg, responding to a dare by a girl he wants to impress and the taunting of a group of young acquaintances, attempts to climb a vertical ladder on an old gasometer, a storage tower in a deserted gasworks. The reader experiences the event through the consciousness of the climber, living through the various perceptions and changing emotions of the performer as he undergoes a wide gamut of feelings from foolish bravado to sheer terror and dreadful isolation.

The group of three boys and two girls are probably teenagers because they are apparently old enough to be given considerable freedom, yet young enough to have little sense of responsibility. They have walked out the back gate of a public park into a run-down, almost deserted section of town, wandered on to the abandoned gasworks, and started throwing bricks at the rusty iron gasometer, towering above all the other structures. The protagonist is showing off, casting his bricks higher than the others, claiming that he knows something about throwing grenades. Then comes the shout from one of the girls: "Bet you can't climb as high as you can throw!"

The boys immediately take up the derisive, taunting tone. The playful psychological game quickly pushes Flegg into a position of bravado from which he cannot gracefully retreat without losing face.

There are two ways of ascent, one known as a Jacob's ladder, bolted flat against the side of the tower, the other a zigzag staircase with a safety railing. Flegg saunters toward the safer stair, but the boys call him a sissy and insist that he climb the vertical ladder.

The ladder looks solid enough except that some twenty feet of the lower rungs are missing. A wooden painter's ladder is propped up against the vertical ladder, however, making it perfectly accessible. One of the girls, no longer vicious but actually encouraging and admiring, gives him her handkerchief to plant at the top of the tower like a banner.

He starts off jauntily enough, practically running up the wooden ladder but slowing significantly when he reaches the vertical ascent. Flakes of rust drop in his face, and he finds that he cannot remove a hand long enough to brush them off. He shakes his head to dislodge them, but this action makes him feel giddy and brings on the first twinge of fear. By the time he has climbed about fifty feet, he is close to panic and still far from the top.

Not only is he in constant dread of falling, but also everything around him seems unusually large, while he, and certainly his companions on the ground, seems very small. Now there is a new horror: There is a confusion of voices from below and a scream from the one girl who said nothing when the others taunted him. She seems to be shrieking, "Put it back, put it back, put it back!" The terrorized climber glances down for a second—just long enough to realize that someone has removed the wooden ladder. He can see it lying flat on the ground. The girl's hysterics are distracting the others. They are wandering away, abandoning him on the ladder with no way to get down.

He struggles to control his panic, focusing his attention compulsively on one rung at a time and creeping upward, looking neither up nor down. Only when he reaches the last rung does he dare to look up once more. The story ends with his realization that the rungs of the ladder do indeed end, but there are five more feet of impassable space before the top of the tower.

*Themes and Meanings*

As might be expected in a story of suspense in which even the protagonist is undefined except in the most general terms, theme is not prominent in this tale. Particularly noteworthy is the author's control over the reader's attention and the effective expression of psychological nuances in an emotionally packed situation.

The indeterminate ending creates a real cliff-hanger, leaving to the imagination of the reader what the outcome will be. Logic and a realistic mode suggest tragedy; it seems unlikely that the protagonist is going to be rescued. Because those on the ground really know nothing of the actual plight of the climber and may assume, if they think at all, that he can return from the top by the stairway, their return is improbable.

One significant meaning that emerges from the story is that human beings are often, especially at this age, at the mercy of their impulses, with precious little attention to possible consequences. Many an uneasy parent will recognize this volatile combination of peer pressure, ego sensitivity, and inexperience that often leads to tragedy. The unique character of this exploit, different from usual misdemeanors of urban young people, lends a certain irony to the situation. Unlike pure pleasure-seekers, this young man assumes a pseudoheroic task that derives from a more archaic notion of valor: to climb the mountain and plant his lady's banner at the peak. Even the girl who starts the mean goading of the protagonist succumbs to the ancient meaning of chivalric action when she offers her handkerchief.

The story also emphasizes the existential isolation of each person in his or her private perception of experience. The climber has every reason to believe that no one knows the extremity of his distress. He is cut off both literally and spiritually from communication with his peers or anyone who might help or even sympathize with his predicament. If he lives through this experience, he will have learned a sobering truth about human destiny: The most stressful experiences of life are often the most solitary, and certainly every person does his or her own dying utterly alone.

### Style and Technique

Any story depending heavily on suspense, rather than on more leisurely sources of reader interest, requires a fast opening to engage the reader's attention and a swift closing after suspense has attained its peak. The climber's abandonment on the tower where he can neither ascend nor reach the ground again certainly provides the latter. William Sansom achieves the first requirement by jumping into the middle of the climb, then backtracking to explain the situation.

> As he felt the first watery eggs of sweat moistening the palms of his hands, as with every rung higher his body seemed to weigh more heavily, this young man Flegg regretted in sudden desperation but still in vain, the irresponsible events that had thrust him up into his present precarious climb.

This promise of excitement-to-come sustains the reader for the several paragraphs of preliminary events. These lend credibility to the situation, showing how it arises from the natural self-absorption, sexual rivalries, jealousies, and insecurities of young people everywhere. The brief reference to the protagonist's aspiring to "the glamour of a uniform" when he pretends to throw bricks with the special lobbing action of throwing hand grenades suggests a wartime milieu in which heroic action is even more a part of young male psychology.

Sansom is adept at describing how the appearance of an object changes radically from different perspectives. When Flegg first looks up from his position on the vertical ladder, the effect is quite alien to the impression it gives even a few yards away from the tower. The precision of this passage is remarkable for both its visual accuracy and its psychological effect.

> From this angle flat against the iron sheeting, the gasometer appeared higher than before. The blue sky seemed to descend and almost touch it. The redness of the rust dissolved into a deepening grey shadow, the distant curved summit loomed over black and high. Although it was immensely stable, as seen in rounded perspective from a few yards away, there against the side it appeared top heavy, so that this huge segment of sheet iron seemed to have lost the support of its invisible complement behind, the support that was now unseen and therefore unfelt, and Flegg imagined despite himself that the entire erection had become unsteady, that quite possibly the gasometer might suddenly blow over like a gigantic top-heavy sail.

The downward view is also distorted: "His friends appeared shockingly small. Their bodies had disappeared and he saw only their upturned faces." Such surrealistic appearances contribute to his impression of utter isolation. What is close at hand seems unnaturally large: "Even now the iron sheeting that stretched to either side and above and below seemed to have grown, he was lost among such huge smooth dimensions, grown smaller himself and clinging now like a child on some monstrous desert of rust."

The psychological realism of the story, rooted both in the special effects of an unfamiliar perspective and the tricks of an active imagination, eventually approaches archetypal imagery. Flegg's view of the top, still inaccessible at the end, seems more frightful even than the abyss below him. He sees it as "something removed and unhuman—a sense of appalling isolation."

> It echoes its elemental iron aloofness, a wind blew around it that had never known the warmth of flesh nor the softness of green fibres. Its blind eyes were raised above the world. It was like the eyeless iron visor of an ancient god, it touched against the sky having risen in awful perpendicular to this isolation, solitary as the grey gannet cliffs that mark the end of the northern world.

At this moment, if at no other, the frivolous escapade undertaken on a dare seems to suggest the mythic quest of the epic hero to the end of the world. Sansom does not allow this impression to remain, however, for poor Flegg is not cutting a very heroic figure: "Flegg, clutching his body close to the rust, made small weeping sounds through his mouth." At the end, when he realizes he cannot attain the top, he is staring and circling his head like a lost animal. Whatever impression one might have had about the romantic connotations of such an adventure, they dissolve in grim reality.

*Katherine Snipes*

# A VERY OLD MAN WITH ENORMOUS WINGS

*Author:* Gabriel García Márquez (1928-    )
*Type of plot:* Fable
*Time of plot:* The twentieth century
*Locale:* A Latin American village
*First published:* "Un señor muy viejo con unas alas enormes," 1968 (English translation, 1972)

> *Principal characters:*
> PELAYO, a villager who discovers the old man with wings
> ELISENDA, his wife
> FATHER GONZAGA, a village priest
> AN OLD MAN WITH WINGS

*The Story*

One day when Pelayo, a coastal villager, goes to dispose of crabs that have washed ashore onto his property, he discovers an old man with wings lying face down in the mud. The toothless creature is bald and dressed in rags. As Pelayo and his wife, Elisenda, carefully examine the creature, looking for clues to its origin, it responds to their questions in a tongue that they cannot identify. They suspect that he is a castaway from a ship. Other villagers who see the old man offer theories about his origins and appearance. The couple plan to set him adrift on a raft, but they first imprison him in a chicken coop. When a large crowd gathers around the coop, Pelayo and his wife decide to charge admission to view him, thereby creating a circuslike atmosphere.

The local priest, Father Gonzaga, is disturbed by rumors that the mysterious winged creature might be an angel, so he comes the next day to investigate. When the old man fails to understand Latin, the priest denounces him as an impostor. Nevertheless, curious people travel great distances to see the creature, and a carnival arrives to take advantage of the large crowds. Father Gonzaga, in the meantime, writes to the pope in an attempt to ascertain the church's official position on the creature and the apparently "miraculous" occurrences that the crowds associate with the old man. The Vatican demands to know if the old man knows Aramaic, if he can fit on the head of a pin, and if he has a navel. Meanwhile, the sick and the handicapped come to the old man in search of cures. The old man does seem to perform miracles, but these miracles are gratuitous in that they are unrelated to the sickness involved. A blind man, for example, grows three new teeth.

The crowds begin diminishing after the carnival puts on display a woman who was transformed into an enormous spider for having attended a dance without her parents' permission. Nevertheless, Pelayo and his wife have profited so greatly from their enterprise that they purchase a new house and fine clothing. After their chicken coop collapses, the old man moves into the couple's home, where he becomes a nuisance.

Over the years the old man makes feeble attempts to fly, but not until the end of the story does he finally gain sufficient strength and altitude to fly away.

## Themes and Meanings

"A Very Old Man with Enormous Wings" treats two issues: interpretation and invention/imagination. After the discovery of the stranger, six interpretations of his significance arise within the story. Once Pelayo recovers from his initial astonishment, he concludes that the old man is a lonely castaway. The basis for his conclusion is that the man speaks in a strong "sailor's voice." This explanation is merely arbitrary, however, because basic logic rejects the interpretation and makes Pelayo's explanation merely humorous. The second interpretation is made by a neighbor woman who is thought to know "everything about life and death." The humor of her interpretation arises in the certainty with which she pronounces that the old man is an angel.

The next three interpretations are proposed by various innocent and ingenuous villagers. According to them, the stranger may be either the mayor of the world, a five-star general, or the first of a race of winged wise men who will take charge of the universe. Although Father Gonzaga believes that the old man is not an angel, it is noteworthy that as the "official" interpreter in the town, he is the only one who refuses to offer a concrete interpretation; instead he merely sends a letter to the pope.

In the final analysis, the text offers no rational explanation for the enigmatic man. If fact, the text defies rational explanation or analysis. It is suggested, however, that the old man may be purely imaginary because he is described as disappearing in an "imaginary dot" on the horizon at the end of the story. Although critics have argued that the old man leaves because of his disillusionment with the exploitation surrounding his visit, at no time is this interpretation substantiated within the narrative itself.

"A Very Old Man with Enormous Wings" thus becomes a parody of the interpretive process itself. Appearing as the first story in the volume *La increíble y triste historia de la cándida Eréndira y de su abuela desalmada* (1972; *Innocent Erendira, and Other Stories*, 1979), it also functions as a kind of warning to the reader. The story's implication is that one must take extreme care when attributing rational laws of cause and effect to innately irrational occurrences. The story also affirms Gabriel García Márquez's right to invention, to the creative process, and to the life-affirming value of the human imagination.

## Style and Technique

In "A Very Old Man with Enormous Wings," García Márquez makes use of several highly inventive diversions from the basic story line to make interpretation even more elusive. In these narrative diversions theme and technique become inseparably intertwined. Although the old man/angel is central to the story, and every event bears on him, his appearance, behavior, identity, fate, or effects, the attention focused on the old man is frequently interrupted by shifts of focus to other characters, who are sometimes named and described at length. The obtrusiveness of the narrator, who is both at one with and apart from the other characters, also functions to distract the reader. The story, in fact, vacillates between the perspective of the omniscient narrator and that of the villagers, individually and collectively. When Father Gonzaga enters, for example, he reveals his suspicions about the old man, his observations about him, his sermon to the assembly of villagers, and his promise to seek advice from higher authorities. A few pages later, there appears a synopsis of his correspondence to the pope about the old man, and after another few pages, the waning of the old man's popularity seemingly cures Father Gonzaga of his insomnia. Then the old man disappears from the narrative altogether.

The full history of the carnival woman who was transformed into a spider for disobeying her parents constitutes another episode and provides a similar distraction, as do the imaginative excesses of the ailments suffered by those who seek the old man's help and the cures he provides: A blind man remains blind but grows three new teeth; a leper has sores that sprout sunflowers; a paralytic does not recover the use of his limbs but almost wins the lottery. Such details call attention to themselves, rather than to their cause. Thus, the episodic structure and narrative commentary within the story combine purposefully to distract the reader from the old man, thereby making rational interpretations of his arrival and departure impossible.

The reader of the story occupies a position superior to that of its characters, who view odd persons as clowns and believe that their neighbors possess supernatural powers. This sense of superiority is important to the story's humor, but it is only a minor aspect of the reader's total response. More significant is the reader's attitude regarding the role of interpretation and invention. The reader appreciates invention in itself and learns to accept its privileged position in the story. The diversions from the main story line give invention precedence over action or closure. The reader approaches interpretation cautiously, as attributing symbolic values to either the old man or his mysterious disappearance will merely be acts of pointless interpretation. Thus, the Magical Realism of García Márquez's style—a blurring of the division between the real and the fantastic—is used to underscore the notion (indeed, the seeming contradiction) that the irrational is a natural part of life and must be accepted on its own terms.

*Genevieve Slomski*

# THE VERY THING THAT HAPPENS

*Author:* Russell Edson (1935-    )
*Type of plot:* Fable
*Time of plot:* Anytime
*Locale:* A farmhouse
*First published:* 1960

> *Principal characters:*
> FATHER, a farmer
> MOTHER, his wife

*The Story*

This skewed and brief fable begins with a man, father, galloping into the kitchen of his house on an imaginary white horse. He is beating himself with a horsewhip and screaming joyfully at his wife to look at what he has done: He has invented for himself a new head that is a horse's head, he roars. His wife, mother, acknowledges that he has indeed done something, but that she is not at all pleased with whatever that something might be. Father goes on to explain with delight that this new horse's head that he has created is a heroic head. It has taken the place of his intrinsic head—the man-head with which he was born—which is now in his left buttock. The inversion of the usual man/animal hierarchy is here apparent: Father's posterior seems a natural location for his man-head, as the horse's head is clearly more majestic. Also, now that father has two heads, he is compelled to repeat every phrase as though two separate mouths were speaking. Rather than serving to reinforce what he is saying, however, this repetitive-ness serves only further to confuse and muddle his already muddled attempts at com-municating to his wife the essential importance of his deed.

In frustration mother finally yells, "Why is what is what?" Father replies in appar-ent justification—though in a detached manner, as if his head were not a part of him-self—that his head had simply to think of a horse and it became one. That, he says, would seem to be the only explanation of how such things happen. This implication of existential ambiguity and randomness does not sit well with mother as she grows in-creasingly agitated. To her frenzied cries of why this has happened at all, father ends the story with the rejoinder, "Because of all things that might have happened this is the very thing that happens."

*Themes and Meanings*

This half-page-long story was also published as part of Russell Edson's collection *The Very Thing That Happens: Fables and Drawings* (1964). The themes that the story presents are much clearer when taken in the context of the whole collection. As is evident from the above synopsis of his tale, Edson is not a fabulist in the traditional sense. His prose poems, as they are sometimes called (a description that he claims to abhor), do feature animals prominently, and they do attempt to convey some sort of lesson. It would be an exaggeration, however, to call them moral messages, as they define an amoral world that is more threatening, dehumanizing, and misanthropic than the world described in Aesop's classic fables. Instead, Edson uses the experiences of animals and objects to parallel human events as he performs a sort of ontological probing into the nature of this thing called life. Edson's primary themes here are the unstable arbitrariness of existence and the inanity of endless human attempts to make sense of it, order it, and control it.

Edson's universe may be irrational, but it is not without meaning. While poking fun at humankind's sense of superiority and the need to believe in some semblance of control, Edson also pities this human condition and in fact justifies it. After all, without this sense of arbitrariness, there would be no process of logic. That is to say, if everything were cut and dried, orderly and sensible, there would be no need to figure things out, to draw distinctions and conclusions, or to find a niche for oneself in the universe. Self-exploration would go no further than mindless faith.

It is ironic that the search for meaning in life is what is assumed to set human beings apart from other animals. However, it is through this search that human beings are struck by the loneliness, isolation, and meaninglessness of existence and experience such great angst that they ultimately are rendered indecisive, unadventurous, and hopeless. By conflating or interchanging father's head with the horse's head, Edson is suggesting that the typically pejorative "horse sense" is not in fact so senseless. Once humanity has embarked on its journey for wisdom and truth, through whatever ontological means, perhaps it should accept its inability to know the truth, or if that truth even exists.

By accepting that its perspective cannot go beyond the arbitrary, random, and chaotic, humanity becomes free to go where its instincts and perceptions lead it—to do what it does and get on with it—like the story's horse. The human system for knowledge need not be forsaken in order to accept, and does not preclude a simultaneous realization, that any system for knowing will never fully explain the nature and workings of the universe. Things do happen. Father thinks of a horse's head and he becomes one. There comes a time for acceptance and surrender, which is necessary to struggle through the inherent search for self and meaning in life. This acceptance allows father to break out of the frozen stasis of waking, eating, and sleeping that is his function as a human.

By blurring the distinctions between man and horse, head and ass, heroic and banal, Edson manages to obviate hierarchy. Good and bad become meaningless. The playing field is leveled, and all things—both animate and inanimate—share equal weight. Importance or unimportance thus becomes a matter of perspective. In Edson's world, everything is contingent on the reference frame, or one's visual scale. Everything is part of the same reality in a skewed platonic sense. All things are shadows of images of shadows endlessly, so far removed from the absolute that it scarcely matters if the absolute even exists. Human beings are confined by their perspective and their unwillingness to stray beyond the fragile boundaries of their own psyches. This notion explains in part the animal motif, especially that of barnyard animals, in Edson's work: It offers another perspective. People tend to think of such animals as confined, as one-dimensional, and as extensions of themselves to be used as tools toward human ends. The point is that all things—people, animals, and objects—are part of the same fabric, which weaves the disparate threads of free will, fate, and chance. It is how humans modulate these strands that determines their reality and whether their particular confined perspectives are a comfort or a curse. In this story father pushes against the false boundaries of reality and finds comfort in accepting that although unexplainable things happen, his perspective is limited only by his imagination.

*Style and Technique*

In Edson's surreal world, not only is the seemingly impossible possible—it literally Is. The matter-of-fact, casual tone that he employs to convey a wildly outrageous reality underscores this notion. His stories are brief snapshots of moments that are absurd, perverse, capricious, horribly grotesque, and frequently hilarious. His tightly packed stories are nutshell commentaries on the human condition, which he treats in a detached, oblique, and austere manner. His syntax is dry and elegant, and rhythmically his work has the poetic effects of fine verse. By combining quaint rhythms and subjects with grotesque images and horrible madness, he creates an imaginary world that is almost silly.

The impetuses in Edson's stories are narrative and dramatic, rather than descriptive. Description is too static as a technique to hold up against the constantly changing realities that his tales convey. His stories bleed energy, and all things are alive. Images jump off the page, changing and intertwining in a fictive realm where a character need merely entertain a possibility, and his head becomes that of a horse. Edson engages the reader, relying on the reader's ability and willingness to suspend disbelief and allow for all possibilities, no matter how great the absurdity.

Edson writes short prose pieces that blur the borders of a grossly general reality. He says his work is "always in search of itself, in a form that is always building itself from the inside out," as though the author is consumed by the story as an entity larger than himself. His is a form that discovers itself and constantly re-creates itself through the act of writing.

Edson's style is experimental; his imagination revolutionary. He combines all the fantasy of Lewis Carroll's *Alice In Wonderland* (1864) with the ribald psychedelic meanderings of Hunter S. Thompson's *Fear and Loathing in Las Vegas* (1972). The resulting brew is a new genre of zany fiction that explores fundamental human anxieties.

*Leslie Maile Pendleton*

# VICTORY OVER JAPAN

*Author:* Ellen Gilchrist (1935-    )
*Type of plot:* Domestic realism
*Time of plot:* 1945
*Locale:* Seymour, Indiana
*First published:* 1984

> *Principal characters:*
> RHODA MANNING, the narrator, who recalls a moment when she
> was in the third grade
> HER MOTHER
> BILLY MONDAY, her third-grade classmate, a rabies victim

*The Story*

When the story opens, Rhoda is enthralled with imagining particulars about Billy Monday's "tragedy": He is to have "fourteen shots in the stomach as the result of a squirrel bite." With ghoulish awe, Rhoda describes the ritual of the school principal and Billy's mother coming to get him every day when it is time for his shot. Using the pronoun "we," she speaks for the whole class in her descriptions. She and her best friend Letitia joke with each other about how they themselves would react to such a situation. By contrast, Billy Monday sits on a bench by the swings not talking to anybody. He is a small, pallid boy whom everyone ignored until he was bitten.

Although Rhoda is disgusted by the fact that Billy can barely read and that his head falls on the side of his neck when he is asked to do so, she is also fascinated by him. Rhoda is the only third-grader to have had an article published in the elementary school paper, and she determines to interview Billy for another article. Her first efforts at this during a noon recess cause Billy to withdraw into the shape of a human ball. Mrs. Jansma comes over to comfort him, sending Rhoda off to clean the chalkboards.

Meanwhile the school is gearing up for another paper drive to help the war effort. Rhoda jumps to her feet to be the first volunteer and to claim Billy Monday as her paper-drive partner. At home, Rhoda's mother rewards her for volunteering to be Billy's partner by baking her cookies. Rhoda feels pleased and goes outside to sit in her treehouse with cookies and a book. As she daydreams about becoming like her mother, it becomes clear how much she wants and needs her mother's approval, especially with her father off fighting in the war. Her mother has been painting liquid hose on her legs, getting ready for a visit from the Episcopalian minister, and Rhoda thinks about what an unselfish person her mother is. Later she overhears the adults talking about her approvingly, in intimate tones. Rhoda smugly returns to her book with a fresh supply of cookies and loses herself in the dialogue of a romance meant for adult readers.

On the Saturday of the paper drive, there is a slight drizzle, and Mr. Harmon, the school principal—who was shell-shocked in World War I—gives the children assembled on the school playground a patriotic pep talk. The third-grade class is leading the drive by seventy-eight pounds.

As Rhoda and Billy begin pulling a red wagon into the neighborhood assigned to them, Rhoda interviews Billy for the article she plans to write. Billy gives her a few unsensational answers and she continues to make herself the heroine by pulling the wagon and going up to the doors by herself. They are so successful that Mrs. Jansma later says "she'd never seen anyone as lucky on a paper drive" as Billy and Rhoda. They all decide to make one more trip.

As it gets dark, Rhoda and Billy decide to try a brick house that looks to Rhoda like a place where old people live; she thinks that old people are the ones with the most newspapers. This time she urges Billy to go to the door with her because she is tired of doing it herself. A thin man about Rhoda's father's age answers the door. This time Billy asks the man for papers; it is the first time that he has spoken to anyone but Rhoda all day. They follow the man through the musty house to the basement stairs, where he says they can have all the papers that they can carry. The children feel lucky when they find a large stack of magazines. Excited about winning the competition, Rhoda eagerly goes up and down the stairs filling the wagon. When she returns, Billy beckons her to look at what is inside one of the magazines: nude photographs of young children. They leave the house immediately, not closing doors or stopping to say thank you. Outside they discover that all the magazines from this house are of the same kind. After throwing them away, they part company and Rhoda tries to comfort Billy by saying that at least he will have something new to think about when he gets his shot the next day. Then she twice urges him not to tell anybody. Uncharacteristically, he keeps his head raised and looks straight at her when he says that he will not. He also asks if she will really be writing about him in the paper.

On the way home, Rhoda struggles with the images left in her mind by the photos and picks irises in an effort to please her mother. She writes her article about Billy, and it appears in the school paper. However, she never does get around to telling her mother about the magazines.

One day in August Rhoda is walking home from the swimming pool, and the man who gave her and Billy the magazines drives by and looks right into her face. She drops everything and runs home, scared and determined to tell her mother. When she gets home, however, her mother, brother, and several guests, including the minister, are crowded around the radio listening to the news. Her mother tells her to be quiet because they are trying to determine whether the United States has won the war. As they listen to news of the dropping of the biggest bomb in history on Japan, no one pays attention to Rhoda. She goes upstairs to think things over, feeling ambivalent about the war ending because it will mean the return of her father. Wrapped in her comforter, she falls into a nightmarish reverie in which she sits behind the wheel of an airplane carrying the bomb to Japan, but first dropping one on the bad man's brick house.

*Themes and Meanings*

The violent inevitability of both natural and social processes colliding with childhood innocence is a predominant theme in this story. The strongest treatments of this are suggested by the brutal rabies antidote that Billy must undergo and the atom bomb itself. Although precocious Rhoda aspires to be more sophisticated than her years, her innocence is evidenced by the very romanticism with which she attempts to protect herself from the world.

The ironic source of both Rhoda's fantasies and real problems is her desire to gain status with others. The fanatical need to live for and justify larger-than-life purposes, though made somewhat comic in Rhoda's character, is also tragic when it is measured against the larger backdrop of the logic that allowed the United States to end the war by using bombs that brought with them the knowledge that humankind is capable of destroying the planet.

Through Rhoda, the story emphasizes the human tendency to feed and live off drama and suffering, whether big or small, in order to make one's own life seem more important. At the same time, it shows how Rhoda herself is victimized by such a tendency, which she has only learned from the adults around her.

*Style and Technique*

Ellen Gilchrist's powerful and effective use of Rhoda as a first-person narrator helps to bring out these themes without making them hackneyed or didactic. Readers can perceive the hypocrisy in Rhoda's brand of romantic idealism, but she cannot—which makes her delivery of it that much more effective. Gilchrist effectively combines character development with narrative tone that makes the telling of the story inseparable from understanding Rhoda as a character. Although she lives for such drama, the irony is beautifully rendered as her own shock at the magazines overtakes her love of the sensational, and finally, although perhaps it has affected her more profoundly than Billy's rabies shots ever did or will, she does not disclose it in the same way at all. In fact, the narrative technique is one in which the disclosure is ironic. It is revealed by virtue of the fact it was never something she could figure out how to tell her mother, unlike the other things with which she rushed home in the hope of gaining approval.

There are also images in the story emphasizing the titillating sexual disclosure more blatantly exposed in the magazines: a glimpse of underpants from the monkey bars, the liquid hose that Rhoda's mother paints on her legs, a bathing suit and towel thrown down on the sidewalk. Juxtaposed with these images of vulnerability is the rhetoric of combat used to fuel both the paper drive and Rhoda's ambitions and fears. The rabies shot and the bomb are the core images around which this juxtaposition takes place.

*Maria Theresa Maggi*

# VICTROLA

*Author:* Wright Morris (1910-1998)
*Type of plot:* Realism
*Time of plot:* 1981
*Locale:* A small American town
*First published:* 1982

> *Principal characters:*
> BUNDY, an old man who lives alone except for his dog
> VICTROLA, his dog
> MISS TYLER, the dog's previous owner
> AVERY, a druggist

## The Story

Bundy is an elderly man who lives alone with his dog. He has had the dog since the death of its previous owner, Miss Tyler, who lived above Bundy. The overweight, asthmatic dog was already old at the time of Miss Tyler's death, several years before. When he lived with Miss Tyler, the dog always snarled when he met Bundy and barked wildly when he opened his mailbox. Bundy had taken the dog in even though he has never liked large dogs with short pelts and "had once been a cat man." Bundy does admire the dog's "one redeeming feature": He sits whenever he hears the word "sit."

Bundy and the dog have gotten along since the time they went to the park and the dog began furiously digging a large hole, only to have Bundy give him a sharp crack with the end of the leash. The dog turned on him with a look of hatred, but Bundy had "just enough presence of mind to stand there, unmoving, until they both grew calm." After this incident, they reached what Bundy considers a permanent truce.

The focus of the story is a shopping trip taken by the two of them. They go to a drugstore for Bundy's medicine and a vitamin supplement for the dog's itching. Passing an antique warehouse, Bundy realizes "that he no longer wanted other people's junk. Better yet (or was it worse?), he no longer *wanted*—with the possible exception of an English mint, difficult to find." At the supermarket, Bundy ties the dog to a bicycle rack and goes in to do his shopping.

A few minutes later, he is called to the front of the store, where the dog is lying on its side "as if sleeping." A clerk explains that some other dogs rushed it and apparently frightened it to death. When a woman asks the dog's name, Bundy says that it is Victor "since he could not bring himself to admit the dog's name was Victrola." Miss Tyler believed that the dog looked like the RCA symbol: "The resemblance was feeble, at best. How could a person give a dog such a name?"

*Themes and Meanings*

Wright Morris has frequently written about dogs and cats. In *One Day* (1965), a dog wears goggles while riding sitting up in a car, creating the impression that he is driving, and a cat has laryngitis in "The Cat's Meow." Usually what is most important is the animals' effects on humans, as when a cat causes three people to become more alive in "DRRDLA." What is significant in "Victrola" is that the dog and the man share the same problem: old age. Bundy is bothered when Avery, the druggist, never fails to comment on Victrola's age. Bundy notices that as Victrola grows older the younger dogs, one by one, begin to ignore him: "He might have been a stuffed animal leashed to a parking meter." Bundy worries that the owners of these dogs see him in the same way: "The human parallel was too disturbing for Bundy to dwell on it." When Dr. Biddle says that he will miss Victrola, Bundy believes that the retired dentist's eyes betray his fear that the dog's owner will "check out first."

Bundy senses that the other old men he encounters at the supermarket are touchy about whether he looks "sharper" than they do, but he considers elderly women he encounters less suspicious: "Bundy found them more realistic: they knew they were mortal. To find Bundy still around, squeezing the avocados, piqued the old men who returned from their vacations." Still, when Bundy thinks about what will happen "if worst came to worst," he is not certain whether he is thinking of himself or Victrola: "Impersonally appraised, in terms of survival the two of them were pretty much at a standoff: the dog was better fleshed out, but Bundy was the heartier eater." When the dog dies and someone finds Bundy a place to sit down, he remains standing as if to offer firm proof, to himself if to no one else, that he is anything but ready to follow Victrola.

Morris's fiction is full of eccentric old men who wander bemused through a world that they understand much less than they are willing to admit. Sometimes, however, this world seems beyond understanding. In the supermarket, Bundy suspiciously studies "the gray matter being sold as meat-loaf mix." He is not at all nostalgic for the past, but that does not blind him to the shortcomings of what passes for civilization, as when he enters the checkout lane "hemmed in by scandal sheets and romantic novels." For Morris's characters, the vagaries of modern life are something to be passed by rather than fruitlessly grappled with.

*Style and Technique*

One of the most notable aspects of Morris's approach to fiction is his objective tone. He is more amused than angered by what Bundy encounters on his shopping trips. Morris is more concerned with reporting changes in American society than in mourning the loss of anything, realizing that hindsight makes the past seem better than it was. He always avoids sentimentality as well, choosing to shift the focus at the end of the story from Bundy's response to Victrola's death to something comic: An elderly woman who always keeps the shopping cart to ferry home her purchase of two frozen dinners this time allows a police officer, arriving to investigate the dog's demise, to escort her across the street.

Much of the humor in "Victrola" is derived from Bundy's inability to control the dog as much as he wants. Victrola sits off to one side "so that the short-haired pelt on one rump was always soiled. When Bundy attempted to clean it, as he once did, the spot no longer matched the rest of the dog, like a clean spot on an old rug." Morris reveals the characters of both of his protagonists through humor: "Without exception, the dog did not like anything he saw advertised on television. To that extent he was smarter than Bundy, who was partial to anything served with gravy." Such blending of detail, character, and humor is what makes Morris such a distinctive artist as a short-story writer.

*Michael Adams*

# VIEWS OF MY FATHER WEEPING

*Author:* Donald Barthelme (1931-1989)
*Type of plot:* Antistory
*Time of plot:* A timeless present
*Locale:* Unspecified
*First published:* 1970

> *Principal characters:*
> THE UNNAMED NARRATOR, who may or may not be telling a story
> about the life and death of his father
> LARS BANG, the coachman, who may or may not have recounted
> a story of the death of the narrator's father
> A LITTLE GIRL, who witnesses the death of the father

*The Story*

In "Views of My Father Weeping," there is no realistic plot line based in the conventions of cause and effect and set in some existing time and space. Rather, Donald Barthelme presents the reader with a story about the supposed death of a narrator's father combined with interlineations that present alternating views of a father weeping. To complicate the matter even further, the story about the death of the father may or may not be true because the coachman, who storifies the experience, is reported to be a "bloody liar." In addition, the juxtaposition in the story of the narrator to the coachman suggests a doubling of the two men, an identification that makes the narrator a "bloody liar," too.

Asterisks separate thirty-five paragraphs that constitute the story. Paragraphs range from twenty-five lines to one line, the shortest being the last, which consists of one abbreviated word, "Etc.," which brings the reader back to the beginning of the story in an endless circle or a series of infinite regressions. The retrograde character of the action is consistent with the interlineations where "regression" operates in psychoanalytic terms to suggest a return of the libido to earlier stages of development or to infantile objects of attachment in the case of both father and son.

The opening of the story consists of two sentences establishing a possibly factual situation: "An aristocrat was riding down the street in his carriage. He ran over my father." The presence of an "aristocrat" in a "carriage" suggests a period when noblemen were driven about in coaches by liveried coachmen. The place of the accident, in King's New Square, together with references to the nobleman, the Lensgreve Aklefeldt, a count who lives at 17 rue du Bac, suggests a European setting. On the other hand, the interlineations refer to, among other things, mail carriers, insurance salespeople, armadillos, Ford Mustangs, television, and the American plains in such a way as to identify a setting in modern times in the United States. Furthermore, in the interlineations, the father is alive, if aged and continually weeping.

The tie between the storified experience concerning the death of the father and the interlineations is the narrator. In the storified experience, the narrator is searching for the "truth" about the killing of his father. In the interlineations, the narrator is searching for the "truth" about his feelings for his father, which will result in his own ego identity.

Having been notified by the police of the accidental death of his father by a hit-and-run carriage, the narrator seeks witnesses to the occurrence so that he can determine for himself the real conditions of his father's death. The first witness that the narrator finds is a little girl, eleven or twelve years old, who says that she witnessed only part of the accident because part of the time she had her back turned. She identifies the man in the carriage as an aristocrat. Later this little girl will inexplicably turn up at the narrator's door to tell him the name of the coachman who was driving the aristocrat's carriage.

The little girl is the first of three females who give the narrator some kind of guidance in his search for his father's executioner. A woman named Miranda will tell the narrator how to get inside the aristocratic quarters where the nobleman lives and how to present himself to the inhabitants of the great house. Another woman makes final comment on the story the coachman, Lars Bang, finally tells the narrator. This woman is the one who points out that "Bang is an absolute bloody liar." The only other female in the story is the narrator's mother, who apparently is at some distance from her husband and son because she is not present at the burial, and the son telephones her with the news of his father's death.

Stories told to the narrator by various witnesses to the accident differ. According to the witnesses, either the father was drunk and was himself the cause of the accident or the driver was at fault because he could have avoided the collision had he tried. The narrator says that he smelled no alcohol on his father at the scene of the accident. Lars Bang, in telling his version of the story, says the father was thoroughly drunk and attacked the horses in such a way as to cause them to rear in fright and to run headlong over the father, dragging him forty feet over the cobblestones. Bang says that he tried but could not stop the horses.

The interlineations present the distress of a son with a father who cannot control his weeping. The fact that the son is not sure that the weeping father is his own suggests an archetypal father figure who may be "Tom's father, Phil's father, Pat's father, Pete's father, Paul's father." This archetypal figure desires in the son's mind to be thanked for his contribution to the life of the son and worshiped by the son in the manner demanded by a god. The son alternately sees himself before his father in a ceaseless attitude of painful supplication and as his father's avenger, someone who, if only he knew what was causing his father to weep, could try to do something about it:

> Father, please! . . . look at me, Father . . . who has insulted you? . . . are you, then, compromised? . . . ruined . . . a slander is going around? . . . . an obloquy? . . . . a traducement? . . . . 'sdeath! . . . . I won't permit it! . . . . I won't abide it! . . . I'll . . . move every mountain . . . climb . . . every river . . . etc.

Juxtaposed to images of the father weeping are images of the father not weeping but in absurd situations, such as straddling a very large dog, writing on a white wall with crayons, shaking pepper into a sugar bowl, knocking down dolls' furniture in a doll's house, and playing shoot-'em-up with his son with real guns.

Both lines of narration—the storified experience of the death of the father and the interlineal comments on and description of the behavior of the weeping father—come to the same conclusion, expressed in the final paragraph: "Etc."

### Themes and Meanings

There is no way for a reader of "Views of My Father Weeping" to tell whether anything described in the story has actually taken place. Nor can any reader tell anything objective about the father. What the reader does experience is the author's subjective expression on a surrealistic plane of a son's feelings about his father that are strong, but ambiguous. The son's nightmare vision of the father's continual weeping suggests that fathers can do nothing but weep and sons can do nothing to alleviate their weeping, though sons may feel compassion for fathers who weep. On the other hand, weeping fathers can get on the nerves of youthful sons (who are not yet fathers). Sons can desire their fathers dead and project visions of accidents that kill them. The sons themselves (because the visions are theirs) murder the fathers.

In this way, the two narrative lines of the story are joined. Lars Bang is a projection of the narrator, who kills the father whom the son desires dead. Lars Bang is a liar, as is the son who covers up his desire to rid himself of his father by projecting it into a dream context. Nothing the son can do, however, will rid him of the vision of the weeping father, and nothing the son can do will stop the passage of time from transforming the murderous son into a weeping father himself.

### Style and Technique

Characterized by a surreal surface that combines in varying degrees elements of the fantastic, incongruous, absurd, and clichéd, this story owes much to writers, such as the great nineteenth century Continental novelists Nikolai Gogol, Fyodor Dostoevski, and Charles Dickens, and the great modernists, such as Franz Kafka, Vladimir Nabokov, James Joyce, and Jorge Luis Borges, whose novelistic dreamscapes provide a suprarational way of knowing that is distinctly different from a "realistic" view of the everyday world as apprehended through the senses. In Barthelme's story, as in others characteristic of the postmodernist mode, the ordinary or existential gives way to the fabulous; fact and fiction, as ordinarily conceived, are blended, and the story draws attention to itself not only as artifact but also as an epistemological act, a valid way of knowing. For Barthelme, as for other postmodernists, fiction is not mimetic, not an imitation of life. Rather, fiction is an act of creation, a shaping and a forming of reality that defines self. One is, according to Barthelme, what one makes. One defines oneself in one's art. Thus, changes in aesthetic structures can lead to changes in the world around the artist.

*Mary Rohrberger*

# A VILLAGE SINGER

*Author:* Mary E. Wilkins Freeman (1852-1930)
*Type of plot:* Regional
*Time of plot:* The 1880's
*Locale:* New England
*First published:* 1889

> *Principal characters:*
> CANDACE WHITCOMB, the soprano in the church choir for forty
> years
> ALMA WAY, her replacement in the choir
> WILSON FORD, her nephew and Alma's fiancé
> MRS. NANCY FORD, her sister and Wilson's widowed mother
> REVEREND POLLARD, the minister of her church
> WILLIAM EMMONS, the choir leader

*The Story*

One Thursday, about eight o'clock in the evening, Candace Whitcomb receives a visit from all the members of the choir in which she has sung for forty years. They bring cake and oranges for what Candace thinks is a surprise party. After they leave, she finds a photograph album addressed to her from her many friends. Inside the album is a letter informing Candace that she has been dismissed from the choir.

Candace is angry at being discarded and at the way in which she was removed. The following spring Sunday is warm, so the little church at which Candace used to sing has opened all its windows. When Alma Way, the new soprano, begins her solo, Candace (whose cottage stands close to the church) begins playing loudly on her parlor organ and singing to drown out Alma's voice. All the members of the choir rally around Alma after the service to express their anger at Candace and their sympathy for the new soprano. The choir director and minister are particularly solicitous about the new singer and critical of her predecessor.

Reverend Pollard visits Candace to try to prevent any recurrence of such a disturbance. He finds that she is using the photograph album as a footstool, and when he suggests that she inadvertently sang a bit too loud during the morning service, she replies that she did so intentionally. She further informs him that she intends to continue to sing against her rival every Sunday. During that afternoon's service, Candace repeats her performance during Alma's solo.

Candace's nephew, Wilson Ford, loves Alma and hopes to marry her someday. Infuriated by his aunt's treatment of his fiancé, he rushes into Candace's cottage and threatens to throw her parlor organ out the window if she again disturbs Alma's singing. Candace replies by telling him that because of his outburst, she will rewrite her will to disinherit him. Then he will not have her money or her house, without which he will not be able to marry.

Candace will not, however, disrupt Alma's singing again. Her rebellion has so drained her that she becomes fatally ill. On the evening of her rebellion, she looks outside to see a fire in the distance consuming the spring foliage. This conflagration mirrors the fever that is destroying her. Her sister, Mrs. Nancy Ford, who comes to tend her, thinks that the illness is trivial. The wiser Candace knows that it is mortal. During her last week of life, she regrets her hostility to Reverend Pollard, and she asks her sister to brush off the photograph album to remove the signs of the function to which she initially consigned it. She tells her nephew that he can have her house and money, and she even asks Alma to sing a hymn for her: "Jesus, Lover of My Soul." Though dying and repentant, Candace's spirit has not been totally crushed; when Alma finishes her song, Candace's last words to her are, "You flatted a little on—soul."

*Themes and Meanings*

Like Mary E. Wilkins Freeman's other stories of this period, such as "A Church Mouse" (1889) and "A Poetess" (1890), "A Village Singer" places a woman in conflict with male hierarchy, represented in all three stories by a minister. Here the Reverend Pollard and Candace Whitcomb have both served the same church for forty years. He sometimes hesitates in his speech, and Candace indicates that his sermons lack the freshness they once possessed. Yet no one gives him a photograph album and asks him to leave his post. The choirmaster, Williams Emmons, has held his position for decades and is older than Candace. If her voice has deteriorated, logically his must have also. Yet no one gives him a farewell photograph album. Again, as a male, he can remain choirmaster as long he as he likes.

Candace rightly feels betrayed on various levels. As an artist, she knows that her voice is still good. Moreover, she tells Reverend Pollard that salvation does not depend on anyone's hitting a high note. A church should exhibit Christian charity. She also is hurt as a woman. For decades the choirmaster had sung duets with Candace and had walked her home after Saturday night choir practice. Villagers expected him to propose marriage to her. Instead, he supports her dismissal and sides with Alma in the ensuing conflict.

Even her nephew turns on her. He knows that her will leaves him all she owns, and both know that this legacy will allow him to obtain the happiness that eluded Candace. Still, he shows no sympathy toward her or even a willingness to discuss her grievance. He reacts to her pain with threats of violence.

Again like other Freeman heroines, Candace refuses to succumb to this male hierarchy. Here her triumph is short-lived because her resistance drains all her energy. Still, she has not gone gently into that good night, and on her deathbed she exhibits a mixture of Christian forbearance and independence that allows her to retain the reader's sympathy. She takes no revenge on her nephew, apologizes to the minister, and seeks reconciliation with her rival. At the same time, when William Emmons comes to inquire about her, she lets him go away without seeing her; and she criticizes Alma's singing. Candace's strength is evident also in her nephew's dependence on her. He would like to earn enough to buy a house and support a wife, but he has been unable to do so. He needs a woman—his aunt—to supply the means that permit him to live as he wants. Candace yields to illness, but no man could have stopped her from pursuing her independent course, from refusing to surrender to the men who would render her superannuated.

*Style and Technique*

Candace's deathbed criticism of Alma's singing highlights a key concern of the story. Alma's name means "soul" in Latin, but as Candace's last words state, Alma lacks something in that department. By agreeing to replace Candace, Alma has sided with the church's male hierarchy, which in turn supports her against her independent predecessor. Alma sacrifices her freedom—she is going to marry Wilson—for male approval that requires her to supplant Candace.

Alma's failure to live up to her name results not only in her betrayal of a woman in siding with the village patriarchy but also in her rejection of the past. Candace, in her conversation with the minister, notes that manners and tastes are changing: "Folks are gettin' as high-steppin' an' fussy in a meetin'-house as they are in a tavern, nowadays." Even in an isolated New England village, new attitudes are intruding to banish reverence for old ways and old people. Candace is evicted from her post; her sister will be left to live alone when Wilson marries Alma and moves into Candace's cottage.

Local color stories seek to preserve a vanishing world. In "A Village Singer," Freeman achieves this goal by recording the language and life of rural New England. Candace speaks in the cadences and dialect of her native place. In this village, social activities revolve around the church. Freeman's description of Candace's house also captures the past as it links Candace to the Old World. Candace has hung looped lace curtains at her window and grows lilacs—the quintessential New England flowering shrub—and a rose tree in her garden. She receives the minister in her parlor, which is furnished with a rocking chair and another seat upholstered in haircloth. Significantly, the choir gives Candace a photograph album to hold the images of her past. Freeman's stories such as "A Village Singer" serve this same purpose of capturing between covers snapshots of what was but no longer is.

*Joseph Rosenblum*

# VILLON'S WIFE

*Author:* Osamu Dazai (Shūji Tsushima, 1909-1948)
*Type of plot:* Social realism
*Time of plot:* 1946
*Locale:* Tokyo
*First published:* "Viyon no tsuma," 1947 (English translation, 1956)

*Principal characters:*
MRS. OTANI, the narrator and wife of the celebrated poet
MR. OTANI, the celebrated poet
THE RESTAURANT OWNER
THE OWNER'S WIFE

*The Story*

"Villon's Wife," set in the dark years of the early postwar era, is narrated by the wife of a writer who has been much celebrated but who has given himself over to drunkenness and debauchery. The story opens late on a winter night as the woman, asleep with her retarded son, hears her husband come home, drunk as usual. With uncharacteristic tenderness the husband asks if the child still has a fever. At this point a man and woman arrive at the front door and call for the writer, Mr. Otani. An argument ensues and the wife tries to intervene, but Otani pulls a knife and rushes out of the house, "flapping the sleeves of his coat like a huge crow," and disappears into the darkness.

The wife invites the two visitors into the shabby house and learns of the difficulty between these people and her husband. The couple explain that they run a small restaurant and drinking place where Otani has been a regular customer for several years, accompanied by a succession of women friends. He has run up a huge debt, but what is worse, on this particular evening, he has stolen five thousand yen that the owner needs in order to pay his wholesalers before the end of the year. Not wanting to make a scene in public, the couple have followed Otani home, hoping that they can persuade him quietly to return the money. Instead, he threatens them with a knife and runs away.

On hearing this story, the wife's only response is to burst out laughing—they are so poor she cannot even afford to take her sick child to a doctor, much less pay back the five thousand yen her husband stole or pay off the debts he has accumulated. The wife, however, reassures the couple that everything will be settled the following day and asks them not to file charges against her husband quite yet.

The next morning, the woman takes her child and wanders aimlessly for a time, then goes to the restaurant where her husband stole the money. Not knowing what else to do, she once again reassures the owner and his wife that someone will come soon with the money, and says that to show her good faith, she will stay at the restaurant as a sort of hostage until the debt is paid. The wife keeps herself busy waiting on customers. She is quite popular with the customers, who are in a festive mood since it is Christmas Eve. That evening, a man and woman came in dressed and masked for a masquerade party. Although realizing that it is her husband, the wife treats him as she would any other customer. His friend speaks briefly with the owner and pays back the five thousand yen that was stolen.

When the owner thanks Mrs. Otani for helping to get his money back, she offers to stay on and continue working until her husband's drinking debt is also paid. At first, she finds her life wonderfully transformed now that she has found a way to deal actively with her problems rather than simply sit at home and worry. The enthusiasm, however, does not last long, and after working for twenty days, she concludes that all men are criminals and that as poorly as her husband treats her, he is not the worst of the scoundrels she has come to know. One evening a customer follows her home, and when she shows some sympathy for him, he rapes her.

The next morning, she goes to work and finds her husband already at the restaurant and already drinking heavily. He shows her a review in the newspaper where he is referred to as a monster. He asks if she thinks he is a monster and explains that he stole the five thousand yen in the first place to buy New Year's presents for her and the child so that they could have "the first happy New Year in a long time." The wife's only response to this excuse is that there is nothing wrong with being a monster as long as one somehow manages to survive.

*Themes and Meanings*

Osamu Dazai, who had always been a social rebel, found himself in a paradoxical situation when Japan surrendered in 1945. For years, he had been preaching the message that accepted social values were bankrupt. With the loss of the war, society at large came to agree with him, and, indeed, saw him as something of a prophet. Although he offered no new set of social values to replace the old, with this story and some postwar novels, he became a major spokesperson for the values and attitudes of Japanese society at that time.

Typically for Dazai, the two central characters, Otani and his wife, represent contrasts at every level. In this regard, they become spokespeople for two different approaches to Japan's postwar condition. The wife is industrious, nurturing, practical, and willing to deal with problems. Otani, on the other hand, is frivolous, irresponsible, dissolute, and self-indulgent. In the end, the wife has the strength to recognize her situation and to adapt, accept, and endure it, although her husband cannot. For the wife, the most important thing is survival at any cost, no matter how degrading or dehumanizing that survival turns out to be. The husband cannot accept life on those terms, and for him there is only flight and despair. Although the wife understands and accepts her condition and changes her way of living to ensure survival, the husband fails to come to terms with his desperate condition. It is typical of Dazai to depict strong, enduring women who nurture weak, feckless men. In this story, the women are practical realists, and the men are idealistic dreamers.

The title of the story alludes to a work written by Otani that has the title "Francois Villon." There are certain parallels between events in Dazai's story and the life of the French poet. Villon was a romantic and a poet who was accused of stealing five hundred gold crowns from the College of Navarre shortly before Christmas in 1456. His ballads, like Dazai's story, depict his helpless entanglement in shameless vice and are known for their grim humor and their expression of the vanity of life. At another level, the reader can see Dazai depicting himself in the character Otani, who sees himself as the Francois Villon of Japan. This is particularly true in the sense that Dazai's position was similar to that of Villon, who was loved by all of Paris for his poetry even while his personal life was a disreputable shambles.

*Style and Technique*

Dazai's favorite techniques for depicting the human condition are paradox and black humor. One sees examples of this when the restaurant owners arrive at Otani's house and fall back on social convention, telling him what a nice house it is. In fact, the mats are rotting, the paper doors are in shreds, and the cushions are filthy and torn. Again, one sees Dazai's sardonic humor when the restaurant owner refers to Otani as a genius, an aristocrat, and a man of unlimited capability, whereas the wife, immune to flattery, knows perfectly well that her husband is a drunkard, a thief, and a lecher who is brazenly unfaithful to her.

By creating the character of the wife as being an unflinching realist and giving her the narrator's role, Dazai is able to contrast Otani's self-pity with the absence of self-pity on the part of the wife, giving the work its terrible power. This effect is created because the narrator does not pass judgment on the events she recounts; she simply states the facts and her own determination to go on surviving.

*Stephen W. Kohl*

# A VISIT OF CHARITY

*Author:* Eudora Welty (1909-2001)
*Type of plot:* Didactic
*Time of plot:* The 1930's
*Locale:* An American nursing home
*First published:* 1941

> *Principal characters:*
> MARIAN, a young Campfire Girl who visits a nursing home
> ADDIE, an elderly female occupant of the nursing home
> OLD WOMAN, who is Addie's roommate

## The Story

The action of "A Visit of Charity" is deceptively simple. Marian, a young Campfire Girl, reluctantly visits an "Old Ladies' Home" to gain points for her charity work. While there, she meets two old women, one who chatters on in an obsequious way and another, old Addie, who, confined to bed, resents the little girl's visit as well as her own babbling roommate. When Marian leaves the home, she retrieves an apple that she hid before entering and takes a big bite out of it. Thus the story ends in a seemingly inconclusive way, leaving the reader to wonder if it is really a story at all. When one looks beneath the slight surface action of the story, however, one sees that "A Visit of Charity" has a complex structure based on a series of metaphoric devices, all of which serve to evoke the dreamlike grotesque atmosphere within the nursing home.

As Marian enters the home, the bulging linoleum on the floor makes her feel as if she is walking on the waves, and the smell in the building is like the interior of a clock. When the mannish nurse tells Marian that there are "two" in each room, Marian asks, "Two what?" The garrulous old woman is described as a birdlike creature who plucks Marian's hat off with a hand like a claw, while old Addie has a "bunchy white forehead and red eyes like a sheep"; she even "bleats" when she says, "Who—are—you?" Marian feels as if she has been caught in a robber's cave; she cannot even remember her own name. In her dreamy state, Marian cannot think clearly. When the old woman rocks faster and faster in her chair, Marian cannot understand how anyone can rock so fast.

The climax of the story occurs when it is discovered that it is old Addie's birthday. When the babbling roommate tells Marian that when she was a child she went to school, Addie lashes out in the single long speech in the story, telling her roommate that she was never young and that she never went to school: "You never were anything—only here. You never were born! You don't know anything. . . . Who are you? You're a stranger—a perfect stranger." When Marian goes over to Addie, she looks at her very closely from all sides, "as in dreams," and she wonders about her as if "there was nothing else in the world to wonder about. It was the first time such a thing had happened to Marian." When she asks the old woman how old she is, Addie says "I won't tell" and whimpers like a sheep, like a little lamb. In the last paragraph of the story, Marian has escaped her terrifying experience; when she jumps on the bus, she takes a big bite out of the apple that she hid, seemingly unaffected by her nightmarish experience with the old women.

## Themes and Meanings

The basic theme of the story is suggested by the obvious irony of the title, for Marian's visit is not one of true charity, but rather a formal, institutionalized gesture. It certainly does not represent the biblical notion of charity in 1 Corinthians, which is interpreted in the Revised Standard Version of the Bible as "love," or sympathetic identification of one person with another. From the beginning of the story, Marian does not think of the two old women as people like herself. She not only is aware of the strangeness of the old ladies, but she also has become a stranger to herself. Thrown out of her familiar world, where she belongs, she is in a grotesque dreamworld, where she intensely feels her difference from the old ladies and thus her own separation and isolation. This symbolic sense of alienation explains the strange, dreamlike effect of the nursing home on Marian.

If the story were concerned only with Marian's difficulty in identifying with the old women, it would be easier to dismiss, for one might legitimately ask how it is possible for a girl to feel empathy for these strange and grotesque old women. Thus, to show that the feeling of charity, in the New Testament sense of "love," is totally lacking in the story, Eudora Welty establishes the relationship between the two old women. Why do they not love each other? It should be easy for them to perceive their common identity and thus maintain a sense of unity instead of one of total separation. However, they do not; they seldom speak except to contradict each other; as old Addie says, they are strangers: "Is it possible that they have actually done a thing like this to anyone— sent them in a stranger to talk, and rock, and tell away her whole long rigamarole?" Addie's tirade against her roommate becomes the thematic center of the story: In a world without love, all people are strangers, for they cannot break through their own sense of separation to perceive their commonality and thus their oneness with one another. When Addie says that the other old woman is empty, she recognizes that this is so both because she is not loved and because she has no love to give. Without love, she is a stranger, just as without love all human beings are strangers to one another and to themselves.

The crisis for Marian occurs soon after the climactic moment of old Addie's tirade, for she then asks Addie how old she is and looks at the old woman very closely from all sides "as if in dreams." As Marian looks at Addie, she "wondered about her for a moment as though there was nothing else in the world to wonder about. It was the first time such a thing had happened to Marian." However, this opportunity for identifying with the old woman is a fleeting one, for when Addie refuses to tell her age and begins crying, Marian jumps up and escapes.

*Style and Technique*

"A Visit of Charity" is typical of Welty's early short fiction, both in its use of a tight metaphoric structure and in its focus on the problem of love and separateness, which Welty has made her most predominant fictional theme. Symbol, metaphor, and biblical allusion are the primary devices that Welty uses to give depth and resonance to this seemingly simple story. The story is not merely a social criticism of institutional charity; it is about the difficulty, in any context, of following the biblical injunction to "love thy neighbor as thyself." Marian's final act—retrieving the apple she hid before entering the home and taking a big bite out of it—is the final symbolic gesture that unifies all the other metaphors and allusions in the story. Her biting the apple, recalling the biblical story of Adam and Eve, suggests both the sense of separation that follows the Fall and the difficulty of healing that separation through love, as mandated by the New Testament. In the Gospel of John, Jesus three times asks Peter if he loves Him. When Peter replies that he does, Jesus says, "Feed my sheep."

When one recalls that Addie, the old woman who desperately needs love, is constantly referred to as a sheep or a little lamb, the implication of Marian's bite into the apple is clear. She has refused to feed the sheep—literally by refusing to give the apple to Addie and symbolically by refusing to give her love. Thus, by means of the central metaphors and the biblical allusions, the story illustrates both the Old Testament loss of union as depicted in the Genesis story and the difficulty of following the New Testament injunction to regain that union through loving the neighbor as the self. Marian takes the bite of the apple and the story is over; the reader is left with the echo of old Addie's despairing cry, "Who are you? You're a stranger—a perfect stranger. Don't you know you're a stranger."

*Charles E. May*

# A VISIT TO GRANDMOTHER

*Author:* William Melvin Kelley (1937-    )
*Type of plot:* Social realism
*Time of plot:* The 1940's
*Locale:* New York City and the American South
*First published:* 1964

*Principal characters:*
>DR. CHARLES DUNSFORD, a black, middle-class professional with festering childhood memories
>CHARLES "CHIG" DUNSFORD II, his eldest child
>GL DUNSFORD, the doctor's spontaneous, hedonistic older brother
>MAMA EVA DUNSFORD, Dr. Dunsford's mother

*The Story*

Although the title of this story sparks images of loving company and comforting surroundings, it actually is a presage of disaster. Dr. Charles Dunsford has left his New York home to attend his twenty-year college reunion in Nashville, Tennessee. Accompanied by his oldest son, Charles "Chig" Dunsford II, he spends a festive week in the South. Then he decides to prolong their vacation, suggesting to the teenage Chig that they visit his mother, who has not seen her grandson since he was a small boy.

Once the pair arrives at "Mama" Eva Dunsford's home, their journey becomes an unpleasant one. Plied with questions and pampered by attentive relatives, Chig settles in with ease. His father, however, becomes taciturn and withdrawn. The constant, mesmerizing stories about his fun-loving brother, GL Dunsford, open old resentments that Charles had buried under his kind, gentle exterior.

Finally, unable to listen to the tales anymore, the jealous brother blurts out his anger during the family's dinner. Complaining to his mother that she never really loved him at all, he voices the familiar lament of the overdisciplined, overachieving sibling: "If GL and I did something wrong, you'd beat me first and then be too God damn tired to beat him. At dinner, he'd always get seconds and I wouldn't. You'd do things with him . . . but if I wanted you to do something with me, you were always too busy." The astonished Mama justifies her behavior, arguing that she loved all of her children even though she may have treated them differently. However, Charles remains distraught. After repeating that it is too late for mending wounds, he runs upstairs to his room. Sadly, who should then appear at the door, "smiling broadly [with], an engaging, open, friendly smile, the innocent smile of a five-year-old," but GL himself, eager to reunite with his brother.

*Themes and Meanings*

When "A Visit to Grandmother" was published, one reviewer castigated it for not being "concerned enough with the race problem." Two years earlier, William Melvin Kelley himself had asserted that dealing exclusively with racism was not his intent: "A sixteenth of an inch of skin is nothing either to crow about or to feel ashamed of. If you are a human being, and know it, you will remain a human being even if you are brainwashed, deprived of food, clothes and shelter, drugged, beaten or shot." Kelley's preface to *Dancers on the Shore* (1964) underscores this thought with his vow to "depict people, not symbols or ideas disguised as people." However, at least in this story, Kelley breaks his own pledge. Although the Dunsfords' individual motives and personalities are shallowly developed, taken as a group they deftly reveal the universal strengths and sorrows of human families.

Foremost, Kelley illustrates that the bedrock of human families is their unity. In contrast to Charles's physical separation from his birthplace and acquired bourgeois lifestyle (he sends his children to exclusive schools and summer camps), his extended family members still live in the same town. (In fact, Mama's very hands "were as dark as the wood" of her chair "and seemed to become part of it.") The adult Dunsfords even mimic one another in their colors of hair and clothing, white and brown, as if to externalize their shared experiences and dreams. They further demonstrate their solidarity by welcoming Charles and Chig, who are veritable strangers, without hesitation.

This sense of kinship that defies time and distance becomes most prominent in the story's final scene. As the dinner conversation focuses on family memories, some of the Dunsfords—Chig, his aunts, and Mama—ask, answer, or direct questions. The two remaining men, Charles and his voracious brother Hiram, listen. By accounting for every member's behavior, regardless of vigor or passivity, Kelley emphasizes the importance of each individual's participation in order to make the family vibrant. Thus, Aunt Rose keeps piling food on Chig's plate, despite his polite refusals, as though in some way the sustenance of the very least among them is necessary for the survival of the others.

Even the conflict between Charles and GL exposes a truth about family unity. These two men are so unlike each other that it seems unfathomable for them to have shared even one parent. GL, "part con man, part practical joker and part Don Juan," is the family's black sheep who has never established a career and family, constantly brushes the wrong side of the law, and cultivates his wits for survival as much as for trend-setting eminence. On the opposite end of the social spectrum, Charles, a soft-spoken, long-married father of three, owns his own home and maintains a successful medical practice. Ironically, though, both men exist on the family's periphery. Just as Charles leads a self-imposed exile in New York, GL flits from place to place outside his home. Foreigners to their own kin, GL looms as the roguish hero of the family memoirs while Charles puzzles his mother when she tries to identify him. Such similarities suggest that these two are brothers, with something in common, no matter what comes between them. Having sprung from the same bloodline and shared the same upbringing, they have more potential for ignoring their differences than first appears.

*Style and Technique*

Kelley's style here is unembellished and direct, almost reportorial. His typical descriptions, presented in loose, choppy sentences, are nearly juvenile in their simplicity: "She squinted. She looked like a doll, made of black straw, the wrinkles in her face running in one direction like the head of a broom. Her hair was white and coarse and grew out straight from her head. Her eyes were brown . . . and were hidden behind thick glasses." Instead of detracting from the story, however, this language is appropriate, because the action is related through the young Chig's eyes. At seventeen, he is on the threshold of adulthood, but he is an innocent in this story with regard to his father's relationship to GL and the rest of the family down South.

Unfortunately, the author neglects an opportunity to use this naïve point of view to heighten suspense. With Chig's uninformed observations, he could have deftly alerted readers to the angry confrontation that ends the tale. Instead, Kelley undercuts the plot by revealing the outcome too soon. For example, during the dinner-table discussion of GL, Chig sees his father's "face completely blank, without even a trace of a smile or a laugh." The youth is too absorbed with the fun and food to conclude that something has gone awry. However, the impact of his description is weak because it lacks subtlety. In the very first sentence of this story, Chig discloses that "something was wrong" between his father and grandmother. Additionally, his early comments about his father's "far too offhand" manner and reticence about his childhood forebode disaster. Thus, Chig's half-conscious glance at his father during the meal is simply another part of the climax, rather than an unsettling, masterful harbinger of it.

*Barbara A. McCaskill*

# THE VISITOR

*Author:* Russell Banks (1940-        )
*Type of plot:* Psychological
*Time of plot:* 1986 and 1952
*Locale:* Tobyhanna, Pennsylvania
*First published:* 1988

> *Principal characters:*
> THE NARRATOR, a forty-six-year-old man
> HIS FATHER
> HIS MOTHER
> GEORGE RETTSTADT, a restaurateur

*The Story*

"The Visitor" is an account of how a man's past has shaped his present. As the story begins, the anonymous narrator tells of his recent trip from his home in New York City to East Stroudsburg University in Pennsylvania to deliver a lecture. The university is a short distance from Tobyhanna, where he lived as a boy; on an impulse, he drives the extra miles to visit the town.

Paragraphs about the narrator's childhood in Tobyhanna—his parents and their rage, a visit to the local bar, and the home in which his family lived—are interwoven with paragraphs about his more recent past—his adult visit to the town—both narrated from his mature perspective. The year that the narrator and his family lived in Tobyhanna was a time of frustration for his parents. His father drank heavily, womanized, and lied to his wife about how he spent his evenings. As his drinking increased and he spent more time away from home, he became increasingly violent. The narrator's mother was stuck with three small children in a house five miles from town.

As the adult narrator arrives in Tobyhanna, he pulls up to the bar on the main street and goes inside. The smell, look, dampness, and dirty feel of the place are so unchanged that reentering it makes the narrator recall a visit that he, his father, and his brother made there thirty-four years earlier. This bit of memory is the beginning of a longer one about a specific Saturday during one winter; throughout the remainder of the story the remembering and telling about that visit parallels the events and details of the narrator's recent visit. The locals gathered in the bar in 1986 remind him of those present on that distant Saturday—his father and his cronies and a woman with red lipstick to whom his father gave his complete attention.

The bartender asks the adult narrator if he wants another beer; this abruptly pulls the story forward into the more recent past. The narrator declines and leaves. When he is back in his car, his story again goes back in time, and he is a young boy riding home from the bar with his father and brother. His father invents an alibi to explain their long absence to his wife and gets his son (the narrator) to support his story when his mother questions them. The father knows that of the two sons, he is the one whom his mother will question.

Approaching the same house thirty-four years later, the narrator notices that aside from its color, it is unchanged. A sign identifies the house as Rettstadt's Restaurant. Now he recalls facing the door that opened into the kitchen when he was a child. He feels weak, his heart beats hard and fast. He is going back into memory, into the past.

On that winter Saturday those many years ago when the narrator, his father, and his brother arrive home, it is snowing, and his mother is in the kitchen. His father delivers his story: His car got stuck in the snow, and he had to do some work at the depot. Mother knows that he is lying; his threadbare excuse demands that she challenge his story. She rejects the lie, telling him that she can smell the bar and another woman on his clothes. They argue; their shouts grow louder and more pained.

Slipping from this painful memory but still on its scent, the adult narrator describes the house as he sees it in 1986—the changes made to convert it to a restaurant. A man scrubbing cooking utensils looks up, sees his visitor, and introduces himself as George Rettstadt. The narrator tells him that he used to live in the house. Rettstadt focuses his gaze and pronounces the narrator's last name; he mistakes the narrator for his father.

During a brief tour of the house, the narrator sees it as it was and steps deeper into the cave of memory of that long-ago Saturday. He remembers fleeing the kitchen, going upstairs to his bedroom, lying on his bed, his mother bursting into the room to demand the truth from him. She screams at him to admit what she already knows: that they went to the bar and that there was a woman there. The boy nods his head in assent.

The narrator declines Rettstadt's invitation to see the upstairs; instead he goes outside to look around the yard. He walks to the back of the house to stand beneath the window of his old bedroom. Thrown again into the distant past, he hears the sound of his father's steps on the stairs. The child knows what is about to happen, knows the depth of his father's rage and violence. Remembering the beating that he received from his father that day ends both this memory and his visit to the house.

From the ground below the bedroom window, the narrator leaves for the university, where he delivers his lecture to a small group of teachers and students and then dines with them at a local restaurant. Afterward he drives home to New York.

### Themes and Meanings

The meaning of "The Visitor"—the problem that Russell Banks explores in this story—is expressed in its title; however, violence is an integral component of the ideas of a visitor and of visiting. Although the story tells of a profound experience of one man revisiting a place and moment from his past, the narrator explicitly states that it is violence that makes his visit possible and necessary and that it is violence that makes the man a "visitor."

It is telling that the adult cannot re-create the details of his beating by his father in the same representative, clear prose that he uses to describe the incidents that preceded the beating—the bar, the drive home, and the escalating argument between his parents. Instead, his account of his father's violence against him is told with distanced language and an analytical objectivity. He does not explicitly state that his father hit him in the head, slammed him in the ribs, or threw him to the floor; rather, he says: "When you are hit in the head or slammed . . . or thrown . . . by a powerful man."

Compounding this distance, while at the same time providing a rationale for the story, is the narrator's analysis and theory of violence: that it produces "white light and heat inside the head"—an "extraordinary immolation . . . worth any price." An act of violence demands perpetuation and visitation, so that the boy who is beaten will become a man who beats, so that the boy who is beaten will become a man compelled to return to the scenes of his violence, whether he was beaten or he beat someone else there. Violence locks one into the past, into itself. It has made this man a constant visitor of places and of memories.

The necessity of anyone's return visits and participation in the perpetuation of violence is expressed in significant ways. Just as the narrator's mother felt compelled to challenge her husband rather than accept his lie, so too the adult narrator is compelled to perform violence. Banks calls violence a "narrative whose primary function is to provide reversal," so that a weak, victimized boy becomes a strong, violent man.

Illustrating the necessity of the visit, the settings in which the narrator finds himself are more powerful than he, drawing him paradoxically forward into his past. He is compelled; images plunge him into the past, into memory; light and smell affect his body, which seems to know the past and the memory before his mind does. The narrator emphatically insists on this necessity, saying to the reader, "Listen to me: you are locked into that narrative, and no other terms . . . are available."

*Style and Technique*

Giving the story a provocative dimension is Banks's use of images and metaphors that double. Just as the distant past of the narrator's childhood echoes his recent visit to Tobyhanna, there are several other instances that reinforce this mirroring quality. In the downtown bar the narrator orders a beer from a woman whose "double—her twin" sits on a barstool. Later he refers to this as a "doubling image" that replicates, "doubling the place itself with" memory.

As he drives up to the farmhouse, the narrator notices two stone chimneys that are "matched" by a pair of maple trees, all of this suggesting doubleness and symmetry. The child narrator and his brother share a room with a pair of windows and twin beds—the twin beds perhaps suggesting that the brother, too, was a victim of the father's violence.

More to the point, however, is the incident in which the narrator is mistaken for his father. When Rettstadt first sees him, he calls him by his father's name, and the narrator equates himself with his father, writing that he was "more likely my father than my father's son." All of this enriches the point of the story, that violence repeats itself and that because of violence the past and present must visit each other.

*Julie Thompson*

# VIY

*Author:* Nikolai Gogol (1809-1852)
*Type of plot:* Folktale
*Time of plot:* The eighteenth or early nineteenth century
*Locale:* In and near Kiev
*First published:* 1835 (English translation, 1887)

### Principal characters:

KHOMA BRUT, a philosophy student at the seminary in Kiev
KHALIAVA, a theology student
TIBERIY GOROBETS, a rhetorician
THE "VEDMA," a witch, who takes different forms
THE "SOTNIK," the commander of the Cossacks
YEVTUKH,
SPIRID, and
DOROSH, Cossacks
VIY, the chief of the gnomes, whose eyelids droop down to the
earth

## The Story

In "Viy," a description of student life in the seminary of the Bratsk Monastery in Kiev is followed by an introduction to three students who are hiking home for the summer. They are the philosopher, Khoma Brut, the theologian, Khaliava, and the rhetorician, Tiberiy Gorobets. The three students lose their way in the dark and are unable to find the road. Being hungry and afraid of wolves, they ask for lodging at the first farmyard they come on. An old woman at first refuses to take them in, saying that she fears "such great hulking fellows." The three students swear that they will behave themselves, however, and Khoma falsely promises to pay her "the devil's bit" in the morning. The old woman invites them in, saying "What fine young gentlemen the devil has brought us!" She gives them all separate places to sleep. Khoma is given a place in the sheep pen.

In the middle of the night, Khoma is awakened by the entry into the sheep pen of the old woman. She reaches out her arms toward him. Khoma tries to reject her advances, saying that she is too old for him and that it is a time of fasting. However, he finds himself strangely powerless to move away from her. She leaps onto his back with the swiftness of a cat and begins to ride him, beating him on his side with a broom.

To his amazement and horror, Khoma carries the old woman out into the wide plain, which seems to him to be at the bottom of a clear sea. The sun replaces the moon, and he sees a beautiful water nymph floating pale and naked before him. He feels an exhausting sensation that is at the same time voluptuous and exhilarating.

Realizing that he is in the power of a witch, Khoma begins to recite all the prayers he knows, all the exorcisms against evil spirits. The old woman's power seems to fade, and he, as quick as lightning, stops carrying her and jumps onto her back instead. As she starts to carry him, he picks up a piece of wood from the roadside and begins to beat her with it. The moon comes back into its former place, and as they soar over the plain, the old woman's angry howls become fainter and sweeter until they sound like delicate silver bells. Khoma, still beating her severely, wonders if she is really an old woman at all. At last, he hears her murmur, "I can do no more," as she sinks exhausted onto the ground. As Khoma looks at her, she is transformed into a lovely young woman with luxuriant tresses and eyelashes as long as arrows.

Khoma, shaken by his experience with the old woman, runs all the way back to Kiev, forgetting his companions. In Kiev, he passes whistling through the market three times, finally winking at a young widow in a yellow bonnet, who takes him home to regale him with her food and her favors. That same evening, he is seen in a tavern smoking his pipe and throwing a gold coin to the keeper. He thinks no more about his extraordinary adventure.

Meanwhile, rumors are circulating everywhere that the daughter of one of the richest Cossack sotniks (commanders), who lives some distance from Kiev, has returned one day from a walk, severely injured, hardly able to crawl home to her father's house, and is lying at the point of death, expressing the wish that one of the Kiev seminarists, the philosopher Khoma Brut, should read the prayers and the psalms over her for three nights after her death.

Hearing from the rector of the seminary about the sotnik's daughter's request, Khoma has a presentiment that something evil is awaiting him. He tries to excuse himself from the task and even plans to run away. The rector turns him over, though, to a detachment of the sotnik's Cossacks, who transport him in a large chaise to the sotnik's village, stopping along the way at a tavern to get drunk.

When they arrive at the sotnik's house, Khoma is informed that the daughter has died. The sotnik, despondent and angry over his daughter's death, leads Khoma to her body. Khoma almost panics as he recognizes in the beautiful young woman the luxuriant tresses and the eyelashes as long as arrows of the witch he killed earlier. He tries to excuse himself from the task of reading prayers over her body, telling the sotnik that he is sinful and unworthy, that he even "paid the baker's wife a visit on Maunday Thursday." The sotnik, however, will not relent. He insists that Khoma is to read the prayers each night from dusk to dawn.

Before the first night's reading, Khoma talks to the Cossacks Yevtukh, Spirid, and Dorosh, who eagerly affirm that the sotnik's daughter was indeed a witch. Spirid tells a chilling tale about Mikita the dog-keeper who withered and spontaneously burst into flame after the witch rode on his back all over the countryside. Then Dorosh relates how the witch, in the form of a dog, attacked the baby of Sheptun's wife, sucking its blood and even killing its mother. From these stories, Khoma is frightened, but, fortified by vodka, he goes to read the first night's prayers.

The body of the sotnik's daughter has been taken into the village church. There, at dusk, Khoma begins to read his prayers, but soon the girl's body rises up out of the coffin and walks around the church: It is the witch, reaching out her arms for him. Khoma draws a circle around himself and fervently reads all the prayers and exorcisms he has been taught. The witch is unable to penetrate the circle and, at dawn, she returns to her coffin.

The next day, Khoma witnesses the Cossacks playing a strange game, similar to skittles, called "kragli." The winner of the game gets the right to ride on the loser's back. This reminds him of the witch, but he is confident that his prayers will protect him. It is not until he is locked up for the second night in the church with the now-putrefying corpse that fear again seizes him. Indeed, the corpse does again rise to walk around the church, muttering unintelligible words and trying to possess him. He hears the wings and claws of other demons trying to enter the church, but he survives by staying within his drawn circle and reading his exorcisms with desperate zeal. In the morning, a local Cossack coquette notices that his hair has gone completely gray.

Before the third night's reading, Khoma confronts the sotnik with the knowledge of his daughter's witchcraft, trying one more time to be excused from reading the prayers over her body. The sotnik responds by threatening to flog Khoma if he does not complete his task. Khoma tries to run away, but he winds up running in a circle, back to where Yevtukh finds him and leads him back to the church at dusk. The third night's vigil is the worst of all. The witch's corpse rises as before but is now more terrible. Other monstrous demons crash through the windows of the church and scurry about, trying to find him. The witch shouts, "Bring Viy! Go get Viy!" Viy does indeed arrive: a thick-set, bandy-legged figure covered with black earth, and with eyelids drooping to the ground. "Lift up my eyelids. I do not see!" he says. The demons all rush to lift his eyelids. Now Viy's terrible gaze is fixed on Khoma. "There he is!" he shouts, and all the demoniac company pounce on Khoma, who falls expiring to the ground, his soul fleeing his body in terror. The cock then crows to signal the dawn, and the demons panic. They wedge themselves into the doors and windows of the church while trying to get out. The priest is subsequently forced to close the church, which in later years is so overgrown with weeds that it is forgotten.

In the final scene, Tiberiy Gorobets and Khaliava are back in Kiev. Some time has passed; Khaliava is now the bell-ringer of Kiev's highest belfry, while Tiberiy Gorobets is now a philosopher, as Khoma was. At a tavern they drink to Khoma's memory, concluding that "all the old women who sit in our market in Kiev are witches."

## Themes and Meanings

Especially in his earlier stories, Nikolai Gogol adapted the folktales told to him as a youth by his mother. These folktales spring from the oral tradition of the Ukraine, where Gogol was born. They involve peasant legends of the supernatural and the everyday customs of the ethnic groups that inhabit the Ukraine, most notably the Cossacks. Thus "Viy" is rich in Ukrainian folklore and the boisterous character of the Cossacks. The religious undercurrent represented by the seminary and the prayer vigil is a reflection of the influence of Gogol's father, a strictly religious man who died when Gogol was still young. The clear sexual symbolism of "Viy"—being ridden by a witch until a "voluptuous" state of exhaustion is achieved—has been interpreted as evidence of Gogol's own ambivalent sexuality, feeling sexual urges but being convinced, perhaps for religious reasons or out of a misidentification with his mother, that indulgence of them leads to damnation.

## Style and Technique

In general, Gogol's style is to deluge the reader with detail that seems digressive at first, but that relates to the main plot in psychologically supportive ways. He presents stories-within-stories, creating seemingly inconsequential characters who are born and are given names, lives, and interesting deaths, all within a paragraph. "Viy" is no exception to this pattern. Other interesting narrative techniques can be seen here as well—for example, the technique of triplication, which derives from the telling of folktales. The story is written in two distinct parts, each with parallel structure, yet there are three students, three "riding" incidents, and three night vigils, among other examples. In addition, there is an inordinate focus on eyes, the "windows of the soul," and on visual processes. In her beautiful forms, the witch has eyelashes as long as arrows. Khoma perishes when his eyes meet the gaze of Viy, that long-eyelidded gnome whose very name is a contraction of the Russian verb *videt*, which means "to see."

*Lee B. Croft*

# THE WAIT

*Author:* Rick Bass (1958-    )
*Type of plot:* Domestic realism
*Time of plot:* The late twentieth century
*Locale:* Houston and Galveston Bay, Texas
*First published:* 1990

>    *Principal characters:*
>        THE NARRATOR, a bachelor
>        KIRBY, his best friend, a real estate appraiser
>        JACK, Kirby's friend, a dentist

*The Story*

The unnamed narrator's girlfriend, Marge, has recently left him, so he goes from Montana to east Texas to fish with his friend Kirby and Kirby's friend Jack. As they drive through downtown Houston in the early morning rain, the narrator sees the buildings as "like tall jails . . . the shutdown of a life." Depressed, he feels unable to measure up to the Texas myth that "the world can be tamed—it's a bull that can be wrestled, and with strength and courage and energy you can lift that bull over your head and spin it around and throw it to the ground." Moreover, because he is unready to take on the responsibilities of being a husband and father, he feels like an imposter, trying to live a "strong" life, "fast and free, scorning weakness." Both Jack and Kirby are married and have children, and the narrator envies them.

As they drive, they hear animal noises in a box in the back of Jack's jeep. When Jack tells them it is a coyote, the others assume that he is joking. Later, they launch a boat in Galveston Bay and notice a billboard showing a beautiful, smiling woman named Renee Jackson who is missing; the narrator finds himself on the verge of tears, presumably because he associates her with his own missing girlfriend. This time Marge has left him not for the usual reasons, but because she was tired; the narrator admits to himself that he does sometimes get really wild. Jack tells the narrator it is all right to cry over the missing woman and recalls how Kirby cried over a large pregnant redfish that they caught the previous year that died despite their efforts to release it alive. The narrator thinks that he will be ready to settle down someday and be a good husband and father, and "the wait will make it nicer," as he thinks about the missing Renee, who he hopes will return and make her parents all the happier after they have long waited for her.

The men's fishing is successful and even the stormy weather, which charges the sky all around them, never hits them. The only threats to their pleasure are the "popdicks," other fishermen who crowd them when they find a good spot. The narrator himself never catches a fish; when his friends fail in their efforts to help him, he concludes that "like most things, it's just something that I am going to have to work out by myself."

As the men drift back toward shore, they discuss sex, but the narrator feels uneasy about it. When Jack describes his wife as a "hellcat in bed," the narrator is relieved that Kirby does not talk about his own wife. As they near the billboard again, Jack says that he thinks they found Renee's skeleton the previous spring. This observation and the lateness of the hour make the narrator feel overwhelmingly lonely and tired.

The story ends when Jack stops the jeep and releases a coyote, which he caught in his backyard. Despite being cooped up for hours, the coyote heads north (the direction from which the narrator has come); it runs "without looking back, as if it knows exactly where it is going." The narrator sees the freed animal as "the most beautiful thing."

*Themes and Meanings*

Although the narrator says he thinks he and his girlfriend will get back together "because we have been together far too long *not* to come back together," he has little confidence in his own prediction because this time "it was a little different." His response is to get out of the house. Although his wildness has in the past necessitated escaping from domesticity, which may be associated here with the feminine (Marge goes back home to Virginia, a state that is symbolically feminine), the narrator has a desire for home and family, and the domesticity of his two fishing buddies is attractive to him.

In the course of the story one senses that male companionship is not sufficient. Part of what makes Jack and Kirby best friends, the narrator realizes, is that their wives are also each other's best friends. None of the feminine figures alluded to in the story are actually present, but their absence prompts desire; they include Marge, Kirby's and Jack's wives (Tricia, who has made lunches for them, and Wendy), the missing Renee Jackson, the pregnant redfish, Kirby's seven-month-old daughter (also named Kirby, which suggests a close father-daughter relationship), and Jack's dental assistant (whose "bosoms" Kirby claims he can see when she leans over the dentist's chair). Even one of the strawberry-colored artificial shrimp that they are using as bait looks "like a woman coming out of her slip." Near the end of the story the narrator describes the sky as "a lurid black, a horrible purple, like the bruise on the inside of a woman's thigh." One might question, at this point, how "wild" the narrator has been with Marge. He has never been married, and he sees himself as being even less ready to be a husband than to be a father. Perhaps his weeping over the missing Renee is not so much a display of his compassion and sensitivity as an expression of guilt.

The men in this story are generally associated with a sort of bestial wildness. The narrator associates himself with bulldogging; when he runs off into the mountains in Montana, he sees himself as lying in the sun "like a dog." Kirby tells Jack that he has dreamed that his friend was "a raccoon, banging around in the garbage." Jack, who is associated with the coyote, describes his wife as a "hellcat." Jack's seventy-nine-year-old father is mentioned at one point as ranting, raving, and "howling" when his son had engine troubles with a boat. The shameless "popdicks" who invade the men's fishing spot come from a "black squall line, savage thunderstorms, wicked cold streaks of lightning."

In short, the men in this story appear to be so concerned with not looking like "sissy-pants" shore fishermen that they risk "the shutdown of a life." Early in the story the narrator says that he feels "like an outlaw, an alien" because the two men riding in the front of the jeep are husbands and fathers. When Jack takes over the throttle of the boat, the narrator sees that he, too, has become an outlaw, but a happy one, and then he recognizes that "the longer you go without something, the happier you are when you finally get it." This truism applies to the coyote at the end of the story and may eventually hold true for the narrator as well.

*Style and Technique*

"The Wait" does not appear among the ten stories that make up Rick Bass's first collection, *The Watch* (1990), but it has much in common with its stories. (Kirby and Tricia, in fact, appear in three stories in that book.) Like many of Bass's stories, "The Wait" shares what has been called the "minimalist" style. In an article in *Harper's Magazine* (April, 1986), Madison Bell lists as characteristics of minimalism a trim or closely cropped style (which applies especially to sentence structure), concern for surface details (as opposed to elaborate or lush description), a tendency to ignore nuances in character portrayal, and "a studiedly deterministic, at times nihilistic, vision of the world." Bell does not admire the minimalist trend, which can be traced back to Ernest Hemingway, and perhaps even to Anton Chekhov, and which finds adherents in such writers as Raymond Carver, Ann Beattie, and Richard Ford. Nevertheless, this kind of spare realism has become an important mode in American fiction, and it offers an option to the fantasy and Magical Realism that have become especially popular in postmodernist and Latin American fiction.

Most of Bass's stories fit the definition of minimalism fairly well. One never sees a character vividly in his stories; one rarely knows how a character looks—in contrast to character descriptions in Charles Dickens, for example. There is a flatness to the picture's finish. For some readers, however, such surfaces are superior to one that might be described as "busy" and overwrought. Certainly, though, this story is neither nihilistic nor deterministic. As in many Chekhov stories, its ending is not absolutely resolved; the door remains open. For many readers, the open ending, the rejection of the pat conclusion, is preferable because it is more lifelike.

*Ron McFarland*

# WAITING

*Author:* Joyce Carol Oates (1938-     )
*Type of plot:* Psychological
*Time of plot:* The 1960's
*Locale:* The United States
*First published:* 1974

> *Principal characters:*
> KATHERINE ALEXANDER, an unmarried woman in her thirties who works in a welfare office
> HER MOTHER
> BOB MOTT, who is in his late forties, married, and on welfare

*The Story*

As the story begins, the reader is caught in the middle of miscommunication. Bob Mott is trying to explain to Katherine Alexander why he has lost his job. She is distracted; he is embarrassed. She is suspicious, slightly disgusted by Mr. Mott. The narrator abruptly shifts attention to Katherine's life story. She has grown up barely admiring her retired father, frightened of becoming her struggling, unattractive mother. Her older sisters have married; her older brother, returned from the navy, works in a parts factory. Katherine supports her mother, yet she has saved enough to earn a degree from the university in the School of Social Work.

In her senior year, Katherine meets a young man who is studying to become a dentist. Although at first he is "on the rebound" from a love affair, he eventually falls in love with Katherine. As they begin to plan for marriage, Katherine's mother becomes ill. The consequent gall bladder operation is "a vast and complicated affair" that interrupts the young couple's plans. Katherine begins her social work; the young man strains over his studies; the mother becomes nervous for her daughter. Impatient after months, then years, of delay, the young man ends their relationship. Katherine is devastated—mostly by his "weakness."

After this happens, at age twenty-six, it seems that Katherine grows closer to her mother—sharing a loneliness. Her energies are devoted almost exclusively to work. She becomes expert at distinguishing the truth from lies. She also distances herself emotionally from the suffering that she sees; her idealism descends into cool distrust. She feels uncomfortable "with those certain women." At one point she takes an unhealthy pleasure in humiliating a prostitute; her victim, enraged, lashes back, calling her an "ugly bitch." It is then that she meets Mr. Mott.

The narration returns to the moment at the beginning of the story: Mr. Mott tries to explain himself; Katherine, disturbed by the prostitute's curse, cannot understand his problem. Mr. Mott makes himself clear—he has lost his job and plans to abandon his pregnant wife.

The narrator, once again, shifts back into Katherine's private life. Her mother sickens and dies, leaving "everything" to Katherine. Out of a sense of loyalty to the memory of her proud, bigoted, mother, she refuses to sell the family house to "colored." She gives herself completely to her job. By choice, she distances herself utterly from the people she had once hoped to help. She no longer meets the "candidates," but, shut off in her own office, she judges them. Her social life is bleak—meeting "awkward, polite bachelors" who quickly disappear from her life.

In a chance meeting, Mr. Mott reenters her life. Cheerful, newly employed, he offers her a ride home in his new car. Katherine, nervous, clutching her purse, is uncertain of herself and embarrassed by him, but she accepts. As they approach her mother's house, she is ashamed, defensive, maintaining that she keeps the house out of respect for her dead mother. She invites him in to "chat." She is repulsed by his manners, his language; her glances judge his every action.

With cruel abruptness, Mr. Mott turns on Katherine. He humiliates her for earning so little, for living in a neighborhood that is mostly black, for her sentimental attachment to "mommy," for her condescending demeanor in the welfare office. He tells her that he witnessed the incident with the prostitute who had cursed her; he himself calls her an "ugly dog-faced bitch." He confesses that he has been waiting for six years to "get" her. He strikes her several times. As she begins to weep, the entire tragic emptiness of her life descends on her—but she cannot understand it.

### Themes and Meanings

Joyce Carol Oates makes an insistent comparison between Katherine's public and private lives. Initially, she seems to be completely selfless in both—supporting her wreck of a family, giving her life to the service of others. However, soon the public and private dimensions of her life become ironically reciprocal: The less competent she becomes in gratifying her personal desires, the more competent she becomes at managing the lives of other unfortunates.

However, "competence" in her job entails achieving a productive distrust for humanity. The more she is hurt personally, the more readily she can detect true suffering from camouflage: "With frightened people, lies were obvious because they never looked up at Katherine; with the bold and brazen, lies were obvious because they tried to stare her down. The only people who puzzled her were those who couldn't remember the truth, who didn't know themselves if they were lying." A passage such as this, placed in the very center of Katherine's story, gradually accumulates layers of irony as the story proceeds. In her domestic and professional capacities, Katherine lies to herself without knowing it. Katherine helps others because she feels better when she does. Her fiancé becomes like one of her welfare "people" in her mind; her mother's medical expenses "equaled so many hours of her job." When Katherine "investigates" a poor neighborhood, the narrator slyly creeps into her mind, where it becomes obvious that she uses her job to prop herself up: "Wasn't she maybe, from a well-to-do family, dedicating herself to helping people? And wasn't she pretty?" This is what Katherine hopes her "people" will think of her. The brutal truth (that she is despised for her distant distrust) is revealed to her by Mr. Mott as the story ends.

Katherine feels "nervous" and "vaguely ashamed" in the presence of the prostitutes who frequent the welfare office. Does she humiliate the prostitute because she despises her, or is it more likely that her vague shame has to do with self-recognition? After her violent confrontation with the prostitute who curses her, Katherine prays "My God, don't let me get like that." Significantly, "her mind was so jostled, she didn't know whether she was thinking of her mother or of the prostitute." These two women represent possibilities to Katherine—whore and mother, both psychological and economic hostages to an unfriendly world, to the world of Mr. Mott.

Mr. Mott is the catalyst for the story's meaning; he psychologically violates Katherine. Throughout her life, Katherine has deluded herself about family, sex, loyalty, and her "social work." She has so resented the inadequacies of her private life that her public life has become a sham, a show of power. Mr. Mott explodes the distinction between what she is and what she wants the world to believe she is. He is one of her "people," someone who has "succeeded." While his success entails abandoning his wife and children, Katherine seems to resent him not so much because of his callousness as because of his success: He no longer looks up to her.

As the insults begin, the scene resembles a dog turning on a master; this is Katherine's perception of the relationship. The truth is displayed to Katherine; she weeps after many years of repressing the tears. However, just when it seems that the truth may render Katherine whole, may heal and renew her pathetic life, the reader realizes that Mr. Mott's hatred has instead intensified Katherine's confusion. The reader is in the middle of the same miscommunication with which the story begins.

*Style and Technique*

The title of the story reflects its form. Oates subverts the reader's expectations: namely, that Katherine is the only character "waiting." Everyone around Katherine has been waiting: The mother waits for her daughter's success; the fiancé waits for his lover's acceptance; the welfare "candidates" wait for the social worker's attention; Mr. Mott waits for revenge.

Oates uses this important verb twice in the final paragraphs of the story. Mr. Mott reveals: "For six years I been waiting to run into one of you—" After Mr. Mott has beaten Katherine, the narrator states very simply that "she waited." He has been waiting to vent his rage; she has been waiting to weep. The reader has also been waiting: The title of the story works as a kind of riddle, solved in the story's conclusion. Through shifts in the narrative focus, Mr. Mott remains a peripheral concern to the story. He seems an annoyance, a diversion from the main story line; yet in the final scene he overwhelms Katherine and the reader with a ruthless reality that has been lurking in the background for pages.

*Mark Sandona*

# WAKEFIELD

*Author:* Nathaniel Hawthorne (1804-1864)
*Type of plot:* Fable
*Time of plot:* The 1800's
*Locale:* London
*First published:* 1835

> *Principal characters:*
> WAKEFIELD, an average, middle-class man
> MRS. WAKEFIELD, his wife

*The Story*

Wakefield is a middle-aged man living in London, in a comfortable home with his wife of ten years. He has an "inactive mind," a peculiar "vanity," a "harmless love of mystery," a certain "selfishness" and "strangeness." One October evening, he tells his wife good-bye before leaving by coach for a journey into the country. Knowing his love of mystery, she does not inquire into the details of his trip. He tells her not to be alarmed if he does not return for three or four days but to expect him on Friday evening. She later recalls the "crafty smile" on his face as he departs.

Instead of going on a journey, he takes an apartment on the next street with a vague plan of observing the effect of his absence on his wife. Alone in the apartment, he seems to realize the inanity of what he is doing. However, as time goes by, he is overcome with curiosity about the effect of his disappearance. Vanity lies at the root of his project. He watches his house to see how life proceeds without him but is fearful of being recognized. Consequently, he buys a red wig and unusual clothes to effect a disguise. Three weeks after his disappearance, Wakefield observes a physician entering his house; he knows that his wife is ill, but he tells himself that he must not disturb her at such a time. He expects that she may die and even seems to desire subconsciously to harm her. He cannot bring himself to return. When his wife recovers, Wakefield is vaguely aware that an "almost impassable gulf" separates him from her and from his former life. In due time, Mrs. Wakefield settles her husband's estate and proceeds with her life as a widow. Nathaniel Hawthorne comments that Wakefield has virtually no more chance of returning to his old life than if he were actually dead.

For ten years, Wakefield watches his house and observes his wife as best he can. He loses any feeling that his actions are strange. One day, he sees Mrs. Wakefield on her way to church. Jostled by the crowd into bodily contact, they look into each other's eyes, but she fails to recognize him. Returning to his lonely room, he falls on the bed and passionately cries out that he is mad. It is the only time that he seems to be emotionally moved. He has postponed his return from month to month, year to year, with one feeble excuse or another, until now he is in limbo, neither dead nor truly alive. He has retained "his original share of human sympathies," is "still involved in human interests," but has lost "his reciprocal influence on them." However, he has no clear concept of how he has changed and continues to think that he could return home the same man who departed years earlier.

In the last scene, twenty years after Wakefield's departure, he takes his usual walk to his house, which he still considers his own. Again it is autumn, and he sees through a window a fire on the hearth and on the ceiling, a "grotesque shadow" of Mrs. Wakefield, a "caricature." When a chilling rain begins to fall, he suddenly considers it ridiculous to stand outside when the comforts of his home are just beyond the door. He enters with the same "crafty" smile on his face that he wore when he first left. Instead of following Wakefield inside, the author comments: "Stay, Wakefield! Would you go to the sole home that is left you? Then step into your grave!" The story then concludes with a moral such as Hawthorne promised at the beginning:

> Amid the seeming confusion of our mysterious world, individuals are so nicely adjusted to a system, and systems to one another and to a whole, that, by stepping aside for a moment, a man exposes himself to a fearful risk of losing his place forever. Like Wakefield, he may become, as it were, the Outcast of the Universe.

*Themes and Meanings*

Many Hawthorne characters destroy themselves, or others, by some unusual action that separates them from the mainstream of life and eventually destroys their human ties. Aylmer in "The Birthmark" seeks scientific success and an abstract ideal, but in the process he kills his wife. Wakefield, more or less on a whim, abandons his domestic tranquillity and is doomed to a solitary life. When he finally wishes to return home, he discovers that the only home prepared to welcome him is the grave. The outline of the story, which Hawthorne claims in the first paragraph to have borrowed from a newspaper, he changes in the end to convey his belief that the breaking of human ties is evil and irrevocable. The man in the news article, he says, returned after twenty years to the bosom of a loving wife and became a loving husband until death. Wakefield, however, by the end of the story is an outcast of his own making.

Wakefield's sins are his changing, for selfish reasons, the course of another person's life and his withdrawing, for no good reason, from his established relationship with his wife and with society. Of all people, his wife is the one in whose life he should actively participate. Instead, he removes himself and coldly observes. By breaking his ties with his wife, his home, and the customs of his former life, he separates himself from everything that binds him to humanity and to life itself—hence Hawthorne's references to him as dead or as a ghost and Hawthorne's leaving him on the threshold of his house. Wakefield is physically alive, but in all other respects he is dead; though he may enter his house, he cannot reenter his old life. Although he intended to withdraw for only a short time in order to observe the effect, he remains aloof so long that he loses his position in the scheme of things.

"Wakefield" contains two concepts often found in Hawthorne's stories—the isolation of a man from the world and the cruel attempt of one person to alter another person's life. The "crafty" smile on her husband's face that Mrs. Wakefield observes as he leaves reveals the beginning of his sin—deliberate estrangement from his former life and from the world. This estrangement, which initially is little more than a whim or a joke he intends to play on Mrs. Wakefield, becomes his destruction. It becomes obsessive as he watches his house and wife for twenty years, powerless to return and confess the truth of his actions. While she makes a normal adjustment to his absence, he is, ironically, trapped by his plan into becoming an outcast. Wakefield neither realizes nor anticipates how unimportant his disappearance will be in terms of the larger world. Hawthorne comments that it is dangerous to separate oneself even from loved ones, for their lives go on and one is quickly forgotten. Hence he refuses to allow a happy reunion for Wakefield and prepares the reader for the theme stated at the end of the story.

*Style and Technique*

The structure of "Wakefield" is quite simple. An unusual event, a husband's self-imposed absence, is expanded into a brief moral allegory, a type of story Hawthorne often employed. By claiming in the first paragraph that he took the initial incident from an old newspaper, he lends an air of reality to the strange event. Continuing to address the reader directly, Hawthorne welcomes him or her to an excursion into the remarkable anecdote, for an unusual incident often produces ideas worth considering, he claims. He concludes the introduction with an idea that points to the theme at the end of the story, giving the effect of a neatly wrapped package.

Throughout the story, Hawthorne uses a technique of prompting and leading the reader's reactions concerning what is happening with the characters. When Wakefield vacillates in deciding to return home, Hawthorne comments, "Poor man!" When Mrs. Wakefield falls ill after her husband's disappearance, the author injects, "Dear woman! Will she die?" The effect is that the reader is always conscious of the author's presence and of his guiding the reader's thoughts. This effect is strengthened by the numerous moralizing passages interspersed throughout the story. The author states early that unusual incidents such as the one on which the story is based have a "moral"; he then scatters didactic passages throughout the story as well as stating the clear moral message in the conclusion.

One characteristic of most stories that is virtually lacking in "Wakefield" is dialogue. Even the parting scene, in which Wakefield leaves his wife for the supposed journey, is not dramatized. Instead, Hawthorne describes everything for the reader, sometimes preparing for the next event with a phrase such as, "Now for a new scene!" Occasionally, Wakefield's thoughts are expressed within quotation marks, but these passages are as close as Hawthorne comes to using dialogue. Thus, the loneliness of Wakefield's situation is emphasized. By breaking all of his ties with his former life for the sake of a foolish whim, Wakefield condemns himself to the life of an outcast. From the climactic scene near the church in which his wife fails to recognize him,

Wakefield clearly can never return to his old life. The following events and the lack of dialogue all convey the fact that Wakefield is permanently separated from the social fabric of life.

"Wakefield" shares several characteristics of the classic fable. The results of a single incident are investigated in a relatively brief narrative of about six pages. The characters do not have complete names and are not roundly defined. Mrs. Wakefield is the stereotypical widow, and Wakefield is motivated by a single obsession. Especially reminiscent of the fable are the didactic tone, the reader's constant awareness of the author's presence, and the author's insistence that here there is "much food for thought." Everything in the story is designed to make that thought clear, and it is flatly stated in the concluding paragraph.

*Louise S. Bailey*

# THE WALK

*Author:* José Donoso (1924-1996)
*Type of plot:* Psychological
*Time of plot:* The 1950's
*Locale:* A South American city
*First published:* "Paseo," 1959 (English translation, 1968)

> *Principal characters:*
> THE NARRATOR, an adult recalling his childhood
> MATILDE, his aunt
> PEDRO, his father
> GUSTAVO and
> ARMANDO, his uncles
> A MONGREL WHITE DOG, Matilde's pet and companion

*The Story*

Many years after the events related in the story, the narrator passes by the house in which he grew up and attempts to reconstruct the circumstances that led to the mysterious disappearance of his aunt Matilde. As a child, he lived in a home that included his widowed father, his unmarried aunt Matilde, and two bachelor uncles, Gustavo and Armando.

Aunt Matilde originally moved into the house in order to take care of the narrator after his mother passed away when he was four years old, but once she settled in, most of her attention went to caring for her own three brothers. Managing the household with a firm and steady hand, Matilde re-created the household in her own image—with more order than warmth, and more impersonal efficiency than human affection.

Surprisingly, one day Matilde took in a stray white dog, which she had found on a street after it was hit by a car. In her devotion to nursing the injured dog back to health, Matilde began to neglect her regular household duties and routines. Gradually the mongrel bitch replaced the brothers as her principal companion. When she stopped joining her brothers for a game of pool every evening in order to take the dog for a walk, it was clear that the life of the family was no longer the same.

This change put Matilde's brothers in the same situation as the narrator, who had always been neglected by his aunt. It was not in the brothers' nature to say anything to Aunt Matilde about the disruptive impact of her relationship with the dog. As the narrator remarks, it became "more important than ever not to see, not to see anything at all, not to comment, not to consider oneself alluded to by these events." Thus, instead of voicing their concerns, they tried to ignore the changes in their lives. As the dog became not just Matilde's companion but her "accomplice," Matilde's walks got longer and longer, and she often came home dirty and disheveled. Finally, one day she went out for a walk and did not return. Although the brothers tried to discover her whereabouts, they had no success. Nevertheless, as the narrator states, "Life went on as if Matilde were still living with us."

*Themes and Meanings*

A principal theme in this story, as in several José Donoso novels, is the complicated relationship between order and chaos, between rationality and irrationality. Before the appearance of the mongrel bitch, the narrator's household was a perfectly ordered world in which nothing was left to chance, with no room for anything new or unexpected. At several points in the story, the witness-narrator compares his childhood home to a closed book. This comparison highlights the closure and confinement that characterize his family's life.

Once the mongrel bitch appeared, however, that "world of security" that Aunt Matilde and her brothers had so carefully constructed began to fall apart. Coming from the streets, the dog represents a worldliness that began to crack open the "closed book" of the house. The dog brought into the house the element of chance—she was a foreign body, an agent of worldliness that shattered the sanitized peace and security of the family. One evening, when the dog urinated on the floor of the room in which Matilde and her brothers gathered after dinner to play billiards, the three brothers got upset and retreated to their bedrooms. Although nobody said anything about the incident, it was clear that the family's life was no longer what it had been.

In order to dramatize the destruction of the household's order, the author insinuates parallels between events in this story and the biblical story of the Fall. For example, the narrator compares his childhood house not only to a closed book but also to a "heaven," an artificial paradise shut off from the dangers of the outside world—a world that he knew only through the lights and foghorns of ships in the nearby harbor. Then, much as the serpent entered Eden and seduced Eve, the dog strayed into the house and won Matilde's affection, changing the family's life beyond repair.

The reader may well wonder, however, whether what happens in the story constitutes a fall or a redemption, as the dog's intrusion into Matilde's life also had salutary consequences. Although the rigid routines of the household kept everything in order, they also stifled feelings. As the narrator remarks about the older members of his family: "With them, love existed confined inside each individual, never breaking its boundaries to express itself and bring them together. For them to show affection was to discharge their duties to each other perfectly, and above all not to inconvenience, never to inconvenience." The other side of order, the author seems to say, is sterility. If the house is a paradise, it is also a stifling, airless one, into which the vitality of the real world cannot penetrate.

When Matilde undertook to nurse the dog back to health, she broke the house rules—choosing an elective pastime over duty, thereby inconveniencing her brothers—but she was also getting in touch with a side of her that had not expressed itself before. In caring for the dog, she displayed a warmth and tenderness that she had never shown in her dealings with members of her own family. Paradoxically, the mongrel bitch brought out Matilde's humanity in a way that her brothers and nephew never did. When Matilde abandoned the house, she may have been choosing a more vital, if less tidy, existence. The stray dog thus may not have been Matilde's temptress but her redeemer.

A related theme of the story is the fragility of excessive order. When people try to impose too rigid an order in their lives, they make themselves more vulnerable to the intrusion of disorder. If the narrator's house had been less of a closed book, the outside world would not have subverted it so easily. If Matilde had had other outlets for her human feelings, perhaps she would not have become so strongly fixated on the dog. In addition, it is clear that because they always led such sheltered lives, Matilde's brothers were not prepared to deal with the crisis precipitated by the intrusion of the dog and her subsequent disappearance. Instead of taking effective action, all they did was retreat behind the massive door of their study and discuss what had happened.

*Style and Technique*

As one might expect from a writer whose favorite author is the American novelist Henry James, the handling of point of view is crucial to the overall significance of Donoso's story. His narrator's perspective on the events is affected not only by the circumstance of his reconstructing the story many years after it happened, but also by the fact that he was only a child at the time of his aunt's disappearance and thus not privy to the conversations among the adults. As sometimes happens in James's novels, Donoso's narrator has only a partial and limited access to the story he wants to tell. Indeed, much of what he reveals he did not personally witness but only overheard by standing outside the closed door of the library, where his uncles gathered to discuss Aunt Matilde's disappearance.

For this reason, the narrator's account contains guesswork and speculation. The central mystery of Matilde's disappearance thus remains unresolved. Not only was she never heard from again, but the narrator can never learn precisely why she left. Alternatively, he may know why she left but—like his father and uncles—is incapable of coming to terms with the real reasons for her disappearance. It is significant that the first word of his account refers to her disappearance only as *Esto*, "It"—a vague, imprecise designation that may betray his difficulties with coming to grips with the disappearance of his aunt. By the end of the story, he is no closer to the truth. Appropriately, the story ends not with an explanation of the mystery, but with a confession of uncertainty: "The door of the library was too thick, too heavy, and I never knew if Aunt Matilde, dragged along by the white dog, had got lost in the city, or in death, or in a region more mysterious than either."

Although in one respect the narrator's function is to open the "closed book" of his family's life and discuss publicly the story of his aunt's disappearance, in another respect he cannot—or will not—disclose much: He opens the book only to shut it again, leaving the reader in the dark about the causes and results of Aunt Matilde's last "walk."

*Gustavo Pérez Firmat*

# THE WALK

*Author:* Robert Walser (1878-1956)
*Type of plot:* Antistory
*Time of plot:* 1917
*Locale:* Switzerland
*First published:* "Der Spaziergang," 1917 (English translation, 1957)

> *Principal character:*
> THE WALKER, the narrator and protagonist, a writer

*The Story*

One morning, the narrator, a writer, leaves the melancholy confines of his room to take a walk. Pleased with his suddenly "romantic and adventurous frame of mind," he rejoices at the beauty, freshness, and goodness of the day.

His first encounter on the street is with Professor Meili, a famous scholar with a forbidding, yet sympathetic figure. Various other people catch his attention: a priest, a chemist on a bicycle, a junk dealer, an army doctor, children at play, two elegant women in short skirts, and two men in straw hats.

Pretending to be a fussy connoisseur of books, he visits a book shop and asks in well-chosen words what is the most widely read and popular book of the day. When the book dealer returns with the treasured book in his hands, the writer, whose books do not enjoy such success, coldly leaves the shop with barely a thank-you.

Entering the next bank that he comes on, he is pleasantly surprised to find that several anonymous benefactresses have credited his account with one thousand francs. The bank clerk notes the smile of the poor, disregarded writer, who rejoices in the unexpected gift as he continues his walk. In an aside, he calls attention to a luncheon date he has at one o'clock with Frau Aebi. He passes a bakery and is disturbed by its flamboyant gold lettering, which he sees as a symptom of contemporary egotism, ostentation, and fraudulence, where everything is allowed to appear to be more than it really is. Gone is the modesty of the baker who merely baked an honest loaf of bread.

At the sight of a busy foundry, he is at first ashamed of the fact that he is not working but is only out for a stroll. However, in his bright yellow English suit he feels like a lord in his park, even though the country road is dotted with factories and simple houses and there is nothing really parklike about it. Two children who are playing in the street enchant him for a moment before a loud, rushing automobile disturbs their idyllic game. He looks angrily at the car's occupants, for he loves quiet and the moderate pace of walking and abhors the unnatural haste and pollution of the automobile.

He asks his readers for their indulgence as he announces in advance two significant figures on his walk, a supposed former actress and an alleged budding singer. The first woman turns out not to have been an actress after all, but as she responds pleasantly enough to his rather forward questions, he proceeds to tell her that when he arrived in the area not long ago, he was at odds with himself and the world. Slowly he overcame his hopelessness and anxiety and underwent a rebirth, so that now he is quite happy and receptive to the good around him.

After paying his respects to her, the writer once again sets out on his way. A charming milliner's shop elicits a shout of joy from him. He finds its rural setting so attractive that he promises to himself to write a play entitled "The Walk," in which it will appear. A nearby butcher shop similarly enraptures him, but he is too easily distracted and needs to reorient himself and regroup his forces, like a field marshal trying to gain an overview of circumstances and contingencies. Parenthetically, he adds that he is writing all of his elegant sentences with an imperial court pen, which gives them their brevity, poignancy, and sharpness.

Continuing his stroll past vegetable and flower gardens, orchards, wheat fields, meadows, streams, and all manner of other pleasant things, he is suddenly confronted by a particularly unpleasant and sinister being—the giant Tomzack, whose terrible appearance disperses all of the writer's happy thoughts and imaginings. The writer knows him well, this half-dead phantom superman without home, love, fortune, friends, or country. Without looking back, the writer enters a fir forest, whose quiet, fairy-tale interior gives him back his joy and sense of well-being.

When he leaves the forest, he hears the voice of the singer, a young schoolgirl with a captivatingly beautiful voice. He tells her that she has a dazzling future as a great operatic singer and advises her to practice diligently. She barely comprehends his lengthy encomium on the virtues of her voice, a speech, he admits, that was given mostly for his own pleasure. In the distance he sees the railroad crossing that will be so important to him later in his walk, but before crossing it he must attend to three other important matters: trying on a new suit at a tailor's shop, paying his taxes at the town hall, and depositing a noteworthy letter at the post office.

First of all though, as it has just struck one o'clock, he has to dine with Frau Aebi. Declining conversation, she watches him devotedly as he eats. She insists that he keep eating as much as possible, for she claims that his main reason for coming was not intellectual discussion but to prove that he has a good appetite and is a hearty eater. When she persists, he leaps up from the table, asking how she dares to expect him to stuff himself. She laughs and says it was only a joke to show him how certain housewives can be overindulgent toward their guests.

His next stop is the post office, where he mails a caustic diatribe to a gentleman who has betrayed him and whose only concern is money and prestige. He then takes up battle with the tailor, whose botched work confirms the writer's worst fears. Instead of finding a faultlessly tailored suit, he finds his suit ill-fitting, misshapen, unimaginative, and amateurish. Faced with the tailor's vehement counter protests, the writer quickly withdraws and marches to the tax office, where he hopes to correct a gross error on his tax bill.

Rather than possessing the considerable income that the tax accountants suppose, he has only the most meager income of a writer whose books find no echo among their intended readers. However, "one always sees you out walking," remarks the tax collector. Indeed, the writer answers, walking invigorates him and keeps him in contact with the world. Deprived of his walks, he could not write a single word, for the studies, observations, thoughts, and insights that he gathers during his walks are essential to his work and well-being. He persuades the official that attentive walking is indeed a serious occupation and is promised as a result careful examination of his application for the lowest possible tax rate.

The writer at last reaches the railroad crossing, which seems to him like the high point or center of his walk. Here he waits with a crowd of people as a train filled with soldiers passes by and each group greets the other with patriotic joy. After the crossing clears, his surroundings seem transfigured: The country road, the modest houses and shops, the gardens and meadows are surrounded by a silver veil. He imagines that "the soul of the world has opened, and all evil, sadness, and pain are about to disappear." Having lost its external shell, the earth becomes a dream, and time seems to exist only in the present.

One delightful scene follows another, but as he continues his walk, his romantic exuberance gives way again to sharper observation of the landscape and its buildings and inhabitants. He meets a black dog, a stiff, finely clothed man, and a disheveled laundrywoman, passes several historically interesting buildings, reels off a lengthy list of everyday things and occurrences, and reads a placard advertising a boardinghouse for elegant gentlemen.

It is now evening, and his walk comes to an end at a lakeside. Two figures appear in his mind: a beautiful young girl and a weary and forsaken old man. He is filled with melancholy thoughts and self-reproaches and picks flowers as it begins to rain. He lies down for a long time and then remembers the pretty face of the young girl, who long ago left him without returning his love. The flowers fall out of his hand. He rises to go home, and everything is dark.

*Themes and Meanings*

"The Walk" is the longest and most famous of the more than fifty sketches of walks that Robert Walser wrote after his return from Berlin to Switzerland in 1913. Walking for Walser, who is clearly visible behind the transparent persona of his narrator-protagonist, was an essential creative activity and served a far different function from a normal recreational and diversionary stroll. As Walser's walker tells the tax collector, it is his principal connection to daily life, the only real means that a solitary individual has to confront and communicate with the everyday world.

Walking is also Walser's narrative means of creating space (the German word for "take a walk"—*spazieren*—means literally "to space") for the free flow of ideas and perceptions. The walk itself is the only element that binds together the numerous observations, reflections, and soliloquies that make up the story. The external world is little more than a set of slight and fleeting encounters that provoke a wide range of emotional, perceptual, and philosophical responses. In the moment of the epiphany at the railroad crossing, the narrator comments that the inner human being is the only one that truly exists. Thus, the conversations and images in the story can be seen as outward projections of inner needs and fantasies—particularly, the need for recognition as an honest, unpretentious writer in search of enduring relationships and connections. The men in the story are almost all ostentatious, dishonest, or threatening figures, whereas the women and girls are alluring, witty, and artistic. Similarly, the moments of joy, contentment, and euphoria occur usually in conjunction with images of women and are constantly threatened by memories of a frightening past (embodied in the giant Tomzack) and fear of future loneliness (the figure of the forsaken man in the forest). The celebration of the details of everyday life in "The Walk" may thus be viewed as an attempt to ward off the threats of a crude, male-dominated society and to keep open a more benign aesthetic space for future imaginative and literary excursions.

### Style and Technique

The first-person narrator takes great pains to undermine conventional modes of narration, for the story that he has to tell is not a reconstruction of external events that are reputed to have occurred, but rather the willful linking together of episodes, philosophical reflections, lengthy monologues, and playful asides to the reader within the constructed framework of a day's walk. By parodying conventional foreshadowing and chronological sequence, Walser underscores the accidental nature of his peripatetic imaginative encounters.

Despite an occasional touch of sentimentality and melancholy, a light, self-ironic tone sustains the work. Walser never loses sight of his potential readers and lets his narrator remark at one point that "probably no other author has ever thought of the reader with such gentleness and tenderness as I." Without a sustained plot structure, developed characterization, or linear time flow, however, the reader's task is not easy. Nevertheless, it is not the larger structures that count here, but rather Walser's close attention to detail, a technique that has been termed an "immersion in the minimal." What results is a very personal vision that is both poignant and compellingly unaffected.

*Peter West Nutting*

# A WALK IN THE SUN

*Author:* Geoffrey A. Landis (1955-      )
*Type of plot:* Science fiction
*Time of plot:* The near future
*Locale:* The Moon
*First published:* 1991

*Principal character:*
TRISH MULLIGAN, an astronaut

*The Story*

   *Moonshadow,* never meant to be a landing vessel, crashes on the Moon. Trish Mulligan, the only survivor, tries the radio, but Earth is behind a mountain range. She inventories her assets: Her solar-powered vacuum suit works, and plenty of food packs remain unbroken. The lunar maps are gone, except for a small, global map that was meant to be used as an index to the others.

   To call for help, Trish needs to get the radio and the three-foot antenna dish to a mountaintop with a view of Earth. Climbing is easy in the low gravity, but the dish is awkward to carry. She has only five minutes before Earth goes below the horizon, but that is enough for communicating her situation. It will take them a month to launch a rescue mission. Lunar sunset is just three days away, and the Sun is her only source of energy for life support. She starts loping toward the Sun.

   After just eight hours, Trish's voltage monitor warbles. She cleans the dust from her solar array, but has to find a walking pace that avoids stirring up dust. Fighting boredom, she talks to her late sister Karen, commenting on the pretty but dry terrain. She bounds over the small hills and craters and detours around the larger ones. After twenty hours, she stops and finds a way to sleep without damaging her solar arrays. They can be detached, but their cable is short. She dreams that Karen is not really dead but just playing a joke on her. When she awakens, Earth is just a hand span above the horizon. On her way again, she feels her feet starting to blister. When alive, her sister Karen had hiked on blistered feet and had no patience with those who complained and lagged behind.

   On about the sixth day of her trek, Trish passes through Tranquility but does not see the historic Tranquility Base landing site. She laments to Karen about missing the only tourist attraction in the area. She continues westward, racing the Sun. She passes south of Copernicus, picking her way past jumbles of rock. She tells nonexistent companions that the footing is tricky, so they should pay heed to her foot placement.

   Later, jogging through the smoothness of Oceanus Procellarum, Trish looks around to see if Karen, who died years ago, is there and notes that Earth is low on the horizon. The space suit chafes; it is unfair that she has to wear one and Karen does not. Karen tells her she does not wear one because she is dead. Trish asks how Karen can be here if she is dead, and Karen replies that she is not actually here but present only in Trish's imagination. Trish looks, and there is no Karen; she asks her sister to come back. Distracted, she stumbles and falls. Frantic, she stays face down to protect the fragile solar arrays on her back. When she gets up, a long scratch mars her faceplate, but it holds. One strut of the solar array has buckled, but she is able to bend it back and splint it.

The terrain has turned mountainous again. Karen tells Trish it is about time she woke up. Trish starts to get overconfident, but Karen warns her that the hard part is yet to come, her suit is damaged, and she cannot afford any more problems. She passes beautiful scenery but has to keep going. Karen tells her she cannot rest now. The Sun starts gaining on her. After more slogging along, her air system malfunctions. She has to spend more than half a day finding and fixing the problem. She resumes walking, with Karen walking beside her. Karen tells her she is dead, but Trish denies it. They converse about childhood memories. At length, Trish agrees to try to say goodbye to Karen.

Eventually, with darkness overtaking her, Trish reaches the crash region but cannot find the crash site. She climbs the tallest nearby mountain, to get the last bit of sunlight. The rescue mission arrives at the crash site, having heard nothing from the stranded astronaut for a month. They see her westbound footprints, then they hear her suit radio. She has seen their lights. Finally, rescued, she makes her peace with Karen.

## Themes and Meanings

"A Walk in the Sun" hinges on the cleverness of astronaut Trish Mulligan who determines to walk around the Moon to stay in the sunlight and keep her solar-powered life-support systems in operation. Once this solution to her predicament is presented, the rest of the survival story focuses on how she copes with the utter solitude of her situation, hundreds of thousands of miles from the nearest living human, with no possible communication other than the sound of her own memories. Early in the story, author Geoffry A. Landis introduces Trish's older sister Karen. Karen had always pushed her "bratty little sister" to keep up, to accomplish more. Although she resented her older sister's pushing, Trish nonetheless idolized her. Trish did not realize that Karen had to struggle to keep ahead of her sister. Karen left her sister behind after dying in a wilderness fall.

The gradual buildup of Trish's dependence on Karen, which reaches a climax in her settling of unresolved issues with her dead sister, fits well in the survival tale. The adventure side of the story presents the thrill of whether Trish will make it clear around the Moon and get rescued, and the psychological side presents the increasing dependence on her imaginary sister, which must lead to either madness or a resolution.

## Style and Technique

"A Walk in the Sun" actually tells two stories, one of the astronaut's survival effort and the other of her relationship with her sister Karen. It is never implied that Trish is going crazy; Karen is a mirage, appearing somewhat real to Trish, even though she knows that Karen is not really there.

To tell the survival story, Landis neatly interweaves admiration of the scenery, the progress of Trish's race with the Sun, the difficulties in trekking across the varying lunar terrain, and a few small crises such as foot blisters and equipment failure.

Landis introduces Karen gradually, on the second page of this sixteen-page story; the first mention of her is when Trish asks herself what Karen would have done in this predicament. Two pages later, when the radio fails, she again asks what Karen would have done. It is another two pages later when she first starts talking to Karen. Here again, Landis edges into Karen's added presence in Trish's mind; Trish just comments on how beautiful the scenery is. Later, when she sleeps, she dreams of Karen. The next day, her blistered feet bring more thoughts of Karen, who had gone on despite her own blisters. When she misses Tranquility Base, she comments about it to Karen. As the lunar hike continues, Trish talks more and more to Karen, warning her of treacherous footing and asking advice about how to negotiate an upcoming hill.

It is not until halfway through the story that Landis begins to tell us some of the history between Trish and Karen. She would not let Trish be the hike leader and called her a "bratty little pest." Even the family dog followed Karen around, despite Trish being the one who fed and watered him. However, just in time for the reader to know that Trish is not really losing her mind, she confronts the fact that Karen is long dead, and then Karen vanishes. This bothers Trish, though. She still wants the company of her sister, even knowing that it is imaginary.

The next day, faced with another challenge, she finds that Karen is with her again, chiding and urging her to go on. Later, Trish is in pain and wants to stop, but Karen will not let her. Still later, Trish's rationality recovers somewhat, and Karen tells her "I'm dead. . . . Let me go." They discuss Karen's difficulty in living up to her little sister's idolatry, then Trish's subsequent difficulty in growing up with a dead sister. After facing up to these issues, Trish finally says goodbye to Karen.

*J. Edmund Rush*

# WALKER BROTHERS COWBOY

*Author:* Alice Munro (1931-    )
*Type of plot:* Domestic realism, coming of age
*Time of plot:* The mid-twentieth century
*Locale:* Lake Huron, Ontario
*First published:* 1968

> *Principal characters:*
> THE NARRATOR, a preadolescent girl
> BEN JORDAN, her father
> NORA CRONIN, her father's boyhood friend and possible lover

*The Story*

"Walker Brothers Cowboy" is told in the first person from the point of view of an adult woman recounting a significant formative experience from her preadolescent girlhood in which she meets a woman her father dated before marrying her mother. Through the encounter, she comes to view her father in a new light by realizing that he is not only a family provider but also a man with a colorful emotional history all his own.

The opening scene of "Walker Brothers Cowboy" establishes the geographic and psychological landscape of the story—rural Canada in the decade following World War II, where the narrator's family and most of their neighbors have fallen on hard times and struggle to maintain their dignity in the face of declining fortunes. As the story begins, the narrator describes her mother making homemade school clothes for her because her family can no longer afford store-bought ones. Her father, Ben Jordan, was earning a respectable living raising foxes for their fur but the fur market bottomed out, and he has had to take a job as a door-to-door salesperson. The narrator's father invites his daughter to join him for a walk along the shores of Lake Huron. This rare bonding experience unites the pair, who seldom share any time together because of the demands of Ben's work.

The narrator's mother—a disillusioned and emotionally reserved woman—minds to the everyday needs of her daughter and son while Ben spends long days on the road. Ben views his time with his children as precious and seizes the chance to spend an evening alone with his daughter. Although the narrator describes her relationship with her father in the ambivalent terms of a girl poised at the edge of adolescence, viewing their relationship as both nurturing and tedious, it is clear that the narrator appreciates her father's attempts to spend meaningful time with her. On the shore of the lake, he describes to her how it was formed thousands of years ago by a receding glacier—a shallow but memorable pretext for a chance to share a moment with a daughter with whom he fears losing important connections.

In a further effort to remain an active force in the lives of his children, the next day, Ben invites them to accompany him on the road for a day's selling. Disillusioned by the abject poverty of the farm households to which he peddles everything from laxatives to soft drink syrups, the narrator likens her father's sales territory to the Depression-era country of the 1930's. She observes that "this kind of farmhouse, this kind of afternoon, seem to me to belong to that one decade in time." Because of her age, the narrator's conception of the 1930's can only have come from history books and classroom anecdotes. Nonetheless, she views the daylong trip with foreboding and disdain, at least until the threesome embarks on an unexpected diversion.

Near the end of his run, her father takes the children to visit the home of Nora Cronin, an unmarried woman who single-handedly runs her family farm and cares for her blind, elderly mother. Their familiarity with each other clearly implies that at some point in the distant past Ben and Nora were good friends, possibly even lovers. Nora welcomes his company eagerly, implying that this is more than a sales visit. Once Nora has invited the Jordans into her home, she excuses herself briefly to her bedroom, where she dons a conspicuously attractive dress and generously applies perfume.

As her father shares a round of drinks and comfortable banter with Nora, the narrator begins to realize that Ben also possesses a distinct identity separate from that of the father and provider she knows. He is a man with a past—one that he feels compelled, particularly now, to revisit. The narrator discovers something she had never even considered before—that her father has a life separate from her mother, her brother, and herself. He drinks whiskey with Nora despite the fact that her mother has told the narrator previously that her father never imbibes. Likewise, Ben has serious acquaintances of which the narrator has never before heard any mention. At the story's close, the narrator contemplates how such revelations have altered her perception of the differences between the worlds of the child and the adult, bringing her one step closer to growing up.

*Themes and Meanings*

"Walker Brothers Cowboy" primarily concerns three major themes: the consequences of economic decline on middle-class families in rural postwar Canada, the dilemmas and epiphanies of a young girl on the brink of adolescence, and the multiplicity of identities even the most commonplace of individuals may possess and even cultivate as a way to deal with material hardship and accompanying feelings of relative powerlessness. Alice Munro interweaves these themes into a tale that extends beyond the bounds of a mere coming-of-age story and explores how all people—regardless of age—deal with the struggle to assert and confront their ever-evolving notions of self.

The story paints a picture of life in rural Ontario in the 1940's and 1950's that is far from nostalgic. The narrator unflatteringly describes it as reminiscent of the Great Depression. Every locale in "Walker Brothers Cowboy," from the Jordans' home to the countless doorsteps on which Ben peddles his wares are described in terms of regretful decline. Ben has had to give up the family business as a fur trader and is forced to make ends meet through commission sales. Prospects are similarly bleak for his peers; Nora mentions that her brother-in-law also struggles to stay steadily employed and that she herself is struggling to support herself and her disabled mother. Her home is filled with furnishings that are well past their prime, and her front door threatens to fall from its hinges for want of repairs she cannot afford to make. Such revealing details say much about the economic landscape of this story; "Walker Brothers Cowboy" is set in a place where the residents struggle to hold onto what they have rather than hope for the promise of prosperity.

The narrator looks on the declining fortunes of her family and neighbors with regret and disillusionment. Although one might expect a story told from the point of view of a preadolescent girl to be naïvely hopeful, the tone of "Walker Brothers Cowboy" is far from being playful or capricious. This suggests that life on the brink of poverty, especially when it comes after having tasted the fruits of even meager prosperity, forces people to seek gratification and fulfillment in the most desperate of places. The narrator seeks it in a sales run with her father, while Ben seeks pleasure in an unannounced visit to an old friend—even at the risk of such a visit looking suspicious to his wife. Although the narrator seems to apprehend little else about her father's motives for taking his children to see Nora, near the end of the story she remarks—after exchanging a knowing glance with Ben—"that there are things not to be mentioned" about their afternoon digression. These are things the narrator will come to understand in time, perhaps as the result of composing this narrative as an adult.

*Style and Technique*

The most prominent stylistic achievements of "Walker Brothers Cowboy" include its particularly distinctive use of first-person point of view and its tendency to communicate through implication rather than overt statement. Munro relates the story through the eyes of a child even though no child could adequately comprehend the dynamics of its principal actions. The narrator, for example, is too young to fully understand the nature of Ben's relationship to Nora. Any adult, however, would gather from the details she observes about them that Ben and Nora share a familiarity with each other that could have resulted only from a teenage romance left unresolved by time and circumstance. Thus, the central consciousness of "Walker Brothers Cowboy" is clearly adult despite the fact that its narrator is ostensibly a preadolescent child. This lends a marked sense of irony to the story that underscores its somber, pessimistic tone.

Munro exploits this irony to remarkable effect, using it as way to contrast the difference between the way children and adults perceive the world. A child relates the tale, but its intended audience is clearly adult. No child would see the need to revisit the past, particularly a person's distant and perhaps obscured past, the way an adult would. However, exploring why people sometimes need to resurrect long-lost feelings and experiences is the thematic locus of the story. Thus, Munro writes "Walker Brothers Cowboy" from the unlikely point of view of a child to reinforce the paradox already inherent in her subject matter. In this way style and theme mirror each other perfectly in the story, which is both bold and memorable in its attempt to merge form and content in highly innovative ways.

*Gregory D. Horn*

# THE WALL

*Author:* William Sansom (1912-1976)
*Type of plot:* Psychological
*Time of plot:* World War II
*Locale:* London during an air raid
*First published:* 1947

> *Principal characters:*
> THE NARRATOR, a firefighter
> LEN,
> LOFTY and
> VERNO, three other firefighters

*The Story*

This very short story of less than four pages describes what goes on in the narrator's mind as he perceives that a huge wall is about to fall on him and his fellow firefighters. After an initial impression of the scene and the nature of the work that has been going on in a typical, hellish night during which firefighters are trying to control fires during air raids in London, the lapse of time covered by the story is a very few minutes or even a matter of moments.

It is 3:00 A.M., and this is their third major blaze—a huge, brick warehouse, five stories high. The men are cold, wet, exhausted, almost mindless in their persistent, stubborn pouring of water into one crimson window after another. The narrator holds the icy nozzle while two other men share the weight of the heavy hose behind him. The fourth man of the team is off to the side, looking at the squat trailer pump that is roaring and quivering with effort. No one is thinking.

Then comes the long, rattling crack, sounding above the throb of the pump, the roaring of the flames, the background hum of aircraft. The narrator knows instantly that the wall is falling. The ratio of thought to action is immediately reversed; the protagonist is rooted to the spot, but his mind snaps alert. His vision becomes preternaturally sharp, recording every detail of the huge, black wall of brick with evenly spaced oblong windows that are bulging with fire, as well as noting and assessing with peripheral vision the possibilities of escape on either side. They stand in a narrow alley with limited access. On one side, the fire-fighting equipment blocks the way—the other side is free. He could yell "Drop it," and they could race up the free side, though the long wall leans over that area as well. He cannot move and says nothing. He meditates about the many ways a wall can fall—swaying to one side, crumbling at the base, or remaining intact and falling flat. The three men crouch, and the wall falls flat, miraculously framing the group of three in one of those symmetrical, oblong window spaces. The fourth man is killed, but the three are dug out with very little brick on top of them.

*Themes and Meanings*

This is a story almost purely of sensation—what it feels like to be in such a situation, how the mind works in the face of almost certain death. Although one might extract a theme from it or an observation about human experience, the particular event itself is enough. The remarkable escape from death is too unusual to warrant any generalization, except that sometimes strange things happen. They do not occur for any moral reason, for example, because the men who were saved were better, wiser, or more skillful than he who died. They do not provide evidence of an interfering God or predestined fate. In fact, the "accidental" survival of the men is perhaps more a technical convenience to lend realism than a thematic device; after all, how could one know what the narrator was thinking if he had not survived to tell the tale?

One might suggest a somewhat existential observation: how even the most dreadful experience becomes infinitely valuable, or at least notable, when the mind recognizes that death is imminent? The color, the shape of things, the significance of the environment attain some kind of absolute distinction; the "thingness" of objects that were before only vague and peripheral to existence suddenly comes into focus, concentrating time and awareness in a few vivid moments.

Such a story has some kind of significance or meaning partly because it gives the impression of undeniable authenticity, not a gothic exercise such as Edgar Allan Poe's "The Pit and the Pendulum," in which one enjoys the goosebumps of sustained suspense without believing a word of it. William Sansom was, as a matter of fact, a firefighter in London during the German Blitzkrieg of World War II. While such firsthand experience is not always necessary to an imaginative writer, it certainly lends verisimilitude to a story that depends not so much on plot as on the subjective experience of an event.

"The Wall" departs from a somewhat romantic, popular assumption that in the moments before death one's life passes in review. The protagonist does indeed live in a mentally expanded space between the time when the wall leans above him and when it crashes around him, but that space is filled with very practical, realistic observations and reflections—not an ounce of nostalgia or regret over lost loves. In that, too, the story gives the impression of relentless realism.

*Style and Technique*

In her introduction to Sansom's collection of short stories, Elizabeth Bowen says, "A Sansom story is a tour de force." That statement certainly applies to "The Wall," which is technically flawless, plunging the reader into experience immediately and holding that attention while he expands a moment almost, but not quite, to the breaking point.

He manages to convey not only the intensity of the crisis but also the weary tedium of the unremitting struggle to contain fires in an air raid. What would be exciting, perhaps even exhilarating in small doses, becomes simply exhausting to the body and stupefying to the mind under constant, night-after-night effort. The initial description conveys this tedious acceptance of the firefighter's nightly chore, creating an effective contrast to the feeling tone of what follows later in the story.

> Until this thing happened, work had been without incident. There had been shrapnel, a few enquiring bombs, and some huge fires; but these were unremarkable and have since merged without identity into the neutral maze of fire and noise and water and night, without date and without hour, with neither time nor form, that lowers mistily at the back of my mind as a picture of the air-raid season.

The narrator offers a series of descriptive details that would typify their experience. Although each is sharp and clear, it is prefaced by "I suppose" or "Probably" or "Without doubt," suggesting that these were every night occurrences, so familiar as almost to be unnoticed.

> I suppose we were drenched, with the cold hose water trickling in at our collars and settling down at the tails of our shirts. . . . Probably the open roar of the pumps drowned the petulant buzz of the raiders, and certainly the ubiquitous fire-glow made an orange stage-set of the streets.

Such things happened so often that "they were not forgotten because they were never even remembered."

When the telltale crack of the bursting brick and mortar herald the collapse of the wall, however, the wandering mind snaps to attention. "I was thinking of nothing and then I was thinking of everything in the world." The sudden expansion of the narrator's powers of observation is metaphorically expressed: "New eyes opened at the sides of my head so that, from within, I photographed a hemispherical panorama bounded by the huge length of the building in front of me and the narrow lane on either side."

There follow two-and-a-half pages of dense, precise description of what he thought and saw between the time when the building heaved over toward them and the few moments it took for the wall to come crashing down. There is no particular sense of panic, though the men seem rooted to the spot. Perhaps there is simply acceptance of the inevitable, with only a touch of hindsight irony.

> We dropped the hose and crouched. Afterwards Verno said that I knelt slowly on one knee with bowed head, like a man about to be knighted. Well, I got my knighting. There was an incredible noise—a thunderclap condensed into the space of an eardrum—and then the bricks and the mortar came tearing and burning into the flesh of my face.

Bowen suggests in the introduction that "what rivets one to a Sansom story is a form of compulsion, rather than 'interest' in the more usual, leisurely or reflective sense." Certainly the characters here are not "interesting"—in fact, the reader knows nothing at all about them. He is so caught up in the sensations of the moment that it does not matter who they are. Nor does the event have any particular moral dimension; the reader must accept the protagonist's simple judgment that they were "lucky."

*Katherine Snipes*

# THE WALL

*Author:* Jean-Paul Sartre (1905-1980)
*Type of plot:* Psychological
*Time of plot:* About 1937
*Locale:* Spain
*First published:* "Le Mur," 1937 (English translation, 1948)

> *Principal characters:*
> PABLO IBBIETA, the narrator, a political prisoner during the
>     Spanish Civil War
> JUAN MIRBAL and
> TOM STEINBOCK, his fellow prisoners
> A BELGIAN PHYSICIAN

*The Story*

Set during the Spanish Civil War of 1936-1939, "The Wall" sets forth the predicament of three men who are taken prisoner without warning or explanation by Falangist forces operating under General Francisco Franco; the story is narrated in the first person by Pablo Ibbieta, an erstwhile political activist who considers himself the most lucid of the trio, no doubt with good reason.

After a summary interrogation, the three captives are sentenced to death by firing squad. As they begin to confront their fate, Pablo finds himself increasingly preoccupied with the reactions of his fellow prisoners, implicitly comparing their behavior to his own. Tom Steinbock, a former comrade-in-arms, betrays his nervousness by talking too much; the third man, hardly more than a boy, is one Juan Mirbal, who repeatedly protests his innocence, claiming that the Falangists have mistaken him for an anarchist brother.

Throughout the long night preceding their planned execution at sunrise, the three men continue to respond in different manners as a Belgian doctor, ostensibly sent in to comfort them, records their behavior with a clinically observant eye. Pablo, meanwhile, is watching also, observing the doctor. Gradually it occurs to Pablo that the physician, not affected by the death sentence that hangs over the prisoners, in fact belongs to a different order of being; unlike them, he is sensitive to cold, and to hunger, no doubt because he can look forward to "tomorrow." The captives, slowly but surely, are losing touch with their bodies, with a loss of control that goes well beyond simple fear. Pablo, in moments of total recall, revisits the small pleasures of his life and political career, only to note that such moments are not utterly devalued by the immediacy of his death: "I had understood nothing. I missed nothing: there were so many things I could have missed, the taste of manzanilla or the baths I took in summer in a little creek near Cadiz; but death had disenchanted everything."

Reminded by Tom of his mistress Concha, whom he had once mentioned to Tom in a rare moment of weakness, Pablo reflects with some amazement that he no longer misses Concha, either: "When she looked at me something passed from her to me. But I knew it was over: if she looked at me now the look would stay in her eyes, it wouldn't reach me. I was alone." In Pablo's current state, even the wild fantasy of a reprieve leaves him strangely cold; as he explains, "several hours or several years is all the same when you have lost the illusion of being eternal."

Toward dawn, Tom and Juan are led from the cell to be shot; Pablo, however, is detained for further questioning concerning the activities and whereabouts of the anarchist Ramon Gris, of which he had previously denied any knowledge. Although he no longer values Gris's life any more than he does his own, Pablo will still refuse to divulge what he knows, if only out of stubbornness. Finally, overwhelmed by the apparent absurdity of his captors' fancy uniforms and self-important airs, Pablo tells an elaborate lie about Gris's supposed whereabouts: As he spins his improbable tale of Gris hiding in a nearby cemetery, he imagines the stuffy, beribboned officers running about among the graves, lifting up tombstones, and the look on their faces when they perceive that the prisoner has tricked them.

The officers have been gone for no more than half an hour when one of them returns, ordering Pablo to be turned loose among the other prisoners, those still awaiting sentence. It is from one of the latter, a baker named Garcia who has "had nothing to do with politics," that Pablo will learn the truth: Ramon Gris, improbably, had taken refuge in the cemetery after an argument with the cousin who had been hiding him; unable to seek refuge with Pablo because of the latter's arrest, he could think of no place else to go. The Falangists, reports Garcia, found Gris hiding in the gravediggers' shack, and when he shot at them they killed him with return fire. As the news begins to sink in, Pablo collapses to the ground in a fit of helpless laughter.

*Themes and Meanings*

Anticipating by nearly half a decade the full development of Jean-Paul Sartre's existentialist philosophy, "The Wall" presents in imaginative form some of the major themes of that philosophy, giving concrete illustration of seemingly abstract ideas.

The "wall" of the story's title is the wall of the prison courtyard against which the prisoners are lined up to be shot; by extension, however, it comes to symbolize the boundary between life and death, between "being" and "nothingness." Pablo Ibbieta, although he will survive physically at least long enough to tell his ironic tale, is, in fact, as good as dead from the moment that he first perceives and appreciates the immediate prospect of his "nothingness." The human capacities for love, friendship, and political activism have all died in him as he has passed, as it were, through the "wall" to the other side.

Awaiting execution during the small hours of the morning, Pablo has reviewed his life and found it strangely wanting: "I wondered how I'd been able to walk, to laugh with the girls: I wouldn't have moved so much as my little finger if I had only imagined I would die like this. My life was in front of me, closed, shut, like a bag and yet everything inside of it was unfinished." Like many of Sartre's later characters, Pablo senses that most of his planned actions will die with him, unperformed, with little trace of him left to posterity. Notwithstanding, he persists in observing his stubborn code of honor, in his implied commitment to the liberal cause, and in his determination to die "cleanly" and "well," in contrast to his fellow prisoners. For Sartre, there is no afterlife, no trace of individual human passage on earth save for the sum total of accomplishments to be recorded after death.

## Style and Technique

Couched in the first person, limited solely to Pablo's individual perceptions and opinions, "The Wall" serves as an object-lesson in the literary and critical theories that Sartre was then developing. There is no God-like, omniscient narrator; the style is less literary than conversational, even "earthy," with frequent recourse to rough language and profanity in description, metaphor, and dialogue. Except for Pablo's random recollections, the characters and their actions are described entirely "in situation," with little attention paid to possible background or motivation. To further underscore Sartre's attempt at "authenticity," at least insofar as is possible in art or literature, the story's setting and "atmosphere" are evoked entirely through the immediate, often graphically rendered perceptions of the narrator's five senses. The story's "trick" ending, however sensational, is nevertheless amply prepared for throughout by the nature of the tale to be told, and by Pablo's awareness of contingency and irony in life.

*David B. Parsell*

# WALTER BRIGGS

*Author:* John Updike (1932-    )
*Type of plot:* Domestic realism
*Time of plot:* The late 1950's
*Locale:* The Boston area
*First published:* 1959

> *Principal characters:*
> JACK, the protagonist
> CLARE, his wife
> JO, their two-year-old daughter
> WALTER BRIGGS, a character from their past

### The Story

Driving home from Boston (a fifty-minute trip), Jack and his wife, Clare, entertain their daughter Jo with a version of a familiar nursery rhyme while their infant son sleeps. After Jo also falls asleep, they talk about the people they have met at a party, which leads into an extended memory game in which they try to remember names and details about people they had known when, newly married, they had worked together at a YMCA family camp in New Hampshire for a summer five years before. Their conversation, mostly commonplace and trivial, reveals hidden conflicts. One name out of their past that eludes both of them is the surname of a man called Walter who stayed all summer and played bridge every night.

Lying in bed after arriving home, Jack starts recalling poignant details of their early married life at the summer camp, particularly of their cabin and of his habit of reading Miguel de Cervantes's *El ingenioso hidalgo don Quixote de la Mancha* (1605, 1615; *The History of the Valorous and Wittie Knight-Errant, Don Quixote of the Mancha*, 1612-1620; better known as *Don Quixote de la Mancha*) every evening before dinner. Thinking of his tears at the conclusion of the novel, Jack suddenly recollects the name that had escaped them; he turns to his sleeping wife and says, "Briggs. Walter Briggs."

### Themes and Meanings

The themes of "Walter Briggs" are revealed mainly through the character of the protagonist and the nature of the conflict with his wife. Beneath the surface of the memory game in the car there is a quiet but strong undercurrent of resentment and jealousy. Jack begins the marital hostilities by remarking that Clare's comments at the party about Sherman Adams (a controversial figure in President Dwight D. Eisenhower's administration) were "stupid." Then, talking about another person at the party, Jack observes that Foxy "loves you so."

This comment is followed by a series of exchanges in which Jack remembers attractive physical features of females at the camp, which provoke responses from Clare. He recalls the girl "with the big ears who was lovely," and then defends her pride in her ears when Clare disparages the girl's wearing of "those bobbly gold gypsy rings." Jack also calls to mind a mentally disturbed girl who was "awfully good-looking," and a woman named Peg Grace who had "huge eyes." Clare counters with the observation that Peg had a "tiny long nose with the nostrils shaped like water wings" and further remembers that Peg's boyfriend was sexy in his "tiny black bathing trunks." Jack then recalls a German kitchen boy "with curly hair he thought was so cute." Clare, in response, explains, "You didn't like him because he was always making eyes at me." Jack says that he really did not like the German kitchen boy because he had beaten him in a broad-jump competition and that he was pleased when the German was, in turn, beaten by someone else.

Jack's competitive instinct is one reason for the exchanges between Jack and his wife. Early in the story, the author explains that Jack found the memory contest deficient: "A poor game, it lacked the minimal element of competition needed to excite Jack." In this light, the comments about other women are designed to make the memory game more exciting by provoking Clare to respond. On a deeper level, however, the form that this provocation takes suggests that Jack is indeed quite receptive to the charms of other women and subconsciously, out of a sense of inadequacy, wants to let his wife know of this attraction.

Jack's sense of inadequacy is also brought out by Clare's obvious superiority in the memory game. He does not have her talent for accurate and vivid recall, and he believes that he has "made an unsatisfactory showing." Although he is jealous of "her store of explicit memories," he is also pleased that she so generously shares with him reminiscences from their mutual past.

In the final scene, after they are in bed and Clare is asleep, Jack's memory begins to become more precise and intense. Spurred by her statement that the German boy had made eyes at her, he begins to recollect loving details of their early married life: "Slowly this led him to remember how she had been, the green shorts and the brown legs, holding his hand as in the morning they walked to breakfast from their cabin, along a lane that was two dirty paths for the wheels of the jeep." His memories increase in poignancy: "Her hand, her height had seemed so small, the fact of her waking him so strange."

Jack finally recalls that he had spent the whole summer, in the half hour between work and dinner, reading *Don Quixote de la Mancha* in a chair outside their cabin and how he cried at the conclusion when Sancho Panza urges his master to go on another quest, perhaps to find "the Lady Dulcinea under some hedge, stripped of her enchanted rags and fine as any queen." It is at this point that Jack triumphantly remembers the lost last name of Walter Briggs and says it softly to the sleeping Clare.

This ending, then, represents a triumphant moment of joy for Jack. He has not only scored a small victory in the memory game by recovering the name of Walter Briggs, but also he has achieved something much more substantial. He has been able to recover his early feelings for his wife and the details of their life together in the modest cabin. Moreover, the allusion to *Don Quixote de la Mancha* suggests another new dimension to their relationship. He now sees Clare as the Lady Dulcinea, a desirable and splendid woman, just as Sancho and his master perceived Dulcinea. Jack experiences a moment of epiphany, a new and deeper awareness about his feelings for his wife. He becomes aware, through the power of memory, of precious hours in his life, which, as the story suggests, come from little things, from commonplace shared experiences.

*Style and Technique*

The plot of "Walter Briggs" is a straightforward sequence of events, starting in the car in the drive from Boston and ending late that same night. The bulk of the action, however, is retrospective in that it takes place in the memory of the main character. Still, the emphasis is not in the events themselves, but on what they reveal about the protagonist and the effect they have on him. The journey as a plot device is a common one, and it is appropriate here in that it serves as a metaphor for Jack's journey into a part of his past self that had been forgotten.

Jack's character is revealed primarily through the exchanges with Clare. However, it is a very subtle dialogue in that the thrusts and parries of the conversation as well as the underlying hostility between Jack and his wife are artfully concealed beneath the banal observations of a somewhat bored couple on a tedious automobile trip. As often occurs in real life, the major issues between Jack and his wife are not directly stated but are indirectly brought out and then passed by as the conversation quickly shifts to another person or incident. In the end, Jack is revealed as a complex and dynamic character with very human failings yet also a person to like and perhaps admire. The author shows Jack as a person capable of change who manages to extract something permanently valuable from an unpromising evening in a car.

The point of view is limited omniscience; the story is told in the third person through the eyes of Jack, the protagonist. Although characterization mostly emerges from dialogue concerning memories from camp, the final important insight into Jack's character comes from the author's direct recording of what Jack is thinking and feeling, which permits one to see the intensity of Jack's new awareness. Because the point of view is restricted to Jack's consciousness, the reader learns about Clare only by what she says and does and by what Jack thinks of her, not through any authorial revelation of her thoughts.

"Walter Briggs" demonstrates those aspects of style for which John Updike is widely praised. Among these are the strong sense of time and place in modern America, created here by the references to contemporary religious and political figures, by his knowledge of everyday practices of Americans, and even by his mention of brand names and common commercial products. Updike also has a careful ear for the way people speak and for the rhythms of conversation. In the dialogue between Jack and Clare, Updike expertly captures the ebb and flow, repetitions, and interruptions of two people who know each other intimately. The opening conversation between Clare and her daughter Jo is a masterpiece of mother-child dialogue.

Above all, Updike is notable for a poetic style, which in a single telling phrase or in the perfect word or image evokes the essence of a character or a scene. The following description, for example, captures the bleakness of the summer cabin, which stands in contrast to the remembered richness of the experience there: "All around the cabin had stood white pines stretched to a cruel height by long competition, and the cabin itself had no windows, but broken screens."

Finally, the title itself serves a dramatic function by creating a sense of mystery. Who is this character, Walter Briggs, one wonders, whose name Jack and Clare are so desperately trying to recollect? At the end, the name, fully shown again in the last two words of the story, is a helpful instrument for the revelation of Jack's new awareness.

*Walter Herrscher*

# WALTZ OF THE FAT MAN

*Author:* Alberto Ríos (1952-    )
*Type of plot:* Fable
*Time of plot:* Unspecified
*Locale:* Unspecified
*First published:* 1991

>           *Principal character:*
>           NOÉ, an overweight butcher

*The Story*

Noé is a middle-aged man who pays precise attention to the details of his appearance—his trim mustache and creased clothing—and the details of his house, which has blue trim and a blue door that will stand against spirits. Noé's existence, however, is one of utter loneliness, with a complete lack of social and emotional contact with other human beings. His profession as a butcher brings him sadness, even though he chose this profession in an effort to do good things. Noé considers that the townspeople's polite disregard of him might be because he is overweight, but he does not think of himself as fat. He considers his body as a heaviness that has come from the inside out. He attends wakes in the town simply for the opportunity for human contact, but he receives only obligatory common courtesy from others. He simply wishes to be part of the town.

To find a release from his loneliness, Noé dresses in a blue suit and dances outside of the town. Noé dances with the faceless wind and encircles his arms around the branches of black walnut trees; the trees are as unyielding as women's arms, but they at least cannot leave to gossip about him. He feels free to let out his "thin girl"—a partner who will not ignore him. Together, they dance the dance of weddings through the night.

In an attempt to become more of a regular man and be in the mainstream of human relations, Noé begins to wear his blue suit to his butcher shop. He also devises a small plan to shake the hands of women vigorously in order to see some movement of their bodies—some indication that he is recognized as another human being. By attending wakes, he can kiss the cheeks of the bereaved, but even this clumsy attempt often meets with failure.

As a further antidote to his unwanted loneliness, Noé begins to collect clocks, even hanging them on his butcher shop walls. He collects the clocks because they have hands, "and in so many clocks was a kind of heaven, a dream of sounds to make the hours pass in a manner that would allow him to open up shop the next day." He perceives of them as women—giving them women's names—and imagines that they are beckoning and speaking to him. Despite the townspeople's objections to this strange behavior, Noé is left alone. One winter evening, however, Noé hears the blue clock, his favored "Marina," hesitate. He hurries to the clock that is calling to him as "a wife in pain." Even though he tells himself that Marina is only a clock, he is disconcerted, and after examining her, he wraps her up in butcher's paper like a piece of meat, an act that seems to bring him comfort.

As Noé quickly walks home in the darkness, cradling his precious Marina, he hears an oleander call to him as he passes by the stand of walnut trees where he has danced before. He hesitates as he hears his name called again, searches through the leaves, and then puts down the clock to investigate. It is a whispered voice that he recognizes, the voice of Marina, "who had made so many places for herself in his life. . . . She was the blueness inside him, the color of his appetite, the color both of what filled him and what he needed more of." The voice asks Noé if she loves him, and if so, to act like a horse. After hesitating, Noé obeys the voice, stamping and snorting, willing to do anything for Marina, the embodiment of his loneliness and desire. The laughter of soldiers hiding in the oleanders forces Noé to turn for home, without Marina, bereft of even this small comfort in his desolate existence.

The loss of Marina causes Noé to sell his butcher shop, buy a brown horse, and leave the town. He rides into the future, feeling that he has "become an exponent to a regular number." All he really wanted was to belong and for everyone and everything to be nice, for people to follow the Golden Rule of common courtesy and humanity. This, he now knows, is too much to ask. In the final section of the story, Noé meets up with a circus and feels as if he has finally found his real career with a "company of half-size men, two-bodied women, and all the rest of the animals who danced." Within this group of supposed misfits, Noé reaches a place where he is free to dance and free to be himself.

### Themes and Meanings

Alberto Ríos, a writer who has won many prestigious awards for his poetry and fiction, has said: "I was born on the border of Mexico to a Mexican father and an English mother. I write often about this background, especially the Mexican/Chicano aspects." In this story, however, the theme of loneliness transcends culture and gender to convey an archetypal portrait of an Everyperson who is at first immobilized by the abject alienation imposed on him by others. The poignancy of the story is that Noé's desire is so seemingly simple: the need for involvement, both social and emotional, with other human beings. Because Noé is different, perhaps, overweight and viewed as suspect by others, he cannot belong in a "normal" small town. Instead, he must free himself by leaving and joining a circus peopled by beings who are viewed as equally strange, but in reality, are perhaps more humane than those considered normal in ordinary society.

Within Noé's large body, he carries characteristics that are both male and female, a fact that makes him even more identifiable as an Everyperson searching for a place to belong. This theme of androgyny can be found in Noé's dance with the wind and the trees when he is free to let his "thin girl" out, his hidden desire to socialize and make emotional contact with other human beings. Also, in two instances in the story, Noé feels as if he "were his own mother." With familial bonds absent in the story, Noé must embody this absent motherhood. In fact, Noé's large body of "slow bones" seems to encompass the desire of all humans—both male and female—to feel as if they belong.

Noé attempts to fit in by keeping a neat house trimmed in blue, wearing a blue suit to become a "regular man," and finding comfort in the hands of his numerous clocks—especially in his blue Marina. However, it seems as if this recurring blueness is a reflection of Noé's isolation; blueness does not bring him comfort or solace. However, Noé does contain the capacity to free himself in the final section of the story when he reaches the circus people standing near the road. He realizes that they "called him without telegraph or telephone. Something stronger." Everyone, in his or her own way, is a misfit, and perhaps the ultimate satisfaction in human experience is the ability to connect emotionally with others. With the circus, finally, Noé achieves this.

*Style and Technique*

Ríos has said that his writing is often narrative, and he thinks of his books as "talking to each other." Furthermore, Ríos's multilingual experiences and work with translation have given him an astute appreciation for the richness and complexity of all languages. The seven short sections of this story clearly show his powers of lyricism. The language itself seems to waltz off the page, with each carefully crafted phrase contributing to fluid images. The language lends a strange beauty and complexity to the character of Noé, the fat man who is so much more than his outward appearance: the Everyperson who can succeed in a cold world.

This story also has a quality of Magical Realism; nothing is quite what it seems to be on the surface. Noé, an overweight butcher, encompasses both genders and the desire to be respected and loved. At the end of the story, he is beginning a transformation process when he catches up to the circus: "He arrived as a beast, almost, something crazed and unshaven, out of breath. Or as a beast on top of a man, as if the horse itself were more human, and asking for help." No longer confined within the parameters of what passes for "appropriate" or "courteous" behavior, Noé is released. After an existence that can only be defined by its loneliness, Noé has ridden to a new life where there is the promise of emotional bonding and the freedom to dance.

*Laurie Lisa*

# THE WANDERERS

*Author:* Alun Lewis (1915-1944)
*Type of plot:* Realism
*Time of plot:* The 1930's
*Locale:* Wales
*First published:* 1939

> *Principal characters:*
> MICAH, a small boy
> THE GIPSY, his father
> MAM, his mother
> JOHNNY ONIONS, a French peddler

*The Story*

Although this story focuses primarily on the marital relations of a Gypsy and his Welsh wife, the central character is the small child, Micah, for he is the one most affected by his parents' passions. The plot is simple. A Welsh woman has married the Gipsy, obviously because she was pregnant with the boy Micah, but also because, as she says, she does not like to live in houses. Their life, which gives the story its title, is one of wandering, peddling, haggling, and hiring themselves as laborers out whenever possible.

The central event of the story occurs when the wife sees her husband coming out of a barn with a farm girl and soon after becomes sexually attracted to a French peddler and has sex with him while her husband sleeps. The next morning, Micah tells his father that the peddler took his mother into the meadow during the night. While the Gipsy goes off with the peddler, presumably to beat him, the wife leaves to meet the peddler in another town.

After walking for hours, the wife gives up her quest, returns to the caravan, and has a physical fight with her husband, which sends Micah running in terror into the meadow. When the Gipsy finally tires of the fight, he and his wife have sex. When Micah returns and finds them asleep, he is content, knowing that when they awake everything will be the way he likes it.

The actions and passions of the story are reminiscent of the fiction of D. H. Lawrence, whose influence is clearly apparent here. This is a story of primitive desires, involving people practicing a wandering lifestyle. It depends on a stereotype of Gypsies as dark, violent, sexual creatures, homeless and almost animalistic in their desires— dark strangers that more civilized folk use as bogeymen with which to frighten young children. The story also depends on other reductive stereotypes. For example, when the Gipsy goes into town to pawn his wife's earrings, he deals with a "shrivelled little Jew" with a pointed nose and an ingratiating manner. It is similarly stereotypical that the Gipsy would have a literal "roll in the hay" with a somewhat mindless farm girl and that the man who is so alluring to the wife is a Frenchman.

Even the use of the little boy Micah as a central figure, slapped by his mother, boxed by his father, and terrified that his mother will be taken away by the peddler, is a convention based on the notion that children are often the bewildered victims of adult passions that they do not understand but instinctively fear. Micah intuitively knows that the Frenchman is a threat, for as he watches his mother talk to the peddler, Micah puts his arms around her and bites into the flesh at the nape of her neck, only to be thrown off quivering like an animal. Above all, he desires stability, the reassurance of the status quo, although the life that he has known with his wandering parents has hardly been ideal.

### Themes and Meanings

"The Wanderers" evokes a lifestyle that may appear romantic from a distance but that, close up, is seen to be merely sordid and animalistic. When the Gipsy sees the farm girl, what he responds to are her breasts, strong and round, pressing against her cotton blouse, and his composure melts into an "aching tumult of desire." His wife almost as immediately responds to the French peddler. The story suggests that she is not simply trying to avenge herself, but that she has become "infected" by her husband's own powerful passions. The language used to describe her desire for the peddler is almost identical with that used to describe her husband's desire for the farm girl. She feels that she has never burned like this before.

Alun Lewis, whose death in World War II cut short a promising career, is best known as a poet. "The Wanderers" appeared in a collection of stories, *The Last Inspection* (1942), most of the stories in which deal with life during the early years of the war in England, when air raids were a nightly horror. In "The Wanderers," he shifts away from the wartime setting, but the rootlessness depicted in this story is akin to that felt by the soldiers whom he more often takes as his central characters. At the same time, the story depicts the uncontrollable force of sexuality—a force that Lewis evidently regarded with a mixture of fascination and guilt.

The basic irony of the story is that the wife of the Gipsy, who is himself the archetypal wandering character, runs away from him with another wandering character, a reversal that somewhat domesticates him and makes him the cuckolded husband. Perhaps the most profound irony of the story is that as Micah strives to maintain the stability of his life with his parents, the reader must reflect that Micah's life has nothing resembling genuine stability at all.

### Style and Technique

Although the story centers on Micah, it is not told from his point of view but rather from an omniscient third-person approach in which the narrator alternately enters the mind of the brutal and sexually aroused husband, the wildly inflamed wife, and the bewildered child. By this narrative strategy, and by other means as well, Lewis sought to give the story something of the violent authority of a ballad or a folktale—an attempt not entirely successful.

The language of the story is generally straightforward, but there are traces of Lewis the poet: At the crucial sexual moment between the Gipsy and the farm girl, Lewis describes the luminous darkness of the barn as if it were "cloudy with purple, intangible grapes." In several nearly voyeuristic scenes, the wife is naked—getting ready for bed, bathing in the stream, looking in the mirror—and here the description is simple but powerfully suggestive. Many readers, it should be noted, will object to the attitudes that inform the story, particularly the link between violence and sex.

*Charles E. May*

# WANDERING WILLIE'S TALE

*Author:* Sir Walter Scott (1771-1832)
*Type of plot:* Gothic, epistolary
*Time of plot:* The mid-1760's
*Locale:* Dumfries, Scotland
*First published:* 1824, as an episode in the novel *Redgauntlet*

> *Principal characters:*
> DARSIE LATIMER, a law student taking a walking vacation from
>     his studies in Edinburgh
> ALAN FAIRFORD, his correspondent, a fellow law student
> WILLIE STEENSON (STEVENSON), a blind itinerant fiddler
> STEENIE (STEVEN) STEENSON, Willie's grandfather
> SIR ROBERT REDGAUNTLET, a nobleman who dies before giving
>     Willie's father a receipt for his rent
> SIR JOHN REDGAUNTLET, Sir Robert's heir
> DOUGAL MACCALLUM, Sir Robert's butler and assistant
> HUTCHEON, Sir Robert's serving man

*The Story*

While taking a break from his studies in Edinburgh, Darsie Latimer is roaming the border country in western Scotland, staying at an inn in Dumfries. There he encounters Willie Steenson and his wife walking in the same general direction, on the road toward Dumfries. Willie's wife says that Willie is a good teller of tales, so Latimer asks him to tell one as they walk. What follows is Willie's tale.

When Steenie Steenson, Willie's grandfather, went to Redgauntlet Castle to pay his rent, he was taken by Dougal MacCallum to meet Sir Robert Redgauntlet, sitting alone in his oak parlor, except for his pet jackanape, Major Weir, and suffering from a painful attack of gout. Willie explains that Sir Robert was wearing a sword and pistols for protection against Whigs who might want to take vengeance on him for his part in supporting Jacobite uprisings. Steenie handed a bag of silver, his rent money, to Redgauntlet, who instructed MacCallum to give him some brandy while he counted the money and wrote out a receipt.

Just as Steenie and MacCallum left the room, however, Sir Robert yelled out, crying for water for his feet and wine for his throat. When his feet were plunged into a tub of water, the liquid boiled. Sir Robert accused MacCallum of giving him blood to drink instead of wine and threw the cup at him (the next day, the maid washed blood from the carpet). When the jackanape caused a commotion, Steenie ran from the room, forgetting both the silver and his receipt. As he fled, he heard that the laird (lord) was dead and afterward hoped that MacCallum would remember seeing his money bag and Sir Robert's saying that he intended to write a receipt for him.

Preparation for Sir Robert's funeral fell to MacCallum, who slept in a room next to the one in which Sir Robert lay in state. MacCallum asked Sir Robert's servant Hutcheon to share the room, partly because he was still hearing Sir Robert's paging whistle calling for him during the night. On the night before the funeral, the whistle sounded again, and both old serving men went toward the coffin. Hutcheon saw "the foul fiend in his ain [own] shape" sitting on Sir Robert's coffin and lost consciousness. When he recovered, he found MacCallum lying dead.

The new estate owner, Sir Robert's son John, came from Edinburgh and discovered that the rent payment record book had no entry for Steenie for the previous year. He therefore pressed his tenant for payment or for a receipt showing that payment had been made. Steenie protested at length that he had indeed made the payment, but both its recipient and the only other witness were now dead. He offered to produce witnesses from among those from whom he had borrowed the money for his rent, but Sir John insisted the evidence he wanted had to be a receipt from his father. When Steenie suggested someone else in the household may have seen the money, Sir John questioned all the servants but concluded that they had seen nothing.

Sir John pressed Steenie further, telling him that he must either pay or quit his land. Steenie insisted that he was an honest man, but Sir John accused him of trying to cheat him. He asked Steenie where he supposed the money to be, and Steenie, driven to desperation, said, "In hell, if you *will* have my thoughts of it . . . with your father, his jackanape, and his silver whistle." Steenie then ran again, as Sir John called for law officers.

Steenie approached his chief creditor, only to be further abused by being called a thief and a beggar. He then began to ride home through Pitmurkie wood, stopping at a hostler-wife's cottage long enough for a quick brandy. There he proposed two toasts: the first to Sir Robert's memory that he might not rest quietly until he had set things right with his tenant; the second to "Man's Enemy," that he might get back the silver for him or tell him where it was. Soon a strange horseman appeared and said that although he was misunderstood in the world, he was a great one for helping friends. He told Steenie that the dead laird was disturbed by Steenie's curses and by his family's wailing and that if Steenie would go to him, the laird would give him his receipt.

Steenie agreed to the stranger's proposal and followed him deeper into the woods to a great house very much like Redgauntlet Castle. There, the door was opened by Dougal MacCallum, who said that Sir Robert had been crying for him. He warned Steenie not to take anything from anyone there—neither meat, drink, nor silver, but only to take the receipt that was due him. Amid much wine-drinking and revelry among people who had participated in the Jacobite uprisings, Steenie was called by Sir Robert, while someone said that Major Weir would be there in the morning.

Sir Robert, "or his ghaist [ghost], or the deevil in his likeness," asked Steenie if he had settled the rent matter with Sir John. When Steenie insisted that he needed Sir Robert's receipt, the laird said he would give it if Steenie played a tune on the pipes. He asked for a tune that Steenie had learned from a warlock, who heard it during a Satan-worshiping meeting. Bagpipes were brought, but because they were made of white-hot steel, Steenie said that he had no breath to play the pipes. He also declined food and drink, saying that he had come only for the receipt. Sir Robert gave a receipt to Steenie and told him to tell Sir John to look for the money in the Cat's Cradle. He also told Steenie that he must return in a year to pay homage for the protection Sir Robert was giving him. However, Steenie said that he relied only on God, and the entire vision of hell disappeared.

Some time later, Steenie awoke in the churchyard near Redgauntlet Castle, receipt in hand, which he delivered to Sir John, who acknowledged that he must have gone to Hell for it. Hutcheon identified the Cat's Cradle as a long unused turret, accessible only by ladder, and Sir John took one of his father's pistols and went there. A shot rang out, followed by Sir John's flinging down the body of the jackanape and calling out that he had found the silver, as well as several other missing objects. Steenie agreed with Sir John that no word could go out about the events of his "dream," except that Steenie might speak with the local minister, who assured him that if he walked a straight path thereafter, Satan would not bother him.

*Themes and Meanings*

After Willie finishes his tale, he tells Latimer that his purpose has been to convince the younger man that it may not be safe to take up with a stranger while traveling—which is exactly what Latimer is doing in accompanying Willie and his wife. Like much of Sir Walter Scott's work, the story presents a sympathetic treatment of many supporters of the Stuart claims to the throne of Britain, a historical reality during Scott's time, as was the historical clan warfare to which he alludes. The story introduces the Redgauntlet family, to which Darsie Latimer, in the course of the longer novel, discovers that he belongs. Suggestions that the family has been marked by supernatural events occur throughout the novel. The tale's central theme is the political and sectarian conflict in late seventeenth century Scotland and England after the Glorious Revolution of 1688. Various references give a context of Covenanters, Roman Catholics, Quakers, and members of the Church of England; however, Scott does not proselytize.

*Style and Technique*

Scott's novel *Redgauntlet* is made up of correspondence between Darsie Latimer and Alan Fairford—with most of the letters written by Latimer—and is supplemented by journal entries written by both men. The episode of Willie's tale is reported by Latimer to Fairford, as related to Latimer by Willie. The tale is rendered in Scots dialect, which Latimer faithfully records—a regular feature of Scott's writing style.

The story makes many references to "the forty-five"—a code name for the Jacobite uprising of 1745 that supported the monarchical claims of the Young Pretender, Charles Edward Stuart. Willie appears again late in the novel when he fiddles the tune, "The Campbells Are Coming," to alert those attending a Jacobite conspiracy meeting in time for them to be prepared for the law to enter.

*Carolyn F. Dickinson*

# WAR

*Author:* Luigi Pirandello (1867-1936)
*Type of plot:* Social realism
*Time of plot:* About 1916
*Locale:* Fabriano, Italy
*First published:* "Quando si comprende," 1919 (English translation, 1939)

> *Principal characters:*
> A MOTHER, whose son is about to go to war
> A FATHER, whose son has been killed in the war

*The Story*

Some travelers from Rome are obliged to spend most of the night aboard a second-class railway carriage, parked at the station in Fabriano, waiting for the departure of the local train that will take them the remainder of their trip to the small village of Sulmona. At dawn, they are joined by two additional passengers: a large woman, "almost like a shapeless bundle," and her tiny, thin husband. The woman is in deep mourning and is so distressed and maladroit that she has to be helped into the carriage by the other passengers.

Her husband, following her, thanks the people for their assistance and then tries to look after his wife's comfort, but she responds to his ministrations by pulling up the collar of her coat to her eyes, hiding her face. The husband manages a sad smile and comments that it is a nasty world. He explains this remark by saying that his wife is to be pitied because the war has separated her from their twenty-year-old son, "a boy of twenty to whom both had devoted their entire life." The son, he says, is due to go to the front. The man remarks that this imminent departure has come as a shock because, when they gave permission for their son's enlistment, they were assured that he would not go for six months. However, they have just been informed that he will depart in three days.

The man's story does not prompt too much sympathy from the others because the war has similarly touched their lives. One of them tells the man that he and his wife should be grateful that their son is leaving only now. He says that his own son "was sent there the first day of the war. He has already come back twice wounded and been sent back again to the front." Someone else, joining the conversation, adds that he has two sons and three nephews already at the front. The thin husband retorts that his child is an only son, meaning that, should he die at the front, a father's grief would be all the more profound. The other man refuses to see that this makes any difference. "You may spoil your son with excessive attentions, but you cannot love him more than you would all your other children if you had any." Therefore, this one insists that he would really suffer twice what a father with one son would suffer.

The man with the two sons at the front continues by saying that a father gives all of his love to each of his children "without discrimination," and, even if one son is killed and the other remains, this is a son left "for whom he must survive, while in the case of the father of an only son if the son dies the father can die too and put an end to his distress." Thus, the situation of a man with two sons would still be worse than that of a man with one son.

Another man interjects that this argument is nonsense because, although parents belong to their sons, the sons never belong to their parents. Boys at twenty, "decent" boys, consider the love of their country greater than the love of their parents; when they go away to fight, they do not want to see any tears "because if they die, they die inflamed and happy." One should therefore rejoice that they have thus been spared the ugly side of life, its boredom and pettiness and its bitterness and disillusion. He says that everyone should therefore laugh as he does, "because my son, before dying, sent a message saying that he was dying satisfied at having ended his life in the best way he could have wished."

The woman whose son is being sent to the front to "a probable danger of death" is stunned by the stranger's words. She suddenly realizes that her deep sorrow lies in her inability to rise to the height of all those fathers and mothers who have the ability to resign themselves to the departure and even the death of their sons. She listens with close attention to the man's account of how his son has fallen as a hero, and she believes that she has suddenly stumbled into a world "she never dreamt of, a world so far unknown to her." Moreover, she is greatly pleased when it appears that everyone else seems to feel the same and congratulate the "brave father who could so stoically speak of his child's death." However, reacting as if she had just heard nothing, she asks the man, "Then . . . is your son really dead?" Everyone stares at her, including the old man who has lost his son.

He tries to answer but cannot speak. The silly, incongruous question makes him realize, at last, that his son is, in fact, really dead and gone forever. His face begins to contort, and, reaching for a handkerchief, he, to everyone's amazement, breaks down "into harrowing, heart-rendering, uncontrollable sobs."

### Themes and Meanings

This is a world of crumbling values, made all the more vapid because of the intense desire to rationalize attitudes and live in a mist of illusions. The characters are overwhelmed by events that they cannot control and little understand, but they pretend otherwise. The woman, who has just arrived, is somewhat of an outsider; she apparently has not had time, or is not yet willing, to submerge her natural emotions under a mask of acceptable public sentimentality.

The passengers reflect the lack of enthusiasm of the Italian people for the Great War, in which their country became involved because of a greedy backroom deal to acquire a few more chunks of territory that only few thought worth spilling blood to get. The lands would most likely have been theirs as the price of staying out. Italy's participation was conditioned by no great outpouring of national sentiment, nor because the national interest demanded it. However, a pretense has to be made. One character says, "Our children do not belong to us, they belong to the Country." His words, however, lack conviction. These people, despite their boastful facade, are not preoccupied with the great forces of history. They want to make it through life causing as little damage to their dignity as possible. They want to preserve the only thing that gives their life meaning and ensures their link with immortality: the lives of their offspring. One character says, "Is there any one of us here who wouldn't gladly take his son's place at the front if he could?" Everyone nods approval, but in fact such a question is academic because the premise on which it is built is so farfetched. However, the concern is genuine.

In a sense, the war is far removed from this provincial railway siding—there is no mention or description of any actual fighting—but the war's presence is nevertheless overpowering, conveyed in the characters' pathetic attempts to maintain appearances through worthless intellectualizations, hollow gestures, and futile attempts to sublimate anxiety. If none of the characters is swept away by a sense of participation in a great national crusade, none seems to turn to religion for comfort; indeed, the absence of any meaningful reference to religion is remarkable for people living in such an avowedly Roman Catholic country. Nothing is accepted as being in conformity with God's plan, or with his grand design for the Italian nation. No sacrifices are sanctified by their relation to a higher purpose. One gets the impression from these people that none of the sons sacrificed in this war will have died on the field of any honor.

Luigi Pirandello's characters are prisoners of their own subjectivity and their own lack of imagination. They are morally featureless. However, their stale words and feeble efforts to communicate, coming from their boredom and trepidation, reveal a genuinely human need. They must convince themselves of their own intrinsic worth to alleviate their desperation.

### Style and Technique

Pirandello uses a well-established literary device to tell his story: He contrives a restricted setting for his characters and lets them share their thoughts with one another. Such constraint—Pirandello even honors the three classical unities of time, place, and action—more dramatically reveals a world in which all progress and hope of progress has ceased. This atmosphere is as dull, oppressive, and intrusive as yesterday's lifeless beer. Pirandello is trying to represent human experience as realistically and banally as possible and could hardly be considered a symbolist; nevertheless, the imagery is there. His characters sit in an old-fashioned train in a small railway station in a small Italian province and wait to be taken to an even more remote and backward part of their country. They wait for something to happen with the dread that it might. They wait with the same spirit of resignation in which they struggle to accept and minimize the ultimate loss of their sons.

Pirandello lets the characters speak for themselves. He offers the barest of description, saving himself the trouble by relying on the reader's own knowledge of his locale. In thus downplaying the surroundings, Pirandello is able to intensify the characters' relationships to one another. This intensification is necessary because his characters are so essentially colorless, with features made deliberately unpleasant. Consider how Pirandello describes their eyes: One has "bloodshot eyes of the palest grey"; another has "eyes small and bright and looking shy and uneasy"; still another has "his eyes [that] were watery and motionless"; and yet another has "bulging, horrible watery light grey eyes": These are people in decay.

Pirandello's style is lean, remarkably lacking in metaphors and imagery. His descriptions are sparse and gray. He seems to be repetitive and not very original, dealing almost in clichés. He reveals no great philosophical or psychological insights, perpetually distancing himself from his characters. The story ends with a sort of double resolution: The woman, after listening to the man's description of how his son had fallen for king and country "happy and without regrets," believes that she can at last come to terms with her grief. However, her period of reconciliation will be all too brief. The man, whose son was slain, who until now has successfully been able to suppress his loss, suddenly has all of his illusions swept away. He will bear the scars of his grief for the remainder of his days. Pirandello makes a skillful use of irony: The father's damnation is also his salvation. The realization that he no longer will be able to protect himself by self-deception brings to an end his artificiality and restores his humanity. Whether a similar catharsis will affect the others is doubtful.

*Wm. Laird Kleine-Ahlbrandt*

# WARD NO. 6

*Author:* Anton Chekhov (1860-1904)
*Type of plot:* Psychological
*Time of plot:* The 1890's
*Locale:* A provincial Russian town
*First published:* "Palata No. 6," 1892 (English translation, 1916)

> *Principal characters:*
> ANDREI EFIMYCH RAGIN, a doctor
> IVAN DMITRICH GROMOV, a patient in a mental ward
> MIKHAIL AVER'IANYCH, a postmaster
> EVGENII FEDORYCH KHOBOTOV, a doctor

## The Story

Anton Chekhov begins his tale by taking his readers on a tour of the mental ward of a hospital in a provincial Russian town. His initial description stresses the filth and disorder prevailing in the institution, as well as the cruel barbarity that the caretaker Nikita shows toward the helpless patients in the ward. One patient in particular draws the narrator's interest. This is Ivan Dmitrich Gromov, a polite but very agitated young man who suffers from a persecution complex. The narrator recounts how Gromov came to be placed in the mental ward: As a sensitive individual acutely conscious of the backwardness and hypocrisy permeating rural Russian life, he began to fear that he could be arrested and imprisoned through someone's error or through a miscarriage of justice. Increasingly paralyzed by this irrational anxiety, he was eventually institutionalized in Ward No. 6, where he now languishes with the other patients, neglected by the medical authorities.

As the narrator continues, he states that one man has unexpectedly begun to visit Gromov. This is the doctor in charge of the institution, Andrei Efimych Ragin. Now the reader learns of Ragin's life and personality. A heavily built, powerful man, Ragin possesses a curiously passive disposition. When he was appointed to the post of medical supervisor for the hospital, he was appalled by the primitive, unsanitary conditions he found there. However, he lacked the strength of character to push for reform, and after an initial period of zealous work he "lost heart" and ceased going to the hospital. Gradually he developed a consoling rationalization for his own failure to strive for change: Illness and death are an inevitable part of the human experience; the current state of medical knowledge is relatively limited; therefore, there is no real point in trying to improve things—he himself figures as only a minor element in an entire system of inescapable social injustice. Bored and disillusioned, Ragin discovers one day that an interesting individual is lodged in the mental ward. Thus, he begins visiting Gromov to conduct extended discussions with him about life and philosophy.

The conversations between Ragin and Gromov provide the ideological core of the story. Ragin tries to convince Gromov that the human intellect is a self-contained organ that allows one to find peace of mind in any environment, even prison. Gromov counters this notion by pointing out that humans are made up of flesh and blood, and that to reject the pains of the flesh is to reject life itself. Descrying, in Ragin's words, an empty philosophy of expediency, he accuses Ragin of laziness and of ignorance about real life. Caustically he declares that Ragin may talk about intellectual peace of mind, but that if the doctor were to squeeze his finger in a door, he would certainly scream at the top of his lungs.

Gromov's prediction is borne out when Ragin himself is forced into the mental ward after antagonizing his friend the postmaster and a fellow doctor with a streak of erratic and unsociable behavior. Now Ragin undergoes a chilling awakening. Staring through the bars of the asylum window, he sees the blank stone walls of a nearby prison and the dark flames of a distant bone mill. In a flash he realizes that this is true reality. Panicked by his discovery, he tries to leave the ward, but he receives a beating from Nikita instead. The next day he suffers a stroke and dies. Chekhov concludes his gloomy tale by commenting that only the postmaster and Ragin's maid attend the doctor's funeral.

*Themes and Meanings*

In Gromov and Ragin, Chekhov depicts two individuals who are ill-suited to deal with the reality of contemporary life. Gromov may be the more sympathetic of the two. His confessed zest for life—"I want to live!" he exclaims at one point—contrasts favorably with Ragin's intellectual retreat from experience. On the other hand, he, too, finds it easier to talk about life than actually to live it. Neither man possesses the strength or confidence to combat injustice in the world; in the end, they are both defeated by their internal weaknesses.

However, while both Gromov and Ragin are shown to be inadequate to the task of living meaningful and productive lives, they both seem more sensitive and alert than the rest of the people in their provincial town. Indeed, Gromov remarks that there are scores of madmen walking freely outside the asylum while people such as himself are imprisoned. Ragin concurs and asserts that such a fate is merely a matter of chance. His own relationship with his supposed friend the postmaster and his colleague Dr. Khobotov adds support to this view. The postmaster is an idle chatterer with no true understanding or compassion for anyone else's woes but his own, and Dr. Khobotov is a dull lackey who secretly covets Ragin's position and finally manages to replace him. Nor does the situation seem much better beyond the borders of this rural town. Ragin journeys with the postmaster to Moscow and Warsaw, but he finds nothing of stimulation in either locale. The atmosphere of unrelieved vulgarity and banality that Chekhov creates in this story led a fellow writer to declare that Ward No. 6 is Russia itself. Chekhov's tale provides vivid evidence that Russian society was prey to the twin vices of ignorance and indolence. Mere words and philosophical theories are insufficient to combat this pernicious affliction.

*Style and Technique*

Chekhov's narrative is structured in such a way as to lead the reader gradually into the world of the rural mental asylum. The charged descriptions at the outset of the story communicate his indignation over the way society has traditionally dealt with the emotionally disturbed. His portraits of the patients in the ward, from the intellectual Gromov to a man who once sorted mail at the post office, convey his compassion for the plight of those who suffer from mental illness. Then, with the incarceration of Ragin in the ward at the end of the story, the reader perceives directly the true horror of the setting. Chekhov endows Ragin's view from the asylum window with symbolic dimensions: The prison walls he sees echo his own involuntary confinement, and the bone mill also in sight stands as an emblem of impending death and destruction.

This symbolic mode of description surfaces again after Ragin suffers his fatal stroke. Ragin thinks for a moment about immortality, then dismisses it. Suddenly, he sees a vision of an extraordinarily beautiful herd of deer that race past him and disappear. Although Chekhov does not explain the significance of this vision, it is possible that the deer represent those aspects of life that Ragin himself ignored or overlooked. In his arid intellectual meditations he became divorced from the real world, from nature, and from living beauty. Only at the end of his life, when it is too late to change, does he undergo a mystical epiphany. This moment of beauty swiftly passes, however, just like Ragin's life itself.

Not only do Chekhov's descriptions of the natural environment carry symbolic associations; his descriptions of people, too, add depth to the reader's understanding of character and personality. The fact that Ragin is physically imposing yet walks softly and cautiously mirrors the contradictions in his psychology, too: Although he is in charge of the hospital and possesses the power to try to make changes in the system, he is too timid to utilize his strength.

Complementing Chekhov's charged descriptive passages are the passages in which Gromov and Ragin exchange opinions on life. As in several other of the short stories he wrote in the early 1890's, Chekhov constructs a situation in which two individuals with differing approaches come together and conduct a debate with each other. Chekhov himself does not take sides in any obvious way. He prefers to let the reader evaluate the two viewpoints and decide for him- or herself the merits and flaws of each. In this tale, though, Ragin's arguments are clearly exposed as the weaker of the two, because as he himself discovers, the sufferings one encounters in real life are not as easily dismissed as they are in an intellectual debate. Taken together, Chekhov's evocative descriptions and his passages of intellectual exploration culminate in a striking indictment of the shortcomings of rural Russian society.

*Julian W. Connolly*

# THE WARRIOR PRINCESS OZIMBA

*Author:* Reynolds Price (1933-    )
*Type of plot:* Sketch
*Time of plot:* A Fourth of July around 1955
*Locale:* Southern United States
*First published:* 1962

> *Principal characters:*
> AUNT ZIMBY, an aged African American woman, blind and
>     almost deaf
> VESTA, her daughter
> MR. ED, the narrator

*The Story*

Events unfold slowly: Mr. Ed, a southern white man, visits Aunt Zimby every Fourth of July—the date that she has designated as her birthday. His purpose is to give her a birthday present, a new pair of blue tennis shoes, although she has never played tennis and is now blind and cannot discern the color. He annually reenacts this tradition, following the example of his father, who has been dead for two years.

Aunt Zimby, who was born around the time of the Civil War, has "belonged" to this family of whites through four generations, being passed down and along to them as a matter of duty, care, and heritage. In her blindness and old age, Aunt Zimby confuses Mr. Ed, the narrator, with Mr. Phil, his dead father. She sits on the front porch of the shanty, which will scarcely keep out a gentle rain, chews snuff, and reminisces about her overlong life. She retells one story from earlier years of a time when she herself was Mr. Phil's accomplice in eating mulberries against his parents' instructions. A second recollection is of a night when Mr. Phil went dancing with the white girls, and came home in the rain and mud, wearing only his underwear; he had to undress in order to protect his new clothes.

Lost in age and place, the ancient woman who survives only as a relic from the past asks when Mr. Phil will show up with her new shoes for a birthday present. Ed neither tries to explain that his father is dead nor even tries to answer her; rather, he sits silently with the new shoes in a state of contemplation and is transfigured and transposed to another time and existence. After Aunt Zimby falls asleep, Ed gives the shoes to Vesta, her daughter, and leaves, wiping tears from his eyes.

*Themes and Meanings*

Essentially a work of sentimentality for the South's heritage, Reynolds Price's story is at once a character sketch of a figure from the past as well as an intense expression of a contemporary southerner coming to terms with his heritage and that past.

"The Warrior Princess Ozimba" is a story in which the past meets the present, white meets black, father meets son, and youth meets age. Aunt Zimby, who is described as the "oldest thing any of us knew anything about," is one of the last surviving vestiges of the Old South. Mr. Ed, in contrast, is the modern white man replete with good intentions and symbolic gifts.

Aunt Zimby was named "Princess Warrior Ozimba" by Ed's great-grandfather, after a character in a book that he was reading during the Civil War era. After being freed, she and her own family remained connected to the narrator's family, as was the case with many slaves after their emancipation. She was then more or less handed down from generation unto generation, first as a slave, later as a servant and as an employee, and now as a relic—a kind of embodiment of an antique that does not die.

Ed, the central consciousness of the story, though not its central figure, is by all counts a good man who would not only honor family tradition but also try to do what is right by giving Aunt Zimby her due respect, as symbolized by the blue tennis shoes that he brings. He makes the annual trip out to her shanty, walking up the creek with respect, though perhaps not love, to discover that she somehow plays a role in defining his own existence. Though he evidently sees her only once each year, he enacts the family duty to her, even though she no longer even knows who he is.

Aunt Zimby has been a warrior against time itself. In her old age and confused mind, she cannot recognize that she is talking to Ed rather than his father. Somehow, the two men are intermingled, not because Aunt Zimby is mistaken, but because they are so much alike. Ed learns that he has become his father; something is thus accomplished as he comes to terms with his own identity and selfhood. It is his lot to replace his dead father; he succeeds in doing so by honoring Aunt Zimby in this yearly ritual with the tennis shoes. At first, this mixing up of characters is only a matter of confusion in Aunt Zimby's mind; but as Ed sits on the porch listening to her stories about his dead father (who, for Zimby, is not even dead), he realizes that he may as well be his father. Eventually, he realizes that for all intents and purposes he has become his father. Nothing is lost or gained in Zimby's mind and mistake. Similarly, nothing is lost or gained in Ed's new awareness that he is now his father in some sort of spiritual manner.

"The Warrior Princess Ozimba" resembles many southern stories and novels that are dominated by characters who possess an intense longing for the past. Ed learns that he is a product of that past, which is not yet dead and will not be dead even with the imminent passing of Aunt Zimby. He perceives and attains, through the character of the old black woman, a connection not only with his father, but with his grandfather and great-grandfather. His own being thus antedates the Civil War.

Similarly, revealed here is the meaningful relationship between the children of the white master and the "black mammy" figure. There is, perhaps, no racial equality depicted in this story, but there is shown interracial love and respect. For Zimby, the most important event of her life is the presentation of those tennis shoes, of value only because they prove she is remembered, honored, respected, and loved by her "white folks." For Ed, there is the fact that this woman has functioned as an archetypal Earth

Mother figure for him and his forebears. Peace and love, though not equality, exist at least on some individualized basis and for these two characters.

*Style and Technique*

Like other southern writers who followed William Faulkner, Price has always tried to distance himself from the greatest of these so that his own works would not be seen merely as pale imitations of Faulkner's fiction. Nevertheless, in terms of subject matter, structural syntax, and literary sensitivity, Price's works are inescapably reminiscent of Faulkner's writing; such is especially the case with "The Warrior Princess Ozimba."

The main subject here is personality (what it means to be defined by the culture and heritage of the American South) and personhood. Although Price's technique may be independent of Faulkner's influence, it is a parallel to it. The story's confusion of the past with the present, its sentimentality for days and times gone past, its intense longing for a life that should have been but is no longer, all surface here as main elements holding this short story together. In *Intruder in the Dust* (1948), Faulkner wrote that "the past isn't gone, it isn't even passed"; remarkably and exactly, such is the case here with Aunt Zimby, a relic of the Civil War who has survived past the middle of the twentieth century.

The syntax of Price's writing also inevitably reminds one of Faulkner's own: Sentences perambulate, becoming successfully unwieldy with an occasional, out-of-place big word that momentarily throws the reader, but then is seen as appropriate, correct, and masterful. The story's first two paragraphs contain five different parenthetical thoughts and observations, all given in the manner of Faulkner; they provide insight and provoke thought. The dialogue of characters also echoes the sentimentality of the Old South rather in the same way as Faulkner would have rendered it.

These obvious and undeniable parallels to Faulkner's style do not distract from Price's own value as a writer about life, the human heart, and the South. Clearly, Price is not consciously attempting to imitate Faulkner; his own closeness to his subjects is garnered in such sensitivity that his fiction is far more than mere imitation.

*Carl Singleton*

# WASH

*Author:* William Faulkner (1897-1962)
*Type of plot:* Psychological
*Time of plot:* 1872
*Locale:* Sutpen's Hundred, Yoknapatawpha County, Mississippi
*First published:* 1934

> *Principal characters:*
> WASH JONES, the protagonist, a poor white man
> THOMAS SUTPEN, an arrogant, ambitious, disillusioned owner of
> a ruined plantation
> MILLY JONES, Wash's granddaughter
> MILLY'S NEWBORN DAUGHTER
> AN OLD BLACK WOMAN, a midwife

## The Story

The opening page and a half, set in 1872 at dawn on Sunday morning, presents all principal characters except Wash Jones. It begins with Thomas Sutpen standing above the pallet where Milly Jones and her child lie; Sutpen's arrogance is seen in his stance, with whip in hand, as he looks down on the mother and child. His mare has also given birth; the contrast between his attitude toward the colt and toward his and Milly's child presents the central problem of the story: The mare has borne a male; Milly, a female. If Milly were a mare, he would provide better quarters for her. Leaving the run-down fishing shack, he walks past his rusty scythe, which Wash Jones, Milly's grandfather, borrowed three months earlier. The scythe will become important both as a symbol and as an instrument of death.

The third-person narrator now embarks on a six-page digression, recounting events from 1861, when Colonel Sutpen rode away to fight in the "War Between the States," until his return to a ruined plantation in 1865, and through the years 1865 to 1870, when Sutpen and Wash together ran a country store and drank "inferior whiskey." There is reference to Sutpen's son, "killed in action the same winter in which his wife had died," and to Wash's grandchild. Emphasis is placed on the deterioration not only of Sutpen's property but also of his person. Even though he still rides the same black stallion and presents, at least to the naïve, worshipful Wash, a proud image, he is now a storekeeper best characterized by misplaced pride, unconcern for others, and habitual drunkenness.

Wash is characterized throughout this section as a poor white in both the literal and the connotative meanings of the term. For many years, he has lived in the deteriorated shack by the slough on the plantation, the object of scorn by whites and blacks alike. While Sutpen was away, Wash pretended to have the responsibility of taking care of Sutpen's place, but he was careful never to enter Sutpen's house. After the return, he achieved entry by carrying the drunken Sutpen in and putting him to bed. Wash has closed his eyes to the fact that Sutpen has been seducing Milly, as evidenced by the pretty ribbons she has worn around her waist. When Wash confronts Sutpen with the fact of Milly's new dress, the subject changes to whether Wash is afraid of Sutpen. The conversation and the digression end with Wash saying that Sutpen will make it right.

The last nine pages return to 1872 and the main narrative, the scene at the cabin on that Sunday when the mare's colt and Milly's girl are born. As Wash watches Milly and the black midwife, he thinks of Sutpen, admiring the man, and of the new relationship that will exist between him and Sutpen. He hears the sound of Sutpen riding up; the midwife announces that the baby is a girl; and it is dawn. Wash's pride in being a great-grandfather is balanced against the problem of telling Sutpen that the newborn child is a girl.

The words Sutpen speaks and the attitude he shows toward Milly and the baby cause Wash to realize Sutpen's true character for the first time. As Wash approaches, Sutpen lashes him with the whip. Wash then kills Sutpen with the rusty scythe. Wash is occupied through the day with tender care for Milly and with watching at the window. After a white boy discovers the body, Wash waits for the men to come. After dark, the gentle Wash once again becomes violent, killing Milly and the baby with a butcher knife, setting fire to the cabin, and attacking the sheriff's posse silently with the rusty scythe.

*Themes and Meanings*

The theme comprises the contrast between the arrogance of Thomas Sutpen and the lowliness of Wash Jones, and the ultimate consequences of this contrast. Sutpen's arrogance is everywhere evident, especially in the two parts that make up the main narrative. He rides a stallion, he carries a whip in his hand, and the story opens with him looking down on Milly and his newborn daughter. He is callous and unfeeling toward the girl he has seduced and toward his own child. He cares more for the mare and newborn colt; in fact, Wash comes to realize that Sutpen has arisen early because of the stable birth, not because of the one in the cabin. Sutpen's statement that if Milly had been a mare he would have provided a stable for her and his stalking out of the cabin without any recognition of his daughter further emphasize his arrogance.

Similarly, with Wash, Sutpen displays only arrogance. When the man who has been his companion in the store and in drinking bouts, the man who has put him to bed on occasion, confronts him with the fact of his seduction of the fifteen-year-old Milly, Sutpen's only response is to note that Wash is afraid of him. He offers no explanation of his conduct nor does he accept any responsibility for Milly or her newborn child. Wash's assurance that Sutpen "will make hit right" is never confirmed; it later proves to be misplaced confidence. One can speculate about whether Sutpen would have done better had the child been a boy, but in the story he only makes a passing remark to the midwife to do whatever is needed. When Wash approaches him about his attitude, he lashes out with the whip, thus driving Wash to the act of violence with the scythe. Nowhere in the story does Sutpen express any concern for the feelings of Wash, Milly, or anyone else. He is entirely self-centered, reacting to the lowered status of the storekeeper by closing the store when his ego can stand no more and drowning his shame in alcohol.

Wash, on the other hand, has come up in the world through his association with Sutpen. He is of the lowest caste of southern whites, living in a shack in which the blacks would never live. When he pretends to responsibility for the property of Sutpen, the blacks as well as the whites laugh at him in scorn, at a time when the former are still slaves to a white man. The borrowed scythe is a reminder that Wash owns nothing. The fact that it is rusty and has stood unused for three months among the tall weeds indicates that he is lazy and irresponsible. His admiration for Sutpen (in the latter's deterioration) is misplaced at best. His inattention to the seduction of his grandchild and his acceptance of the fact when he hopes to achieve higher status through the birth of Sutpen's child mark him as weak and devious.

Sutpen is a static character, unchanging to the end. Wash, however, is dynamic, undergoing radical change at the moment of truth. He becomes courageous, violent, tender, and patient, no longer the passive character of the past twenty years. Given the fact of such change, one senses the inevitability of swift retribution on Sutpen for his many real and imagined injuries to Wash and his family.

*Style and Technique*

In this story, as in much of his work, William Faulkner attempted to telescope present and past time into the present moment. In "Wash," he employs the epic techniques of *in medias res* and digression. The basic style is third-person, past-tense, direct narrative throughout, with little attention to psychological nuances except through suggestion. There is the almost objective viewpoint of reporting only what can be seen and heard. Even though Wash is followed as protagonist throughout, his inner thoughts and motivations are often inferred from words and deeds, although there is limited direct statement of such. The viewpoint, then, would seem to be limited omniscient third-person narration from the viewpoint of Wash, but with some of the qualities of objectivity.

Basic simplicity of structure is seen in the three parts of direct narrative, long digression, direct narrative. Intensity is achieved through the contrast of the two men and through the irony of their incongruous relationship. Compactness in the story is achieved through the focus on one day in one place, the classical unities of time and place, and through the coincidence of Wash's recognition of the true nature of things with his reversal of intention (the classical unity of plot).

"Wash" may be read on two levels. As a short story it has all the internal ingredients for enjoyment and evaluation. The mass of information about Faulkner's other writings and about his fictional county of Yoknapatawpha, as well as occasional references to Thomas Sutpen in the novels, enhances such reading. Knowledge of the doctor on whom Sutpen is based and of the genesis of the Sutpen narratives might also be helpful. On another level, "Wash" may be read against the background of complete knowledge of the greater context within which the author later placed it, for it eventually came to be part of a chapter within the novel *Absalom, Absalom!* (1936). This longer context reveals a young Thomas Sutpen of humble origins in the coal fields of what is now West Virginia, where everyone was considered equal; his deeply traumatic experience of being treated as poor white trash at a plantation house in Tidewater, Virginia; the deep psychological scars that resulted; his obsession with building a plantation of his own, first in Haiti, later in Mississippi; and his equal obsession with building a family dynasty, thwarted first through the revelation that his first wife was part black, later through the tragic consequences of relationships between his mulatto son and his white son and daughter. The reader would know that the younger son Henry had killed his half brother and was in perpetual hiding at the Mississippi plantation. Also helpful would be the knowledge that Sutpen had once proposed marriage to his young sister-in-law Rosa Coldfield provided she would first bear him a son. In the short story, Sutpen's worst qualities are emphasized, while the best, where mentioned, are tainted as seen through the eyes of Wash. In the novel, the full motivations of this driven man are delineated.

*George W. Van Devender*

# THE WATCH

*Author:* Rick Bass (1958-   )
*Type of plot:* Social realism
*Time of plot:* The 1980's
*Locale:* Seventy miles south of Jackson, Mississippi
*First published:* 1988

> *Principal characters:*
> BUZBEE, an old man who has run away from home
> HOLLINGSWORTH, his sixty-three-year-old son
> JESSE, a bicyclist in his early twenties

*The Story*

Buzbee is a seventy-seven-year-old man who has spent his entire life in a tiny community settled by his parents. Hollingsworth, his son, is only fourteen years younger; the two men have lived together primarily as friends for sixty-three years. One summer, Buzbee runs away to live in the thick, mosquito-infested woods alongside the bayou, and Hollingsworth posts an offer of a thousand-dollar reward for his father's return.

Hollingsworth is lonely without Buzbee and has to fight down feelings of wildness, especially in the evenings when the two used to talk. The town was once well populated, but epidemics of yellow fever have killed everyone but Buzbee and his son. They have buried family and neighbors in cemeteries across the countryside and lost an edge of some sort because nothing again would ever be as intense as holding out against death. Even so, Hollingsworth is not sentimental about losing Buzbee. He does not offer a larger reward for his father because he does not want people to think he is sad.

Hollingsworth runs an old barn of a store, which attracts so little business that some cans of milk have stayed on the shelves for forty years. The Coke machine still has old-formula Cokes in bottles, and it is for these that a young bicycle racer named Jesse stops by. The first time that Jesse visits, Hollingsworth is speechless with excitement. He begins waiting for Jesse to appear, and even has the driveway paved to look like a snake in the green grass that makes a path straight to the store.

Jesse is slower than his teammates because he has an older bike. He begins each day by checking the wind; the slightest breeze means his ride will be harder, that he will slide along the roads looking for paths of least resistance. He is the only rider on his team to stop at Hollingsworth's for a cold soda; the other cyclists are too serious about their sport to take such breaks.

One day, Jesse mentions Buzbee. He has seen the reward posters, and wants the money. He tells Hollingsworth he has seen a man who looks like him, describing an old man wearing dirty overalls crossing the road with a live fish tucked under his arm.

Jesse suggests they use Hollingsworth's tractor to run Buzbee down and lasso him; Hollingsworth suggests they use the neighbor's wild hounds.

As the summer progresses, Jesse stops racing in order to help Hollingsworth catch Buzbee. He builds a go-cart so he can drive to the store, eat old cans of food, and listen to Hollingsworth talk. Even though Jesse cannot stand to listen to the man for more than twenty or thirty minutes at a time, he returns each day, growing soft and fat. Hollingsworth, on the other hand, thinks of Jesse as his true love; he hopes the cyclist has an accident so that he cannot return to racing. The older man talks endlessly about his life, and practices roping a sawhorse with a lasso, dragging it across the gravel, reeling it in as fast as he can.

Meanwhile, Buzbee knows that his son wants him home, but he has no intention of returning. He has found the remains of an old settlement near the bayou, where he keeps a small fire going to ward off mosquitoes and to smoke catfish and small alligators. He hangs his food from the trees by looping vines through their jaws and stringing them up "like villains, all around in his small clearing, like the most ancient of burial grounds: all these vertical fish, out of the water, mouths gaping in silent death, as if preparing to ascend."

He brings a rooster and four chickens to his camp, and the birds locate the precious quinine berries that Buzbee's father planted long ago during a malaria epidemic. After women hear about Buzbee's settlement, they arrive a few at a time. They are middle-aged laundresses from such abusive situations that Buzbee's camp seems luxurious by comparison. They laugh and talk together, "muscled with great strength suddenly from not being told what to do, from not being beaten or yelled at."

As the women grow comfortable around Buzbee, they stop wearing clothes, and he sits in a tree above them, watching them move around naked, talking happily. At night, they all sit around the fire, eating roasted alligators and smearing the fat over their bodies to repel mosquitoes. The women begin sleeping with Buzbee, and one becomes pregnant. Another contracts malaria, but all of them prefer life on the bayou to life in town.

Several attempts to catch Buzbee fail. Hollingsworth and Jesse try to sneak into the settlement, but Buzbee and the women hear them coming and run through the swamp to hide in the trees. Hollingsworth and Jesse dig large pits and cover them with branches, hoping to catch all of them, but the women find a pit after it traps a deer. Finally, Hollingsworth borrows his neighbor's hounds. They muzzle the dogs and lead them into the swampland after Buzbee. Jesse brings an extra lariat and rope to truss him up, because he figures the old man will be senile and wild. The dogs are nearly crazed; they jump and twist at their leashes until they are too hard to hold. Then they silently and swiftly race straight into Buzbee's camp.

Jesse buys a new bike with his reward money and begins riding by himself, growing faster than ever. He now rides by Hollingsworth's store without stopping, disgusted by the sight of Buzbee chained to the front porch. Trapped by his over-talkative son, Buzbee squints at the trees in the distance and thinks only of breaking free again, for good.

*Themes and Meanings*

"The Watch" follows an American literary tradition of describing men who break free of responsibility to taste freedom and act young again. This freedom is poisoned by a sense of loss: The cemeteries are a constant reminder that all one's neighbors have died. In this story, even the alligators hanging in Buzbee's camp are reminiscent of a burial ground. Buzbee feels free in the silence of his camp, and the women's admiring glances make him feel young again, but at night he looks up at the moon through "bare limbs of the swamp-rotted ghost trees, skeleton-white, disease-killed." His freedom is marred by the feeling of being trapped. In constant danger of being caught, Buzbee discovers that he is not free after all.

Recurrent images of snakes in the story underscore the theme of entrapment. Hollingsworth's driveway is compared to a snake in the grass, and his porch, too, is black as a snake that has just shed its skin. Jesse is the prey in this case; Hollingsworth's driveway is the path of least resistance, and the path swallows him up for an entire summer. Afterward Jesse becomes a predator, camping with Hollingsworth in the cool grass the night before they catch Buzbee.

Buzbee's chickens disappear one by one until he finds a corn snake in the rooster's cage that is swallowing the rooster—only its thrashing feet are showing. Buzbee kills the snake, but the rooster dies when it is pulled back out. Metaphorically, the scene foreshadows Buzbee's being caught. Like the rooster, Buzbee is trapped in the woods, an easy target for a mad son with hounds. At the end of the story, Buzbee plans his final escape, sure that this time he will get away completely. This time, however, his only sure escape may lead directly to a nearby cemetery.

*Style and Technique*

Rick Bass learned the art of storytelling as a child in south Texas, listening to his grandfather and other relatives spin yarns at the family hunting lodge. This experience infuses much of his work with an oral quality, as though he is talking directly to the reader; critics often praise Bass for his comfortable use of a vernacular idiom. Best known for writing about the connection between man and nature, Bass often uses animals and setting symbolically, as he does in "The Watch."

The text of this story has a restless quality; although the story is long, its scenes are short. Point of view switches from one character to another, and the plot moves abruptly through time. Conflict is left unresolved. Realistic characters are confronted with bizarre situations, as when Jesse sees Buzbee with a live carp under one arm. "And listen to this," Jesse says to Hollingsworth, then suggesting that Buzbee has been "eating on that fish's tail, chewing on it." Bass has said that it is important to surprise the reader with unexpected twists in the plot; "The Watch" demonstrates his agility in doing so.

*Mary Pierce Frost*

# THE WATCHER

*Author:* Italo Calvino (1923-1985)
*Type of plot:* Neorealist
*Time of plot:* 1953
*Locale:* Turin, the Cottolengo Hospital for Incurables
*First published:* "La giornata d'uno scrutatore," 1963 (English translation, 1971)

> *Principal characters:*
> AMERIGO ORMEA, the protagonist, a poll-watcher
> LIA, Amerigo's friend and mistress
> THE CHAIRMAN,
> THE WOMAN IN ORANGE,
> THE WOMAN IN WHITE, and
> THE THIN MAN, other poll-watchers

*The Story*

This story focuses on the observations and reflections of a Communist Party worker, Amerigo Ormea, on a day in which he is participating as a "poll-watcher" during the 1953 Italian election. The voting place to which he has been assigned is Turin's Cottolengo Hospital for Incurables, a shelter for the mentally and physically afflicted. The voters at Cottolengo are its staff and, primarily, its inmates, and Amerigo's responsibility, especially as a Communist, is to see that the voters are all mentally capable of voting on their own without being guided by nuns and priests of the institution (who would be supporters of the Christian Democrat Party, opposing the Communists in the election). Working with Amerigo are five other volunteers—a chairman, a clerk, and three other watchers.

This is a psychological drama, in which the conflicts and resolutions are intellectual, occurring in the mind of the protagonist; the external action provides the context in which Amerigo faces the political, moral, and religious questions that are central to the story. The complexity of the story exists in Amerigo's intensely sensitive and ethical mind, which wanders through labyrinthine paths of speculations. The actual events are straightforward.

Amerigo leaves home at five-thirty in the morning and walks in the rain to Cottolengo. Throughout the day, Amerigo vacillates in his feelings about the election—whether, for example, taking the election to an institution for the mentally infirm and disabled helps democracy or harms it. However, he begins positively, with a simple determination. He recognizes what he regards as

> The moral question: you had to go on doing as much as you could, day by day. In politics, as in every other sphere of life, there are two important principles for a man of sense: don't cherish too many illusions, and never stop believing that every little bit helps.

At the polls, the task he is assigned is that of checking the voters' identity papers. One of the watchers, a woman in orange, questions the validity of a voter's medical certificate that claims that the man is blind. She notices that the voter is able to see that he has accidentally taken two ballots. A priest accompanying the voter defends the medical certificate, and Amerigo enters the argument, stating that the certificate is valid "if it tells the truth." He suggests that they test the voter's ability to see. The chairman, the two other watchers, and the priest outnumber Amerigo and the woman in orange, and the priest has his way, accompanying the voter into the voting booth to assist him. Amerigo and the woman record their protest, and Amerigo goes out for a smoke.

Amerigo feels a personal crisis at this point, in which all action seems futile: "[M]orality impels one to act; but what if the action is futile?" Progress, liberty, and justice seem the privilege of the healthy, and not universal, because the afflicted cannot share in them. The only practical attitude for the Cottolengo unfortunate seems to be a religious one, "establishing a relation between one's own afflictions and a universal harmony and completeness." Society creates the institution to help the afflicted, but nothing can really be done, so that "Cottolengo was, at once, the proof and the denial of the futility of action." Amerigo finally returns to his work as poll-watcher, believing that the only right action is to behave well in history, "even if the world is Cottolengo." Pessimistically, however, Amerigo muses that being right is not enough.

Amerigo returns to his home during his lunch break and begins reading a passage from the early writings of Karl Marx, on the relationship between humans and nature. Lia, Amerigo's mistress, telephones him, interrupting his reading. They have a pointless argument about her belief in horoscopes, which Amerigo regards as irrational. They hang up, and Amerigo calls her back to tell her that she is "prelogical," but Lia will not let him speak, asking him instead to listen to a recording that she is playing. Amerigo, frustrated at not being able to speak, argues again with her and they hang up again. Lia calls back and informs Amerigo that she thinks she is pregnant. Amerigo reacts in horror and suggests abortion, which angers Lia, and she hangs up again. Amerigo makes a last call, to soothe her, and again is not able to speak because Lia wants him to listen to another recording. He feels fatalistic about their differences, illustrated for him by this interchange.

While Amerigo anguishes over their future, Lia is passive. Amerigo thinks, "[F]or her it's nothing, for her it's nature, for her the logic of the mind doesn't count, only the logic of physiology." However, Amerigo feels reassurance in Lia's consistency: She is always irrational, always unpredictable. During this episode, Amerigo feels largely disappointed in himself for not living up to his model of behavior, which is to maintain a calm, lucid mastery of situations. Depressed about Lia's pregnancy and how lightly she seems to take it, he thinks of Cottolengo, "all that India of people born to unhappiness, that silent question, an accusation of all those who procreate."

Returning to Cottolengo, Amerigo joins the other voting officials in visiting a ward of inmates who cannot leave their beds. Amerigo objects to allowing the vote of a paralytic man who cannot express himself. After arguing with the mother superior and a priest, Amerigo prevails, and his objection is subsequently applied by the priest in charge to the remaining bedridden inmates in the ward. Amerigo has taken action that has made a difference.

Observing a peasant farmer who is visiting his paralytic and apparently noncommunicative son, Amerigo considers the quality of love. Unlike the mother superior, who attends the afflicted for no recognition other than "the good she derived from them," the father "stared into his son's eyes to be recognized, to keep from losing him." Amerigo thinks, "Those two . . . are necessary to each other. . . . Humanity reaches as far as love reaches; it has no frontiers except those we give it." This reflection leads Amerigo to acknowledge his love for Lia, and in a moment of revelation he hurries to call her. Her line is busy, and when he finally does reach her they end up arguing over her busy line and a trip she is planning, apparently in response to something Amerigo had carelessly said the day before. Amerigo is both furious at his inability to control his interactions with Lia and relieved that Lia never changes. He feels an impulse to hang up and at the same time a fatalistic sense that he is caught.

At the end of the day, Amerigo makes his last significant observation in Cottolengo, when he meets a fifty-year-old man who grew up in the hospital and has lived his whole life there. The man is without hands but manages to overcome his handicap with skillful manipulation of his arms. Amerigo's final response is a positive one: "Man triumphs even over malign biological mutation." He sees in the Cottolengo man a fitting symbol of the human as *homo faber* ("man the maker"); in Cottolengo itself, which the Cottolengo man describes as being like a small city, Amerigo sees a symbol of all cities, which are to be respected for the human will and ingenuity that creates them. Thus, at the end of the story Amerigo feels a response to a question that opened the story: "[A]re institutions, which grow old, of no matter; is what matters only the human will, the human needs . . . restoring verity to the instruments they use?" His feeling now is that

> *Homo faber*'s city . . . always runs the risk of mistaking its institutions for the secret fire without which cities are not founded and machinery's wheels aren't set in motion; and in defending institutions, unawares, you can let the fire die out.

*Themes and Meanings*

In the protagonist's contemplations, many issues are raised: the nature of democracy, progress in history, blessedness (that is, the sensation of universal harmony in which one takes part) versus personal dissatisfaction (which can be a stimulus to action and creativity), religion as the acceptance of human smallness, humanity's triumph over adversity, and the importance of personal experience over abstraction. The number and variety of these issues demonstrate the fecund restlessness of Amerigo's mind, and resulting as they do from Amerigo's observations during his day as pollwatcher, they dramatize the insistence in Italian neorealism of looking at events in the context of the environment.

These issues, however, are not so much thematic in the story as illustrative of how Amerigo's mind works. It is a characteristic of his mind that he can always perceive the antithesis of an idea and is challenged by the consequent conflict. Contemplating his reasons for going to Cottolengo, Amerigo observes how "his thoughts raced in such an agile objectivity that he could see with the adversary's own eyes the very things he had felt contempt for a moment earlier." This process itself—conceiving an idea, constructing its opposite, or opposition, and working toward a resolution—is a parody of Communist dialectic, with its thesis, antithesis, and synthesis.

The central theme of the story arises out of Amerigo's struggle with the ironies and paradoxes of a voting day in Cottolengo. He begins the day feeling self-confident, within his limits, and fairly positive about democracy, despite his "slightly pessimistic" outlook on politics. Watching the setting up of the polling place and reflecting on the tendency of institutions to forget the inspirations that created them and settle into meaningless bureaucracy, he senses an absurdity. The prospect becomes even bleaker when he observes the mental deficiency of most of the Cottolengo inmates and imagines history as decline, a sort of reverse march of progress, by which brilliant generations are replaced by increasingly dull ones. Finally comes a feeling of the futility of action, for as a watcher, there is nothing Amerigo can do to "stop the avalanche" of abuse as one inept voter follows another. Even the blessedness of the nuns is depressing, inasmuch as it seems to remove them from the real world of action: "Amerigo would have liked to go on clashing with things, fighting, and yet achieve at the same time . . . a calm above it all." This ideal, however, is still inaccessible to him. Moreover, his enthusiasm for Marx's early writings, in which he seeks something positive to "channel and accompany his reflections," turns sour; Amerigo reflects that Marx's notion of human universality is pointless unless it can promise legs to the lame and eyesight to the blind.

The turning point occurs when, in spite of his frustration with trying to communicate with Lia, Amerigo begins to admire her courage in facing the possibility of her pregnancy. His overwhelming impulse then is to express his feeling of tenderness toward her. It is from this experience that Amerigo slowly climbs out of his depression. He becomes more active in enforcing the law in the election, and finally, through his observation of the peasant father visiting his son, and the Cottolengo man, he arrives at his vision of *homo faber* and his city. The story thus dramatizes the view that humanity can arrive at a positive vision through direct, personal experience, which includes both an intellectual interaction with events as well as empathy and love.

### Style and Technique

"The Watcher" is told from the third-person-singular point of view, which facilitates approaching the protagonist objectively while still revealing his thoughts. The clearest impressions in the story are those of Amerigo's mind. Other impressions are less detailed, or vague. Though the voting officials play dramatic roles in the story, their names are not mentioned, and they are drawn in only the harshest of outlines. The major character of Lia is never seen, and her voice is heard only over the telephone, accompanied by undescribed music. All of this serves to intensify the focus on Amerigo's thoughts and swings of mood. The world of the story is, in fact, presented only as a perception of Amerigo's. Even the rain at the outset of the story, rather than being presented objectively, independent of Amerigo, is presented as one of his perceptions: "It looked like rain." Soon afterward is the image of Amerigo "tilting his umbrella to one side and raising his face to the rain."

Paradox and symbol in this story are basic to Calvino's theme, and are obvious rather than subtle. The significant symbols are well explained: Cottolengo represents human society as a whole, and the Cottolengo man who was reared in the hospital is *homo faber*—representative, that is, of the spark within a man that accounts for his humanity.

The most outstanding stylistic trait of the story is Calvino's mirroring in his sentence structures the complexity of Amerigo's thoughts. In the story's second chapter, it is learned that

> At times the world's complexity seemed to Amerigo a superimposition of clearly distinct strata, like the leaves of an artichoke; at other times, it seemed a clump of meanings, a gluey dough.

What follows is a tour de force, a one-sentence paragraph that is nearly two pages long. To create many layers of subordination (Amerigo's qualifying comments and retakes), Calvino utilizes thirty-eight commas, nine pairs of parentheses, four sets of colons, two sets of dashes, and a semicolon. The sentence, about Amerigo's role as a Communist, is filled with contradictions and paradoxes. Within the sentence, he describes himself, by turns, as pessimistic, optimistic, and skeptical. The paragraph is, itself, like the complexity of Amerigo's world, an artichoke, each set of leaves enfolding another inside itself.

Another example of Calvino's artistry occurs in the fourth chapter of the story. The second paragraph ("It was a hidden Italy that filed through that room . . . ") is another lengthy, one-sentence paragraph. This time, the sentence is periodic rather than cumulative, in order to create tension. It describes the inmates of Cottolengo as the "secret of families and of villages," poverty's "incestuous couplings," and "the mistake risked by the material of human race each time it reproduces itself." The sentence is rhythmically interrupted with the parenthetical disclaimers, "but not only," which emphasize Amerigo's caution and fastidiousness as a thinker and build up suspense toward the climax in the image of mutants, products of poisons and radiation, and the insistence on randomness as the governing agent in human generation.

*Dennis C. Chowenhill*

# WATER LIARS

*Author:* Barry Hannah (1942-      )
*Type of plot:* Psychological
*Time of plot:* The 1970's
*Locale:* Farte Cove in west central Mississippi
*First published:* 1976 as "Homeless," one of three stories published under the overall
   title of "Behold the Husband in His Perfect Agony"; as "Water Liars," 1978

*Principal characters:*

THE HUSBAND, the narrator
THE "WATER LIARS," a group of fishermen who gather at Farte
   Cove
A FISHERMAN, a sixty-year-old newcomer who tells a
   disconcerting story

*The Story*

"Water Liars" is told in first person by an unnamed married man who recalls his reaction the previous year when he learned that his wife had had sex with other men before their marriage. As the story begins, he is still trying to determine why he was, and
apparently still is, unable to handle that knowledge. He realizes his tendency to constantly relive every "passionate event" and finds himself driven wild by thinking
about his wife's former lovers even though he acknowledges that her sexual history is
no different from his.

On the morning following his thirty-third birthday, after a night of extensive drinking, he and his wife awake to a truth telling that leaves the narrator in great shock and
dismay. After several weeks of trying unsuccessfully to deal with his newfound
knowledge about his wife's sexual experiences, the narrator, on the pretext of going
on a fishing trip with a friend, takes off for a week at Farte Cove. Typically, when
things go wrong for the narrator, he finds escape and comfort in going down to Farte
Cove off the Yazoo River in Mississippi to fish, drink, and listen to the old liars who
gather on a fishing pier and tell tall tales and ghost stories. In addition to his unresolved agony about his wife, he also leaves behind worries about bill collectors and
money problems.

When he reaches Farte Cove on Friday evening, he sees a combination of old and
new faces, but the stories begin as always—a tale of sexual relations with a ghost, a
yarn about numerous large fish caught with bare hooks, and an account of the ghost of
the Yazoo himself wandering the area. Then one "old boy" tells of having to chase
away from their pier hundreds of high school students who were drinking, using
drugs, and swimming naked. This story immediately leads the narrator to recall his
personal agony and to envision his wife back in 1960 as part of such a high school
group. He becomes enraged with jealousy even while recognizing the illogic of his

emotion. He knows that as a teenager he had forced girls into sexual experiences, only to berate them afterward.

The narrator finds himself jolted back to the events at hand when a newcomer about sixty years old, younger than most of the old liars, begins a tale of a fishing experience that occurred late one night with a friend in a small cove nearby. He says that the two fishermen began hearing such unnatural moans and sighs that they became terrified. Finally, with a large flashlight, they discovered over in the brush on the bank the story-teller's own daughter and a man, both half-naked, making the ghostlike noises. The older fishermen become visibly upset by the newcomer's story, and two of them complain that it is not an appropriate story.

The narrator, however, recognizes that the storyteller has related a truthful experience, an experience from which he has never recovered. Therefore, he takes the story-teller back to the cabin with him and his fishing buddy, Wyatt, and they all get drunk. The next morning they go out fishing in the same cove in which the storyteller had seen his daughter. The narrator, recalling this event, says he felt a strong kinship with the storyteller, and he ends "Water Liars" with en epiphanic declaration, "We were both crucified by the truth."

*Themes and Meanings*

Inherent in the title "Water Liars" is a theme that dominates much of Barry Hannah's fiction—the dishonesty that pervades human life and the difficulty humans have in facing truth. The "water liars" tell stories that are, by mutual consent, always outrageously improbable, often involving the supernatural, and never about themselves or known persons so that no one will be hurt. The storytellers prefer to live in a world of illusions, a world in which it is permissible to tell stories of humans having sexual relations with ghosts, but not stories involving the sexual activities of their daughters or wives. When faced with a story that concerns a real incident, they recoil and shun the storyteller.

Like most of Hannah's protagonists, the narrator is lonely, wounded, and self-reflexive. Because of his recently discovered private truth that his wife was not a virgin when they married, he is particularly vulnerable and unable to retain objectivity about the stories he hears. His knowledge and private suffering therefore color both his hearing of the stories and his telling of them for the reader. Awareness of his wife's sexual history comes at a crucial time in his life. Thirty-three years old, confronted with money problems, he obviously needs to feel heroic and tries to think of himself, like Jesus, "coming to something decided" in his life, something free from ambiguity, unquestionable, fully resolved.

However, the truth-telling session with his wife, after a night of drinking, accomplishes the opposite, providing him with more ambiguity and uncertainty. The narrator has to face not only the truth of his wife's sexual history but also the truth of his reaction to it. He acknowledges intellectually the illogic of his having expected her to be a virgin while he himself was sexually active, but emotionally, psychologically, he cannot rid himself of the sense that he has been betrayed.

Tension thus comes from within the protagonist who is conscious of the destruction of a dream based on the cultural expectation of the sexually dominant male hero who marries the pure virgin. Even though he recognizes the sexism, even perhaps the immorality, of such a dream, he cannot let go of it. Instead he feels an "impotent homicidal urge." His own sense of manliness has been severely damaged. He wants to destroy those he holds responsible, those who "trespassed" his wife, but he finds himself utterly helpless.

Both the original title of the story, "Homeless," and the title of the longer work in which it was incorporated in its first publication, "Behold the Husband in His Perfect Agony," suggest that the truth damages and perhaps even destroys the narrator's marriage. Unlike the "water liars" who tell stories to escape reality, however, the narrator is apparently telling his story now, as the man who told the story of his daughter did, not to escape truth, but to try to understand it. Confronting the truth brings him agony and little real understanding; however, he comes nearer to facing truth than most of Hannah's narrators. He also finds some comfort in recognizing that he is not completely alone in his suffering.

*Style and Technique*

Unlike most of Hannah's fiction, "Water Liars" has no violence, has a fairly straightforward plot, and even includes a traditional epiphany. Yet the greatest strengths of the story are those found in most of his writing—the style, the voice, and the language. "Water Liars" is replete with word play that develops character, theme, and tone. In the opening sentence the narrator refers to himself as being "flocked around by the world," an unusual word choice that indicates a sense of being surrounded like an animal, trapped and helpless. Even though he later proclaims he is not "poor-mouthing" and that he does not want pity from anyone, he clearly feels betrayed and regards himself to be a victim.

Another significant use of word play in the opening paragraph is the reference to the old liars "snapping and wheezing at one another." "Wheeze" suggests not only the difficulty the old men have breathing, but that they are telling familiar jokes or tales, stories that enable them to escape rather than face reality.

Some of the word play turns, as it frequently does in Hannah's fiction, into scatological humor. The scatological imagery reflects the bleakness, the negativity of life; at the same time, the accompanying humor provides one means of coping with that bleakness. The narrator's place of escape is Farte Cove, and the narrator focuses attention on the implications of the name so that they do not escape the reader. He notes that the family for whom the cove was named insisted on pronouncing their name Far*tay*. The narrator also reveals that the composition of the crowd gathered there continually changes as men are "always dying out or succumbing to constipation." He continues the joke by making a remark about the men carrying bran cookies in their coats.

References to Christianity are also frequent in Hannah's work, and in this story he uses an allusion to Jesus' crucifixion as a framing device for the narrator's epiphany.

The narrator makes a direct comparison of himself to Jesus near the beginning of the story when he refers to his thirty-third birthday celebration. Then he reiterates the connection with his comment about being crucified in the concluding sentence of the story. The comparison is ironic, however, because the narrator's agony results from an acknowledged selfishness, from his inability to accept sexual experiences by his wife even while acknowledging committing similar actions himself. However, unlike the "water liars," he at least recognizes and confronts the truth even when he does not fully understand it.

*Verbie Lovorn Prevost*

# A WAY OF TALKING

*Author:* Patricia Grace (1937-    )
*Type of plot:* Social realism
*Time of plot:* The 1970's
*Locale:* New Zealand
*First published:* 1975

> *Principal characters:*
> ROSE, a university student who returns home after a long absence
> HERA, her sister and the narrator
> JANE FRAZER, a seamstress

*The Story*

Told in the first person by Hera, "A Way of Talking" focuses on the narrator's older sister Rose. Hera is to be married soon, and Rose has come home to her Maori family so that she can take part in the wedding. She has been studying at the university in Auckland, New Zealand's largest city, for an extended period. When members of the family meet her at the bus station in the village, they find that Rose has not changed and can still make them laugh with "a way of talking" that is distinctive to her. When they arrive home, Rose and the family have their evening meal, referred to as tea. After tea, they stay up talking into the night. This scene, although brief, creates a communal warmth in which three generations of the extended family participate.

The next day, the sisters drive over to the home of the local seamstress, Jane Frazer, to order Rose's dress for the wedding. Jane is a Pakeha, the disparaging name the Maori have adopted for the European settlers they consider interlopers, so Hera fears that there may be an ugly scene once they meet because of Rose's reputation for being outspoken. At first, all goes well as Rose and Jane talk about the university and about life in Auckland. While Hera listens, she suspects that Jane may be jealous of Rose's freedom and her life in the city, even though the seamstress has a beautiful house and ostensibly all that she needs to be happy.

The narrator's worst fears materialize when Jane makes a casual remark about her husband getting some Maoris to cut scrub. Although Rose remains calm, Hera knows that her sister will not let the remark pass unchallenged. After a pause, Rose asks if the Maoris have names. When Jane admits that she does not know any of their names, Rose asks her why she has never bothered to find out. Jane mumbles something about how difficult the names are to remember. During this exchange, Rose has taken on what Hera describes as a "Pakehafied" way of talking.

The sisters immediately climb in the family station wagon and head home. Hera is so angry that at first she cannot speak, but she finally manages to tell Rose how much she had embarrassed them in front of Jane Frazer. Rose tells her sister not to worry, then assures her that Jane was not offended because "she's got a thick hide." She also notes that Jane will still want to be their friends because Maoris are fashionable these days. When they return home, Rose becomes her cheerful self again, mocking Jane's walk and continuing to talk in a "Pakehafied" manner, imitating the condescending remarks she imagines Jane would make about their Maori family.

The clash between the two women and Rose's harsh remark about "a tough hide," followed by her comic rendition of the incident, deeply affect the narrator, who has always considered herself weak. The experience serves as a turning point in her life, and she pledges that she will never leave her sister alone in the pursuit and defense of Maori dignity.

The story closes with another family scene around the table as the three generations joke and talk and laugh and eat the simple meal of Maori bread and corn.

*Themes and Meanings*

"A Way of Talking" displays a mischievous and comic quality in spite of its serious condemnation of racial prejudice in New Zealand. The story treats the contemporary conflict between the Maoris, the original New Zealanders who have lived on the remote islands for centuries, and the European colonizers who arrived in the nineteenth century and displaced them from much of their land.

This conflict between Jane the Pakeha seamstress and Rose the Maori student does not initially seem very significant or even particularly abusive. Certainly Jane has no intention of offending Rose by her casual remark about "the Maoris" and by her lack of concern over names. Yet to Rose, the statement represents a thousand other insults and indignities, some unintentional, others deliberate, that she and her people have suffered over the years. Rose's derogatory remark about the seamstress having "a tough hide" epitomizes the insensitivity the Maori recognize in the treatment they receive from the Pakehas, who too often take for granted their superiority over those they have marginalized.

That Rose stands up for her people is admirable, but her stand is not the most important part of the story. Hera reveals that Rose has always been blunt and forthright in her relations with the Pakehas. In contrast, Hera and the rest of the family have simply suffered the humiliations, countering them to a degree by their private ridicule of the Pakeha. After the incident with the seamstress, Hera experiences an epiphany, fully aware that she will no longer remain silent, but, like Rose, find her own "way of talking." This transformation came about when Rose said, "Don't worry Honey she's got a thick hide." Hera reacts to Rose's frank assessment, thinking "it made her seem a lot older than me, and tougher, and as though she knew much more about the world. It made me realize too that underneath her jolly and forthright ways Rose is very hurt." So Hera pledges never again to leave Rose, or her Maori community, alone.

"A Way of Talking" is the opening story in Patricia Grace's first collection, *Waiariki* (1975). Placed in context with the nine other stories in the volume, its title takes on a fuller resonance. Grace, one of the most admired of Maori writers, shapes the ten stories so that they progress toward a discovery of a Maori "way of talking." Like Hera, the Maori must learn to talk so that they can show who they are. In the book's final story, "Parade," the Maori gain this ability and confidence. Grace believes that one way to accomplish the objective lies in fiction that is not confrontational but that represents the truth about the Maori. In the impressive body of work that has appeared since *Waiariki*, Grace views Maori culture in its social and spiritual context and hopes for a reconciliation between that culture and the one imposed by the European settlers.

### Style and Technique

Grace's fiction has often been called simple or lyrical, descriptions that fit "A Way of Talking." She frequently employs the first-person narrative, as she does in this story. She is always skillful in capturing a voice that rings true, whether the voice is that of a shy young woman like Hera or the smart aleck narrator of "The Hills," a story in another of Grace's collections, *Electric City, and Other Stories* (1987). In these first-person narratives, the characters speak in their own way, tell a simple story about an experience in their lives, and then come to a realization.

Through the simplicity and lyricism of a narrative such as "A Way of Talking," Grace moves toward a subtle complexity. In the four pages that the story covers, she opens up an entire world, showing that the Maori culture is a rich one, especially in its emphasis on family. Both of the scenes with the family eating, although only suggestive in detail, are striking in their representation of community, which is an essential element in Grace's work. The character of Rose is immediately established through the eyes of the narrator. In turn, Hera evolves into a strong character as she analyzes her sister's action and her own weakness.

The way Hera tells her story also brings to mind the Maori oral tradition, which like all such traditions relies in part on a storyteller relating an experience and concluding with a moral. Although the story related by Hera just hints at Grace's use of this tradition, much of her fiction incorporates chants and other borrowings from the rich Maori oral tradition.

*Robert Ross*

# WAY STATIONS

*Author:* Harriet Doerr (1910-2002)
*Type of plot:* Realism
*Time of plot:* March of 1963 or 1964
*Locale:* Concepción and Ibarra, Mexico
*First published:* 1990

> *Principal characters:*
> SARA EVERTON, an American living in Mexico
> RICHARD EVERTON, her husband, who operates a mine
> KATE, their longtime American friend, who is visiting them
> STEVE, Kate's estranged husband
> INOCENCIA, an elderly beggar woman
> LOURDES, the Evertons' cook
> THE CURA, a local Roman Catholic priest

*The Story*

A train from the United States border arrives two hours late in Concepción, Mexico. Sara and Richard Everton are at the station expecting the arrival of their friends from the United States, Kate and Steve. They worry that something is awry when neither friend emerges from the sleeping car. After a search, Kate is spied at the top of the train's rear platform, seemingly unwilling to disembark. Kate announces that she has come alone. Without prying, the Evertons load her luggage into their car, and they travel the road to Ibarra.

During the ride it becomes clear that Kate visited Ibarra three years earlier with her husband. Indeed, Kate is a frequent traveler who has lived in several different time zones. As Richard points out changes in the landscape since her last visit and Sara informs her that they all have been invited to attend a program for the upcoming day of the priests, Kate remains unresponsive. When she does speak, it is to inform her friends that she and her husband have separated. The reader learns that there was an accident: In an unsupervised moment Kate and Steve's two-year-old son toddled into the street in front of their home and was killed by a passing motorist. Kate's feelings of guilt and the long-lasting depression in the aftermath of her child's death have led to the breakup of her marriage.

During the first three days of her visit, Kate rises from bed only after the Evertons have gone out of the house. She spends the late mornings with the cook, Lourdes, who recognizes Kate's troubled condition and spreads talismans around her effects in an effort to reverse her ill fortune and will her spiritual redemption. Kate spends the balance of her days lying in a hammock, deep in sleep or sorrow. When Sara and Richard conspire to think of ways to lift Kate out of her depression, Sara suggests a trip by riverboat or railroad. Richard removes the hammock, and Sara takes Kate for a walking excursion to a ruined monastery at Tepozán. Kate recalls a picnic they had together at Tepozán during her previous visit with Steve.

In their continued attempts to move Kate out of her unhappiness, Richard takes her on a tour of his mine and shows her the shafts of abandoned mines in the hillsides. Sara brings her into the village, where they meet the cura and go into the newly repainted church. There they see a renovated statue of the Virgin, which came from Spain and was moved from one closed chapel to another until its arrival in Ibarra. "For her, Ibarra is only a way station," Kate observes. Sara sees this statement, along with Kate's memory of the earlier picnic, as a sign of her friend's returning abilities to remember, perceive, and feel.

Kate and the Evertons attend the priests' program as guests of honor. It is literally a watershed event. Although Kate has been repeatedly told that she will not need the umbrella that she brought with her since the rainy season does not begin until June, it begins to rain during the proceedings. Parish children perform two plays that illustrate responsibility in marriage and the various incarnations of a child who grows in faith and as he matures, commits his life to the priesthood. The plays lead Kate to question aloud the direction of her own destiny. Her itinerary lies outside the security of the Evertons' parental presence and the hierarchies of the church, in which each person has a place in a link that leads to God.

The next morning Kate brings her train ticket to the breakfast table. The story ends as it began, at the train station in Concepción. Two trains arrive at the station, one southbound and the other headed to the north. While Richard negotiates Kate's ticket inside the station office, Kate disappears. Instead of returning to the United States she takes the other train, leaving the Evertons a note saying "I've gone on." Sara and Richard imagine where Kate might go, and Sara thinks of La Chona. In that town an ambitious gardener has pruned trees into the shapes of Ferdinand and Isabella receiving Christopher Columbus, with his three ships sailing behind.

*Themes and Meanings*

This story is in effect a missing chapter from Harriet Doerr's 1984 novel, *Stones for Ibarra*. Set during 1960 to 1966, that novel chronicles the Evertons' move to Ibarra, the diagnosis of Richard's fatal illness (which is only briefly alluded to in "Way Stations"), and the couple's increasing acculturation to Mexican life and sense of belonging, ending with Richard's death and Sara's departure from Mexico. Both the novel and the short story focus on the themes of fate and chance or accident, intimacy and selfhood, multiculturalism, and the calamity and heroism of everyday life. Doerr uses "Way Stations" to explore the meanings of time and space, the nature of faith, the contrasts between modern or scientific perceptions and syncretic folk beliefs and practices, and most important, the conflicts between human will and divine plan or destiny.

Communication is an important theme, and, as in the work of Carson McCullers, the ability or inability of characters to communicate and understand is a metaphor for the essential loneliness of the individual and also for the human capacity to empathize with, relate to, and improve the lives of others. The sense of accident or fate and the blending of the secular and the spiritual, rational and magical worldviews, also are central to Doerr's work. These themes are related to the story's main metaphor, that of movement or transformation. "Way Stations," which begins and ends with a train at the station, is filled with images of and references to travel and metaphors of life as a passage or trip with several stages. Death or passing is coupled in these images with rebirth.

The many "way stations" in the story include the train station; Ibarra as a temporary place for Kate to heal from her sorrow; the church as a spiritual way station, with its stations of the cross; and the Evertons' home as a stopping point for local people passing by. Marriage has proven to be a temporary way station for Steve, while Kate thought of it as a lifelong effort. Kate is identified with the statue of the Virgin Mary, which has been moved from one country to another and then from one chapel to another, and in turn with Columbus and his voyage into the New World. Lourdes is concerned with another form of passage, the spiritual one of Kate and the Evertons' souls into heaven—in this case, the earth itself is the way station.

*Style and Technique*

Although the story is not written in the first person, Sara is effectively the narrator of the story, and the series of scenes unfold out of her experience of the events. The story is told in an objective tone and in episodic form, with descriptions of events and the use of dialogue between the characters coupled with Sara's inner thoughts, feelings, and observations.

The story line of "Way Stations" in effect echoes that of *Stones for Ibarra*: Both story and novel are framed by the loss of a husband and begin and end with their female protagonists arriving at and departing from Ibarra.

The landscape is important in Doerr's work, and the tension between will and fate are reflected in it. Sara's gardening and pruning of her yard is an attempt to control her life and maintain order, in contrast to the sometimes harsh serendipity of the surrounding arroyos. Religious imagery pervades the story: For example, when Richard shows Kate the abandoned mines, Sara thinks of them as like beads on a rosary, each successive one representing a new hope or prayer.

The story follows a metaphorical path of rebirth and transfiguration. It begins with conception (at the town of Concepción), and Kate's time in the hammock at the Evertons' is a womblike period of gestation. When Kate and Sara enter the church, it is described with multiple images of water, like a baptism, or as if the two women were deep in an ocean or surrounded by amniotic fluid. The return to the train station at the end of the story is a kind of rebirth for Kate, as she chooses her own independent path and embarks on it. Her choice involves a play on words of the story's title, as she chooses her own way at the station, accepting that the previously planned route of her life (represented in her train ticket that was purchased before the breakup of her marriage) has been changed and that she needs to go on, to her own voyage of discovery.

*Barbara J. Bair*

# THE WAY WE LIVE NOW

*Author:* Susan Sontag (1933-     )
*Type of plot:* Social realism
*Time of plot:* The 1980's
*Locale:* Unspecified
*First published:* 1986

*Principal characters:*
MAX, a man with AIDS
HIS FRIENDS

## The Story

The plight of Max, a victim of acquired immunodeficiency syndrome (AIDS), is told entirely through the voices of his friends. They observe his first reactions to his illness—denying that he has it and delaying a trip to the doctor for the blood test that will establish his condition definitively. Each friend reacts differently to Max's dilemma. Some sympathize with his state of denial; others worry that he is not seeking medical attention early enough. Aileen thinks of herself, wondering if she herself is at risk. She doubts it, but her friend Frank reminds her that AIDS is a totally unprecedented illness; no one can be sure they are not vulnerable. Stephen hopes that Max realizes he has options; he should not consider himself totally helpless at the onset of the disease.

When Max is hospitalized, Ursula says that Max has received the AIDS diagnosis almost with relief after his months of anxiety. Friends wonder how to treat him. They decide to indulge him with the things he likes, such as chocolate. They visit him frequently, and his mood seems to lighten.

Does Max really want to see so many people? Are they doing the right thing by visiting him so frequently? Aileen asks. Ursula is sure they are; she is certain that Max values the company and is not judging people's motives. Friends such as Stephen question Max's doctor, trying to assess the gravity of each stage of Max's illness. The doctor is willing to treat Max with experimental drugs, but she tells Stephen that the chocolate might bolster Max's spirit and do as much good as anything else. Stephen, who has followed all the recent efforts to treat the disease, is disconcerted by this old-fashioned advice.

Kate shudders when she realizes that Max's friends have started talking about him in the past tense, as if he has already died. Several friends suspect that their visits are palling on him, while other friends argue that he has come to expect their daily presence. There is a brief respite from anxiety as Max's friends welcome him home from the hospital and observe that he is putting on weight. Xavier thinks they should stop worrying about how their visits affect Max; they are getting as much out of trying to help him as he is. They realize that they are dreading the possibility that they might also get the disease, that it is just a matter of time before they or their friends succumb to it. Betsy says that these days everybody is worried about everybody, that just seems to be the way people live now.

Max's friends think about how he has managed his life. He practiced unsafe sex, saying it was so important to him that he would risk getting the disease. Betsy thinks he must feel foolish now, like someone who kept on smoking cigarettes until he contracted a fatal disease. When it happens to you, Betty believes, you no longer feel so fatalistic; you feel instead that you have been reckless with your life. Lewis angrily rejects her thinking, pointing out that AIDS infected people long before they knew they needed to take precautions. Max might have been more prudent and still have caught AIDS. Unlike cigarettes, all that is needed is one exposure to the disease.

Friends report the various phases of Max's reaction to the disease. He is afraid to sleep because it is too much like dying. Some days he feels so good that he thinks he can beat the disease. Other days he thinks that the disease has given him a remarkable experience. He likes all the attention he is getting. It gives him a sort of distinction and a following. Some friends find his temperament softened and sweetened; others reject this attitudinizing about Max as sentimental. Each friend clings stubbornly to a vision of Max, the story ending with Stephen's insistent statement, "He's still alive."

## Themes and Meanings

"The Way We Live Now" is a brilliant orchestration of voices, showing how AIDS can change the lives of everyone who knows a victim. As Max's friends speculate about what he is going through, it is as though they are suffering from the disease themselves, trying to keep him alive in their thoughts and wishes. How they react to his disease depends very much on the kind of people they are. They argue with one another and sometimes support one another, desperately seeking ways to cope with the imminence of death. Max's approaching fate forces them to confront their own mortality, although they rarely acknowledge that they are indeed thinking of themselves as much as they are of him.

Death has many faces, many manifestations, Susan Sontag seems to be implying. For some, it is to be shunned. Some of Max's friends visit him rarely—one supposing that they had never been close friends anyway. Other friends, such as Stephen, almost seem to want to take over the fight against death—quizzing the doctors, boning up on the latest medical research, and conducting a kind of campaign against any capitulation to the disease. Very few friends are fatalistic; almost all of them hope that a medical breakthrough will come in time to rescue Max.

They live in fear. One friend finds out that his seventy-five-year-old mother has contracted AIDS through a blood transfusion she received five years earlier. No one is immune to the disease; even if everyone does not get it, everyone will probably know someone close to them who does. It is the extraordinary vulnerability of these people that makes them argue with or reassure one another and question what is the best behavior. Everyone encounters an ethical dilemma about how to lead his or her life and how to respond to those who are afflicted with the disease.

## Style and Technique

Sontag allows the portrait of Max and the responses of his friends to his disease to filter gradually through the many voices of her story. No voice is dominant. Max is rarely heard speaking in his own voice, although his plight is discussed in nearly every sentence of the story. Consequently, the blending and clashing of voices reveals a society in argument with itself, testing ways of responding to AIDS, advancing, then rejecting, certain attitudes.

As in real conversation, voices overlap one another so that one statement is interrupted by another, and one speaker merges into another:

> He seemed optimistic, Kate thought, his appetite was good, and what he said, Orson reported, was that he agreed when Stephen advised him that the main thing was to keep in shape, he was a fighter, right, he wouldn't be who he was if he weren't, and was he ready for the big fight, Stephen asked rhetorically (as Max told it to Donny), and he said you bet.

In this example, the views of several friends are heard, and dialogue is recapitulated in what Max tells Donny. Sentences contain speeches within speeches, a complex layering of social and psychological observation that is emphasized by long sentences that continually switch speakers, so that a community of friends and points of view is expressed sentence by sentence.

It is the rhythm of these voices, of the ups and downs in their moods, of the phases people go through in responding to the disease, that is one of the most impressive accomplishments of Sontag's technique. She presents the tragedy of one man, yet from the first to the last sentence the story is about society's tragedy as well. The speakers retain their individuality, yet they also become a chorus, almost like one in a Greek tragedy. They do not speak the same thoughts at once, but the syntax of the sentences makes them seem bound to one another—as enclosed by their community of feeling as the clauses in Sontag's sentences are enclosed by commas. The speaker's thought at the beginning of a sentence is carried on, refuted, modified, or added to by speakers in later parts of the sentence. The sentence as a grammatical unit links speakers to one another. Whatever their attitudes toward the disease, they cannot escape the thought of it. Thinking of it is, as one of them says, the way they live now.

*Carl Rollyson*

# WE BLACKS ALL DRINK COFFEE

*Author:* Mirta Yáñez (1947-    )
*Type of plot:* Social realism, psychological
*Time of plot:* The 1960's or 1970's
*Locale:* A family home in Cuba
*First published:* "Todos los negros tomamos café," 1976 (English translation, 1989)

> *Principal characters:*
> THE MOTHER
> HER TEENAGE DAUGHTER

*The Story*

The story begins in the middle of a fight between a mother and her daughter in the family home. Through the daughter's stream of consciousness, it is revealed that the teenager wants to go pick coffee in the mountains with a school volunteer group. However, her mother fervently protests the co-ed excursion that will take a sheltered fifteen-year-old girl away from her home for a forty-five-day period. During the dispute, the mother tries to keep her temper in check, does not yell, and closes the windows so as not to be overheard by the neighbors. However, when the daughter continues to dismiss her mother's reasons for disallowing the trip, the argument escalates into a contained rage.

What the daughter considers ridiculous excuses for not granting permission, the mother cites as good reasons that will avoid grave consequences. The mother reminds the teenager of the behavior expected of young white girls with good upbringing. Taking off to the mountains without parental supervision is unprecedented and unacceptable behavior within the extended family. Besides, the mother argues, the teenager may encounter all sorts of dangers out in the country, contract a disease, turn into a sickly burden, or become the object of town gossip. Sarcastic remarks by the daughter about guarding the family honor, getting pregnant, or falling in love with a black boy suggest just how out of date and exaggerated the mother's worries seem to the teenager.

The daughter's stream of consciousness reveals that coming into womanhood fuels her longing for independence from a home environment that she finds stifling. In the struggle for control, the daughter confronts the mother on her racial prejudice by questioning the family's lily-white ancestry. Centuries of intermarriage between dark-skinned Moors and Spaniards in the mother country, the daughter contends, makes it difficult to prove any claim to a lineage of pure Spanish blood. After this final bull's-eye blow to undermine the family name and the heritage it holds dear, the mother relents and tells the daughter that she is free to do as she pleases.

## Themes and Meanings

Like the rest of the stories in the collection *Todos los negros tomamos café*, the title story "We Blacks All Drink Coffee" deals with young people serving the Cuban government as brigadiers in the coffee harvest. The Cuban Revolution and the resultant break with capitalism resulted in the virtual closing of Cuba's borders to exchanges with the West, including free trade. The country needed a cheap labor force, so it initiated a widespread push for people to participate in community service. The government's adherence to Marxist ideology provoked profound changes in longstanding traditions, many stemming back to when Spain colonized the island.

As implied by the daughter, the new revolutionary society is tolerant of boys and girls going on extended work trips together, accepting of pregnancy out of wedlock, and nonjudgmental about mixed marriages. However, the mother's response indicates that pre-revolutionary values still linger among the older generation.

Embedded in the story's conflict, which on the surface captures young people's universal cry for independence, lies the tension between the traditional family values of Cuba before the Marxist revolution and the liberal social values that have evolved since then. The mother symbolizes old world Cuba, in which gender roles were conventional, racial segregation common, and protection of women's virginity was considered essential for maintaining a family's reputation and an untarnished white racial lineage.

Fear that the daughter may commit improprieties that will compromise the family name is really what the mother means when she points out the potential dangers that the teenager may encounter in the mountain coffee-growing region. Notably, the mother's references to the bush, forest, and wild countryside allude to the unleashing of sexuality, and the daughter compares the four constrictive walls of her room to the cloistered cell of a nun. Moreover, at the core of the mother's trepidation is the dread of her daughter forming a liaison with a nonwhite male, a pervasive prejudice in Cuban society that the communist regime has tried to eradicate. The story's original Spanish title refers to an old Cuban song, "Ay mamá Inés." The song's refrain chants "Ay mamá Inés, Ay mamá Inés,/ todo los negros tomamos café" (Oh mammy Inés, Oh mammy Inés,/ we blacks all drink coffee).

The mother's attempt to dissuade the daughter from joining the brigadiers enacts the struggle to preserve a belief system that her offspring does not share and the government does not support. Her measured tone of voice during the argument and her closing of windows so as not to be overheard by neighbors suggest that she maintains the proper feminine demeanor demanded by tradition. The mother's exaggerated claim that the teenager's volunteer activities will raise the blood pressure of her grandmothers and aunts to near fatal levels and that she herself will soon be underground and eaten by worms, signals the death of traditional values from a middle-class point of view.

For this teenager, coming into womanhood is tied to becoming a conscious "daughter" of the revolution. Hence, in her opinion, her mother is standing in the way of her full integration into the revolutionary community. Staunch defenders of conservative ways such as her mother put family interest over the common good—in this case, helping to harvest the coffee crop. The daughter's defiance of parental authority turns into a political act of rebellion. In the closed house turned metaphorical boxing ring, the mother finally throws in the towel when she recognizes that their difference in perspective is ideological and irreconcilable. Symbolically, in this bout, the revolutionary family has won over another "daughter" for its cause.

*Style and Technique*

In "We Blacks All Drink Coffee," as in the other stories in the collection, collaborating with the revolution makes for praiseworthy citizens. Although endorsement of communist ideals is not overtly political, nothing less than a sympathetic perspective would be publishable in the highly censured society in which Mirta Yáñez writes.

The narrators in this collection are often young brigadiers who, while on volunteer detail, witness life in the coffee-growing town of Florida Blanca, and as a result of this experience develop a personal understanding of people and communities different from those back home. The story "We Blacks All Drink Coffee" differs in that the narrator/protagonist is a would-be brigadier whose sympathies for people and behavior considered unworthy by her mother spark a family crisis. Unlike Yáñez's predilection for external settings, this story remains contained within the household in which the quarrel erupts.

Typically, in Yáñez's stories, a lack of clear dialogue leaves the reader to surmise who is doing the talking. This is further complicated in "We Blacks All Drink Coffee" because the narration is filtered through the direct interior monologue of a teenage girl. The unsuspecting reader must figure out from bits and pieces of conversation that an argument is underway.

In Yañez's clever rendering of the daughter's stream of consciousness, the voices of both teenager and mother mingle, are cut in mid-sentence, and stop and continue as characteristic of a dispute. The teenager's constant shifting of pronouns—"she" and "my"—when referring to the mother suggests the ambivalence of the narrator's feelings. For example, by using the third-person pronoun "she," the daughter distances herself from the antagonizing mother. When the teenager then identifies her as "my" mother, she restores the personal relationship between them. At times the teenager also abandons the first-person pronoun "I" and refers to herself in the third person as "her," "this child," "a girl," "a daughter," thus conveying her lack of control and self-ownership in the face of the mother's manipulation.

Yáñez circumvents the volatility of sensitive themes such as sexuality, politics, and racism via the use of symbols and metaphors. The wild bush, menstruation, brigadiers, the mother-daughter conflict, the protective home, all hold meaning beyond their apparent definitions. The Cuban Revolution is never mentioned or contextualized, for instance. Yet without this information, the reader would be at a great loss to interpret deeper meanings in this story. Although it may seem ironic that the powerless teenager is the one who controls the narration as both narrator and protagonist, her role is symbolic. Like the revolutionary underdogs who fought in the mountains of the region where she wants to go pick coffee, the daughter ultimately wins against great odds. The story's characters are anonymous because beyond representing a dysfunctional mother-daughter relationship, their disagreement represents tensions within the country.

By contrast, Yáñez skillfully attributes the characters with traits that anchor them to reality and thus keeps them from becoming purely symbolic. The author infuses the teenager's remarks with sarcasm and those of the mother with exaggeration to capture each character's stance. Reasonably in keeping with their ages, and as filtered through the teenager's perspective, the daughter comes across as a smart aleck and the mother as terribly old-fashioned. After all, it is their run-of-the-mill bickering, although rich in symbolism, that mounts in ever-increasing tension until the story's denouement leads to the surprising resolution.

*Gisela Norat*

# WEDDING NIGHT

*Author:* Tommaso Landolfi (1908-1979)
*Type of plot:* Fable
*Time of plot:* The mid-twentieth century
*Locale:* Northern Italy
*First published:* "Notte di nozze," 1939 (English translation, 1963)

## Principal characters:

A YOUNG BRIDE
A CHIMNEY SWEEP

### The Story

The arrival of a chimney sweep brings a wedding banquet at the bride's house to an early end. As the sweep changes his clothes and proceeds to clean out the chimney in the kitchen, slowly working his way up the chimney shaft three times, the bride exits the kitchen in embarrassment. After the sweep finishes, he changes his clothes again, eats breakfast, and sends out to the bride, who is seated outside, a gift of a small bouquet of edelweiss. The family briefly converses with the sweep after his meal; then he leaves, after which the bride places the edelweiss bouquet under portraits of her dead relatives.

### Themes and Meanings

Virtually all details of plot, characterization, word choice, figurative language, and symbolism in this brief story help convey the theme that life contains a paradoxical blend of innumerable opposites or oppositions: male-female, upper class-lower class, experience-innocence, knowledge-ignorance, age-youth, life-death, daring-shyness, animate-inanimate, public-private, light-dark, bestial-refined, cleanliness-dirtiness, and white-black. The bride, whose inexperience and youth are stressed by the use of the word "young" eleven times, feels a kind of feminine shyness from the intrusion into the privacy of her home by the never-immaculate sweep, who must partially undress in order to do his job. The sweep also feels shy before his employers, however, although he knows more about them than they know about him. Concerned about his privacy, he wishes "to hide himself behind . . . words" and "let the curtain of words fall in the same way that the cuttlefish beclouds the water." Tommaso Landolfi's typical concern about whether language clarifies or obscures reality or relationships is suggested here, as well as tension between the social classes. The lower-class sweep is thus protecting himself linguistically from his employers.

During the sweep's work, the inanimate chimney comes alive for the bride, who empathizes in pain with its penetration, the "rhythm of a dull scraping which gnawed at the marrow of the house and which she felt echoing in her own entrails" and then with the sweep's cry sounding "from the stones of the house, from the soul of the kitchen's pots and pans, from the very breast of the young bride, who was shaken by it through and through." Paradoxically, what the bride first hears as a "bestial howl of agony" when the sweep finally breaks through to the roof "proves to be a kind of joyous call," suggesting a complex intertwining of opposites in life, love, and the sexual act. Moreover, the earthy sweep, never completely free from black soot and repeatedly described with animal imagery, gives to the bride the delicate, white edelweiss—a flower whose name means "noble white."

Death and life are also paradoxically mingled. Although the abundant soot's appearance and smell remind the bride of death, and the sweep standing on a pile of soot reminds her of a grave digger, the clearing out of the chimney and its penetration give it new life, just as the imminent death of her own sexual innocence will lead to the lives of her children and descendants. Ironically, the sexual act itself, leading to new life, results in a sort of death, in the participants' peaking and then decline in emotion and in physiology, as suggested by the sweep's cry of agony and joy in breaking through to the roof, his "black foot . . . of a hanged man" that emerges from the "slit" of opening to the chimney, and his appearance on the soot pile "like a gravedigger on a mound of earth" at his reemergence on finishing the job. The sexually suggestive word "slit" is significantly repeated, implying—as much else in the story does—the influence of Sigmund Freud on Landolfi's writing. Finally, the activity of chimney cleaning, which represents two kinds of "death" to the bride, and prompts her to place her edelweiss bouquet under the portraits of dead ancestors, represents the continuation of life to the sweep and his descendants, for he reveals immediately before he leaves that he is about to bring his son into his business. A link is also suggested here with the child that the bride will likely bear as a result of her married nights, if not the impending wedding night. Though set in winter—the season of death, echoing "deaths" in the story—the actions of the plot will ultimately contribute to new life.

*Style and Technique*

Landolfi's word choices and sentence structures differ from some of his other short fiction in being simple in this story, helping to impart to it a fablelike quality. While some of Landolfi's other fiction uses more polysyllabic and abstract words, almost all of his work has the same kind of vivid symbolism as this story. In this tale, for example, almost all the details of the sweep's clothing are evocative, from the earthiness suggested by the brown of his corduroy suit's hue of "linseed oil" and his brown shirt, to his "two huge mountain boots." The weight of his boots also suggests the earthbound, though they also hold him "erect," counteracting his stoop, and point, contradictorily, to both aspiration and rising sexuality. The name of the material in his suit evokes aristocracy, as "corduroy" was originally thought to mean "cloth of the king"—a sharp contrast with the sweep's social class. In its liquid stickiness linseed oil suggests the by-products of lovemaking; in its hardening property, which is used for protective coating in paint and varnish, it suggests the coating of the chimney and the bride's ignorance, to be assailed by sweep and groom, respectively.

The coating that the sweep dons—ironically, in order to uncoat the chimney—is a black "gag" resembling a mask that covers his nose and mouth; it suggests the opposition between articulate and inarticulate, plus sweep and groom as masculine rapacious, intrusive robbers of a sort. The sweep's revelation that he violated prohibitions against picking edelweiss is an analogue of the groom's imminent violation of a much different sort of flower. Moreover, the bride's difficulty in summoning the courage to speak to the sweep and her difficulty in understanding his words on the two occasions that he speaks to her suggest the problems of language and communication, including their involvement in the relationship between the sexes. To maintain his own privacy, the sweep speaks opaquely obscuring sentences that resemble the cuttlefish's ink and recall his black gag.

After the bride retreats outside the kitchen the third time, the fact that she seats herself on a millstone suggests a rural setting, in which people grind their own wheat and corn; it also suggests her imminent induction into domestic life, after the wedding night. Also implied is the bride's being ground down by what lies ahead. The tool that the sweep uses to scrape out the chimney (apart from its vague phallic overtones) resembles the implement used to scrape kneading troughs. These, like the millstone, may be associated with bread—the staff of life and the focus of daily activities of family life.

In the bride's metaphoric conception, from the first moment that she meets the sweep, of his "caterpillar nature" is implied his humility, or shyness, in the presence of the affluent; his ability to crawl up chimney walls; and new life and transformation after the chrysalis stage. The bride's conception, in simile, of the sweep resembling a crab louse, suggests not only his dark environment but also sexuality, echoing the caterpillar imagery. Ironically, although this caterpillar-natured person begins the destruction of the bride's insulation from the social and sexual worlds, he also gives her a flower bouquet, the beautiful edelweiss. Growing only in mountainous wildernesses, edelweiss is collected only with difficulty analogous to the difficulties of the sweep and bride. Its plucking, as the sweep admits, has been outlawed, analogous, the story implies, to the forbidden aura of the chimney sweep's and the groom's activities. Finally, the flower's structure contains a protective covering of woolly bracts; this covering is implicitly related to the story's focus on penetrating the surfaces of things. This last concern is metaphysical, transcendent, and perhaps the crux of all Landolfi's fiction.

*Norman Prinsky*

# WELCOME TO UTAH

*Author:* Michel Butor (1926-    )
*Type of plot:* Antistory
*Time of plot:* The early 1960's
*Locale:* United States
*First published:* "Bienvenue en Utah," 1962 (English translation, 1963)

*Principal character:*
AN ANONYMOUS TRAVELER

*The Story*

"Welcome to Utah" is a chapter excerpted from *Mobile: Étude pour une représentation des États-Unis* (1962; *Mobile: Study for a Representation of the United States*, 1963), a larger work that attempts to render the essential quality of each American state. Like an imaginary guidebook to the United States, this work takes readers through all the states in the Union, in alphabetical order according to the alliance of place-names: From Lebanon, New Jersey, it switches to Lebanon, Ohio, and then to towns with the same name in Indiana and Illinois, for example. There are no characters or plot in the conventional sense; its fifty chapters—each devoted to one of the fifty states and covering a forty-eight-hour time span—provide an abundance of descriptive and interpretive material about the country.

The chapters are linked by the mere invocation of town names duplicated in several states as well as by the longer continuing text of the narrator's running commentary on American history, the history of American Indians, and African American history. Comments on the time in each place and secondary material (such as catalogs, advertisements, road signs, restaurant menus, and quotations from famous historical figures) are incorporated into the text.

There is no action in the story, merely the illusion of interstate travel. The reader is carried along by the chain of associations, both temporal and spatial, provided by the narrator and by his imaginative use of quotations. The reader gains an impression of the United States that is at once startling and accurate: startling because of the frequent reminders of the suffering of America's many disfranchised peoples at the hands of white colonists, and accurate in its history and quasi-statistical evocations.

Because the chain is continuous, the complete book can be read, beginning anywhere, and readers are free to plan their own tours of the United States. "Welcome to Utah" can thus be understood on its own as a series of associative mobilizations. The town of Wellington, Utah, at sundown is the starting point for the narrator's journey of associations that propel him forward. This eventually leads to a moment early on in the chapter when Utah is abandoned for points east. Beginning with Wellington and an accompanying quote that describes the arrival of the Latter-Day Saints to the basin of the Great Salt Lake, the narration abruptly shifts to the town of Wellington, Nevada, a small town identified briefly by the presence of the Summit Lake Indian Reservation. The narrative then makes a detour back to Utah to take up the town of Huntsville, justifying this deviation with a passage quoted from textbook American history citing Huntsville as Brigham Young's chosen spot for founding his new Mormon city.

The main narrative line is then punctuated by fragments of factual information, snippets of banal conversation, quotations from road signs, and advertisements in a Sears, Roebuck and Co. catalog for a schoolbag illustrated with a colored map of the United States. Next, the history of the Mormons and their missionary zeal remind readers that they are still in Utah.

Shortly thereafter, the narrative travels in time and place to New England, where an account from the trial of Susanna Martin, one of the women implicated in the Salem Witch Trials of 1692, is presented. This account is less of a digression than a bridge leading back to the East Coast and eventually to New York City. Discussion of New York evokes a report on the numbers of European-language newspapers printed in this country, lures readers into restaurants serving French, Indonesian, Italian, and Irish cuisine, and evokes images of this city's architectural icons, the Empire State Building and the Seagram's Building. Readers are bombarded by big-city advertising, urging them to drink Coca-Cola, to fly Sabena and KLM, and to tune into WBNX for broadcasts in Ukrainian.

Eventually readers are transported back in time and space to the South by way of Danville, New Hampshire, and then to Danville, Virginia. The chapter closes with several brief descriptions of the interiors of Monticello, alternating with lengthy extracts from Thomas Jefferson elaborating his belief in the inequality of race. A final associative leap jumps from Vienna, Virginia, to 11:00 P.M. in Vienna, Maryland, near Chester in Maryland. After all these imaginative deviations and detours, the welcome to Utah ends with an arrival back on the East Coast.

*Themes and Meanings*

In Michel Butor's travelogue of Americana, evocations of cities and cultural and political history are developed as themes on multiple levels: temporal, spatial, historical, and physical. His efforts to capture the sensation of travel transport readers backward in time, as well as forward in space, as they move from state to state, town to town, and century to century. The first word of the title of the large work, "Mobile," suggests Alexander Calder's whimsical mobile sculptures, which, like each state or historical landmark, may be read from a variety of perspectives. Road signs introducing new states and town names are reminders that America is the land of mobility in which people move from place to place in automobiles. Distilled quotations and advertising reveal other significant aspects of American culture. Recurring Howard Johnson's ice-cream flavors and advertisements from the Sears catalog echo the American mail-order catalog mentality. The names of cities that reappear in different states duplicate America's pattern of mass production. The use of juxtaposition conveys a feeling of speed as the reader travels down the highway of Americana.

This story also works as a social document of the more disturbing aspects of American history. Butor draws attention to the mistreatment of American Indians at the hands of America's white inhabitants, whom he calls "Europeans." The Indian, the "expression of this scandalous continent," posed a great menace to white colonists as they tried to replace the wilderness and build grids of roads and farmlands. To juxtapose the history of white America with its own cultural shame is, for Butor, to offer a realistic panorama of a country. It is certainly no accident that Butor pairs the name of each city with the name of a corresponding Indian reservation.

*Style and Technique*

Butor's dedication of *Mobile* to the American painter Jackson Pollock suggests that he seeks to scatter haphazard fragments of Americana throughout his travelogue. However, this suggestion is deceptive when one realizes how much controlled chance goes into the fabric of this story. Indeed, Butor intended *Mobile* to be composed like a patchwork quilt, piecing together the patchwork iconography of America to create his story. His purposeful juxtapositions, digressions, and quotations create the feeling of a patchwork, working rhetorically to guide the reader along prosaic roadways.

Alternating typefaces provide a crucial map for reading this travelogue. For example, geographical information, details of local flora and fauna, and advertisements are printed in roman type and serve as the story's framework. The welcoming signs that introduce different states and town names are printed in roman capital letters. County names, times, road signs, and brief physical descriptions of individual states are printed in lowercase roman letters. Around this framework Butor groups a wide selection of materials in italics. Short italicized phrases, often concerning American colonial history or containing banal dialogue, describe the natural and cultural features characteristic of each region. Longer italicized texts, including commentaries, catalogs, and selections from writings of famous Americans convey what is distinctive in American culture as a whole. The opposition of the shorter, fragmented italic elements with longer italicized texts may be viewed as dialogue or even distinction between rich local diversity and national cultural identity.

Butor's reliance on a disjointed form is much more than a compendium of impressions of the United States by an outsider. The quiltwork form of *Mobile* is neither symmetrical nor definitive. It is instead an experimental work that renounces a central narrative consciousness in favor of one that approximates the experience of movement through time, history, and space. The varieties of typefaces, as well as blank spaces and margins, provide readers with greater mobility as they make their way across the page over the vast American landscape. This rejection of linearity provides a compelling solution to the abundance of heterogeneous information that assails the cross-country traveler and inquiring cultural historian.

*Constance Sherak*

# WELDING WITH CHILDREN

*Author:* Tim Gautreaux (1947-    )
*Type of plot:* Realism
*Time of plot:* The 1990's
*Locale:* Gumwood, Louisiana
*First published:* 1997

> *Principal characters:*
> BRUTON, a grandfather and part-time welder
> NU-NU,
> MOONBEAN,
> TAMMYNETTE, and
> FREDDIE, his four grandchildren

## The Story

"Welding with Children" is a comic, "feel-good" story about a welder with four unmarried daughters, each with a child, who tries to "weld" what he sees is broken about his four grandchildren. The story opens when the welder's casino-bound wife leaves him to take care of all four grandchildren: Nu-Nu, Moonbeam, Tammynette, and Freddie. While he is trying to weld a bed rail for one of his daughters, the children get in the way and play with his welding tools. Bruton is ashamed of his trashy yard with a greasy auto engine hanging from a tree. When the children start screaming for an Icee, he drives them down to the Gumwood Pak-a-Sak. When he hears an older man say, "Here comes Bruton and his bastardmobile," he is embarrassed. One of the men tells Bruton that maybe he can do better with this batch than he did with his own children.

On the way home, one of the children uses a curse word that makes Bruton pull over and tell him that children do not use language like that. When they get home, another child uses a four-letter word, and Bruton tells them to stop talking like white trash. He asks them if their mothers ever talk to them about God. This initiates a comic dialogue between Bruton and the children about the Bible, which makes him understand that the children know nothing about it. He gets out his old Bible stories book and begins telling them about the creation and Adam and Eve.

As the children ask questions about what Bruton reads, he realizes that the only knowledge they have about religion comes from films and television. He fantasizes about packing them up in his car and heading out to the Northwest to start all over again. However, he recognizes that you cannot drive away from yourself and that whatever bad was going to happen was partly his fault. He goes into town the next day and asks the man who called his car the bastardmobile how to fix things so his grandchildren do right. He is advised to take the children to Sunday school and church every Sunday and to clean up his yard. After Bruton talks to the Methodist preacher, he goes home and starts cleaning up the yard, calling a salvage company to take away four derelict cars, six engines, four washing machines, and more than two tons of scrap iron. "Time for a change," he says.

When his oldest daughter brings Nu-Nu and Freddie over to spend the night, she tells him Nu-Nu said his first word, which was "Da-da." Bruton tells Freddie he is going to put up a tire swing on the oak tree. When Nu-Nu says "Da-da," Bruton thinks the child may never be able to face the fact that Da-da, whoever he was, is never coming back. When Freddie says even Nu-Nu can ride the tire swing, Bruton says, "He can fit the circle in the middle."

## Themes and Meanings

Tim Gautreaux's milieu is the rural farm country of south central Louisiana. Although his characters are often down on their luck, their moral values are sound. Gautreaux writes about working-class men and women who meet a challenge to their humaneness and usually manage to handle it with courage and grace. Comparing him to Flannery O'Connor, critics have praised his stories as being morally complex in their depiction of human frailty and deceptively simple in their lyrical style.

"Welding with Children" exhibits Gautreaux's typical focus on a working-class man who has made a few mistakes and tries to start afresh. There is nothing shiftless about Bruton, but he does have a tendency to let things slide a bit. The reader is not given any information about how he brought up his four daughters, but the fact that each of them has an illegitimate child suggests moral laxity somewhere. The fact that his wife seems more interested in going to the local casino than helping with the grandchildren suggests that he gets no moral support from her either.

In his "Contributor's Note" to *The Best American Short Stories, 1998,* Gautreaux says that Bruton is typical of grandparents all over the country who are raising their grandchildren because they did not raise their children right in the first place. However, Gautreaux is not trying to teach any social message here but to create a comic tour de force in which a grandfather is stymied by the video store and MTV influences that threaten to make his grandchildren the "white trash" that neighbors think he and his wife and daughters are.

The central section of the story is a comic dialogue between Bruton and the four children as he tries to read to them out of a Bible storybook. When he asks if their mothers read Bible stories to them at bedtime, one child says that she rented *Conan the Barbarian* once. When Bruton says that is not a Bible story, the child asks why not, saying, "It's got swords and snakes in it." This film-inspired assumption is reinforced when the children see a picture in Bruton's book of the serpent in the Garden of Eden. When Bruton tells them the snake is the devil in disguise, one child says that is just an old song she heard on the radio.

Bruton's decision to clean up his yard and try to teach the children by example is indicative of the rural southern notion that only white trash have lots of junk lying around in plain view. The story ends with an idyllic image of Bruton fixing the children a tire swing in the yard and putting the baby Nu-Nu in the middle of it, who will swing there like some angelic innocent while the proud grandfather looks on smiling.

This story has no intention of being realistic or socially responsible. It is simplistic of Bruton to think that by cleaning up his yard and reading the children Bible stories he will make everything right. It is unrealistic to think that putting up a tire swing will woo the children away from their videos and television shows. It is naïve to think that his four daughters will change their ways just because their father is trying to change his.

However, social realism is not what Gautreaux is after here. He simply wants to write a story about how humans hope to start anew, to be forgiven for the past, and to have possibilities to do better in the future. Although the dialogue between Bruton and the children about religion and the Bible exists primarily to give Gautreaux the opportunity for a comic encounter, the basic theme of the story is essentially Christian.

*Style and Technique*

Gautreaux has said he got the idea for this story one day while he was in the Wal-Mart and heard a middle-age man's voice complaining to a friend about his three daughters who kept having children out of wedlock and bringing them over so that he and his wife could take care of them. What caught Gautreaux's attention was the old guy's great voice, "southern, smart, and full of humor." Indeed, what makes "Welding with Children" a pleasure to read is the first-person voice of Bruton. The voice is colloquial but not corny. It is the voice of a man who has had all the best intentions, but who has been careless about his parenting, just as he has been careless about what litters his yard.

The story is deceptive in its simplicity, meandering along without apparent formal tightness. For example, at one point Bruton spends several paragraphs recollecting the few months he spent in college before flunking out. Although this section may seem irrelevant to the story's theme, it is actually part of the foundation for Bruton's central view that feelings are more important than intellect. He says that one semester in college gave him his money's worth learning about people with hearts no bigger than birdshot.

Heart is exactly what Bruton communicates in his comic, yet poignant, lament about how his grandchildren are hopelessly ignorant about religion, and thus morality, and how it must be his fault. For this story to work, the reader has to like Bruton as much as Gautreaux does. Gautreaux's masterful, yet seemingly simple, control of the first person point of view makes it clear that Bruton is a simple man who has a good heart. At the end of the story, both Gautreaux and the reader can only wish him well.

*Charles E. May*

# A WET DAY

*Author:* Mary Lavin (1912-1996)
*Type of plot:* Domestic realism
*Time of plot:* The twentieth century
*Locale:* Ireland
*First published:* 1944

> *Principal characters:*
> THE NIECE, the narrator, an educated and independent thinker
> HER AUNT, an older woman who respects the clergy
> FATHER GOGARTY, a priest plagued by ill health

*The Story*

"A Wet Day" is a subtle story that explores several conflicts. The first is between the young narrator and her aunt. This young person has been to the university and has acquired ideas that are considered radical in her small Irish village. The most radical of these is her lack of respect for the Roman Catholic clergy. Her estimate of a person's worth does "not allow credit for round collars or tussore." She judges the person and not the office, and thus contrasts with her aunt, who is afraid to offend the local priest, Father Gogarty. The aunt respects the priest because of his position and never questions his moral character.

In the first scene, Father Gogarty visits the aunt to get some vegetables from her. The aunt carefully keeps her niece away from the priest so that she will not make a troublesome scene, even though doing so results in her and her niece getting wet.

The garden setting is repeatedly described as wet and sodden. This troubles the priest, who spent his early years studying for the priesthood in the balmy confines of Rome and now suffers greatly from the wet and unhealthy environment in which he lives. A diabetic, Father Gogarty can eat only vegetables—primarily cabbage and rhubarb. This wins him the sympathy of not only the aunt, but also her niece and the whole village.

Mike, the gardener, is also fond of Father Gogarty and goes out of his way to provide him with vegetables. He sympathizes with the priest's plight and encourages him to persevere. Father Gogarty occasionally despairs about his condition and diet, but, with Mike's encouragement, he comes to see that it is his duty to take care of himself.

The story changes after Father Gogarty asks Mike about a friend from his home town of Mullingar who has died recently. The young man was engaged to marry Father Gogarty's niece Lottie. During a visit the young man became seriously ill and Lottie wanted him to stay at Father Gogarty's rectory because it would be dangerous for him to return to Dublin in a cold car. Father Gogarty revealed his selfish nature by denying the young man shelter in order to protect his own health. After everyone agreed to decide the issue by the question of whether the young man had a temperature, Father Gogarty lied about not having a thermometer and sent the sick man away in a cold car. The young man had pneumonia and soon died.

This scene revealed Father Gogarty's character. Selfish rather than pastoral, he is interested only in protecting himself. This exposure of his true nature changes the attitude of the aunt about Father Gogarty, and her relationship with her niece improves. They have fewer fights and resolve their earlier conflicts after both judge Father Gogarty to be an ineffectual priest.

*Themes and Meanings*

A major theme of "A Wet Day" is the contrast between the priest's official role and his moral nature. Should the priest be respected because of his clerical position, or should he be judged as others are? Eventually the story reveals that Father Gogarty lacks precisely those qualities of caring that a priest should have. Possessing no pastoral qualities, he is concerned only with selfishly preserving his own health. This judgment is rendered not in words but in the rejection of lettuce by the aunt at the end of the story. Earlier she honors Father Gogarty because of his office; at the end she sees him merely as a man—and a deficient one.

Another way the story conveys its meaning is through imagery. It is filled with images and references to wetness, sodden plants, and dripping skies. The aunt and her niece live in harmony with this wet environment. For example, the aunt keeps a dripping fuchsia bush for its beauty on the rare sunny day that comes. In contrast, Father Gogarty thinks the bush should be cut back or eliminated because he thinks it increases the danger of catching cold. He is more worried about catching an infection and disease than about caring for others.

A conflict that begins the story is between the traditional aunt with settled views and the more modern, educated niece. The young niece has no respect for institutions, especially the Roman Catholic clergy that is so important in Ireland. By the end of the story, however, she forgets about the revelation of Father Gogarty's character, which now has less significance for her. The aunt changes her own view more dramatically. She is clearly upset at Father Gogarty's showing himself to be a poor shepherd to his flock. As a result of this change, the aunt reconciles with her niece, and they agree on how to judge a person.

Another important conflict is between the "duty" that the priest feels to protect and care for himself and the necessity of being concerned with and caring for others. In obeying one dictate, he ignores the other, giving his own health and comfort priority over the urgent needs of the sick young man. The priest even goes so far as to lie about not having a thermometer in his house.

*Style and Technique*

"A Wet Day" is narrated by one of the major characters, the young niece, who reveals her own thoughts and observations, but no one else's. She describes the few key scenes in the story without expressing judgments on Father Gogarty.

The story's setting is also worth noticing. It is set in a small and clearly traditional Irish village. The people in the parish respect and sympathize with Father Gogarty because of his medical problems and the "cabbage" and "rhubarb" that he must eat. They endure his dry sermons uncomplainingly since they seem to conduct their spiritual lives without much help from him. They also accept the wet and cold of the church as penances that they endure for their spiritual benefit. By contrast, Father Gogarty is concerned primarily with his own comfort; he is not in tune with his setting or his parishioners. Completely oriented to the prevention of disease and infection, he has little sense of the spiritual. The aunt calls him a "martyr," but no true martyr would be willing to sacrifice the life of another to his or her own comfort and quiet.

The priest's style is clearly different from any of the other characters in the story. When introduced, he is complaining about the slugs that are ruining the lettuce on which he depends. His conversation is filled with negative comments about the weather and the possibility of disease. Self-pitying about his condition, he speaks about dying from deliberately eating a steak in order to gain sympathy from others. He is also cunning and calculating in the way that he forces the young man from Mullingar to agree to a fatal car trip. However, he seems not to be aware of the negative effect of the revelation of his character.

The lettuce is an important symbol that shows the changes occurring within the aunt. At the end, when she says "Take it away," she shows her rejection of the priest and his world of vegetables. Earlier in the story, she gladly gives lettuce to the priest to help sustain him. Now she wants nothing to do with it. In contrast, the niece could eat a "bowlful" of lettuce and is annoyed at her aunt's rejection of it. However, she does see its significance, and she and her aunt are reconciled as a result.

*James Sullivan*

# WET SATURDAY

*Author:* John Collier (1901-1980)
*Type of plot:* Satire
*Time of plot:* The 1930's
*Locale:* Abbot's Laxton, England
*First published:* 1938

> *Principal characters:*
> MR. PRINCEY, a head of a family who despises his family
> MRS. PRINCEY, his hysterical wife
> MILLICENT PRINCEY, their daughter and a killer
> GEORGE PRINCEY, their son and a failed medical student
> WITHERS, the local clergyman, a murder victim
> CAPTAIN SMOLLETT, a neighbor

*The Story*

On a rainy July day, Mr. Princey gathers together his family, which he abhors, because his daughter, Millicent, has done something so stupid as to threaten his way of life. Mr. Princey's pleasures are simple: He loves his house; likes to walk through the village, where his prestige is acknowledged; and enjoys reminiscing about the lost pleasures of his childhood.

As he addresses his family, he mercilessly lashes at Millicent for her as yet unnamed error. If caught, he explains, she will be hanged or committed to an asylum for the criminally insane. He also insults George, his son, when he asks the young man whether his abortive career as a medical student has enabled him to tell whether Millicent's crime can be disguised as an accident. George says that it cannot. Millicent has hit the victim several times with a croquet mallet.

Calming his wife with direct abuse and his daughter with threats of asylums and hanging, Princey asks Millicent to describe the afternoon's events. Millicent, it turns out, had been packing up the croquet set in the stable on that wet afternoon when the young neighboring curate, Withers, on his way for a walk to Bass Hill, cut through the property and stopped to talk, sheltering himself in the stable away from the heavy rain. Millicent had long loved this young man (George interjects that the local pub has been laughing at her infatuation for the past several years), and so, when Withers said that he was now in a position to be married, she assumed that he was about to propose to her. She was wrong. Apologetically, he gave her the name of another girl with whom he would be married and turned his back to leave, at which point Millicent struck him several times with a croquet mallet. Then she returned to the house, trusting her family to shelter her. In this, she was correct.

They are still discussing the death of Withers when Captain Smollett, with only a tap at the door, walks in. Clearly, he has been in a position to hear some of their conversation, but he assumes that they have been joking about Withers's death. He admits that, at the moment, he is none too fond of that young man himself because he, too, has been courting the young woman whom Withers won.

This admission gives Princey an idea, and he calls George to the stables. A few minutes later, Princey returns and asks Smollett if he would like to see something interesting. When they reach the stables, Princey aims a gun at Smollett and tells him that, while he and George came out to shoot a rat, they might well have an accident and shoot Smollett instead. Holding Smollett captive, Princey explains that Withers's accident must be smoothed over. Smollett, he says, would remember the conversation that he had walked in on when he heard that Withers had met with a fatal accident that day. Smollett, an apparently honest man, admits that he probably would.

Princey explains that he does not want Millicent arrested because he would be forced to leave the village. Smollett offers a promise of silence, but Princey insists that he must ensure the neighbor's silence by other means. He considers killing Smollett, having no more compunction about two corpses than about one, but he finds another way out. Smollett, after all, has admitted his own jealousy of Withers and thus has a motive for killing him. Therefore, offering Smollett the choice of death or compliance, he implicates Smollett in Withers's death. He orders George to hit Smollett in the face hard enough to leave traces of a struggle, and he forces Smollett to leave his own fingerprints on the murder weapon and on the ring by which the flagstone over the sewer is raised. Withers's body is deposited in the sewer.

Princey mops his brow with relief. Because no one knew that Withers would stop on his way to Bass Hill, investigators are hardly likely to check the Princey sewer. The group returns to the drawing room, where Mrs. Princey gushingly thanks Smollett for his cooperation. She still has tears of gratitude in her eyes as Smollett goes down the drive.

Princey has one last talk with his wife and daughter and, after the rain ends, one last look around the stable. Reassured, he picks up the telephone to call the Bass Hill police station and report the murder. The story ends here, but the reader has watched the evidence being manufactured and knows that Princey has done a very thorough job. Smollett will most assuredly take the blame.

### Themes and Meanings

"Wet Saturday" is one of a group of stories in which John Collier satirizes social institutions, including marriage. Marriage, like the professions of law and medicine, tends, in Collier's view, to be governed by conventions and acquisitiveness, not by integrity and concern. In "Wet Saturday," the family's last name and the father's behavior alike suggest that this is a family that carries the belief that an Englishman's home is his castle to an insane extreme.

Essentially, this tightly knit but unhappy family is waging war against the community in which it resides. Princey despises his family; in him, Collier has deftly sketched the lines of a man who deeply resents adult responsibility and who yearns for the privileged world of childhood that he attempts to re-create. Despite his domestic emotions, however, Princey will defend his obviously deluded daughter, even if her defense allows her the freedom to prey on the community in the future.

Every detail of the story points to the family's narrow self-interest. A young man of God eagerly on the brink of success and marriage is, to this family, no more than refuse to be crammed down a sewer; at no point in the story does any member of the family utter any word of concern or remorse at his death. In the family's treatment of Smollett, the members give ample evidence that they honor no promises and no bonds of friendship; Smollett may well hang for a crime that he did not commit and that he vowed to conceal. The family, though, has gained its end: Its standing in the community will remain untainted. The Princey family, then, provides a typical Collier microcosm of an acquisitive and power-hungry society at its very worst.

*Style and Technique*

Collier creates horror by emphasizing the ordinariness of the Princey family. It could be any family dominated by a tyrannical father; this is Collier's point. Collier creates his effect by an intricate flattening out of events so that no single event—such as the death of a man of God—seems more significant than any other to this family, and by the flat, cold, emotionless language with which the story is told. The language is that of journalism, and it creates the illusion of truth to life. It reminds the reader that horror can lurk anywhere, even in the tightly knit circle of a pleasantly respectable family on an ordinary rainy Saturday afternoon.

The language of Mr. Princey dominates the story and sets the tone. Whether he is giving his family a tongue-lashing or discussing the death of Withers and the possible death of Smollett, his words are totally devoid of any emotion. He can speak without pity of his daughter's hanging, and he debates killing Smollett in the same language as he mentions shooting a rat. After George hits Smollett at his instruction, Princey politely apologizes; only a little while later, he frames Smollett for the clergyman's murder.

*Betty Richardson*

# WHAT IS THE CONNECTION BETWEEN MEN AND WOMEN?

*Author:* Joyce Carol Oates (1938-    )
*Type of plot:* Psychological
*Time of plot:* The 1960's
*Locale:* The United States
*First published:* 1970

> *Principal characters:*
> SHARON, a widow, thirty-four years old, who works in a
>   department store
> HER HUSBAND, now dead, whom she remembers
> A MAN, unnamed, who follows her home

*The Story*

Joyce Carol Oates's story is an experimental rendering of guilt and sexual repression. Through an alternation between a series of questions (in italics) and answers (in roman), she exposes the rawness of a very vulnerable personality: a woman unable to understand her own desires and fears. The reader's burdensome task is to understand this neurosis, even if the central character never will. The rather curt, at times clinical, questions seem to come from a male universe; the irrational, at times utterly disjointed answers seem to emanate from the female narrator's defense of another woman—a woman as broken as she is. The title of the story (also one of its questions) seems to support this reading.

Sharon, this miserably unhappy woman, spends a sleepless night vaguely waiting for something or someone to happen to her. She brings into her memory a young boy from her high school days who "had died of insanity." She thinks of her mother, miles away, whose snoring disgusts her; throughout the story her mother appears as a bittersweet but inaccessibly distant memory. In the middle of these scattered reminiscences, the reader is uncomfortably aware that Sharon is terrified by the possibility that the telephone will ring.

She then recalls an unspecified afternoon before this sleepless night. She had met an old friend of her father-in-law. He reminds her of all the dead men in her life: father-in-law, father, husband, and the insane high school boy. She successfully shakes him off. A stranger confronts her; he expresses concern that the old man was harassing her. Something about this man stuns her. She begins to confuse this man with her husband—reminding herself that he could not be her husband, yet considering that perhaps the stranger is a survivor of the automobile accident in which her husband had died. It becomes clear that the psychological stability of this woman is, to say the least, tentative.

She continues on her way home, stopping at a grocer's, obsessed with the stranger. The man has followed her to the store; she is oddly terrified by the coincidence. She is frightened by, yet attracted to, the stranger.

Periodically she recalls her life with her husband, his death, and her meager survival. Since her husband's death, the world has become desexualized, dehumanized: "a world of bodies, directed clumsily by thoughts, by darting minnowlike ideas." Periodically the reader returns to her sleepless night; it seems that much of this woman has died with her husband.

At 4:30 in the morning, the telephone rings—as she had feared. She is certain that the stranger followed her home that afternoon. She answers; after a breathy hesitation, the voice asks: "Hello, is this Sharon?" He identifies himself as "someone you just met." Hysterical, she slams down the telephone receiver.

She spends another restless night and early morning in anticipation. The telephone rings at five o'clock; she does not answer. There is a knock at the door; the man calls her by name. In a turmoil of emotional contradictions she opens the door, "and everything comes open, comes apart." With these words the story ends.

*Themes and Meanings*

The very form of "What Is the Connection Between Men and Women?" is the most important aspect of its meaning. A distance establishes itself between question and response. This distance can be translated into male/female, outside/inside, sane/insane—any number of dichotomies that reflect the basic paradigm of cage/prisoner.

However, this paradigm does not invite the reader to share a simplistic moral judgment—that women are innocent victims of thoughtless male imprisonment. To a certain extent, Sharon has created her own prison. She has translated the death of her husband into the death of her sexual desires. She feels unfaithful to him because she is attracted to another man; the fact that her husband is dead means nothing, for she is "permanently" married to him—and he is "permanently" dead.

The questions asked about Sharon vary in intensity from "*How does it feel to lie awake all night?*" to "*What does a woman feel while a man makes love to her?*" At times the female answers are completely disjointed from the male questions. For example, in answer to the second question above, one reads, "Barefoot, she is standing at the door" or "She walked quickly home, threading her way around people." All but one of the questions are asked more than once—at times with serial insistence, at other times intermittently, as if the questioner is returning to a topic with renewed hope. The very disjunction between question and answer seems to be the central theme of the story: The connection between men and women is one of repeated misunderstanding.

Oates does not make it easy for the reader to understand or to sympathize with Sharon, this widow perpetually at the edge of a breakdown. The questions asked from outside remain unanswered. Readers start to ask their own questions: How can an incident as ordinary as a conversation in a grocery store represent such anguish for this woman? What has she become? As terrifying as the stranger is to her, the real terror is Sharon's own sexuality.

In one of the answers to the question concerning a woman's feelings during love-making, one reads what seems to be an authentic response: "A violent penetration to the heart: up in the chest." However, what momentarily seemed to be sexual gratification quickly turns to violence: "A sense of suffocation. Strangulation . . . with her mind broken up into pieces of white, terrified glass." Sex is death for Sharon.

Thus, the final paragraphs represent the ultimate invasion of privacy. Until the conclusion, the questions might have come from anyone, anywhere, outside this distracted personality. As the story ends, however, Oates explicitly identifies the questioner with the stranger whom Sharon has encountered. He asks: "Are you in there?" The response is: "He said that. He said something—she did not hear it exactly." Although on the surface the question has to do with whether Sharon is behind the door, the question resounds with meaning. The stranger, embodying sex, death, and experience, knocks at the door of a self-made prisoner; he comes to confront this vulnerable woman, wondering what is "inside." His next question is simply formed by her name: "Sharon?" Her name is "like a stab deep in her belly." Once again she conflates sexuality with violent self-destruction.

The ending provides the reader with no easy resolution. As Sharon opens the door to experience, the reader knows only that "everything comes open, comes apart." Is she destroyed by this invasion of experience? What could she lose? Is she saved by this potential assault? What could she gain? Oates's story is strategically open-ended.

*Style and Technique*

"What Is the Connection Between Men and Women?" maintains a double vision; one of its major experiments is in point of view. The questions are asked directly; the answers are indirect, third-person narration. However, the paradox is that the questions of a skeptical exterior confront the answers of a sympathetic interior. Sharon does not speak for herself—the reader knows her through a mediating narrator who keeps her in steady focus. The implication is that she cannot speak for herself.

Repetition is forcefully used to convey meaning. For example, Sharon's neurotic obsession with a dead husband emerges from the repetitions within the following passage: "She is married permanently to that man. Married. Married permanently. She is in love with that man yet, a dead man. Married, In love. When she sleeps, she sleeps with him; his body is next to her, in sleep." Later in the story, these repetitions reemerge: "She was still married. She was married permanently."

The repetition comes from outside as well; the questioner repeats himself almost maniacally. The question asked only once is: "Are you in there?" He has only thirteen questions in his repertory, yet he speaks twenty-seven times.

Repetition on each side of the double vision is a stylistic response to the title question: The connection between men and women, between experience and fear, between the outside and the tormented interior, is tenuous.

*Mark Sandona*

# WHAT WE TALK ABOUT
# WHEN WE TALK ABOUT LOVE

*Author:* Raymond Carver (1938-1988)
*Type of plot:* Domestic realism
*Time of plot:* The 1970's
*Locale:* Albuquerque, New Mexico
*First published:* 1981

*Principal characters:*
MEL MCGINNIS, a cardiologist
TERRY, his wife
NICK, the narrator
LAURA, Nick's wife

*The Story*

Nick, who is Mel's close friend, recounts a conversation that the two men and their wives had over gin and tonics in Mel and Terry's kitchen. The remembered dialogue is dominated by Mel, who is determined to articulate a definition of real love. Nick occasionally departs from recounting the conversation to remark briefly on the room, or on the progress of their drunkenness, or to give background information about himself or whoever is speaking. The story begins with Nick's suggestion that because Mel was a cardiologist, that sometimes "gave him the right."

Nick says, as background information, that Mel spent time in a seminary before going to medical school. Mel thinks that real love is nothing less than spiritual love. Terry recalls Ed, the man with whom she lived before she lived with Mel. Ed, she says, loved her so much he tried to kill her. She describes his brutal treatment of her, and she wonders what can be done about love like that.

Mel disagrees strongly with Terry's contention that Ed's feelings for her were love. As they argue about it, Mel accuses Terry of being a romantic. Nick and Laura are reluctant to judge, but when Terry says that when she left Ed, he drank rat poison, Laura is shocked. Mel tells them that Ed is dead and begins another story about Ed's violence and his death, to which Mel was privy because he was on call in the emergency room. Mel emphasizes how Ed regularly threatened them. Laura in particular wants to know the end of the story of Ed. Terry and Mel disagree about whether it was right or not for Terry to sit with Ed when he died grotesquely as a cumulative result of his suicide attempts.

When Nick and Laura make physically romantic gestures toward each other, Terry cynically teases them, saying that only because they have been together for the short time of a year and a half do they still feel romantic. They break the tension by refilling their glasses and toasting to love.

At this stage in their drunkenness, Nick describes the yard outside as an enchanted place. Mel continues, wondering what anyone really knows about love, talking about how fleeting "carnal, sentimental" love is. Mel maintains that if any one of them died, that person's partner would go off and find someone new. Mel is also bewildered at how he could once have loved his first wife and now so thoroughly hate her. Terry worries that he is getting drunk. The situation becomes tense for a moment, and Laura dissipates the tension by claiming they all love him. Mel does not seem to recognize her as the wife of his friend, but he says that he loves her too.

Getting increasingly drunk, Mel tries to illustrate the concept of real love by telling a gory story about a car accident in which a couple in their mid-seventies is critically injured. Terry interrupts him again, then tells him that she loves him, and he says that he loves her, something they repeat throughout the story as they disagree or ridicule each other. Mel goes off on tangents about wearing seat belts, finishing the gin, and wishing to be a knight. He confuses "vassals" with "vessels." His language and manner get more belligerent and careless. He is temporarily quieted by Nick's observation that sometimes knights suffocated in their armor. Laura asks Mel to finish his story about the old couple. Terry gets sarcastic about Mel's behavior and they exchange words. The room grows darker as the sun sets.

When Laura again asks Mel what happened, he makes a drunken pass at her, saying if they were not all in their present situation, he would carry her off. Terry tells him to finish his story so they can go to dinner. The story ends like a bad joke, bringing drunken despair for Mel, who still cannot explain what he is saying. He is depressed and wants to call his children. Terry talks about Mel's hated former wife, Marjorie, and reminds him that she might answer the phone. It is clear Terry also hates Marjorie, and Mel fantasizes that he would like to go to her house in a beekeeper's suit and release a swarm of bees, to which she is allergic. He would, he muses, only do this if the children were not home. He also wishes that she would get married again.

Mel is too drunk to do anything. In fact, everyone is too drunk to rise and go to eat, although Laura says she is hungry. Mel turns his glass over and spills his drink on the table. They all sit in the dark, listening to their hearts beat.

*Themes and Meanings*

Raymond Carver's story bears many calculated, ironic resemblances to Plato's *Symposion* (388-368 B.C.E.; *Symposium*, 1701), a dialogue meant to showcase Socrates' views on love. Carver uses the same frame that Plato does, that of a friend recounting a story. Carver, however, twists this frame, which is meant to give added validity to the opinions expressed in *Symposium*, to suit his own more ironic purposes. Among these is that trying to understand the nature of love through talk is at best a tale twice removed from its own point. In *Symposium*, Socrates walks away from a table of drunken, sleeping men whom he has bested with his wisdom, but in Carver's story a drunken Mel pours his gin out on the table, then sits in silence and darkness. Mel, an ironic Socrates, has bested no one and has not successfully defended his ideas about love. No one, least of all Mel, is able to walk away after the discussion is over.

They are all too drunk. Mel is unable to arrive at any statement wiser than "gin's gone."

One of Carver's themes is that talking about love does not bring people any closer to understanding the experience of love. This idea is complemented by the ironic implication that talking about love seemingly inevitably involves telling stories of lovers' entanglements or situations filled with gruesome extremes. Carver cleverly dramatizes a philosophical point made by Socrates in the middle of *Symposium*: that because love seeks absolute goodness and beauty, love must therefore be the state of lacking these qualities. The characters in Carver's story are examples of this lack. They seek but do not find absolute goodness and beauty. In contrast to the *Symposium*, Carver emphasizes the carnal, physical nature of love as intrinsic to its power. Carver implies that love almost never manifests itself apart from the tortures it brings.

*Style and Technique*

Carver's strong reliance on dialogue gives readers a sense of immediacy. This immediacy is as deceptive and illusory as the definition of love is for the characters. The story, after all, comes to the reader secondhand; moreover, the story is modeled on a fiction that concerns itself with the truth. The emotional escalation of a conversation, masterfully rendered, emphasizes the urgency of the human needs to love and be loved. The conversation shows that conversation is the medium through which love continually eludes those who would capture it and define it.

Many critics refer to Carver's writing style as "minimalist." He did not particularly like the term, given its connotations of smallness and inadequacy. Whether or not one assigns such a label or quibbles about how it should be defined, there is no question that each character is drawn sparingly, although with the essential details. For example, although Mel's drunken torpidity increases as the story develops, readers are also aware that Mel is a surgeon, and that "when he was sober, his gestures, all his movements, were precise, very careful." This observation is essential to establishing the significance of Mel's behavior during the conversation about love. A favorable definition of minimalist writing is that in it there is nothing extraneous—such a definition applies to Carver's stories.

*Maria Theresa Maggi*

# WHAT YOU HEAR FROM 'EM?

*Author:* Peter Taylor (1917-1994)
*Type of plot:* Social realism
*Time of plot:* The early 1920's
*Locale:* Thornton, a small town in Tennessee
*First published:* 1951

>*Principal characters:*
>AUNT MUNSIE, an African American woman who was the nanny
>   for the Tolliver children
>THAD and
>WILL, her two favorites of the Tolliver children
>MISS LUCILLE SATTERFIELD, a white woman who understands
>   her

*The Story*

Aunt Munsie is the town character, an old black woman who makes her way daily through the streets of town pulling a small wagon in which she collects slop to feed her pigs. Sometimes she stops traffic when she enters the square. She walks in the middle of the street, and most townspeople, when driving in town, simply call out to her until she moves out of the way. Only newcomers to town and ill-mannered high-school boys ever toot their horns at her.

As she makes her daily rounds, stopping at the houses of white women who hand her packages of garbage scraps for her slop wagon, she often calls out, "What you hear from 'em?" Her question is misunderstood by people who do not know her. Some even think she is an old beggar woman who calls out, "What you have for Mom?" Aunt Munsie knows these people laugh at her behind her back, but that does not bother her. She considers them ignorant people of "has-been quality."

The white patrons who know Aunt Munsie understand that her question is related to her history with the Tollivers, a prominent family in town. They know that she single-handedly raised the Tolliver children after their mother died. She wonders when Will and Thad, her favorites among the children, plan to return from Memphis and Nashville, where they have successful careers, and take up residence in Thornton, their hometown.

Thad and Will have made unannounced visits to Aunt Munsie's house separately over the previous ten years. During their brief visits, their children would go through her house into the backyard to see the pigs and chickens. Aunt Munsie would hug the children and fuss over them and soon be asking Thad or Will when they were coming back. They always told her that someday they would leave their businesses, buy property on the edge of town, and move back to Thornton.

Miss Lucille Satterfield, the widow of Judge Satterfield, understands Aunt Munsie's maternal feelings for the Tolliver children, and she shares any news of them when she can. At the same time, Miss Lucille and some of her neighbors are concerned that Aunt Munsie, who is thought to be nearly deaf and blind, may be struck by an errant automobile on her daily rounds. Her refusal to stop pulling her old wagon around town leads the Tollivers and others in town to come up with a plan to stop her daily activities on the streets of Thornton. The Tollivers consult with the mayor and discover that Aunt Munsie is one of only three people in town who own pigs. The Tollivers buy the pigs from the other two owners, and then the town passes an ordinance forbidding the ownership of pigs in the town limits.

When Aunt Munsie's daughter Crecie tells her about this new ordinance, Aunt Munsie sells her pigs to a neighbor who lives just outside the town limits. She never talks about the conspiracy to anyone. She lives another twenty years, outliving Crecie by many years. She begins to act like other old black women in town. Her character and manners become less harsh and offensive. She often reminisces with Thad and Will, who still visit her, but never again asks them when they are coming back.

*Themes and Meanings*

Aunt Munsie's story is in many respects a tragedy involving her loss of a clearly defined role and her loss of status as an African American in a southern culture dominated by prominent white families. The high point of her life was the years that she spent raising the Tolliver children after Mrs. Tolliver died. Although she was an illiterate old woman, she persevered and raised the children with affection and discipline. She was proud of them, particularly Thad and Will, who became successful professional men in Memphis and Nashville. She was more than their nanny; she felt that she was almost a mother to them.

Because of her bond with the Tollivers, she thinks that she has achieved an elevated status in the town. She believes she has the right to ask about Thad's and Will's welfare and their future plans. Her constant refrain, "What you hear from 'em?" is meant to remind people of that bond. Until she is forced to get rid of her pigs, she is in charge of her destiny and has a place in the social geography of the town.

Long after Thad and Will left Thornton, Aunt Munsie harbored the hope that they would return for good. Their return would signify a recognition that her role as surrogate mother is vital and meaningful to them. Their return would mean that they respect and honor her, and still need her maternal care. When she learns that the Tolliver men have conspired to take away her pigs, she is grief-stricken. Realizing they never had any intention of returning to Thornton for good, she feels betrayed. She learns that she has no role in their lives beyond that of a nanny. She is no different to them from the other old black women on the square in Thornton who spend their days spinning yarns and "talking old-nigger foolishness." Before their betrayal, Aunt Munsie is a woman living in the present, a force to reckon with. Now she is broken by events and becomes a docile, obedient old black woman, an "Aunt Jemima" figure, wearing a bandanna around her head, a nonthreatening image of a harmless old woman who reminisces about the good old days.

The author suggests that Aunt Munsie is living an illusion in thinking that the Tolliver men will return to Thornton. In effect, she refuses to accept the social and economic realities of her life and invents a fantasy life regarding her role in the Tolliver family. When she faces the fact that Thad and Will are not coming home, she rejoins her social and ethnic group and functions in the real world for the last twenty years of her life. The narrator seems to imply that colorful town characters such as Aunt Munsie are cast aside by the forces of progress and social conformity.

*Style and Technique*

The narrator tells this story some thirty years after the events described. There is a bittersweet irony in his tone of voice. Apparently he represents the point of view of the townspeople of Thornton. His story is based on the strands provided by the various storytellers with access to the facts of the case. Although the narrator is sympathetic toward Aunt Munsie, he recognizes that her vision of the future was illusory and self-defeating.

The little wagon that Aunt Munsie pulls through the town functions as a symbolic object. It is shaped like a coffin, and the author writes that she pulls the tongue of the wagon as if it "were the arm of some very stubborn, overgrown white child she had to nurse in her old age." The wagon represents the death of her dream to reclaim her vital maternal role. It is like a burden she drags through town to remind people of who she was and what she has lost. She would give anything to take care of Thad and Will if they returned to Thornton, but that role has been lost, and at the end of the story Aunt Munsie is forced to give up her dream.

*Robert E. Yahnke*

# WHEN I WAS THIRTEEN

*Author:* Denton Welch (1915-1948)
*Type of plot:* Domestic realism
*Time of plot:* Probably 1928
*Locale:* A Swiss Alpine village
*First published:* 1948

> *Principal characters:*
> THE NARRATOR
> ARCHER, a university student
> THE NARRATOR'S BROTHER

## The Story

The narrator recalls that, when he was thirteen, he went on a skiing trip to Switzerland with an older brother, spent an enjoyable day skiing with an older youth, and, for no reason he could understand, was accused of scandalous behavior of a kind unfamiliar to him. Staying at the same lodge as the narrator and his brother, a student at Oxford University, is Archer, also a student at Oxford. The brother does not like Archer. The narrator, however, is very impressed by Archer's physique and bearing when, for example, he sees him skiing bare-chested in a cavalier, robust fashion.

He is of the impression that Archer takes little interest in him until the two meet on a sun terrace, where the narrator has gone to read a book, drink hot chocolate, and eat "delicious rhumbabas and little tarts filled with worm-castles of chestnut puree topped with caps of whipped cream." That afternoon tea illustrates the sensibility of the narrator—although he is only thirteen, he is a devotee of the luxurious.

The book the young man is reading is one by Leo Tolstoy. He is puzzled by Tolstoy's description of one of the characters as an illegitimate child. After Archer initiates conversation, the younger youth ventures to ask what the term means, but in his profound innocence he cannot believe the explanation that Archer gives him—that an illegitimate child is one born out of wedlock. The books Archer says he likes to read indicate that he is rather more worldly than the young narrator. One, he says, was entitled *Flaming Sex*; it "was by a French woman who married an English knight and then went back to France to shoot a French doctor." He calls such a book a "real life" story, but it, like others he describes, appears worldly to the point of being slightly sordid and risque.

Archer is, then, similar to the narrator in that both gravitate toward the hedonistic. He invites his new young friend to ski with him the next day. The next morning, the narrator's infatuation with Archer is apparent; he recalls that when Archer slung their skis across his shoulders, "he looked like a very tough Jesus carrying two crosses." During the outing, Archer provides for his less robust companion with food and physical support. He also initiates him into some common luxuries of adulthood: hot black coffee, a glass of sweetened rum, and cheap Swiss cigarettes. The younger boy takes readily to the role of the initiate; when Archer hands him pieces of a tangerine on his outstretched palm, he has to restrain himself from licking them up as a horse would do. While skiing, Archer urges the young narrator to unusual boldness; when the narrator falls, Archer "hauled me out of the snow and stood me on my feet, beating me all over to get off the snow."

That paternal but curious physical intimacy continues after the two return to Archer's rooms, which are in an annex some distance from the chalet, and take baths, scrubbing each other's backs. The younger youth massages Archer's legs, which are cramped after the day's skiing. The narrator apprehends no threat from the older youth, and it transpires that he need fear none. It is clear, however, that his infatuation with Archer makes him willing to try anything that Archer recommends. The element of physical attraction that has been developed gradually and unobtrusively by Denton Welch has blossomed. The narrator remarks, for example, that Archer's "thigh, swelling out, amazed me."

The meal the two youths then eat in a restaurant is, like everything else they have eaten, almost decadently luxurious. By the end of it, the younger youth has drunk a mixture of lemonade, lager, and creme de menthe and is tipsy. After he and Archer have returned to Archer's room—Archer sings "Silent Night" in German along the way—he is quite drunk and falls asleep, grateful that Archer has thoughtfully taken off his shoes, undone his tie, and loosened the braces holding up his pants.

The next morning, the two go to the chalet for breakfast. They meet the narrator's brother, who has unexpectedly returned early from his own extended skiing expedition. Archer clearly is aware that the older brother will have cause to suspect that inappropriate activities have taken place and tries to provide an explanation for his and his friend's arrival at the chalet so early in the morning. The older brother swallows neither his nor the narrator's explanation. After the narrator returns to his room with his brother, he vomits as a result of what he had drunk the night before. His older brother beats him with a slipper and shouts at him. The narrator, who has been recalling the incidents several years later, remembers that the violent outburst made him think that his brother had gone mad.

### Themes and Meanings

The narrator describes how he became unwittingly infatuated with Archer during the brief time they spent together. He was young, impressionable, and naturally given to infatuation, though he had as yet developed neither a capacity for full-blown sexual passions nor even an understanding of the kinds of friendship that exist between members of the same sex. He had, however, developed an appetite for worldly, sensual pleasures—one unusually keen in so young a youth, and of a kind that apparently struck Archer as indicative of a proclivity for homosexual love.

The motivations of Archer, however, are not clear. Nothing he does with the boy is clearly improper, but it is clear that he is homosexual, motivated by a paternalistic sentimentality, and manipulative of the young narrator.

This story, like virtually all of Welch's writing, is evidently largely autobiographical reminiscence. Interestingly, Welch, as a narrator with a clearer, more mature notion of what transpires between Archer and himself, appears to relish the experience and does not suggest that it was in any way injurious. He does not impute questionable motivations to Archer; in fact, he paints him as benevolent and caring, and he depicts his experiences with Archer as wholly enjoyable, at least up to the point at which he vomits and is beaten by his older brother.

As the reader sees the friendship between Archer and the young man gradually develop, the natural tendency may be to question its propriety. Welch handles this aspect of his story carefully. The narrator at age thirteen is not totally ingenuous. At dinner after the skiing expedition, he is aware that Archer is encouraging him to do things he ordinarily should not be doing. Archer offers him a cigar, and "I had the sense to realize that he did not mean me to take one and smoke it there before the eyes of all the hotel." However, the young man's awareness is limited. When he massages Archer's leg, for example, he is impressed by its physicality but does not realize that what impresses him are its sensual qualities, its firmness and sponginess.

Here the young man is ingenuous, and his innocence, along with the way Welch manipulates the action to resemble at many points a sexual encounter, makes the reader expectant of a breaching by Archer of that innocence. It could be said that Welch is almost titillating the reader. From another perspective, however, it can be said that Welch is presenting a tale of first love—one in which boy meets boy, rather than girl.

*Style and Technique*

The central technique of the story is the narrative stance adopted by Welch. His narrator is telling a story about himself and understands the significance of the events about which he is writing, but his description makes it clear that he did not understand their significance at the time they occurred. By treating the encounter as a pleasant day of eating fine foods and skiing, Welch also suggests that in one sense it was simply that.

It is important to note that it is Welch, or his narrator, who places the narrator's experiences in a positive and idealized light. To do this, he has to provide many details that would most probably not have occurred to the narrator at age thirteen. When, for example, he refers to Archer, who is carrying two pairs of skis, as "a very tough Jesus," it is surely the adult narrator, or Welch, recalling the incidents of several years earlier, who supplies this interpretation, not the thirteen-year-old who was too naïve to know what sort of friendship Archer fancied.

The character of the precocious thirteen-year-old boy is an unusual one. The degree to which his appetite for finery is developed is almost too great to credit. More subtly drawn is his surprising independence. For example, he never refers to the older brother by name, and he never describes him. This nameless facelessness throughout the story makes his actions at the end of the story appear all the more intrusive. This intrusive personality serves Welch's purpose well, for it places in sharper focus the narrator's ultimate innocence; it seems that Welch considers it almost a failing in the suspicious, unspontaneous brother that he is morally upright.

*Peter Monaghan*

# WHEN THE LIGHT GETS GREEN

*Author:* Robert Penn Warren (1905-1989)
*Type of plot:* Regional
*Time of plot:* About 1914
*Locale:* A farm in the South
*First published:* 1936

### Principal characters:

THE UNNAMED NARRATOR, Mr. Barden's grandson
MR. BARDEN, a veteran of the Civil War
AUNT LUCY, Mr. Barden's daughter
UNCLE KIRBY, Aunt Lucy's husband

*The Story*

The first-person narrator of this story—a young boy when its events take place—remembers his grandfather from an unspecified time after 1918 and the old man's death. The memories (his own and his grandfather's, both imperfectly understood) lend depth to the tale and at the same time determine its loose-jointedness.

The story begins appropriately with a recurrent but inaccurate memory—"My grandfather had a long white beard"—and the shock the boy used to feel when he came home from school and watched his grandfather trimming his beard before the mirror: "It is gray and pointed, I would say then, remembering what I had thought before." As memories will, the boy's memories combine to create an ideal morning home for the summer from school, but even in the familiar routine of beard-trimming, ceremonious dressing (black vest, gold watch and chain, corncob pipe), and breakfast—always the same—the boy finds himself reminded of his grandfather's mortality; significantly, this is contrasted with his having been a soldier, "like General Robert E. Lee": He recalls noticing how "shrunken" his grandfather's "hips and backsides" were and the way his own stomach tightened at the sight, "like when you walk behind a woman and see the high heel of her shoe is worn and twisted and jerks her ankle every time she takes a step."

The domestic comedy of breakfast, related as another never-changing given in the boy's life, reveals a set of tensions and obstinacies not consciously understood by the boy. The laborious explanation of why Uncle Kirby called grandfather Mr. Barden indicates a clannishness perhaps not even recognized by the boy and, ironically, suggests that the grandfather is still in charge, though he clearly is not: "It was because my Uncle Kirby was not my real uncle, having married my Aunt Lucy, who lived with my grandfather." The matter of the cob pipe becomes a test of authority between husband and wife and between father and daughter, but Uncle Kirby's grin, "like a dog panting," and Mr. Barden's "Don't it stink" leave the test unresolved.

The story proceeds with three scenes. The first introduces contingency for the first time ("If it had rained right and was a good tobacco-setting season . . . "). The tobacco-setting occasions a detailed and idyllic description of the lot, the cold stream that runs through it, the rise with its sassafras and blackberries, the fields, and the setting itself, but here, as in what went before, the idyll is undercut by the grandfather's mortality and by displays of ineffectual authority. The boy notes that his grandfather rides "pretty straight for an old man" and sees "the big straw hat he wore waggle a little above his narrow neck." Later, at the field, Uncle Kirby's "Get the lead out" only brings grins to the faces of the "little niggers," and Mr. Barden's "Why don't you start 'em, sir?" has no effect at all; the work apparently begins despite, not because of, these two men, and "about ten o'clock" Mr. Barden "would leave and go home."

As in the scene that follows, the narrator's memories of his own experience of his grandfather lead into memories of Mr. Barden's more distant past. As a young man, Mr. Barden raised and showed horses, but now (because "horses were foolishness") tobacco has become his single care. Once he tried to be a tobacco buyer but lost his warehouses and their contents in a fire. The failure is explained as bad luck by the boy and as inevitable by Mr. Barden's daughters; Mr. Barden himself shrugs it off as just as well. Now he watches as the crop is set, suckered, plowed, or wormed, and he worries, "nervous as a cat," when a summer storm threatens.

In the second scene, the narrator describes Mr. Barden's mornings when he does not go to the fields. He sits under a cedar tree, smokes his cob pipe, and, on most days, reads a book. The narrator's account of the history his grandfather reads and the poetry he recites leads into memories of the old man's more distant past by identifying him with Napoleon Bonaparte, Mr. Barden "having been a soldier and fought in the War himself." The boy listens to the history, to the poetry, and to the stories of the Civil War, and he wants to be proud of his grandfather, but he feels shame, thinking that his grandfather never killed any Yankees—his boyish explanation for his grandfather's never having been promoted beyond the rank of captain.

During the afternoons, Mr. Barden would sleep, and that is how the narrator usually remembers him. Alternatively, he says, he remembers him "trampling up and down the porch, nervous as a cat, while a cloud blew up and the trees began to ruffle." This generalized memory quickly narrows to a particular time, in 1914, when "the leaves began to ruffle like they do when the light gets green, and my grandfather said to me, 'Son, it's gonna hail.'" It did hail, and this time Mr. Barden had a stroke. As the narrator sits by the bed in the shadowy room, his grandfather speaks again, "Son, I'm gonna die," and again, "I'm on borrowed time, it's time to die," and finally, "It's time to die. Nobody loves me." The narrator's response, "Grandpa, I love you," is a lie: "I didn't feel anything." However, outside again in the sunny yard, watching a hen peck at a hailstone, wondering whether the tobacco has been damaged, still "not feeling anything," he says it again "out loud, 'Grandpa, I love you.'"

Mr. Barden lives four more years: "I got the letter about my grandfather, who died of flu, but I thought about four years back, and it didn't matter much."

*Themes and Meanings*

Unlike the narrator of Robert Penn Warren's poem "Safe in Shade," who takes from an apparently identical communion with his grandfather a memory of safety and of "Truth—oh, unambiguous," the narrator of "When the Light Gets Green" carries with him a sense of disillusionment and, perhaps unconsciously, offers the reader a powerful argument against the ability of humanity to control its present environment, past, or future.

The remainders of humankind's mortality and of the limits of authority in the early parts of the story suggest how powerless humanity is to control or to keep its present, but the scene under the cedar tree and what follows it focuses this theme and adds the past and future to the story's purview. Mr. Barden's obsession with history has a double significance. On one hand, his subjects are all illustrative of battles won or lost: Flodden Field, where James IV of Scotland was slain on the field, the sack of Constantinople by the Ottoman Turks, Napoleon Bonaparte's ill-fated Russian campaign. On the other hand, Mr. Barden attempts to rewrite his own history and that of the South with hypotheses modeled on his readings, asserting, for example, that "if they had done what Forrest wanted and cleaned the country ahead of the Yankees, like the Russians beat Napoleon, they'd whipped the Yankees sure."

Unlike history, Mr. Barden "never read poetry, he just said what he already knew," and what he already knows emphasizes the ironies of man's pride and his failure to control. The narrator remembers and quotes snippets from two poems by George Gordon, Lord Byron, but he does not finish the stanzas he recalls. The first is from *Don Juan* (1819-1824), Canto III, stanza 86, and though it begins in a celebratory vein, its last lines strike a different note: "Eternal summer gilds them yet,/ But all, except their sun, is set." More disturbing still is the second bit of poetry, from *Childe Harold's Pilgrimage* (1812-1818), Canto IV, stanza 179. The narrator quotes only the stirring first line, "Roll on, thou deep and dark blue ocean, roll," but Byron's stanza continues:

> Ten thousand fleets sweep over thee in vain;
> Man marks the earth with ruin—his control
> Stops with the shore;—upon the watery plain
> The wrecks are all thy deed, nor doth remain
> A shadow of man's ravage, save his own,
> When, for a moment, like a drop of rain,
> He sinks into thy depths with bubbling groan,
> Without a grave, unknell'd, uncoffin'd, and unknown.

As Warren's story moves on from the cedar tree to 1914 and then to 1918—another war, another human failure to control—through love affirmed but nonexistent to Mr. Barden's death, the reader is reminded again of Warren's poem "Safe in Shade" and its finally grim view:

> That all-devouring, funnel-shaped, mad and high-spiraling,
> Dark suction that
> We have, as the Future, named.

*Style and Technique*

The cluster of images attracted to the color in the title of this story creates a peculiarly appropriate ground for the tale of memory told here. Three images are particularly important. The first is the green light of the title, though it is not met again until late in the story. It is, literally, a natural phenomenon anticipating the onset of a hailstorm, but framed as it is by the other two images, it becomes a fitting portent of Mr. Barden's death. The second image is the mirror that opens the story and is reintroduced after the hailstorm: "the wavy green mirror, which in his always shadowy room reflected things like deep water riffled by a little wind." Later, as the narrator waits in his grandfather's room after the old man's stroke, he notices again "the mirror, which was green and wavy like water." This green mirror becomes an emblem of Mr. Barden's life with its depths of unhelpful, even inaccurate, memory, and its likeness to water lends it further depth—the depth of the frightening and watery world of the unconscious.

The third image is the narrator's rather than his grandfather's, the green of the cedar boughs where he listens to poetry and stories of the Civil War: "I lay on my back on the ground . . . and looked upside down into the cedar tree where the limbs were tangled and black-green like big hairy fern fronds with the blue sky all around, while he said some poetry." Again, his grandfather had told "how the dead men looked in the river bottoms in winter, and I lay on my back on the grass, looking up in the thick cedar limbs, and thought how it was to be dead." In this third image, the grandfather's long look downward into the wastes of memory becomes his grandson's upward and not yet frightened gaze into what any human being can expect of the future: at best something tangled and at last something dead.

*Jonathan A. Glenn*

# WHEN WE WERE WOLVES

*Author:* Jon Billman (1968-    )
*Type of plot:* Social realism, regional
*Time of plot:* The 1950's
*Locale:* High plains of Wyoming
*First published:* 1996

*Principal characters:*

PASTOR LIVERANCE, the chaplain of the Wyoming state prison
WARDEN GORDON, a warden of the Wyoming state prison
THE CZECH, a 500-pound goliath hockey player for the Cheyenne
    Buffalos
RICH BELECKI, an embezzler and forward on the Wolves hockey
    team

*The Story*

"When We Were Wolves" opens in a Wyoming state prison with the narrator reminiscing about convict life in 1949 and how inmates were forced to wear the Oregon boot, a heavy iron device designed to discourage their escape. This device is turned into a training tool by him and the other men who play on the prison hockey team, the Wolves. To condition themselves for the game, they wear the boot and also don ice skates when walking and running across the exercise yard. They learn to think and act as a team and adopt a pragmatic version of Christianity in the hope of improving their lot in prison, gaining privileges, and perhaps winning quicker release. The Wolves adopt brotherly love out of necessity to avoid fighting among themselves, which is punished by solitary confinement in "the hole," and so that they can play hockey in the Oil League. They are in pursuit of the Oil Cup, awarded to the best team in the Rocky Mountain Oil League, while Pastor Liverance, their prison chaplain, a former Canadian hockey player, team coach, and a man possessed, is in pursuit of the Holy Grail. By playing hockey, the Wolves believe that they are on their way to improving their lot as prisoners. Pastor Liverance becomes so convinced of the merits of prison hockey that he begins to write a book on the subject.

The context is the oil boom of the 1950's when Wyoming created oil barons, some of whom supported city hockey teams and leagues, providing uniforms, coaches, and salaries. The Wolves, however, depend on the prison garment shop to make their uniforms out of canvas in the color of "atomic orange," picked by Warden Gordon. Few of the team members know much about hockey, but they work hard to get in condition and practice hard to execute the fundamentals, only to be defeated by every team they face. Pastor Liverance provides spiritual guidance to team members, teaching them the Bible, including stories about Cain, David, and Goliath. As a result, they become men, a team committed to one another as well as a means by which league team owners profit by scheduling their hockey teams to play against the convict team.

The Wolves play their final game with the Cheyenne Buffalos, a team that Pastor Liverance wants very much to defeat and that has "the Czech," an unstoppable player of mythic proportions, nine feet tall on skates and weighing five hundred pounds. The Wolves are badly beaten by the Buffalos, but when the Czech brutally body checks and kills Rich Belecki, an embezzler and the Wolves' best skater, Pastor Liverance leads the Wolves onto the ice, where as a pack, a team, they bring down and kill the giant. The governor then sees to it that the team—including Pastor Liverance—are "buried" in the prison system. That is where the narrator, now nearing seventy, and Liverance reminisce about the Wolves and how they became men.

*Themes and Meanings*

"When We Were Wolves" asks whether men convicted of every crime from murder to embezzlement can create hope and meaning for their lives even in prison. Jon Billman does not give a simple or sentimental answer to the question. Instead, he builds on Christian parables and sports clichés to develop themes of sacrifice, cooperation, and compassion in this complex allegory for the human condition, a "prison" from which death is the only escape. However, the hope of "deliverance"—from evil, pain and suffering, and death—is offered through action and faith. Here action is the ritual combat codified and afforded by hockey. By playing hockey, the group of prisoners becomes first a gang, then a team, and finally apostles, a progression over three distinct sorts of brotherhood and community. The Wolves progress from being animals to becoming men by developing a willingness to sacrifice themselves individually for the good of the larger group. Faith is brought to the men by Pastor Liverance who promises "better time" (prison argot for ways of serving one's sentence with a degree of safety and comfort and, perhaps, relief from boredom) to those men who will play for a penitentiary hockey team.

If crime violates the social order by breaking the bonds of community and brotherhood, then acts that restore or create such bonds may be useful in restoring the convict, one convicted of a crime, to the community and harmony with it. The Wolves are promised that by skating for Jesus, they may be born again. Indeed, they do learn in Purgatory, the home of the (fictional) state prison, how to work together as a collective social unit, to love and sacrifice for one another, and to act and think as a team, as apostles. Pastor Liverance, their chaplain, is an ironic Christ figure, flawed by his ambition; nevertheless, he offers his own life and sacrifices his own freedom to lead the charge of retribution against the Czech giant, the Goliath of the Cheyenne Buffalos, who has killed Belecki, perhaps the only "innocent" on the Wolves team. Pastor Liverance thus joins his team to do "hard time" in prison. The ironies, of course, are many, not the least of which is the violent nature of ice hockey, especially in the Oil League, in the context of the violent and venal nature of the larger community in which it is played. Billman is a wry and severe critic of his culture, as is clear from the name of the Wyoming State Penitentiary Christian Wolves. Because wolves are, in the context of the story, extinct in the lower forty-eight states, their fate is foretold in their name; there is, ultimately, no escape from mortality.

*Style and Technique*

The story is told from a retrospective first-person point of view by the unnamed narrator, who writes with the authority of one of the convict members of the Wolves. Billman couples convincing knowledge of the historical facts about Wyoming's various oil and uranium booms with stories about prison hockey. Billman seems familiar with the efforts in the 1950's of Leonard "Oakie" Brumm, who, as the athletic director for the state prison at Marquette, Michigan, once arranged for his team of hard-core convicts to play hockey against the Detroit Redwings—instead of rioting. The result of Billman's research and powers of observation is a realistic yet mythically compelling and insightful narrative about the human condition, rendered in a crisp and colloquial style that moves subtly into allegory. Billman weaves together elements of Christian myth and legend with such gritty details of prison life in Wyoming as the Oregon boot. Billman provides rich additional details about Wyoming small-town life and the hockey played in cigar-smoke-filled arenas by teams that are owned and sponsored by sleazy newly rich oil barons before audiences who shower opposing teams with beer, cigarettes, and mustard.

Billman's style is clear, colloquial, concrete, and rendered in a voice at once laconic and stoic. The narrator is never named, his "outside" identity submerged completely in his role as spokesperson. The story thus takes on the quality of folk legend, anonymous yet profound. The narrator is the voice for his gang, his pack. As one of the apostles, his function is to set down this "epistle" to the world, this story of a group of men led by their redeemer not to a life of fame and fortune but to a life of sacrifice and insight and powerful bonding. Religious allegory is often risky business for a writer, but Billman succeeds because he gets the details of prison life and small-town hockey right. He is totally in control of the tone, set by the low, even voice of his narrator who was there and lived to testify to the truth of the events. Billman signals his deepest thematic intentions clearly in the first sentence of the second paragraph, which articulates the progression of gang-to-team-to-apostles.

*Theodore C. Humphrey*

# WHERE ARE YOU GOING, WHERE HAVE YOU BEEN?

*Author:* Joyce Carol Oates (1938-    )
*Type of plot:* Allegory
*Time of plot:* A summer Sunday during the 1950's
*Locale:* A suburban community in the United States
*First published:* 1966

> *Principal characters:*
> CONNIE, the fifteen-year-old protagonist
> ARNOLD FRIEND, her demon-lover

*The Story*

The world in which Connie lives is dominated by Hollywood, popular music, shop-ping plazas, and fast-food stands. For Connie and her friends, evenings spent with a boy, eating hamburgers, drinking Cokes, and making out in a dark alley seem like heaven, filled with promises of love sweet and gentle, "the way it was in the movies." Clearly, Connie's parents do not understand the significance of her adolescent day-dreams and activities. Her mother constantly nags at her for spending too much time in front of a mirror and for not being as steady and reliable as her twenty-four-year-old, unmarried sister. Her father appears as uninvolved in her life as the other fathers who drop off their daughters and friends at the local hangout never question their eve-ning's activities when they pick them up.

One hot summer Sunday, Connie chooses to remain at home alone while her par-ents and sister go to a barbecue at an aunt's house. Suddenly "an open jalopy, painted a bright gold" comes up the driveway. Her heart pounding, Connie hangs on to the kitchen door as she banters with the two boys in the jalopy, who invite her for a ride. The driver, Arnold Friend, saw her at the drive-in the night before and had "wagged a finger and laughed," saying "Gonna get you, baby" in response to Connie's smirk. At first, Connie is tempted by his invitation; she "liked the way he was dressed, which was the way all of them dressed: tight faded jeans stuffed into black scuffed boots, a belt that pulled his waist in and showed how lean he was." His clothes, his talk, and the music blaring from his radio are all familiar to her. Then she begins to notice that he seems much older than her friends and that he knows too much about her, even where her parents are and how long they will be away from home.

As the story proceeds, Arnold moves closer to the porch but promises not to come in the house after Connie. Apparently, he wants her to join him of her own free will. His tone becomes more menacing, nevertheless, even as he promises to love her: "This is how it is, honey: you come out and we'll drive away, have a nice ride. But if you don't come out we're gonna wait till your people come home and they're all going to get it." With this threat to her family, Connie begins to lose control; sick with fear, she calls for her mother and starts to pick up the phone, then puts it back on Arnold's command. "That's a good girl. Now you come outside," he continues, and she slowly pushes the door open, "moving out into the sunlight where Arnold Friend waited."

## Themes and Meanings

On a literal level, "Where Are You Going, Where Have You Been?" is a spine-chilling tale of rape and murder with a plot carefully controlled to create suspense. On a figurative level, it is an allegory of lost innocence, the screen door symbolizing the fragile threshold between childhood dreams and adult experience, between romantic illusions of love and the brutal reality of adult sexuality. Connie's "friend" turns out to be a "fiend"; her vague dream-lover arrives masked in the familiar trappings of her world, only to reveal the face of lust and violence beneath the false facade.

On a still deeper symbolic level, Connie's experience itself becomes a metaphor for American naïveté and vulnerability. In this story, as in much of her fiction, Oates explores the moral poverty of American popular culture and the ways in which it leaves her characters defenseless against powerful forces of evil. For Connie, "the bright-lit, fly-infested restaurant" is a "sacred building" and the omnipresent music is like a "church service" always in the background, something on which she can depend. As if to parody Christian symbolism, Oates describes the "grinning boy," holding a hamburger aloft, which caps the bottle-shaped restaurant. It is here that Connie finds the "haven and blessing" otherwise missing in her life. Oates shows her readers how teenagers have created a strict code of dress, behavior, and language to fill the void left by the absence of conventional religion and adult authority. The inauthenticity of such a code is revealed by Arnold's ability to ape it so easily; its impotence, by Connie's absolute inability to defend herself against his attack.

In this story, Oates pays special attention to the mother-daughter relationship and the lack of meaningful communication between them. Their bickering, as described by Oates, is itself an empty ritual: "Sometimes, over coffee, they were almost friends, but something would come up—some vexation that was like a fly buzzing suddenly around their heads—and their faces went hard with contempt." In the end, it is her mother for whom Connie cries; her last thought before she finally pushes open the door is that she will never see her mother again. As she crosses over into the "vast unknown," Connie shuts the door on childhood. Oates seems to suggest that if either one of them had made the effort to communicate, Connie might have remained safely a child until old enough to choose the future. Ironically, it is Arnold Friend who promises to teach Connie about "love," typically the mother's role, while threatening to kill the entire family if she does not permit him to do so.

## Style and Technique

Oates's masterful mixing of literal and figurative, psychological and allegorical levels makes "Where Are You Going, Where Have You Been?" a powerful and fascinating story. This mix is particularly evident in her depiction of both Connie's and Arnold's double identities. Connie carefully pulls her sweater down tight when she leaves home: "Everything about her had two sides to it, one for home and one for anywhere that was not home." Arnold stuffs his boots in order to appear taller and more attractive or perhaps to hide the cloven feet of his satanic self. In Connie's action, the reader recognizes the adolescent beginning to break away from her family and to test the powers of her emerging sexuality. In Arnold's, the reader sees the devil's traditional role as archdeceiver and seducer. On a still deeper psychological level, Arnold Friend is the subconscious nightmare version of Connie's waking desires and dreams, erotic love as her sister June might suppose it, not "sweet and gentle" as promised in Bobby King's songs. Allegorically viewed, Friend brings the vehicle that will lead Connie to the "vast sunlit reaches" of the future, a metaphor that expresses the vagueness of her dreams while also representing an unknown—attractive, perilous, and as inevitable as death.

Though the story is heavy with thematic significance and symbolism, it also reads quickly because of Oates's skill in building suspense. Each stage of Arnold Friend's unmasking and Connie's resulting terror and growing hysteria is carefully delineated. When Arnold first arrives, Connie cannot decide "if she liked him or if he was just a jerk." The reader becomes more suspicious than she does as she notices his muscular neck and arms, his "nose long and hawk-like, sniffing as if she were a treat he was going to gobble up and it was all a joke." Gradually, Connie realizes that all the characteristics she "recognizes" in him—dress, gestures, the "singsong way he talked"—do not come together the way they should. Her heart begins to pound faster when she questions his age and notices that his companion has the face of a forty-year-old baby. Worse yet, Arnold seems to possess preternatural vision to the point of describing all the guests at the family barbecue, what they are doing, how they are dressed. As he states more explicitly what he wants from her, Connie's terror and the story's suspense mount. When Arnold promises not to enter the house unless Connie picks up the phone, the reader may recall that the devil as evil spirit cannot cross a threshold uninvited. At this point, the end seems inevitable; in her presumed murderer's words, "The place where you came from ain't there any more, and where you had in mind to go is cancelled out."

It is no wonder that "Where Are You Going, Where Have You Been?" is the most frequently anthologized and critically acclaimed of Oates's short stories. Its popularity is ensured by the famous Oates blend of violence, sex, and suspense; its place in the American literary canon by its thematic importance, Oates's frightening vision of the contemporary American inability to recognize evil in its most banal forms.

Though many critics have complained about the gratuitous violence of Oates's work and seem to distrust her extraordinary fluency (she produced more than thirty-five volumes of stories, novels, and literary criticism in her first twenty years as a published writer), this particular story demonstrates her ability to achieve tight compression and careful stylistic control. From the first line, "Her name was Connie," to the last, "'My sweet little blue-eyed girl,' he said, in a half-sung sigh that had nothing to do with her brown eyes," this is a story in which every word counts.

*Jane M. Barstow*

# WHERE IS THE VOICE COMING FROM?

*Author:* Eudora Welty (1909-2001)
*Type of plot:* Psychological, impressionistic
*Time of plot:* Summer, 1963
*Locale:* Thermopylae, a small southern town
*First published:* 1963

> *Principal characters:*
> THE NARRATOR, an angry, resentful white man
> HIS CRITICAL WIFE, the wage earner of the family
> ROLAND SUMMERS, an African American civil rights activist

*The Story*

In "Where Is the Voice Coming From?" plot becomes subordinate to character as an anonymous speaker, the "voice" of the title, reveals his innermost thoughts in a stream-of-consciousness monologue. The action of the story is largely internal, in the mind and memory of this narrator, as he recalls recent conversations with his wife as well as his role in the death of Roland Summers, an African American civil rights leader in the small town of Thermopylae. The story concludes with the only external action in present time as the speaker begins to play his guitar.

The narrator, a white southerner in the early 1960's who has been pushed beyond his limits by the growing Civil Rights movement, is filled with rage and insecurity as the traditional rules of his society begin to give way. The possibility of murder first occurs to him when he sees Summers's face once too often on television, calling for equal rights for African Americans. He realizes that he has the power to eliminate that face permanently, even though he must borrow a delivery truck from his brother-in-law to carry out his predawn mission. He hides and waits for the black man's new white car to approach the lighted garage and paved driveway of his home. Although the narrator has never seen Summers in the flesh, only his picture, he recognizes him instantly in spite of the darkness and shoots him down. Both he and Summers are trapped in the moment as he shoots, but now he can be certain that the dead man will never be his equal. At the same time, the narrator admits his envy of Summers's green lawn and garage light, the shiny new car, and a standard of living that he himself cannot meet, as well as the waiting wife who rushes to the body.

The speaker's own wife is not so loyal. She wonders why the shooting did not occur earlier for the good of the town, as a local white columnist suggested, and warns the narrator that the assassination will put Summers's name back in the news. Worse, she has heard that the National Association for the Advancement of Colored People (NAACP) is going to send a more important official to Thermopylae; killing this official might have caused a greater impact. After her husband admits that he threw his rifle into the weeds, she accuses him of carelessly dropping it. In self-defense, he justifies the murder of Summers because he knows he has prevented some impulsive and careless teenager from doing the same thing and getting caught.

In the aftermath of the shooting, Summers's face does indeed appear on television and in the newspapers; in contrast, the narrator has never even had a photograph taken. Rumors fly, including the possibility that the NAACP has killed Summers in order to create a martyr. However, the narrator is consoled by the fact that he is now worth a five-hundred-dollar reward, while Summers, the dead man, is worth nothing. The speaker is ready, even eager, for a fight between the races, ready for chaos and rebellion against the teachers, preachers, and courts who are so eager to tell him how to live. He believes that people like himself are ready to take control, to tell the courts, the police, and even the president when they have gone too far. Alone, he reaches for his guitar and begins to play.

*Themes and Meanings*

In her fiction, Eudora Welty rarely takes a political stance or comments directly on her society, but in this departure from her often warm and affectionate examination of life in the American South, she plunges directly into the harsher reality of the civil rights era and the tumultuous shift in the social structure of her native region. The complexity of the problem and the ongoing effects of this shift become a major theme of "Where Is the Voice Coming From?" as African American citizens demand equal treatment and those at the bottom of white society fear their own displacement.

The white speaker is dangerous in his frustration. He comes from the lowest economic stratum, with no indication that he is employed, although his wife does hold a job. Apparently he does not own a car because he has to borrow a truck. Although he is outraged by the small black schoolchildren who have previously demonstrated for civil rights, much of his anger seems personal, directed especially at the vocal and visible leader, Roland Summers. Envy chokes him: Summers's picture is in the paper, his street is paved, his grass is green and well watered, and his wife leaves a welcoming light on for him. (The narrator's own wife could not afford to pay for such things.) Roland Summers personifies for the white narrator the injustice of a system that has failed to respect him as a man and now threatens to place ahead of him others who he believes are less deserving. He refuses to yield to a group that he has been taught to regard as inferior.

The narrator also thinks, correctly, that even his wife belittles him, not giving him full credit for what he has accomplished by ridding the town of an unwelcome agitator. She assumes that he got the idea from the newspaper columnist, when actually he thought of it himself. Even though he recognizes that his status is low—lower even than that of his sarcastic wife—the narrator needs to believe that he is still better than a man such as Roland Summers. His whole history, his identity, is at risk, threatened by this social upheaval, and he cannot submit quietly.

*Style and Technique*

This story has a background in fact. Welty wrote it on the night she learned of the murder of Medgar Evers, a local black civil rights leader much like the fictional Roland Summers, which took place in 1963 in her hometown of Jackson, Mississippi. Unaware of the killer's identity, yet familiar with the bitterness of racism and class resentment, she created a poor white narrator who so closely resembled the real murderer that several details of the story had to be altered before its publication in *The New Yorker*, in order to avoid prejudicing the case.

A major strength of the story is the speaker's voice, rich in local dialect, which also reveals him as uneducated and self-righteous. A proud man, he feels himself betrayed by everything in which he has believed. Clearly, he is a man overwhelmed by a growing movement he does not comprehend and cannot prevent. By allowing this narrator to tell his own story, Welty does not treat him as a stereotypical villain but presents him with understanding and even a certain level of compassion.

The credibility of the story is increased by passing references to historical persons, including Governor Ross Barnett of Mississippi; Caroline Kennedy, the young daughter of then-president John F. Kennedy; and James Meredith, the African American student whose enrollment integrated the University of Mississippi. In addition, sensory details are plentiful. When the narrator describes his early morning journey to Summers's neighborhood, he offers a litany of typical street and business names, locating the familiar railroad tracks and the lighted bank sign that gives the time and temperature. He notes the brutal heat, even at night; the intense emotional pressure that he experiences; and his sudden relief when Roland Summers falls.

Perhaps the most obvious symbol is the gun. Although the gun bestows temporary power on a powerless man, the narrator tells his wife that he threw his rifle in the weeds because the barrel was scorching hot and because there was really nothing worth holding on to anymore. At the story's end, he has replaced the gun with his old guitar, an enduring part of his own past, while he plays and sings "a-Down" to comfort himself—a mindless refrain and a foreshadowing, for now he, not Roland Summers, is going down.

*Joanne McCarthy*

# WHERE IS THE VOICE COMING FROM?

*Author:* Rudy Wiebe (1934-    )
*Type of plot:* Historical, metafiction
*Time of plot:* The 1890's
*Locale:* Prince Albert District, Saskatchewan Territory
*First published:* 1971

*Principal characters:*
THE NARRATOR, the story maker
ALMIGHTY VOICE (JEAN-BAPTISTE), a young Cree Indian

## The Story

"Where Is the Voice Coming From?" raises the question of how an author can make a story tell the truth when basing his or her work on so-called facts that do not agree. The story is written in the narrator's voice, which may well be taken as the author's own voice, as he ponders the various historical traces of an event that occurred more than one hundred years ago.

A young Cree Indian, Jean-Baptiste, best known as Almighty Voice, is arrested for stealing and killing a stray cow owned by the U.S. government. He is held in the police guardroom at Duck Lake, Saskatchewan Territory, in the charge of Constable R. C. Dickson. Somehow he manages to escape. Dickson is later cited for negligence and punished.

While being pursued, Almighty Voice shoots and kills Sergeant Colin Campbell near Prince Albert, after warning him three times not to advance. Almighty Voice becomes a much-wanted fugitive. Although a reward of five hundred dollars is offered for his capture, he succeeds in eluding his pursuers for more than eighteen months.

The escape ends in a standoff on May 27, 1897. On a poplar bluff near the Minnechinas Hills in the Prince Albert District, Almighty Voice and two friends face an armed force of more than one hundred police officers, civilians, and Prince Albert volunteers. With two Winchester rifles between them, the three fugitives manage to kill two police officers and one civilian volunteer, while, incredibly, holding the opposition at bay for three days and two nights. Then a voice rises from the bluff: "We have fought well. You have died like braves. I have worked hard and am hungry. Give me food." A crow falls out of the sky onto the bluff.

A short while later, an unforgettable voice rises over the exploding smoke and thunder of guns, "high and strong in its unending wordless cry." It is the death chant of the Almighty Voice, memorable in its beauty and in its "incomprehensible happiness."

It is a "wordless cry," explains the narrator, for he lacks a reliable interpreter who understands Cree. However, it is an understanding of Almighty Voice that the narrator is after and that eludes him here, for not all the records the narrator so assiduously investigates tell the same story. In the end, the very elements of the story run the story maker aground and shift him from his carefully controlled role as spectator of what has happened to a participant in the story. The element that impels this change is a picture of Almighty Voice himself. Two official descriptions accompany that picture. Besides some minor contradictions, one description accords his face a "feminine appearance." The narrator is stunned, for the face in the picture strikes him as devastatingly masculine, "a face like an axe" with a look in the eyes "that cannot be endured." It is this face, so different from the official description, that irresistibly draws the narrator into the drama of the event whose truth he tried to render impersonally. Now the question is, what really did happen here? Who was the real Almighty Voice? Where did his voice come from, and what did he really say?

### Themes and Meanings

The opening sentence, "The problem is to make the story," indicates at once that this will be no ordinary tale, centering on character and plot. Instead, Rudy Wiebe's story is about writing a story. It is also a story about the death of a rebellious young Indian who stole a cow and killed a police officer, but that story's main use is as illustration for the larger story: the artist's struggle to transmute the cold facts of history into the elements of fiction, a story that must nevertheless render the truth of what happened.

It all starts with gathering the facts. There are the names of the star players and the supporting cast on the fringes. There are proclamations, notices, descriptions, and pictures. There is a piece of white bone from the skull of Almighty Voice in a glass showcase. Another glass showcase holds the rifle he used, its upkeep noticeably neglected in contrast with the lacquered and varnished cannon standing close by. There are the gravestones of those who died in action, though the burial place of the Indians is unknown. Also, there is the place, Minnechinas Hills, where it happened. Assembling these facts seems simple enough. However, facts, rubbing against one another, rarely remain inert. Even facts from a hundred years ago have a way of acquiring human significance. They have a way of rubbing off on the writer as well, of drawing in the human agent who tries to assemble them into the elements of a story.

Such personal involvement is perhaps inevitable, even desirable, if the story is going to make an event of history come alive and signify. However, there is always the danger that the writer might shift from serving the facts of history to having the facts serve him or her. This danger grows acute when the facts fail to add up. When the picture of Almighty Voice and its descriptions turn out to be at odds, the writer finds himself shifting from spectator to story element, proving French philosopher Pierre Teilhard de Chardin, whom he quoted at the outset, right, and Greek philosopher Aristotle wrong. Now he cannot simply let the "facts" speak for themselves. He must examine those given "facts" and select the ones that have the most truth-telling power.

Wiebe's concern in all of his historical fiction is to break down the old distinction between fact and fiction. That is not meant to diminish the importance of fact; on the contrary, his conscientious respect for fact is borne out by his painstaking research. Good fiction will not falsify the facts but release their power to bring the reader close to the characters and conflicts and truths of the past and experience their ongoing significance.

Wiebe does that in the story of Almighty Voice by making the death chant the central, controlling image. It is in his dying that the young Cree voices the greatness of his people. The magnificence of his death chant is the narrator's attribution, to be sure, but it does not falsify the facts so much as it interprets them and releases their power. The reader hears that voice and begins to comprehend something of the mystery of its power and beauty, even when neither author nor reader will ever fully understand the Cree himself and will never fully know "where the voice is coming from."

*Style and Technique*

Wiebe is well known as an author whose writing, especially his historical fiction, makes considerable demands on its readers. His novel *The Blue Mountains of China* (1970), for example, is a deliberately disjointed narrative, employing a variety of narrative techniques, multiple voices, and radical shifts in point of view and time. Wiebe's stylistic variety and structural inventiveness honor serious readers for the commitment and intelligence they bring to the task.

"Where Is the Voice Coming From?" violates expectations that a reader normally brings to the reading of a short story: a beginning, middle, and end that include setting, character, and plot. Instead, Wiebe's story begins more like an essay on the problem of story making. There are relevant quotations from philosophers Teilhard de Chardin and Aristotle and from English sociologist Arnold Toynbee. There are names and exhibits and buildings and a scattering of data that initially confuse because no context for them has yet been provided. They are just so many fragments of some event whose nature the reader can only guess, pieces of a puzzle whose final design is still a mystery.

By using this technique, Wiebe's intent is to engage the reader as a participant in the narrator's challenge, namely to look closely at everything from the event that may be of importance. That search for all relevant facts takes the reader past the names of Indians and police officers and past showcase exhibits and places where the action occurred, and finally ends with the discovery of the discrepancy between the picture of Almighty Voice and its accompanying descriptions. In this way, the reader has simulated and shared in the narrator's search for meaning.

The picture stirs the narrator's creative dissonance: the tension between his task as historical reporter and as artistic interpreter or story writer. It functions as catalyst for the conclusion of this story, an ending that shifts to a vividly descriptive style and is passionately felt and eloquently rendered. In the end, all the fragments come together to create a powerful climax in the voice of the dying Cree, making audible once more the voice of the Great Spirit of his people.

*Henry J. Baron*

# WHERE THE JACKALS HOWL

*Author:* Amos Oz (Amos Klausner, 1939-    )
*Type of plot:* Psychological, social realism
*Time of plot:* The late 1950's or early 1960's
*Locale:* A kibbutz in southern Israel
*First published:* "Artsot hatan," 1963 (English translation, 1981)

*Principal characters:*
GALILA, a beautiful, headstrong young woman
SASHKA, her father, an intellectual first-generation kibbutz resident
TANYA, her mother, a first-generation kibbutz resident
MATITYAHU DAMKOV, a blacksmith and second-generation kibbutz resident

## The Story

The first of this story's ten numbered sections provides an overview of a land in transition from summer to fall, as a cool wind cuts through the warm "khamsin" wind. The focus then cinematically changes to Sashka writing at his desk and then to his daughter Galila showering and thinking about an invitation from Matityahu Damkov to visit his room to inspect gifts of artists' supplies and a pattern requested by Damkov from his cousin Leon in South America.

Sunset spreads over the plain and the kibbutz, overtaking the older, first-generation kibbutzniks (residents) still on their deck chairs. Damkov leaves his room to go to the communal dining hall. Damkov's body is described, along with his present and former occupations on the kibbutz. Again the story's roving point of view shifts, this time to Damkov's worries about whether Galila will accept his invitation.

Kibbutznik behavior at the dining hall is described, including communal discussions and division of the newspaper, as well as Tanya's complaints to the kibbutz work organizer and then to Damkov about his overdue repair of a lock. As night falls on the kibbutz, generators keep electric searchlights going, and a wary jackal cub is caught in one of the steel traps laid around the kibbutz. The circles of the plowed fields and lights flow into a description of the opposition between the inner circle of founding kibbutzniks, symbolized by the circle of light around Sashka at his writing desk, and the outer circle of second-generation kibbutzniks, represented by the Holocaust refugee Damkov, who is now hosting Galila in his bachelor's quarters. Damkov prepares imported coffee and makes small talk with Galila, going into sexually suggestive detail about his former horse-breeding job with his cousin Leon in Bulgaria before Damkov fled to Israel and Leon to South America.

Using the first-person plural, the narrator contrasts the founding kibbutzniks with newcomers, such as Damkov, who search for acceptance at all levels, including female companionship. Meanwhile, outside the kibbutz, the captive jackal cub struggles with the trap and a group of bedraggled jackals gathers, exults, sorrows, and disperses.

In Damkov's room, Galila appreciates the artists' supplies and sensuously applies brush to canvas. Something not described suddenly happens as a result of sexual "waves" between Galila and Damkov. Damkov summons one of his terrible daydreams; Galila awakens on the floor amid scattered art supplies. When she threatens to tell Sashka about Damkov's overfamiliarity or even shout out the window, Damkov wrestles with her and sensuously whispers in her ear the secret he has longed to tell her: He claims to be her father, through an affair with her mother, Tanya. Although Galila first argues with him—calling attention to her own blond hair, which is mentioned repeatedly throughout the story—she finally acquiesces.

In contrast to the beginning of the story with the sunset, the story closes with the narrator's description of sunrise over the land in a transition from summer to fall, and reference to the many eternal cycles that inhere in time and nature.

## Themes and Meanings

"Where the Jackals Howl" is pervaded by opposites or oppositions, which appear to have an underlying link comparable to that between the jackal cub and the steel trap or that within the eternal cycles of nature from night to day or from summer to winter. Intellect, rationality, language loving, handsomeness, towheadedness, foundation-laying, rootedness to Israel, and communal orientation, as represented by Sashka, are contrasted with the opposite qualities in Damkov. His eyes repeatedly redden with blood like those of the stud horses he raised. Called "mad" by Galila and other kibbutzniks, he distrusts language, has an ugly body and deformed left hand, is dark-haired, is a relative newcomer, and wishes to flee with Galila to South America.

Many hidden connections, such as those between Sashka and Damkov, pervade the story and underlie the oppositions. For example, Damkov wins over Galila using language in his story of horse breeding. He also uses language in whispering his secret into her ear, despite his clumsiness with and mistrust of words.

Also suggested is a hidden bond between Israelis and Arabs. The Arabs are never named, but their presence is conveyed through one of the symbolic meanings of the jackals as well as the story's references to the darkness and "foe" or "enemy" lying beyond the circles from the kibbutz's searchlights.

## Style and Technique

The story's point of view shifts often and sometimes abruptly, ranging from first-person plural (revealed to be the founding kibbutzniks, as opposed to latecomers or later generations) to the interior consciousness (without quotation marks) of Galila, Damkov, the jackal cub, and Sashka. It also ranges from third-person descriptions of conversations to a mysterious second-person voice in the reporting of Damkov's apocalyptic flood daydream.

This shifting helps convey the hidden connections among persons and polarities, the conjunction of all things within one land in a story whose Hebrew title, "Artsot hatan," is literally "the jackal's lands." Along with symbolism, the pervasive figure of speech personification suggests cumulatively, as well as in individual instances, covert ties among apparent divergences, even including, as the narrator points out repeatedly, the animate and inanimate worlds.

If the jackals symbolize the surrounding "foe," the jackal cub symbolizes Galila, who like the cub warily approaches the bait—artists' supplies—in Damkov's quarters but is caught. As the cub licks its steel trap, so Galila finally fawns on Damkov, who in repeated metal imagery—including his own metalworking—is associated with the steel trap and the lock for Tanya, which has significant Freudian symbolism.

Galila, whose Hebrew name literally means "ring," "circuit," or "territory," is captured by the lure of gifts from Damkov, whose Hebrew forename, Matityahu, means "gift of God." Ironically, like other first-generation pioneers, Sashka is said to have been "forged" in fury, longing, and dedication to establishing the kibbutz, the metaphor equating him to Damkov in the latter's metalworking and the recurrent imagery associating Damkov with heat. The recurrent polarity of heat versus cold is initiated in the story's opening paragraphs, as a blast of cool sea wind, in a sexually suggestive metaphor, "pierces" the massive, dense sirocco wind.

Abundant twists and ironies of plot help express the idea of a concealed "current," a repeated word in the story, connecting antipodes. For example, early in the story is a description of Sashka as having "fatherly assurance," which seems to apply to him both as a founding kibbutznik and as an actual father. A little later comes the narrative feint of identifying Galila as the daughter of Sashka and Tanya. In the third section, Damkov and Tanya converse in the distanced tone of kibbutz colleagues rather than as former lovers, including Tanya's complaint about Damkov not having fixed her lock. In the fifth section, Galila, identified as Sashka's daughter, thinks gratefully to herself that Damkov has no children because he is ugly and not one of her circle.

Also, when Galila readies to leave because of Damkov's reference to the wickedness of her mother, Damkov calls her as "daughter," which appears to be the address of an elder to a youth rather than a literal assertion of paternity. While Damkov is responding to Galila's upset at the sexual overtones of his description of horse breeding, Damkov's voice is described as almost fatherly. Later in the story, Galila and Damkov refer to opposites in the word "father" when she says that her father will kill Damkov and Damkov replies that her father will take care of her from now on. Additionally, though Damkov's room and his ugly appearance are referred to as "sterile," his first work was horse breeding, and he has been, in some sense, more fertile than Sashka, in an example of one of the story's polarities, between sterile and fertile.

Both opposition and reversals may be seen in the forenames of the main characters. Ironically, the pioneers most committed to the kibbutz and the state of Israel, Sashka and Tanya, have retained their European forenames. In contrast, Matityahu and Galila, representing latecomers and the later generation, have adopted or been given Hebrew forenames, appropriate to the Holy Land of the Bible.

Galila is partly drawn to the Europe-New World side of the polarity between what Amos Oz calls "Asia" (including the Middle East) and the West (Europe and the Americas), regarding her attraction to the painters' supplies. Damkov, with his offer of gifts to Galila from South America (coffee and painting equipment) and the United States (cigarettes from Virginia), as well as his European background, desires to take his daughter, so much an opposite to him, and flee with her to live with his cousin Leon in the New World, which Damkov considers a world away from the harsh land of the Bible and society of the kibbutz.

However, the eternal cycle of oppositions detailed in the short story's brief final section—sunset versus sunrise, heat versus cold, dry versus wet, summer versus winter—suggests that escape is not possible. What remains is the continual striving in life, embodied in the very etymology of the name "Israel"—which means "man who saw God."

*Norman Prinsky*

# WHITE ANGEL

*Author:* Michael Cunningham (1952-    )
*Type of plot:* Domestic realism, coming of age
*Time of plot:* The 1960's
*Locale:* Cleveland, Ohio
*First published:* 1988

*Principal characters:*
ROBERT "BOBBY" MORROW, nine years old, nicknamed "Frisco" by his brother
CARLTON MORROW, his sixteen-year-old brother
ISABEL MORROW, their mother, a teacher of exceptional children
THEIR FATHER, a music teacher
CARLTON'S GIRLFRIEND

*The Story*

"White Angel" is the story of the coming of age of two brothers. The nine-year-old narrator, Robert Morrow, enjoys a close and happy relationship with his sixteen-year-old brother, Carlton. Their parents, both teachers, had several children between Bobby and Carlton, but only these two have survived.

The white angel in the story's title refers to a monument in the graveyard behind the Morrow's unpretentious tract home. Bobby and Carlton often enter the cemetery because they have hidden a bottle of whiskey in the veranda of what Bobby calls a "society tomb." They go there to smoke pot and drink from their stash.

Carlton also drops acid, taking it with his orange juice in the morning as his mother prepares breakfast. He shares his acid, called windowpane, with Bobby, although, ever protective, he limits Bobby to half the dose he himself takes. Thanks to Carlton's tutelage, Bobby considers himself the most criminally advanced nine-year-old in the fourth grade.

The boys' mother, suspecting Carlton's involvement in illicit drugs, is uneasy because police officers drive past their house, stop, make notes, and then go on. She attempts to worm information out of Bobby, but he denies that his brother takes drugs. He walks away from his mother to avoid further confrontation, but she pursues him, demanding that he not walk away from her.

Minutes before, Bobby had come from the cemetery, where he unexpectedly encountered Carlton and his girlfriend in the process of losing their virginity. Bobby hovered behind the white angel monument. Carlton saw him there and was startled but eventually winked and continued his impassioned lovemaking.

Both Bobby and Carlton are captivated by the memory of Woodstock, which they have romanticized as only a person who had not attended that historic rock concert could. For them, Woodstock symbolizes freedom—everything to which they aspire and admire. As Bobby evades his mother's interrogation, walking east in the house, he fantasizes that every step takes him nearer to Yasgur's farm, where the concert at Woodstock, New York, was staged.

When Carlton returns from the cemetery and from his first sexual encounter, he rejoices that his brother was indirectly involved in this landmark event in his life, declaring that Frisco, as he calls him, is now a man. Elated by his conquest, Carlton suggests that he will find his brother a girl because, at nine, Frisco has been a virgin too long. Carlton's shoes are covered with mud that he tracks through the house, provoking his mother. She is unforgiving about his dirtying her house.

The father, however, is more detached. He labors away in the basement assembling a grandfather clock from a kit he bought so that he can pass an heirloom on to his children. He takes Carlton's breach of cleanliness calmly, suggesting only that Carlton clean up the mess he has made, thereby minimizing the problem.

All of this is a prelude to the story's central event: Carlton's accidental death. The Morrows are holding their annual party to celebrate the return of the sun after a long, dark winter. The party is a staid affair attended by their teacher friends. The boys help serve the drinks. The tone of the party changes this year, however, when some of Carlton's friends crash the party and add life to it. Soon everyone is mellow. Teenage boys dance with aging female teachers. Everyone imbibes liberally.

One adolescent boy, Fred, thinks he sees an unidentified flying object (UFO) in the yard. The guests flock into the yard but conclude that the object can be explained and is not a UFO. They return to the house, whereupon Carlton, quite high, returns to the yard. He crosses into the cemetery, then returns and heads toward the house. Not realizing that the sliding glass door is closed, he walks through it, sending jagged glass in every direction. A shard lodges in his throat and pierces his jugular, causing him to bleed to death before medical help arrives.

As the story ends, Bobby is now his parents' only child. The mother is grief-stricken to the point of being inconsolable. She and her husband occupy separate bedrooms. Carlton's girlfriend, after numerous psychiatric sessions, moves to Denver with her family. Following the accident, Bobby cannot bear to look her in the face.

*Themes and Meanings*

Love and death are pervasive themes in American fiction, and both of these elements permeate "White Angel." Michael Cunningham based this story on newspaper reports of an actual event that occurred near Cincinnati in 1965. The Morrow house is close to a graveyard, which becomes a symbol of both death and love. The graveyard is where Carlton first makes love to his girlfriend and where he and his brother smoke the pot and drink the whiskey that help unite them in an unusually close fraternal bond.

Death hovers over the story from start to finish. In its third paragraph, the narrator reveals that Carlton is going to die, although the means of his death is withheld until near the end of the story. Isabel Morrow suffered the loss of her first husband, who was killed in action during World War II. She has also given birth to stillborn babies or has lost children in their first days of life.

The love theme in "White Angel" is less pervasive than the death theme, although the close relationship between Carlton and Bobby is clearly one of fraternal love, with Carlton acting almost parentally toward his younger sibling. Cunningham also makes clear that Isabel loves Carlton unconditionally, even though his actions perplex her. On one level, he does things such as track mud through the house. On another, more serious level, Isabel fears he is leading a secret life that she correctly assumes is related to his involvement with drugs.

The boys' father attempts to remain the neutral parent. He views his sons as living examples of genetic continuity. They will preserve the family name. His hard work in assembling a grandfather clock from a kit is his nod to future generations. He wants to have something tangible to pass on to his heirs. When he is drawn into the conflict between Isabel and Carlton after Carlton tracks mud into the house, he suggests a practical solution that will put the matter to rest, something Isabel is too irritated to do.

Cunningham deals skillfully with the two major themes that pervade "White Angel." He interweaves them and uses the theme of fraternal love to project the irony of Carlton's assuming the role of surrogate parent, even though what he teaches Bobby is far from what conventional parents would teach a child.

*Style and Technique*

Cunningham's approach to "White Angel" is notably visual. The setting in a middle-class suburban neighborhood evokes images of manicured plots with one- and two-story tract homes on them. One can easily visualize the gully behind the Morrow house that separates it from a cemetery whose monuments—particularly the one of the white angel—are visible from the house. After Carlton's death, the small gray finger of his tombstone rises among the others, within sight of the white angel's marble eyes, quite visible from the house.

Although Bobby is the narrator, his narration is not that of a nine-year-old. Cunningham makes clear that Bobby is telling the story some years after Carlton's death. Seemingly his parents still live under one roof but quite apart, his mother in her bedroom, his father in his. Cunningham does not disclose the narrator's age. Perhaps he is not still living at home.

Just as his parents forced Bobby to go to bed before the party ended on the fateful April night on which Carlton died, one year after Carlton's death, Bobby finds his father wandering in the kitchen, presumably lost in thought on this anniversary of the tragedy, and has to put him to bed. Bobby, in a notable role reversal, sits nurturingly on the edge of the bed until his father falls asleep. The implication the story leaves is that the Morrows will endure, but that they are very different people from who they were before Carlton's death.

*R. Baird Shuman*

# A WHITE HERON

*Author:* Sarah Orne Jewett (1849-1909)
*Type of plot:* Realism, regional
*Time of plot:* The late nineteenth century
*Locale:* Rural Maine
*First published:* 1886

> *Principal characters:*
> SYLVIA, the protagonist, a nine-year-old girl
> MRS. TILLEY, her grandmother
> A YOUNG HUNTER, who is from the city

*The Story*

Sarah Orne Jewett's "A White Heron," the most popular of her short stories, is a prime example of a "local color" story in its depiction of the life of a particular region—in this case, her native Maine. Jewett explores the internal conflict that a transplanted city girl experiences between her newly acquired love for nature and her natural and awakening interest in the opposite sex. Sylvia, who knows where the rare white heron has its nest, must decide between an allegiance to the things of nature and the gratitude and friendship of the young hunter who seeks to add the white heron to his collection of stuffed birds.

In the first part of the story, Jewett establishes Sylvia as a "child of nature" who is somewhat wary of people. After having spent the first eight years of her life in a "crowded manufacturing town," where she had been harassed by a "great red-faced boy," she is now at home in the "out-of-doors." Her grandmother, who rescued Sylvia from the city, believes that Sylvia had never been "alive" until her arrival at the farm. According to her grandmother, "the wild creatur's counts her one o' themselves." In fact, when Sylvia first appears, she is driving home a cow named Mistress Moolly, which is described as Sylvia's "valued companion." Sylvia feels more at home with her "natural" society than she does with "folks."

As a result, when she hears "a boy's whistle, determined, and somewhat aggressive," she is "horror-stricken," but the young man overcomes her fear and accompanies her to her grandmother's farm. Having spent the day hunting, he seeks food and shelter for the night, and Mrs. Tilley obliges him. The young hunter discusses his collection of birds, listens to Mrs. Tilley talk about her son Dan's hunting, and learns that Sylvia "knows all about birds." He then offers ten dollars for information about the whereabouts of the white heron. The next day, Sylvia accompanies him as he hunts, and his "kind and sympathetic" behavior wins her "loving admiration," although she cannot understand why he kills the very birds he professes to like.

The second part of the story concerns Sylvia's decision to climb the "great pine-tree" in order to gain a vantage point from which she can discover the white heron's nest, which she apparently plans to reveal to her new friend. Rising before her grandmother and the hunter, Sylvia sneaks out of the house and makes her way through the forest to the tall pine tree. After climbing the nearby white oak, she negotiates the "dangerous pass" from the oak to the pine and finally reaches the top, from which she can see both the "vast and awesome world" and the white heron's nest, which holds the white heron and his mate. (Jewett thereby balances the two worlds: nature and the "outside" world beyond the farm.) When she returns to the farm, however, Sylvia will not reveal the location of the nest, despite the rebukes of her grandmother and the entreaties of the hunter, who thought he had won her over.

### Themes and Meanings

In "A White Heron," Jewett presents her readers with a series of conflicting values, all of which may be included under the theme of the country versus the city. By having Sylvia choose nature over civilization, Jewett clearly indicates her own preference while she also acknowledges the cost of making that choice.

Jewett's comparison of Sylvia to the "wretched dry geranium that belonged to a town neighbor" is instructive, for Sylvia thrives, as would the geranium, on being transplanted from town to country. When she first meets the hunter, Sylvia hangs her head "as if the stem of it were broken." Clearly, Jewett means to suggest that Sylvia is indeed a flower, a part of nature. She not only is accepted by the wild animals but also feels "as if she were a part of the gray shadows and the moving leaves." Sylvia's ties to nature are also reflected in Jewett's description of her bare feet and fingers, which are like "bird's claws," a simile that identifies her with birds and helps explain her decision to save the white heron.

The hunter who pursues the white heron is from the city and is therefore tainted by civilization. In fact, like the "great red-faced boy," he represents a threat to Sylvia: He may not physically harm her, but he can corrupt her by enticing her to "sell out" nature by taking money for information. Jewett does not condemn the hunter for hunting in itself; Mrs. Tilley obviously understands that hunting produces game birds ("pa'tridges," for example) to be eaten in order to survive. On the other hand, hunting all kinds of birds (including thrushes and sparrows) simply in order to stuff them for one's own "collection" is a notion "foreign" to Mrs. Tilley and incomprehensible to Sylvia: "She could not understand why he killed the very birds he seemed to like so much." In effect, her first perception of him as the "enemy" is correct.

The "persuasive" young man's corruption is signaled by his situation when Sylvia meets him. Like many other moral wanderers in dark woods (Nathaniel Hawthorne's Young Goodman Brown comes immediately to mind), the hunter is "lost." When he is guided to a hermitage and receives Mrs. Tilley's hospitality, he repays it by attempting to exploit Sylvia's obvious fondness for him and Mrs. Tilley's equally obvious need for money. He is successful in enlisting Mrs. Tilley's support, but Sylvia has grown and learned important lessons from her climb up the pine tree.

In many ways, "A White Heron" is an initiation story with mythic overtones. A young girl who lives in cloistered innocence is exposed to temptation from the outside world. The agent of temptation uses her developing interest in the opposite sex to seduce her into betraying the natural world to which she belongs. Although her "woman's heart," which had been "asleep," is "vaguely thrilled" by the young hunter, she also gains new insights into herself and the world of nature. Her morning journey, which takes her through the dangerous bog, and her subsequent climb up the pine tree both test her and teach her. When she negotiates the "passage" from the oak to the pine, she undertakes a "great enterprise," one at once challenging and fulfilling. From the top of the pine she can see the "vast and awesome world" that lies beyond the safety of the farm. Unfortunately for the hunter, she also sees the white heron and his mate. The two worlds are in conflict, and the parallel between the herons and her own situation is readily apparent to the "sadder but wiser" Sylvia: Her happiness at helping the object of her infatuation can be achieved only at the expense of destroying another "domestic" situation, which may be more significant. In a kind of epilogue Jewett writes, "Were the birds better friends than their hunter might have been—who can tell?"

*Style and Technique*

In her depiction of the often-reiterated conflict, Jewett is not objective; the "scales" are heavily weighted in favor of nature. Besides using stereotypical characters in a Good-versus-Evil confrontation of mythic dimension, she uses sentimentality to invest both vegetable and animal worlds with human characteristics. Sylvia's "valued companion" is not the hunter, but Mistress Moolly, the cow, who is capable of "pranks." The birds and beasts "say good-night to each other in sleepy twitters," thereby making their deaths seem more like "murder" and helping to account for Sylvia's final decision. Even the pine tree is personified and depicted as an ally in her quest for knowledge. The tree is "asleep"; it even stands still and holds away the wind as Sylvia climbs. Sylvia's very name, with its "sylvan" suggestions, indicates that her true home is in nature (she is known as "Sylvy" rather than the more formal "Sylvia"). Similarly, Mrs. Tilley, who "tills" her farm, is also in her proper habitat. On the other hand, the unnamed hunter is seen as an interloper who does not belong.

In order to elicit sympathy for Sylvia, Jewett uses the third-person-limited point of view, so that Sylvia's perceptions become the readers' perceptions. Her choice seems inevitable, but at the end of the story Jewett gains some distance from Sylvia and editorializes about the decision: "Dear loyalty, that suffered a sharp pang as the guest went away disappointed later in the day, that would have served and followed him and loved him as a dog loves!" The slavish, servile behavior Jewett describes is "puppy love," unworthy of the white heron's death. On the other hand, the epilogue concludes with the cost of Sylvia's decision: "Bring your gifts and graces and tell your secrets to this lonely child!" Jewett's last words suggest that the child needs human companionship and that nature's "gifts and graces" may only partially compensate for "whatever treasures" ("whatever" tends to undermine the value of the "treasures") she lost through her decision.

*Thomas L. Erskine*

# A WHITE HORSE

*Author:* Thom Jones (1945-    )
*Type of plot:* Philosophical realism, absurdist
*Time of plot:* The 1990's
*Locale:* Bombay, India
*First published:* 1992

> *Principal characters:*
> "AD MAGIC," an amnesiac advertising writer
> A BOY, with a monkey
> A DOCTOR

*The Story*

"A White Horse" follows an amnesiac who calls himself "Ad Magic" as he slowly regains his memory within a phantasmagoric landscape of beachfront Bombay, India. The story begins when the tour bus in which Ad Magic is riding crashes into a truck. Ad Magic has had a premonition of the accident, but that does not stop him from hurtling down the center aisle of the bus. A candy on which he was sucking becomes trapped in his throat, and he is saved by the Bahraini tourists with whom he has been traveling. The event is another source of humor to the other tourists, who have been laughing at him all day. Earlier, at a cave containing a statue of Buddha, they had managed to scare a huge group of bats into flight, sending them swooping toward Ad Magic and causing him to fall into an inch-deep layer of bat guano.

Ad Magic leaves the bus and heads toward the beach. He meets a young boy who carries a monkey dressed in a red uniform. Ad Magic gives the boy an expensive sweater and so much money that his tour guide insults him. He begins walking away from the tour, past advertisements, a drainage ditch, and a shantytown.

He spies a white horse, which appears about to die. At that moment, he realizes he has once again stopped taking his medications, which has led him to wander away from his daily life, this time to India. He has no idea what his real name is, only that his nickname is Ad Magic. His pockets contain a huge roll of money and a hotel room key. He knows he can determine his identity back in that room, but he does not yet want to know.

As Ad Magic sits with the boy and his monkey, bits of his memory return. He recalls a doctor telling him that he has epilepsy and that it periodically causes him to forget his identity, disappear, and rush about the world, much like a character in a soap opera. Ad Magic knows he has periods of deep depression, in which he feels hatred for everything and everyone, but at this moment, his concern is for the white horse and its suffering.

He determines that the horse used to work for the circus that once occupied the area into which he has wandered. He calls for a doctor and returns to the remains of a Ferris wheel that might have once been turned by the horse. The sight brings back another memory, this time of a childhood visit to a fair, where he had climbed out of a bumper car, fallen, and then been rescued, perhaps by his father.

A doctor arrives, and Ad Magic offers him five hundred dollars, then a thousand, to save the horse. The doctor begins to examine the horse and Ad Magic as well. Ad Magic discovers he has a terrible black eye, and the doctor gives him some pills that make him sleep while the doctor's boxer dog watches over him.

When Ad Magic awakens, the horse is beginning to look better. The doctor has removed some abscessed teeth and cleaned up its sores. He goes for a swim with the boxer dog and begins to feel a moment of happiness. When he and the dog return, Ad Magic hugs the horse, and the doctor asks what "Ad Magic" means. Ad Magic explains that he writes advertisements and that he sometimes feels he connects with magic, with inspiration. He quickly offers up a few possible ads and says that his ability to create ads is connected to the white horse. He offers the doctor six hundred dollars a month if he will take care of the horse, and more money to watch after the boy.

Ad Magic returns to his hotel room. He looks in his wallet, at a photo of his family, and his identity returns to him. Immediately he begins pouring ideas onto a pad of paper and soon has enough ad ideas for a year. He spends the night writing, and the story ends with him calling his wife.

*Themes and Meanings*

"The White Horse" is about the search for inspiration and for meaning in life. Suffering from terrible depression, Ad Magic tries to obliterate himself with drugs and alcohol in order to escape from his life. He is afflicted with a form of epilepsy that causes him to regularly disappear from his normal life and wander the globe. He has found himself in places such as Zanzibar; American Samoa; Lima, Peru; and Lusaka, Zambia. Ad Magic explains that he essentially runs away whenever he feels a complete hatred for the world. Once on his journeys, he begins to find some inner peace only when he starts thinking about something other than himself, for example, when he takes care of a white horse that has been abandoned on the beach, and, indirectly, a young boy who wanders there as well.

Though Ad Magic realizes early in the story that he has had another relapse and that clues to his identity are at his hotel room, he avoids returning there, back to his life. He appears to be a figure of humor, spending his money wildly, but his connections with the white horse and the young boy enable Ad Magic to become a protector. His ability to create is connected to a purpose deeper than just selling things.

In the story, the white horse reminds Ad Magic of a white horse that figured in the final emotional breakdown of European philosopher Friedrich Nietzsche. (In 1889, Nietzsche saw a man beating a white horse in the street. Nietzsche threw his arms around the neck of the horse to save its life.) However, instead of figuring in deepening emotional problems for Ad Magic, the horse and its survival connect Ad Magic with his identity, a sense of creative magic, and a meaning in life.

"A White Horse" is also about pain and the struggle to escape it. As the doctor explains to Ad Magic: "Animals don't experience pain in the same fashion humans. . . .

Pain for humans is memories, anticipation, imagination." Ad Magic's amnesia causes him to experience the pain of life in much the same way that the doctor argues an animal does. When Ad Magic disappears on one of his fugues, he lives without memories. The memories in this story are painful for Ad Magic; they are of people who loved him but are no longer alive. He recalls events and places, but the kind people within his memories have no faces. The settings of these memories are vivid, and his emotional attachment to these people—a doctor and perhaps his father—is strong, but his ability to truly recall them is limited.

By the end of the story, Ad Magic has reconnected with the deep, unconscious sources of inspiration, and he has shifted from the one who needs care to the person caring for others.

### Style and Technique

Thom Jones uses a variety of techniques to capture the experience of an amnesiac. The story begins *in media res*, or "in the middle of things." This technique means the author does not begin with an explanation of upcoming events or at the actual onset of the story. To capture the bewilderment of someone whose memory has been disrupted, the story begins in the middle of the action, at the moment of a bus crash. Ad Magic is described as a human cannonball as he flies down the bus's center aisle.

Throughout the story, different characters and events mirror and double one another. The opening bus accident leaves Ad Magic pantomiming his need for help. Soon after, Ad Magic meets a young boy and his monkey, which also performs a meaningless little set of gestures. He offers to look after the boy, which triggers his memories of adults who looked after him when he was a boy. The boy and the trained monkey initially appear to be a source of comedy, as Ad Magic has been throughout the day, for the other tourists.

On first impression, the settings appear to be filled with unusual sights, generally humorous or surreal. However, they serve to support the deeper, sadder mood of the story. At first, the tone is humorous, as the story describes Ad Magic's pratfall into bat guano, but this incident happens during a visit to a statue of Buddha, which is a source of meditative peace. The setting in which Ad Magic meets the horse contains a broken-down Ferris wheel. At first, it seems another outlandish setting, but with its endless circling, the wheel also represents his endless roaming search. Ad Magic goes for a swim in the bay, which is a moment of pure joy; however, he cannot help but notice that the water contains human waste. Earlier he has watched people wash their clothes in the same channel that others are using as a toilet. Everywhere the story is filled with images of duality.

At first, Ad Magic seems a ridiculous figure, as he offers hundreds and hundreds of dollars to take care of a horse he spotted only hours before. However, beneath the humor of the unfolding events of the story is a deep pathos, a deep sadness, as well.

*Brian L. Olson*

# THE WHITE HORSES OF VIENNA

*Author:* Kay Boyle (1902-1992)
*Type of plot:* Social realism
*Time of plot:* 1934
*Locale:* The Austrian Tirol
*First published:* 1936

> *Principal characters:*
> THE DOCTOR, a country physician who is nevertheless
>   sophisticated and widely traveled
> HIS WIFE, a trained nurse
> DR. HEINE, a young Jewish intern from Vienna

*The Story*

The fictional account of events in the Austrian mountains (Tirol) in the summer of 1934 is directly related to the political events of the period. These include the rise of the Nazi Party in Austria and the murder of the Austrian chancellor, Engelbert Dollfuss, on July 25, 1934, by right-wing elements undoubtedly encouraged and financed by the German chancellor, Adolf Hitler, who was eager to annex Austria to the German Reich.

A country doctor has injured his knee while climbing at night with a group of local men near his mountain chalet. As his injury may take weeks to heal, he requests a student-doctor from the hospital in Vienna to help service his patients. When the young doctor arrives, his appearance is noted with disapproval by the country physician's wife. His "alien" appearance indicates his Semitic origin, his "black smooth hair . . . the arch of his nose." However, both the doctor and his pet red fox seem relatively unaffected by the student-doctor's racial origins and initially accept him. The country doctor is more sophisticated than his wife. He has traveled widely and lived in large cities throughout the world, and thus tends to reserve judgment even while agreeing with her that an urban, Jewish physician will not be easily integrated into the society of this isolated mountain valley. The student-doctor, Dr. Heine, tries hard to cooperate with both the doctor and his wife, who assists him as his nurse. He listens carefully to instructions, "taking it all in with interest and respect." Dr. Heine even enlists the sympathy of the doctor's wife when his clothes are accidentally burned by the sterilizing lamp during a dental operation.

Dr. Heine gives no cause for criticism in his manner or his conversation. He solidifies his bond with his mentor by demonstrating his interest in high culture: music, painting, and books. The older man, forced to be inactive, amuses himself by carving wooden puppets ("his dolls"). The walls of the house are lined with books and his own paintings and drawings, dating from his imprisonment in Siberia and Dalmatia in World War I. After dinner one evening, Dr. Heine relates to the doctor, his wife, and their two sons a story of the purchase of a famous Viennese Lippizaner horse by a maharaja and how a groom destroys the horse and then commits suicide rather than see the beautiful animal sent off to a foreign owner in an alien land.

Two weeks after the student-doctor's arrival, the doctor invites his family, other children, and friends to attend a performance of his marionette theater, featuring the newly created characters fashioned during his illness. The play begins at eight, and it features a "gleaming" and impressive grasshopper. The strong, "green-armored" grasshopper is engaged in conversation by a small, dwarfish clown with a human face and carrying a bunch of artificial flowers, tripping at every step on his oversized sword. The clown seems powerless and ridiculous when compared to the powerful grasshopper, self-confident "and perfectly equipped for the life he had to lead." Dr. Heine's amusement evaporates when he realizes that the grasshopper is being referred to in the text as "The Leader," and the clown as "The Chancellor." The power and conviction of the grasshopper's oratory completely overcome the diminutive clown, who maintains his belief "in the independence of the individual" before falling over his sword into a field of daisies.

A few days later, Dr. Heine takes an evening walk from the chalet to view the mountain peaks. They seem cold and forbidding to him, and he yearns for the warmth and intellectual conversation he was accustomed to in Vienna. A moment later, he notices lights moving up toward the house from the valley. He sees them as "beacons of hope" come to rescue him from this bare northern environment of rock and "everlasting snow." Mentally he bids the lighted chain to come to him "a young man alone, as my race is alone, lost."

Actually, the local constabulary troops (*Heimwehr*) have come to arrest the doctor, who is suspected of clandestine antigovernment activities. The Austrian chancellor has been assassinated. Dr. Heine offers his help to the doctor, who leaves in good humor but, because of his leg, must be carried to the town hall (*Rathaus*) on a stretcher. He jokes about fruit and chocolate that his wife would throw up to his cell window from the street. He has been imprisoned before—during the riots and unrest in February. As the doctor is carried away, Dr. Heine recalls again the proud white horses of Vienna "bending their knees" to the empty royal box "where there was no royalty any more."

## Themes and Meanings

Kay Boyle, an American expatriate writer who lived in Europe from the late 1920's until the early 1940's, wrote on political themes in several of her best-known stories. Boyle here focuses on the summer of 1934, a period of political unrest in Austria that followed the riots of the previous winter, when the Dollfuss government had used troops and artillery against workers in the Karl Marx Hof apartment complex in Vienna. All the events of Boyle's narrative, though completely fictional, closely relate to the actual historical accounts. The elapsed time is about one month, from the end of June until July 25 (the day of Chancellor Dollfuss's murder).

The resident doctor, who has been spending so much time climbing the mountain near his house and returning late in the evening, is one of the right-wing Nazi sympathizers who have been accused of burning fiery swastikas on the mountain heights and are being investigated by the *Heimwehr*. The mountain setting ("snow shining hard and diamond-bright on their brows") is an appropriate backdrop for the action, a Wagnerian setting for the Aryan supermen of Nazi legend. However, the fiery symbols on the mountain are only one aspect of the doctor's personality, which combines "tenderness and knowledge," "resolve" and "compassion." Even his wife is seen in a more humanitarian light when the student-doctor's coat catches fire (the Wagnerian fire of purification?) and she helps save him from serious injury. Later, the young doctor feels "defenceless" as he watches the mountain beacons of "disaster"; the silver swastikas on the black uniforms resemble too closely the burning emblems on the black mountainsides.

As the Nazi doctor is political and draws strength from the barren, snowcapped mountain peaks that symbolize the land and its heritage, so the young Jewish intern seems closely related to his urban origins and the intellectual and cultural background from which he springs and in which he feels comfortable. Young Dr. Heine is no less a product of Austrian tradition than his older and more experienced colleague. This fact is demonstrated by his story of the white horses, symbols of a graceful but impractical past. Like the Germans who want to unite the two German-speaking peoples, the maharaja who buys the white Lippizaner wants to possess what he admires but cannot understand the aristocratic cultural background, the love of something uniquely beautiful, which leads the groom to wound the horse and, finally, to destroy himself. The powerful, affluent forces of Germany seek to possess something that to the young doctor is intangible—the spirit and heritage of Austria.

In contrast, the symbolic values of the Nazi doctor are represented explicitly in the marionette play he produces for the local children. The grasshopper, sleek and green (the color of German army fieldpieces and regular army uniforms), overpowers and seduces the humble, silly clown dancing nimbly to what appear to be native tunes (by Wolfgang Amadeus Mozart, Austria's most illustrious composer). The clown is on his way to his own funeral. The sheer physical power of the grasshopper makes the clown appear as inconsequential as a local hairdresser. In the political allegory presented by the doctor, Hitler, as the armored grasshopper, must triumph over the foolish clown (Dollfuss), whose strong religious faith (Christian Socialist Party) is no match for the ruthless practical politics of the Nazis.

Dr. Heine, who recognizes both the opposition and the inherent anti-Semitism of the older doctor and his wife, also realizes that the doctor has a more compassionate and intellectual nature beneath his doctrinaire political creed. He deplores the blackness that is closing in on his country, a world in which beauty and integrity will be lost ideals. He reaches out to the doctor, now being carried off by the *Heimwehr*, and recalls the powerless but supremely graceful white horses bowing to the empty royal box. He realizes that his thoughts and inclinations are "small and senseless in the enormous night" which is descending. However, in the world now dominated by powerful political forces, the finer feelings of intellectual men appear to be out of place.

*Style and Technique*

The narrative is divided into three distinct parts. The first section recounts the fact of the doctor's injury and his hiring of a student-doctor. In the second section, which deals with the two stories told by the physicians (first about the white horses, then about the grasshopper and the clown), the omniscient narration shifts temporarily to the limited view in the thoughts of the wife, then the student-doctor. The shift from limited to omniscient continues throughout the remainder of the narrative. The major part of the interior monologue, however, is concerned with the thoughts of Dr. Heine. The senior physician's thoughts are never revealed except through dialogue. The third section is the shortest and is concerned only with the events of July 24 and the final significant thoughts of Dr. Heine.

The most important symbolic aspect of the narrative is the setting, and without its specific chronological frame the events would be largely meaningless. Even seemingly minor facts significantly affect the characterization. The fact, for example, that the older doctor was a prisoner of the Russians ("in Siberia") during World War I influences his political ideas and suggests motivation for his Nazi sympathies.

Boyle skillfully uses a totally uninflected (almost documentary) style in the initial sections of the tale, only gradually exposing the thoughts of the wife and the young Jewish doctor; she finally abandons the earlier narrative mode in the third and final section as the emotional development of the author's idea reaches its climax.

It may be pertinent to Boyle's purpose that only Dr. Heine, the student-doctor, is given a specific personal identity. The other characters in the story, both major and minor, are identified only as "the doctor," "his wife," "the *Burgermeister*," "the *Apotheker*" (druggist), and so forth. This device tends to focus the reader's attention and sympathies more exclusively on the young doctor's view of events, which is clearly the intention of the author.

*F. A. Couch, Jr.*

# WHITE NIGHTS

*Author:* Fyodor Dostoevski (1821-1881)
*Type of plot:* Impressionistic
*Time of plot:* About 1848
*Locale:* St. Petersburg
*First published:* "Belye nochi," 1848 (English translation, 1918)

Principal characters:
THE UNNAMED NARRATOR
AN INSOLENT GENTLEMAN
NASTENKA, a seventeen-year-old girl
HER GRANDMOTHER
FEKLA, their charwoman
THEIR LODGER
MATRENA, the narrator's landlady

*The Story*

This work takes its title from the long twilight periods that, during the warm months of the year, last nearly until midnight in northern lands, including some parts of Russia. The unnamed narrator has lived in St. Petersburg for nearly eight years and knows very few people in the capital city. During bright, clear spring nights, he has habitually walked down major streets and alongside the canals; recently, he has been troubled by vague misgivings he cannot entirely identify. Quite by chance one night, he happens on a fetching young well-dressed girl leaning against an embankment. She is preoccupied; from time to time muffled sobs escape from her. She is set on by an older gentleman in formal evening attire, evidently with dubious intentions. Stricken with fear, the girl takes flight instantly; the narrator quickly interposes himself between them and drives back the assailant by brandishing his thick, knotted walking stick. When the girl returns, her eyes still moist from weeping, the narrator takes her arm and awkwardly asks her indulgence for his shyness. He confides in her at some length and confesses that, although he is twenty-six years old, heretofore he has only dreamed of women; he has not known any of them apart from two or three old landladies. Before they part, he extracts from her a promise to meet again the next night. He declares that he is overwhelmed with happiness. Throughout their conversation, he is moved and fascinated by her small, delicate hands and gentle laughter.

On the second night, the girl receives the narrator warmly; she apologizes for being overly sentimental and asks him to tell her the whole history of his life. To encourage him, she introduces herself as Nastenka and tells him that she lives with her old, blind grandmother, who is perpetually knitting stockings and is invariably solicitous about the young girl's acquaintances and whereabouts. The narrator unabashedly confesses that he is a dreamer. He is happy only during the evening, when his work is done and familiar sights are invested with heightened, highly personal qualities. His life has passed almost entirely in idleness and solitude; the return to his workday pursuits brings numbing and morose sobriety. Nastenka, who has been listening patiently and attentively, recounts her life with her grandmother and Fekla, their deaf charwoman, at their boardinghouse. Once Nastenka had been shown particular attention by a lodger, and her suspicious grandmother insisted on a strict accounting for all of her movements. Several times all three of them went out to the theater and the opera. When their tenant concluded his business in the capital about a year earlier and went on to Moscow, Nastenka was left isolated again. She had understood that he would write to her but doubts that she will ever hear from him again.

As the third night begins, the narrator fears that there will be no meeting, and for a time he waits in agonizing anticipation. When Nastenka appears, their conversation is confused and inconclusive; she is recurrently troubled by fears that her former lodger has vanished for good. The narrator is awkwardly torn between his growing affection for Nastenka and his concern about the other man.

On the fourth night, all is ended. Nastenka, who still has heard nothing from her erstwhile companion, feels abandoned and betrayed. The narrator offers to intercede for her and suggests that she write a letter that he will take to the lodger. She is troubled that her unrequited love for the other man may have compromised her relations with the narrator; he reassures her that his love for her is undiminished. If the lodger may bring her happiness, on her behalf he will be the more pleased for it. As the narrator weeps, Nastenka bursts into tears, and she lays her hand on his shoulder. Then, each comforted by the other's suffering, they discuss the future; they consider houses where they could live together, and the narrator lightheartedly suggests that they could go to the opera. As they talk over such fondly envisioned projects, Nastenka is suddenly transfixed: She has seen the young man from their boardinghouse. He repeats her name; without a word she takes the narrator by the neck with both hands, kisses him warmly and tenderly, and then hastens to join her lover.

The next day, the narrator is awakened by Matrena, his landlady. He has received a letter from Nastenka; in it, she beseeches his forgiveness and affirms that their love, though short-lived, was sincere. She will be married to the lodger in a week, but she will remember the narrator always. The narrator, with no regrets or recriminations, thankfully invokes his recollections of her as the one ray of happiness in his dreary life.

## Themes and Meanings

Love, both fleeting and permanently held dear, is presented in this narrative of four nights and a day. The narrator's chance meeting with Nastenka brings about an exchange of self-revealing confessions on the part of two isolated souls; as they unburden themselves and discover that they are kindred spirits, their mutual attachment grows. As in many affairs of the heart, much takes place over a relatively short period of time, while events of much longer duration are referred to in passing. Both the narrator and Nastenka experience marked emotional vicissitudes, alternately haunted by melancholy and transported with joy. Each senses the other's mood, which then is quickly and deeply reflected in the other's outlook. Moreover, the shared feelings that have drawn them together are not dissipated by the sudden, albeit long-awaited, appearance of Nastenka's lodger.

The narrator describes his relationship with Nastenka as a single blissful moment that redeems an otherwise unhappy life. This brief and illuminating period, which has infused in him a single, transcendent vision of romantic love, foreshadows the author's later concerns with religious insight and redemption. In this instance, the narrator is enthralled by the depth of feeling summoned forth during his meetings with the girl; it is this revelation that matters to him, rather than the ultimate resolution of their romantic situation. This aspect also distinguishes this story from romantic works in which it does matter whether relationships are continued and consummated and in which parting yields grief rather than elevation of the spirit.

*Style and Technique*

The relationships recorded here constitute what must be one of the happier love triangles on record, and the curious charm of the ending is a result, in the main, of certain forms of characterization. For all of Nastenka's own misgivings, the narrator is only too pleased that she has found love in her friend the lodger. This peculiar working of love's alchemy, by which the narrator's attraction to the girl is transmuted into ardent hopes for her happiness with another man, can occur because of the narrator's peculiar traits: He is a professed dreamer, and much of everyday experience passes him by; he has reconciled himself, for the most part, to a drab and uneventful existence. Only a certain number of people and sights inspire his imagination, and then only during the later periods of the day. For him, therefore, even a brief and evanescent relationship with a young woman seems disproportionately precious. He is gentle and accepting by nature; in most senses he is not a possessive sort. Thus, he may cherish his memories of Nastenka as the most fondly felt of his nocturnal reveries.

This work itself has a fragile, dreamlike quality that imbues the narrative with a light, romantic air; in some ways it seems insubstantial. The point of view is largely that of the narrator; his story is told in the first person and is presented almost as a diary, with a series of entries for the four nights and the day he wishes particularly to recollect. It is impressionistic but also highly focused: He refers to familiar buildings almost as though they were persons. Clouds and bright stars that appear during the warm spring nights have a special meaning for the narrator, but there is also much, notably his background and the details of his daily work, that appears, if at all, only in passing.

Much of the story is given over to conversation, and indeed for the most part the narrator's relationship with Nastenka is established in long passages of dialogue in which each one's dreams and aspirations are set forth at length. Many of the facts that are known about the narrator come to light in this manner; Nastenka's past association with the lodger is evoked entirely from her exchanges with the narrator. In this fashion, basic concerns of the major characters are raised directly and immediately.

*J. R. Broadus*

# WHITE RAT

*Author:* Gayl Jones (1949-    )
*Type of plot:* Psychological
*Time of plot:* The 1970's
*Locale:* Kentucky
*First published:* 1977

> *Principal characters:*
> WHITE RAT, the narrator
> MAGGIE, his wife
> LITTLE HENRY, their son
> J. T., Maggie's lover
> COUSIN WILLIE, a black woman who tells White Rat where
>     Maggie is
> GRANDY, White Rat's grandmother

*The Story*

"White Rat," a first-person account by White Rat, a light-skinned African American man, begins in the present, then switches to the narrator's experiences of "passing" as white, even when he does not want to, and then returns to the present.

When the story begins, Cousin Willie tells White Rat where he can find Maggie, who has run off with J. T.; and White Rat goes to get his wife. When they get home, Maggie kisses little Henry, her three-and-a-half-year-old clubfooted son, and fixes dinner. She says she is pregnant, and White Rat offers to give his last name to the child even though J. T. impregnated her, and tells her that no one has to know that the child is not his. She responds, "You know. I know." White Rat and Maggie sleep in the same bed but do not have any physical contact.

In the next part of the story, White Rat recounts his experiences as a light-skinned African American. He explains that he got his nickname because his mother said that he looked like a white rat when he was born. When he attempts to call little Henry "White Rabbit" because of how he looked when he was born, Maggie objects, claiming that the boy might develop a "complex." He then describes how people assume that he is white, which causes problems when he goes to black "joints." He describes what happens as he and some of his friends are arrested and jailed for being drunk and disorderly. When they are locked up, the police, assuming that White Rat is white, put him in a cell with a white man, while the other African Americans are put in another cell. The police ignore White Rat's protestations, but when he threatens his white cellmate, the police put him in a separate cell. When his grandmother Grandy arrives at the police station, she tells the officers that she has come for her two grandsons. When the police realize that White Rat is indeed an African American, they are reluctant to admit their mistake and tell her that he was put in a separate cell because he started a "rucus." After she pays ten dollars for the release of the two cousins, they are freed.

White Rat's "other big 'sperience" occurs when he and Maggie go to the court-house to get a marriage license. The clerk, assuming White Rat is white, says, "Round here nigger don't marry white." After White Rat tells him that he is an African American, the clerk "just look at me like I'm a nigger too, and tell me where to sign." After their marriage they move to Huntertown, and Maggie gives birth to Henry, who has a clubfoot. White Rat says the trouble between him and Maggie began with this birth. He blames Maggie for Henry's problem, believing she did something wrong that caused their son to be born with a clubfoot. In the ensuing argument, White Rat blames Maggie's side of the family for the deformity, and Maggie retaliates by attacking him for his "whiteness." When he tells her he is leaving, she asks about Henry; he replies, "He's your nigger." He then goes to a "hoogie joint" (white bar), where he tells the bartender his story in altered form: He becomes a priest who renounces his vows and marries a woman who bears a clubfooted child. The priest believes he is responsible for the child's clubfoot because he broke his priestly vows of celibacy. When a drunken White Rat returns home and finds Maggie and Henry gone, a neighbor gives him a note from Maggie, who writes that she left with J. T. because of White Rat's drinking and took Henry only to protect him. The next day Henry returns, and White Rat figures that Maggie thinks he will have to be sober to take care of Henry and himself.

The last paragraph of the story occurs two months after Maggie left, which is when White Rat finds out where she is and brings her back home. She tells him that when the baby comes, "we see whose fault it was," but two months after her return, White Rat has seen "no belly change."

### Themes and Meanings

White Rat's narrative exposes him as a violent, abusive, alcoholic husband with mixed feelings about his racial identity. He acknowledges that he has always "been a hard man, kind of quick-tempered" but denies that he has changed since the marriage. Maggie claims that he started drinking after they were married and that the drinking makes him quick to anger, causing him to verbally abuse her. Afraid that the verbal abuse may lead to physical abuse, Maggie leaves him: "She say one of these times I might not jus' say something. I might do something." She takes Henry with her because she is afraid that White Rat might hurt him, a fear that is validated by White Rat's statement that Henry "know what it mean when you hit him on the ass when he do something wrong." Her return home may, in fact, have been prompted by her desire to protect her son.

Although he claims that he has been sober for two months, White Rat is a heavy drinker. After he leaves Maggie, he goes to a white bar, where he passes for white and tells the bartender two versions of his marriage to Maggie. In the first, he tells the bartender about a black priest who is punished for renouncing his vows of celibacy; his punishment is having a clubfooted son. In the second, he describes a white priest who also breaks his vows, but his punishment is that he has a "nigger" for a child. In the second version, White Rat can also be seen as the child who is the punishment for miscegenation. Even though he claims that he hates the "hoogies" (whites) as much as his father did, Maggie disagrees and states that he marred her because she is "the lightest and brightest nigger woman" that he could get and "still be nigger." When he returns from the bar, he finds Maggie has gone and declares, "She the nigger." He may complain about the problems involved in being a light-skinned African American, but some of his comments suggest that he enjoyed some of the privileges and status that used to be given to light-skinned African Americans: "I kept telling Maggie it get harder and harder to be a white nigger now specially since it don't count no more how much white blood you got in you."

Because of the first-person narration, the reader gets only White Rat's perspective on the action. What is not related is Maggie's situation as a black woman abused by her husband, abandoned by her lover, and forced, either by concern for her child or for economic security, to return to a husband who expects to be fed the morning after she returns to him. He is, as Cousin Willie puts it, "the lessen two evils." Maggie can only retaliate by mentioning the child she will soon have, if, in fact, she is pregnant.

*Style and Technique*

White Rat's narration contains African American speech patterns and exposes his faults and shortcomings. Like all unreliable narrators, he reveals more to the reader than he is aware of, and like Gayl Jones's other narrators, he appears to be mentally and emotionally unstable. He feels superior to the branch of his family that comes from the hills, but he is as superstitious as he claims that they are. Corrected when he uses "pronounced" instead of "renounced," he then just uses "'nounced" because he does not like being corrected or because "renounced" is not in his vocabulary. It appears that he suffers from the "complex" that Maggie fears Henry would experience. Driven to rationalize his behavior, albeit in an altered story, to a white audience, he almost comes to terms with his own behavior, but he lacks the insight to empathize with Maggie, who claims that he "treats her like dirt," or to understand that his actions drove her to leave him. Like Maggie, who seems imprisoned in her exploited situation, White Rat is in his own cage, incapable of change.

*Thomas L. Erskine*

# THE WHITE STOCKING

*Author:* D. H. Lawrence (1885-1930)
*Type of plot:* Domestic realism
*Time of plot:* The early twentieth century
*Locale:* A small town in England, probably in the Midlands
*First published:* 1914

> *Principal characters:*
> TED WHISTON, a young traveling salesperson
> ELSIE WHISTON, his wife
> SAM ADAMS, an admirer of Elsie

*The Story*

When the smooth married life of a rather ordinary young couple is disrupted by the intrusion of a third person, the couple find themselves swept into an explosive situation that is beyond their capacity to control. There is certainly nothing remarkable about the protagonists, Ted and Elsie Whiston. They have been married two years, and live in a small, homey dwelling, their first house. She is a former factory worker, small and pretty, but also coquettish and superficial ("she seemed witty, although, when her sayings were repeated, they were entirely trivial"). He is a traveling sales representative, slow but solid, totally confident in the love of his wife, in whom he seems to find his whole being enriched and made whole. She has grown bored, however, and now tends to take him for granted, even mocking and jeering at him, although in spite of this she feels a deep attachment to him. It is the tension between these two contradictory attitudes that propels the story along its course.

The story begins on the morning of Valentine's Day. Elsie is excited to find in the mail a package addressed to her. She discovers that it contains a long white stocking, in which a pair of pearl earrings has been placed. She puts them on immediately, and her vain pleasure at the sight of herself in the mirror sets an ominous tone for the remainder of the story. Hiding the earrings, Elsie pretends to her husband that the white stocking is only a sample, but at breakfast she feels compelled to admit that this was a lie. Throughout the story, her naïveté, her insensitivity to the subtlety and delicacy of the feelings with which she is dealing, and her vacillation and duplicity contribute to the story's violent climax.

It transpires that the stocking was a gift from her former employer and admirer, Sam Adams, and she unconsciously goads her husband more by telling him that earlier in the year Adams sent her another stocking, but she concealed it from him. Concealment followed by later confession is her regular pattern of behavior. Worse is to follow (at least from Ted's point of view). She has been seeing Sam Adams, but only, she says, for coffee at the Royal. As Ted goes to work, they part in a state of unresolved tension, caught in a situation that neither of them has the maturity to grasp fully or to resolve. Cut adrift from their stable, day-to-day moorings, they are now at the mercy of powerful subconscious forces.

The middle section of the story is an extended flashback, revealing the significance of the friendship that Elsie had with Sam Adams and the uneasy triangle it formed with Ted. The flamboyance of Adams, the factory owner, is in sharp contrast to the dour steadiness of Ted. Adams, a forty-year-old bachelor, is a ladies' man, fashionably dressed and possessed of considerable charm. He is at home on the dance floor, in contrast to Ted, who does not dance. This is one of the critical points of the story and is highlighted by an incident, recalled in a flashback, that leads directly to the gift of the white stocking. Ted and Elsie attend a Christmas party given by Adams. Adams invites Elsie to dance, and she finds the experience completely exhilarating. Something about Adams, "some male warmth of attraction," ignites her; the rhythm of the dance and the close physical presence of her partner seem to transport her away from herself, into the deepest recesses of her partner's being. It is a new state of consciousness for her, and a pure physical pleasure. Adams has touched a vein of feeling, sensuality, and physical response in her that is quite beyond the reach of dull Ted, moodily playing cribbage in another room, and Elsie becomes momentarily aware of a grudge against Ted for failing to satisfy this aspect of her being. However, she is also disturbed by Adams. Even as she dances with him, she cannot quiet the voice of conscience. The intoxication of the dance is not free of tension. On the contrary, it strains her, and some part of her remains closed to Adams and will not be opened. That part belongs to Ted. What she loves about him is his permanence and his solidity, yet part of her being is closed to him. She will not allow him to penetrate her feelings. Although the situation is temporarily resolved in a flood of tenderness and compassion as they return from the dance, she is nevertheless caught between the attractions she feels toward both men. The seeds of the story's climax have been sown.

Now, however, the couple have married and Adams appears to have been forgotten. The narrative resumes as Ted returns home from work tired and depressed. The love Elsie undoubtedly feels for him is masked by her awareness of his inability to give her everything she needs, and her behavior becomes outrageously provocative. Putting on the stockings, she cruelly and deliberately taunts him, dancing around the room, lifting her skirt to her knees and kicking her legs up at him. They exchange bitter words, and the situation becomes full of barely suppressed hatred. His anger becomes uncontrollable. She is frightened but insists that she will not return the stockings. As the language becomes abusive, Ted threatens his wife with physical violence, which finally erupts as she tells him the truth about Adams's earlier gifts of earrings and a brooch. Striking her across the mouth, Ted is filled with the desire to destroy her utterly. A final catastrophe is avoided, however, as he is overcome with weariness and disgust at the whole situation. Slowly and deliberately, he locates the offending jewelry, packs it up, and sends it back to Adams. Returning to the sight of his wife's tear-stained face, he is moved to remorse and compassion. As she sobs a half-completed retraction and apology, "I never meant—," a flood of tenderness envelops them both, and the story ends on a note of anguished reconciliation.

*Themes and Meanings*

At the time of writing "The White Stocking," D. H. Lawrence was immersed in a reading of Arthur Schopenhauer's works, particularly "The Metaphysics of Love" in *Die Welt als Wille und Vorstellung* (1819; *The World as Will and Idea*, 1883-1886). He double-underlined a passage that referred to the falsity of the harmony that lovers suppose themselves to feel because this "frequently turns out to be violent discord shortly after marriage." This is exactly what happens in the "The White Stocking"; the story reveals how hard it is for a man and a woman to attain stability and wholeness in a close relationship, and the destructive and irrational behavior that results when the attempt fails. It suggests that sexual love carries an undercurrent of hostility, even hatred. The sexual overtones of the story are clear from the outset. The reader is made aware of Elsie's "delightful limbs" and how the sight of her bare flesh excites and disturbs Ted. Elsie's dance with Adams is described in highly erotic terms, and unbridled sexual taunting immediately precedes the story's climax.

The basic issue is one that Lawrence was to address throughout his writing career: How was an individual to preserve his or her integrity, freedom, and separate identity when intensely involved in a union with another human being? Ted and Elsie Whiston can be seen as Lawrentian pioneers—even though they are largely unaware of it—in the attempt to attain the "star equilibrium" that Lawrence described in *Women in Love* (1920): "a pure balance of two single beings," like "two single equal stars balanced in conjunction." This ideal state of perfect union and perfect separateness is glimpsed momentarily by Elsie. In the enhanced sensuality of the dance, which anticipates the mystic sexual unions of Lawrence's later novels, Elsie finds that "the movements of his [Adams'] body and limbs were her own movements, yet not her own movements." However, she cannot maintain this union, either with Adams or with Ted, because she has found no stable center within herself. She oscillates wildly between two poles of her being, both of which she needs: the rich vitality and dynamism of the dance, but also the "enduring form," the sense of permanence, that Ted gives her. Because she can find no way of synthesizing the two within herself, the couple seem doomed to a series of temporary reconciliations, each followed by another outburst of hostility and mutual incomprehension.

*Style and Technique*

"The White Stocking" is one of Lawrence's earliest stories. It was originally entered in a competition offered by the *Nottinghamshire Guardian* in 1907, when Lawrence was twenty-two. It did not win, and the judges commented that it was "lacking finish." Like most of Lawrence's early stories, it is marked by a down-to-earth realism, and this makes an important contribution to its effectiveness. The commonplace setting, for example, the Whistons' small, "seven and sixpenny" dwelling, and the homeyness and simplicity of their daily routine, is disturbingly limited and ordinary. This is reinforced by the effect of the diction. The predominance of short sentences containing a high proportion of monosyllabic words has a simple, almost childlike effect, suggesting that the characters are undeveloped in their understanding of life;

they lack sophistication and self-knowledge. (This changes only in the rich, flowing prose used to describe the dance, which ably conveys the new reality that Elsie has discovered.) The presence of an omniscient narrator, who sees so much more than any individual character is able to see, tends to emphasize for the reader the smallness and inadequacy of the Whistons' own perspective.

These stylistic elements effectively highlight, by contrast, the surging, primeval forces that the characters unleash in themselves and in one another, for which they are totally unprepared. It is as if they are living only on the surface of life. The bewilderment expressed in Elsie's final reconciling words, "I never meant—," is highly significant. The rational, everyday world that they inhabit makes them helpless before the dark and irrational psychic forces that they unwittingly arouse. They might well echo the cry of St. Paul in Romans 7:15: "I do not understand my own actions. For I do not do what I want, but I do the very thing I hate."

*Bryan Aubrey*

# A WHOLE LOAF

*Author:* Shmuel Yosef Agnon (Shmuel Yosef Czaczkes, 1888-1970)
*Type of plot:* Autobiographical
*Time of plot:* The 1930's
*Locale:* Jerusalem
*First published:* "Pat Shelema," 1933 (English translation, 1957)

> *Principal characters:*
> THE UNNAMED NARRATOR, the protagonist
> DR. YEKUTIEL NE'EMAN, a writer and sage, an acquaintance of
> the protagonist
> MR. GRESSLER, a wealthy landowner and favorite acquaintance of
> the protagonist

*The Story*

At the beginning of "A Whole Loaf," the narrator's suggestive comment, "I had made no preparations on Sabbath eve, so I had nothing to eat on the Sabbath," explains why he leaves his home in search of a meal. Other reasons for going out are the hellish heat at home and his sense of loneliness, for his wife and children are still abroad and he has to see to his own needs.

The protagonist thus joins other strollers at the end of the Sabbath day, partaking of the cool Jerusalem air. Soon he is distracted from his search for a restaurant by the great sage Dr. Yekutiel Ne'eman, sitting by his window. Expecting a word of wisdom, he hears Dr. Ne'eman rebuking him for not doing something to reunite the family back in Jerusalem.

The narrator then tells of Dr. Ne'eman's book, which has raised heated debate concerning its authenticity but which the sage claims to be a record of the words of Lord. Some believe that the book is authentic, whereas others hold that it is merely Dr. Ne'eman's own writings, attributed by him to an unknown and never-seen Lord. One undisputed effect of the book, observes the narrator, has been that people have bettered themselves by it, whereas others devote themselves heart and soul to keeping every word in it. Praising the book, the hero is surprised and grieved when Dr. Ne'eman leaves the window. Returning soon, however, he gives the hero a packet of letters to be posted. Accepting the task, the hero promises to mail the letters as asked.

When the Sabbath is over, the hero heads for the post office to mail the letters, all the while debating whether he should not go and eat first. He finally resolves first to fulfill his obligation to Dr. Ne'eman and finds himself standing before the post office. Just as he is about to enter, he is distracted by the strange sight of a carriage driven by his acquaintance from abroad, Mr. Gressler, making its way down the sidewalk. The pedestrians, far from being upset, appear to enjoy the danger of being nearly run over by the carriage.

Recalling the close, pleasure-filled friendship he has had with Mr. Gressler abroad and in Jerusalem, the narrator remembers how his friend was instrumental in amusing him and teaching him a knowledge to counter all other kinds of wisdom. Their close relationship was halted for a while when, still abroad, Mr. Gressler persuaded the hero's downstairs neighbor to set fire to his stock of cheap goods and collect the insurance. The fire, however, spread and consumed the hero's home as well, burning up his uninsured books and belongings. The remainder of his wealth was squandered on the ensuing litigation urged on him by Mr. Gressler. Blaming Mr. Gressler for his losses, the hero abandoned him, immersing himself in Dr. Ne'eman's book and leaving for the Land of Israel. On the boat, he noticed that Mr. Gressler was headed for the same destination, but his cabin was in the first-class section, whereas the hero was spending the journey in the lowliest class. On landing, Mr. Gressler helped him through customs and the journey to Jerusalem, whereupon their friendship was renewed and became even stronger after the hero's family went abroad.

Now, joining Mr. Gressler on the carriage, the hero forgets the letters and his hunger. Soon they encounter Mr. Hofni, the inventor of a better mousetrap, whom the hero dislikes. He grabs the reins to lead the horses away from Mr. Hofni, causing the carriage to overturn. Both riders roll in the dirt, and the hero, his body aching, proceeds to the nearest hotel dining room and orders a meal (after a long and hungry wait) but insists on having a whole loaf to go with it.

Now the waiting truly begins, for many meals are served to others while he does not receive his—in part because of the search for a whole loaf. Hearing the clock strike half past ten, the hero leaps to his feet to go and mail the letters, and he collides with the waiter, spilling his own meal. The manager comforts the hero and promises that a new meal will be soon prepared for him.

With his soul flying between the restaurant kitchen and the already closed post office, the hero awaits the meal he was promised. The last of the diners having left, the lights are turned off, leaving the hero still waiting for his food. When he hears the doors being locked, he knows that no one will return until morning. Although trying to sleep, the protagonist is disturbed by a mouse gnawing at some bones left on a table. He soon becomes convinced that it is he who will eventually become a meal for the mouse. Seeing a cat, he hopes that the mouse will run, but neither pays attention to the other and the cat's eyes take on an eerie green color that frightens the hero. The sound of a passing carriage prompts the hero to call on Mr. Gressler for help, but no help comes.

When the servants arrive in the morning, they are astonished to find the hero still waiting for his meal, and they laugh when the waiter identifies him as the one who ordered a whole loaf. The hero gets up, feeling dirty, sick, hungry, and thirsty, and makes his way back home, still unable to mail the letters as the post office is closed on Sunday. He washes and goes out to get some food, for he is still alone; his wife and children are abroad and the burden of providing for his own needs is still on him.

## Themes and Meanings

"A Whole Loaf" is perhaps the most frequently cited of Shmuel Yosef Agnon's *Sefer hama'asim* (1932; book of deeds), an anthology of short stories characterized by unreal, dreamlike situations and categorized as materialistic stories—namely, tales, or episodes within larger works, whose connotational import is in a higher (timeless) sphere than the denotational plot.

The key to this story's meaning has been identified by scholars as its title, with particular emphasis on the possible connotations of the term "loaf." There are a number of possible interpretations of what the loaf and the narrator's hunger for one represent, ranging from a yearning for spiritual, religious nourishment to one for selfish, material rewards, all the way to a desire by the hero to practice idolatry.

The difficulty with explaining the meaning of the term "loaf" may be skirted by focusing on the title's adjective. Thus, one may say that the protagonist's insistence on having a loaf (whatever it may mean) that is whole constitutes the crux of the difficulty in providing him with one, thereby leaving him hungry physically, but even more so existentially, for an unattainable wholeness.

The story focuses on the hero's state of loneliness and his inability to commit himself to a specific set of values. He is of two minds about issues such as Dr. Ne'eman's book, his desire to eat or carry out the promise to mail the letters, and his inability to take steps to reunite the family. These, and others, are all encapsulated in the narrator's opening statement about being unprepared for the Sabbath (or for anything else), thereby having to bear the consequences of not enjoying the rewards of prior preparation. The penalty for his inaction is also an emotional one, represented by the hellish existence in his room, where flames of fire appear to torment him (an expression of his sense of guilt) on the Sabbath day.

The character of Yekutiel Ne'eman has been said to represent Moses or some Mosaic figure on the evidence of his name, both the first and last parts of which have been attributed by Jewish lore to Moses, and of his influential and controversial book. The letters, then, would compose that which was handed down by Moses—the commandments or the healing, spiritual, and ethical values contained in the Five Books—ostensibly recorded by Dr. Ne'eman as spoken by Lord, namely God (who is referred to in the story with four dots that stand for the tetragrammaton YHWH, God's unique four-letter name).

In respecting Dr. Ne'eman's claims regarding the book's authorship and by agreeing to mail the letters, the hero would be identified as a man of faith, eager and willing to pass the tradition on to others and into the future. His ambivalence about his ways in life, though, makes his mission to the post office dubious. His sense of responsibility to two distinct missions—the collective, religious one represented by Dr. Ne'eman and the selfish, individualistic view indicated via the restaurant and Mr. Gressler—leaves him caught in the middle, experiencing a spiritual starvation, as of the proverbial ass dying of hunger between two bales of hay because he cannot decide of which of the two to eat. Thus torn between two impulses, the hero remains perpetually in a state of imperfection, unable to have his whole loaf.

*Style and Technique*

In "The Whole Loaf," Agnon characteristically transformed real events into a powerfully evocative literary gem. The story's opening recaptures Agnon's own experience when, in 1925, renting a room in Jerusalem, he had yet to arrange for the immigration of his wife and children, who were still living with his wife's family in Germany. Agnon's separation from the family, his sense of guilt at not heeding his wife's urging to arrange for their speedy reunion in Jerusalem, and the constant dependence on the postal service for linking him with his loved ones are but the most visible biographical details from that period incorporated into this tale of the struggle between modernity and tradition for the soul of the hero. For example, in a letter to his wife dated March 18, 1925, Agnon recounted the unusually hot spring weather in Jerusalem that prevented him from remaining in his room, because its outer walls were covered with sheets of metal.

Eight years later, Agnon drew on these memories to embellish and reflect the spiritual torments of his protagonist, whose sense of loneliness is greater than the mere pain of being apart from his family. Agnon generalized and abstracted his own loneliness, hunger, and discomfort to indicate the existential predicament of the tradition-sensitive hero, who has become skeptical about the very existence of Lord and about the origins of Dr. Ne'eman's book (details mostly omitted by Agnon in the revised and translated version of the story).

The protagonist's shaken faith may also have been suggested by Agnon's decade-long exposure to modernism as manifested by the broad array of German intellectual life, at that time a new and unprecedented experience in the author's life (whether in Galicia or the Land of Israel), leaving a deep and lasting impression on his worldview and his literary creativity. Thus, Agnon observes in this story the bipolarity of modern-day Jewry, a conflict expressed in the rift within the hero's personality between allegiance to a Mosaic way of life (as represented by the character with the Hebrew name, Yekutiel Ne'eman) and allegiance to the life of secularism (indicated by the character bearing the German name, Gressler).

Furthermore, the fire that consumed the hero's books and household belongings, the outcome of the satanic temptation of Mr. Gressler, is a transmutation of an emotionally traumatic fire in 1924, which burned Agnon's library (and never-to-be-published book) while he was living in the German city of Homburg.

In the story, the events reflect the hero's sense of guilt for associating with Mr. Gressler and living abroad; his reaction to the fire, for example, was a break with Mr. Gressler and his secular lifestyle, an immersion into Dr. Ne'eman's book, and immigration to the Land of Israel.

"A Whole Loaf" thus bears out the point that Agnon's approach to writing stories was an intimate fusion between his experience and his imagination, the latter working on the former to condense and refine it and reflect the ideas and values he hoped to relay to his readers.

*Stephen Katz*

# THE WHORE OF MENSA

*Author:* Woody Allen (Allen Stewart Konigsberg, 1935-    )
*Type of plot:* Parody
*Time of plot:* The 1970's
*Locale:* New York
*First published:* 1974

> *Principal characters:*
> KAISER LUPOWITZ, a private detective
> WORD BABCOCK, his client, a blackmail victim
> FLOSSIE, the blackmailer
> SHERRY, the title character, a prostitute of the mind

*The Story*

Kaiser Lupowitz, a New York private detective, is hired by Word Babcock to thwart a blackmail scheme. Babcock, who builds and services joy buzzers, considers himself an intellectual but does not find his wife intellectually stimulating: "She won't discuss Pound with me. Or Eliot. I didn't know that when I married her." He hears about a call-girl service providing female college students who will discuss intellectual matters for a fee, and he becomes a regular customer. Flossie, the madam, wants ten thousand dollars, or else she will turn over to his wife tapes of his "discussing *The Waste Land* and *Styles of Radical Will*, and, well, really getting into some issues" with a girl in a motel room. Babcock needs help because his wife "would die if she knew she didn't turn me on up here."

Lupowitz calls Flossie, who sends him Sherry to discuss the works of Herman Melville in a room at the Plaza. After some pseudointellectual banter, Lupowitz threatens to have Sherry arrested unless she tells him where to find Flossie. Sherry begins to cry, saying that she has reached her current state because she needs the money to complete her master's degree: "I've been turned down for a grant. Twice."

Sherry sends Lupowitz to the Hunter College Book Store, a front for Flossie's operation. The detective discovers that Flossie is really a man. Flossie explains that he wanted to take over *The New York Review of Books* and went to Mexico for an operation that was supposed to make him look like Lionel Trilling: "Something went wrong. I came out looking like Auden, with Mary McCarthy's voice. That's when I started working the other side of the law."

Lupowitz disarms Flossie before the male madam can shoot him. Taking him to the police, Lupowitz learns that the FBI is after Flossie: "A little matter involving some gamblers and an annotated copy of Dante's *Inferno*."

*Themes and Meanings*

Literature, philosophy, intellectual pretensions, sex, and parody are the most common elements in Woody Allen's fiction, and all are on display in "The Whore of

Mensa." The story is Allen's second parody of the kind of detective fiction associated with Dashiell Hammett and Raymond Chandler. In the first, "Mr. Big," Kaiser Lupowitz is hired to prove or disprove the existence of God. Allen's intellectual satire can also be seen in such diverse works as "Spring Bulletin," "The Irish Genius," "No Kaddish for Weinstein," and, especially, "The Kugelmass Episode."

Allen has frequently been criticized for filling his stories, plays, and films with in-jokes aimed at a limited audience, but that audience is simply anyone reasonably well read. Allen's satire depends on his reader recognizing the comic incongruity of Sherry's being arrested for reading *Commentary* in a parked car, Lupowitz's threatening to have Sherry tell her story at Alfred Kazin's office, the detective's asking, "Suppose I wanted Noam Chomsky explained to me by two girls?," and Sherry's attempting to bribe Lupowitz with photographs of Dwight Macdonald reading.

Allen's humor is aimed at intellectuals while making fun of them. Lupowitz responds to his first sight of Sherry: "They really know how to appeal to your fantasies. Long straight hair, leather bag, silver earrings, no make-up." Like Alvy Singer's first wife in Allen's film *Annie Hall* (1977), Sherry is a cultural stereotype: "Central Park West upbringing, Socialist summer camps, Brandeis. She was every dame you saw waiting in line at the Elgin or the Thalia, or penciling the words 'Yes, very true' into the margin of some book on Kant."

As with all of Allen's humor, a serious purpose lurks beneath the surface gags. Allen equates the need for intellectual stimulation with prostitution because so many people approach sex, emotional involvement, and intellectuality on the same shallow level. Thus, Lupowitz prepares for his meeting with Sherry by consulting the Monarch College Outline series so that he can fake his way through their Melville encounter. Sherry also fakes her responses just as a prostitute would: "Oh, yes, Kaiser. Yes, baby, that's deep. A platonic comprehension of Christianity—why didn't I see it before?" This superficiality is what Word Babcock wants: "I don't want an involvement—I want a quick intellectual experience, then I want the girl to leave."

Allen's point is that shallowness in one segment of life is likely to spread into others. The interrelatedness of all aspects of life is emphasized when Lupowitz goes to Flossie's and learns that for three hundred dollars he can get "the works: A thin Jewish brunette would pretend to pick you up at the Museum of Modern Art, let you read her master's, get you involved in a screaming quarrel at Elaine's over Freud's conception of women, and then fake a suicide of your choosing—the perfect evening, for some guys."

*Style and Technique*

"The Whore of Mensa" celebrates the clichés of hard-boiled detective fiction. Sometimes Allen presents these clichés straight: "I turned and suddenly found myself standing face to face with the business end of a .38"; "He hit the ground like a ton of bricks." Sometimes he adds a touch of silliness, as when "a quivering pat of butter named Word Babcock walked into my office and laid his cards on the table" and when Sherry arrives "packed into her slacks like two big scoops of vanilla ice cream." Occasionally, he gives the expected a small twist: "I pushed a glass across the desk top and a bottle of rye I keep handy for nonmedicinal purposes." Allen tops it all off by having Flossie arrested by a Sergeant Holmes.

Allen no doubt chose the detective form as the vehicle for his satire not only for its appropriateness for the prostitution plot and the literary allusions but also because of the importance of the vernacular in American crime fiction. Like Mark Twain, S. J. Perelman, and numerous other humorists, Allen enjoys distinctively American ways of saying things such as "I owned up" and "A five-spot cools him." It is fitting that "The Whore of Mensa" ends with a parody of the master of the laconic, staccato American style, Ernest Hemingway: "Later that night, I looked up an old account of mine named Gloria. She was blond. She had graduated cum laude. The difference was she majored in physical education. It felt good."

*Michael Adams*

# WHY CAN'T THEY TELL YOU WHY?

*Author:* James Purdy (1923-    )
*Type of plot:* Social realism
*Time of plot:* Several years after World War II
*Locale:* An unspecified American city
*First published:* 1957

*Principal characters:*
PAUL, a sickly and lonely boy
ETHEL, his widowed mother

## The Story

Paul is a frail, pathetic child who lives with his mother, a frustrated and bitter woman who spends her days working and her evenings complaining on the phone to her friend Edith Gainesworth about the trouble of caring for a sick son. Paul is so desperately lonely, however, that even this kind of attention excites him. Paul has discovered photographs of his father, who died in the war, in old shoe boxes. He has transferred them to two clean candy boxes and now spends his time looking through them on the back stairs as he listens to his mother ask advice from her friend, who studied psychology at an adult center. Ethel cannot understand why Paul wants to play with these photos instead of with toys like normal children—especially since she has told him so little about his father. Despite her insistence that Paul give up the photos and overcome his obsession with his father, Paul continues to seek companionship through the black-and-white images of his father, watching him grow up from a boy his own age to a man and a soldier in the army. When his mother laments that her days at work are hard but being home in the evening with such a sick child is even worse, Paul enters the room with the pictures and attempts to distract her with airplane and bird sounds. He has been home from school for two months; Ethel is certain that his preoccupation with the photos is making him ill.

One night Ethel awakens suddenly. Paul is not sleeping in his cot and his blanket is missing, so she looks for him anxiously and resentfully. She first goes to the kitchen, but remembers Paul rarely eats anything. Finding him asleep on the back stairs with the photos, she angrily asks him why he is sleeping there, if it is to be with his photos. When Paul fails to answer, Ethel seizes his boxes of photos. She is repulsed by him; when she notices an ugly mole on his throat, she compares him to a sick bird. Paul inadvertently calls her "Mama Ethel," though she has told him never to refer to her as his mother because it makes her feel old. A black substance spews from his mouth. He apparently has tried to eat the pictures, but the omniscient narrator says that it is as if Paul has disgorged his heart, blackened with grief.

## Themes and Meanings

James Purdy first published "Why Can't They Tell You Why?" in a collection of short stories called *The Color of Darkness* (1957)—a title suggesting that its stories are about emptiness and failed relationships. This story's theme is loneliness, which is reflected in both Ethel's and Paul's feelings of isolation from each other and from the rest of society. Ethel is an embittered widow who rarely even mentions Paul's father. She feels that her days of hard work with the public and standing on her feet all day are surpassed in misery only by her evenings spent caring for an ill child, yet she actually spends that time complaining to a friend on the telephone. The story's chief concern, however, is the alienation of Paul, who is denied the love that he needs from his mother and is even robbed of the surrogate that he seeks in the old photographs of his dead father. At an intense moment in his confrontation with his mother, his fear emanates from the idea that he and Ethel are the only two people in the world.

When Ethel charges Paul with preferring his dead father to his living mother, the irony is that Paul's father is more alive to him than his cold, uncaring mother. Paul's efforts to annoy his mother by looking at his father's photos while she talks about him on the phone are desperate attempts to construct the only family unity he has ever known.

The title of the story reflects the story's use of language as a marker of these failures of communication. The man to whom Ethel always refers as "your father" differs greatly from the man in the pictures whom Paul comes to think of as "Daddy." Paul is frightened by her calling him a "little man," not knowing what she means by it but feeling that it forebodes more suffering for him. Paul cannot articulate why he is so drawn to the photos because he does not understand his own needs, the real nature of his illness. He craves love, but because he has never been shown any, he cannot explain to his mother what he seeks. Ethel insists that Paul not call her "Mama," because it makes her feel old, yet the clear implication is that she also does not want to admit that Paul is her child. When she looks at him she is revolted and cannot believe that he is her son. This denial develops into an inability even to see him as human. Indeed, she herself is dehumanizing him, robbing him of his humanity, by refusing to show him any love and by destroying the only source of love he has found in his life.

*Style and Technique*

Purdy's work draws much of its impact through understatement and implication. He presents little visual description but conveys vivid images through his use of metaphor. Although Ethel never actually strikes Paul in the story, its details strongly suggest that she has often locked him in the basement for punishment and that she has been physically abusive. When Ethel jerks Paul toward her by his pajamas, he pleads for her not to hurt him. She pulls his hair, and Paul winces when she raises her hand. He is apprehensive at the thought of being punished, but being sent to the basement is even more terrifying to him. That Paul is neglected is reflected in his unmended nightshirt and the strange excitement that he feels when he hears Ethel talk about him on the phone.

Paul is afraid of his mother, yet each character perceives the other as distant and even nonhuman. To Paul, Ethel is a monster; to Ethel, Paul is an animal and a burden.

Purdy often describes Paul in terms of sick, starving, scared animals. Paul debases himself by pathetically petting the fur on his mother's slippers to persuade her to let him keep the photos. At the end of the story, when he goes completely mad, Paul hisses like a trapped animal. There is, Purdy tells the reader, no chance of bringing him back.

Ethel is described in equally unattractive images, often demoniac, involving fire and smoke. When she takes some of the photos from him, she tells him that she will burn them. She then heads toward the basement while Paul clutches her legs and shrieks wretchedly. Ethel recoils at his touch, feeling as if a mouse were crawling under her clothes. Threatening to send Paul away to a mental institution as was his Aunt Grace, Ethel looks down at Paul crying pitifully at her feet, stroking her furry house slippers. She demands that he throw the pictures in the furnace, but after a brief period in which his fear quiets him, the boy starts running around the room in panic. His voice is strange to both of them, and unusual gurgling sounds seem to come from his lungs.

As Ethel throws pictures into the fire, she turns to look at Paul, who is crouched over the pictures like a threatened, wounded animal. Her bathrobe smells of smoke; her face is lighted by the fiery furnace. Further, any suggestions of tenderness in Ethel are always qualified as being menacing or false. The candy boxes are symbolic of what the photos signify to Paul. Literally Paul is starving, as he will not eat; he is emaciated and pale. Metaphorically starving for affection, he is getting sustenance only from what he keeps in the candy boxes. Because his mother will not nurture him, he seeks his father's love. Paul's attempt to swallow the pictures completes this metaphor.

The story's omniscient point of view allows the reader to see the isolation of both Paul and Ethel from each other—she in repugnance, he in terror. They are strangers as well as antagonists. Their communication is infrequent and fraught with tension. Ethel's language is full of nuances that confuse and frighten Paul. He does understand, however, that when she says, "All right for you," Ethel is indicating that any attempt at communication is abruptly halted.

*Lou Thompson*

# WHY DON'T YOU DANCE?

*Author:* Raymond Carver (1938-1988)
*Type of plot:* Antistory
*Time of plot:* About 1980
*Locale:* Somewhere in the United States
*First published:* 1981

> *Principal characters:*
> A MAN
> A GIRL
> A BOY

*The Story*

As he pours himself a drink in the kitchen, a man looks out the window to his front yard, where the bedroom furniture has been arranged almost precisely as it was arranged in the bedroom. There is the bed, flanked by two nightstands and two reading lamps; a chiffonnier; a portable heater; a rattan chair. The kitchen table stands in the driveway, and on top of it are a record player, a box of silverware, and a potted plant. The rest of the furniture is also on the lawn: a desk, a coffee table, a television set, a sofa and chair. Earlier in the day, the man had run an extension cord from the house to the lawn, and now all the electrical items can be operated as well outdoors as they were inside the house.

Later, after the man has gone to the market, a boy and a girl stop at the house, thinking that the furniture on the lawn must signal a yard sale in progress. They begin to examine the items in the yard, and soon the boy turns on the television set and sits down on the sofa to watch it. The girl tries out the bed and invites the boy to join her; though it makes him feel awkward, he gets on the bed with her because there seems to be no one in the house. After a while, the boy decides to see if anyone is at home who can tell him the prices of the items in the yard. The girl instructs him to offer the owner ten dollars less than the asking price for each item.

Meanwhile, the man returns from the market. The boy says that they are interested in the bed, the television, and the desk, and they haggle, settling on forty dollars for the bed and fifteen for the television. The man pours drinks for all three of them. While drinking his glass of whiskey, the man drops a lighted cigarette between the sofa cushions, and the girl helps him find it. The three sit together drinking whiskey in the dark.

The man decides that the young couple should buy the record player. He refills their drinks. Finding a box filled with records, he asks the girl to pick one, which she does at random, unfamiliar with any of the titles. The boy, by now slightly drunk, is writing a check when the man suggests that the boy and the girl dance to the phonograph music. Though the boy is reluctant, the couple start dancing together in the driveway, and before long the man joins them. The girl notices that the neighbors are watching, but the man seems not to mind, telling her that the neighbors only thought that they had seen everything at his house. The girl and the man start to dance closer together.

Some weeks later, the girl tries to describe what happened at the man's house that night. For a time, she talks about the incident frequently, trying to get it out of her system.

*Themes and Meanings*

Like many of Raymond Carver's short stories, "Why Don't You Dance?" is about an ordinary man moved to desperation by reversals of fortune. Though the reader is uncertain about what recent events have caused the man's bizarre behavior, there are broad hints in the text about a marital breakup. At any rate, the home is in crisis, probably as a result, at least in part, of the man's heavy drinking—he is never without a drink in the story, and he mixes beer and whiskey with ease. Similarly withheld is what happens after the man and girl start dancing together, but certainly it is something that the girl, weeks later, would like to be able to forget. The suggestion is of exhibitionism and voyeurism, though the act itself is less important than the reader's knowledge that the man is at the breaking point. Twice during the story the girl calls the man "desperate," though his behavior throughout is less frenzied and irrational than it is eerily calm. He is a man with nothing left to lose.

Much of the effect of this story is attributable to the very ordinariness of the characters, the surroundings, and the dialogue. In its ability to exploit the potential horror of the everyday, "Why Don't You Dance?" can be called surrealist. The setting, a suburban lawn, is made unfamiliar and grotesque because it is covered with furniture obsessively arranged as it was indoors. Routine objects take on weird significance in the context of the story: A garden hose dispenses water to dilute the girl's drink; a phonograph and a set of old record albums provide the musical accompaniment to the story's climax; a used bed becomes a symbol of two marriages. The characters themselves are wholly without surface distinction. Nameless, almost generic, they speak in flat, simple sentences, the tragic weight of which is apprehended by the reader only at the end of the story. The physical and emotional landscape is like that of a painting by René Magritte (1898-1967): deceptively ordinary, but charged with submerged anxiety and despair.

The namelessness and banality of each of the story's elements serves another purpose, however, and one ultimately more chilling. Their lack of differentiating characteristics makes these characters into Everyman and Everywoman, forcing the reader to realize that this situation could befall anyone. In front of the empty house, the couple, who are "furnishing a small apartment," act out a grotesquely compressed pantomime of middle-class married life. The girl tests the bed while the boy shyly demurs. The boy sits on the couch watching television, and the girl tries the electric blender. Finally, at the man's prompting, they begin to dance, setting the stage for the story's unspeakable climax. In this sense, they are the man's heirs and his successors, and the tragedy that has ruined him seems destined to impinge on their young lives.

*Style and Technique*

Much of what would be called exposition and characterization in a more conventional story is omitted from "Why Don't You Dance?" The reader knows little about the man or about the young couple, and this deliberate vagueness forces the reader to speculate, to fill in the gaps in the narrative. What has become of the man's marriage? Why has he emptied the contents of his house onto the lawn? Most important, what happens at the end of the story? By posing but refusing to answer such questions, the story leaves everything to the reader's imagination, thus producing not one but an infinite number of possible narratives. Paradoxically, this story—which is superficially so brief and so simple—is highly complex, subject to almost limitless interpretation.

Unlike many of Carver's short stories, "Why Don't You Dance?" is less a realistic portrayal of middle-class life than a parable of human relationships and human suffering. In this most minimalist of narratives, a writer famed for his spareness of style succeeds in evoking a tragedy as universal as it is disturbing.

*J. D. Daubs*

# WHY I LIVE AT THE P.O.

*Author:* Eudora Welty (1909-2001)
*Type of plot:* Wit and humor
*Time of plot:* The early 1940's
*Locale:* China Grove, Mississippi
*First published:* 1941

> *Principal characters:*
> SISTER, the obsessed narrator of the story
> STELLA-RONDO, her sister, a returned prodigal
> MAMA, Sister and Stella-Rondo's mother
> PAPA-DADDY, their grandfather
> UNCLE RONDO, their uncle
> SHIRLEY-T, Stella-Rondo's young daughter

*The Story*

This comic story is an extended dramatic monologue told by Sister to an unnamed visitor to the post office, where she now lives after having left her home because of the return of her sister Stella-Rondo. As the title suggests, the story is an apologia in which Sister attempts to explain why she has decided to live in the post office of the small town of China Grove, where she is postmistress. The first line of the story establishes the problem quite clearly: "I was getting along fine with Mama, Papa-Daddy and Uncle Rondo until my sister Stella-Rondo just separated from her husband and came back home again." Ostensibly, Sister's decision is a result of all of her family turning against her after the return of Stella-Rondo, who earlier ran off with a traveling photographer, who, to hear Sister tell it, was her own boyfriend before Stella-Rondo stole him from her.

What makes the story both comic and complex is that the reader hears only Sister's side of the story. As she says, Stella-Rondo broke up her and Mr. Whitaker by telling him that she was one-sided. To this Sister, in her own twisted logic that dominates the story, replies, "Bigger on one side than the other, which is a deliberate falsehood: I'm the same. Stella-Rondo is exactly twelve months to the day younger than I am and for that reason she's spoiled." It is this petty and petulant point of view of Sister that makes "Why I Live at the P.O." a tour de force of southern idiom, one of Eudora Welty's most admired stories.

Indeed, Sister is one-sided, and as she recounts the events that take place around the Fourth of July in China Grove, the reader sees through her seemingly banal defense. Sister is a childish woman obsessed with trivia and her persecution complex. She is also a delightful fictional creation made up of lovely illogic, and that is the key element in this hilarious story. The family comedy begins when Stella-Rondo claims that her two-year-old daughter, Shirley-T, is adopted; Sister denies this by saying that

Shirley-T is "the spit-image of Pappa-Daddy if he'd cut off his beard." Beginning with this remark by Sister, Stella-Rondo methodically turns each member of the family against Sister until Sister, unable to bear it any longer, systematically goes through the house taking everything that belongs to her and setting up housekeeping in the post office. The list of the things that Sister gathers up—a sewing-machine motor, a calendar with first-aid remedies on it, a thermometer, a Hawaiian ukulele, and bluebird wall vases—is in itself a wonderfully comic catalog.

Thus, the plot of the story is minimal, even trivial. In fact, trivia is what seems to characterize this extended monologue, for it is difficult for the reader to take seriously any of the events of the story that Sister tells. The reader feels superior to the characters in the story, as is typical of comedy, because he or she can laugh at the foolishness of the values they embody. At the end of the story, when Sister says that she likes it at the "P.O.," with everything cater-cornered, and that she wants the world to know that she is happy, the reader perhaps suspects that she protests too much. At this point, one must look back on the story and try to get beneath Sister's own stated justification for her actions. Only then can the reader answer the basic question: Why does Sister live at the P.O.?

*Themes and Meanings*

It is often difficult to discuss the theme of a comic story such as this one, for to explicate comedy too often puts one to the thankless task of explaining a joke. What makes "Why I Live at the P.O." amusing, however, according to many readers (it is one of Welty's best-known fictions) is that Sister is a comic example of the schizophrenia of obsession, that she thus becomes almost mechanical in her reactions to her persecution complex. The reader laughs at the story because the characters seem so obsessed with trivia; yet, as is typical of most comedy, there is something serious beneath the laughter: The reader despairs to think that people can be so obsessed with such petty matters.

Many of Welty's fictional characters seem isolated in some way; this story is one in which the reader must discover the nature of that isolation. Thus, one might say that this story is about the reader's gradual discovery of why Sister does live at the P.O., and that this reason goes beyond what Sister says, although what Sister says is all the reader really has. Indeed, the reader must analyze Sister's situation as she herself describes it and develop a dual perspective: a sympathetic identification with Sister followed by a detached judgment of her actions and speech. The problem of the story is that of Sister, who is the kind of character who cannot do things herself, but instead must have someone else act out her own desires. In this story, it can be said that Sister is the thinking side of the self, while Stella-Rondo is the acting side. Thus, it is true when Sister says throughout the story that she does nothing and everything is Stella-Rondo's fault, but at the same time the reader is right to suspect that everything that happens is Sister's doing.

For example, it is Sister who first dates Mr. Whitaker, but it is Stella-Rondo who marries him and moves away from the family; Sister wants to do both but cannot act on her desires. According to Sister, Stella-Rondo turns the other members of the family against her, but what Stella-Rondo actually does is act out Sister's feelings. Sister communicates everything in an oblique way, never expressing her feelings directly but always manipulating events and people diagonally through Stella-Rondo. Consequently, she can cause many events to occur yet disclaim responsibility for any of them. Thus, because Stella-Rondo is the objective side of Sister's subjective self, it is inevitable that the more that Sister attempts to drive out Stella-Rondo, the more she herself is driven out.

Stella-Rondo is the female version of the biblical prodigal son returned. Sister desires to remain safe at home and manipulate the family from her position as dutiful daughter. Ironically, however, Stella-Rondo becomes the favorite when she returns, while Sister becomes the exile. The irony of the story is that although Sister spends the whole tale explaining why she lives at the P.O., she really does not know why. Although she talks throughout, no one listens to what she says, not even herself. No one listens to anyone else in this story, especially Sister. As she says in the last line, if Stella-Rondo should come to her and try to explain about her life with Mr. Whitaker, "I'd simply put my fingers in both my ears and refuse to listen." In a metaphoric sense, Sister has told the entire story with her fingers in both her ears; that is, she cannot hear her story from the dual perspective that the reader can.

*Style and Technique*

The method of "Why I Live at the P.O." is that of a dramatic monologue. Thus, its closest literary analogue is the dramatic monologue of Robert Browning, in which there is always a gap between the way speakers perceive themselves and the way listeners perceive them. A dramatic monologue is a work in which speakers reveal themselves unawares. In such a form, the speakers, even as they seem to damn another character, actually only succeed in damning themselves. Perhaps the literary character that Sister resembles even more than a figure from Browning's poetry is Fyodor Dostoevski's Underground Man in his short novel *Zapiski iz podpolya* (1864; *Notes from the Underground*, 1954). As it is for Dostoevski's nameless antihero, Sister's logic is not so much insane as it is the rational pushed to such an extreme that it becomes irrational and perverse. It is indeed the style of her speech—that is, the whole of the story—which reveals this problem.

"Why I Live at the P.O." is different in both tone and technique from Welty's usual fiction. In most of her best-known stories, reality is transformed into fantasy and fable, and the logic is not that of ordinary life; here, in contrast, things remain stubbornly real. Many readers have noted that the dreamlike nature of Welty's stories depends on her ability to squeeze meaning out of the most trivial of details. Here, however, in a story that depends on the triviality of things, there is no dreamlike effect; the trivial details are comically allowed to remain trivial. Regardless of the difference in style, however, here as elsewhere in Welty's fiction, the focus is on the isolation of the self.

*Charles E. May*

# WICKED GIRL

*Author:* Isabel Allende (1942-    )
*Type of plot:* Domestic realism
*Time of plot:* The late twentieth century
*Locale:* South America, probably Chile
*First published:* "Niña perversa," 1989 (English translation, 1991)

> *Principal characters:*
> ELENA MEJIAS, an eleven-year-old girl
> HER MOTHER, the owner of a boardinghouse
> JUAN JOSE BERNAL, a boarder

*The Story*

Elena is a nondescript, self-absorbed eleven-year-old who helps her mother run a boardinghouse. No one, including her mother, notices her unless some chore must be done. One of Elena's responsibilities is to spy on guests to ensure that their behavior conforms to her mother's standards. Elena and her mother speak to each other infrequently, but when they do, their conversations revolve around Elena's reports. Her mother, as crafty as Elena, knows when the girl embellishes what she overhears and sees.

Their routines begin to change when a singer, Juan Jose Bernal, nicknamed "the Nightingale," comes to board with them. He is different from the usual boarders, civil servants or students who lead quiet lives. Bernal needs special food, quiet hours during the day, long baths, and extra telephone service. Knowing her mother's concern with her reputation, Elena is surprised when she rents the room to the flamboyant Bernal, but she says nothing, remaining as invisible as ever.

Although dealing with Bernal's hours and demands means more work, Elena sees her mother begin to change. She wears perfume and buys new underwear, and she sits opposite Bernal in the kitchen, listening to his stories, smiling and laughing. Because Elena is used to spying, nothing her mother buys or does escapes her notice. Elena begins to hate the man who has claimed her mother's attention, seeing him as a cheap scoundrel and fake artist.

One evening, Bernal appears on the patio with his guitar and begins to sing. Despite his unremarkable voice, his singing sparks a new festive air in the quiet boardinghouse. Suddenly, Elena's mother grabs her hand and pulls her up to dance. After a moment, Elena sees that her mother is entranced by the music. Elena's mother pushes her away and sways on the floor alone, absorbed in the mood of the night.

After that, Elena sees Bernal in a new way, as a sexual being who can evoke such response. She watches him even more intensely, going over and over his body in her mind. She becomes obsessed with him, waiting for him to see her, yet almost dying of pleasure if he speaks to her or touches her. At night, she stays awake thinking about him and even goes to his room, touching his possessions and lying naked in his empty bed to absorb every bit of his essence into hers.

One day, Elena sees Bernal touch her mother and senses what the touch means. This realization so disturbs her that she begins to spy even more on her mother. She discovers that instead of singing every night, Bernal spends the night with her mother, making love. One night, she slips quietly into her mother's room and watches them. Elena notes her mother's every movement, believing that if she uses these same techniques, she can win Bernal herself.

Absorbed in this fantasy, Elena goes about her work routinely but becomes more and more immersed in the plan she is weaving. She eats little, a fact that her mother attributes to her approaching puberty. One day, she purposely stuffs herself with peas and cheese, becoming too ill to stay at school. Returning home at a time when her mother is marketing, she goes immediately to the room of the sleeping Bernal. Removing her clothes as she has done often when alone in his room, she slides into bed with him and begins to use the techniques she saw her mother execute so successfully. Bernal responds until he feels her light body on his. Realizing it is not his lover, he screams that she is a wicked girl, slaps her face, and leaps from the bed. The door opens to reveal another boarder standing outside listening.

Elena spends the next seven years with nuns, then goes to college and begins working in a bank. Her mother and Bernal marry, give up the boardinghouse, and retire to raise flowers in the country. Although Elena's mother occasionally visits her, Bernal does not come along. He thinks of her constantly, however, and becomes obsessed with the image of her and of all young girls. He even buys children's clothing and frequents school yards. His fantasy of that one day takes hold of his whole being.

When Elena is twenty-six years old, she and a boyfriend visit Bernal and her mother. Bernal spends hours on his appearance and rehearses every possible conversation many times in his mind. Instead of the fantasy child, he finds a shy, rather insipid young woman and feels betrayed. When the two are alone in the kitchen getting wine, Bernal tells her of his consuming passion and what a mistake he made to reject her on that morning long ago. She looks at him speechlessly. She has overcome the pain of her first rejected love. She does not even remember it.

*Themes and Meanings*

"Wicked Girl," with its ironic ending, focuses on two of Isabel Allende's favorite themes: the power of passion and the strength of ordinary Latin American women such as Elena and her mother. Males dominate Latin American society, and Bernal seems to have everything under control. He makes the boardinghouse adhere to his schedule of demands by seducing the owner and bewitching her daughter. When he almost succumbs to Elena's seduction techniques, he calls her "wicked" for tempting him to break ancient taboos about having sex with young girls.

What he is not prepared for, however, is the effect of this seemingly inconsequential event involving a nondescript young girl. The power she has over him becomes his obsession, making him an outcast from mainstream society, sneaking around spying on young girls exactly as Elena spied on him and the other boarders.

Elena, on the other hand, prospers. Being sent away from her oppressive home situation opens up opportunities. She goes on to college and gets a job in a bank, certainly better than waiting on roomers in a boardinghouse. When she returns to visit Bernal for the first time, she is still shy and not attractive, but the young man with her is begging to marry her, and she has a successful career. She, not Bernal, is in the position of power. She shows her real strength at the end of the story, when Bernal pours out his years of pining for her. She is astounded. She has forgotten the incident, filing it away with life's other learning experiences. This strong woman has developed coping skills that Latin Americans usually associate with men.

In the women's lives, passion is important. Throughout the story, love transforms. Elena's mother, who had grown unattractive from years of hard work, blossoms under Bernal's caresses, acting like a young girl in love. Elena shows the immature obsession of a first awakening to sexual feelings as she stalks her prey around the boardinghouse and watches her mother make love. Love and sex are a part of women's lives. The strong woman enjoys these things but does not let them rule her life.

*Style and Technique*

Isabel Allende is a master storyteller, and "Wicked Girl" illustrates her narrative abilities well. She uses an especially interesting technique, very long paragraphs that relate many events. Some cover almost two pages. All include imagery enhancing the emotions that arise from the events.

The plot begins immediately with a brief description of Elena, followed by the foreshadowing statement, "Nothing about her betrayed her torrid dreams, nor presaged the sensuous creature she would become." At the beginning of the second paragraph, Bernal enters and things move steadily along, as Allende chronicles Elena's growing obsession with Bernal. Dialogue appears only once, in the key scene in which Bernal realizes that it is Elena, not her mother, making love to him.

Images add to the sensuality of the plot. Flowers appear frequently. Before Bernal sparks the passion in the two women, the geraniums are dusty and give off no fragrance. As their passion for him unfolds, making women out of both of them, the sensations become stronger. Elena's mother wears perfume. On the Sunday evening Bernal plays his guitar and her mother dances erotically, it is hot and the scent of flowers hangs heavily in the air. The sensuous details build as Elena notices all the smells in his room when she lies on his bed, absorbing his presence with all of her senses. On the day that Elena comes to him, it is white-hot in midday.

The details are different in the last two pages, which cover the aftermath of her sexual encounter. Allende covers these events in a cool, factual style. Bernal hopes to rekindle Elena's desire on the patio where the scent of carnations hangs in the air, but the last encounter between Elena and Bernal takes place in the cool kitchen. The story ends with a twist of irony, bringing the narrative to a direct closure in the very last sentence: "She could not remember any particular Thursday in her past."

*Louise M. Stone*

# THE WIDE NET

*Author:* Eudora Welty (1909-2001)
*Type of plot:* Psychological
*Time of plot:* The early twentieth century
*Locale:* Dover, Mississippi, on the Natchez Trace
*First published:* 1942

*Principal characters:*
WILLIAM WALLACE JAMIESON, a recently married farmer
HAZEL JAMIESON, his pregnant wife
VIRGIL THOMAS, William Wallace's bachelor friend and neighbor

*The Story*

As the vernal equinox approaches, Hazel Jamieson, three months pregnant, refuses sexual relations with her husband, William Wallace Jamieson. Mystified and hurt by this rejection, William Wallace spends a night out, drinking with his bachelor friend Virgil Thomas. On returning home in the morning, he finds a note from Hazel announcing that she will not put up with him any longer and has drowned herself in the Pearl River. William Wallace and Virgil then organize a party to drag the river for her, using the wide net that belongs to the local patriarch, Old Doc. The scholarly Doc questions the pair closely to be sure that they have a good reason for using the net, because William Wallace has used it within the last month, and it is not his turn. When Doc believes it possible that Hazel may have drowned herself, he reflects that "Lady Hazel is the prettiest girl in Mississippi . . . A golden-haired girl." He decides to join the search.

As the search gets under way, it takes on a mystical, ritual quality. Doc observes that this is the equinox, the time of change from fall to winter, when all of creation seems made of gold. William Wallace responds by thinking of Hazel as "like a piece of pure gold, too precious to touch," then asks, mysteriously, for the name of the river they all know so well. Like Hazel, the river, though familiar, becomes mysterious, "almost as if it were a river in some dream." William Wallace's search of the river becomes a metaphor for his attempt to fathom the mysterious depths of Hazel's character.

Other ritual elements include the two black boys who push Doc in an oarless boat, the mysterious objects dredged up from the bottom, Virgil's refusal to allow strangers to watch them, William Wallace's deep dives, the fish feast, William Wallace's phallic dance with a catfish attached to his belt buckle, and their subsequent "vision" of "The King of Snakes," a large water snake that seems to be evoked by William Wallace's dance. The search ends just in time for a violent thunderstorm, which transforms the benign golden landscape temporarily into a terrifying, agitated silver landscape.

Of these ritual elements, William Wallace's deepest dive seems especially significant: He dives below the normal muddy world of the river into the "dark clear world of deepness." The narrator asks whether he found Hazel in this deepness: "Had he suspected down there, like some secret the real the true trouble that Hazel had fallen into, about which words in a letter could not speak . . . how (who knew?) she had been filled to the brim with that elation that comes of great hopes and changes . . . that comes with a little course of its own like a tune to run in the head, and there was nothing she could do about it—they knew—and so it had turned to this?" Diving deep into the river, William Wallace might also dive deep into Hazel, there to confront the same mystery that lies at his own center—"the old trouble" that all people share but that they cannot articulate. Newly married Hazel, confronting the changes of marriage, of the season, of motherhood, is shown at the beginning of the story as inarticulate but filled to the brim with golden life: "When he came in the room she would not speak to him, but would look as straight at nothing as she could, with her eyes glowing." Her mystery is like the fish of the Pearl River, infinite and familiar at the same time.

When the quest is finished, Old Doc reflects that he has never been on a better river dragging: "If it took catfish to move the Rock of Gibralter, I believe this outfit could move it." Virgil replies that they did not catch Hazel,but Doc replies in turn that girls are not caught as fish are; they are more mysterious. William Wallace returns home to find a moon-made rainbow over his house and Hazel waiting for him. He tries to assert control over her, to prevent her behaving so whimsically again, but she evades him, asserting that her self belongs to her. He feels again the elation he felt on winning her consent to marry, feeling in her loving assertion of selfhood the mystery of self that is at the center of their love and union as well as of their separation and sorrow.

*Themes and Meanings*

As she does in her novel/story cycle *The Golden Apple* (1949), Eudora Welty uses ideas and images from William Butler Yeats's "The Song of Wandering Aengus" in "The Wide Net." Aengus is a fisherman who went fishing with a hazel wand as a pole and caught a silver trout that was later transformed into a glimmering girl. The girl called his name and ran, "and faded through the brightening air." He has spent his life trying to find her again, dreaming of a union with her in some paradise where, until the end of time, he will pluck "The silver apples of the moon,/The golden apples of the sun." The minor coincidences of images suggest a connection with the poem. The two works share the theme of a man trying to fathom and thus achieve an ideal union with a woman. This ideal union is unattainable in this world, but the fascination of the mystery of the human soul, which cannot be captured in words and which seems to separate lovers, also draws the lovers together in an endless pursuit that gives depth and richness of meaning to life.

Ruth Vande Kieft, in an essay on Welty, describes this theme as central to much of Welty's fiction: "Welty shows how the most public things in life, love and death, are also the most mysterious and private, and must be kept so. Though privacy requires the risk of isolation and loneliness, it is a risk worth taking in order to achieve the proper balance between love and separateness." William Wallace and Hazel are attempting intuitively to achieve such a proper balance. The ritual of the wide net seems central to William Wallace's success, Just as it is the ritual itself rather than its products that William Wallace and his friends value, so it is the process of interaction in tension with Hazel, rather than achieving control over her, which makes their marriage rich and golden.

### Style and Technique

Perhaps the central characteristic of Welty's style in this story is its evocative quality. In outline, the story is simple and realistic, the account of a marital misunderstanding that sends the young husband off on a compensatory masculine adventure. However, in the telling, Welty evokes a deeper, even more universal layer of meaning. By means of suggestive images and carefully constructed narrative commentary, Welty points to and suggests the meanings of the ritual aspects of the whole expedition. For example, as William Wallace and Virgil plan to gather the men, William Wallace catches a rabbit. He demonstrates how he can "freeze" the animal, making it stand for a moment under his hand. Welty makes it clear that in exercising a kind of hypnotic control over it, he is expressing his wish to control Hazel in this way. Virgil's reaction points at the paradox of William Wallace's desire, setting up the meanings that will emerge from the ritual elements of the quest: "Anybody can freeze a rabbit, that wants to . . . as you out catching cottontails, or as you out catching your wife?" To control Hazel would be to reduce her to a relatively uninteresting animal.

One of the evocative images is William Wallace's phallic fish dance. The men have finished their search without finding Hazel's body. After eating and napping on a sandbar, William Wallace feels exuberant. Doc attributes this joy to the pleasure of the chase: "The excursion is the same when you go looking for your sorrow as when you go looking for your joy." William Wallace then hooks a catfish to his belt buckle and begins to dance, "tears of laughter streaming down his cheeks." Then, a giant water snake appears, looped out of golden light rings on the river, evoking from the usually silent Malone men the cry, "The King of Snakes!" Among other possible meanings, one seems to be the celebration of their masculinity, which they affirm in the pursuit even of the essentially mysterious and uncapturable woman. They confront their own mystery simultaneously in a meaningful ritual, an acting out of what they cannot put into words.

Welty describes her motive for writing as a lyrical impulse "to praise, to love, to call up, to prophesy." Ruth Vande Kieft says that Welty's fiction may be seen "as a celebration of so many pieces of life with the mysteries rushing unsubmissively through them by the minute." In "The Wide Net," Welty's evocative style points to and lights up some of those rushing mysteries in the lives of rural Mississippians.

*Terry Heller*

# THE WIDOW

*Author:* Beth Lordan (1948-    )
*Type of plot:* Magical Realism
*Time of plot:* The 1990's
*Locale:* The American Midwest
*First published:* 1987

> *Principal characters:*
> WARREN BOYD, an American farmer
> ANN BOYD, his wife

*The Story*

"The Widow" is a lyrical exploration of the secret magic of the individual when one is able to see it. The story begins by flatly stating that the morning Warren Boyd dropped dead, he was the only living person on his farm. The second paragraph just as flatly describes Warren's wife, Ann, who has been dead for three years, hovering in the upstairs bedroom watching.

After this somewhat unsettling opening, Beth Lordan's magically realistic fantasy then narrates the life of Warren and Ann, which is quite ordinary, except for those moments when Ann sees Warren transfigured by shimmering bubbles of light. The first time she sees Warren transformed, she is in the upstairs bedroom thinking about jelly when he walks out of the milk-house slowly and gracefully, as if he were walking under water. Tiny air bubbles, gleaming like glass pearls, cling to his body.

The second time Ann sees him illuminated, he does somersaults in the yard as she watches from the bedroom window. She does not see the magical transformation again the rest of the year, although she keeps watch for the miracle. Then, in a sudden tragedy, Susan, the couple's five-year-old daughter, catches a cold and dies at the end of the summer, and they are stunned by the "simplicity" of her death. In the spring, Warren returns from a trip to town, and Ann sees him get out of the car with a soft brilliance around his body, like mist off a barn roof. He turns in slows circles on the gravel driveway and stands with his arms lifted to the sky.

Although Lordan describes only three transformations, Ann watches Warren transformed again and again, although never completely. When Ann dies suddenly of a stroke or heart attack at age seventy-one, she understands that the three wishes that everyone always talks about are not given out until the moment of death; her first wish is that she remain with Warren until his death, watching him, hoping that at the moment of his death she might understand what the splendor of his transformations means.

In the three years before Warren's death, she sees his mysterious illumination a few more times and discovers that she sees the visions only when he goes hatless; however, the morning that he dies, one of his hats is firmly on his head. Ann waits by his body watching until she realizes that, without even knowing she was there, his own first wish was to go. Disappointed and feeling empty and alone, she starts back upstairs and, remembering how Warren shimmered that first time, the sweet smell of raspberry jelly cooking comes to her. She goes to the bedroom and stands by the open window and makes her second wish, for tears.

*Themes and Meanings*

The central theme of Lordan's magical story is the mystery of the other. The premise of the parable is that often one spends one's life focused on ordinary, everyday things and never sees the special magic of the person with whom one lives. Ann's life often seems endless and perverse to her, designed to keep her from finding out about Warren; she has felt this great excitement the first time she saw him transformed and knows it is an excitement that ordinary living has kept pushing aside. Before it happened the first time, she knew some things about Warren—that he was fussy about his eggs, that he would always sleep on the side away from the wall, and that he got corns on his left foot and not on his right. However, when she first sees him illuminated, he is transformed from the ordinary to the extraordinary, and she feels something like a "deep memory" about the magical transformation.

After the vision, Ann's life goes back to its normal rhythm. In some way, she is glad the vision fades and the "real" Warren returns. When their daughter is born, she thinks these are good "ordinary" years—a wholesome, sturdy, serious time. However, when she sees the vision of Warren again, this time doing somersaults on the grass, she feels triumphant and breathless because he seems released from the everyday like a childlike creature.

Ann and Warren's everyday life is broken up again by tragedy, the death of their child, which leaves a void that makes Ann welcome a third manifestation of Warren's magical illumination. After this time, Ann begins to understand that her ability to see Warren in its special, secret nature, is love, although she does not think of it that way.

At the end of the story, when Warren, unaware that Ann is there, makes his first wish to leave, he can do so because Ann is already gone, and all he wants is to join her. At first, Ann can feel only a heavy weight of loneliness and a sense of disappointment. However, on thinking about her situation, she knows she still has two wishes. Her first one, for tears, expresses her sense of poignant loss of all the time past, the nostalgic sense of those moments when life could have been special; her second wish, unstated, but assumed, is to join Warren. Thus, the story ends with a sweet sense of the fulfillment of the promise of lovers—that they will never leave each other.

*Style and Technique*

The central technique of Magical Realism is to present incredible events usually associated with fairy tales and fables in a straightforward, realistic way. Thus, the term suggests a duality in which the ordinary and the extraordinary intersect. Although usually associated with such Latin American writers as Jorge Luis Borges, Gabriel García Márquez, and Julio Cortázar, such writers as Franz Kafka, Isaac Babel, and

Eudora Welty have written stories that have many of the characteristics of Magical Realism.

Lordan's story is a creative working out of people's intuitive knowledge that someone whom they love has special characteristics that, if asked, they might be unable to articulate. Can the question of who a person really is be answered by merely itemizing and totaling up all the ordinary, everyday things that the individual does or says? Or is there some secret self that other people sense but cannot quite identify or name? Lordan's task in this story is to suggest that to truly see the other person as he or she really is, people must be still and watch, for too often, caught up in the trivial activities of everyday reality, they fail to see. The fact that Ann sees Warren in this special illumination only without his hat suggests that he loses his specific individual identity when he is transformed, becoming instead a universal, archetypal emblem of the special spiritual nature in everyone.

As the basis for her story, Lordan makes use of a distinction that anthropologists say characterizes the primitive mentality: a distinction between the sacred and the profane. The profane includes all the everyday responsibilities and activities of human life—the need to eat, work, and procreate—whereas the sacred is that human belief that there is more to life than merely the sum of the everyday. The parablelike style of Lordan's story reflects this basic mythic distinction.

Lordan also makes use of a formalist theory of art that suggests that human beings get so caught up in the familiar world of everyday reality that they miss the magic of life around them. The world becomes "familiarized," and thus people respond habitually until what they experience is not the concrete real world, but rather the abstractions they create. The role of the artist then is to "defamiliarize" the world, make people see it as it really is, not as their stale habits have defined it. This is a central romantic view that informs all of Magical Realism and that infuses "The Widow" from the first time Ann sees Warren as his secret, special self to the point when she makes her final wish to join him.

*Charles E. May*

# THE WIDOW'S SON

*Author:* Mary Lavin (1912-1996)
*Type of plot:* Fable
*Time of plot:* The early twentieth century
*Locale:* Rural Ireland
*First published:* 1951

> *Principal characters:*
> THE STORYTELLER
> AN UNNAMED WIDOW
> PACKY, her fourteen-year-old son
> AN OLD MAN, her neighbor

*The Story*

In "The Widow's Son," the storyteller presents two versions of the same story, with different endings. A poor, illiterate widow in an isolated village has one son who is her "pride and joy," "the meaning of her life," but when he is fourteen and about to reward her sacrifices and her hope by winning a scholarship, he dies in an accident outside their home. The boy is cycling home, faster and faster down a steep hill, and at the bottom he swerves to avoid one of his mother's hens. The mother is dismayed at the absurdity of the event and simply asks, "Why did he put the price of a hen above the price of his own life?" Her neighbors try to comfort her with "There, now." Her question and their response may imply that the event is beyond comprehension, as if it must simply be accepted as fate; nevertheless, the mother's cry reveals her impatience and irritation with a human error, her son's poor judgment when he swerved.

Earlier in the story, the widow was sketched as a person who had not only accommodated herself to her limited circumstances but also had triumphed over them. Her poverty is compounded by nature, but she is not fatalistic, and by her own industry she has made her small patch of land as productive as a larger farm. Her fierce will to make the best of her situation seems to achieve her triumph until the absurd accident ends everything.

There is a suggestion, however, that this is a story with a form of cruel justice. Perhaps she is too self-centered in her pursuits, too arrogant in the face of a fate that has already made her a widow. She tries to conceal her obsessive love for her son with a gruff exterior, as if she fears the ridicule of her neighbors for the single-mindedness of her devotion. Nor does she discuss her hopes with her son; instead, she threatens him and tries to encourage him to fulfill her goals by making him fearful. Her neighbors, who know her character well, seem to conclude that it is the boy's fear of her that brought him to his death.

This suggestion, that she has been blinded in her dealings with her son by the harsh persona that conceals her sentimental nature, is made explicit in the second version of the story. It begins in the same way as the first and "in many respects . . . is the same as the old." In the conversation between the widow and the old man as they await the son, she denies "in disgust" the suggestion that she has doted on the boy and spoiled him, a "ewe lamb." As if to prove the truth of her denial, when Packy kills the hen rather than himself, she attacks him, beating him over the head with the bleeding hen. This display of anger, which becomes a self-conscious display in front of her neighbors, compromises her; when he reveals that he was rushing home to tell her that he has won a scholarship, she wants to hug him, but she "thought how the crowd would look at each other and nod and snigger," and she does not want to "please them" by demonstrating her joy. Trapped by her own harsh, public persona and angry at the perversity of the situation that has denied her the social respect that the scholarship should have brought her, she begins to attack Packy, to humiliate him, even as she inwardly grieves at the price she is paying for maintaining her pride. The story ends this time with the disappearance of the son, who never returns to her, although he does forward her money as repayment for her sacrifices.

The storyteller presents this second version as if it were the product of the neighbors' gossip and secret speculation, for it reflects their shrewd sense of the woman's character. The narrator now generalizes in the form of a moral, which is usual at the end of a fable or, perhaps, a folktale: that "the path that is destined for us . . . no matter how tragic . . . is better than the tragedy we bring upon ourselves."

*Themes and Meanings*

The story invites the reader to join in the game of speculating about a road not taken in life and to share the pleasure of the storyteller by inventing an alternative outcome. There are severe limits placed on that speculation, however, for the story seems to imply that the choices made in life are mostly determined by character and by life itself—that there is little free choice. While the first version is granted the reality of action, the second is simply a daydream of what might have been; in each case, though, the outcome is remarkably similar: The mother loses her adored son and the story challenges the reader to wonder if the widow could have avoided her tragic fate.

The simplicity of the folktale in the first version gives prominence to actions that follow as inevitably as the bicycle gains momentum coming down the steep hill. The brevity of the first narrative leaves little room for character analysis; what is added are the shrewd psychological hints that suggest that the widow's motivation is complex and deeply embedded. A comparison of the two versions reveals that the angry confrontation between the widow and her son simply uncovers a hidden well of "disappointment, fear, resentment, and above all defiance." These impulses spring up "like screeching animals" at the sight of blood. The widow, who had appeared as a simple person with a single purpose going calmly about her business, now appears to have an ungovernable character that predetermines her fate; the action, which seemed to be shaped by accident, now seems to mirror the natural anarchy of her own inner self. Most poignant and most frustrating is that she cannot stop herself once the violent energy has been released.

Can this fate be avoided? The narrator offers consolation in the concluding paragraph: "It is only by careful watching, and absolute sincerity, that we follow the path that is destined for us." This path is preferable, even if it is tragic, to the self-made tragedy that issues from one's own blindness or willfulness. In an odd twist, the reader is encouraged to stand back from the obsessive, enclosed world of the proud widow and share in the gossip of her neighbors. Storytelling itself is a form of "careful watching"; the play of invention, of speculating on motive, character, and outcome, demonstrates "the art of the gossip" as well as the art of the storyteller. Both activities, it is suggested, may free people from self-deceptive blindness. The wisdom of the folktale or intuitive psychological speculation contributes to the hope that one may discover one's natural path in life.

### Style and Technique

This story seems to break all the rules of modern narrative technique, yet its combination of folktale and self-conscious philosophical speculation is disarming. The mode of country storytelling with a cast of village stereotypes, nameless widow, and grass-sucking old man, is mixed with a more literary dramatization of the same situation, and the risks to the fictive illusion are increased by the intrusive comments of a writer/narrator. The effect of a comment such as this is to deflect the reader's resistance to repetition: "After all, what I am about to tell you is no more fiction than what I have already told, and I lean no heavier now upon your credulity than, with your full consent, I did in the first instance." Writer and reader are united in a conspiracy, in the cooperative process of finding meaning in a fable. The brisk tone of presentation and inquiry keeps the momentum of the narrative from flagging, especially in the second version, and the writer's deference to the reader is flattering and involving, as in the process of gossiping.

Mary Lavin's choice of this technique reflects her thematic interest. If the widow ends by appearing to be a mean and self-destructive character, it is the result of her isolation from other people. The story implies that "careful watching, and absolute sincerity" are encouraged in the confidential and cooperative exchanges of gossip or storytelling.

*Denis Sampson*

# THE WIFE OF HIS YOUTH

*Author:* Charles Waddell Chesnutt (1858-1932)
*Type of plot:* Social realism
*Time of plot:* The 1880's
*Locale:* Groveland, Ohio
*First published:* 1898

> *Principal characters:*
> MR. RYDER, the protagonist, a light-skinned, socially prominent
> African American
> MRS. MOLLY DIXON, an educated, light-skinned African
> American from Washington, D.C.
> LIZA JANE, an older, uneducated, dark-skinned African American
> from the South

*The Story*

The story begins with a description of the Blue Vein Society, a social club of mixed-blood African Americans living in the North after the Civil War. While membership criteria were ostensibly based on a person's social standing, everyone in Groveland, Ohio, knows that only those persons whose skin is light enough to show blue veins are asked to join. Mr. Ryder, a single, light-skinned man who has achieved a respected position in the railroad company over twenty-five years, is called "the dean of the Blue Veins." Possessing impeccable manners, a passion for British poetry, and a tastefully furnished and comfortable house, Ryder has arrived at the height of social standing and is ready to ask the beautiful, educated, and accomplished widow, Mrs. Molly Dixon from Washington, D.C., to marry him.

Not only is Ryder attracted to this young woman, but he also sees such a marriage as his social responsibility to "lighten" the race—the only means available for mixed-race people to assimilate into the larger white society. He explains that he is not prejudiced toward those of darker complexion, but that he regards mixed-blood people as unique: "Our fate lies between absorption by the white race and extinction in the black. The one doesn't want us yet, but may take us in time. The other would welcome us, but it would be for us a backward step." The joining of two such respected and accomplished mulattoes as Ryder and Molly Dixon is, for Ryder, a serious social and political obligation.

To honor Dixon, Ryder decides to give a ball in her honor; this will give him an opportunity to propose to her and also allow him to host an event that will mark a new epoch in the social history of Groveland. Only the best people—those with the best standing, manners, and complexion—will be invited. Critical of the growing laxity in social matters among even members of his own set, he wants to demonstrate to the community the standards that he considers proper to maintain.

On the day of Ryder's great ball, he relaxes on his porch as he debates which passage of Alfred, Lord Tennyson's love poetry about fair damsels would most honor Dixon. An old black woman wearing a blue calico dress and a red shawl, who looks like a bit of old plantation life, approaches Ryder and identifies herself as Liza Jane, a former slave from Missouri. Before the Civil War she was married to a free-born mulatto named Sam Taylor, who was indentured to her master and nearing the end of his commitment. Her unprincipled master was so desperate for money that he planned to sell Taylor, although he did not legally own him. When the woman discovered her master's plan, she urged her husband to flee to freedom. Taylor promised to return for his wife, but her angry master sold her down the river and she never saw Taylor again. For twenty-five years, however, she has been looking for him: first all over the South—from New Orleans to Atlanta to Charleston—and now in the North. Liza Jane asks for Ryder's help in locating her long-lost husband.

After listening patiently and patronizingly to the old woman while examining her old daguerreotype portrait of her missing husband, Ryder tells her that he cannot help her. He promises to look into the matter, then goes upstairs to his bedroom and stands for a long time, gazing thoughtfully at his own reflection in a mirror.

That evening, Ryder's home is filled with the most prestigious of Groveland's African American citizens—teachers, doctors, lawyers, editors, and army officers. Although they are considered "colored," most of them would not attract even a casual glance because of any marked difference from white people. When Ryder finally stands to deliver his toast to Dixon, he does not quote Tennyson. Instead, he recounts his afternoon visit with the old black woman. Then, to the surprise of his guests, he poses a hypothetical question: What would any of them do if they were the young man for whom Liza Jane was looking? What if this young mulatto man had made his way in the world from his humble beginnings, had educated himself, had established himself in his community, had achieved a high social position, and had become a different person than he had been when he married as a young man? Discovering that his wife—who is older than he, uneducated, dark-skinned, and lowly—what would any of them have done? Would they have claimed their spouse?

After an uncomfortable silence, Dixon states, "He should have acknowledged her." It is then that Ryder, turning to his afternoon visitor, who is now neatly dressed in gray, and wearing the white cap of an elderly woman, announces to the elite Blue Vein Society, "Ladies and gentlemen, this is the woman, and I am the man, whose story I have told you. Permit me to introduce to you the wife of my youth."

### Themes and Meanings

In "The Wife of His Youth," Charles Waddell Chesnutt presents the struggles of mixed-blood African American people in the latter part of the nineteenth century as they sought to define their place in American society. Despite their educations, their economic achievements, and their social positions, they remained at the margins of both black and white societies. A great many sentimental literary works of the post-Civil War period portray such people as tragic figures who, in their desperate attempt to pass for white and their desire to enter white society undetected, in denial of their

African roots, meet a terrible end. In these romanticized tales, women sacrifice themselves to a great cause or to death, and men pose a threat to the racial purity of white society. In his story, Chesnutt rejects the tragic mulatto stereotype and insists that his readers see his characters in their individuality. Ryder and the other Blue Veins anticipate, as critic William L. Andrews has observed, the "New Negro" of the 1920's—men and women who would claim their African heritage proudly and create their own unique culture with its own art, music, literature, and philosophy.

Chesnutt's characters are forerunners of African American philosopher W. E. B. Du Bois's "Talented Tenth," the top 10 percent of the African American people who would attend universities, assume positions of power and influence, and lead their people to their proper place in American society. Ryder's decision to acknowledge the dark-skinned wife of his youth is one man's affirmation of his past and his culture. Chesnutt, as Andrews points out, makes the abstract issue of racial identity a "personal ethical decision, to be judged on an individual basis in light of the social, economic, and psychological factors that most affect the persons concerned."

*Style and Technique*

Chesnutt first gained public attention by writing dialect stories of the South in the vein of popular writer Joel Chandler Harris's Uncle Remus tales. Chesnutt's early stories, the best known of which is "The Goophered Grapevine," present the clever former slave, Uncle Julius, who tells his new Northern master and mistress tales of voodoo, haunting, and plantation life. Unlike Harris's sentimentalized portraits of antebellum slavery, Chesnutt's stories are accounts of courage, wit, and survival; however, Chesnutt found the dialect stories confining. "The Wife of His Youth" is his first piece using standard vocabulary and style. While the cunning Uncle Julius of his earlier stories could criticize society using wit and humor, Chesnutt's more conventional stories were not easily accepted. Readers found his discussions of miscegenation, prejudice, and class distinctions discomforting. He refused to return to the popular images of the Old South that were so profitable to him. Chesnutt insisted on examining the difficult issues of race and color, of morality and social responsibility, that interested him, what he called "the everlasting problem."

The prominent novelist and editor William Dean Howells called Charles Chesnutt a literary realist of the first order. Chesnutt published sixteen short stories, along with a group of poems and essays, between 1883 and 1887. In 1899, two collections of his short stories appeared. Though he continued to write into the new century, producing three novels between 1900 and 1905, his works of social criticism never found the audience that his dialect stories had enjoyed. Chesnutt is important in the history of African American literature, initiating its short-story tradition. In 1928, he received the NAACP Spingarn Medal for "pioneer work as a literary artist depicting the life and struggles of Americans of Negro descent, and for his long and useful career as scholar, worker, and freeman."

*Laura Weiss Zlogar*

# A WIFE'S STORY

*Author:* Bharati Mukherjee (1940-    )
*Type of plot:* Social realism
*Time of plot:* The late twentieth century
*Locale:* New York City
*First published:* 1988

*Principal characters:*
PANNA BHATT, a Ph.D. candidate at New York University
HER HUSBAND, who is visiting from India
CHARITY CHIN, her roommate
IMRE, her friend, a male Hungarian immigrant

*The Story*

Panna Bhatt is attending a performance of David Mamet's play *Glengarry Glen Ross* (1983) in New York City with Imre, another immigrant separated, as she is, from his mate. They are not lovers, but they share the intimate friendship that only alienated foreigners in an adopted country can know; theirs is the mutual bond of strangers in a strange land. She thinks the play insults her culture and also insults her as a woman. She is so offended that she decides to write to Mamet to protest his depiction of East Indians.

She and Imre discuss her sensitivity to these issues, and he assures her that she must learn to be more flexible and adjust. Panna, however, is both resentful and disillusioned to realize that as a temporary immigrant already acculturated to certain American ways of being, she is caught in the middle, a mediator between cultures and cultural perceptions.

Panna gradually perceives differences between her old and new cultures that are in some ways freeing and expanding, and, in other ways, jarring and unnerving. For example, she is able to hug Imre in the middle of the street, an informal, spontaneous show of affection that she could not demonstrate toward her husband in India, where cultural restraints do not allow such personal displays. In India, Panna was not even allowed to call her husband by his first name.

The second part of the story briefly addresses the wide gap that separates Panna from Charity Chin, her roommate, who is a "hands" model. This short section underscores some of the emphases of the story at large, focusing on yet another immigrant who responds in her own unique way to the problem of adapting to another culture. Each immigrant undergoes the acculturation process, but it not only is different for each person, but also reflects the relativity of cultural values. In the United States, Charity is a model with high ambitions, but in India, she would just be a "flat-chested old maid."

The third sequence of the story concerns Panna's husband's visit. Panna shifts back and forth between seeing the United States from the tourist's point of view—her husband's ravenous shopping sprees, for example—and her own sense of disintegration and fragmentation. She views herself as already alienated and different from her husband and the culture and country he represents. They tour Manhattan and take the ferry to a dingy snack bar at the base of a scaffolded, and therefore forlorn, Statue of Liberty. Her husband is disappointed by the disparity between America's image and its reality; he thinks New York is no better than Bombay.

At the end of the story, Panna confronts herself naked in the mirror, a person singularly transformed by her experience as a foreigner and temporary immigrant in the United States. Her old life is really gone, and she recognizes this fact, not with rue or remorse, but with an exhilarating sense of metamorphosis. However, it is a transformation both miraculous, like a butterfly, and strangely disorienting and disturbing, as she watches, simultaneously, herself and someone who is a stranger to herself: "I am free, afloat, watching somebody else."

*Themes and Meanings*

"A Wife's Story" is aptly titled because it is the story of one wife who finds that her sense of self—as woman, as spouse, as cultural being—is being transformed by the culture she now inhabits. Bharati Mukherjee not only indicates the particular and rarefied state of mind and being of an immigrant undergoing a definite process of acculturation within a specific culture, but also produces, through the comments and meditations of her narrator, the sense of alienation and strangeness it creates. In this story, the alienation is not merely cultural, but also takes the form of a vast alienation along sexual lines. Panna is an East Indian transforming into an American—with altered cultural awareness and values—but she is also transforming into a new woman: a female with a vision that is miles away from her husband's world and universes beyond her grandmother's restricted female being.

The other major theme addressed in "A Wife's Story" is the sometimes humiliating process of adapting to a new culture. Panna envisions herself as a new woman at the end of the story, and it is a positive, even if disorienting, expansive image. Throughout the story is interwoven the sense of irony at what the immigrant must undergo to effect a cultural transformation. The initial image of the story is the narrator watching herself being parodied and insulted by characters in an American play. She goes on to rebel at the subtle racism, the misjudgments, the stereotyping inherent in any culture clash between races and ethnic groups. She wants to write to Mamet. She will even write to Steven Spielberg to tell him that Indians do not eat monkey brains. Through the juxtaposition and, ultimately, the union of the universal theme of a global acculturation process, Mukherjee produces the picture of a mixed blessing for the individual immigrant struggling to make his or her way through a new world defined by differing and bewildering cultural codes. It is a complex and exhilarating opportunity for personal growth, but it separates the stranger in a strange land from family, spouse, and previous conceptions of self.

*Style and Technique*

This story carefully pairs a universal statement about the process of growth, which is often accompanied by humiliation, that occurs in any collision between cultures, with a personal statement of a first-person narrator undergoing that process. The first-person point of view is a primary means by which modern writers communicate the very nature of reality, that is, any sense of "absolute" truth actually residing in the relative world of personal perception. Thus Panna's metamorphosis, along with its disturbing elements, must be seen through her particular focused eyes. The reader is drawn into her unstable, mutating world. Through her comments, sometimes ruefully ironic, at other times determined and directed, Panna places order and meaning on this instability.

Mukherjee focuses her themes stylistically by incorporating character. It is her people who make meaning. The variety of her characters, named and unnamed, all serve to generate and further her themes. In opposition to them, Panna defines and creates herself. She is who she is—unlike them—and who she is becoming—often like them. She is estranged from a fat man in a polyester suit in the theater who "exploits her space," and yet she is like Imre when he exults in his freedom on a New York city street.

Finally, Mukherjee produces the underlying structure of her themes through her use of language. She intermixes incongruent, yet relevant terms: "Postcolonialism" (an intellectual, historical term) is somehow fitting in the same sentence with "referee" (a sports term employed metaphorically). The image of the city's numerous mixed races as astronauts possesses a certain truth. Interjected comments about her characters tend to reflect the American culture of which they are becoming a part: "Love is a commodity, hoarded like any other." Through her use of the first-person point of view, character, and diction, Mukherjee creates a world of fluctuating and transforming immigrants grounded in the personal adventure and vision of her narrator, who straddles not only two worlds, but two selves.

*Sherry Morton-Mollo*

# WILD SWANS

*Author:* Alice Munro (1931-    )
*Type of plot:* Psychological
*Time of plot:* Possibly the late 1940's
*Locale:* West Hanratty, a small town outside Toronto
*First published:* 1978

> *Principal characters:*
> ROSE, the protagonist, a high school student
> FLO, her garrulous, motherly adviser
> A UNITED CHURCH MINISTER, her traveling companion on a train

*The Story*

Before leaving for the first time by herself on a trip to Toronto, paid for from the prize money she won in her school essay competition, young Rose, the protagonist, is warned by Flo against various sexual dangers that could befall a young woman traveling alone. Flo, a motherly, talkative woman—Rose's stepmother in *Who Do You Think You Are?* (1978), Alice Munro's collection of linked short stories from which "Wild Swans" is taken—warns Rose particularly against white slavers who commonly disguise themselves as ministers of the Church. Rose is skeptical, refusing to believe anything the garrulous Flo says on the subject of sex. She recalls an incredible story Flo told her about a retired undertaker who traveled around the countryside seducing women with chocolates and flattery and making love to them in his hearse.

Though Rose is skeptical, Flo's cautionary anecdotes about sexual seduction are very much on her mind. As the train leaves Hanratty, the small town where she lives, she is sitting by herself, absently staring at the passing countryside and thinking of what she will buy in Toronto. The train gradually fills up, and at one of its station stops, a man in his fifties takes the seat beside her. Chatting idly about the spring weather, he casually mentions that he is a United Church minister. He is not wearing a collar, explaining its absence by observing that he is not always in "uniform." He tells her about seeing a magnificent flock of wild swans during a recent drive through the country.

Rose responds to him courteously but briefly, discouraging conversation. Because the morning is cold, she covers herself with her coat. The minister turns to his newspaper and soon falls asleep or appears to fall asleep. His newspaper lies on his lap, adjoining Rose's coat. Rose becomes aware of the tip of the newspaper touching her leg just at the edge of her coat. She wonders if it is in fact the man's hand that is touching her and muses that she often looks at men's hands, wondering what they are capable of. Hands become, in her musing, a metonym for the sensual male, and she recalls fantasizing about being used as a sexual object by a virile French teacher.

In this frame of mind, she becomes aware that it is indeed a hand, not the tip of the newspaper, that is touching her leg. The hand is gradually moving to her thigh. She wants to protest, but initially curiosity and then sexual excitement weaken, then suppress, any protestation. The hand titillates her and brings her to a climax, which is described in terms of a flock of wild swans explosively taking to the sky. Munro's account of this seduction is replete with ambiguity. The reader is never certain whether the hand is imagined or actually there. Is it possible that Rose is fantasizing? She does say at one point that her "imagination seemed to have created this reality," an observation that, however, with its use of "seemed," encourages rather than eliminates ambiguity.

As the train pulls into Toronto, the passengers begin to stir and the minister awakens or appears to awaken. He offers to help her with her coat, and when she declines, he hurries out of the train ahead of her. Rose is never to see him again in her life, the narrator states, but she is often to recall him and his "simplicity, his arrogance, his perversely appealing lack of handsomeness." She speculates as she leaves the train on whether he is actually a minister, and for the first time since meeting him, she consciously recalls Flo's warning about white slavers disguised as ministers.

Munro provides a postscript to this incident. As Rose steps off the train, she remembers Flo mentioning a woman named Mavis who works at the Toronto station. Flo told her that Mavis once went for a weekend to a Georgian Bay resort, pretending to be the actress Frances Farmer. Flo, observing that she could have been arrested for impersonation, admired her "nerve." Rose, too, in the final sentence of the story, expresses admiration for Mavis's daring act: "To dare it; to get away with it, to enter on preposterous adventures in your own, but newly named, skin." Munro evidently intends this as Rose's conscious or unconscious comment on her own preposterous adventures on the train.

### Themes and Meanings

Munro believes that the individual's true emotional, psychological, moral, and cerebral motivations are complex and elusive. Consequently, human experience cannot really be portrayed in any objective, categorical way. The brief but poignant incident from Rose's life illustrates clearly Munro's artistic credo. She inclusively suggests various ways of interpreting Rose's experience, leaving readers to draw their own conclusions.

In her deliberate and skillful use of ambiguity in depicting Rose's response to the liberties taken by the United Church minister, Munro wants the reader not only to know but also to experience how difficult it is at times for the individual to separate fantasy from reality. Narrated strictly from Rose's point of view, the story allows the reader into her consciousness, making it possible to experience vicariously the overwhelming force of fantasy and imagination.

Responding to the story as a portrayal of an actual seduction leads the reader into a consideration of society's immorality and hypocrisy and, more important, of Rose's motivations in reacting the way she does. Is she an innocent experiencing awakening sensuality? The narrator suggests that her acquiescence to the minister's probing hand is not sensuality or passivity but an overpowering appetite for experience: "Curiosity. More constant, more imperious, than any lust. A lust in itself, that will make you draw back and wait, wait too long, risk almost anything, just to see what will happen." Munro, in an interview, reiterated explicitly this interpretation of Rose's inaction. She said that the story describes how the individual reacts to "something unthinkable" and that Rose exhibits not "passivity but curiosity."

In the first published version of this story, Munro did not include the concluding episode concerning Mavis's impersonation of Frances Farmer. In appending this ending to the later version published in *Who Do You Think You Are?*, Munro added another contiguous dimension to Rose's experience. Rose, who at the beginning of the story is portrayed as acquiescent to the milk vendor whom Flo challenges, now shares Flo's admiration for Mavis's audacity in pretending to be Frances Farmer, and, by extension, she perhaps reluctantly admires the minister's boldness as well. Given Munro's deliberately ambiguous portrayal, Rose quite likely also admires her own nerve in indulging in sexual fantasizing on a crowded train. Mavis's "preposterous adventure" in her "own, but newly named, skin" parallels Rose's own just-concluded adventure experienced in actuality or perhaps in her own young, vibrant imagination.

*Style and Technique*

In James Joyce's short story "Araby," a work with which Munro is familiar, the young narrator moves effortlessly between his real and imagined worlds, often not distinguishing between the two. In a crucial scene relating a conversation between the narrator and the girl he loves, Joyce uses deliberate ambiguity to allow the reader to feel the intensity of the boy's imagination. The reader is never categorically sure whether the conversation actually takes place or is fabricated by the highly imaginative youth.

In the crucial scene of her story, Munro also employs the technique of ambiguity to point up, like Joyce, the thin demarcation between fantasy and actuality and to induce the reader to share vicariously in the protagonist's experience. There are several ambiguous phrases and images. Many sentences overtly suggest that initially it is Rose's imagination that perceives the tip of the newspaper to be the minister's hand: "She thought for some time that it was the paper. Then she said to herself, what if it is a hand? That was the kind of thing she could imagine." Immediately after, she wonders: "What if it really was a hand?" Perhaps the sentence that most emphatically persuades the reader to acknowledge the possibility of ambiguity in Rose's perception of the seduction is this one: "Her imagination seemed to have created this reality, a reality she was not prepared for at all."

Rose's perception of the man's reclining posture is equally ambiguous. Could he be actually sleeping? As she looks at him, she observes that he "had arranged the paper so that it overlapped Rose's coat. His hand was underneath, simply resting, as if flung out in sleep." When the train reaches Toronto, Rose notes that the minister, "refreshed," opens his eyes. Is he refreshed from actually sleeping or from the sexual encounter? Rose assesses his offer to help her with her coat as "self-satisfied, dismiss-ive." Is this because of the unprotested liberties he took with Rose, or is it simply an aspect of his personality?

Munro has sharp eyes and ears for particulars of the individual's traits and behavior. For example, she alerts the reader to Flo's pronunciation of the words "bad women," which are run together like "badminton." Some details have only tenuous thematic and narrative significance and are included essentially to create authenticity of people and places. A good example of this Chekhovian technique is the account of Flo's ac-costing the vendor of sour milk at the Hanratty station. Munro effectively uses details of nature to convey the protagonist's feelings: The reference to the sensual wild swans in the title and the story is appropriate, and Rose's imagined or real orgasm is poeti-cally conveyed through a host of natural (and artificial) images that flash by the train window.

*Victor J. Ramraj*

# WILDGOOSE LODGE

*Author:* William Carleton (1794-1869)
*Type of plot:* Realism, horror
*Time of plot:* The 1820's
*Locale:* Near Dundalk, County Louth, Ireland
*First published:* 1830

### Principal characters:

THE NARRATOR, a member of a Roman Catholic secret society
PATRICK DEVANN, the Captain of the secret society

## The Story

"Wildgoose Lodge," a nineteenth century tale of terror based on an actual event, begins with the narrator receiving a summons to attend a meeting of a Roman Catholic secret society called the Ribbonmen. In the middle of winter, on a gloomy, stormy day, the narrator, filled with apprehension about the summons, goes to the meeting in the parish chapel. Forty people are waiting for him there, but the welcome he receives is not the hearty greeting to which he is accustomed. Although he does not know the reason for the meeting, he knows that it involves something terrible.

The leader of the Ribbonmen, Patrick Devann, a schoolmaster who teaches in the chapel and on Sunday is clerk to the priest, gives the narrator a glass of whiskey to drink, but the narrator holds back because they are in a church. As more men enter, all are made to drink the whiskey as a sign of their commitment to the act that Devann, called the Captain, has planned, although no one knows what that act is. The Captain reads the names of a group of members of the society who have betrayed the organization and says that all those assembled are brothers on a sacred mission to punish the traitors. The Captain takes the Missal on the altar and swears by the sacred and holy book of God that he will perform the action they have met to accomplish. When he strikes the book with his open hand with a loud sound, the candle goes out and the chapel is thrown into darkness; there is the sound of rushing wings that makes all the men pull back in horror at what they perceive is a supernatural event. However, someone explains that the candle was extinguished by a pigeon and that the sound of rushing wings resulted from the many pigeons roosting in the rafters having been frightened by the loud noise.

Although not all the men swear to participate in the punishment of the so-called traitors, all of them swear to keep secret what happens on this night. A small number of men, whom the narrator calls the Captain's gang, swear to participate and then affirm their oath by yelling and leaping in triumph around the altar. Afterward, all the men—one hundred thirty strong—go out into the stormy night, at one point fording a flooded area around the house of the family to be punished by leapfrogging over one another. When the men reach the house of the accused traitors, the Captain immediately sets it afire and tells his men "No mercy is the password for the night."

When a woman puts her head out the window of the burning house and begs for compassion, the Captain and his gang pierce the woman's head with a bayonet and push her body back into the flames. When a man with his clothes burned off comes out of the house, he begs that his child, an infant, be spared. The Captain calls him a "bloody informer" and shoves him back into the flames. When a woman with an infant in her arms appears at the window, the Captain thrusts his bayonet into the infant and throws it into the flames also. Throughout these atrocities, the narrator is filled with horror, but no one does anything to stop the slaughter. Finally, all the victims are dead, and the house is quickly consumed by flames.

### Themes and Meanings

Originally appearing in 1830 in *The Dublin Literary Gazette* as "Confessions of a Reformed Ribbonman," the story was retitled "Wildgoose Lodge" in the second series of William Carleton's *Traits and Stories of the Irish Peasantry* (1830-1833). Although Carleton was not actually present at the atrocity, in the last paragraph, he addresses the reader directly, saying that a few months later he saw the bodies of the Captain and all those actively involved in the massacre hanging from a gibbet near the scene of the horror. In a final footnote, he says, "This tale of terror is, unfortunately, too true." He explains that the reason for the punishment was that shortly before the fatal night, the murdered family accused and convicted some of their fellow Ribbonmen of theft and assault. "Wildgoose Lodge" is therefore not a story of Irish sectarian conflict; both the murderers and the murdered family are Catholic. Carleton's purpose in this story is not to make a political point but rather to horrify the reader by combining an account of actual events with the conventions of the nineteenth century tale of terror.

Carleton creates a thematically appropriate atmosphere surrounding the events by describing the day as gloomy and tempestuous. Moreover, the fact that the meeting in which the murders are planned takes place in a church and involves ceremonies of brotherhood is perceived to be bitterly ironic to the narrator. This ironic contrast between the church and the men is further emphasized when the narrator describes the devilish malignancy of the Ribbonmen captain as "demon-like," "Satanic," "supernatural," and "savage." When the Captain slams his fist down on the altar Bible to swear an oath, a sound of rushing wings fills the church. Although the sound of wings has a natural explanation—pigeons in the rafters frightened by the leader's striking the Bible—the act communicates a sense of mockery of Christian values. The ironic contrast between brotherhood and barbarity persists throughout the story.

The actual scene of the revenge murders is described symbolically, for the torrential rains have created a lake in the meadow where the house lies, isolating it on a small island in the middle so that the Ribbonmen have to create a human bridge over which they can travel to reach it. The description of the murders is graphic and horrifying. When a woman leans out the window and cries for mercy, her hair aflame, she is "transfixed with a bayonet and a pike" so that the word "mercy" is divided in her mouth. When another woman tries to put her baby out the window to safety, the Ribbonmen Captain uses his bayonet to thrust it into the flames. The story ends with the narrator affirming that although the language of the story is partly fictitious, the facts are close to those revealed at the trial of the murderers, which resulted in between twenty-five and twenty-eight men being hanged in different parts of County Louth.

*Style and Technique*

Carleton's choice of the first-person point of view of an observer, although he himself did not see the events described, is a romantic literary device—typical of such writers as Washington Irving, Edgar Allan Poe, and Nathaniel Hawthorne—to emphasize the reactions of the teller. Although ostensibly merely an eyewitness report of an event, the account reflects the kind of self-conscious patterning of reality that is characteristic of the modern short story.

The first nineteenth century tale-of-terror device Carleton uses to fictionalize the actual is the premonition the narrator has about the meeting, although the summons he receives has nothing extraordinary or startling about it. He has a sense of approaching evil; an "undefinable feeling of anxiety" pervades his "whole spirit," very much like the undefined sense of anxiety that pervades the spirit of many of Poe's narrators, such as the unnamed narrator of "The Fall of the House of Usher" when he first rides into view of the ominous house. Moreover, like many Poe narrators, Carleton's narrator says he cannot define the presentiment or sense of dread he feels, for it seems to be a mysterious faculty, like Poe's "perverse," beyond human analysis.

A completed action, treated as if it were an action in process, "Wildgoose Lodge" is a classic example of how the modern romantic short-story writer developed techniques to endow experience with thematic significance without resorting to allegorical methods of symbolic characterization and stylized plot construction. What makes "Wildgoose Lodge" a modern story is the heightened perception of the engaged first-person narrator, who is both dramatically involved and ironically aware at once. Moreover, the story's selection of metaphoric detail with the potential for making an implied ironic moral judgment—the atmospheric weather, the ironic church setting, the physically isolated house, and the imagery of the leader as Satanic and his closest followers as fiendish—shift the emphasis in this story from mere eyewitness account to a tight thematic structure. It is just this shift that signals the beginning of the modern short story most commonly attributed to Hawthorne and Poe in the following decade.

*Charles E. May*

# THE WILL

*Author:* Mary Lavin (1912-1996)
*Type of plot:* Domestic realism
*Time of plot:* The 1940's
*Locale:* Rural Ireland
*First published:* 1944

> *Principal characters:*
>> LALLY CONROY, the disinherited daughter and protagonist
>> KATE CONROY, the oldest child and the family leader
>> MATTHEW CONROY, the only male child
>> NONNY CONROY, the youngest child

*The Story*

Mary Lavin's "The Will" is set in rural Ireland; in such a rural locale, the people tend to be excessively concerned about respectability and to be afflicted with a meanness of spirit. The story begins soon after the mother's will has been read by a solicitor. The four children then discuss the consequences of the mother's cutting Lally out of the will. What follows is a series of contrasts, and some conflicts: between the children who remained in the rural Irish town—Kate, Matthew, and Nonny—and Lally, who left home at an early age for the city and marriage.

The first contrast is between the practical, and socially respectable, desire of the other children to provide Lally with some of the money taken away from her by the will and Lally's steadfast refusal to violate her mother's wishes. Kate takes the lead and prods Matthew to suggest that each of them will contribute to Lally a part of the money they received. Their concern seems, for the most part, to be for what people will say rather than for their sister. Matthew says, "We won't let it be said by anyone that we'd see you in want, Lally." Lally, however, resists their attempt to circumvent their mother's will; she believes that such a plan would be in violation of her mother's wishes and that, if her mother did not wish her to have the money, she should not have it. Lally has a sense of fairness and justice that contrasts with the others' attempt to preserve respectability.

Such a contrast can also be seen in her reaction to the next proposal by Matthew. Matthew offers to pool their resources and purchase a hotel in the city for Lally to run. In his eyes, a hotel would be more respectable than the boardinghouse that Lally now has: "It would be in the interests of the family," he tells Lally, "if you were to give up keeping lodgers." Lally rejects this proposal as well. She thinks of her departed husband rather than respectability. "I'd hate to be making a lot of money and Robert gone where he couldn't profit by it." She is interested in fulfilling people's desires and does not worry about what people think.

Another contrast is that Lally, although an exile from the house, is the only one to display any feeling for her mother's death. She cries when she remembers her mother and their relationship before she left home, "but the tears upset the others, who felt no inclination to cry." She also cries when she hears that her mother's last words were "blue feathers"—Lally had worn those blue feathers the day she left home to go to the city. It is obvious that the mother felt much affection for Lally. She could not, however, rise above her social prejudices. Kate says that the mother "might have forgiven your marriage in time, but she couldn't forgive you for lowering yourself in keeping lodgers." In contrast, Lally overcomes her mother's attitude and continues to love her.

The next contrast is that all the family members except Lally treat appearance(s) as reality; Lally consistently refuses to do so. Nonny is worried that people will think that the family has quarreled about the will, but Lally responds, "What does it matter what they say, as long as we know it isn't true." Appearances mean nothing to Lally; what matters is what people know. Both Matthew and Kate, on the other hand, take their stand for, as Kate says, "keeping up appearances." The others also have a "grudge" against Lally for her run-down appearance, which reminds them of what they, too, will someday be. Kate says, "You're disgusting to look at." Nonny joins in, "I'd be ashamed to be seen talking to you." Lally does not answer them or even acknowledge their insults; she has things to do in the city and must go. The others oppose her leaving on the same day of the burial, but this is more for appearance's sake than Lally's:

> All of them, even the maid servant who was clearing away the tray, were agreed that it was bad enough for people to know she was going back the very night that her mother was lowered into the clay, without adding to the scandal by giving people a chance to say that her brother, Matthew, wouldn't drive her to the train in his car, and it pouring rain.

The story shifts its focus from the conflict between Lally and her family to Lally's own thoughts as she leaves the house to return to the city. She recalls her earlier dream of escaping from the town and finding "the mystery of life." Now she realizes that she was not changed by marriage, or her life in the city, or by keeping a boardinghouse: "You were yourself always, no matter where you went or what you did." Lally does, however, believe in one change: The change of death and what happens after death is the mystery. She begins to remember tales of souls being tortured from the catechism and suddenly becomes troubled by the state of her mother's soul. She rushes into a church and asks the priest to say some masses for her mother's soul. She tells the priest, "She was very bitter against me all the time, and she died without forgiving me. I'm afraid for her soul." The priest tells her that Mrs. Conroy has left three hundred pounds for masses, but Lally believes that "it's the masses that other people have said for you that count." What is needed is a sacrifice by one person for another, not the performance of a ritual.

She rushes to catch the train, but her thoughts are still with her mother as she sits in the train. She thinks that she may have some money left after buying food for herself and her children, and this money will be used for ten masses and to light some candles at the Convent of Perpetual Reparation. Lally is confused, even feverish, but what is important is the contrast between her feelings and concern for her mother and the coldness of the others. Even Mrs. Conroy is cold and calculating, with her three hundred pounds for masses, while her daughter lives in poverty. Only Lally cares.

### Themes and Meanings

The most important theme of "The Will" emerges from the contrast between outward appearance and inner reality. All but Lally are concerned with social respectability, with appearances only. Nonny says, "I don't know why you were so anxious to marry him when it meant keeping lodgers." Only Lally knows what is real and what is primary: "It was the other way around, . . . I was willing to keep lodgers because it meant I could marry him." For her, the unchanging self within, relationships with others, and the feeling and knowledge of others are real. The others can never act without an eye to what others will say or think, and therefore they can have no immediate or spontaneous feelings. They are trapped by their worship of mere appearance. In contrast, Lally remains free to do what seems right and important, whether it be helping a new lodger move in, marrying someone of whom her family does not approve, or trying to lift her mother out of Purgatory with her dearly bought masses.

### Style and Technique

One important technique in the story is the shift of point of view. In the first part of the story the point of view is third-person limited. The narrator describes the characters or the place but refuses to enter the thoughts of those characters. When Lally leaves the house, however, the narrator enters the mind of Lally and records her thoughts. The narration mirrors the change from a social scene to a personal and reflective one. It is essential that the reader know Lally's thoughts in the second part of the story in order to evaluate her actions in the first part, and only a change in the type of narration can accomplish this.

One element of style needs to be mentioned: the use of imagery at the end of the story. The images of darkness and those of red ("the dark train," "through the darkness," "red sparks," and "burning sparks") fill Lally's mind and remind her of the mother's suffering in Purgatory and make her feel confused and feverish, and these feelings impel her to take some action to relieve her mother's suffering. The penultimate paragraph begins with Lally feeling some "peace," but that peace is driven out by the images.

*James Sullivan*

# WILL YOU PLEASE BE QUIET, PLEASE?

*Author:* Raymond Carver (1938-1988)
*Type of plot:* Psychological
*Time of plot:* The 1970's
*Locale:* Eureka, a town in Northern California
*First published:* 1976

> *Principal characters:*
> RALPH WYMAN, the protagonist, a high school teacher
> MARIAN WYMAN, his wife

*The Story*

The first few pages of "Will You Please Be Quiet, Please?" run quickly through ten years in the life of Ralph Wyman, a young man whose father tells him, on Ralph's graduation from high school, that life is a "very serious matter" and "an arduous undertaking," which, despite its difficulties, can still be rewarding. Early in his college career, Ralph finds himself discarding potential careers he had envisioned for himself—law and medicine—when he finds the work too difficult or emotionally stultifying. He turns to literature and philosophy, in which he finds some stimulation. Most of his first college years, however, he spends aboard a stool in the local pub, until one special teacher, Dr. Maxwell, changes his life. Maxwell's influence reshapes Ralph's sense of his own future, and he becomes a "serious student," joins a variety of campus organizations, finds himself a wife, Marian, and diligently prepares himself, during his last year, to become a teacher.

Before taking teaching positions in a small town in Northern California, Ralph and Marian marry. One afternoon on their honeymoon, Ralph walks up the road below their hotel and catches a glimpse of his new wife standing with her arms over the ironwork balustrade, her long black hair spun out by the breeze. The image is stunning, but the memory of her pose haunts him later because somehow he cannot see himself as part of the exotic world in which he imagined her for only that moment.

Five years pass quickly, and Ralph and Marian have two children. Marian teaches music at the local community college, but Ralph continues at the high school. One Sunday night, the only event to shock the quality of their relationship emerges from a memory that each has tried to bury, a memory that has reinforced Ralph's fearful image of his wife on their Mexican honeymoon. When Marian, quite whimsically, brings up the matter of her leaving a party one night with another man two years earlier, Ralph pursues her lead and tries hard to pin her down on what it was, exactly, that had happened between them. Two years before, she had claimed that nothing at all had occurred.

Ralph's paranoia becomes evident as he pushes his wife, almost mercilessly, to reveal the truth. Slowly and painfully, the story unravels itself, and Ralph discovers that the worst fears he has carried with him since that night are warranted. Very emotionally, Marian confesses her guilt.

The second half of the story opens later that night, as Ralph has begun a drinking binge. He has left the house to drink, and he finds himself wandering in and out of downtown bars. As he staggers down the street, he picks up pieces of conversations that haunt him with their application to Marian's confession of her infidelity. He wanders through bars jammed with people, across steamy dance floors, and into restrooms where walls are marked with lurid obscenities. In his confusion, things he sees and hears strike him as haunting moral lessons only half-understood.

For a few minutes, he takes refuge in the back room of a bar, where a card game is in progress. After playing a few hands with the men around the table, he blurts out what had happened in an almost matter-of-fact tone, but the card players appear untouched by his trauma. He leaves and heads out to the pier, where, as he imagines, Dr. Maxwell, his favorite professor, would likely sit and watch the waves to try to come to some understanding of his problem. Ralph finds no solace near the water, however, as he is beaten by a man in a leather jacket.

It is almost morning when he opens his eyes and realizes that he has nowhere to go but home. When his children awaken, they find him sitting up, his face laced with dried blood. He runs to the bathroom to hide. Marian, obviously distraught from his absence and the specter of his bloody face, begs him to come out. He simply tells her to be quiet and prepares to take a bath. Once the children are gone, he leaves the bathroom and gets into bed. Still unsure of how he must react to his wife, he lies perfectly still when she comes to him and tries to get him to talk. When she moves toward him sexually, he tries to stay away as long as he can, but finally he cannot battle what he feels growing within him and he turns to her, "marveling at the impossible changes he felt moving over him."

### Themes and Meanings

Raymond Carver is sometimes unjustly accused of creating only the kinds of characters who lack cunning and insight. Ralph Wyman may lack the ability to understand how to deal with what is, for him, a very traumatic moment in his life, but his inability to deal with his wife's confession cannot be blamed on stupidity. Ralph's drunken wanderings occur because he is slowly discovering the basic truth of what his father had told him years before, that life is a very serious matter.

This idea is the basic theme of Carver's story: Ralph's own initiation into the very serious matter of life itself. As the son of a grade-school principal, as a college kid with too grandiose visions of his own ability, even as a student who drops out of the mold for awhile, and as a converted "serious student" who then marries and tries, not unsuccessfully, to take a respectable position in a comfortable small town, Ralph Wyman still must learn the horrors of living in a world in which one's expectations may not always be met, in which weakness is a given, and in which deceit, like a bad memory, thrives in the silence of a guilty, human heart.

The most interesting twist that Carver administers to his very traditional initiation story is the way the story ends, Ralph's surrendering to his own physicality in turning to respond to his wife's attention. Readers often expect that initiation stories will end in what James Joyce called an "epiphany," a moment of seeing the whole truth. Carver sets the reader up for such a revelation but then concludes not with clarity but with more complexity, the mystery of that dynamic human force, desire. Trying to stay away from his wife completely, Ralph cannot keep his body from responding to her when she wants his forgiveness. He is, in fact, powerless in the surge of desire that rises in him. As confused as he is in trying to know how to act toward Marian, he cannot stop from turning to meet her. He stands in awe as he sees how very little he understands.

Does Ralph understand more about himself and Marian at the end of the story? He probably does not. However, the limits of his experience have been reset, and he knows much more about "this serious matter" of life.

*Style and Technique*

Carver is often associated with those contemporary writers who have been described as "minimalists." The term is meant to describe, among other characteristics, a style that lacks amplitude, which handles both emotional extremes in monotone, as if true joy and pain do not exist. In this story, however, Carver's protagonist feels deeply the pain of his wife's revelation, even though the pain is dulled for a few hours by his drunkenness.

Another characteristic of the minimalist technique is often thought to be an extremely short and abrupt style. Carver's word choice never reaches beyond very ordinary, contemporary language, and his sentences are often short, giving the texture of his fiction an almost machine-gunlike, staccato touch and sound. However, there is little about this story to make it anything more or less than traditional. Time is used realistically throughout; the style, while short and abrupt, never stands in the way of the story line. Carver's descriptions are never vapid and emotionless, but instead are sharp and convincing, especially when he follows Ralph's trek to a greater sense of his own mystery in those vivid scenes that capture the reality of dizzying drunkenness prompted by self-destroying paranoia.

*James C. Schaap*

# WILLIAM WILSON

*Author:* Edgar Allan Poe (1809-1849)
*Type of plot:* Parable
*Time of plot:* The 1820's and 1830's
*Locale:* An unnamed village, Eton College and Oxford University in England, and Rome, Italy
*First published:* 1839

> *Principal characters:*
> WILLIAM WILSON, the narrator and protagonist, an infamous criminal
> WILLIAM WILSON, the rival and opponent of the narrator

*The Story*

"William Wilson" is a tale narrated by an infamous criminal who is on the verge of death. He is ashamed to reveal his name; William Wilson is an admitted pseudonym. As death approaches, he tries to explain the momentous event that led to his life of misery and crime. His greatest fear is that he has forfeited heavenly bliss as well as earthly honor.

The path to the single event responsible for Wilson's criminality begins in an ancient, dreamlike English village whose memories alone now afford him pleasure. The village includes the church and academy that Wilson attends from age ten to fifteen. Dr. Bransby, the pastor of the church, is also principal of the academy, and Wilson marvels at the "gigantic paradox" that allows one man to be both a benign clergyman and a stern disciplinarian. The academy is set apart from the mist-enclosed village by a ponderous wall and a spike-studded gate. Old and irregular, with endless windings and subdivisions, the school building becomes for the narrator a palace of enchantment. Even the low and dismal classroom is a source of spirit-stirring and passionate excitement.

At the academy, Wilson wins control over all of his fellows but one—a classmate with the same name as his. The two William Wilsons are identical in height and figure, move and walk in the same way, and dress alike. In fact, they were born on the same date and enter school at the same time. They seem to differ only in voice: The narrator speaks in normal tones, his namesake in a low whisper.

As time passes, their rivalry intensifies. They quarrel daily because of what the narrator calls his namesake's "intolerable spirit of contradiction." However, the narrator admits in retrospect that his rival was his superior in moral sense, if not in worldly wisdom, and that he would be a better and happier man today had he more often taken the advice given him.

Late one night, bent on a malicious joke, the narrator steals through narrow passages to his namesake's room. There, as he looks into the sleeper's face, he is overcome with such horror that he nearly swoons: The face he sees is identical to his own. Awestruck, the narrator flees to Eton College, where he soon dismisses what he has seen as an illusion. During an evening of prolonged debauchery, however, he encounters a shadowy figure who admonishes him with the whispered words "William Wilson" and then vanishes. This scene is reenacted at Oxford University. Just as the narrator's cheating at cards brings Lord Glendinning, an aristocrat, to the brink of financial ruin, a stranger of the narrator's height mysteriously appears. He points to evidence of the narrator's cheating and, before disappearing, leaves behind a coat that is the duplicate of the narrator's own.

The narrator leaves Oxford, but he flees in vain. In Paris and Berlin, in Vienna and Moscow, he is thwarted by the figure he now regards as his archenemy and evil genius. However, even as the narrator acknowledges his namesake's elevated character and majestic wisdom, he vows to submit no longer. The confrontation occurs in Rome at the masquerade party of Duke Di Broglio, an aged Neapolitan nobleman. As the narrator threads his way through the crowd to seduce the young and beautiful wife of the duke, he feels a light hand on his shoulder, hears a low whisper in his ear, and sees a figure attired in a costume identical to his own. In a voice husky with rage, he orders the figure to follow him to an antechamber or be stabbed on the spot.

Inside the antechamber, they struggle briefly before Wilson repeatedly stabs his namesake through the bosom. However, it now seems as if there is a mirror in the room where none had been before, because Wilson sees his own image—spattered with blood—directly in front of him. Wilson soon realizes that what he sees is not a reflection; it is the blood-dabbled figure of his namesake. With his dying words, no longer in a whisper, the namesake says that Wilson has murdered himself and, in doing so, has lost all hope for happiness on earth or in Heaven.

*Themes and Meanings*

Edgar Allan Poe often deals with the theme of the divided self or the split in personality, and "William Wilson" is his most obvious story of the war within. Poe links the two William Wilsons—they have the same name, common physical traits, and identical histories—to show that the two are doubles or twins or parts of the same self. What part of the self does each represent? The story's epigraph suggests the identity of the second William Wilson: "What say of it? what say [of] CONSCIENCE grim,/ That spectre in my path?" The second William Wilson, who comes and goes like a specter or apparition, represents the conscience or moral sense; that is why, as the gentle but persistent voice within, he speaks only in a low whisper and why no one other than the narrator ever sees him.

Since the second William Wilson stands for the spiritual or heavenly part of the self, it is appropriate that his death costs the now-soulless narrator all chance for an afterlife: The narrator represents the earthly, mundane, physical part of the self that above all seeks pleasure, power, money, and conquest. So long as the conscience or spiritual self is present to restrain its earthly counterpart, Wilson's villainy is limited to drinking, swearing, and cheating at cards. Once the spiritual self is destroyed, however, there occurs a "sudden elevation in turpitude," and the earthly self turns to serious crime. The civil war in "William Wilson" ends with the triumph of the physical self over the spiritual self, but the price of victory is the loss of eternal life.

## Style and Technique

One of Poe's favorite techniques is to tell a story in such a manner that the reader is not quite sure what happens. In "William Wilson," for example, it is not easy to know what Wilson actually sees when he looks into his namesake's face or, in the final scene, when he confronts the blood-spattered figure that may or may not be his reflection. Poe refuses to make his tales transparent for two major reasons. First, he is convinced that, in the nature of things, truth is difficult to know because it is difficult to separate appearance from reality. William Wilson admits that he may have hallucinated the events of his story and that his entire existence may be a dream. Second, Poe deliberately blurs events so that the reader will question the story's literal level and look beneath its surface to discover allegorical meanings.

On a literal level, William Wilson and his namesake are distinct individuals; on an allegorical level, the two represent the warring parts—the physical and the spiritual—of the divided self. Allegorically, it makes sense that William Wilson does not become aware of his namesake's existence until age ten, the age, according to Poe, at which psychic wholeness is lost and the split in consciousness emerges. It makes equally good allegorical sense that William Wilson sees less and less of his spiritual self as the split in consciousness widens and intensifies with age.

The story's major events and characters all have allegorical significance. That Dr. Bransby is both a benevolent pastor and a rigid schoolmaster underlines the theme that all human beings are made up of contradictory impulses. That William Wilson spends his early years in a remote, circumscribed, and dreamlike setting suggests, allegorically, that the child's vision has not yet been compromised by contact with the mundane world. That the final confrontation between the earthly Wilson and his spiritual counterpart occurs during a masquerade is allegorically appropriate; indeed, Poe uses this pattern in "The Cask of Amontillado," "Hop-Frog," and "The Masque of the Red Death" as well. In Poe's writings, to cover oneself with a mask or a veil or a costume is to retreat temporarily from consciousness of the outer world to consciousness of the inner world, site of the civil war that rages in every human breast. Poe's deliberate obscurity both points to the complexity of truth and invites the reader to look for allegorical meanings beneath the surface of the tale.

*Donald A. Daiker*

# WILLIS CARR AT BLEAK HOUSE

*Author:* David Madden (1933-    )
*Type of plot:* Historical
*Time of plot:* March 21, 1928, with flashbacks to 1860-1867
*Locale:* Knoxville and Holston Mountain, Tennessee; various sites in Virginia; and
   out west
*First published:* 1985

> *Principal characters:*
> WILLIS CARR, the protagonist, a veteran of the American Civil
>    War and a sharpshooter during the siege of Knoxville
> GENERAL JAMES LONGSTREET, Confederate general and
>    commander of Rebel forces during the Knoxville siege
> WILLIAM PRICE SANDERS, a Union general subordinate to
>    General Ambrose Burnside at Knoxville

*The Story*

David Madden sets Willis Carr's stories about his experiences as a soldier during
the American Civil War within the framework of a meeting of the Knoxville chapter
of the Daughters of the Confederacy on March 21, 1928. Indeed, the entire story takes
the form of the report of the organization's secretary. Introduced by Professor Jeffrey
Arnow, a member of the history department at the University of Tennessee, Carr tells
the women gathered in the music room at Bleak House what he remembers about the
siege of Knoxville (in November and December of 1863), part of which he spent as a
sharpshooter in the tower at Bleak House itself.

Carr's story is rambling, slightly unfocused, and structured by the process of asso-
ciation. He is roughly eighty-two years old, having been born on Holton Mountain,
Tennessee, in 1846, and he was fourteen when he served under Confederate General
James Longstreet in what his hostesses prefer to call "the War Between the States."
Carr remembers that he was suffering from a fever when he reached Knoxville in
1863, which accounts for the haziness of his recollections. He does remember Bleak
House clearly and tells his audience that there was a man painting a fresco on a wall
downstairs during the military action. He remembers, too, that he was one of four
sharpshooters sent up in the tower of the house. When one of them was killed and the
other two wounded, Carr sighted an officer on a white horse dashing back and forth
between the Yankee and Rebel lines. He remembers thinking that this was a hallucina-
tion induced by fever, for no officer on either side would behave so recklessly, and he
shot at the man, thinking that he could do the phantom rider no harm.

Two years after the war was over, Carr returned to Tennessee from the West.
Stopping in some small town—he thinks that it was Pulaski—he met and sketched a
man introduced as the killer of General Sanders during the fight at Knoxville. Having

returned to Holton Mountain and swept the decomposed body of his great-grandfather into the fireplace, Carr remembered one day while hunting bear the officer on the white horse in Knoxville. It came to him that this might have been General Sanders, and he remarks to his audience that he has walked all the way to Knoxville to revisit Bleak House in an attempt to determine if he, Willis Carr, is really the sharpshooter who killed the Union general.

To this point in the story, Carr has the characteristics of the kind of heroic figure his audience might be expected to admire. He goes back to the start of the war in his speech, however, and in explaining his involvement destroys his potential for heroic status in their eyes. He explains that his East Tennessee family, with the exception of his mother, were Union sympathizers. His grandfather, father, and brothers took part in raids against railroad bridges instigated by Parson Brownow to handicap the movement of Rebel troops. Carr himself ended up in Longstreet's army because he was picked up in Knoxville as a Union sympathizer and agreed to join the Confederate troops to keep himself from being hanged. He intended to desert to the Federals as soon as possible, he remarks, but he enjoyed being a sharpshooter so much that he remained with Longstreet and served at Gettysburg and in the Wilderness.

Carr remembers the actual Confederate attack on the fort, renamed in honor of General Sanders, in Knoxville, and describes how helpless he felt watching his comrades being slaughtered. When General Longstreet himself was shot, during the Wilderness Campaign in Virginia, by one of his own troops, Carr got discouraged and deserted in a Yankee uniform. Picked up by Confederate soldiers and taken to Andersonville Prison, he was saved from execution as a deserter only because he was recognized as a sharpshooter by one of the Federal prisoners. Carr was made a guard by the Commandant of Andersonville, Captain Wirtz. A black Yankee soldier, formerly the slave of a Cherokee plantation owner, told him about the Indian Sequoyah, who invented an alphabet for Cherokee, preserving it as a written language, and this encouraged Carr to want to learn to read and write. The prisoner taught him, but one day the prisoner stepped over the dead line and was shot by his pupil.

Carr is not sure why he killed this man, just as he is not certain if he is the sharpshooter who picked off General Sanders. He has read much about the war in the years since it ended, and he tells the members of the Knoxville Daughters of the Confederacy that he cannot believe that he was really a part of the Civil War until he can answer both questions. He notes that he remembers sketching the faces of his three fellow sharpshooters on the west wall of the tower in Bleak House, and if the sketches are still there, they would provide him with firm evidence of his participation. Still, he remarks, he does not think that he has the strength to climb all those steps.

*Themes and Meanings*

On its most fundamental level, Madden's story deals with the relationship between historical fact and individual experience. Willis Carr's difficulty in finding the connection between events in his own life and statements accepted as historical truth dramatizes the problem that concerns Madden. The death of General Sanders is an event either totally separate from Carr's life or intimately part of it. The alternatives suggest differing philosophical conclusions. If Carr can prove that he was part of the war, that he did kill Sanders, then he can conclude that his actions have meaning and that he has some control over events in his life. If he cannot obtain that assurance, he must conclude that he lives in an absurd universe in which an individual is acted on by events and cannot shape them.

Madden does not provide a clear resolution of the dilemma that his protagonist faces. Carr is aware that there are two competing historical accounts of the death of General Sanders. In the first, the general is shot while, mounted on his white horse, he leads troops along the Kingston Pike. In the second, an English adventurer named Winthrop was mounted on that horse, and the general was shot while standing on a hill overlooking the battle. If the first account is true, the man at whom Carr shot was General Sanders, and he can claim a place in history. If the second account is true, however, Carr has no place in history, even if he was present during the skirmishing around Knoxville in 1863.

"Willis Carr at Bleak House" also has its fighter side. Madden is enjoying the idea of Carr, an irreverent East Tennessee hillman, speaking to the Daughters of the Confederacy and failing to confirm any of the conventional notions about the War Between the States. Carr does not see himself as serving a noble cause; his were Union, not Confederate, sympathies, and he stayed with General Longstreet because he enjoyed shooting people, not because he believed in the Confederacy.

*Style and Technique*

Madden places Willis Carr's account of the past within the framework of a meeting of the Daughters of the Confederacy, and the humor of the story arises from the juxtaposition of Carr's narrative and the impersonal framework of the secretary's report. In addition to the implied comment about the unsatisfactory role Carr fills as speaker to this organization, Madden employs a broader humor in the story. The anecdote about Carr sweeping great-grandfather into the fireplace seems material straight out of folklore, as does Carr's account of himself outrunning the horses of his grandfather, father, and brothers on the way to Knoxville.

More significant is the fact that Madden makes Willis Carr an artist. Even while working as a sharpshooter in Longstreet's forces, he sketches the faces of his companions on the west wall of the tower in Bleak House. After the war, he tells his audience in Knoxville, he supported himself for two years out West by sketching men he met in bars. Several times during his speech, he refers to the man painting a fresco in Bleak House during the fighting going on outside. These details give substance to Carr's statement that he has come back to Knoxville to attempt to answer questions that will enable him to feel a part of the war. Like a painter, he is attempting to see the face of truth and to fix it permanently. The story suggests that both Carr's desire for certainty and his failure to attain it are inevitable.

*Robert C. Petersen*

# THE WILLOWS

*Author:* Algernon Blackwood (1869-1951)
*Type of plot:* Horror
*Time of plot:* 1905
*Locale:* Hungary
*First published:* 1907

> *Principal characters:*
> THE UNNAMED NARRATOR, the protagonist
> HIS COMPANION, a Swedish man

## The Story

The first-person narrator and his companion, a Swedish man, are on a canoe trip, intending to travel the entire length of the Danube River to the Black Sea. The river is in flood and has swiftly carried them into Hungary and a completely wild and uninhabited area. As far as the eye can see, there is nothing on either bank but limitless clusters of large willow bushes.

They decide to stop overnight on one of the many small islands dotting the river, and on setting up camp are almost immediately confronted by two odd sights that serve to set the tone for their stay. A strange creature, almost like an otter, is seen floating down the river turning over and over, while shortly afterward they see a "flying apparition" traveling rapidly down the river, resembling a man in a boat who seems to be making the sign of the cross and shouting wildly at them. These odd events serve as a stimulus to the narrator's imagination, and he realizes that the beauty of the wild landscape also contains weirdness, even terror, such as the howling wind, raging water, and especially the constantly moving willow branches.

Later that night, the narrator undergoes stranger encounters. Peering out of his tent, he sees in the moonlight a column of odd shapes or beings rising out of a clump of willows and disappearing into the sky, the figures appearing to melt in and out of one another. The sight is so strange and majestic that the narrator almost gets down on his knees to worship. Later that night in his tent, he hears a pattering sound, as of innumerable tiny steps, coming from outside his tent, and also feels as if a great weight is pressing down on him. He goes out and looks around and realizes that the willows seem to have moved closer to the tent during the night.

The next morning, the narrator hopes to have his staid and unimaginative traveling companion convince him that he has been dreaming, but instead he hears the astonishing revelation that a canoe paddle is missing and there is a tear in the bottom of the canoe. Adding to this ominous note, the companion divulges his feeling that mysterious forces in the area sense their presence and will try to make them victims. Increasing their tension is the discovery of small conical holes in the sand all over the island.

The damage to the canoe means that they will have to spend another day and night on the island for repairs, which is disquieting news. That night at supper, they find that the bread is missing from their provision sack. It is just at this time that a sound like a ringing gong is heard coming from the sky, although it also seems to come from the willow bushes and even from inside their bodies. They are now fully convinced that these sounds and the other manifestations can only be nonhuman in origin and are almost certainly threatening.

The narrator's companion, believing that they have trespassed on the grounds of another world, explains that they must keep quiet and especially not think about the alien forces; otherwise the two will be found and sacrificed. As if in corroboration, when one of them shouts, a strange cry is heard in the sky directly overhead and the gonging comes nearer.

Late that night, they go out hunting for firewood and see a sight so frightening that it makes one of them faint. Looking back at the camp that they have just left, they see a large, dark, rolling shape almost like the willow bushes in appearance, apparently looking for them and starting to come in their direction. They are saved only because one of them has fainted while the other is distracted by a sudden pain, thus preventing their minds from dwelling on the approaching entity, causing it to lose their location. When they get back to their camp, they see that the sand around it is completely riddled with the same conical holes.

The final confrontation comes later that night, when the narrator awakens and discovers that his companion is missing, while the gonging and pattering noises are louder than they have ever been. He finds his friend in a trance, about to jump into the river, and drags him back into the tent. At this point, all sounds cease and his friend suddenly grows calm, says that "they" have found a victim, and falls asleep peacefully.

The next morning, much relaxed, the companion repeats that a victim evidently was found and they will see evidence of this if they search. They indeed discover the corpse of a man in the water, caught in the willows. When they touch the body, the same gonging sound rises up into the air from it and fades away. To their horror, they see the same conical holes in the body that are in the sand and realize that these are the marks of the beings or entities into whose territory they have accidentally ventured.

*Themes and Meanings*

Algernon Blackwood was the foremost exponent of the outdoor supernatural story, although he also wrote the more claustrophobic indoor (haunted house) variety. Set in a free and untrammeled wilderness, "The Willows" luxuriates in a near-pantheistic treatment of nature; the river, the wind, and the willows are described in personifying terms and can frighten as well as charm. There is an accompanying idea, openly expressed by the narrator, that this world of nature is pure and human presence only spoils it.

However, there appears in this story a related but more radical theme: that there is an unseen world pressing close to common reality. The story turns not on nature spirits or deities so much as on another world or dimension that intersects that of the reader and is completely unrelated to the human scheme of things. In this, "The Willows" differs from most of Blackwood's nature stories, in which the preternatural phenomena are nature spirits or demons (as in "The Wendigo" and "Glamour of the Snow"). "The Willows" is typical of Blackwood's other stories, however, in its setting in the middle of a virgin wilderness, given Blackwood's underlying idea that nature is separate from the human sphere and contact with civilization can only spoil it.

An interesting feature is that the beings or forces inhabiting this other reality are dangerous but not actually threatening to the human world if left alone, an idea differing from Arthur Machen (1863-1947), another English outdoor specialist, and especially the American H. P. Lovecraft (1890-1937), whose beings are ready to destroy the earth. Again, this idea is a reflection of Blackwood's near-worship of nature and his dim view of human presence in it. Interestingly, the narrator feels almost like worshiping the entities he sees ascending to the sky.

*Style and Technique*

Blackwood's stories have been most famous for their style, and it is the use of suggestion rather than literal depiction or explanation that has contributed most to his style. This use of suggestion and ambiguity adds greatly to atmosphere and tension. Lovecraft labeled Blackwood as the supreme master of weird atmosphere, and this story is regarded as Blackwood's best.

The nature of the forces that assault the travelers is never clarified, and the conception of these forces grows and changes as the story progresses. The relationship of the various things seen (the beings ascending to the sky, the dark, rolling shape) to one another is not explained, nor is it clear which of these entities is the controlling force from the other world. Even the view the author gives of these various visions is filled with ambiguity. The narrator sees an otter where the companion sees a manlike creature; the ascending beings are seen very hazily; the dark shape is seen by the narrator as "several animals grouped together, like horses, two or three, moving slowly," and by the companion as "shaped and sized like a clump of willow bushes, rounded at the top, and moving all over upon its surface."

A favorite technique of the author is to make his protagonist a visionary who is open to, and even invites, experience with another world or reality, while a second character is a man of science or at least of down-to-earth nature whose function it is to rescue the hero from the charms or dangers of the vision. Blackwood gives an interesting twist to this idea in "The Willows" when the down-to-earth character, the Swedish companion, is the first to acknowledge the presence of the supernatural and even reverses the situation when he admits to having long had a theory about another world. Aside from this, Blackwood utilizes the different viewpoints of his two characters to give alternate descriptions of the various phenomena they see, contributing to suggestion rather than literal depiction.

*James V. Muhleman*

# THE WIND AND THE SNOW OF WINTER

*Author:* Walter Van Tilburg Clark (1909-1971)
*Type of plot:* Psychological
*Time of plot:* The early twentieth century
*Locale:* The desert mountains of Central Nevada
*First published:* 1944

> *Principal characters:*
> MIKE BRANEEN, an elderly prospector
> AN UNIDENTIFIED YOUNGER MAN

*The Story*

Mike Braneen has been looking for gold in the rugged desert mountains of Central Nevada for fifty-two years, roughly the last quarter of the nineteenth century and the first quarter of the twentieth century. He apparently has found enough gold to support his meager lifestyle, but he has long since ceased expecting to strike it rich.

Mike's life has become routine to the point of ritual; he spends eight months of every year—from April to December—in the mountains, and when the first snow falls he takes refuge in the little mining town of Gold Rock. For eight months, Mike is alone, with only his burro for company. However, in his loneliness be perpetually relives the social phase of his life. Though comfortable with his solitary life, Mike's self-identity is clearly defined by his human relationships.

As the story begins, Mike is descending from the mountains on the rugged old wagon road, into the sunset, and toward Gold Rock. It is late December, and snow flurries are in the air. Mike is keenly attuned to nature's cycles, and he knows that this will be the first storm of winter. He picks his way down the old Comstock road, avoiding the new highway, the cars and trucks, and all other manifestations of the new era that has passed him by. Alone with his burro Annie, there is nothing to interrupt the flow of Mike's memories.

Mike thinks about the burros he has had—eighteen or twenty in all. He can remember the names of only a few, those with some unique characteristic, and for the past twenty years he has gradually felt less personal about them. He has begun to call all the jennies "Annie" and the burros "Jack."

Mike remembers women he has known, usually fleetingly, like the "little brown-haired whore" with whom he spent one night in Eureka. He cannot remember anything about her in bed, but he remembers standing with her by the open window of the hotel, listening to piano music from below. He also remembers her heart-shaped locket with the two hands gently touching. Her name was Armandy, and Mike remembers with pleasure this brief moment of human contact.

The sun sinks lower, and Mike and Annie climb the last rise before the final descent to Gold Rock. He remembers the town: John Hammersmith's livery stable, where he will take Annie; his room in Mrs. Wright's house on fourth street; the International House, where he will go for their best dinner; and most of all the Lucky Boy Saloon, where he will find the proprietor, Tom Connover, and the rest of his old friends. He relives the ritual of his arrival, how he will trim his beard, put on his suit, and go down to the Lucky Boy, how Tom will look up and greet him warmly. From somewhere in the recesses of Mike's memory, however, comes an alternate picture of a nearly empty town, of strangers who work for the highway department or talk of mining in terms that Mike does not understand.

Mike and Annie reach the summit, stop, and look down. Instead of a bright string of orange windows, Mike sees only scattered lights across the darkness, producing no "communal glow." Mike realizes that this is how Gold Rock is now, a town grown old like himself, a town that, like him, is going to die. As Mike and Annie descend into Gold Rock, a highway truck swerves to miss them. Mike stops in front of the Lucky Boy; the saloon is boarded up and dark.

A younger man approaches, and the bewildered Mike stops him. Mike learns that the Lucky Boy has been closed since Tom Connover died in June. Confused, Mike asks directions to Mrs. Wright's place. The stranger tells Mike kindly that Mrs. Wright has been dead for some time and reminds him that it was at Mrs. Branley's house where he stayed last winter. Mike is afraid to ask about John Hammersmith, afraid that he, too, is dead. Mike recognizes that he has outlived his time, that his death is also approaching. As the man and the burro turn up the street, their "lengthening shadows" are obscured by the snowflakes.

### Themes and Meanings

It is clear from the beginning of the story that Mike Braneen is nearing death. He is an old man with physical debilities, approaching senility. His memories run together, though the reader might attribute this to fifty-two years of routine rather than to senility. Mike himself, however, is well aware that he has outlived his era. The transitoriness of life is thus a central theme. Mike, the town of Gold Rock, and the era of the solitary prospector are all dying.

However, neither Mike nor Walter Van Tilburg Clark is overly sentimental. Mike's life has been good. His chosen lifestyle has given him both freedom and social contact, both of which his personality requires. Though a loner, Mike defines himself by human relationships; his self-concept as rugged individualist requires the admiration of his friends, and during his eight months of solitude he relives the memories of human contact in Gold Rock, Eureka, and other Nevada towns.

Mike is comfortable with solitude, too. He is close to nature, reads her signs, and lives in harmony with her cycles. Just as Mike brings his social memories with him to the mountains, he also brings his habit of retrospection with him back to town. Suddenly Mike's friends are gone, the Lucky Boy is closed, and memories are all that Mike has left—and memories alone are not enough. The wind and snow of winter are about to claim Mike, too.

*Style and Technique*

"The Wind and the Snow of Winter" is a highly symbolic story. The title introduces the season of death, and the story begins "near sunset." Myriad images convey the sense of impending death, of the transience of life, of the end of Mike's era.

Mike is descending into a dying town, a town where his friends are already buried, where the social institutions that enriched his life have faded, where the prospector and his mule have been replaced by highways and trucks. Mike walks into the setting sun, it is the time of winter solstice, and the snow that covers all for the season of death is beginning to fall.

That Mike has little future left is poignantly conveyed by his living in the past. Though he does not remember that Mrs. Wright is dead, it is obvious that he has been hardened by loss and death. That he has learned from the pain of broken attachments is apparent in his increasing detachment from his burros.

Mike's introspection is prompted by what he calls "high-blue" weather. In spring high-blue, he used to think about women, to anticipate the future. Now he is more responsive to fall high-blue; he thinks of the past, of old friends—and he watches the weather carefully because he has begun to fear getting caught in a storm.

As Mike approaches the last pass, it is "getting darker rapidly." Mike looks at the sunset and remembers God. He anticipates the view from the summit of his "lighted city," the Gold Rock of his memories as well as the "lighted city" that he anticipates beyond death.

Thus the imminence of Mike Braneen's death is clearly established by Clark's symbolism. The reader is not especially surprised to look down with Mike on the dim, scattered lights of Gold Rock. One is prepared for the death of Mike's friends, for the closing of the Lucky Boy, for the approaching death of Mike himself, and one sees one's own shadows lengthen, one's own life obscured.

Mike is at peace with himself, with nature, and with his society, but he is also mortal. Clark's story not only exploits the universal symbols of human mortality and transience but also explores the human need to hold off the blast of winter—and to accept winter when it comes.

*Jerry W. Wilson*

# WINTER DREAMS

*Author:* F. Scott Fitzgerald (1896-1940)
*Type of plot:* Domestic realism
*Time of plot:* Several years before and after World War I
*Locale:* Black Bear Lake, Minnesota, and New York City
*First published:* 1926

> *Principal characters:*
> DEXTER GREEN, the protagonist, seen first as a fourteen-year-old
> youth and later as a successful businessperson
> JUDY JONES, the woman Dexter loves
> DEVLIN, a business acquaintance of Dexter

*The Story*

F. Scott Fitzgerald divides "Winter Dreams" into six episodes. In the first, fourteen-year-old Dexter Green, whose father owns the "second best" grocery store in Black Bear Lake, Minnesota, has been earning thirty dollars a month pocket money caddying at the Sherry Island Golf Club. He is responsible and honest, touted by at least one wealthy patron as the "best caddy in the club." His decision to quit his job comes suddenly—proclaimed, to incredulous protests, to be the result of his having got "too old." Such public excuse masks the real and private reason: Dexter has just been smitten head-over-heels by the willful, artificial, and radiant eleven-year-old Judy Jones, who, with her nurse, shows up at the club carrying five new golf clubs in a white canvas bag and demanding a caddy. Dexter watches her engage in a sudden and passionate altercation with the nurse, which piques his interest and works to align him with Judy. He not only sympathizes with her but also senses that an equally sudden and violent act on his part (his resignation) can be the only possible response to the "strong emotional shock" of his infatuation.

In the second episode, which takes place nine years later, Dexter has become a successful entrepreneur in the business world. His laundries cater to moneyed patrons by specializing in fine woolen golf stockings and women's lingerie. Playing golf one afternoon with men for whom he once caddied, Dexter contemplates his humble past by studying the caddies serving his party, but the reverie is broken when a golf ball hits one of the men in his party in the stomach. It was driven by Judy Jones, now an "arrestingly beautiful" woman of twenty, who, with her partner, nonchalantly plays through Dexter's foursome.

After an early-evening swim, Dexter is resting on the raft farthest from the club and enjoying strains of piano music from across the lake. Judy approaches by motorboat, introducing herself and requesting that Dexter drive the boat so that she can ride behind on a surfboard, making clear that she is dallying to delay returning home, where a young man is waiting for her. The encounter ends with her offhand invitation to Dexter to join her for dinner the following night.

In the third episode, visions of Judy's past beaux flit through Dexter's mind as he waits downstairs for Judy, dressed in his most elegant suit. When she does appear, though, Dexter is disappointed that she is not dressed more elaborately. In addition, her depression disturbs him, and when, after dinner, she confides that the cause of it lies in her discovery that a man she cared for had no money, Dexter is able to reveal matter-of-factly that he is perhaps the richest man of his age in the Northwest. Judy responds to this information with excited kisses.

The fourth episode forms the culmination of Judy's tantalizing and irresistible charm. It shows a dozen men, Dexter among them, circulating around her at any given moment, always entranced, alternately in and out of her favor.

After experiencing three ecstatic days of heady mutual attraction following their first dinner, Dexter is devastated to realize that Judy's attentions and affections are being turned toward a man from New York, of whom she tires after a month. Thereafter, she alternately encourages and discourages Dexter, and when, eighteen months later, he realizes the futility of thinking that he could ever completely possess Judy, he becomes engaged to a girl named Irene Scheerer, who never appears as an actual character in the story. In contrast to the passion and brilliance that Judy inspires in him, Dexter feels solid and content with the "sturdily popular" and "intensely great" Irene.

One night when Irene has a headache, which precludes her going out with him, Dexter passes the time by watching the dancers at the University Club and is startled by the sound of Judy's voice behind him. Back from Florida, Hot Springs, and a broken engagement, she seems eager to tantalize Dexter again and asks if he has a car. As they drive around the city, Judy teases him with "Oh, Dexter, have you forgotten last year?" and "I wish you'd marry me." Dexter is confused about whether the remarks are sincere or artificial, but when, for the first time, she begins to cry in his presence, lamenting that she is beautiful but not happy, Dexter is passionately drawn to her once again, despite his better judgment. When Judy invites him to come inside her house, Dexter accepts.

The fifth episode takes place ten years later. Dexter reminisces about how the passion rekindled from that one night lasted only a month, yet he feels that the deep happiness was worth the deep pain. He knows now that he will never really own Judy, but that he will always love her. At the outbreak of the war, having broken off his engagement with Irene and intending to settle in New York, Dexter instead turns over the management of his laundries to his partner and enlists in an officer's training program.

The final episode occurs seven years after the war. Dexter is now a very successful businessperson in New York City. Devlin, a business acquaintance from Detroit, makes small talk by remarking that one of his best friends in Detroit, at whose wedding Devlin ushered, was married to a woman from Dexter's hometown. At the mention of Judy's name, Dexter pumps Devlin for more information and learns that Judy's life has become an unfortunate one indeed—her husband drinks and runs around with other women while she stays at home with the children. Worst of all, though, is the fact that she has lost her beauty. When Devlin leaves, Dexter weeps, not so much for the fact that Judy's physical beauty has faded, but that something spiritual within him has been lost: his illusion, his youth, his winter dream.

## Themes and Meanings

In being heralded as the "laureate of the Jazz Age," Fitzgerald struck in his very American writing a balance between romance and disaster, glitter and delusion. His characters include the petted and popular and rich, who both dream and live recklessly and who have as their biggest enemy time, the time that ages and changes. The aging process is signified by the word "winter" in the title, but "winter" also signifies a transition that is more tragic than physical deterioration; by the end of the story, Dexter's emotions have become frozen. He has lost the ability to care or to feel. His "dream" of Judy had kept him energetic, passionate, and alive, and now the dream has been taken from him.

The reader cares about Dexter at the beginning of the story and wants him to succeed in career and in love. One myth associated with the American Dream is that even the poor, by spunk and luck, have a chance of making it big, and Dexter, whose mother "talked broken English to the end of her days," has worked hard to raise himself out of the poor immigrant class to which he was born. However, the dream of material success finally proves unsatisfying to Dexter, who comes to know that money cannot buy his real dream. In contrast, Judy was born into wealth and takes it as much for granted as she does her good looks. Judy, the spoiled little rich girl, gets what she deserves. She has been a merciless flirt, using her attraction to break hearts for sport. When the story reveals that she has become careworn and commonplace, married to a bully who deceives her, it is obvious that the tragedy is not hers but Dexter's, who most wanted not riches, but a woman he could never have. What is the most tragic of all, the woman was not worth having.

## Style and Technique

Fitzgerald's direct narrative style is as clear and straightforward as Dexter's romantic purpose. The flashbacks and gaps in the story mirror Dexter's on-again, off-again affair with Judy, though his unswerving obsession with her and the chronicle of it is emphasized here. Fitzgerald's tale uses poetic language and diction, yet it does not imply more than it states, and, in the story's episodic structure of fits and starts, it is loose enough to accommodate some things that are almost irrelevant. Dexter's business success, for example, is fortuitous; the real attraction and attention of the protagonist and the reader is his private life.

The third-person limited omniscient point of view allows the reader to know Dexter's story exclusively through Dexter's thoughts and reactions to what is happening. It is necessary to remember that Dexter is a romantic idealist and that his temperament is responsible for both his idealization of Judy and his subsequent disillusionment.

Dexter's enchantment with Judy and the vitality he draws from her are symbolized by the color and sparkle Fitzgerald uses to present her and to create a context in which

Dexter can contemplate her. When he first sees her as a young woman, Dexter notices the blue gingham edged with white that shows off Judy's tan; then, later in the afternoon, the sun is sinking "with a riotous swirl of gold and varying blues and scarlets" and Dexter swims among waters of "silver molasses." The author establishes the painting motif when Dexter stretches out on the "wet canvas" of the springboard, which suggests that Judy's seeming art of beauty and charm is all really superficial artifice. With Judy's blue silk dress at their first dinner and her golden gown and slippers at their last dance, Dexter swoons "under the magic of her physical splendor."

During his engagement to Irene, Dexter wonders why the fire and loveliness and ecstasy have disappeared. The very direction of his life, which he let Judy dictate by her casual whim, is gone as well, until she appears to play his heartstrings once more. Irene quickly fades from Dexter's romantic imagination because there is nothing "sufficiently pictorial" about her or her grief to endure after he breaks up with her. Judy is the picture of passion and beauty, energy and loveliness, the true love and true dream that are with him until, learning of Judy's decline, he recognizes it as a signal of the demise of his own dreams.

*Jill B. Gidmark*

# WINTER NIGHT

*Author:* Kay Boyle (1902-1992)
*Type of plot:* Social realism
*Time of plot:* The 1940's
*Locale:* New York City
*First published:* 1946

> *Principal characters:*
> FELICIA, a seven-year-old girl
> A WOMAN, the baby-sitter for the evening
> A MAID
> FELICIA'S MOTHER

## The Story

As the evening darkens one winter night, the maid tells Felicia that once again her mother will not be coming home to their apartment until after Felicia is asleep. Felicia's father is away in the war. As usual, a baby-sitter will come when it is time for the maid to leave. The maid defends the mother's absence on the grounds that, after working hard all day, she deserves her freedom at night. The maids and the baby-sitters change frequently, allowing no time for Felicia to become attached to any of them. They do their jobs, providing no emotional nourishment for the little girl.

This night, the baby-sitter is early. She is a dark-haired, sad-eyed woman who immediately shows an interest in Felicia. Unlike the other sitters, this one offers to clean up after the girl's dinner so she can be alone with her sooner. Whereas other sitters perfunctorily take care of Felicia, moving through a routine that gets her to bed as soon as possible, as if she were merely something that has to be disposed of, this sitter breaks the routine. She tells Felicia that she reminds her of another little girl whose birthday this happens to be. Always attentive to Felicia, the sitter talks to her about the other little girl. Felicia, in her innocence, is never aware, but the reader quickly realizes that the woman is talking about her experiences in a German concentration camp. Felicia interprets everything she hears according to her own experience, reflecting her own anxieties, brought on by the extended absence of the father, whom she hardly remembers, and the nightly absences of her mother.

The little girl in the concentration camp could not understand what was happening to her, why her mother was taken away, why she could not go to her ballet lessons. The baby-sitter took care of her after she was separated from her mother, until they, too, were separated; the baby-sitter assumes that the little girl died in the camp. Felicia falls asleep in the woman's arms, and that is how Felicia's mother finds them when she returns after midnight. The sight of the two of them in each other's arms shocks her.

## Themes and Meanings

The first sentence of the story states the theme: "There is a time of apprehension which begins with the beginning of darkness, and to which only the speech of love can lend security." Children live with this concern continuously; adults have repressed it. In a world at war, the darkness is pervasive. Children and adults alike in this story suffer from the dearth of words of love. Both Felicia in New York and the little girl in the concentration camp are innocent victims of a world in which the adults are themselves too insecure to provide security for others. The kind baby-sitter can provide affection to both girls, but she cannot save either of them from the darkness of the adult world in which men kill children in the name of ideology and mothers spend their evenings in search of pleasure. Felicia's mother could stay at home; the frequency of her absences, however, indicates that she is herself the victim of needs beyond her control. The maid says that the mother is buying her freedom and that nobody gets hurt by this. Regardless of the success of the mother in achieving this nebulous goal, Felicia is clearly being hurt by her neglect. Whatever freedom the mother gains is at a cost to her daughter. The kind baby-sitter knows that there is no escape and offers herself as a temporary stay to the darkness for Felicia. Through her own suffering she reaches out to Felicia for what solace, fellowship, and compassion she can provide.

Whether the mother leaves her child out of her own need or out of callous disregard, the result to Felicia is the same: No one is there to comfort her. Only the woman with the experience of the concentration camp understands the girl's fear.

*Style and Technique*

The constant danger to authors of stories about suffering children is that they will overstep the boundary between pathos and sentimentality, as most of them do, turning pathos into bathos. The effectiveness of "Winter Night" derives in part from Kay Boyle's skill at counterpointing Felicia's plight with that of the other little girl without losing any of the specificity that makes them worthy of compassion.

Such details as the "golden fur" on their limbs, the lilac of their eyes, and the interest they have in ballet not only unite them in the mind of the sitter, but also make them real for the reader. Felicia's plight is individualized by the details of her apartment and of her nighttime routine, by the dialogue of the maid, and by the questions she asks the sitter. When the sitter speaks of the crying of the girls in the camp, Felicia asks whether they cried because their mother had to go out to supper. Such questions ring true because they are derived from Felicia's experience. In the same fashion, the story of the girl in the camp escapes sentimentalization by the understated manner in which the woman sticks to the factual details of that experience.

The story of the other little girl, more dramatically sensational, has the potential to make Felicia's story mundane or trivial, yet in Boyle's hands it has rather the opposite effect. The failure of Felicia's mother to try to comfort her daughter in a world in which such things happen to little girls deepens the pathos of her situation. Felicia and all the other children have reason to be apprehensive.

*William J. McDonald*

# WINTER: 1978

*Author:* Ann Beattie (1947-    )
*Type of plot:* Social realism
*Time of plot:* 1978
*Locale:* Los Angeles and Connecticut
*First published:* 1981

> *Principal characters:*
> NICK, the protagonist, age twenty-nine
> BENTON, a painter and Nick's friend, also age twenty-nine
> OLIVIA, Benton's girlfriend
> ELIZABETH, Benton's former wife
> JASON, Benton's and Elizabeth's young son
> ENA, Benton's mother
> UNCLE CAL, Benton's uncle

*The Story*

The story begins in Los Angeles, where the protagonist, Nick, who grew up with Benton in New England, now works in the recording industry. When Benton, with his girlfriend Olivia, flies to Los Angeles to sell his latest batch of paintings to a wealthy, eccentric patron, he calls on his old friend Nick for moral support. Nick has had trouble adjusting to the deals, drugs, and flamboyance of Southern California, but Olivia, who is constantly experimenting with drugs, seems at home with the decadent Hollywood scene. At the news that Benton's younger brother Wesley has drowned in a boating accident, the three fly home, too late for the funeral but fortunate to find a flight at all so close to Thanksgiving.

They join what remains of Benton's family (his mother Ena, his former wife Elizabeth, his son Jason, and his Uncle Cal), who are assembled at the dead Wesley's house in the Connecticut countryside where Wesley had recently moved, it has been speculated, either to return to simplicity or to assuage some sort of guilt Ena has caused. Nick, too, finds rural New England serene and natural, a return to simplicity and tradition, with pumpkins, apple orchards, and picturesque graveyards, a place where "snow" means not cocaine but the real thing; he wishes he could live there again. The family reunion promises to be anything but peaceful, for when the three arrive from the West Coast, the other family members have already begun taking Wesley's belongings, and they rush to confess, exposing their own self-interests. Between the traditional Elizabeth and Olivia, who is often under the influence of drugs, the atmosphere is understandably charged, a situation not helped by Olivia's tendency to monopolize the bathtub.

Benton's mother entertains an impossible fantasy, that her family will gather harmoniously in front of the fireplace, but she cannot manage to get everyone together at the same time. Perhaps to compensate, she insists that they wait for Hanley Paulson to deliver a load of firewood; although he charges too much, he has always delivered her wood in the past and she finds that she "can always count on Hanley." Her brother-in-law and secret admirer, Cal, bickers with her whenever he is not worrying about his health or the vegetarian foibles of his interior decorator. The child Jason seems determined to have his divorced parents reconciled.

Wandering among these miniature dramas, taking everything in but not really involved emotionally in anything (not even in the brief sexual interlude with Elizabeth), Nick is free to observe the family as a whole and to recall Wesley's influence. Wesley, a photographer, had once taken a picture of Nick's hands that transformed them into something strange, soft, and priestlike; Nick contemplates Wesley's death as a strange still life.

When the firewood finally arrives, not Hanley but his surly son delivers it; he demands extra compensation to stack it, then carries off most of Wesley's pumpkins. Toward the end of their time together, the family joins around the table to eat Ena's large dinner, which is supposed to replace the Thanksgiving dinner she never prepared, but she cannot make pumpkin pie because, she claims, all the pumpkins are gone. During the meal, the tension that has been smoldering finally flares up, sending young Jason from the table in tears. Benton puts Jason to bed with a story about evolution, in which dinosaurs turn into deer but remember their change with sadness.

*Themes and Meanings*

It would be difficult to find a more traditional symbol of America than the New England family gathered together at Thanksgiving to celebrate physical survival and spiritual renewal. In this case, however, what is in addition intended to be a reaffirmation of the family in the face of the loss of one of its members becomes instead such an occasion for internal competition that it drives young Jason symbolically from the family table.

On one level, then, the story follows the disintegration of a family as a result of the internal conflicts of its members: competition of egos and lifestyles. On another, broader, level, the theme becomes one of evolution, competition, and survival. Particularly in the light of Ena's rigid insistence on ritual (no matter how empty) and her subsequent disillusionment (in Hanley, her family, and civilized behavior in general), the American family can be seen as a rather cumbersome cultural institution that must try to compete successfully with the newer and self-indulgent, amorphous, anesthetic culture represented, in the story, by Southern California. Certainly this family seems already stretched to its limits, barely able to accommodate two divorces, a wife and girlfriend under the same roof, erratic electrocardiograms, Yoga, alcohol and drugs, casual sex, and the needless death of a young man.

Even if the family does manage to adapt and survive, its individual members have already begun paying a personal price for change: guilt and a sense of loss. As times and lives continue to evolve from one form into another, the family becomes like the creatures in Benton's bedtime story, whose eyes grow "sad . . . because they were once something else." Each of the characters, yearning for a return to simplicity and security, searches for some ritual, formality, or father-confessor, as if some symbolic act might absolve guilt and restore what was lost. Wesley's death is only the catalyst for his family's private fears. Divorced Ena wants a world where fate ordains "what's in the cards," where people behave in benevolent and predictable ways—all guaranteed to relieve her of the responsibility of real choice: "I would have made pumpkin pie, but the pumpkins disappeared." Uncle Cal is so afraid of dying that he resorts to an almost superstitious regime of diets, exercises, fads, and devices in an attempt to forestall the inevitable. Olivia retreats from pain and responsibility into her drugs. Benton attempts to return to childhood innocence through little Jason. Elizabeth seduces Nick (whom she sees in the role of a priest) in order, he suspects, to exorcise Wesley's ghost. Even Nick, as he contemplates the changing relationship between Benton and himself, imagines a phone booth to be a confessional; back in New England, he wishes that he could return to a time before he learned that his father had once wanted to send him away, before he realized that death could be casual and unpredictable, before he found himself using people and burdened with the ensuing guilt.

As the characters struggle helplessly between desire to regain innocence or security and their inability to do so, Ann Beattie offers no clear-cut answer to their dilemma, though she does suggest the paradoxical metaphor of the still life: the composition that remains of what once existed. Over the whole story hangs its title, like a photographer's caption denoting still-life order and a single, graspable point in time, all the while contrasting sharply with the theme of change or evolution, and with the particular turbulence and conflict of the characters' lives. Nick expresses the story's central irony, admitting that he is fascinated by photographs given simple still-life captions when the subject matter is alarming, disturbing, absurd: "Photograph gets a shot of a dwarf running out of a burning hotel and it's labeled 'New York: 1968.'" He goes on to caption an imagined shot of the capsized boat and floating orange life vests, all that remain of Wesley's death; "Lake Champlain: 1978." This image serves both as a colorful arrangement of objects and as evidence of the absurdity and needlessness of Wesley's death—he should not have been boating in November, and he should have been wearing a life preserver. At the same time, the still-life metaphor becomes, finally, Nick's attempt to impose order, however arbitrary, on an event that cannot be comfortably explained using reason; an expression in lieu of any explanation; an attempt to bridge the gap between present and past, between change itself and what cannot be changed. Only Nick (though perhaps Elizabeth as well) has clearly begun to understand something about his own motives in an absurd and transient world, but this growth process allows Wesley's death to be not completely in vain.

## Style and Technique

Beattie's style is deceptively simple. Related as a collection of very human, often hilarious details, this story gives (as do Wesley's photographs) the effect of life spontaneously observed rather than arranged or posed, reported rather than judged. Into the zany and poignant moments of the characters' lives are woven dozens of smaller anecdotes and observations, some experienced by the characters, others merely repeated at second hand. Irony and humor work side by side. The sequence of events seems less important than their accumulation.

However, on closer inspection, the seemingly random details add up to a subtly structured and solid whole. Even small anecdotes and details carefully support (and often offer substantive clues to) the main themes. For example, the cat that Nick and Elizabeth pick up at the side of the road and take to their motel room manages to adapt comfortably to whatever surroundings in which it finds itself, reinforcing the animal secret of survival. In a detail from the past, Nick recalls Benton's feeling trapped and tossing his wallet out of the car window; Nick retrieves the wallet, which falls open on the seat to Elizabeth's picture: Benton can no more easily discard his changing identity and credentials (marriage, impending fatherhood) than he can control change itself. Ena takes the dead Wesley's chain of keys, though they open nothing she can find; still, she keeps trying, hoping perhaps to unlock an answer to her son's needless death.

In image after image, the themes reappear in major and minor variations; as they do, a single picture begins to emerge. Just as Wesley's photographs transform the ordinary into something of mystery and beauty, so the story transforms disparate and ordinary elements into a single artistic vision of contemporary life whose harshness is softened by the human touch.

*Sally V. Doud*

# WIRELESS

*Author:* Rudyard Kipling (1865-1936)
*Type of plot:* Fantasy
*Time of plot:* 1902
*Locale:* An unnamed English seaside town, possibly Teignmouth
*First published:* 1902

> *Principal characters:*
> THE NARRATOR, identified only as "I"
> MR. CASHELL, SR., the proprietor of a chemist's shop
> MR. CASHELL, JR., his nephew, an amateur electrical
>    experimenter
> JOHN SHAYNOR, an assistant in the shop
> FANNY BRAND, a girl with whom Shaynor is infatuated

*The Story*

"Wireless" is on one level the story of a failed experiment. Mr. Cashell, Jr., has invited the narrator to join him in an attempt to send radio transmissions between his uncle's shop and an operator in Poole, some distance away. At first, Poole does not come through, and by the time it does, the narrator has lost interest and has decided to go home. In the interim, all that has been heard on Cashell's radio receiver is the sound of two warships failing to communicate with each other—their transmitters working but their receivers out of tune—ending with the phrase "Disheartening most disheartening." On the scientific level, then, nothing happens in "Wireless"—though one should note that everyone in the story accepts that these mishaps will be corrected soon, if not immediately, and that this scientific failure is purely temporary and will ultimately prove insignificant.

More significant, and potentially more disheartening, is what happens while Mr. Cashell is waiting for his signal. The narrator passes the time by talking to the young shop assistant, John Shaynor. It is soon clear that Shaynor is dying of tuberculosis. He will not admit it to himself, blaming his cough on a sore throat from smoking too many cigarettes, but Cashell does not expect him to live a year, and the narrator silently agrees. Shaynor is also, equally pathetically, infatuated with a girl who comes into the shop and takes him out—into a bitingly cold east wind, the last thing one would recommend for a tuberculosis patient—but who will clearly outlive and very probably forget him. Shaynor is a doomed nobody.

However, for a few brief hours he is also a focus, the human "receiver" (perhaps) for a message that comes through from Somewhere. This message appears to consist of the poetry of John Keats. As Shaynor slumps into a coma—caused perhaps by his illness, or possibly by the lethal alcoholic concoction the narrator has devised to warm everyone up—he starts first to declaim, and then to write, garbled versions, fragments, even whole sections, mostly of Keats's poem "The Eve of St. Agnes," but also of "Ode to a Nightingale" and the ode "To Autumn." When Shaynor comes out of his coma, the narrator establishes that he has never heard of Keats. He is not remembering, then. Where has the poetry come from? Furthermore, how does this mysterious and supernatural event relate to the equally mysterious but scientific event (or nonevent) taking place in Cashell's makeshift signal station next door?

*Themes and Meanings*

The central theme of the story is clearly the inexplicable. Twice the narrator asks Cashell for an explanation of what he is doing, asking first what is "electricity," and second what is "induction." Both times, Cashell replies by telling him, not what these phenomena are, but how they work. The propagation of radio waves through empty space remains itself mysterious to the characters, and is referred to more than once as "magic."

It is worth noting how very up-to-date Rudyard Kipling was, both in his science and in his sense of amazement. "Wireless" was first published in 1902, but even if this fact were not known, the story could be precisely dated on internal evidence. Its first sentence, from Shaynor, is: "It's a funny thing, this Marconi business." This comment clearly dates the story as occurring after 1896 (the year of the first arrival of Guglielmo Marconi in England) and probably after 1901—for it was in December of that year that Marconi created a sensation with the first transatlantic radio transmission. In the center of the story, however, is a clear description of a device known as a "coherer." This was the work of Edouard Branly, and was used in the early Marconi transmissions but was supplanted after 1904 by the diode. The incident of the warships signaling further recalls an event of 1899. However, by 1910, it is safe to say, such contacts were too regular to be any longer a matter of amazement. "Wireless" accurately records the first impact of a major new technology on popular consciousness. That impact is one of awe and fear.

The central thought of Kipling's story, then, is that if an inexplicable "Power" can send impalpable messages through the dimension of space, then maybe it, or another, can send messages through time. Radio's messages can be received only after careful preparation and "tuning." Messages from the dead, perhaps, need something analogous. What the narrator records is the tuning of Shaynor—as it were, a human "coherer"—to receive the signals of Keats.

Keats and Shaynor are alike in many respects. Both are apothecaries, both are victims of tuberculosis, both are in love—one with Fanny Brawne, the other with Fanny Brand. The chemist's shop in the story is also curiously similar to the setting of Keats's "The Eve of St. Agnes." Instead of having windows with stained glass, it has the giant colored bottles of the old-fashioned apothecary. Outside it, at the game shop, hang the dead birds and hare, ruffled by the searching wind like the animals at the start of Keats's poem. When Fanny Brand takes Shaynor out, she takes him to the church of St. Agnes. The bitter cold; the sleet on the windowpanes; the red, black, and yellow cloth; the fear of death; and the frozen churchyard are common to both poem and story.

A kind of plausibility accordingly thickens around Shaynor's unconscious recording of Keats's poem (which he does like a man in the throes of composition). The radio messages give a scientific analogue. The immediate circumstances argue that this could be an unrepeatable coincidence, an ideal man and moment for "reception." Shaynor, furthermore, is dying, perhaps drunk, certainly near somnambulism, all traditionally favorable states for moments of insight. Finally, the whole house—this is told twice—has been "electrified" by Cashell's primitive antenna. The reader is given every reason for suspending disbelief. However, the event at the heart of the story remains inexplicable, unexplained.

It is also, in several ways, sad or disheartening. This kind of communication will not be improved. It is a "one-off." Soon, Shaynor will be dead. What he has received is in any case a travesty, a garble of brilliant lines—just as Fanny Brand and the chemist's shop appear common, cheap, and vulgar compared with Madeline and the magic setting of Keats's poem. Is it poor reception? Is it a ghost unable to recapture its own greatness? A final thought is the possibility—worst of all—that Shaynor is not a receiver but a transmitter: that it is his agony and his peculiar circumstances (hare, colored bottles, colored blanket, and so on) that in some way "went out" to Keats to be transmuted into poetry. This theory would depict creativity itself as derived from a failed experiment; it would be merely subordinate art and magic (as Keats feared) to the progress of science.

## Style and Technique

The main point here is Kipling's famous compression. It can safely be said that no detail in "Wireless" is without significance and, furthermore, that no reader has ever read this story with full comprehension on first attempt. The early details of birds and hare make no sense until one comes on the explicit references to "The Eve of St. Agnes." Similarly, Shaynor's cough cannot be recognized as terminal until he starts to cough blood. Once the general frame of the story has been recognized, however, the reader is challenged to return and discover every trace of explanation, hinted allusion, dramatic irony—an activity that requires a reading not only of Kipling but also of Keats. Thus, the narrator's apparently casual remark that Shaynor's eyes "shone like a drugged moth's" takes on more meaning when one remembers Keats's line near the heart of "The Eve of St. Agnes" comparing stained glass to the wings of a tiger-moth—and Shaynor indeed becomes "a tiger-moth as I thought" a few pages later. The moth imagery is, however, not only one of color but also one of doom: Fanny Brand kills Shaynor with her little excursion to the church like a candle tempting a moth to burning. Shining eyes, too, are a symptom of tuberculosis. One phrase, therefore, can work on three levels.

It is also significant that Shaynor's Keatsian language starts just before his coma, as if triggering it, and further, that as he starts to come out of the coma, the lines he quotes start to go wrong. A sense of failure and degradation is in fact vital to the story, suggesting that Shaynor's visions of love and beauty—wherever they come from—are illusions. He literally adores Fanny Brand; Cashell sees her as "a great, big, fat lump of a girl"; the narrator sees both perspectives, but on the whole sides with the latter, as he is conscious of the commercial ugliness of much of his setting.

The story's final power stems, however, from Kipling's unique ability to describe. There is hardly a better description of cold and deepening solitude in English than in this story, and it is brilliantly set off by the rich evocation of color and scent within the chemist's shop. "Wireless" is a tour de force by a prose artist determined to show what his medium could do even in rivalry with poetry at its greatest.

*T. A. Shippey*

# THE WISH HOUSE

*Author:* Rudyard Kipling (1865-1936)
*Type of plot:* Fantasy
*Time of plot:* The early twentieth century
*Locale:* A small village in Sussex, England
*First published:* 1924

> *Principal characters:*
> MRS. ASHCROFT, an old countrywoman
> MRS. FEETLEY, her friend

*The Story*

On a pleasant March Saturday in the Sussex countryside, Mrs. Ashcroft entertains her old friend Mrs. Feetley for afternoon tea. At the outset, talk quickly turns to memories of the past, and the story unfolds entirely through the ensuing dialogue. Mrs. Ashcroft recalls the death of her husband many years earlier. She hints that it had not been the happiest of marriages, and that both sides carried their share of the blame. Her husband had warned her on his deathbed that retribution lay in store: "I can see what's comin' to you." However, this ominous note does not fully prepare the reader for the strange story, involving mysterious and supernatural events, that Mrs. Ashcroft now relates to her spellbound friend.

After her husband's unlamented death, Mrs. Ashcroft, who combines the practical worldliness of Geoffrey Chaucer's Wife of Bath with the simplicity of the country-woman, traveled to London, finding a job as a cook in an upper-class home. It was an easy life, and she fared well. After a year, she moved back to Smalldene, a village in Sussex, where she worked on a farm. It is there that she met Harry Mockler, and their lives were destined to become entwined in a curious and baffling manner. Mrs. Ashcroft regarded Harry as her master, although, looking back, she certainly holds no illusions about romantic love. "What did ye get out of it?" Mrs. Feetley asks. "The usuals. Everythin' at first—worse than naught after," is the reply. Although she loved Harry unquestioningly, far more than she had ever loved her husband, eventually he deserted her, and she suffered greatly.

Now her story takes an unexpected turn. She relates that one day, suffering from a bad headache, she found the playful company of young Sophy Ellis, the daughter of the local charwoman, irksome. Sophy, having discovered the reason for Mrs. Ashcroft's irritability, immediately promised to relieve her headache, as if to do so was the easiest thing in the world. She promptly left the house. Within ten minutes, the headache vanished. Mrs. Ashcroft naturally assumed this to be a coincidence, but Sophy insisted on her return that it was she who was responsible for the cure, and that she was now suffering from the same headache herself. As Mrs. Ashcroft questioned the child, she heard with increasing amazement about the Wish House, a deserted house in nearby Wadloes Road, in which a spirit, known as a Token, lived. The Token had the power, if asked, to transfer an affliction from one person to another. No one, however, could wish good for himself; the spirit dealt only in bad.

Some months elapsed, during which this incident lay at the back of Mrs. Ashcroft's mind. The next summer, she traveled once more to London, and then again to Smalldene. By chance, she met Harry, whom she still loved, but found that he was tragically changed from his former self. Having sustained a bad leg injury, which had turned poisonous, he was a broken figure and was not expected to live more than a few months. Acutely distressed, she urged him to see a doctor in London, but he refused. In desperation, Mrs. Ashcroft decided that there was only one thing that she could do for him. In the evening, single-minded in her purpose, she set off for the Wish House. On her arrival, she rang the bell boldly and immediately heard the approach of shuffling footsteps. The footsteps reached the front door, where they stopped. It was an eerie moment. Mrs. Ashcroft leaned forward to the letter box and said, "Let me take everythin' bad that's in store for my man, 'Arry Mockler, for love's sake." She heard nothing from behind the door except an expulsion of breath. Then the footsteps returned downstairs to the kitchen.

For several months nothing appeared to happen, but in November, Mrs. Ashcroft learned that Harry had fully recovered and returned to his job. Her own troubles, however, were about to begin. The following spring, she developed a boil on her shin that refused to heal. At first, she made no firm connection between this event and Harry's earlier recovery. Later, however, when Harry suffered a kick from his horse, her wound got worse, and she believed that it was drawing the strength out of her. Harry got better. At that point, she knew the truth and uttered a shout of triumph that was also a prayer: "You'll take your good from me 'thout knowin' it till my life's end. O God, send me long to live for 'Arry's sake!"

As the months and years went by, Mrs. Ashcroft learned to regulate the pain and discomfort from her wound. Sometimes the wound appeared to clear up, and she learned that this was an indication that Harry would be in good health for a while, so she conserved her strength. When the wound got worse, she knew that Harry was in need. This continued for years. She gained nothing from this strange situation because no one knew of it except herself; Harry took little notice of her, although, to her relief, he did not take up with another woman.

The final twist in the story takes place when Mrs. Ashcroft reveals that her wound has turned cancerous. She is slowly dying. In a moment of uncertainty, she seeks reassurance from her friend that the pain she endures is not wasted, that it keeps her Harry safe. Mrs. Feetley willingly concurs. Finally, Mrs. Ashcroft asks her friend to look at the wound before she leaves. At the sight of it Mrs. Feetley shudders but kisses Mrs. Ashcroft with sympathy and understanding. The story ends on this note of compassion for the dying woman, who has selflessly taken on the troubles of a man to whom she is devoted and who has given her nothing in return.

*Themes and Meanings*

"The Wish House" was originally published with two obscure poems, one of which, "Late Came the God," provides important commentary on the story. It relates how a vengeful God inflicts continual pain and distress on a woman in payment of a debt. This theme of divine retribution for past sins, real or imagined, forms a minor element in "The Wish House." However, the last lines of the poem reveal the first of the story's main themes, the redemptive, self-sacrificial love of woman for man: "Alone, without hope of regard or reward, but uncowed,/ Resolute, selfless, divine/ These things she did in Love's honour."

This love is unrelated to merit or desert; it sees no fault in the object of love, or seeing, chooses to disregard. There is nothing romantic about it. It is a practical, even instinctive, orientation of the will and heart, in obedience to an inner impulse. The theme has profoundly Christian implications. Mrs. Ashcroft is almost Christ-like in her ability, and her willingness, to take on herself the sins and burdens of another, motivated by the highest love. The wound in her leg will suggest, for the Christian reader, the stigmata of the Christian saint, the wounds received in imitation of Christ. The old Mrs. Ashcroft, chattering away to her friend in country dialect, is perhaps an unlikely figure to remind one of the divine, but the implication of the story is that the simplest folk become godlike, and possess godlike powers, when motivated by a pure desire for the good of another and a resolute will to endure physical hardship and pain without complaint.

The second major theme of the story is what T. S. Eliot appreciatively called its "pagan vision" of country life lived close to nature. This "vision of the people of the soil" is of a world in which magic, in the form of spirits, spells, and curses, still exerts its age-old power. The world that the two old women inhabit consists of an intuitive, prescientific sense of the interrelationship of all creatures at all levels of existence. It is a way of seeing which unquestioningly accepts the fluidity and transferability of spiritual forces, in contradistinction, as Eliot points out, to the modern, materialistic temper. Eliot's suggestion that such a vision must be regained if "the truly Christian imagination is to be recovered by Christians" is apt commentary on "The Wish House." This is because the "pagan vision" underlies the Christian implication of the story: Individual pain and death is not random or wasted but in a mysterious way nourishes the larger good; it is part of the interwoven fabric of pain and joy in which the life of the universe consists.

*Style and Technique*

Somewhat less cryptic and obscure than many of Rudyard Kipling's stories, "The Wish House" skillfully blends realism and fantasy in a way that suggests that the supernatural order is coextensive with the natural. This lends force to the story's themes, with their implication that in spite of surface appearances to the contrary, no part of life is in fact separate from any other part.

The realism is especially noticeable in the country dialect in which both women speak, which has the effect of grounding them in a particular locality and a particular class of character. It also suggests a lack of sophistication, a lack of exposure to modern, homogenizing culture, which makes their acceptance of ancient folk beliefs immediately plausible to the reader. After all the trappings of a March Saturday in southern England—football buses, church visitors, afternoon tea—have added to the realistic flavor, the supernatural, fantastic element creeps in unobtrusively, seemingly enfolded within the natural order. The Wish House is not placed in a mysterious, unspecified setting, but at 14 Wadloes Road, on the way to the greengrocer. There are more than twenty houses in the street exactly like it. The reader's suspension of disbelief is assured. Even the spirit itself is curiously mundane, sitting on a chair in the kitchen and shuffling upstairs, Mrs. Ashcroft observes, as if it were "a heavy woman in slippers."

The effect of this subtle interpenetration of natural and supernatural becomes clear at the end of the story. The sordid reality of the exposed wound that Mrs. Ashcroft displays to her friend remains uppermost in the reader's mind, but it no longer stands alone, without wider significance. It has become the focal point for the mysterious trading of blessing and curse that has been woven into the fabric of the old woman's life.

*Bryan Aubrey*

# WISSLER REMEMBERS

*Author:* Richard G. Stern (1928-　　)
*Type of plot:* Psychological
*Time of plot:* The 1970's
*Locale:* A large university in the United States
*First published:* 1980

> *Principal characters:*
> CHARLES WISSLER, a professor of literature

*The Story*

At the end of yet another academic semester, and the dissolution of yet another group of students of whom he has become extremely fond, Professor Wissler finds himself reminiscing about his thirty years in the teaching profession. His nostalgic odyssey, full of amusing anecdotes and delightful vignettes, forms the core of the story.

He recalls how at the age of twenty-one, immediately after World War II, he won a Fulbright scholarship to teach at a school in Versailles. His French was little better than the boys' English, but the students were respectful and his stay was pleasant enough. The following year had seen him working in Heidelberg, decoding cables for the army and supplementing his income by teaching English language and literature at the university. Heidelberg was full of American soldiers, and the war was a vivid presence in his mind, as he taught the sons and daughters of those who had recently been his enemies. He recalls the beautiful, exquisitely courteous Fraulein Hochhusen, with her "heart-rending popped blue eyes," and "hypnotic lips." His amorous feelings toward her are clear enough to him ("I love you") but carefully shielded from the girl herself. Wissler is always conscious of the sexual charms of his female students, but he has carefully trained himself to feel love "with the sexuality displaced." That, he thinks to himself, has been "priestly excruciation."

At the start of the Korean War, he moved to Frankfurt, to take up a higher-paying job teaching American soldiers. Most of them could hardly read or write, yet there he had the most enjoyable and rewarding experience of his teaching career. He found the willingness and sincerity of his ragged class deeply moving.

Following his return to the United States and sojourns in Iowa and Connecticut, he found himself at a "great Gothic hive of instruction and research" where he has remained ever since. He recalls the hundreds of classes and the myriad students who have passed through his hands and who are now scattered across the globe in a host of different occupations and professions. He recalls particular individuals, such as the "dull, potato-faced" Miss Rabb, who wrote a paper that was so obscure it made sense only when she explained it in person, but this was too late to save her from a C grade.

Everywhere on his travels, from Kansas to Kyoto, New York to Nanterre, there had been wonderful, expressive faces. Even the bored and the contemptuous had their stories to tell. Underlying all of Wissler's experience was love, not only of individuals but also of the class itself, what he calls the "humanscape." The group as a whole was like a complex organism and generated a unique collective consciousness.

Reminiscence over, the story comes up to date. It is December, and the last class of Wissler's current course is in session. There is the sense of "amorous ether" in the room, but Wissler's lecture does not show any trace of it. He recommends a scholarly book on the history of education in antiquity. Like the good academic that he is, he speaks intelligently and interestingly; he is alert to his students' needs and tries to remain objective. The class closes, and there are polite expressions of thanks and gratitude from both professor and students.

One last, simple episode closes the story. Outside, after class, snow falls, and the paths are covered with ice. Wissler slips and falls, only to find his attractive student Miss Fennig on hand to help him up. The simplicity and pleasantness of their brief exchange reveals mutual respect and affection. Outside the formality of the classroom, and beyond the limiting roles of teacher and student, there is only the simplicity of human contact, one hand helping another.

*Themes and Meanings*

It would perhaps be pedantic and heavy-handed to insist on extracting too serious a theme from such a delightful and deft story as "Wissler Remembers." It is more like a series of entertaining snapshots of the pleasures and frustrations of the teaching profession: the opportunities it gives, the restrictions it imposes. Wissler's deep commitment to and quiet love of his chosen profession is clear throughout the range of his remembrance, from the fullness of a class in full swing to the sadness of conclusion and parting.

Nevertheless, throughout the story there is a recurring motif: the gap between what Wissler thinks, what he wants to say—as he allows the reader into his uncensored mind—and what he actually does say. Early in the story, this problem of communication, or noncommunication, is symbolically and amusingly represented in the episode at the French school. Wissler gives his students a French translation of an American poem and asks them to retranslate it into English. Only five of the twenty-five students even understand the assignment, but he offers a reward to anyone who gets within twelve words of the original. Needless to say, the one effort that Wissler recalls was completely unintelligible.

In the same manner, something happens to Wissler's own thoughts in the act of translating them into words, particularly with respect to the deeper feelings that he has for his students. His reminiscences are generated by his desire to tell everything to his students: how much he has grown to love them, and how difficult it will be for him to lose them. He wants to finish the class with a warm and generous tribute: "It has been a splendid class. For me. There is almost no future I think should be denied you. What world wouldn't be better led by you?" However, somehow the words do not come. His farewell comments are polite and restrained: He will have office hours the following week; he wishes everyone good luck.

However, this failure to communicate does not constitute a major character weakness. Wissler is a warm and compassionate man, and his students recognize him as such. The failure arises more from the inevitable restrictions that his position imposes on him. Teacher and student have vastly different roles, and for Wissler to have transgressed his own would have been to fall from the responsibility and sense of duty, which, unstuffily and unpretentiously, he respects. Wissler accepts this limitation without regret. It is in the nature of things that some channels of communication between people may be closed; that is always so in life. Other channels may be open, offering their own kind of reward. This possibility is clear from Wissler's last moments with his students. Although he does not say what he intends to say, there is yet a subtle bond between them, which both sides recognize: "the sweetness of a farewell between those who have done well by each other."

### Style and Technique

Richard G. Stern's diction bears the hallmark of one who began his writing career as a poet before turning to novels and short stories. It is economical, varied, and highly compressed. As one reviewer has commented, "You read a sentence twice not because it is obscure but because you want to make sure you are extracting every nuance." This richness is noticeable in the frequency of short, elliptic sentences, as Wissler's thoughts pile quickly up on one another: "And whoops, heart gripped, I'm heading down, hand cushioning, but a jar," which conveys the sudden shock of slipping on the ice.

Also noticeable in this respect is Stern's frequent use of compounds, which occur in his descriptions of the people who pass through Wissler's mental landscape. Ms. Bainbridge, for example, has a "silver-glassed, turn-of-the-century-Rebecca-West" face; Fraulein Hochhusen is "berry-cheeked"; Herr Doppelgut is "paper-white" and "dog-eyed"; Miss Rabb is "potato-faced"; and the earnest face of Ms. Glypher is "parent-treasured, parent-driven."

The juxtaposition of the formal with the informal, which underlies the story and gives it much of its effect, can be seen stylistically in the first paragraph. As Wissler reviews the names of his current students, no first names come into his mind. He knows them as Miss Fennig, Mr. Quincey, Mr. Parcannis, Miss Shimbel, Ms. Bainbridge, and Miss Vibsayana. The latter "speaks so beautifully." However, in the parentheses that follow (a stylistic device employed frequently by Stern), such formal and correct language gives way to an undercurrent of intense feeling aroused by the thought of Miss Vibsayana and expressed in colloquial, ungrammatical language: "You cannot relinquish a sentence, the act of speech such honey in your throat, I can neither bear nor stop it." The double comma splice and the ellipsis (the omission of the verb in the second clause) convey the sudden rush of feeling and the hurried thoughts that accompany it. This dichotomy between spoken and unspoken thoughts sets the tone for the remainder of the story.

*Bryan Aubrey*

# WITCH'S MONEY

*Author:* John Collier (1901-1980)
*Type of plot:* Satire
*Time of plot:* The 1930's
*Locale:* A small town in the Pyrenees in France
*First published:* 1940

> *Principal characters:*
> FOIRAL, a native of a small town who meets a stranger to the
> village and sells a house to him
> AN UNNAMED AMERICAN PAINTER, who buys Foiral's house and
> is murdered there by Foiral and his friends
> ARAGO,
> GUIS,
> VIGNE,
> QUES and
> LAFAGO, village residents

## The Story

Foiral, having taken a load of cork to his market, is returning to his unnamed village, a tiny hamlet in the Pyrenees-Orientales district of France near the Spanish border. Along the roadside, he encounters a poorly dressed stranger whose mannerisms are eccentric; Foiral assumes that the stranger is a madman. The madman is striding aggressively down the road, but he stops, awestruck, at the top of a ridge as he first looks down on Foiral's village.

On the spot, the madman decides to stay there, perceiving the village as "surrealism come to life." The cork forests, he claims, look like "petrified ogres," while the black clothes of the native villagers make them seem "holes in the light." Foiral, bewildered, tries to remove himself from the vicinity of this lunatic, but the madman detains him, asking for a place to stay. When Foiral claims that there is no such place, the lunatic wanders through the village until he finds Foiral's own vacant property. Forced to admit that the property is his, Foiral finds himself selling it to the stranger, who identifies himself as an American painter who has been living in Paris.

Despite the stranger's appearance, he shows Foiral a wallet containing a number of thousand-franc notes. Having paid a deposit, the stranger returns to Paris for his possessions, while Foiral prepares the house for its new tenant. On his return to the village, the stranger offers Foiral the remainder of the sales price in the form of a check, but the villagers do not understand banking. Foiral recognizes the check only as a billet or note resembling a lottery ticket and is reluctant to take the scrap of paper in payment. Increasingly impatient, the artist refers him to the bank in Perpignan, the nearest city, where Foiral is astonished to learn that the billet can be converted into real cash—and that the bank makes a charge for this transaction. Foiral is indignant at the charge and believes that he has been cheated. Returning to the village, Foiral approaches the artist, hoping that the latter will make up the sum that the bank has charged. The artist, however, says that he, like Foiral, is a poor man. He cannot give Foiral any more money. Foiral assumes this to be a lie. After all, he has seen a little book containing many other billets. Because the one he took to the bank was worth thirty thousand francs, then each one of the others must be worth that amount. Not understanding that these are merely blank checks, Foiral is certain that, by the standards of the village, the artist is an extremely wealthy man.

Nursing his sense of injustice, Foiral speaks with the other village men, assuring them that the stranger admits to having no relatives and describing the little book with its many billets. As a result, these "very honest men" (a phrase not meant ironically) leave their homes late one night to visit the stranger. When they return, they possess the stranger's little billets. They quickly forget the artist himself; even his "final yelp" is forgotten as they would forget "the rattle and flash of yesterday's thunderstorm." Only one man, Guis, who has befriended the stranger, is left out; his decency causes him to be ostracized by the village and berated by his wife.

The billets, or blank checks, which the villagers assume to represent actual cash gradually take control of the town. The community is transformed, but not for the better. Cork concessions and other properties are exchanged for the billets, and the property owners swell with pride and self-importance. Marriages are arranged on the basis of possession of the billets; aging women take young husbands, while young girls become the property of wealthy widowers. Corruption, including gambling and prostitution, flourishes.

Eventually, the villagers feel the need for ready cash. Foiral proposes to lead the village men back to Perpignan, where all expect to exchange their blank checks for money. They go to the city as if preparing for a festival, still unaware that the scraps of paper are worthless, and they mock Guis, who once again has been left behind. Still laughing at him, they enter the bank and are last seen "choking with laughter when the swing doors closed behind them."

*Themes and Meanings*

The self-destructive innocence of the creative artist and the corrupting power of commercialism are recurrent motifs in John Collier's fiction, providing themes for such stories as "Evening Primrose," "The Steel Cat," and "The Invisible Dove Dancer of Strathpheen Island," among others. As in "Evening Primrose," the artist of "Witch's Money" is killed because he is incapable of comprehending the meaning of money to those among whom he chooses to live.

The unnamed artist of "Witch's Money" brings about his own death, much as the villagers later initiate their own catastrophe. Dazzled by the spectacle of the village, the artist forces himself on a reluctant Foiral. However, he speaks to Foiral with curtness and much contempt, impatient with working-class values and oblivious to the dangers presented by those long deprived of money and possessions. The artist fails to imagine Foiral's depth of ignorance concerning banking, and he is unconcerned with the latter's festering sense of injustice. However, the artist openly reveals the contents of his wallet and his checkbook. It is this combination of innocence, impatience, discourtesy, and tunnel vision that brings about his death.

The townspeople are, indeed, "very honest men," until they are corrupted by the prospect of the artist's wealth. From that time on, however, the killers become swollen with pride; they can neither speak to others nor be addressed, not even by their wives. The taint of corruption surrounds the marriages between old and young, while a village widow, in opening her home to "certain unattached young women" and giving "select" evening parties, introduces prostitution to a town that previously could not afford that particular vice. Similarly, the card players can now afford new cards. In short, the town experiences the results of capitalistic emphasis on money and possessions at the expense of human values. Moreover, the townspeople do not know when to stop, and, like the artist, undermine themselves, in this case by the decision to take the checks to Perpignan. As the villagers disappear through the bank doors, the reader is left uncertain as to their fate, but the "swing doors" suggest the doors of prisons and the swinging rope of the hangman.

*Style and Technique*

Collier's style is deceptively simple, his diction crisp and extremely precise. Beneath the seemingly simple language and sentence structure, however, lies a masterful ability to manipulate point of view, to create tone through the use of metaphor, and to exploit every ironic implication of the story.

In "Witch's Money," the tone of horror is maintained by distancing both Foiral and the artist from the reader, who can only watch, fascinated, their single-minded pursuit of self-destruction. The artist—the character with whom the reader can most readily identify—is kept distant from the reader; he is unnamed, and his actions are seen primarily through Foiral's limited viewpoint. When the artist describes his surrealistic vision of the village as a place of sterility and damnation, it is the reader—not the artist or Foiral—who realizes the implications of this vision for the artist's own life.

Ironically, the artist has only an intellectual understanding of surrealism; he does not understand that the barren and decadent landscape reflects the spirit of the place itself and that, if he enters there, he will be living out, not painting, a surrealistic nightmare. Foiral, in contrast, is brought closer to the reader, who is allowed to see the abysmal depths of ignorance and experience that allow Foiral to kill a man whom he does not perceive to be a human being like himself. Not only does Foiral lack comprehension of money and banking, but also his vision of the stranger is fragmentary and incomplete; just as the artist ironically discusses surrealism and the barren landscape without fully understanding either, so Foiral's own aspirations have ironically empty results. When he leads the townspeople to murder, they gain only worthless scraps of paper, while their triumphant entrance into the Perpignan bank will not liberate them but imprison them.

*Betty Richardson*

# WITHIN AND WITHOUT

*Author:* Hermann Hesse (1877-1962)
*Type of plot:* Psychological
*Time of plot:* The 1920's
*Locale:* Germany
*First published:* "Innen und Aussen," 1920 (English translation, 1935)

> *Principal characters:*
> FRIEDRICH, the protagonist, a man who loves rationality and
>     despises superstition
> ERWIN, his friend

*The Story*

Friedrich is described as a man who loves and respects rationality, especially logic and the sciences. In contrast, he has little respect for unscientific forms of knowledge. Though tolerant of religion, he does not take it seriously. He considers mysticism and magic to be pointless and outmoded in the scientific age. In fact, he despises superstition wherever he encounters it, especially among educated people. Those who question the supremacy of science in the wake of recent war and suffering infuriate him. He grows increasingly disturbed as he senses a rising interest in the occult as an alternative to science.

One day, Friedrich visits Erwin, a close friend whom he has not seen for a while. Friedrich thinks that Erwin's smile is indulgent and mocking. He recalls that he sensed a rift between them when they last parted—Erwin was not vehement enough in supporting Friedrich's hatred of superstition. Now they speak awkwardly of superficial matters, and all the while Friedrich is uncomfortably aware of a distance between them, as if he no longer truly knows Erwin.

Then Friedrich spots a paper pinned to the wall, which awakens memories of his old friend's habit of noting an interesting quotation. To Friedrich's horror, however, the line written on this paper is an expression of Erwin's recent mystical interests: "Nothing is outside, nothing is inside, for that which is outside is inside." Friedrich demands that his friend explain the meaning of this sentence and learns that Erwin sees it as an introduction to an ancient form of knowledge, "magic." In disappointment and anger, Friedrich tells Erwin to choose between this superstitious nonsense and Friedrich's respect and friendship. Erwin explains that he really had no choice in the matter—magic "chose him." He begs Friedrich not to part in anger but to accept their separation as inevitable, as if one of them were dying. Friedrich agrees and asks a final favor, to have those mysterious words explained. Erwin tells him that they refer in part to the religious idea of pantheism, in which God is in all things and all things are divine. Also, once one learns to pass beyond the habitual separation of the world into opposites, such as inside and outside, one can be free of such limitations, and that is the beginning of magic. To illustrate this experience, Erwin gives Friedrich a small clay figure, tells him to observe it from time to time, and asks Friedrich to return when the object "ceases to be outside you and is inside you."

Friedrich takes this object, a glazed clay figure of a two-headed god, to his home, where it gradually begins to obsess him. He moves it from place to place in his house, annoyed by its presence, yet finding his eyes continually drawn toward the ugly little idol. Its presence torments him; he grows restless and begins to travel often. After one such trip, he feels especially anxious and unsettled the moment he enters his house. Searching for the cause of his distress, he discovers that his maid broke the idol while dusting and disposed of its shattered remains. Friedrich immediately feels relief that this hateful and annoying reminder of superstition is finally gone, but he soon finds that he misses the figurine. Its absence is almost tangible, causing a growing emptiness within him. From hours of observing the two-headed god, he is able to recall the slightest details of its grins, its crude shape, and the colors and textures of its glaze. Even the word "glaze"—Glasur—upsets him and, spelled backward as "Rusalg," reminds him of a book, Frank Wedekind's *Princess Russalka* (1897), which both horrified and fascinated him.

The loss of the idol so consumes his thoughts that Friedrich wonders if perhaps it was magical. Perhaps Erwin had placed a spell on him through this figure, and Friedrich was a victim of the war of reason against such dark powers. However, he forces such ideas from his mind, thinking that he would rather die than admit even the possibility of magic. He cannot control his terror, however, and he finally wakes in fear one night, to find himself mumbling the words "Now you are inside me." Realizing that indeed the idol is torturing him from within himself, Friedrich hurries to Erwin's house to ask his friend how to remove the idol from inside himself. Erwin patiently explains that Friedrich must learn to love and accept what is now within him and stop tormenting the idol, which is really himself. Friedrich has unwillingly taken the first step beyond such pairs of opposites as inside and outside and now can begin to learn the secret of magic: freely controlling the exchange of inside and outside and becoming free from the slavery to what is inside him.

*Themes and Meanings*

Hermann Hesse often dealt with the need for humanity to overcome dualistic thinking and realize the unity of all reality. For Hesse, the attempt to constrict experience to technological control and objective rationality resulted only in a painful separation from the more sensual aspects integral to the human spirit. He believed that World War I was the result of that sort of spiritual crisis in Europe. Afterward, Hesse devoted himself to urging the German people to turn away from materialistic attitudes toward the inward search for healing and insight. Many of Hesse's postwar works, such as "Inside and Outside" or the later *Siddhartha* (1922), also show his fascination with the spiritual insights of Buddhist and Taoist mystical traditions, which teach the dynamic unity of opposites in one interconnected reality. Everything is related to everything else; each thing is involved in all other things. For Hesse, the recognition of this reality was the key to uniting the diverse aspects of human consciousness into one integrated whole. It was also the key to becoming free from the existential anxieties caused by people's mistaken views of themselves as isolated from one another or from nature.

In "Within and Without," Friedrich is engaged in a struggle, not only against what he perceives as the superstitions of others but also against reality itself. His attempt to mold the world to his conscious ideal of logical reasoning is a war against his own deepest nature and thereby destined to fail. By denying even the possibility of other forms of knowledge, Friedrich enslaves himself to a constant need to reject experiences and ideas that do not conform to his rational attitude. Before he visits Erwin, he is already tormenting himself with the mere idea that others may not share his "enlightened" view of the world.

His internal conflict becomes much more evident once Erwin gives him the two-headed figure. Its apparent power to disturb him reveals to Friedrich the unhappy state of his own mind, as well as his inability to control his anxiety through the means of reason. Once the external form of the idol is shattered, its power over him only increases as Friedrich is left alone with his fears, now revealed as part of his own shattered subconscious. On Friedrich's agitated return to Erwin, it becomes clear that what Friedrich's friend has given him is not simply an ugly clay object but the gift of beginning a journey toward insight and the freedom from his own mental self-torture. This insight into himself and the world is what Hesse means by "magic."

## Style and Technique

The structure of "Within and Without" plays the external events and internal anxieties of Friedrich's life against each other to reveal their interconnectedness. The story moves from an external description of Friedrich's character through Friedrich's experience of the events that lead to the discovery of his internal turmoil. His inner disharmony shapes his world, giving external objects and events their power to disturb him. The outer world allows him to see within himself.

The relationship between these two men with very different attitudes about existence is also a vehicle for the overcoming of the false polarities in Friedrich's mind. As with many other friendships in Hesse's works—Siddhartha's with Govinda, Narcissus's with Goldmund, or Demian's with Emil Sinclair—these two opposed friends represent the rational and sensual poles of human nature. Their interaction allows their underlying union to emerge through the process of their reunion.

The idol plays a striking symbolic role in this piece. Its two opposed heads remind Friedrich of the Roman god Janus, the god of gates and new beginnings. The crude little figure does indeed act as a door to Friedrich's soul and an opportunity for him to overcome his internal conflicts and enter a new life of inner harmony. Even the outer glaze on the clay god is able to reveal his inner conflict and point the way toward its resolution. He becomes obsessed with the memory of the texture and colors of it, seeing its sheen reflected in other objects around him. The idol's surface appearances are thus transcended to reveal the inner depths and interconnections of all aspects of reality. This preoccupation with the glaze also causes him to think about the sound of the word Glasur, relating it to seemingly disconnected bits of his past experiences, such as the sound of a book title, *Princess Russalka*. Frank Wedekind's collection of stories about the unhappiness that results from sexual repression both repels and attracts Friedrich, showing the division between his rational and sensual natures.

This object given to Friedrich, then, symbolizes the polarities within his consciousness and the freedom to go beyond them. His internal conflicts and torments result from his superficial rejection of parts of his subconscious and of reality. His attempt to narrow reality into an external objectivity leads to a painful disconnectedness in his inner life. To become whole, Friedrich must come to recognize the validity of the various aspects of the human mind and the unity of mind and world. The gift of an object outside himself is the gateway through which he is able to enter into himself and begin the process of healing. The line from Johann Wolfgang von Goethe's poem "Epirrhema," which Erwin has taken as his motto, has also proven true for Friedrich: "Nothing is outside, nothing is inside, for that which is outside is inside."

*Mary J. Sturm*

# THE WITNESS

*Author:* Ann Petry (1908-1997)
*Type of plot:* Social realism
*Time of plot:* The mid- to late twentieth century
*Locale:* Wheeling, New York
*First published:* 1971

> *Principal characters:*
> CHARLES WOODRUFF, a retired African American English
>     professor
> DR. SHIPLEY, a Congregational minister
> SEVEN TEENAGE DELINQUENTS
> NELLIE, a teenage girl whom the delinquents abduct and rape

*The Story*

Charles Woodruff, who retired as professor of English from Virginia College for Negroes, was sixty-five when his beloved wife Addie died. His wife's death has made him reluctant to pursue his former plans to spend his retirement as a homebody, so he has accepted an offer from Dr. Shipley, a Congregational minister, to work with seven troubled teens. The sole black in the white picket-fence community of Wheeling, New York, Woodruff does not enjoy his customary, exemplary success with students. After witnessing several unnerving sessions between these bright, demented young men and the authority figures they despise and antagonize (Dr. Shipley and himself), Woodruff impulsively questions their harassment of young Nellie after class. Immediately recognizing the inevitable danger to himself, and keenly aware of his well-founded fear of this devious gang, he instantaneously regrets his effort to intervene, leading as it horrifically does to their assaulting, abducting, and grossly humiliating him, as well. They imprison him in his expensive new coat, wreck his glasses, demobilize him as an auditory witness to their horrendous gang rape of Nellie, and incriminate him by forcing his imprint on Nellie's thigh after she loses consciousness. They leave Nellie in the freezing cold despite his feeble protestations, rob him, and leave him virtually incapacitated—he can hardly breathe or see, and his hands go numb as he searches for the car keys they threw at his head but which dropped in the deep snow. He realizes that as a black man, he is at the mercy of these violent youths, who degradingly address him as "ho' daddy," simply because they are white. He immediately leaves town, rationalizing his abandonment of the nightmare and of its primary victim, Nellie, as he speeds away.

*Themes and Meanings*

Racism and misogyny are intense themes in this story. The delinquents' willful oppression, exploitation, and abuse of both Nellie and Woodruff is institutionally sanctioned: They know, as he does, that no court will accept a black man's word over the lies of seven white males; circumstantial evidence is enough for a white jury to indict a black male, for whom white women are taboo. Nellie is reduced to a mere pawn, an object who embodies the vehicle for enactment of aggressive dominance and coercive submission. Likewise, Woodruff's humanity, professional accomplishments, and hard-won integrity are erased by inequitable power dynamics that objectify and demoralize him. Early in the story, he senses the danger that lurks around these boys when he winces at the gunshot sound their junky car makes as it approaches the Congregational church. He scurries into the building in the hope of avoiding the wrath and resentment he guesses they will express toward his expensive new cashmere coat, which even Addie would have deemed too indulgent.

Ann Petry suggests that these seven delinquents are not entirely evil or solely at fault in their extreme antagonism. They are products of superficial parents and a materialistic culture, and consumers such as Woodruff are its victims, as well. His coat, for example, Petry describes as a straitjacket: It restricts him and his movement and limits his freedom, but it takes a reversal of the authoritative power structure to demonstrate this reality. In turn, the teenage rebels against the mainstream despise the constraints imposed on them and are too intelligent to let their own anger and disgust go unanswered. Everybody will pay for their hateful lives, especially those more disempowered than their egocentric, spiteful selves.

In addition to racial and gender conflicts, there is a generation gap pitting nonconforming teens against their elders, whom they do not respect. Petry layers the conflict and complicates the tension for, although Woodruff is black, he embodies the consumerist values these boys defy. Doubtless, they find his new-car smell, which even Woodruff agrees makes him sniff audibly and greedily, offensive, an affront to their oppositional stance. Petry metaphorically labels their dreadful car a "snarled message" to the adult world. Embittered with their meager scraps, Woodruff assumes, they resent the older generation, which gets more than its share of the goods. Perhaps this disparity is the root cause of the unrelaxed look that Woodruff notes in the eyes of children, cornered by an elusive American Dream. On a satiric level, Woodruff acknowledges that his acquisitions as an older black professional are out of line when he imagines someone calling the state police on him, the scenario of which is both sobering and comical:

> Attention all cruisers, attention all cruisers, a black man, repeat, a black man is standing in front of the Congregational Church in Wheeling, New York; description follows . . . thinnish, tallish black man, clipped moustache, expensive (extravagantly expensive, outrageously expensive, unjustifiably expensive) overcoat, felt hat like a Homburg, eyeglasses glittering in the moonlight, feet stamping . . . mouth muttering.

*Style and Technique*

On the revelation that he is a token, the protagonist demonstrates one of the most memorable narrative devices: parenthetical self-reflections particularly on words or phrases that come to mind. This is a habit fully in character with his having taught English for more than thirty years: "Nigger in the woodpile, he thought, and then, why that word, a word he despised and never used so why did it pop up like that." As Woodruff wonders about other expressions, Petry effectively calls societal assumptions into question. For example, the passage about the hypothetical police bulletin contains a parenthetical aside expressing the racist indictment that any exceptional expenditure by a black man is presumptuous and pretentious.

This technique prepares the reader for the more intense stream-of-consciousness passages touching on preconceptions that language encompasses and the behaviors that accompany them. For example, during the violent rape scene, Woodruff thinks "there are seven of them, young, strong, satanic. He ought to go home where it was quiet and safe, mind his own business—black man's business; leave this white man's problem for a white man." Immediately afterward, Petry illustrates the frustrations experienced by a respectable and educated black man who is compelled to edit himself and guardedly modulate his tone for white hoodlums. Petry's shocking description and relentless detail, especially of the rape scene, interweave poignantly with Woodruff's dismal coming to terms with this unfathomable complex. It is no accident that the pivotal scene occurs in a cemetery: Its gratuitous violence constitutes a dead end for all the parties involved. Petry's symbolism also manifests itself in Woodruff's literal blindness (he is without his glasses), which in turn reinforces his psychological justification for deserting his post and the girl in order to avoid further trouble for himself.

Woodruff is painfully and simultaneously aware of his status and his denial as both his mind and car speed him back to his proper place. Petry's skillful embedding of timeless themes raises significant questions about how this story complicates conventional perceptions of protagonists and adversaries, how the seven troublemakers differ from the students whom Woodruff describes as the "Willing Workers of America," how the boys' violent acts reflect on the community of Wheeling, how Woodruff's relationship with his wife (encapsulated in his memories) affects his decision to leave Wheeling, and how readers might identify with Woodruff's plight at the end of the story. The last question is especially resonant as readers recognize their own complicity in the crimes of varied oppression, their tacit collusion with materialist mainstream culture, and their witnessing of the destruction that ensues when the youths "blackmail a black male."

*Roseanne L. Hoefel*

# THE WOMAN AT THE STORE

*Author:* Katherine Mansfield (Katherine Mansfield Beauchamp, 1888-1923)
*Type of plot:* Psychological
*Time of plot:* About 1908
*Locale:* The bush country in New Zealand
*First published:* 1912

> *Principal characters:*
> Jo, a dapper ladies' man
> THE NARRATOR, Jo's sister
> THE WOMAN, the ugly keeper of the "store"
> ELSE, her daughter, age five
> JIM, a young traveler

## The Story

Three travelers have been caravanning for more than a month in a remote region of the North Island of New Zealand, a wild Maori country: Jim (a guide who knows the environs), the female narrator, and her dapper brother Jo. The heat has been awful, and one of their horses has developed an open belly-sore from carrying the pack. All have traveled in silence throughout the day. They anticipate reaching a "store" in this wild land, a "whare," or home that houses a storehouse of goods to supply wayfarers and that includes a pasture for the horses. Jim has been teasing the two about this stopover; it is run, he promises, by a friend generous with his whiskey, and he also speaks of the man's blue-eyed, blond wife, who is generous with her favors.

At sundown, they reach the whare, and all is not as cheerful as has been represented. The mistress of the store looks scarcely better than an ugly hag; she is skinny, with red, pulpy hands; her front teeth are missing, her yellow hair is wild and skimpy, and she is dressed in little better than rags. She carries a rifle and is accompanied by a scraggly, undersized, five-year-old daughter and a yellow, mangy dog. She claims that her husband has been gone for the past month "shearin'," veers wildly in mood, and appears to the visitors to be "a bit off 'er dot," somewhat unhinged from being too much alone in such a disreputable setting.

After some haggling, the travelers are permitted to stop over. She fetches some liniment for the horse and sends food down to the tent that Jim has set up in the paddock. While Jim is working and the narrator bathes in the stream, Jo, the boisterous singer and ladies' man, "smartens" himself for a visit to the woman at the store. She had once been a pretty barmaid on the West Coast, Jim tells them, and she bragged at having known "one hundred and twenty-five different ways of kissing." Despite her moods and her tawdry looks, Jo is determined to flirt and to venture. "Dang it! She'll look better by night light—at any rate, my buck, she's female flesh!" He returns to her whare while the others dine.

While Jo is gone, the woman's child brings some food, and, though very young, reveals that she loves to draw pictures of almost any kind of scene. Jo returns with a whiskey bottle; he has induced the woman to play hostess to the little party, and they all return to the whare. The adults become slightly inebriated, the child threatens to draw forbidden pictures, and Jo and the woman become more brazenly flirtatious. When a violent thunderstorm ensues, the woman suggests that they all sleep at the house—Jim, the narrator, and the daughter in the store, Jo in the living room, and herself in the bedroom, close by. All are drunk and laughing as they retire.

From their uncomfortable place in the storehouse, surrounded by pickles, potatoes, strings of onions, and half-hams dangling from the ceiling, they can hear Jo rather noisily sneaking into the woman's bedroom. The disgruntled child finally draws for her companions in the store a picture her mother has forbidden her to draft: It reveals the woman shooting her husband with the rifle and then digging a hole in which to bury him. Jim and the narrator are struck speechless. They cannot sleep that night and hasten on their way early the next morning. The narrator laments for her "poor brother." As they are leaving, Jo appears briefly to motion them on; he will stay a bit and catch up with them later. The meager caravan, now minus its dapper gentleman, moves out of sight.

*Themes and Meanings*

"The Woman at the Store" was composed in 1911, when its author was barely more than twenty-one; together with two other tales ("Ole Underwood" and "Millie"), it treats New Zealand scenes and introduces offstage violence to obtain its effect. The repulsive but rather hilarious drinking party abruptly comes to an end when the news of the woman's murder of her "missing" husband is revealed by the small child. At a stroke, the story's meanings are completely turned around. At first, the reader is induced to believe that this is a unique (if somewhat sordid) tale of the wilds—remote, unusual, worthy of being carefully recorded by the narrator. Slowly it becomes clear, however, that, far from being an atypical travelogue, it retells instead "the same old story," albeit askew and in grotesque parody: the dapper and brazen male flirting with and seducing the innocent maid. Then, with a last twist and turn, the author reveals that the woman is quite capable of giving as good as she gets, and the implicit irony becomes evident: The reader is left to contemplate a savage act quite typical of civilization; after all, Greek tragedy has often portrayed family feuds and parricide; one need not travel into the bush to find barbarism, for it is not the Maori tribes that need be feared, but a lonely, bedraggled woman and a smart, egoistic gentleman caller.

Moreover, beneath the glib surface lies the psychological portrayal of loneliness and entrapment. The buxom barmaid has been captured by love, transported to the wilderness, and virtually abandoned by a husband who was always on the run. He often left her for days, even weeks, only to return, demanding a kiss: "Sometimes I'd turn a bit nasty, and then 'e'd go off again, and if I took it all right, 'e'd wait till 'e could twist me round 'is finger, then 'e'd say, 'Well, so long, I'm off.'" Worst of all was her complete transformation. In six years, she has been translated from civilization to isolation, from good looks to ugliness, from sanity to near madness. She has had one child and four miscarriages. Incessantly she reflects on her intolerable life and her intolerable husband: "You've broken my spirit and spoiled my looks, and wot for—that's wot I'm driving at." Again and again, over and over, "I 'ear them two words knockin' inside me all the time—'Wot for!'" That "wot for" is ultimately a question directed to the universe: What is it all about? Why are human beings driven by whim and passion into impossible situations? In murdering her husband, she has at least initiated some action against a cruel force in the world, but she remains caught in its web. Indeed, her fling with the passing Jo is in one sense a refreshment from the cruel grind of her life, but in another, it is merely the reenactment of the servitude she had endured at the hands of her husband. Ironically, the woman at the store continues in a hopeless round, for she is at once barbarian and citizen, rebel and victim. In a miserable little oasis in the wild, amid a plentitude of stores, she has somehow—maddeningly, incomprehensibly—frittered her own small storehouse away.

*Style and Technique*

"The Woman at the Store" is one of Katherine Mansfield's early stories and does not reveal many of the features of her later great tales: extreme subtlety, indirection, tenuous but magical symbolism, impersonation of characters, total mastery of detail and of voice. It is, on the contrary, a straight piece of flatly narrated realism. The narrator herself and Jim are given virtually no personality; all is subsumed by the surface details of travel and encounter with the woman, related with nearly journalistic precision. Indeed, one powerful effect in the tale is achieved when the two learn that the woman is a murderer; understatement prevails, and the characters react almost not at all, expressing no feelings whatsoever. However, it is to be inferred that their response is considerable; Mansfield's employment of indirection here is quite effective.

Best of all, stylistically, are touches of tone and color and atmosphere that presage the coming of a master of the twentieth century short story. Often Mansfield's choice of words is exquisitely appropriate, and her effects are accomplished with the seemingly easy hand of the professional. Such achievement, for example, is clearly evident even in the story's opening paragraph:

> All that day the heat was terrible. The wind blew close to the ground—it rooted among the tussock grass, slithered along the road, so that the white pumice dust swirled in our faces, settled and sifted over us like a dry-skin itching for growth on our bodies. The horses stumbled along, coughing and chuffing.

The story is a masterful display, a surprising performance by a very talented young beginner.

*John R. Clark*

# WOMAN HOLLERING CREEK

*Author:* Sandra Cisneros (1954-    )
*Type of plot:* Domestic realism
*Time of plot:* The twentieth century
*Locale:* Mexico and Seguin, Texas
*First published:* 1991

> *Principal characters:*
> CLEÓFILAS, a young wife full of dreams, living in Seguin, Texas
> JUAN PEDRO, her insensitive, cruel husband
> SOLEDAD, a neighbor woman with a television
> FELICE, the woman who helps Cleófilas to safety

*The Story*

"Woman Hollering Creek" is the powerful narration of the destruction of one woman's dreams told through her consciousness from the days just before her ill-fated marriage to Juan Pedro until the day she escapes his cheating, bullying behavior to return to Mexico. The primary action takes place in Seguin, Texas, a town of nasty gossips, dust, and despair, where Cleófilas gradually learns that the community life she cherished before moving north no longer exists. This town is built so that wives have to depend on husbands for a ride or stay home. There is nothing a woman can walk to: no supportive church, no leafy town square, and no friendly shops.

The story begins in Mexico, the day Don Serafin gives Juan permission to marry his daughter, Cleófilas, and take her to the "other side," across the border. In the emotion of parting, he reassures her that as her father he will never abandon her, a remark that she later remembers for its comfort and hope. The wedding is what Cleófilas has been waiting for her entire life. Through watching films and soap operas, she has learned to desire a fairy-tale existence, the kind she is sure she will achieve with the love of her life, Juan Pedro. Once they settle in Seguin, Cleófilas finds herself drawn to the lovely creek running behind the house. No one knows why the creek is called La Gritona (Woman Hollering). The first time she crosses the creek with Juan, she laughs when he tells her its name. She does not laugh the first time Juan hits her; she does not say a word. Eventually after many beatings and the birth of their son, Juan Pedrito, she sits on the creek bank listening to the high silver voice of the water. It is calling her. She is sure of it. The sounds remind her of La Llorona, a woman who drowned her own children. She wonders if they named the creek for her.

Cleófilas's two friends, Dolores and Soledad, caution her about the dangers of La Gritona, especially after dark. Do not go there, they advise. To take her mind off Juan's nightly drinking at the tavern and his affairs with other women (he was with one woman while she was at the hospital giving birth to their son), she escapes by watching a few episodes of a Mexican soap opera on Soledad's television. She realizes that her life has begun to resemble a soap opera, each episode sadder than the previous one.

When she learns she is pregnant with their second child, her mood changes. She argues with Juan, urging him to take her to the doctor for a prenatal checkup. She promises to tell the doctor that her extensive bruises are the result of a fall down the front steps. When he hesitates, she pressures him. It is for their unborn child, she says. He must relent and drive her for a sonogram. At the doctor's office with her husband in the waiting room, she breaks down. A caring nurse makes a quick secretive phone call to her friend, Felice. The next day, while Juan is at work, Cleófilas takes her baby and walks to the Cash 'N Carry off the I-10 interstate. Felice is waiting in her pickup truck to drive her to the Greyhound station in San Antonio, where she will board a bus for Mexico. As they cross Woman Hollering Creek, Felice lets out a yell and laughs. Soon, much to her surprise and relief, Cleófilas hears the long forgotten sound of laughter coming from her own lips.

*Themes and Meanings*

As its title suggests, "Woman Hollering Creek" explores the emotions contained within one abused woman, Cleófilas, who ultimately becomes a symbol of the many women whose domestic rage simmers quietly before exploding. After moving to Seguin, Cleófilas asks her neighbors about the creek, the woman who hollered. Had she yelled from anger or pain? They shrug. Preoccupied by their own problems with men who have left them, they have little time or energy to consider the creek's name. As Cleófilas's problems intensify and as the beatings become more frequent and severe, she does not fight back or break into tears. Instead she goes to the creek. Although once it had seemed so pretty and full of promise, she now sees it as the darkness under the trees, a destructive force. Eventually, however, after escaping from her oppressive marriage, her own hollering on crossing the creek takes the form of laughter, a light and liberating expression of relief and hope.

To Juan Pedro, his wife's emotional state is of absolutely no concern. Her exhausting efforts to make their house a home by making curtains for the doorways, bleaching the linens, and mopping the floors goes unnoticed. He tires of her suspicious questions, refuses to let her enjoy music or television, and flings one of her romance books in her face from across the room. He even brings another woman into their home while she is in the hospital having Juan Pedrito. When Cleófilas sees the woman's crushed cigarette in a glass, her dreams seem to be equally destroyed.

Although neither her neighbors nor her husband find it in their hearts to help her out of this desperate and depressed state, the kindness of two strangers suggests that a better life for her and her son is indeed possible. When she accepts a ride from Felice, she marvels at the fact that the woman drives a pickup, her very own truck. She is paying for it herself and living on her own. It is as if Cleófilas has seen a new way of being, not the highly romanticized lifestyle she has learned from the Mexican soap operas but one that is grounded in reality and very attainable in her new single condition.

Repeated references to Mexican soap operas occur throughout the story. Cleófilas has paid a heavy personal price for eagerly watching and emulating the characters in the soap operas, who obsess about finding their one great love. Freedom is possible only when she abandons the myth that to suffer for love is good. In the end, no longer a silent martyr, she bursts forth with a long beautiful ribbon of laughter.

## Style and Technique

Often in Sandra Cisneros's works, young women on both sides of the Mexican border wrestle with the pleasures and pains of growing up, falling in love, and facing reality. Often grounding her stories in domestic situations, Cisneros depicts life as a series of heartbreaks and small victories. As readers ride the ups and downs with the characters, they are called on to examine social and cultural situations that give rise to the events of the story. Frequently, as in "Woman Hollering Creek," these are important issues such as wife abuse. In her novel *The House on Mango Street* (1984), she explores a number of social problems such as incest, poverty, latchkey children, and rape. Cisneros deftly presents these themes through skillful characterization, believing that such a technique will create better understanding and empathy than would a heavy-handed examination of the problems.

Cisneros, who is also a poet, differs from other fiction writers in choosing to write small vignettes rather than lengthy prose chapters. This narrative strategy emerges in her short stories as well. For example, "Woman Hollering Creek" has fourteen sections denoting not only shifts in time and space but also in the mood and perceptions of the main character. Appropriately, the final vignette has Cleófilas on the road again, crossing the creek in the opposite direction, heading home to family. She has come to better understand her own dreams and thankfully to celebrate her own strength and wisdom.

*Carol F. Bender*

# A WOMAN ON A ROOF

*Author:* Doris Lessing (1919-    )
*Type of plot:* Sketch
*Time of plot:* A June week during the early 1960's
*Locale:* London
*First published:* 1963

> *Principal characters:*
> HARRY, a maintenance worker, about forty-five years old
> STANLEY, a younger worker, recently married
> TOM, seventeen, the youngest worker
> A WOMAN SUNBATHER

*The Story*

This is the story of seven days during a June heat wave in London. One day, three men repairing the roof of an apartment building in the baking sun see a woman sunning herself on an adjoining roof. Taking advantage of her apparent privacy, she undoes the scarf covering her breasts. When Harry, the oldest worker, leaves to borrow a blanket to put up for shade, Stanley and the seventeen-year-old Tom let out wolf whistles at the woman, but she ignores them. At the end of the day, first Stanley, then Tom, goes to the end of the roof to spy on the woman. Stanley makes a crude remark to the others, but Tom keeps what he sees to himself.

The second day, the men look for the woman as soon as they get on the roof. She is lying face down, naked save for little red bikini pants. When Stanley whistles, she looks up, but then ignores them again. Angered by her indifference, all three men whistle and yell. After Harry calms the other two, they go to work. The sun is even hotter than the day before. That afternoon, while Harry goes for supplies, the other two men scramble over the rooftop until they are looking straight down at the woman. Stanley whistles. She glances at them, then goes back to reading her book. Stanley, furious at her rejection, jeers and whistles, while Tom stands by, smiling apologetically, trying to say with his smile that he distances himself from his mate. He dreamed about her the previous night, and in his dream she was tender to him. When the three workers make their last trip to look at the woman before leaving for the day, Stanley is so angry that he threatens to report her to the police.

The third day is the hottest yet. Harry looks for the woman first, largely to forestall Stanley, and tells the others that she is not there. The men work in the basement. Before going home, however, they climb to the roof to see the woman. Tom thinks that if his mates were not there, he would cross over to her roof and talk to her. Then Stanley screams mockingly, startling her. The fourth day they work in the basement again, but go to the roof at lunchtime for air. The woman is not there. Tom feels betrayed, for in his latest dream she invited him into her bed. The fifth day is hotter still, but the men must work on the roof; there is nothing for them to do in the basement. At midday the woman emerges and goes to a secluded part of the roof. At the end of the day, Tom sees the woman, but tells Stanley that she is not there, thinking that by protecting her from Stanley, he is forming a bond with her.

The sixth morning feels like the hottest of all. The men delay their inevitable climb to the rooftop by accepting tea from Mrs. Pritchett, the lady who has lent them a blanket. After spending an hour at her kitchen table, they reluctantly go up to the roof. There they see the woman and resent her relaxed sunbathing while they work in the brutal heat. Stanley suddenly throws down his tools, goes to the edge of the roof, and starts whistling, screaming, and stamping his feet at the woman. Harry, realizing that Stanley's wild behavior might bring them real trouble, orders the other two men off the roof. Stanley and Harry leave, but Tom sees his chance to meet the woman. He slips into the woman's building, climbs to the roof, and stands before her, "grinning, foolish, claiming the tenderness he expected from her." Tom tries to talk to her, but she dismisses him abruptly and ignores him until he goes away.

Tom wakes up on the seventh day to a gray, drizzly morning. "Well, that's fixed you, hasn't it now?" he thinks viciously. "That's fixed you good and proper." The three men now have the roof to themselves, as they plan to finish the job by the end of the day.

### Themes and Meanings

Doris Lessing gives this story two levels of meaning, one individual, the other social. The individual meaning has to do with Tom's sexual and social confusion. Only seventeen years old, Tom is unsure of himself, envious of his mate Stanley's easy ability to flirt with attractive women. For Tom, the sunbather initially represents the allure of consumer society: "She looked like a poster, or a magazine cover, with the blue sky behind her and her legs stretched out." He feels a powerful sexual attraction: "He had caught her in the act of rolling down the little red pants over her hips, till they were no more than a small triangle. She was on her back, fully visible, glistening with oil."

Tom's sexual desire conflicts with his insecurity; he resolves the tension by romanticizing the sunbather. First, he fantasizes that she is tender with him. Then he dreams an explicitly erotic scene, imagined in the consumer idiom of the 1960's, but romanticized. "Last night she had asked him into her flat: it was big and had fitted white carpets and a bed with a padded white leather headtop. She wore a black filmy negligée and her kindness to Tom thickened his throat as he remembered it." Tom's imaginary trysts with the sunbather become so real to him (for his desire is so powerful) that he thinks he knows her. Moreover, he thinks that she surely must see that he intervenes to protect her from Stanley's crudities. It is all in his head, however, because to the sunbather he is just another ogling worker.

The story's social meaning has to do with the barriers of gender and class that separate the men from the woman. The gender barrier is the more obvious of the two. The woman is physically attractive, but does not respond to the men's calls, even though they think that she is signaling her availability. This angers and insults the men, for their masculinity is spurned. Their feelings relate to the class barrier between them and the woman. Stanley practices a standard of sexual morality that expects men to monitor and control their wives' behavior. His anger at the sunbather stems as much from his belief that women should not be allowed to behave "like that" as it does from the woman's actual rejection. Women who behave "like that," in his view, have husbands who cannot "put their foot down" to keep them from expressing their sexuality. Stanley's view of women reflects the prudery of the British working class.

The class barrier also appears in the theme of work. The work that the three men do is physically hard and demanding; their resentment at having to labor in extreme heat is magnified by the privileged nature of the sunbather's time. Her very presence is a reminder to them that some people do not have to work as hard as others.

*Style and Technique*

"A Woman on a Roof" is told by an impersonal narrator, but from the character Tom's point of view. The narrator knows what is happening in Tom's mind, what his nighttime dreams are, and what he wants from the sunbathing woman. To a lesser extent, one learns of Harry's motives in deflecting Stanley's anger so that the work can go on. However, the narrator's perspective is curiously limited. The narrator tells of Stanley's feelings only by attaching to them labels such as "furious," "bad humour," "bitter." The sunbathing woman is seen exclusively from the outside.

Lessing heightens the story's tension by focusing on the environment of the roof. The reader learns of the basement only that it is gray and cool. The scene in Mrs. Pritchett's kitchen establishes the contrast between the cool flat and the sunbaked roof, between the friendly housewife and the indifferent sunbather. Most striking is the way that Lessing keeps the focus on the roof by revealing next to nothing about the men's lives; it is as if they have no existence beyond the roof. What little information the narrator divulges—that Stanley has been married for three months and that Harry has a son Tom's age—relates directly to the story.

Finally, Lessing uses the image of the heavy boots that the three laborers wear to draw an image of crudity. As Stanley and Tom scramble up the roof levels, they edge along parapets and cling to chimneys "while their big boots slipped and slithered." These big workmen's boots remind the reader of the class and gender contrasts between the relaxed sunbather, her sexually desirable body glistening with sweat and oil, and the three workers, whose own sweat comes from almost unendurable toil.

Lessing's control over the development of this story is superb. The story is spare in the sense that every scene is telling; there are no superfluous words or unnecessary passages. She uses words, dialogue, and description to focus attention where she wants it and nowhere else.

*D. G. Paz*

# THE WOMAN WHO RODE AWAY

*Author:* D. H. Lawrence (1885-1930)
*Type of plot:* Psychological
*Time of plot:* The 1920's or somewhat earlier
*Locale:* Northern Mexico
*First published:* 1925

> *Principal characters:*
> THE WOMAN, thirty-three years old, a "Californian from
> Berkeley"
> LEDERMAN, her husband, fifty-three years old, a rancher in
> Chihuahua, Northern Mexico
> YOUNG CHILCHUI INDIAN, the Woman's guide

*The Story*

In this story of initiation, a Woman from Berkeley—the reader never learns her first name—the mother of two children, is restive and dispirited; her marriage to Lederman, a strong-willed rancher twenty years her senior, has long since lost its physical and spiritual vitality. Devoted to work, Lederman once morally swayed her, "kept her in an invincible slavery." Now she yearns for adventure. Beyond the confines of her ranch live the Chilchui Indians, and she determines to ride out, alone, "to wander into the secret haunts of these timeless, mysterious, marvelous Indians of the mountains."

In part 1 of this story in three parts, the Woman, on horseback, comes on three Indians who seem like figures of fate. One of them, a young man with eyes "quick and black, and inhuman," agrees to guide her to the Chilchui, so that she may "know their gods." Controlling her horse, the Indian leads her to a shelter where other Indians, wearing what appear to be loincloths, are indifferent to her. After a sleep in the "long, long night, icy and eternal," she is aware that she has died to her former self and can never again return to her civilization.

In part 2, she follows the young Indian, descending the slopes until she comes on a green valley between walls of rock. There, an old chief (or medicine man) questions her. After assuring him that she has not come to bring the white man's god, she is led by her guide to an old Indian, who again questions whether she is willing to bring her "heart to the god of the Chilchui." Again she assents. Ordered to take off her clothes, she is ritually touched by the old man, then offered new clothing of cotton and wool. Later, while naked, she is given a liquor to drink, made with herbs and sweetened with honey. At first ill from the potion, she soon lapses into a langorous consciousness in which her senses are sharpened and purified. Although fascinated by the "darkly and powerfully male" young Indian who still guards her, she never is made to feel "self-conscious, or sex-conscious." Instead, after weeks of captivity, while she continues to drink the ritual emetic cup, she is prepared to learn the mysteries of the Chilchui people: They await a white woman who will sacrifice herself for their gods, and then the "gods will begin to make the world again, and the white man's gods will fall to pieces."

In part 3, increasingly distanced from her past life, numbed by the potion (perhaps one containing peyote), she has visions of the Chilchui cosmology. Dressed now in blue, she prepares herself for sacrifice so that the Indian "must give the moon to the sun." Drugged, weary, she is nevertheless unafraid. When the old priest, the cacique, comes to her with two flint sacrificial knives, when she is stripped even of her mantle and her tunic, fumigated, and laid on a large flat stone, she acquiesces to her fate. She understands—she assents: "When the red sun was about to sink, he would shine full through the shaft of ice deep into the hollow of the cave, to the innermost." At that moment, the priest would "strike, and strike home, accomplish the sacrifice and achieve the power."

## Themes and Meanings

Unlike most of D. H. Lawrence's fiction, "The Woman Who Rode Away" does not focus on the theme of mating—of erotic selection. Instead, the long story concerns a psychological and spiritual initiation into the mysteries of primitive religion. As a moral parable that explores religious values distinct from those common to Western cultures, the story resembles other late fiction by Lawrence, notably "Sun" and "St. Mawr" (1925). In these tales, the writer elaborates a moral argument that runs against the grain of his society's moral conventions. In general, the argument holds that spiritual enlightenment—a mystic attainment of pure vital spirit or anima—is superior to any attainment of emotional fulfillment through erotic bonding.

In "The Woman Who Rode Away," the reader is asked to approve the Woman's acquiescence to the act of her own sacrificial slaughter in order to appease primitive gods. More audaciously, the reader is asked to approve the notion that the primitive gods should be restored to their spiritual supremacy, so that the white man's moral order may be overturned.

To understand fully the extent to which Lawrence dares to impose on his readers a different (and, for most, unsettling) consciousness of moral reality, one should compare "The Woman Who Rode Away" with "The Princess," a story begun in 1924 and first published in 1925. Both stories originate from a core idea. Mabel Dodge Luhan records that Lawrence showed her the manuscript of "The Woman Who Rode Away" on or about July 1, 1924; it was also at about that time that the writer made a trip to a cove near the Arroyo Seco in Taos country, a setting that is represented in the story.

Both narratives concern women who escape the spiritual ennui of a Western ranch to ride off, in the company of a Native American guide, in search of adventure. In "The Princess," the guide is Domingo Romero, a Mexican of mostly Indian racial traits, who attempts to rouse Dollie Urquhart to passion (or erotic vitality) through his embraces. His lovemaking, however, is crude, Dollie is indifferent to his sexuality, and she returns to civilization after her love-initiation no longer a physical virgin yet still a spiritual one. The experience has failed to function as a rite of passage to erotic fulfillment. As for Domingo—he is shot down by rangers.

The Woman from Berkeley, on the other hand, completes her initiation, going beyond Eros to the point of self-sacrifice, to Thanatos. Unlike Dollie, whose experience is shallow, the Woman profoundly changes her consciousness. Her Indian guide, unlike Dollie's, demonstrates spiritual strength by initiating her into the mysteries of the primitive gods, not sex; for the Woman, the end result is extinction of ego, rather than a neurotic retention of the old ego, as in Dollie's case. Whereas Dollie remains a civilized woman-child, the Woman from Berkeley "rides" away from the Western world altogether, rides away from life itself, to become moon goddess of the Chilchui cult.

*Style and Technique*

For readers of this story to understand fully, let alone empathize with, the extraordinary mythic journey of the Woman, they must take the same journey in imagination. Through accumulation of details, often hypnotically repeated, and through image and symbol, Lawrence attempts to break down the moral resistance of his readers to accept his thesis; his intention is that the reader acquiesce, no less than the Woman, to a frame of mind that judges her self-sacrifice as morally correct, that absolves her murderer-priest of guilt as a surrogate of the god, that accepts as just and appropriate the fall of Western ethos.

To achieve these tasks, Lawrence creates a psychological pattern of indoctrination that corresponds to the initiation ritual. Perfectly understandable are the stages of the Woman's mental conditioning, so that she alters her consciousness according to the demands of her ritual guide. She is, after all, denied sleep for long periods; stripped of her Western clothing, forced to go naked and then to wear the special garb of the initiate; drugged with mind-altering potions; allowed long periods of silence, times that are alternated with other periods of camaraderie and instruction in the religious cosmology of her captors; finally, exposed to the sun in a ritual of rebirth. Psychologically, the Woman is conditioned to accept her fate.

To support this pattern of mind control, Lawrence's images and symbols lead the Woman (and the reader) from the familiar to the strange, from the material to the spiritual, from reality to magic. The contrasting sensory and visual images of heat and cold, of sun and moon, are brilliantly concentrated in the cave of ice illuminated by a shaft of light from the sun. With great intensity, Lawrence turns attention away from the sacrificial knife lifted over the heart of the Woman and then "deep, deep to the heart of the earth, and the heart of the sun."

*Leslie B. Mittleman*

# THE WONDERFUL TAR-BABY STORY

*Author:* Joel Chandler Harris (1848-1908)
*Type of plot:* Animal tale
*Time of plot:* An age when animals talk
*Locale:* The South
*First published:* 1880

> *Principal characters:*
> UNCLE REMUS, an aged black man who narrates the story
> MISS SALLY'S SON, a seven-year-old and an appreciative audience
> BRER FOX, the villain of the story, determined to catch Brer Rabbit
> BRER RABBIT, the trickster-protagonist of the story, who always gets away

*The Story*

"The Wonderful Tar-Baby Story" is only one of the many tales that Uncle Remus tells Miss Sally's son, but it is perhaps the most loved and most remembered. The story begins with the boy asking whether Brer Rabbit ever gets caught. Uncle Remus proceeds to recount one of the wiley rabbit's closest calls.

His nemesis, Brer Fox, still smarting over being fooled again by Brer Rabbit, mixes tar and turpentine to make a tar-baby. He sets his creation, which indeed looks like a little black figure wearing a hat, beside the road and hides himself in the bushes not far away. Soon Brer Rabbit comes walking down the road and stops in his tracks when he sees the tar-baby. He speaks to it, asks it questions, accuses it of being hard-of-hearing and impolite, and finally yells at it. The tar-baby, of course, says nothing, and Brer Fox stays hidden in the bushes, chuckling quietly to himself. Losing his temper, Brer Rabbit hits the tar-baby, first with one fist, then the other. With both hands stuck in the tar, he kicks it with both feet, getting them stuck as well. In desperation, he butts it with his head, which also sticks firmly in the soft tar. Now Brer Fox emerges from the bushes, laughing so hard at Brer Rabbit's plight that he rolls on the ground.

At this point, Uncle Remus stops his tale to remove a large yam from the ashes. When the boy asks if the fox ate the rabbit, he tells him that the story does not say exactly, although some say that Brer B'ar came along and released the rabbit. Anxious readers will be relieved to know that this dilemma is resolved in a later story, "How Mr. Rabbit Was Too Sharp for Mr. Fox," and that Brer Rabbit does indeed escape.

This second installment with its resolution to the first is often considered an integral part of "The Wonderful Tar-Baby Story" and, thus, should be summarized here as well. Uncle Remus begins by indicting Brer Rabbit as a scoundrel, mixed up in all kinds of shady business. He rejoins the tar-baby story as Brer Fox gleefully celebrates his capture of the wiley rabbit with the help of the still silent tar-baby. He then tries to decide how to kill him. He considers the merits of barbecuing, hanging, drowning, and skinning. Brer Rabbit professes to be in favor of any of these solutions so long as the fox does not throw him into the nearby brier patch. This reverse psychology finally sinks in, and the fox, wanting to do whatever Brer Rabbit would hate the most, flings him by his hind legs into the middle of the brier patch. A few minutes later, the unscathed rabbit jeers from the hill, "Bred en bawn in a brier-patch, Brer Fox—bred en bawn in a brier-patch." He cheerfully leaves the scene. Reading these two stories together gives a sense of completion and closure both for Miss Sally's son and the reader. "The Wonderful Tar-Baby Story" and "How the Rabbit Was Too Sharp for Mr. Fox" allow Brer Rabbit to fool Brer Fox once again, an important theme in almost all the Uncle Remus tales.

### Themes and Meanings

The meanings in "The Wonderful Tar-Baby Story" range from a simple bit of moral advice about not losing one's temper and not having too much pride to complex interpretations from mythology, folklore, psychology, and sociology. On one level, the clever rabbit is an obvious persona for the black slave; inventive, sly, wise, and successful, the physically inferior rabbit inevitably triumphs over the strong, slower, more stupid animals, especially Brer Fox, a worthy opponent, as seen in this story. In Brer Rabbit's world, the weak at least have a chance. The story of the tar-baby, however, offers an interesting variation on the idea of the slave's identification with Brer Rabbit, for the rabbit demands respect from the black tar-baby as the whites expected it from the blacks. This role reversal lets the reader turn against Brer Rabbit and root for the silent tar-baby. In the conclusion, however, the reader once again applauds Brer Rabbit and his clever escape.

"The Wonderful Tar-Baby Story" is not only an entertaining fable for children but also an insightful glimpse into the history, psychology, and folklore of plantation slaves. The lines between black and white, good and evil, comedy and tragedy are blurred and changing. Brer Rabbit, hero and rogue, and Brer Fox, villain and benefactor, meet before the silent audience of the tar-baby (whose role is also ambiguous), shift roles, and rearrange themselves again into the traditional, unresolved conflict between the strong and the clever, the powerful and the powerless.

### Style and Technique

Joel Chandler Harris combines journalistic integrity and an ear for African-American dialect to reproduce authentic oral tradition in print. The tales themselves are remnants or at least reproductions of the tale-telling traditions prevalent in West Africa, yet this story reflects the social experience and historical perspective of African Americans defining themselves through the trickster hero, Brer Rabbit. It is neither the content nor the interpretation of the meaning but the dialect that may cause initial difficulty in reading this story. Harris attempted to reproduce the story the way he remembered hearing it. It was a "language" he knew well, but one that is difficult to read. Read aloud by someone who knows the dialect, however, it is clear and easy to follow.

The dialectal spelling and sentence structure are only two of the stylistic techniques noticeable in this story. The framework of the story-teller, Uncle Remus, and the small boy, there to ask questions, removes the story from direct contact with the reader; thus, the racial message is rendered less threatening. At the same time, this setting provides a context that makes the story more accessible. Miss Sally, the yams cooking in the ashes, the old black man, and the little white boy sharing secrets provide a background for a story about talking animals. The participant-observer quality of the author provides an authentic writing style that is unique to Joel Chandler Harris. "The Wonderful Tar-Baby Story" is a blend of humor, pathos, and realism, far more than simply a children's story.

*Linda Humphrey*

# THE WONDERSMITH

*Author:* Fitz-James O'Brien (c. 1828-1862)
*Type of plot:* Gothic
*Time of plot:* The early nineteenth century
*Locale:* New York City
*First published:* 1859

> *Principal characters:*
> HERR HIPPE, the Wondersmith, also known as Duke Balthazar of
>   Lower Egypt, the protagonist
> ZONELA, Hippe's daughter
> SOLON, a hunchbacked bookseller and Zonela's lover
> MADAME FILOMEL, a fortune-teller and midwife, Hippe's main
>   accomplice in evil

*The Story*

Fitz-James O'Brien's short story "The Wondersmith" is divided into seven sections. The first, entitled "Golosh Street and Its People," establishes the location and dark tone for the tale. The first-person, anonymous narrator is a strong presence in this section, describing the dirty street. The "eccentric mercantile settlement" contains a bird-shop with rare birds, a second-hand book-stall, a shop owned by a Frenchman who makes and sells artificial eyes, Madame Filomel, a fortune-teller, and the shop of Herr Hippe, the Wondersmith.

In section 2, "A Bottleful of Souls," Hippe is described as tall and thin, with a "long, thin moustache, that curled like a dark asp around his mouth, the expression of which was so bitter and cruel that it seemed to distill the venom of the ideal serpent." At a knock on the door, Hippe raises his head, "which vibrated on his long neck like the head of a cobra when about to strike." Filomel, a fortune-teller and midwife, enters with a bottle of fiendish souls. The evil plot of the pair is revealed: The souls will animate the evil-looking wooden soldiers and maidens carved by Hippe, the dolls' swords and daggers will be dipped in poison, and these fatal toys will then be given to little Christian children. Another knock is heard at the door, and Kerplonne and Oaksmith, "true gypsies," enter. The conspirators are all gathered. They animate the manikins, dropping a gold piece among them to provoke a vicious battle. The souls are then gathered back into Filomel's bottle, the manikins are replaced in their box, and the "four gypsies" depart to turn the dolls loose in the bird-shop.

Part 3, "Solon," introduces the second plot, the love story between Solon, the hunchbacked vendor of secondhand books, and Zonela, the child of a nobleman who was stolen by Hippe. Zonela is an organ-grinder with a little monkey named Furbelow. In a song, Solon confesses that he is a poet and that he loves Zonela, and as the girl and the monkey begin to dance, an enraged Hippe enters the room.

In section 4, "The Manikins and the Minos," the four Gypsies are revealed in the bird-shop as they animate the manikins, open all the cages, and turn the savage dolls loose to kill the helpless birds. Hippe expresses his pleasure with the dolls' ferocity, saying: "They spill blood like Christians. . . . They will be famous assassins."

"Tied Up," section 5, cuts back to Solon and Zonela caught by Hippe. Hippe viciously kicks Furbelow into the corner of the room and insults Solon. Solon, at Zonela's touch, experiences the "great sustaining power of love," and finds the courage to speak against Hippe. Hippe responds by telling of his son who was destroyed (inadvertently) through the drinking of brandy with a Hungarian noble; in retaliation, Hippe stole the Hungarian's daughter, Zonela, and destroyed her life through poverty and misery. Now Hippe delights in the prospect of killing her lover. Hippe wraps Solon in a web and locks Zonela in her room.

Part 6, "The Poisoning of the Swords," takes place on New Year's Eve. Children all over the city "were lying on white pillows, dreaming of the coming of the generous Santa Claus." In Hippe's house, the four conspirators are painting the manikins' little swords and daggers with poison and are planning to let the dolls kill Solon for practice. Filomel, when questioned by Hippe, slides the black bottle of souls from her pocket to show that she has it; when she lets it slide back, it does not return to its former place, and "balance[s] itself on the edge of her pocket."

The final section, "Let Loose," opens with Solon locked in his closet, having overheard the plan for the terrible death in store for him. Something leaps from the ceiling and "alight[s] softly on the floor. . . . His heart leaps with joy" when he realizes that Zonela has sent Furbelow with a knife. Solon cuts his cords, opens the door, finds Zonela, and peeps through the keyhole at the four drunk and sleeping conspirators. Filomel's rocking chair gives a sudden lurch, and the black bottle shatters on the floor. The manikins spring to life and begin stabbing the four Gypsies. Maddened and already dying from the poison, the four begin hurling the manikins into the fire; some of the figures escape and set the room ablaze. Solon, Zonela, and the monkey escape, and by morning all that remains of the conspirators and Hippe's home is "a black network of stone and charred rafters."

*Themes and Meanings*

Doubleness in "The Wondersmith" is not simply the enabling mechanism of the plot; it also characterizes the story's overall conception. From the outset, there is an insistence on the underside of the ordinary world. The unattractive environment in which the story is set deftly emphasizes the opposite of metropolitan zest, stimulus, and enterprise. It is in this environment that the story's socially marginal characters ply their quaint but menacing trades and plot their revenge on the conventional world of Christmastime and stable family life. The commitment of Hippe and his underlings to instability evidently derives from the tradition of unsettlement and dispossession that their classification as Gypsies and bohemians connotes. Hippe's scheme seems mindless in its cruelty, and he behaves throughout the story with a demented confidence in his own powers. Nevertheless, there is method in his madness. The scheme's irrational component is its vengeful intolerance of innocence. However, its attack on innocence is located in an exploitation of material reality: Innocence is destroyed through the subversion of toys purchased for the holiday season. The slaughter of the innocents, as conceived by Hippe, certainly out-Herods Herod, but it is to be carried out by making normally dependable and trustworthy playthings duplicitous.

Hippe's murderous anti-Christian designs are precisely counterbalanced or doubled by Solon's loving spirit and capacity for suffering. The Wondersmith's extraordinary artistic talent is negated by the simple integrity of the deformed bookseller. Fascination with Hippe's malevolence is obliged to yield to appreciation for the hunchback's morally upright stance. The author makes it perfectly clear that Solon is more significant for his moral courage, which his behavior unequivocally exemplifies, than for being a poet, a facet of his personality for which no direct evidence is supplied. Those whom Hippe seeks to punish, represented by the innocent and exploited Zonela, are ultimately delivered from degradation by Solon's selfless intervention. As the climax of the story makes clear, deliverance is an end in itself.

The story's double plot assists in establishing its conflict and lends distinctive color and atmosphere to it. "The Wondersmith" may be essentially a retelling, or translation to a New World setting, of standard folktale motifs or dualities such as the struggle between purity and danger, between the beauty and the beast, between artifice and honesty. However, these general, or even stereotypical, considerations are located firmly within the story's specific context and emerge freshly as a result of the author's strong sense of character.

To add depth to the darkness of Hippe's evil mind, O'Brien gives the story a racial dimension. The Wondersmith's obscure origins (he is "one whose lineage makes Pharaoh modern") and his evident chieftainship of an international cabal embody convincingly a sense of otherness and threat. In addition, his access to ancient Gypsy lore and the dukedom with which his intimates invest him make a consistent contribution to a sense of his character's essential foreignness. Drawing, perhaps, on popular superstitions that regard Gypsies as a lost tribe, the descendants of a dispossessed royal house whose ancient rites and usages they now deploy as secret weapons of revenge, O'Brien presents a comprehensive inventory of resources resistant to reason. Supporting the revenge motif is the background to Zonela's captivity, which, interestingly, is Hippe's method of confronting a legitimate "Hungarian nobleman." Moreover, the combination of materials pertaining to foreignness and the nocturnal side of the world enables the author to make an obvious, but nevertheless deft, connection between Romany and romance. In this regard, Solon is not given specific cultural or national origins: His is the spirit of unadulterated beneficence.

While the struggle between Solon and Hippe is for possession of Zonela, a battle between science and poetry is also enacted (and in view of the destructively martial nature of Hippe's carvings, battle does not seem too strong a term). Solon, a poet and reader of books, has learned to interpret the promptings of his heart. His use of a story to declare his interest in Zonela demonstrates what a valuable basis for behavior texts can be. Hippe, on the other hand, uses models and inventions of a more material kind for ends that are a terrifying inversion of Solon's salvific objectives. Hippe's aim is to change the world. Solon, on the other hand, simply wants to make it adequate. The resolution of the conflict, however, does not merely depend on the admirable nature of Solon's personality. Hippe's destruction results from a natural cause, an accident, a species of event that belongs to the ordinary world—which is where Solon desires to take up his natural, rightful place.

Solon's implicit response to Hippe's planned vengeance is to elicit the support of the animal kingdom. In a world controlled, however temporarily, by subversive and malevolent human beings, animals are a last hope, as Solon's rescue by the monkey Furbelow suggests. Prior to this event, the story has already given an unnervingly vivid demonstration of Hippe's powers in the attack on the birds. This episode, as well as confirming the important relationship between the animal, the natural, and Solon, also enacts the murder of song, an occurrence that is paralleled by the captivity of Solon the poet. An attack on nature is tantamount to the elimination of a beautiful attribute that is the natural creature's singular attribute. Nature, for which innocence seems to be a synonym, is vulnerable because it is not duplicitous. Careful to dispel any suspicion of a schematic approach to animal symbolism in the story, O'Brien emphasizes that nature, too, can be cruel and devious by associating Hippe with a serpent. Not only does this association give the Wondersmith a suitably repellent appearance, but also it suggests a familiar link between temptation and destructive knowledge.

The story's invocation of that link facilitates a subtextual consideration on the uses and abuses of knowledge. Hippe's secret lore is capable of imparting poisonous, malevolent life to his artistic creations. He is not, therefore, using knowledge for its own sake, but for the sake of power. Not content to earn his bread by the socially sanctioned use of his talents as a carver, he makes his natural creative ability the vehicle of his blind, destructive urges. His carved models should be a natural source of childish joy. Imbued by the Wondersmith's malevolence, however, they become terroristic automatons. The Wondersmith, thereby, reveals his true, or at least alternative, identity as the horror-monger and reveals O'Brien's themes.

*Style and Technique*

The story is written in the recognizable style of its period, rather than in a style that communicates a strong sense of the author's personality. (Perhaps one reason for O'Brien's comparative neglect by critics is that his work lacks a sense of a strong authorial presence, in contrast to that of his powerful contemporaries Edgar Allan Poe, Nathaniel Hawthorne, and Herman Melville.) The conversational first-person narrative opening is used as a conventional means of access to the plot, and when access has been gained, the narrator no longer functions as an integral presence. The text is perhaps too cautiously anchored in allusions to classical mythology and legend, as well as to works of literature, notably Jonathan Swift's *Gulliver's Travels* (1726). Such references sometimes have the effect of cluttering the pace of the narrative. On the other hand, they also are an economical means of suggesting the archetypal nature of the story's struggle, and they lend weight to that struggle.

Perhaps the most impressive of the story's purely technical achievements is its communication of atmosphere. Beginning with the description of the neighborhood in which the story's dire deeds are planned, there is a consistent air of tension and menace. Even the ostensibly lyrical interlude in which Solon visits Zonela's room has a claustrophobic sense to it, because of the discovery that the girl is Hippe's prisoner and slave. The visit's claustrophobic air is confirmed and intensified when, in turn, the Wondersmith makes the poet his captive. Moreover, O'Brien, as a general strategy, uses deliberately small-scale settings for the action. The use of night also contributes effectively to the prevailing mood of oppression and threat. In addition, once the introductory material has been presented, the story concentrates with impressive consistency on the characters' immediate circumstances, thereby gripping the reader's attention and ensuring that even if the reader is familiar with the general presuppositions of the plot, he or she will be entertained by this reworking of them.

*George O'Brien*

# WORK

*Author:* David Plante (1940-    )
*Type of plot:* Impressionistic
*Time of plot:* About 1980
*Locale:* The Italian countryside
*First published:* 1981

> *Principal characters:*
> ROBERT, an American meeting his lover in Italy
> GIUSEPPE (BEPPO), a neighboring farm boy
> ALESSANDRO (ALEX), Robert's Italian lover, who lives with him
>     in the United States
> THE WIDOW MAZZINI, Beppo's mother, the hardworking head of
>     an Italian farm family
> LA NONNA, Beppo's grandmother, who has an infected leg

*The Story*

Nothing much happens in this story, which won the New York Society of Arts and Sciences O. Henry Memorial Award in 1983. However, the surface details and what little does happen in "Work" suggest great significance. An American named Robert is at the house of his Italian lover, Alessandro, cleaning and preparing it for Alessandro's arrival. Giuseppe (nicknamed Beppo), the young son of the widow Mazzini, spends a lot of time with Robert waiting for Alessandro, or Alex, to arrive. With childlike fascination for violence and the peasant's fatalism, Beppo imagines all the worst things that could have delayed Alex. Beppo rides his horse to Robert's house to take him to the posto publico to receive a telephone call from Alex. Riding bareback behind Beppo, Robert clings to the boy's body. At the posto public, he learns that everyone already knows the message from his lover. The plane has been delayed and Alex will take a taxi from the railway station. Robert and Beppo get back on the horse and stop at the widow Mazzini's house before going to Alex's house to wait for the taxi. When Alex arrives, Robert serves coffee and brandy to Alex and the taxi driver and biscuits to Beppo. Early the next morning, Beppo wakes Robert to ask that he come to the widow's house. Alex cautions Robert not to agree to do anything that he does not want to do; he hints that Robert allows others to take advantage of him.

At the widow's house, Robert, though he protests that he never eats so early in the morning, has breakfast. He talks briefly to La Nonna, the widow's mother, who is suffering from an infected leg and cannot work. He agrees that he and Alex will help the widow and her family pull the tobacco in order to get it to the cooperative warehouse in time to be processed. Alex agrees to help, but makes clear that he thinks Robert has let the widow take advantage of him. In the fields, talk turns to the value of work and the relative advantages of communism and fascism. After the work is completed, the widow says that Robert and Alex must have supper with her family, and though Robert initially declines, Alex tells him that they must go, for the widow "has to feed us for the work we have done."

After supper, which the widow eats while she serves the others, she takes them to the stable to show them her cows. Even at the end of a day's work, she takes advantage of the opportunity to sweep the stable floor. Walking home, Robert says that when he returns to Boston he must begin to work hard to repay his father for all the work he has done. Alex says that they are approaching the ditch with the plank over it, and Robert, a little drunk from the widow's wine, takes his arm. The story ends as the lovers go down the path "to the front of the house, which shone among the elder bushes." Here the story ends.

Nothing much has happened. Everything is very quiet and restrained, but David Plante's few pages of prose establish credible people and some of their relationships. The story makes a significant comment on relative social situations and the possibilities open to some people, closed to others.

## Themes and Meanings

Plante's story is not about homosexuality, although its central characters are a homosexual couple. The relationship between Robert and Alex is simply one of the facts of the story, an important one but not the chief one. The two men's emotional and physical relationship remains implicit. The evidence of the story is that the Italian country people know the nature of the relationship, but they neither express nor imply judgment. The love relationship between Robert and Alex assumes another dimension, at once more generalized than sex and more personal than questions of social conformity. The story is about its announced topic: work. The idea of work or the image of work is present even when the word does not occur.

When Alex arrives, he says that he will make coffee for the taxi driver, but Robert makes and serves the coffee and brandy—calling attention to the division of work. Alex looks over the house and touches a wet wall; he comments that he and Robert will have to get to work on it. He asks why certain things have not been done, but he praises Robert for the work he has done to get the house ready. Robert replies, "Work?" His question raises the issue of the meaning of the word. Is it work to prepare a home for one's lover?

The conversation in the tobacco field concentrates on work and reward. One of the farmhands cannot understand how anybody can work and get nothing for it. The widow and members of her family express the belief that one should get rewards for work, but Alex says that he became a communist because communism "gives our work, however small, meaning in the world." The peasants are amused by his belief, even while they admire it. They have not been able to afford social or political idealism.

At the story's conclusion, Robert tells his lover that he wants to work when he returns to Boston, but the reader is not convinced that Robert will actually fulfill what he seems to regard as an obligation to his aged father. Several Italians have questioned

Robert about his father and why Robert no longer lives with him. Specifically, they want to know, if the old man can no longer work, who works for him. Beppo says that if Robert's father is eighty, he will soon die. La Nonna can no longer work, and will soon die. The implication is that, without work—meaningful activity done for various reasons, including material reward, satisfaction of duty, or love—there is no life.

*Style and Technique*

Plante's work in this short story and in some of his novels comes close to what critics have called minimalism. What he does not say is often as important as what he does say. He resists explanations and commentary and makes the story move forward from specific detail to detail. The action is low-key, and the reader must observe how Plante's selection of details and actions build toward a statement.

The specific details of the story, provided through the subdued voice of a third-person narrator, announce Plante's intentions, and the repetition of some of those details confirms those intentions. Early in the story, Robert is cutting the grass and notices the swifts flying about him: "He thought that there were layers below him of sand and water and rock, and layers above of air and thin cloud, and, above, the layers of the sky, and all the layers rose and fell." Later, the narrator says that "the different levels of earth and air appeared to separate as the daylight lengthened, and the dim upper and lower levels began to disappear." The narrator (thus, possibly Robert) identifies the fine line between the upper and lower levels as the space where "the swifts flew out and back, out and back." The metaphorical import of this central image becomes clear with the accumulation of detail as the story progresses: What fills the gap between the upper and lower levels of day-to-day existence, constituting life, is work.

Plante augments his meaning through repetition. He repeats not only the metaphysical images of the layering of space but also actions (Beppo is always dashing around on his horse; twice the reader sees the boy lead the horse to a large stone so that he can mount it), images of work, attitudes toward work—indeed, the very word "work."

Plante's story is a tone poem and does not depend on resolution of conflict or plot. It plays on repetition of a word and concept central to human experience, but perhaps requiring redefinition or at least reexamination. Robert's brushing away of the spiderwebs in his and his lover's vacation house and the two of them helping the widow in the fields is work of a different sort from that necessary to sustain life. The levels and layers differ, Plante tells his readers, but work has its own dignity.

*Leon V. Driskell*

# THE WORLD ACCORDING TO HSÜ

*Author:* Bharati Mukherjee (1940-    )
*Type of plot:* Social realism
*Time of plot:* 1978
*Locale:* An island-nation off the southeastern coast of Africa
*First published:* 1983

> *Principal characters:*
> RATNA CLAYTON, a thirty-three-year-old journalist
> GRAEME, her husband, a thirty-five-year-old professor of
>   psychology in Montreal
> CAMILLE LIOON, the travel agent, a refugee from Beirut
> JUSTIN, the taxi driver, a native of the island

*The Story*

From Montreal, the Claytons arrive in the wintry June of a recently independent island-nation—perhaps the Malagasy Republic but unnamed and thus serving as a symbol for postcolonial states where coups come with "seasonal regularity"—for what they hope will be a peaceful vacation. They are greeted by an unexpected, unreported revolution in progress; the vaguely leftist government downplays the insurgent "melancholy students and ungenerous bureaucrats" of the neocolonial movement, but the Claytons do not panic, presuming to remain aloof from the rioting, looting, and killing. Beneath their romantic illusions of an escape to an "old-fashioned" paradisiacal retreat, both of them harbor undisclosed motives in taking the trip. Graeme Clayton, while ostensibly wishing to view the Southern Cross, a constellation not visible in Canada, actually hopes to persuade his wife to move to Toronto so that he can accept the chair of the Personality Growth Department, an offer that he has already accepted. Ratna Clayton plans, instead of lolling on the beach, "to take stock" of her previously "manageably capricious" life before the six-month debate over the move.

The narrator, who reflects Ratna's point of view, shows a chaotic world, riddled with divisions of race, religion, class, nationality, and language in seemingly perpetual conflict. Considering Graeme's tendency to lecture at every opportunity, Ratna imagines his clinical account once they return to Montreal; she anticipates that Graeme's colleague, Freddie McLaren, will relate the coup to Catholic-Protestant fighting in Belfast, to religious and political factional strife in Beirut, and to the French separatist movement in Quebec. She recalls their travel agent Camille Lioon's warning against a stop in Saudi Arabia, because of Hindu-Muslim antipathies, and Lioon's accusation that the Saudis are insensitive, even though he is "no less an Arab than they." Ratna contemplates her fear of "Toronto racists," for whom she believes she is "not Canadian, not even Indian" but, in the derogatory "imported idiom of London, a Paki." With a Czech mother, she remembers that even her father's Indian family shunned her "as a 'white rat'" when she was "a pale, scrawny blonde" as a child: The "European strain had appeared and disappeared."

Bearing the anguish of expatriation, Ratna arrives at an intended "refuge" that becomes a "prison," mirroring her own inner turmoil. That turmoil is exacerbated by Graeme's need for "some definitive order." Ironically, as "an authority on a whole rainbow of dysfunctions" and anticipating his direction of studies in personality growth, Graeme maintains a distant perspective on the pain to which he is closest: Ratna's fear of living in Toronto. His marriage is clearly secondary to his career; when Ratna recounts horror stories of Toronto bigots attacking Indian immigrants, Graeme lies: "If you don't want to go to Toronto, we won't go." Further, he dismisses her fears, resenting "this habit she had of injecting bitterness into every new scene." Under Graeme's romantic inclinations for amateur astronomy and photography, there rest the seeds of fascism, a desire for scientifically ordering the chaos around him to suit his own interests: "In place of a heart he should have had a Nikon." Graeme is utterly incapable of understanding Ratna's anxiety as an expatriate.

Both the Claytons, however, deny the events of insurrection and martial law that surround them. They insist on staying at the Hotel Papillon, two blocks away from the center of rioting, against the protests of Justin, their taxi driver and tourist guide, who advises them to stay at the Hilton with other Europeans and Indians. Graeme rejects Justin's stereotyping of himself, accurate as it is, and Ratna, rejecting Justin's pleading that the wealthier Indians are safe there, announces arrogantly that she is a Canadian. The curfew and the closing of the museum, zoo, and school prevent sight-seeing and stargazing; entire sections of the city are sealed off. Paratroopers stop them on their way from the airport to the hotel, searching their luggage; nevertheless, the Claytons insist that Justin drive them through the marketplace.

Furthermore, even middle-class islanders deny the conflict. Justin arranges a bizarre tour to the king's palace, deserted in 1767 when the French deposed the king but still the site of daily recitals by the royal band, which awaits nostalgically the colonial holidays banned after the revolution. Madame Papillon, the proprietess who has remained within her hotel as a recluse for the last thirteen years, depends on Justin for news of the world outside. Indians, as a matter of habitual response, lock their assets in the Hilton's safe even as rioters burn and loot their shops. Ratna, in dwelling on her fears of racism in Toronto, begins to identify with African historical persecution of Indians—who are the Jews of Africa, as Madam Papillon remarks, not altogether innocently. Ratna's uncertainties open her to events around herself, but her focus is on her dilemma in moving to Toronto.

That evening, while the Claytons dine on bad food and good wine, they learn of yet another coup on nearby islands. Their waiter announces the assassination of an ambassador's wife, but the failure of the government-controlled media to report it suggests that the violence on the island is increasing. Graeme, apparently still isolated from the implications of danger, reads a geology article, written by Kenneth Hsü, from *Scientific American*—"his light reading." When Ratna objects to his habit of reading at the table, he replies, "'I'm not reading,' . . . meaning you're free to interrupt me, I'm not advancing my career." Continuing his reading aloud to her, he says, "According to Hsü . . . the last time the world was one must have been about six million years ago" and goes on to explain that the "island is just part of the debris," a result of the continental collision between Africa and Asia. Ratna, besieged by emotions as she reflects on the day almost past and identifying unconsciously with the island as part of the debris, decides that she can be comfortable among the dining guests.

Graeme, still bent on a glimpse of the Southern Cross, persuades the waiter to break curfew, taking him out the kitchen door to see the stars. Before he leaves, he tells Ratna of his decision to accept the job and of having already written to Toronto. He adds, "Don't worry, if anything happens to you there I promise we'll leave." He orders more wine, inviting her to renew the romantic purpose of the trip by seeing the constellation with him. Ratna refuses. After Graeme has left, she translates an entry in French from the menu for an American, numb to the "passionate consequences" of his "unilingualism."

*Themes and Meanings*

In Bharati Mukherjee's introduction to her collection of short stories *Darkness* (1985), she describes her work as an exploration in "state-of-the-art expatriation." By seeking to isolate themselves from the physical violence of the island's coup, the Claytons only intensify, in Graeme's need for clarity and order and in Ratna's aloofness, their emotional inability to understand themselves and each other. Their marriage is a metaphor for misunderstanding between local residents and expatriates; Graeme's self-assured presumption of superiority contrasts with Ratna's urgent need to belong to a society free of racial and nationalistic prejudices. He cannot participate in her emotional disorientation; she cannot desist from the "mordant and self-protective irony" in which she identifies most strongly with the French separatists in Quebec. Only when Ratna resigns herself to following Graeme on yet another path in her journey as an expatriate and finds solace among the mutual English of dining Europeans and Indians (the two halves of her heritage) does she enjoy a momentary sense of belonging somewhere. She does not, however, resolve the difference between immigrant and expatriate: Her fuzzy epiphany in translating for the American both compliments her aloof use of French and undermines the illusory self-protection that it offers. The American, an implicit metaphor for the immigrant, is free to belong to the multiplicity of many cultural heritages; Ratna, explicitly an expatriate, must wonder if she "would ever belong." In her muddled search for "souvenirs of an ever-retreating past," much like Hsü's geological archaeology of unity, and in her aloof detachment, one must conclude that Ratna will "never belong, anywhere."

The irony of telescoping symbols of the marriage, the island's independence, and Hsü's prehistorical world unity for divisive change and inconsequential stability is that however ordered Graeme's worldview may be and however aloof Ratna may remain, they will both be physically and emotionally affected by change and instability. Only by recognizing cultural differences without creating stereotypes and by accepting change within their own lives can the Claytons ever come to terms with the changing circumstances around them, wherever they may be. This recognition and acceptance depends on the cultivated awareness of the immigrant, not the feigned superiority of the expatriate. Ratna fails to gain the immigrant's awareness because she believes that it is an experience restricted to the island and dependent on her own aloofness.

### Style and Technique

Mukherjee's thematic transition from expatriate to immigrant attitudes is achieved not only through her use of irony and symbol but also through her use of specific details laden with metonyms. To portray the island as both a macrocosm of the marriage and a microcosm of the world, she employs a multitude of religions and nationalities. There are references to Christians—Catholic and Protestant—Hindus, and Muslims. European references include the French, English, Germans, Irish, Swedes, Czechs, Hungarians, and Bulgarians as well as Canadian and American characters. Camille is from Lebanon; Graeme's camera is a Japanese Nikon; Hsü is a Chinese name; North Koreans provide foreign assistance; the African troops are "Peruvian-looking"; the World Cup scores originate in Argentina; and there are frequent specific references to India and Indians. The many uses of proper place-names, from Jiddah to Dar es Salaam, in contrast to the anonymity of the island and the capital city (perhaps Antananarivo), establish their universality as symbols for political upheaval everywhere. The brief scene over dinner in which a German teaches "an English folksong to three Ismaili-Indian children" provides a foreshadowing parallel to Ratna's brief experience of immigrant awareness: the song's refrain "row, row, row your boat" itself ironically juxtaposed to Graeme's pseudosophisticated, derivative explanation of continental drift.

Further, Mukherjee's use of language helps sharpen her ironies in the dialogue. When Graeme promises to leave Toronto should anything happen to Ratna, he fails to realize that then it would be too late. When Camille asserts his own Arab identity after calling the Saudis insensitive, he condemns his own insensitivity in the overgeneralized slur. When Madam Papillon complains about not being able to "carry on an honest business," she ignores the colonial exploitation of the past and the neocolonial corruption of the present, both of which she seems to condone. To accentuate the underlying metaphor of geology for politics, Mukherjee shifts the usual context of diction in such phrases as the "epicenter of the looting" and "the plate tectonics of emotions." In another twist of ironic language, the narrator's use of Graeme's borrowed scientific vocabulary itself suggests a missed potential for immigrant awareness; thus, the limited viewpoint of the narrator underscores the pitfalls of the expatriate's shortcomings, suggesting that the language one uses reflects the worldview with which one experiences oneself in the world.

*Michael Loudon*

# A WORLD ENDS

*Author:* Wolfgang Hildesheimer (1916-1991)
*Type of plot:* Fantasy
*Time of plot:* Sometime in the twentieth century
*Locale:* The artificial island of San Amerigo
*First published:* "Das Ende einer Welt," 1952 (English translation, 1960)

> *Principal characters:*
> HERR SEBALD, the narrator and protagonist, who attends the party
> on San Amerigo
> THE MARCHESA MONTETRISTO, the owner of the island and
> hostess of the party

*The Story*

The fabulistic nature of this very brief story is indicated initially by the detached tone of its narrator and by the absence of any social context in which its events take place. There is no plot as such; instead, the story very briefly recounts the narrator's experience at the Marchesa Montetristo's last evening party and the memorable nature of its "extraordinary conclusion," in which the artificial island on which the Marchesa lives breaks up and sinks into the sea. Most of the story focuses on the narrator's recounting of the various important guests he meets during the party.

Perhaps the key word in "A World Ends" is "artificial," for what characterizes the Marchesa and her guests is their allegiance to art and artifice rather than an affirmation of social reality—which is why the Marchesa's home is on an artificial island set apart from the real world. The Marchesa hates the mainland because it is hurtful to her spiritual equilibrium; thus she devotes her life to the antique and the forgotten—qualities that she believes typify the "true and eternal." In fact, the reason the narrator is invited to the party, his one real claim to fame, is that he has sold her the bathtub in which the French revolutionary Jean-Paul Marat was murdered.

All the guests are distinguished by their artistic talents: a woman famous for her rhythmic-expressionistic dance, a famous flutist, a renowned intellectual, an astrologer, a preserver of Celtic customs, a neomystic—all of whom the narrator introduces as if they should be well-known to the reader. In short, as he says, they are the most eminent figures of the age, but all the characters in the story suggest their aesthetic rather than actual existence. Even the Marchesa's domestic servant looks as if he were a character out of the opera *Tosca* (1900). Moreover, the building is described as being of the height of opulence and splendor, representing every period of decor from the gothic onward. Over and over, in describing the place and the guests, the narrator repeats how unnecessary it is to describe, how he need hardly remind the reader of the fame and greatness of those assembled.

None of the people is presented as real; rather, they seem to be artifice itself. The performers are dressed and arranged as if they were a picture by Jean Antoine Watteau. When the servant who looks like a character out of *Tosca* comes to tell the Marchesa of the danger of the island's foundation collapsing, her paleness is described by the narrator in terms of its aesthetic effect; he notes that her paleness suits her in the dim candlelight. Even with that warning, the guests want to go on listening to the music. As the puddles begin to form and the reverberation of the imminent collapse sounds, the narrator says that the guests are sitting upright as if they were long dead already.

The narrator, the only guest to admit his fear and to try to escape, seems to accept what is happening with the same kind of detachment that he has exhibited throughout the story. As he departs and water rises higher, he thinks only that the Marchesa can no longer use the pedals of the harpsichord she is playing and that the instrument will not sound in water. In addition to the narrator, only the servants flee, for they, unlike the guests, have no obligation to the true and eternal culture. The narrator says that no less than a world is sinking beneath the ocean. As he paddles away, the guests rise from their seats and applaud with their hands high over their heads, for the water has reached their necks. The Marchesa and the flutist receive the applause with dignity, although, the narrator notes, they cannot, under the circumstances, bow.

When the building collapses with a roar, the narrator turns around only to note that the sea is dead-calm, as if no island had ever stood there. His last thought in the story is about the bathtub of Marat, a loss that can never be made good—a somewhat heartless thought, he acknowledges, but which he justifies by saying that one needs a certain distance from such events in order to appreciate their full scope.

*Themes and Meanings*

It is not the distance of time that the reader needs to appreciate the full scope of this cryptic and unusual short story, but rather aesthetic distance, for indeed it is aesthetic reality that the story seems to be about. On the most obvious level, the story can be read as a parable of the inevitable fate of trying to live life detached from the reality of social interaction and responsibility. All the guests, after all, seem to exist solely in their devotion to realms of reality apart from the social world—that is, in the world of artifacts and the frozen world of art. The narrator is allowed to survive because, as he says, he is taken up with everyday affairs; it is indeed the everyday that the Marchesa and her guests avoid and deny.

Thus, in terms of a moral-aesthetic parable, Wolfgang Hildesheimer could be pointing out the shaky foundation of such artifice and antiquity, and thus, in a grimly amusing way, illustrating how it must inevitably come crashing down like a stack of cards. Moreover, he does not here offer anything that seems more valuable to take the place of such aesthetic values, for the world of the Marchesa seems to have no social context outside itself. The story is more likely, however, to be one in which Hildesheimer, himself an artist, an art critic, and a stage designer, seems to be creating a world of pure decor and unreality, a world of artifice, for no other reason than to play with aesthetic reality.

The problem is that in such a world of art, one cannot always distinguish between genuine art (whatever that is) and pretension and posturing. There is much name-dropping in this story, a fascination with the antique for its own sake and for its decadent quality. For example, there is the absurdity of valuing the tub in which Marat was killed, and there is the fact that the Marchesa does not seem to know, at least according to the narrator, that the sonata that she and the flutist are playing, supposedly by Antonio Giambattista Bloch, is a forgery, for no such person as Antonio Giambattista Bloch ever lived. In this sense, Hildesheimer is writing an ironic aesthetic fantasy that poses no real moral judgment, but which simply plays with the ambiguity of what is artistic and what is only posturing. Certainly the narrator himself is as guilty of such posturing as are any of the famous guests for whom the world ends at the end of this story.

*Style and Technique*

The story's style depends primarily on the detached and straightforward voice of the narrator, who accepts the values of the Marchesa, even as he escapes her world's final end. The story is very similar to Edgar Allan Poe's "The Masque of the Red Death," for there, too, in a much more ornate style, a world sustained by artifice is destroyed. Even the rooms in the artificial home of the Marchesa are representative of historical stages, not the stages of one's life, as in Poe's story, but rather the stages of architecture and design. As the guests listen to the sonata, the guests move from the Silver Room, which is baroque, to the Golden Room, which is early rococo.

Furthermore, the story is characterized, as other Poe stories are, by the invention of an elaborate world of seemingly real historical figures, with which, as the narrator reminds the reader, one should be very familiar, but which are pure fabrications of the writer himself. In this respect, as well as in the collapse of the foundations of the house, the story reminds one of Poe's "The Fall of the House of Usher," in which Roderick Usher, who also attempts to detach himself from external reality and live in a world of art, collapses within the house that is identified with him. The basic difference between Hildesheimer's story and Poe's stories is that Hildesheimer seems to be, even as he imitates Poe, slightly mocking the aestheticism typical of Poe. Thus, the story is a burlesque of Poe's stories and therefore the aesthetic movement that Poe helped to initiate. The style is a combination of the haughty aloofness of the aesthetes undercut by an authorial tone of gentle mocking. Thus, "A World Ends" has the style and tone of a playful story, for it is an artwork that self-consciously makes use of the ambiguous status and nature of the artwork both to make itself and to mock itself.

*Charles E. May*

# THE WORLD OF APPLES

*Author:* John Cheever (1912-1982)
*Type of plot:* Psychological
*Time of plot:* The 1960's
*Locale:* Italy
*First published:* 1964

> *Principal character:*
> ASA BASCOMB, a poet and the protagonist

## The Story

Asa Bascomb is an eighty-two-year-old American poet living in a villa near the Italian town of Monte Carbone. Except for the fact that he is an expatriate, he resembles the American poet Robert Frost in several ways: He is from Vermont, he has unruly white hair, and he has received many international honors, though not the Nobel Prize. The story opens with him swatting hornets in his study and wondering why this greatest of all literary honors has been denied him.

The only other person living in his villa is Maria, his maid. His wife Amelia has been dead for ten years. Though one of his reasons for living in Italy is to avoid the publicity that would burden him in the United States, fans of his most popular book of poetry, *The World of Apples*, seek him out. Generally, though, his routine is simple and uninterrupted. He writes poetry in the morning; in the afternoon he takes a nap and walks to town to get his mail, which he then goes over at home. Several evenings a week, he plays backgammon with one of the locals.

Bascomb's poetry is as simple and clear-cut as is his life. It has even been compared to Paul Cezanne's paintings. Based exclusively on nostalgia, though, his poetry lacks vision and the impulsiveness that characterized the work of several American poets with whom he is often linked and who committed suicide (one drank himself to death).

The idyllic tenor of Bascomb's life begins to crumble when his memory, the chief source of his poetry, begins to fail him in small ways. He cannot remember, for example, Lord Byron's first name, and he cannot rest until he looks it up. A major difficulty soon presents itself. While on a sight-seeing tour with a Scandinavian admirer, he accidentally discovers a couple copulating in the woods. His memory of this event haunts him, and he is unable to rid his mind of the obscene thoughts that subsequently crowd into it. He goes to bed with his maid, Maria, but though this relieves his urges, it does not drive sex from his mind. Critically interrupting his desire for vision and the Nobel Prize, obscenity becomes the pivot and bane of his work and life. He starts writing obscene poems with literary titles and based on classical models, but he burns them at the end of each morning session. He ends up writing dirty limericks, which he also discards. He travels to Rome to distract himself. This does not work either, for a man exposes himself to him in a public toilet, the art in a gallery Bascomb visits is pornographic, and he finds himself mentally undressing the female singer at a concert.

Back at his villa, he probes for the source of the filth that has invaded his consciousness. Important events in his memory, such as his wife standing in light, his son's birth, and his daughter's marriage, seem linked to this invasion. The "anxiety and love" that define these events for him also seem to be the origin of his lapse from idealism.

Informed by his maid of the statue of an angel in Monte Giordano that is supposed to cleanse troubled souls, Bascomb sets off on foot with a seashell that belonged to his wife, understanding that pilgrimages require these things. He brings an offering for the angel, too—a gold medal awarded him by the Soviet Union. On the way, he watches from concealment a man, his wife, and their three daughters get out of a car. While his wife and daughters line up with their hands over their ears and in a state of delighted excitement, the man fires his shotgun into the air. Then the party gets back in the car and leaves. Bascomb falls asleep in the grass and dreams that he is back in New England, where a boy plays king and an old man gives a bone to a dog. He also dreams of a bathtub full of burning leaves.

A thunderstorm awakens Bascomb. He befriends a dog frightened by the storm and takes shelter with an old man his own age. The old man seems simple, happy, and open, surrounded by his potted plants and holding a stamp album on his lap. Envious of him, Bascomb continues to the shrine. At first the priest in charge of it does not want to let him in because of the communist medal he has brought as an offering. The priest gives in, however, when sunlight comes through a break in the clouds and reflects off the medal, for he regards this as a sign that Bascomb's quest is legitimate. Instead of asking the angel for a personal favor, Bascomb asks it to bless a series of famous writers, all American except for the rhapsodic Welsh poet, Dylan Thomas.

Staying overnight in Monte Giordano, Bascomb sleeps peacefully and awakes renewed, his old sense of clarity and goodness intact. As he walks home, he discovers a waterfall and remembers a similar one in his childhood in Vermont, in which he had once seen his old father bathe naked. He does the same now, after which the police, alerted by his worried maid, find him and bring him home. It is a triumphal return, reminiscent of Christ's entry into Jerusalem on Palm Sunday, and Bascomb sets about writing a new poem in his true style, no longer with his eye on the Nobel Prize.

## Themes and Meanings

The aim of "The World of Apples" is to show that the artist must not only serve himself but also the world around him. Asa Bascomb is disconnected from the world in many ways. He lives virtually alone, having withdrawn from his own country to avoid his public image there. He selfishly broods on his desire for the Nobel Prize and relies more on his memories of human contact than on human contact itself. He keeps the admirers who visit him in Italy at a distance, choosing only a handful to spend any time with at all. The world, in fact, serves him, from his maid and the boy who carries his mail for him to the admirer who takes him on a tour and the official bodies that have given him awards for his poetry. The reason behind all this service is the one book he has written with which people can empathize, *The World of Apples*.

The onslaught of indecent thoughts that Bascomb experiences signals the beginning of his return to an intimate connection with the world around him. These thoughts and the lust they arouse in him challenge his remoteness and abstract purity. The couple copulating in the woods, the man in the public toilet in Rome, and the singer at the concert draw him toward them until he cannot see himself apart from them. Every attempt at escape only brings him closer to the vitality of the physical, including running away to Rome, sleeping with his maid, and writing obscene poetry.

Eventually Bascomb must appeal to a source greater than himself to repair the damage to his sense of self. He must humble himself to a custom not his own, but that of the people among whom he lives. In seeking divine aid, he encounters images of healthy if perplexing human contact such as the man entertaining his family with a shotgun and the old man whose peace and happiness seem to have something to do with the living world in that he grows plants and collects stamps. By now the approach of the rainstorm has awakened Bascomb's senses to his old delight in country things.

After nature has given a sign that it approves of his humble pilgrimage—illuminating his gift with sunlight—Bascomb returns to spiritual health, which his untroubled sleep signifies and which he chooses as his own when he bathes in the waterfall, thus "baptizing" himself—cleansing himself—as one who belongs not only to himself but to the human and natural world at large.

## Style and Technique

The story makes use of the details of setting to dramatize its meanings. For example, in Monte Carbone where Bascomb lives, there are springs that feed the fountains in his garden. He finds the water distasteful, for it is very cold and noisy. The noise is unlike the pure, controlled music of his poetry, but the water's coldness symbolizes his own. The same image of water occurs near the end of the story when Bascomb encounters the waterfall on his way home from Monte Giordano. The waterfall is as cold and noisy as the fountains, but this time the water represents baptism. The noise is a kind of poetry to which Bascomb adds his voice, and the coldness is his own spirit purified through pain.

Other details of setting work in the same way. The signs of age in the buildings in his environment point to Bascomb's own advanced age. The crumbling churches, however, with their still intact artwork, rich and earthy, represent a tradition of human contact with nature and the divine to which Bascomb eventually commits himself. In Rome, the public toilet where the male prostitute exhibits himself echoes Bascomb's own soul at that point, the art gallery represents his mind haunted by obscene images, and the concert hall symbolizes his poetry furtively debased by his lust. Finally, as the thunderstorm dramatizes the turmoil in Bascomb, the sunlight that follows it is an image of his hope, his acceptance by the mysterious forces that govern life, and the generosity he ultimately brings to life.

*Mark McCloskey*

# THE WORLD OF STONE

*Author:* Tadeusz Borowski (1922-1951)
*Type of plot:* Sketch
*Time of plot:* 1947-1948
*Locale:* Warsaw
*First published:* "Kamienny świat," 1948 (English translation, 1967)

> *Principal characters:*
> THE UNNAMED NARRATOR
> HIS WIFE, also unnamed, perceived only from a distance

*The Story*

Very few events take place in "The World of Stone," yet when the conclusion is reached, after five pages, a comprehensive attitude toward the entire world has been described, as well as a resolute course of action toward that world. The story is not impressionistic, although at the outset it seems to register the narrator's stray observations. The reader is presented with two items of information, or building blocks of the story. First, the narrator possesses the "terrible knowledge" that the universe is inflating at incredible speed, like a soap bubble. Second, the narrator enjoys taking long, lonely walks in the city, through its poorest districts. At the beginning, this is all the narrator discloses.

If the reader is tempted to think that these two themes of the story have no relation to each other—that the first is of a purely psychological nature and the second, an innocuous everyday pastime—this is quickly dispelled by the author. Indeed, part of the artfulness of the story's beginning is that the reader is lured into it by a seeming contradiction, only to find that there is none, or that it is not what she or he had expected.

As the narrator takes his daily strolls, he observes the world around him acutely. There is no psychological impressionism here. It is a specific world—a city in ruins, beginning to be rebuilt. The country is unnamed, but it is in postwar Eastern Europe; the details could describe many different European cities after World War II. Fresh grass is already beginning to overgrow the ruins, and people are busy—working, selling wares—and children are playing. The narrator observes this world in its entirety and he feels indifference for it, even contempt. Although some of the first details describing the city and its inhabitants are superficially attractive—peasant women selling sour cream, workmen hammering and straightening trolley-bus rails, children chasing rag balls—the narrator has an unambiguous attitude toward it. It is ugly, meaningless, a "gigantic stew" flowing like water down a gutter into a sewer.

At an important transition midway through the story, the narrator proceeds from one of these walks in the city to the office where he works. It is not any office of a businessman: It is grandiose, with a marble stairway and red carpet "religiously shaken out every morning" by the cleaning ladies. Inside the building is another world, ordered, important, with a hierarchy unmistakably composed of Communist Party members.

At the end of the day, the narrator returns home to his apartment. It has a curious resemblance to the building for party members where he works and which he has just left. He lives there only because of his party position ("it is not registered with any rent commission"). His wife is far offstage working in the distant kitchen, and he goes to his workroom, his desk, where he looks once again out the window, re-creating the world he saw earlier during his walks: the peasant women selling sour cream, the workers hammering rails. He has no feeling whatsoever for any of the people in this world. "With a tremendous intellectual effort," however, he intends to grasp their significance and give them form, chiseling out of stone "a great immortal epic." Although the Western reader might by puzzled by some details, the author states at the end of the story in an unequivocal way that the work he is chiseling from the meaningless world will be great, epic, and immortal because—and only because—it will be a communist world. The ending of the story is a declaration of intention: The narrator intends to create a work giving form to the world. He clearly states that it will have the qualities normally associated with art—epic, immortality, greatness—not because of any craft or compassion or human quality, but solely because of political allegiance.

### Themes and Meanings

Much of the interpretation of the story is done by the narrator himself; it is a story about his "knowledge," which he asserts is not simply opinion but truth. The story operates on a high level of generality. There are no dynamic relations between individual characters, but instead a single point of view (the narrator uses the first-person singular pronoun) looking out at a broad variety of details and people that make up the world. This world is referred to by the title; it is far more important than any single character or living human being, with the exception of the narrator.

The reader will quickly notice that this "world" has two somewhat contradictory qualities: It is both light—ready to dissolve like a soap bubble, insignificant and senseless—and it is heavy, intractable, difficult to grasp, a "world of stone." Other descriptions of this cosmic world fall midway between these two poles: It is an overripe pomegranate, a cosmic gale, a huge whirlpool, a weird snarl, and gigantic stew. This contradiction is one of the most intriguing features of the story. The interpretation of this world, and resolution of Tadeusz Borowski's contradiction, is one of the reader's thorniest tasks. Something is missing, or withheld. There is an irrational element in the story that Borowski partly confronts, and although he stops short of full clarity, this confrontation is one of the most moving concerns of the story. The dominant impression of the narrator's observations of the outside world is not really one of lightness or even "indifference," as the author suggests, but one of disgust. When Borowski claims that the narrator feels "irreverence bordering almost on contempt," he has already created an attitude of full de facto contempt that borders, rather, on hatred. It is not the world, "this weird snarl," that is weird, but the narrator's attitude. What, then is the "stone" of "the world of stone"—what does the author mean by his title? The author does not establish a clear equation, and the reader must interpret the question for himself. It is open-ended, part of the strange and disquieting art of the story. It is possible to follow the author and say that the world is worthy of total indifference and contempt, that it has no objective value and is only a place of stone. The stone can also be interpreted in psychological terms; it is the author's feelings that are petrified.

The single clear, and striking, reference to stone in the story is the description of the Communist Party building in which the narrator works. It is "a massive, cool building made of granite," and its staircase is made of marble. This is the one setting in the story where the world, with its babble and meaningless chaos, is kept at bay.

The title of the story is also the title of the collection of stories; hence, its reference is also outside this particular story. When the reader turns to the other stories—"The Death of Schillinger," "The Man with the Package," "The Supper," "A True Story," "Silence," and above all the stories not about concentration camps but about the postwar, civilian world—the overall feeling of numbness and nihilism is confirmed. Borowski was a survivor of Auschwitz and Buchenwald, and his subsequent fate indicates one path taken by survivors.

An abundant literature has grown up about the concentration camps, as well as the plight of survivors—Elie Wiesel and Bruno Bettelheim are two of the foremost American contributors. Borowski, too, has made one of the most important and lasting contributions to the literature of the Holocaust. American readers often find one of his major themes unpalatable, refusing to accept it, denying it, or sentimentally distorting it: that the human survival instinct is not necessarily a positive value. To survive in the camps often required the willingness to destroy others. (Readers of Wiesel's *Night*, published in 1956, will recall the father and son trying to kill each other for a small piece of bread.) No one has portrayed this better than Borowski, both in his stories and in his life. The "stone" in the title of "The World of Stone" is not only numbness but also destructiveness; it carried over into civilian life after the war and was directed against society as a whole, finding an outlet in the Communist Party. It was also directed against art; after the collection *The World of Stone* was published in 1948, Borowski ceased writing literature and devoted himself to shrill, propagandistic journalism, filled with hatred and largely directed against Americans—no matter that his 1946 book *Bylismy w Oswiecimiu* (we were in Auschwitz) was dedicated to "The American Seventh Army which brought us liberation from the Dachau-Allach Concentration camp." Borowski became consumed by a one-dimensional rage that sacrificed all art to politics. Finally, this hatred was turned against himself; he committed suicide in Warsaw in 1951.

*Style and Technique*

"The World of Stone" is an unusual story in that it has no real characters or plot. It still has considerable art: It is objective, careful, and maintains a very delicate ambiguity throughout; yet it is transitional, marking a point at the end of Borowski's literary career and the beginning of his propagandistic journalism.

One of the best descriptions of the story's style, as well as of Borowski himself, can be found in *Zniewolony umysł* (1953; *The Captive Mind*, 1953), by the Nobel Prize-winning poet Czesław Miłosz; "Beta" is a thinly disguised portrait of Borowski. Miłosz wrote of *The World of Stone*: "The book comprised extremely short stories devoid of almost all action, no more than sketches of what he had seen. He was a master at the art of using material details to suggest a whole human situation."

In the story "The World of Stone," Borowski goes beyond a human situation and reaches a literary cul de sac with no escape. It asserts a destructiveness and contempt that are supposed to inhere in the world, yet the links with their causes are totally severed. "The World of Stone" is almost a work of madness, and this is its eerie, irrational art. The narrator is filled with disgust at the world, and he makes a last effort to present this, to deal with it, in a calm, detached manner. Afterward, he abandoned the calm, the detachment. He found shrill, strident propaganda much more satisfying.

*John R. Carpenter*

# A WORN PATH

*Author:* Eudora Welty (1909-2001)
*Type of plot:* Realism
*Time of plot:* The early twentieth century
*Locale:* Natchez, Mississippi
*First published:* 1941

> *Principal character:*
> PHOENIX JACKSON, a poor and aged black woman

*The Story*

Phoenix Jackson makes her biannual visit to Natchez, walking for half a day in December to reach the medical clinic at which she receives, as charity, soothing medicine for her grandson. Having swallowed lye, he has suffered without healing for several years. Phoenix has made the journey enough times that her path to Natchez seems a worn path. Furthermore, part of that is the old Natchez trace, a road worn deep into the Mississippi landscape by centuries of travelers returning northeast after boating down the Ohio and Mississippi rivers.

Phoenix is the oldest person she knows, though she does not know exactly how old she is, only that she was too old to go to school at the end of the Civil War and therefore never learned to read. Mainly because of her age, the simple walk from her remote home into Natchez is a difficult enough journey to take on epic proportions. She fears delays caused by wild animals getting in her way: foxes, owls, beetles, jack rabbits, and raccoons. She comfortably reflects that snakes and alligators hibernate in December. Thorn bushes and barbed-wire fences, log bridges and hills are major barriers for her. The cornfield she must cross from her initial path to a wagon road is a maze, haunted to her nearsightedness by a ghost that turns out to be a scarecrow. She must also struggle against her tendency to slip into a dream and forget her task, as when she stops for a rest and dreams of a boy offering her a piece of cake. Her perception of these obstacles emphasizes her intense physical, mental, and moral effort to complete this journey.

Despite the difficulty of her trip, she clearly enjoys her adventure. She talks happily to the landscape, warning the small animals to stay safely out of her way and showing patience with the thorn bush, which behaves naturally in catching her dress. She speaks good-humoredly of the dangers of the barbed wire. Her encounter with the "ghost" ends in a short, merry dance with the scarecrow, a celebration that she has not yet met death. Difficult and important as her trip is, she extracts pleasure from it, which further reveals the depth of goodness in her character.

On the trace, a dog knocks her off her path, leaving her unable to rise until she is rescued by a young hunter. Though he helps her, he is also somewhat threatening. He is hunting quail, birds with whom she has spoken on her walk. When the hunter accidentally drops a nickel, she spots it quickly. She artfully diverts his attention by getting him to chase off the strange dog, so she can retrieve this nickel. Her behavior contrasts ironically with the hunter's. She feels guilty about taking the nickel, thinking of a bird that flies by as a sign that God is watching her. Meanwhile the hunter blusters and boasts of his skill and power. He assumes that her long and difficult walk is frivolous in intent, that she is going to town to see Santa Claus. The contrast between their perceptions and the reader's judgments tends to magnify the difficulty and the goodness of Phoenix, emphasizing especially her true courage in contrast to his foolish bravado.

In Natchez, she must find her way by memory, because she cannot read, to the right building and the right office in the building in order to get the medicine. There she encounters the impatience of clinic personnel who are acutely conscious that she is a charity case. Having found the right place, she momentarily forgets why she has come. Her effort and concentration have been so great in making the journey that she has lost sight of its end. When she has the medicine, one worker offers her some pennies for Christmas. She quickly responds that she would like a nickel. Then it becomes clear that she has a specific need for ten cents. She announces that she will buy her grandson a pinwheel and reflects, "He going to find it hard to believe there such a thing in the world. I'll march myself back where he waiting, holding it straight up in this hand."

### Themes and Meanings

In her essay "Is Phoenix Jackson's Grandson Really Dead?" Eudora Welty speaks of "the deep-grained habit of love" that is Phoenix's motive for her trip: "The habit of love cuts through confusion and stumbles or contrives its way out of difficulty, it remembers the way even when it forgets, for a dumbfounded moment, its reason for being." The central motive of Phoenix's quest is true charity, the "deep-grained habit of love" for her grandson. This motive accounts for her apparent lapses in confiscating the lost nickel and in specifying how much money she would like when offered pennies for Christmas. Love also accounts for Phoenix's courage, making it natural and unconscious, simply necessary rather than extraordinary.

Phoenix's courage and true charity are underlined by her encounters with the young hunter and the clinic employees. When the hunter belittles her and boasts of himself because he walks as far as she does when he hunts little birds, with which Phoenix compares her grandson, because he can order his dog to drive off the strange dog that has frightened her, and because he has a gun he can point at her, the reader sees the truer courage of her heart—not merely in her lack of fear of the gun but in her whole journey as well. The hunter's courage comes from his tools and youthful folly, Phoenix's from her love. When the clinic employees remind her twice that hers is a charity case, expecting gratitude for what they give, they contrast sharply with Phoenix who dreams of and delights in bringing her grandson comfort and joy. In approaching true charity, in which love rather than self-praise is the motive, Phoenix achieves true courage. In Phoenix, Welty presents an ideal of goodness.

*Style and Technique*

Winner of an O. Henry Memorial Contest short story award, "A Worn Path" though an early story, is as accomplished as any of Welty's later fiction. This story exemplifies Welty's special power of placing the reader inside convincing and interesting characters without reducing the essential mystery of human character. This power makes her characters seem complete and real. In her essay on "A Worn Path," Welty reveals that the story originated in her vision of a solitary old woman:

> I saw her, at a middle distance, in a winter country landscape, and watched her slowly make her way across my line of vision. The sight of her made me write the story. I invented an errand for her, but that only seemed a living part of the figure she was herself: what errand other than for someone else could be making her go?

Welty also emphasizes that, though it is possible that the grandson is dead, the really important feature of the story is Phoenix's belief that he is alive and that "he going to last." This incentive for Phoenix's quest is central; the possible ambiguity of the grandson's condition is peripheral. Welty's expressed purpose in this story is to focus on Phoenix's habitual goodness.

Crucial to the story's success is Welty's choice of narrative point of view. By confining the reader to Phoenix's perceptions, Welty avoids the danger of sentimentality that she would have risked in a more external presentation of a good person. Though Phoenix may be no better morally than the Uncle Tom in Harriet Beecher Stowe's *Uncle Tom's Cabin* (1852), she seems more real, more in the world—in part because judgments of her character arise from the reader's evaluation of her actions without the insistent help of an intrusive narrator.

Phoenix's thoughts and words are enough to establish her unself-conscious love, courage, and other attractive qualities, but Welty uses the tainted evaluations of the people Phoenix meets to bring out the central qualities of love and courage that illuminate the idea Welty saw in the image that became the origin of her story. That image of a solitary old woman walking across a winter landscape came to mean "the deep-grained habit of love."

*Terry Heller*

# WRACK

*Author:* Donald Barthelme (1931-1989)
*Type of plot:* Psychological
*Time of plot:* 1972
*Locale:* The garden of a suburban house
*First published:* 1972

> *Principal characters:*
> A MAN, recently divorced
> THE LAWYER, representing the divorced wife

## The Story

Two unnamed men are conversing; the text reports only their dialogue, so that the reader must make sense of their remarks as if overhearing them. The opening remarks place the reader in a garden on a day of sunshine and clouds. When the sun is behind a cloud, the first speaker complains of being cold but admits to being consoled lately by the flowers, the Japanese rock garden, Social Security, philosophy, and sexuality.

Then the tone changes. Each man asserts that the other is driving him crazy, and the second man complains of the cold and reports that he still has to "muck out the stable and buff up the silver." He is working for an unspecified "they," who trust him completely. Also, he and the first man have a joint interest in deciding "what color to paint the trucks."

This apparently idle conversation begins to include some odd questions asked by the second speaker: "The kid ever come to see you?" "Where's your watch?" Then he says, "The hollowed-out book . . . is not yours. We've established that. Let's go on." Other items follow, with no system or meaning: doors, a bonbon dish, a shoe, a hundred-pound sack of saccharin, a dressing gown, and "two mattresses surrounding the single slice of salami."

This line of questioning, though obviously not literal and realistic, makes the reader realize that the first man has recently been divorced, that the second man is simultaneously an acquaintance and a lawyer for the divorced wife, and that the two men are establishing the individual ownership of possessions once held in common.

Each item gives rise to a series of remarks, in the course of which the reader learns about "my former wife"—who may not be the one now divorcing the speaker—and Shirley, a former maid. Near the end of the dialogue the lawyer describes the former husband as "too old": "You're too old, that's all it is, think nothing of it," and he denies that description "wholeheartedly" (insisting on that term). The men conclude by raising again the subject of the trucks to be painted.

## Themes and Meanings

The word "wrack" came into modern English from several different sources. As a result, its meanings include destruction, the item destroyed, and that which survives destruction. Donald Barthelme's story, like its title, brings these meanings together.

One of his frequent themes is the beginning of a love affair (as in his short story "Lightning"). A complementary theme is the ending of one, as in the divorce that lies behind "Wrack." One commonly speaks of spouses or lovers as "breaking up," and the breaking up of a marriage constitutes the wrack of this story. The dialogue provides suggestive evidence about many aspects of the breakup. The reader learns about the past (some happy times and a possible earlier marriage that also ended badly), the present (there appears to be no direct contact between the man and his former wife, and his son no longer visits him), and the future (sexuality is a possible consolation, but perhaps he is "too old"). Primarily, however, Barthelme appears to be interested in evoking the low-level pain of breaking up rather than its factual effects.

Another typical Barthelme theme is connected with the items mentioned by the lawyer. Barthelme is perceptive about the persistence of objects in one's life, especially when—as here—they remain after the end of a relationship. At such a time, some once-valued objects appear merely pointless, while others are radioactive with recollections of happiness or sadness. The incoherent formlessness of such objects illustrates literally the breaking up of the relationship that once justified their collection.

### Style and Technique

All Barthelme's stories display his interest in the techniques of storytelling, and the use of dialogue stripped to its barest elements is a technique he has often used. (He is probably indebted to Samuel Beckett's *Waiting for Godot*, [1952], for his earliest interest in the form.) He likes the form because it engages the reader's attention, it lends itself to suggestive patterns, and it permits an almost poetic intensity of language.

The reader's attention is engaged from the start in this story because he must figure out what situation he is witnessing. Then he must continue to read attentively, because clues appear slowly and side issues recur and accumulate emotion.

The speeches are heightened beyond ordinary conversation by their patterns of topic and phrasing. The recurrent topics of divorce—loss, sadness, isolation, alteration, need for consolation—are evoked as each item on the list of possessions is named and discussed. A rough rhythm therefore shapes the conversation. Another rhythm is imposed by the recurrence of specific sentences—for example, "Cold here in the garden" and "Well, you can't have everything." The odd exchange concerning the painting of trucks, which occurs early in the conversation and ends with "Surely not your last word on the subject," recurs almost word for word as the last words of the conversation.

The poetic intensifying of the language is too complex a topic to cover here, but a glance at one passage may suggest Barthelme's technique. At the beginning of the story, when the divorced man is listing sources of consolation, he mentions philosophy. The lawyer oddly says, "I read a book." Then the divorced man adds sexuality.

The lawyer says, "They have books about it." The divorced man says, "We'll to the woods no more. I assume."

The passage is complex and fruitful. "Book" and "philosophy" combine to suggest Boethius's *De consolatione philosophiae* (523 C.E.; *The Consolation of Philosophy*, late ninth century). The lawyer's emphasis on books anticipates his assertion toward the end that the divorced man is "too old"; here that man says relevantly, "We'll to the woods no more"—a bookish response because the line is from a couplet by Theodore de Banville as translated by A. E. Housman. What is more, the story sets these woods against the suburban garden and its neat Japanese formality. This opposition clarifies the divorced man's later description of what he did yesterday: "Took a walk. In the wild trees." Clearly he still hopes to return to the woods of an undomesticated sexuality experienced in life rather than in books. He is "wholeheartedly" resisting age, therefore, as he will insist at the story's end.

Consider one more literary allusion, this one occurring much later, as the breaking up recalls to the divorced man the hopeful beginning. Deep in memories now, he remarks, "In the beginning, you don't know." Here Barthelme is alluding to a sentence from "The Rise of Capitalism," one of his own stories: "Self-actualization is not to be achieved in terms of another person, but you don't know that, when you begin." The divorced man's sad truth is made sadder by this echo.

*J. D. O'Hara*

# WUNDERKIND

*Author:* Carson McCullers (1917-1967)
*Type of plot:* Psychological
*Time of plot:* 1936
*Locale:* Cincinnati, Ohio
*First published:* 1936

> *Principal characters:*
> FRANCES, the protagonist, a fifteen-year-old girl who is
> considered to be a Wunderkind
> MR. BILDERBACH, Frances's piano teacher
> MR. LAFKOWTZ, a violin teacher
> HEIME, Lafkowitz's prize student, also considered to be a
> Wunderkind

*The Story*

The "she" to whom the reader is introduced in the first paragraph, as she enters the living room of Mr. Bilderbach's house, in no way seems to be the Wunderkind of this story. Indeed, as she enters the room her music satchel is described as "plopping against her winter-stockinged legs," her attention is "scattered" by "restlessness," she fumbles with her books, her fingers quiver, and her "sight [is] sharpened [by] fear that had begun to torment her for the past few months." Perhaps, then, this is the story of the young girl as she becomes a Wunderkind. However, she is described as mumbling "phrases of encouragement" to herself, telling herself over and over: "A good lesson—a good lesson—like it used to be." Her name is Frances, the reader learns, and she is fifteen, having arrived for her Tuesday afternoon piano lesson; she is early and must wait until Mr. Bilderbach and Mr. Lafkowitz finish playing a recently acquired sonatina.

Carson McCullers thus sets the stage and situates her characters—with Frances sitting in Mr. Bilderbach's living room—so that, through a series of flashbacks (told from Frances's point of view through a third-person, limited omniscient narrative voice), which extend back to the time when Frances was twelve and began her lessons with Mr. Bilderbach, the author can nudge the reader toward understanding the cause of her protagonist's apparent angst and fear over having lost what "used to be."

This particular Tuesday had begun badly for Frances when, after she had practiced at her piano for two hours, her father made her eat breakfast with the rest of her family: He "had put a fried egg on her plate and she had known that if it burst—so that the slimy yellow oozed over the white—she would cry." This, in fact, had happened, and "the same feeling was upon her now," as she sits in her teacher's living room and looks at a magazine wherein a photograph of her friend, Heime, appears. He had studied the violin with Mr. Lafkowitz, and he had played in a concert with Frances (the critics had praised his performance but criticized hers). He, like Frances, had been called a Wunderkind for his early apparent and great talent. Heime had gone to Pennsylvania (where he is during the time of this story) to study with another, presumably more advanceu teacher than Mr. Lafkowitz. Now he has had his photograph and a brief biography published in a magazine devoted to music and outstanding musicians. Indeed, Heime's obvious and praised success intensifies Frances's growing doubts about her own ability to realize her early promise as a Wunderkind at the piano and to become a professional instead of merely a talented student.

Her dreadful self-doubts began four months before this particular Tuesday afternoon, when the notes she played on the piano began to spring out with a "glib, dead intonation." Initially, she had attributed this, as well as her displeasure over it, to adolescence: "Some kids played with promise—and worked and worked until, like her, the least little thing would start them crying, and worn out with trying to get the thing across—the longing thing they felt—something queer began to happen—But not she! She was like Heime. She had to be."

Unfortunately, it has become increasingly apparent to Frances, as it becomes apparent to the reader of this story, that she is not like Heime. Her technique at the piano is—and was when, three years earlier, she began to study with Mr. Bilderbach— excellent, but he had told her then that technique was not enough: "It—playing music—is more than cleverness. If a twelve-year-old girl's fingers cover so many keys to a second—that means nothing." Naturally, Frances wants to please Mr. Bilderbach, especially since he and his wife, with no children of their own, have treated her like their own daughter over the past three years. For her graduation from junior high school, for example, he had insisted on buying her a pair of new shoes and having Mrs. Bilderbach make her a new dress from fabric he had chosen. She frequently eats dinner with them on Saturdays after her piano lessons, often sleeping at their house and then returning to her home on Sunday mornings, after eating breakfast with them. In some unexpressed way, that "longing thing" in her and the music she plays—that emotion she has been unable to communicate through her piano—is complicated by Mr. Bilderbach's own "longing" for a child.

On Mr. Lafkowitz's departure, Frances goes to the piano for her lesson. "Well, Bienchen," Mr. Bilderbach says to her, "this afternoon we are going to begin all over. Start from scratch. Forget the last few months." She will make a fresh start, then, a renewal. (However, the reader is reminded here of what Mr. Bilderbach had said to Frances during her first lesson with him three years earlier: "Now we begin all over.") He next considers having her play a piece by Johann Sebastian Bach, but then he says, "No, not yet," and instead decides to have her play Ludwig van Beethoven's Variation Sonata, opus 26. The "stiff and dead-seeming" piano keys make Frances feel "hemmed . . . in" and it bothers her that Mr. Bilderbach frequently interrupts her playing with corrections. She asks him to let her play the piece through, without stopping, for then, she says, "Maybe . . . I could do better." He consents, but he is not pleased when she has finished, nor is she pleased: "There were no flaws . . . but the phrases shaped from her fingers before she had put into them the meaning that she felt." She had played this sonata for years; she had also played the *Harmonious Blacksmith* for years, a composition he wants her to play next, "like a real blacksmith's daughter." In other words, he wants her to play what she knows too well, what she plays automatically, and not what would challenge her and force her to grow—as a pianist and an emotional being. His demands on her, seemingly designed to force her into regression or, worse, artistic and emotional paralysis, are too much for her suddenly: "Her heart that had been springing against her chest all afternoon felt suddenly dead. She saw it gray and limp and shriveled at the edges like an oyster." She feels caged, confused. "I can't . . . can't anymore," she whispers to him, leaving the piano to rush past him, grab her books, and hurry out of his house. Once outside, she hurries down the street "that had become confused with noise and bicycles and the games of other children."

### Themes and Meanings

Just as McCullers's *The Heart Is a Lonely Hunter* (1940) and *The Member of the Wedding* (1946) have a frustrated, lonely adolescent girl as a central character, so, too, does "Wunderkind." Similarly, as with numerous other characters in McCullers's fiction, Frances's suffering is largely caused by the manner in which others she cares about perceive her, and by the crippling influence these perceptions have on her own self-image and development.

Called a Wunderkind by Mr. Bilderbach for three years, since their first interactions as student and teacher, then gradually identified as such by the man's older students as well, Frances's potential for greater, more mature personal and artistic growth is undercut because she is understandably hungry for such praise and adopts it as essential to her identity before she understands the great demands and costs such success requires, if it is to be more than merely titular. While McCullers suggests that Frances does possess an extraordinary natural talent as a pianist, she makes it clear that the teacher of such a gifted student must himself have extraordinary professional talent. In this regard, it becomes apparent to the reader that Mr. Bilderbach, because of a significant lack in his personal life, is not equipped to guide Frances toward the realization of mature artistic achievement; he is unable to teach her how to fuse style with content, form with substance.

McCullers points directly to Mr. Bilderbach's professional inadequacy in several cases, the most obvious of which are two scenes: one that Frances recalls as she sits in her teacher's living room and waits for her lesson, and the other occurring near the end of the story, moments before she runs out of his house. The first concerns the night when Mr. Bilderbach demanded that Frances play Bach's Fantasia and Fugue for him and Mr. Lafkowitz, which she did, and did "well," she had thought. However, when she had finished, Mr. Lafkowitz, displeased by her performance, reminds her that Bach, the father of many children, "could not have been so cold," as her rendition of the composer's music would lead one to believe. This comment, she recalls, upset Mr. Bilderbach; during his angry reply, furthermore, she is careful to keep "her face blank and immature because that was the way . . . Bilderbach wanted her to look." The second and more pointed revelation of her teacher's subprofessional perception of her occurs at the end of this story, after Frances has finished playing Beethoven's music and Mr. Bilderbach wants her to play the piece about the blacksmith, "like a real blacksmith's daughter. You see, Bienchen," he confesses, "I know you so well—as if you were my own girl." After a few more words he becomes, "in confusion," silent; then he asks her to play the piece so it sounds "happy and simple." In short, the teacher wants the student to play what he needs and wants to hear, but not what she needs to play in order to grow and develop as a versatile artist independent of her teacher's shortcomings.

*Style and Technique*

One of the most remarkable aspects of "Wunderkind" is its narrative voice and vantage point. While it is that of the third person, with its omniscience limited to Frances's thoughts and perceptions, McCullers communicates the mental and emotional states of her young protagonist by rendering the narrative voice almost neutral where judgments of the other characters in the story are concerned. Because Frances's personality is portrayed at a critical moment of her development—a moment during which she is uncertain about who she is or will be, as she feels a past identity crumbling away from her—the fact that her identity is not fixed precludes her judging others for what they are or are not. In such a transitional state, in fact, Frances is critical of no one but herself.

An excellent example of the above-mentioned neutral narrative perception or portrayal of a character is that of Mrs. Bilderbach. As Frances thinks about her, the reader is told that the woman "was much different from her husband. She was quiet and fat and slow. When she wasn't in the kitchen, cooking the rich dishes that both of them loved, she seemed to spend all her time in their bed upstairs, reading magazines or just looking with a half-smile at nothing." Significantly, the observations with which the reader is presented about Mrs. Bilderbach are nonjudgmental; consequently, the reader is left to decide if any aspects of the woman or her habits are to be seen pejoratively.

Similarly, the portraits of Mr. Bilderbach, Mr. Lafkowitz, and even Heime are all seemingly composed of objective observations, or observations stated objectively. McCullers utilizes this narrative approach for at least three reasons: first, because it gives the reader a sense of Frances's overly self-critical frame of mind, as well as her tendency to observe others (especially adults) in a nonevaluative manner; second, because it portrays a complex psychological struggle, for which there is no easy solution, in a largely impartial manner; and third, because it demands from the reader compassion for both Frances and Mr. Bilderbach as they suffer the effects of her painful growth.

*David A. Carpenter*

# THE YEAR OF THE HOT JOCK

*Author:* Irvin Faust (1924-    )
*Type of plot:* Social realism
*Time of plot:* The early 1980's
*Locale:* Several American cities
*First published:* 1985

*Principal characters:*
PABLO DIAZ, an immigrant jockey from Panama
RAMONA DIAZ, his wife
RAFAEL "RAFE" LAGUNA, a baseball player and Pablo's best
    friend
JEFF KAHN HIALEAH, a horse trainer

*The Story*

Hot jock and jet-setter Pablo Diaz lives a nonstop racehorse life in the greed and lust of the United States in the 1980's. Flying from city to city, horse to horse, woman to woman, and bed to bed, Diaz's way of living parodies that of an American businessman with no morals.

Successful as a horse-race jockey, Diaz is misguidedly proud of his accomplishments and immorality. Living a hollow life with almost no friends or family values, he goes from race to race, winning most of them, only to wind up dead at the end of some sort of spiritual descent. Diaz has plenty of money, goes through women like socks, often buys expensive presents for his wife and two children, snorts cocaine, drives Mercedes and other expensive cars, and prides himself on all of the above. Perhaps with some recognition that something is wrong, he decides to take his son Lorenzo on a racing trip with him to Florida. He is unable to establish a relationship with his son, however, because he does not know how to have a friendship with anyone, and succeeds only at impressing the boy with such particulars of his lifestyle as big cars, women, and tips. He returns home with expensive presents for all, including a three-thousand-dollar Zuni Indian necklace for his wife.

Diaz loses, wins, or places in a series of races, as instructed by his trainer, Jeff Hialeah, and has a string of hotel visits with women such as Helen Stadler, a blond he meets on a plane, and Ginny Gottlieb, his on-and-off mistress. Then the hot jock is visited by his best and only friend, Rafael Laguna. Rafe has not come on a matter of friendship, however, but of business: He asks Diaz to "pull" a race, to make his horse come in second rather than first, in exchange for $100,000. Diaz vocally refuses the offer; nevertheless, his horse does come in second. Afterward, Rafe is arrested, somehow gallantly taking the role of fall guy, and Diaz is left pretending to himself that he did not throw this race for an unknown outsider, that is, the person for whom Rafe is working.

During the next race, Diaz hears a gunshot from the stands. The horse he is riding has been shot, and as the animal collapses, so does the rider. His last thoughts are a wish that his wife Ramona will pray for him. Like a racehorse, the hot jock has simply run himself out.

### Themes and Meanings

"The Year of the Hot Jock" is essentially the story of an immoral man who skids willfully to his own destruction. An embodiment of all that is negative about American society, the great jock Pablo Diaz, like the horses he rides to victory, races thoughtlessly to his own demise.

The story has little to do with jocks or horse racing; rather, it shows the end of a man who, typifying the vision of America and its values of greed and materialism, exists in a state of moral dissolution. Diaz has everything that money can buy: expensive cars; strings of women, including his wife, who satisfy his physical lust but do not give him love; children who are not subjects of love but objects whose affection is to be bought with mopeds and wide-screen television sets; respect and reputation as defined by this society; as well as total self-blindness.

As a jock—in both senses of the word—Diaz not only rides horses and women but also manifests the characteristics of the male muscle without thought or morals. As "The Year of the Hot Jock" is not about horse races or jocks, it is not about sports. Irvin Faust uses the jock here as a representative American type, much as Arthur Miller did with Willy Loman years earlier in *Death of a Salesman* (1949). It is the characteristics of the person, not the job, that are exposed and attacked.

Because Pablo Diaz's immorality is a given, he experiences little in the way of moral choices. For years, he has been following the instructions of his trainer whenever he races, finishing in whatever position he is ordered. When his friend Rafe approaches him with the same deal, he hesitates out of loyalty to his trainer and the danger of not knowing for whom he is working. When Rafe is caught, Diaz resolves to do what he considers to be the right thing, which is to give money to Rafe's wife and kids while he is in prison. Distancing himself from the actual conspiracy of pulling the race, Diaz denies what he has done; nevertheless, he places second in this race as he was asked to do by his friend.

Holding the entire story together is the overall metaphor: Life is like a horse race, and those who run fast and hard will finish close to first. This, in turn, does not mean victory and happiness, but certain and early destruction. Those who live by the sellout will die by the sellout. Diaz's way of life is not only pointless and misguided, but also stupid and evil. Not only does he work his own destruction, but he also lives a hopeless and purposeless life. Diaz, along with his race to the finish, is a comment on the proverbial "life in the fast lane" in America. Ostensible success, as defined by society, is a culprit that not only destroys but also prevents a meaningful life and activity.

### Style and Technique

The most noticeable characteristic of Faust's style in "The Year of the Hot Jock" is the unique syntax. Many sentences are merely fragments; all are short, and those that are longer (perhaps eight or ten words) are always broken two or three times by commas, dashes, or other punctuation. This style is used to replicate the inner workings of a jock's mind. Accordingly, readers are given snippets of thoughts that hold together and make sense, but do not cohere into any thought beyond the shallow.

The entire story is seen from a limited, first-person point of view. Readers know at all times the thoughts and perceptions of Pablo Diaz. The lies he tells others, as well as the lies he tells himself, about his life and his activities are transparent to the reader and should be transparent to the main character himself. His thoughts are on the order of stream of consciousness in a jock's mind.

Faust uses metaphors for life throughout the story. Foremost among these is the racetrack as the road of life. Similarly, women become horses, and horses become women—in a grotesque fashion, both are merely objects that Diaz rides—in this mind of the lustful male who is overcompensating for his shortness and lack of weight by becoming a stud, asserting male primitivity in the most basic of instinctual ways. The story is awash in symbols of a materialistic, greedy, and plastic society: Mercedes cars, Zuni jewelry, big-screen televisions, and so on pervade this man's life. Pablo Diaz exists not so much as a jockey who fixes races, but as a combination and culmination of crass and materialistic stereotypes.

*Carl Singleton*

# THE YELLOW WALLPAPER

*Author:* Charlotte Perkins Gilman (1860-1935)
*Type of plot:* Psychological
*Time of plot:* A summer during the 1890's
*Locale:* Northeastern Atlantic Coast
*First published:* 1892

> *Principal characters:*
> JANE, the narrator
> JOHN, her husband, a physician
> JENNIE, John's sister and Jane's nurse

*The Story*

The story unfolds slowly over many weeks, beginning with the arrival of the narrator (whose name, Jane, is not revealed until the end of the story) at an estate in the country. Jane has gone into a gradual decline, losing interest in her family and her surroundings, since the birth of her baby. Her husband, John, and her brother believe that a long rest is what she needs to feel more like herself. Because both men are respected physicians, Jane believes that they know what is best for her and tries to put on a good face, despite her increasing suspicions that her rest cure may do her more harm than good.

At first, the colonial estate where she is the only guest appears harmless and quaint, with large gardens and spacious rooms. Jane later reveals that her windows have bars and her bed is bolted to the floor. The only people whom she sees are her husband, who comes from the city to check on her, and her nurse, John's sister, Jennie. Jane never has contact with her recently delivered child nor with friends. Her summer home takes on a more sinister tone as her mental condition deteriorates, with the very wallpaper in her room coming to grotesque life.

Jane's husband blames her thinking for all of her problems and forbids her to do anything that will employ her mind productively. Jane rebels at first and keeps a secret journal, but as she weakens, even that endeavor becomes too tiring. She withdraws into her thoughts, which form the running interior monologue of her mental collapse. Apparently accepting the separation from her infant, Jane slowly loses control of her imagination and her motivation to seek human contact. After she collapses and is forced to keep to her room, she becomes fascinated with the patterns on the yellow wallpaper, seeing in the paper's swirls faces and patterns that first amuse and then terrify her.

From her barred window, Jane begins seeing women creeping about the gardens on their hands and knees. Soon she discovers that another woman is trapped behind the wallpaper in her room, something that only she can see. At night, this woman pushes and struggles behind the paper in an effort to escape, rattling and ripping it as she fights to get free.

Jane says that the woman creeps along the walls, and she tries to help free her by gradually peeling back her wallpaper prison. Jane begins to notice signs of deterioration in her room: smears on the wall and bite marks on the bedstead. Gradually she no longer wants to leave her room; when John comes to take her home, she refuses to go and locks herself in with the creeping woman who is now free in the room.

Jane's husband and sister-in-law gain entry and find only Jane creeping around and around the room, surrounded by shreds of wallpaper. The story concludes as she creeps over the form of her husband, who has fainted from the shock of seeing her in her madness.

*Themes and Meanings*

"The Yellow Wallpaper" is partly autobiographical. Charlotte Perkins Gilman wrote it after she fled from her husband with her infant daughter to California. More important than the story's similarities to Gilman's own experience is the larger issue of a woman's right to be creative and autonomous. The story can be seen as advocating a woman's right to act and speak for herself; the alternative clearly leads to madness, as it does for Jane.

At the time of the story, most people believed that women were delicate and prone to madness if overstressed. A common treatment for their presumed mental illnesses combined isolation, rest, and inactivity—the very things that cause Jane's breakdown. From her own account, readers know that Jane enjoys writing and reading, yet John considers these to be dangerous activities to be avoided at all costs. At that time, it was common to remove a depressed woman from all sources of stress or sensory stimulation; women such as Jane were separated from their children, kept in bed, hand-fed, bathed, and massaged. It is precisely this type of treatment that drives Jane to begin hallucinating. The silent madness into which Jane withdraws is not only her reaction to the cure that men prescribe for her, but her only available form of rebellion against these tyrannies.

As Jane becomes more distanced from the world and from any source of sensory stimulation, she begins to hallucinate. Her visions of the creeping women and the woman trapped behind her bedroom's wallpaper symbolize her own binding and oppression. It is the rest treatment prescribed by physicians such as her husband and brother that metaphorically cause the women whom Jane sees to creep like infants rather than walk as independent adults. Jane's rest cure becomes her own wallpaper prison, one that simultaneously drives her insane and pushes her to assert her own rebellious selfhood. By freeing the woman from behind the wallpaper, Jane succeeds in freeing herself. Sadly, however, her mental state has deteriorated so badly that she has become truly insane and will remain utterly dependent on her husband.

At the story's conclusion, the narrator locks herself in her room and ties a rope around her waist so that she cannot be removed. Jane, the woman from behind the yellow wallpaper, creeps about the edges of her prison, a room that she will now use as a fortress. It is significant that Jane waits to reveal her name to readers until after her husband faints in horror at seeing her reduced to a crawling madwoman.

*Style and Technique*

The most prominent technical and stylistic feature of "The Yellow Wallpaper" is Gilman's combining of the first-person narrator and present-tense narration. By allowing readers to see only what Jane sees as she sees it, Gilman duplicates as closely as possible the feelings of entrapment, isolation, and unreality that Jane experiences. Jane's decline into true madness is so gradual and her narrative voice seems so level-headed, even when she describes events that one knows are impossible—such as the creeping women in the garden or the woman struggling to free herself from behind her room's wallpaper—that one might misread this tale as a ghost story rather than as an account of Jane's mental deterioration.

By making the descriptions of the women, the room, and the malevolent shapes and faces in the wallpaper so immediate and realistic, Gilman tricks the reader into seeing Jane as simultaneously mad and in the grips of some haunting supernatural specters. This ambiguity increases the shock that readers experience when they realize that Jane has been talking in metaphors throughout her narrative, that she has been recounting her own sense of intellectual and emotional oppression, rather than seeing actual women crawling about on the ground in the gardens or moving behind her room's wallpaper.

Some readers may be content to let their interpretation of "The Yellow Wallpaper" rest with the supernatural; if left here, however, readers will miss the more important point of Gilman's tale. Gilman forces readers to reconsider Jane's entire narrative by means of the story's conclusion, when Jane finally speaks her own name for the first time as she creeps over her husband's inert body. Little of the story will then make sense unless reexamined. Gilman plants numerous clues throughout the story that express Jane's interior struggle to be herself and to reclaim her independence: her need to be creative by keeping a journal, or the existence of the woman for whom Jane demolishes the yellow wallpaper to effect her escape. Similarly, the information that Jane offhandedly supplies readers in the story's early stages—such as descriptions of the bars on her window, the bite marks on the bed that is bolted to the floor, and her increasing lassitude—now can be reinterpreted as describing the true nature of where Jane has been staying: at an asylum. On second reading, "The Yellow Wallpaper" becomes the story of a woman who, while she may have been depressed, was not insane when she began her cure.

*Melissa E. Barth*

# YELLOW WOMAN

*Author:* Leslie Marmon Silko (1948-    )
*Type of plot:* Folktale
*Time of plot:* About 1970
*Locale:* New Mexico
*First published:* 1974

> *Principal characters:*
> A YOUNG PUEBLO WOMAN, the "yellow woman" of the story
> SILVA, a mysterious Indian male, a rustler from the mountains

*The Story*

On one level, "Yellow Woman" is a simple but haunting story of a young, married Pueblo Indian woman's two-day affair with a maverick Navajo who lives alone in the mountains and steals cattle from white and Mexican ranchers. The story is divided into four brief sections, ranging in length from four and a half pages to less than a page: Section 1 describes the morning after their first night together, and section 4 depicts (sections 3 and 4 are brief) the woman's return to her home and family on the evening of the following day.

When the woman awakens on the first morning, the man is still sleeping soundly, "rolled in the red blanket on the white river sand." She peacefully watches "the sun rising up through the tamaracks and willows," listens to "the water . . . in the narrow fast channel," rises, and walks along "the river south the way . . . [they] had come the afternoon before." She intends to return to her pueblo, but she cannot go without saying goodbye. She goes back to the river, wakes up the man, and tells him that she is leaving. The man smiles at her, calls her "Yellow Woman," and calmly asserts that she is coming with him. The night before, she had talked of the "old stories about the ka'tsina spirit and Yellow Woman," stories of a mountain spirit who takes mortal women away to live with him. The woman apparently had suggested that she was Yellow Woman and Silva was the ka'tsina spirit; now the man's words and actions assert that he is, in fact, the ka'tsina and that she has become the Yellow Woman of the stories: "What happened yesterday has nothing to do with what you will do today, Yellow Woman."

She is drawn to the sexuality, strength, and danger of this stranger and to the potency of the Yellow Woman myths. She allows herself to be pulled down once again onto the "red blanket on the white river sand," and then she leaves with him. It seems that he forces her to come, but she acquiesces complacently: "I had stopped trying to pull away from him, because his hand felt cool and the sun was high." The woman's pueblo has been out of sight from the opening of the story, and the farther she gets from the pueblo, the less sure she is of her identity or of her understanding of reality. As they travel northward, she hopes to meet ordinary people in order to regain her clear, normal perception of reality: "Eventually I will see someone, and then I will be certain that he is only a man . . . and I will be sure that I am not Yellow Woman." They meet no one as they travel through the foothills and into the dark lava hills and finally to his house of "black lava rock and red mud . . . high above the spreading miles of arroyos and long mesas."

In section 2, she enters into his small home and into the rhythms of his life. She cooks for him, makes love to him, sleeps with him. When she awakens to find him gone the next morning, she thinks idly of returning home but waits passively, lost in the silence and beauty of the mountains. She is awed by this man who has assumed the role of a ka'tsina with complete assurance, who has the power to "destroy" her, and who defies the white man and his ways. She knows that life will go on as before in the pueblo: "My mother and grandmother will raise the baby like they raised me. Al will find someone else, and they will go on like before, except that there will be a story about the day I disappeared." She seems to lose interest in going home: "that didn't seem important any more, maybe because there were little blue flowers growing in the meadow behind the store house."

When Yellow Woman wanders back to the house from a peaceful walk in the big pine trees, the man is waiting. He has stolen and butchered a steer and is preparing to go to "sell the meat in Marquez." He expects her to come with him, and she agrees.

In the third section, they descend from the serenity and beauty of the mountains and the myth into the world of harsh and banal reality that the woman has imagined that she had left behind. They encounter an ordinary man, and suddenly this Yellow Woman-ka'tsina story appears to be exposed as a vulgar tale of adultery, theft, and murder. The man is a white rancher who accuses Silva of "rustling cattle" as soon as he sees "the blood-soaked gunny sacks" hanging from the woman's saddle. Silva tells her to go back up the mountain. She rides to the "ridge where the trail forked" and waits. When she hears "four hollow explosions" of the Indian's rifle as he apparently kills the rancher, she takes the trail leading down and to the southeast, rather than returning to the mountain. When she can see the "dark green patches of tamaracks that grew along the river," she releases the horse, first turning it around so that it will return to "the corral under the pines on the mountain," and begins the long walk back to her pueblo.

In the brief final section, the woman follows "the river back the way" Silva and she had come. She drinks the cool river water and thinks about Silva, feeling "sad at leaving" this "strange" man. When she sees the "green willow leaves that he had trimmed" from a branch, she wants "to go back to him—to kiss him and to touch him—but the mountains were too far away now." Moreover, she believes that "he will come back sometime and be waiting again by the river."

She walks into the village in the twilight. When she reaches the "screen door of her house," she can "smell supper cooking" and hear "my mother . . . telling my grandmother how to fix the Jell-O and . . . Al . . . playing with the baby." She decides to "tell them that some Navajo had kidnaped" her and regrets that her Grandpa is not alive to hear a Yellow Woman story.

## Themes and Meanings

At first glance, "Yellow Woman" is a common version of the old story of a married woman seeking to escape from her boring and unfulfilling family life by having an affair with an exciting, unconventional male. The woman here seems to be rather aimless, listless, and irresponsible: She does not really "decide" to go with Silva or to leave him, but rather finds herself doing certain things. She does not appear to have a very strong attachment to her husband or child, nor does she believe that they will mourn her loss very much. When she does return to her pueblo, she holds on to the belief that the "strange" man will come back to get her one day.

Closer scrutiny reveals "Yellow Woman" to be a rich and melancholy story written by a Native American author who is well acquainted with tribal folklore and quite sensitive to the pathos of the American Indian's life in the modern world. The woman longs not so much for a lover as for a richness, a oneness of life that she has heard about in the stories of her grandfather. She lives in the banal poverty of a modern pueblo with paved roads, screen doors, and Jell-O. She seeks to make contact with the vital world of Coyote (a traditional Native American figure of the creator-trickster), ka'tsina spirits, blue mountains, and cactus flowers—a world in which human, animal, spirit, and nature are one, a dynamic world where reality itself is multidimensional and mystical.

"Yellow Woman" is not a simple story of an unfulfilled housewife seeking excitement, nor a tribal folktale of a woman lured out of sight of her pueblo by a spirit (who is linked to Coyote) and who is then unable to escape from his power. Rather, it is a fusion of those stories and more. The woman is not seduced by a man or a ka'tsina spirit so much as by the possibility that "what they tell in stories" may be true in the present, that the world may not have been wholly stripped of its magic and its unity. She is not deceiving herself when she thinks that she might be Yellow Woman; rather, she is trusting to her Indian heritage, which would free her from the white dogma that personal identity is both absolute and final.

She returns to the pueblo somewhat chastened, for she knows that Silva is, among other things, a rustler and a murderer; she knows, too, that he is fierce and free of white domination and that he may be a ka'tsina as well as a man. She has not lost faith in stories, in Yellow Woman or Coyote. It is clear that the poverty of life in the pueblo is spiritual as well as economic, and that the Native American (but not Yellow Woman) is in grave danger of following the white man into his sterile, rational landscape where Mother Earth is plowed up and paved over, Father Sky is polluted with "vapor trails" and acid rain, Coyote is merely a coyote, identity is a prison, and stories are only stories.

## Style and Technique

Perhaps the most striking technical dimension of this skillfully written story is Leslie Marmon Silko's masterful use of a first-person narrator. In fact, the real interest in this story resides not so much in the events of plot as in the character of the speaker. The narrator is absolutely credible as a young Pueblo woman: straightforward, unassuming, and unsophisticated. She is also a natural storyteller with an acute sensitivity to the beauty of the physical world and a deep longing for communion with humanity, nature, and spirit, for a fullness and a resonance of life she fears is lost "back in time immemorial." The simplicity and directness of her prose and the purity of her descriptions are evident from the first line: "My thigh clung to his with dampness, and I watched the sun rising up through the tamaracks and willows." There is a calmness and a wistfulness in this woman's voice that is quite affecting. She brings both the harsh loveliness of the land and the mystery and strength of the man to life seemingly without effort; they are rendered vividly, not because of ornamention or rhetorical skill but because she responds to them in an elemental, deeply felt, manner.

Two other aspects of Silko's technique merit comment: her use of color and the motif of storytelling. Colors play a subdued but important role here. The author draws on traditional meanings and on naturalistic detail to weave a subtle pattern of associations. The woman is linked most strongly to yellow: "Yellow Woman," "the moon in the water," "the deep-yellow petals" of wildflowers, and the "yellow" blossoms of cactus flowers. In the lore of many Native Americans, yellow represents the south (the pueblo is southeast of Silva's home), from which comes summer and the power to grow. During this story, the woman takes root in the alkaline soil of her life, grows, and opens her petals as "moonflowers blossom in the sand hills before dawn." Her beauty, her strength and fragility, her oneness with life, and her ability to grow are all effectively symbolized by her connection with yellow. The man, on the other hand, is associated with life-giving water: the river, willows. He is "damp" and "slippery," and holds an "ancient" and mysterious darkness: His body is "dark"; his horse is "black"; he lives in "blue mountains" in a house made of "black rock." Black is traditionally linked to the west (they travel northwest to reach his house), where the thunder beings live who bring rain, as he brings nourishment to her arid life and parched imagination. The darkness is also suggestive of his violence and sexuality.

The theme of storytelling—the woman's increasingly complex understanding of the relationship between story and reality—is also handled quite skillfully. The woman evolves convincingly from someone who loves to repeat the stories of her grandfather but thinks of them as speaking of a world irrevocably lost, into someone who enters consciously into the reality of a Yellow Woman story and wonders if the first Yellow Woman also "had another name." Finally, she becomes a creator of stories who knows that old stories and new stories and reality are all parts of the same truth. Silko and the woman who returns to the pueblo would agree with Black Elk: "Whether it happened so or not I do not know; but if you think about it, you can see that it is true."

*Hal Holladay*

# YENTL THE YESHIVA BOY

*Author:* Isaac Bashevis Singer (1904-1991)
*Type of plot:* Folktale
*Time of plot:* The late nineteenth century
*Locale:* The villages of Yanev, Bechev, and Lublin, Poland
*First published:* 1962

> *Principal characters:*
> YENTL ("ANSHEL"), a girl who poses as a young man in order to
>     pursue the study of Torah and Talmud
> AVIGDOR, a fourth-year yeshiva student who becomes "Anshel's"
>     study partner
> ALTER VISHKOWER, the richest man in Bechev
> HADASS, Vishkower's daughter, once engaged to Avigdor, who
>     marries "Anshel"
> PESHE, a widowed shopkeeper who marries Avigdor

*The Story*

In the nineteenth century in the shtetls of Eastern Europe, the villages populated almost entirely by Jews, the study of Torah and Talmud is prohibited to females. In the village of Yanev, however, Yentl has pursued such studies, the passion of her life, in secret under the tutelage of her father, who recognizes that his daughter is somehow different from all the other girls of the community. Yentl, tall and bony, has little interest in the running of a household. Rather than cooking or darning socks, studying her father's books is the very center of her life. Yentl, it seems, has the soul of a man.

Dressing herself as a young man and calling herself "Anshel," Yentl leaves Bechev after her father's death to continue her studies formally in a yeshiva, a school for religious teachings. Meeting Avigdor at a roadside inn, she accompanies him to Bechev to study at the yeshiva there. As Anshel, Yentl forges with Avigdor a strong bond, the basis of which is their shared love of Torah and Talmud. Yentl learns that Avigdor has been engaged to Hadass, the loveliest girl in the town and daughter of its wealthiest citizen, that the marriage had been broken off by his prospective in-laws on learning that Avigdor's brother was a suicide. The thought occurs to Avigdor that while he requires a wife and will himself marry the shrewish widowed shopkeeper, Peshe, Anshel should marry Hadass, ensuring that the girl he still loves will not end up the bride of a total stranger.

At first, Yentl dismisses the extraordinary idea, but finding herself drawn ever closer to Avigdor, she warms to his plan, realizing that it will strengthen the bond, now turning to love on her part, between herself and Avigdor. Once Avigdor marries Peshe and spends less and less time with Yentl/Anshel, Yentl asks Alter Vishkower for his daughter's hand in marriage. Considering it an excellent match, Vishkower agrees, and the wedding takes place.

Being completely innocent in sexual matters, Hadass is unaware that her marriage to Anshel is unlike any other, especially since Yentl, in her own way, has even managed to deflower her bride. As time passes, however, aware that Hadass loves her as Anshel, that she loves Avigdor, that Avigdor—whose marriage to Peshe is a disaster—loves Hadass, Yentl realizes that her charade cannot continue. It had begun as a way of exacting vengeance for Avigdor and drawing him closer to herself, but the lives of three people are becoming ever more complex as their fates are further enmeshed. Because Hadass is not yet pregnant after the passage of some months, and Anshel never goes to the baths and never swims with the other men, the villagers begin to gossip about them.

At last, journeying with Avigdor to the nearby town of Lublin, Yentl reveals herself to him as a woman. Avigdor is thunderstruck; he even wonders if Yentl is some kind of demon. Eventually, more sad than angry, he suggests that they divorce their wives and marry each other. Yentl insists that that kind of relationship with him is impossible for her. They have been brought together by their shared love of Torah and Talmud. She can never be wife and housekeeper but must instead continue her studies. However, both of them have come to understand that Yentl must disappear from the lives of Avigdor and Hadass.

Yentl does not return to Bechev but instead sends divorce papers to a bewildered Hadass who takes to her bed, grief-stricken over the loss of her beloved Anshel. Time, however, heals her wound, and Hadass recovers to marry Avigdor, now divorced from Peshe. When Hadass bears him a son, the townspeople, who have been busily pondering the disappearance of Hadass's former husband, can hardly believe their ears on learning at the ceremony of the circumcision that the child is to be named Anshel.

## Themes and Meanings

Isaac Bashevis Singer's entertaining but hauntingly ambiguous little tale does not reveal its meaning easily, nor is it meant to do so. Near the end of the story, the omniscient narrator suggests that the village gossips who insist on prying into the details of Anshel's mysterious leave-taking must finally accept any falsehood as fact: "Truth itself is often concealed in such a way that the harder you look for it, the harder it is to find." This device may be Singer's way of cautioning the reader not to pry too deeply into his characters' motivations, to accept the tale at the simple level of its telling. The truth lies in the story's title, by which the author proclaims that he is recounting the extraordinary circumstances of a girl, Yentl, who is at the same time a boy through her dedication to God's teachings—an androgynous being with the body of a woman and the soul of a man. Yentl herself is confused by the urgings within her that drive her to dress as a man in direct violation of the proscriptions of the beloved Talmud, the words of which have become the very core of her being.

In Singer's stage adaptation of the story, written in collaboration with Leah Napolin and first performed in New York in 1974, Singer clarifies the meaning of a tale that has intrigued but puzzled many readers. In the story, Yentl accepts Hadass's love, but in the play Yentl clearly learns to love Hadass as deeply as she has come to love Avigdor. Singer's intention, it would appear, is to portray in Yentl/Anshel a divided self that is becoming whole through the knowledge of love. Embracing the masculine part of her nature in her love for Hadass and the feminine part of her nature in her love for Avigdor, Yentl, paradoxically, reveals the depth of her love by her sacrifice of that love. Removing herself from the scene, leaving both Avigdor and Hadass, she frees herself for the transcendent love of God, for which she has at last fully prepared herself through a newfound understanding of the joys and despair that accompany human love.

With the birth of the child Anshel, both story and play offer the unstated possibility that Yentl, pursuing her study of Talmud and Torah, becomes an immortal figure to be reborn within the soul of each newborn Jewish child as Yentl herself is transformed into the mythical wandering Jew. The ending calls to mind a reverse myth in a poem by Matthew Arnold to which Singer's story seems related, that of "The Scholar-Gipsy," who deserts books and study to embrace the simple life in his immortal wanderings in the natural world. Yentl, having embraced life itself and released her hold, is finally ready to give meaning to her learning, to live fully the life of the mind as she explores the eternal verities of her God, who accepts her as she has become.

Singer's story has been popularized by the film musical *Yentl* (1983), produced and directed by Barbra Streisand and adapted by her in collaboration with Jack Rosenthal as a vehicle for herself. The otherwise effective film version, however, reverses Singer's original concept. The protagonist of the story is a being who is throughout a figure of androgyny—both Jewish girl, Yentl, and yeshiva boy, Anshel. The Yentl of the play is a young woman who is transformed into an androgynous figure, whereas the Yentl of the film is an androgyne who becomes at last—in the guise of Barbra Streisand—a modern woman with feminist inclinations.

### Style and Technique

Singer's story is a third-person narrative with almost no developed scenes and few extended passages of dialogue. It is charmingly told with utter simplicity, lending it the quality of a matter-of-fact folktale that has been accepted without question by several generations of listeners or readers. The reader never pauses to question the credibility of the tale, for its complex sexuality, even the mechanics of the sexual act between Yentl and Hadass, are never allowed to overwhelm the deceptively simple, seemingly primitive, straightforward style. As the author himself understands, androgyny can be convincing on the page, but perhaps only there. Once the characters are fleshed out, as they must be, for stage and screen, and scenes are added or expanded, an element of titillation intrudes. Singer never allows this element to intrude in the story and attempts to maintain control over this aspect of the play. It is this overt element that finally mars the film version in which he had no hand and of which he disapproves.

*Albert E. Kalson*

# YERMOLAI AND THE MILLER'S WIFE

*Author:* Ivan Turgenev (1818-1883)
*Type of plot:* Social realism
*Time of plot:* The 1840's
*Locale:* Tula Province, 120 miles south of Moscow
*First published:* "Yermolai i mel'nichikha," 1847 (English translation, 1855)

> *Principal characters:*
> THE NARRATOR, a country squire and amateur huntsman
> YERMOLAI PETROVICH, a serf who accompanies the narrator on
> the hunt and is an expert marksman
> ARINA TIMOFEYEVNA, the miller's wife
> SAVELY ALEKSEYEVICH, her husband, the miller
> ALEKSANDR SILYCH ZVERKOV, Arina's previous master, a country
> squire
> HIS WIFE
> PETRUSHKA, a footman

*The Story*

The author-narrator starts with the setting. He is out hunting woodcock with his assistant, Yermolai. The most productive time for such hunting is the spring mating-season of the woodcock. The specific Russian word (*tyaga*, "attraction") that indicates this activity and the hunt conducted by human beings during this season is explained by the narrator. The atmosphere of the setting carries great weight: evening, motionless air, pervasive silence, only weak and occasional sounds, the setting sun, gradual darkness, birds falling asleep, stars, indistinguishable masses of trees.

The description of the atmosphere accompanying the expectation of the woodcock's appearance is followed by a presentation of Yermolai, the narrator's companion on his hunting expeditions. A humble man, a serf owned by a neighbor landowner, Yermolai is a sort of independent type, not yet old, but no longer young either (about forty-five), adapted to and completely familiar with his natural environment, a passionate huntsman, a good shot, and in a way an eccentric. His hunting dog Valyetka is fond of him, but few people are. He does not care much about people, not even his own wife, whom he visits once a week, rarely provides for, and who "managed to get along somehow and suffered a bitter fate." Yermolai himself lives on handouts; his eccentric behavior is tolerated by the peasants, and he enjoys respect only as an expert huntsman.

The locale of the anecdote that forms the substance of the story is near the river Ista, a side river of the Oka in the Tula Province. After minor success with the woodcock hunt on the evening in question, the narrator decides to spend the night nearby and to resume the hunt early the next morning. A lodging for the night is required. A nearby mill seems suitable, but the miller's servant, on his master's instructions, refuses hospitality. After further pleading and an offer of money, both the master and Yermolai are admitted for the night. Before they lie down to sleep, a meal is prepared in the yard on an open fire, where the miller's wife, Arina, gives assistance and the reader detects a certain warmth and attraction between Yermolai and this woman. His occasional "sullen fierceness" is allayed in the company of Arina. He takes an interest in her (her complaint is a tormenting and persistent cough), and she waits on him gladly.

The woman's gentle but sullen demeanor arouses the narrator's curiosity, and he asks a few questions and then informs the reader of the circumstances of Arina Timofeyevna's previous life and the background of her present situation. The child of a village elder, she caught the eye of her master, Zverkov, and his wife, who took her in as a parlor maid, later letting her advance to lady's maid because of her special devotion to her mistress. After ten years of service, the girl asked to be allowed to marry the footman Petrushka. The request was denied. Several months later, the request was repeated, as the girl was pregnant. At this point, she was dismissed from the household and sent back to her village. Here the miller bought her from her previous owners. She brought the marriage certain qualifications, such as an ability to read and write, which were useful in the miller's business. The boy with whom she had been in love, the footman Petrushka, was sent into the army. Her husband, the miller, seems to tyrannize her. She serves and obeys him without love. Their child has died.

Yermolai displays pity and affection for her, which are important in view of the heartless egotism and exploitative treatment of her previous masters, and the surly nature of her husband, the miller. With the knowledge of the hopelessness of the situation of Arina Timofeyevna and the cruel selfishness ruling human affairs, both Yermolai and his master fall asleep under the lean-to before resuming their woodcock hunting early the next morning.

### Themes and Meanings

"Yermolai and the Miller's Wife" was the second in a series of short sketches that Ivan Turgenev published in the late 1840's, largely in the St. Petersburg literary periodical, *The Contemporary*, and that were later collected under the title *Zapiski okhotnika* (1852; *Russian Life in the Interior*, 1855; better known as *A Sportsman's Sketches*, 1932). This collection has been described by critic D. S. Mirsky as "belonging to the highest, most lasting and least questionable achievement of Turgenev and of Russian realism." The sketches gained great popularity with the Russian reading public and were said to have influenced the young heir to the throne, Alexander II, in his decision to abolish serfdom in 1861. In these sketches, the simple man is in the foreground and is presented from a perspective of psychological complexity, which was a novelty at the time. Yermolai is interesting as a person, having both positive and negative features. Such simple folk had not previously been considered worthy of serious literary treatment. Without training and education, they did not seem to possess what were deemed interesting character features. As serfs, they were condemned to a lowly life of drudgery and were viewed with condescension.

Turgenev saw these humble people from a different point of view, foremost as individual human beings, talented, sensitive, and as complex in their emotional life as the members of his own class. He broke with the stereotype of presenting them as a dark, anonymous mass. By showing Yermolai and Arina as gifted and sensitive individuals, the narrator invites the reader to draw his own conclusions about such masters as the Zverkovs and the system of serfdom. He makes his point implicitly, but his lack of sympathy for the self-righteousness, condescension, and egotism of the masters is quite clear. Such people of the upper class see life only in terms of their own comfort and pleasure, remaining totally indifferent to the human needs of others. The elevation of humble people and the indication of the absence of justice in social relations could not help but move Turgenev's readers. However, Turgenev was too perceptive an observer of life, even at a young age, to attribute all ills to social conditions. Human callousness seems to be as much a general condition of life as the result of social causes, as demonstrated by Yermolai's ill treatment of his wife, whom he neglects unconscionably, and the apparent coldness of the miller toward Arina.

*Style and Technique*

Author and narrator appear as the same person and participant in the action. The author-narrator relates, comments, reflects, and treats his reader as interlocutor. This approach creates a feeling of directness and sense of immediacy. The author-narrator directs his voice to the ear of the reader. His voice is pleasant and does not grate. Briefly, a subnarrator appears in the person of Mr. Zverkov, who relates the circumstances of Arina's life in his household. His account and the manner of his speech are used as a negative device of characterization of this man. Modulation is attained by the occasional but sparing use of dialogue. All excess is avoided in this prose style, which aims at clarity and deliberately shuns the use of ornamentation. The descriptions of nature possess a lyrical quality, but these, too, are subdued. The sounds of nature, such as the soft chirping of birds in the enveloping darkness, are gentle and accessible only to the sensitive ear. The prevailing characteristic of nature is silence.

The story has a clear structural design with seven apparent sections, starting with the opening scene in which the narrator and Yermolai lie in wait for the woodcock to appear, up to the moment when they fall asleep. The interval of time between the opening and closing of the story is only a few hours. Moderate use is made of telling names: Zverkov (Arina's insensitive master) is derived from *zver'* ("beast").

The soft narrative voice of the author, the subdued lyricism of its setting, the theme of a lonely existence (Yermolai), and a suggestion of long, inevitable suffering (Arina) let the narrative conclude on a minor key, likely to produce in the reader a feeling of melancholy and mild sadness while also suggesting truth and giving aesthetic pleasure.

*Joachim T. Baer*

# YOU CAN'T GET LOST IN CAPE TOWN

*Author:* Zoë Wicomb (1948-    )
*Type of plot:* Psychological
*Time of plot:* Probably the 1960's
*Locale:* Cape Town, South Africa
*First published:* 1987

> *Principal characters:*
> THE NARRATOR, a young woman, a college student who is
>     designated "Coloured" in the South African racial system
> MICHAEL, her blond lover
> TIENA, a large woman who cooks and cleans for a white family
> MRS. COETZEE, the abortionist

*The Story*

"You Can't Get Lost in Cape Town" is an intense personal interior monologue of a young Coloured woman who aborts her unborn child, the offspring of a two-year relationship with her white boyfriend.

The story begins with the nameless narrator sitting on the bus into Cape Town, South Africa, clutching her purse and worrying about how much the fare is, if she will need change, what the lining of her handbag is made of, and where she should get off the bus. The entrance of two women who cook and clean for white women, on their way home from their jobs, offers her a welcome distraction. The narrator feels a flutter in her womb and thinks that God will never forgive her. She chooses to anchor her mind in the women's conversation, mostly a monologue by the larger and more aggressive of the two who refers to herself as Tiena. The woman is discussing her white mistress, the stupidity and laxness of the white people, and how she manages to outwit them. She shares some chicken she has taken from the house with her friend, while she explains how her exploitative mistress tried to keep her from having any of it for herself. She also discusses the mistress's daughter, who has been having sex with her fiancé but has been using birth control pills, which she assumes the servant is too ignorant to recognize. This girl will be married in white and seen as a blushing innocent by her family, though Tiena sees through her.

As she listens, the narrator becomes anxious again. She thinks of asking for directions, but when the fetus inside her flutters again she feels it is bullying her and decides to leave the bus. She doubts if she will be alive the next day. Having made an arbitrary decision to get off, the narrator is anxious about meeting Michael, who has told her that "you can't get lost in Cape Town." This memory leads her to other memories of their time together, including his response to her pregnancy, which was to ask her to marry him and move to England. However, she feels that he no longer really loves her, and so she has chosen to have the abortion.

The narrator then finds her way to the post office in the city where she is to meet Michael. They go to another part of Cape Town where Mrs. Coetzee is to perform the abortion. The woman questions the narrator about her race, but when the narrator denies that she is Coloured, the abortionist is quite ready to believe her despite the evidence of her own eyes, because the narrator has developed an educated tone and manner. Like the woman on the bus who recognized the birth control pills, the abortionist's Coloured assistant is not fooled and winks at the narrator. Mrs. Coetzee does what is necessary to bring about a miscarriage, and the narrator returns to her home, acting blithe and assured as she tells Michael that it will all be over in the morning.

In the morning, the narrator places the aborted fetus in a garbage can. Simultaneously, she describes God as being absent, having absconded forever as she prepares to discard the newspaper-wrapped package.

*Themes and Meanings*

One of the strongest themes throughout the narrative is that of betrayal, related through imagery that refers both directly and indirectly to the biblical story of the betrayal of Jesus Christ by Judas. While watching the fat woman on the bus discuss her relationship with her employer, the narrator's thoughts flow from the bone the woman waves to the cross of Jesus's crucifixion, and from there to Judas howling in remorse, and finally to Judas's purse containing the payment for his treachery. At the start of the story, the narrator has been obsessing on the cheapness of her handbag, and the unadorned purse she carries within it, which belongs to Michael and contains the money for her operation. When she thinks of Judas, she describes the purse that holds the thirty pieces of silver in the same terms. When she prepares to leave after her abortion, Mrs. Coetzee kisses her on the cheek, as Judas kissed Christ. She almost leaves the purse behind but decides to take it. In the morning, she feels that God has gone. Who represents the Judas figure is not totally clear; is it the narrator betraying her unborn child, Michael betraying their love, the abortionist, or all of them? Certainly the narrator is struggling with her choice to rid herself of this unwanted pregnancy, when, as Michael points out, she wishes to have a family.

Another theme running throughout the story is that of the color system in South Africa, particularly the peculiar position of the Coloured under apartheid: not as totally separated as the black population but decidedly not privileged like the white, rather tolerated at best. The narrator is in this middle state. She can pretend to be white with Mrs. Coetzee, who wants her money and who is unable to see past her educated demeanor, but not in any way is she an equal to whites, though she is obviously not in the same position as the women on the bus. She is also less privileged than the daughter of Tiena's boss, who like the narrator, has been having sex with her boyfriend but who will be regarded as virginal on her wedding day.

*Style and Technique*

The first-person narrative point of view of "You Can't Get Lost in Cape Town" creates a powerful effect on the reader. The narration is highly sensual, beginning with the touch of the cardboard lining in the narrator's cheap handbag and continuing with the sight of the women on the bus, the flutter of the fetus in the womb, the pain of the abortion, and the morning after when she smoothes back the wet black hair of the fetus before depositing the newspaper-wrapped bundle in the garbage. All of this makes the internal viewpoint highly visual and visceral rather than intellectual. The dialogue between the two women on the bus, which dominates the central section of the story, is related as heard, without editorial comment from the narrator, although she does, in the style of stream of consciousness, at times relate the external events with her own internal symbolism and the reader sees more clearly what is driving her.

Cape Town itself plays a minor role in the story, as details of it are relayed while the narrator moves through it to her date with the abortionist. The imagery of the surroundings, the mountains and the ocean, as well as the remembrances of the veld of the narrator's childhood, play off the images of the city, the buildings, shops, roads, and trains: the fertile veld and the city of dustbins, where God has left but the trains run on time.

Interestingly, the tone is on the whole detached. It becomes clear that throughout the story the narrator is trying to detach herself from her decision and its consequences. Therefore, the focus is on the detail and sense impressions, making the story so powerful and concrete that the reader experiences the narrator's internal agony, although it is never referred to directly.

There is a contrast between the proper English, the highly proper quality of the language of the narrator's thoughts and the dialect she hears from the women on the bus. It is clear that there is a large gap between them; however, the women feel comfortable criticizing the narrator when she almost forgets her purse but would never criticize their white employers to their faces. This incident with the purse is metaphoric—it represents the narrator's unacknowledged reluctance to go through with her decision, while at the same time being related to the analogy to the betrayal of Christ by Judas.

*Mary LeDonne Cassidy*

# YOUNG ARCHIMEDES

*Author:* Aldous Huxley (1894-1963)
*Type of plot:* Sketch
*Time of plot:* The 1920's
*Locale:* Florence, Italy
*First published:* 1924

> *Principal characters:*
> THE NARRATOR, an Englishman living in Italy
> SIGNORA BONDI, his landlady
> GUIDO, a peasant boy whom the narrator dubs the "young
> Archimedes"

*The Story*

    The narrator and his wife, a young English couple, rent a house outside of Florence because of its astounding view. When they first consider the property, the landlady, Signora Bondi, seems charming and insists that everything in the house is in perfect working order. Once they move in, however, they discover that the house has many problems. Particularly annoying is a broken pump that makes it impossible to run bathwater. Repeated visits to Signora Bondi's house bring only the answer that she is "out" or "indisposed." The couple are thus forced to communicate with her through certified letters. When even these bring no result, they have the landlady served with a legal writ. Grudgingly, Signora Bondi agrees to replace the broken pump.

    When the narrator unexpectedly meets Signora Bondi's husband in town one day, Signor Bondi apologizes profusely. He knew from the beginning, he says, that the pump would need to be replaced; his wife, however, enjoys sparring with the tenants over minor repairs, and he hopes that the couple will forgive them. A short time later, the couple ask to renew their lease for a year, and Signora Bondi increases their rent 25 percent because of the "improvements" that she has made to the property. Only after extended negotiations does she agree to accept only a 15 percent increase.

    Even while these problems are continuing, the narrator's four-year-old son, Robin, develops a close friendship with Guido, the son of a local peasant family. Although Guido is somewhat older than Robin, he displays patience and affection for the boy. As the narrator comes to realize, Guido is exceptionally bright. At times, he falls silent and stares pensively into the distance. Then, just as suddenly, he resumes the game that he is playing with Robin.

    Signora Bondi also takes notice of Guido and wishes to adopt him. Guido's father asks the narrator for advice. He cautions the peasant against making any agreements with Signora Bondi. Her comments about Guido make it clear that she is not interested in the boy himself, but in how she can mold him. For example, she describes how she wants to dress Guido, almost as though he were a pet or doll. The peasant goes away persuaded that he should keep Guido for himself.

Shortly thereafter, the narrator's gramophone and several boxes of records arrive from England. Although Robin is only interested when his father plays marches or light music, Guido takes an immediate interest in the pieces by composers Johann Sebastian Bach and Wolfgang Amadeus Mozart. From the first, the boy makes a practice of coming to the narrator's house each afternoon to listen to a short concert during Robin's nap. Within a few days, Guido selects favorite pieces and shows a remarkable understanding of harmony.

Impressed with Guido's aptitude for music, the narrator rents a piano and begins to give the boy music lessons. Guido progresses quickly, understanding the structure of canons almost intuitively and finding them easy to write. He is less inventive, however, when it comes to writing other types of music. Reluctantly, the narrator realizes that Guido is not the musical prodigy that he initially appeared to be.

One day the narrator sees Guido explaining to Robin the Pythagorean theorem. On further questioning, Guido reveals that he has not learned the theorem from anyone else, but has discovered it on his own. The beauty that Guido finds in mathematical proofs and the ease with which he learns to compose canons cause the narrator to realize that it is in mathematics, not music, that the boy may be a genius. If Guido is not a young Mozart, he is, in any case, a young Archimedes. The narrator explains that only geniuses such as Guido are "real men" in the world. He notes that most of the ideas taken for granted by humanity were discovered by a few dozen remarkable individuals. In the hope that Guido will grow up to be one of these few extraordinary individuals, the narrator adds lessons in algebra to Guido's ongoing study of music.

As the summer arrives, Robin's health begins to suffer from the intense heat of the Italian countryside. On the advice of a doctor, the narrator and his wife take him on an extended trip to Switzerland. After they have been away from Italy for several weeks, they receive a strange letter from Guido, who says that he is living with Signora Bondi and is terribly unhappy because she has taken away his mathematics books. He has lost his interest in playing music, although Signora Bondi forces him to work at the piano for many hours each day. He ends by begging the narrator to return with his family to Italy.

Only on their return to Florence do the narrator and his wife learn what has occurred in their absence. Immediately after they left, Signora Bondi began pressuring Guido's father to allow her to adopt the boy. When the peasant refused, she threatened to evict him from the land that his family had farmed for generations. Eventually, the peasant acceded to Signora Bondi's demands. They agreed that Guido would live with the Bondis for several months on a trial basis. Although Guido had no desire to leave his family, he went along with the plan because Signora Bondi promised him that they would go to the seaside, a place where he had never been.

When the Bondis returned to Florence from the coast, Signora Bondi did not tell Guido's father that they were back in the area. Convinced that Guido would become a musical prodigy only if he applied himself, Signora Bondi compelled him to practice the piano for extended periods each day and took away his other books, calling them "distractions." When Guido said that he wanted to go home, Signora Bondi told him that his father did not want him anymore. Guido's father, thinking that the Bondis were still at the seaside, never visited him, so Guido believed that this must be true. In despair, Guido threw himself from a window and was killed. Signora Bondi had the boy buried in the Bondi family tomb. When the narrator returns from Switzerland, he learns that he has arrived too late.

### Themes and Meanings

A recurrent theme in many of Aldous Huxley's stories concerns a person who is trapped in a problem beyond his or her control. Most of these stories were written in the 1920's and early 1930's as fascism was spreading throughout Europe and war loomed on the horizon. The predicament in which Huxley's characters find themselves reflects the frustration experienced by many Europeans of that period. Guido's world serves as a microcosm of European history at the time that Huxley wrote.

The character of Guido also represents the universal conflict between intellect and instinct, or between regimentation and unfettered genius. Standing in opposition to Guido's natural creativity are such figures as Signora Bondi herself and the fascist government to which repeated allusions are made in the story. In choosing his favorite pieces among the narrator's records, for example, Guido gives strong preference to Bach, Mozart, and Ludwig von Beethoven—who are viewed by Huxley as composers who achieved the proper balance between natural beauty and mathematical perfection—and he dislikes Richard Wagner, Claude Debussy, and Richard Strauss—who are identified by Huxley with the fascists or with debased emotionalism. In using Florence as a setting and in contrasting northern European "intellect" with southern European "instinct," "Young Archimedes" explores many of the same themes found in E. M. Forster's *A Room with a View* (1908).

### Style and Technique

In a long introductory passage, Huxley sets the mood for his story and describes the continually changing countryside near Florence. This passage foreshadows the shifting moods of the story itself. From its opening account of the narrator's house and the difficulties in dealing with Signora Bondi, readers may conclude that "Young Archimedes" will be a light, comic anecdote. By the end of the story, however, the atmosphere of the work has darkened considerably and the tone has become one of pure tragedy.

The form of "Young Archimedes" is that of a character sketch or "most memorable person" narrative. Examples of this literary form include F. Scott Fitzgerald's *The Great Gatsby* (1925) and Truman Capote's *Breakfast at Tiffany's* (1958). Mixtures of comic and tragic elements are common in works of this sort. Authors use lighter moments to describe the joyous or uninhibited personalities that make their central characters memorable, and they use somber moments to suggest the voids that their characters' departures leave in the lives of their narrators. In order to give such stories greater immediacy, most-memorable-person narratives are almost always told in the first person.

*Jeffrey L. Buller*

# YOUNG GOODMAN BROWN

*Author:* Nathaniel Hawthorne (1804-1864)
*Type of plot:* Allegory
*Time of plot:* The 1690's
*Locale:* Salem, Massachusetts
*First published:* 1835

> *Principal characters:*
> YOUNG GOODMAN BROWN, a Salem householder, the protagonist
> FAITH, his wife
> A MAN MET IN THE WOODS, who may also be the Devil, a
> conductor of a Black Mass in the forest

*The Story*

Young Goodman Brown is bidding his wife, Faith, farewell at their front door. It is evening in the village, and he is going on a guilty errand, a fact that he clearly recognizes and deplores but an errand he has chosen to undertake nevertheless. Taking a route into the forest, he meets, as by appointment, an older man who bears a fatherly resemblance to both Brown and the Devil.

Brown initially considers his decision to go on his unholy errand an exceptional one, but he soon discovers that other presumably exemplary villagers are on the same path, including, to his amazement, Goody Cloyse, a pious old woman who once taught him his catechism but who readily confesses to the practice of witchcraft. With Brown still confident that he can turn back, his older companion departs, leaving behind his curiously snakelike staff and fully expecting that Brown will soon follow.

Brown hides from another group of approaching figures, which includes the minister and deacon of his church and even—to his horror—his wife, Faith. At this point, he yields to despair and sets forth to join in what is obviously a witches' Sabbath or Black Mass. Laughing and blaspheming, Brown rushes toward the throng in the forest. Literally everyone noted for sanctity seems to be gathered together in communion with known sinners before a rock altar amid blazing pine trees. He is led to the latter with another initiate; when her veil is removed, he recognizes Faith. A dark satanic figure welcomes them to "the communion of your race."

Here, conscious that they are standing at the edge of some irredeemable wickedness, they hesitate, and Brown calls out to his wife to resist. A second later, the scene has dissolved, and he finds himself in the forest alone, shivering and confused. The following morning, he returns to the village to find all apparently normal, but he cannot help but shun contact with Goody Cloyse and the other good people—even his own wife.

In his final paragraph, Nathaniel Hawthorne summarizes the later, permanently blighted life of Goodman Brown. He scowls and mutters during prayers, suspects all the pious, recoils from his wife in bed at night, and finally dies without hope.

*Themes and Meanings*

"Young Goodman Brown" is the classic American short story of the guilty con-science. The question Brown confronts is whether his heritage of Original Sin inca-pacitates him for resisting personal sin. In this profoundly ambiguous story, Brown wavers between the desperate cynicism of the corrupt soul and the hopefulness of the believer. At the beginning of the story, he has already made his bargain with the Devil—hardly a token that he is among God's elect but not necessarily a sign of dam-nation, either, if he can reject the consummation in the form of the perverted commu-nion service in the woods. Whether by act of will or by divine grace, Brown appears to have resisted the power of evil at the climactic moment and given evidence of at least the possibility of salvation for his wife and himself.

However, if he has, what can be made of his life thereafter? All family and commu-nity relationships have been poisoned, and if he can be said to retain his faith, he ap-pears to have lost hope completely. If the ability to resist the Devil at his own table is victory, he has triumphed; if he has made the effort at the expense of his capability for human trust, he has met spiritual defeat. Hawthorne raises the question of whether Brown fell asleep in the forest and dreamed the witches' Sabbath. The reader, invited to ponder whether one dream could have such an intensive and extensive effect, may well proceed to wonder why Brown found it necessary to invade the forest at night merely to have a bad dream. If, on the other hand, any part of the forest encounter with the Devil and witches is "real," is Hawthorne to be regarded as a Manichaean who is demonstrating the power of evil?

"Young Goodman Brown" may also be read as a story concerned less with measur-ing the extent of evil in the world and assessing the moral prospects of the guilty than with studying the psychology of guilt. It may be doubted that Hawthorne would exer-cise his creative powers merely to affirm or quarrel with Calvinism, which had largely lost its grip on New Englanders' allegiance by 1835, but he clearly retained a strong interest in the psychological atmosphere fostered by Calvinism. Dilemmas such as the opposition between divine foreordination and free will and that between God's stern and irrevocable judgment and the possibility of his mercy and proffered grace continued to baffle conservative Christians in an era that offered a doctrinally less strenuous alternative such as Unitarianism. The old habits of mind had been chal-lenged, but they were not dead.

Hawthorne's insight into the stages of Brown's guilt is acute. Part of Brown's initial firmness in his resolve to go into the woods and in his confidence that his wife, by staying at home, saying her prayers, and going to bed early will remain unharmed, is his sense of the uniqueness of his own daring. Departing from the ways of the pious and arranging an interview with the Devil lends glamour to his quest. He imagines a "devilish Indian behind every tree" but cannot suppose any other Christian in these precincts. He exudes the confidence of a person who expects to retain control of the situation and pull back if he so decides. When he discovers that he is simply another sinner, simply another member of a corrupt race, he loses all dignity, all capacity for moral inquiry. Giving in to a mindless, emotional indulgence, he is later checked by the awesome finality of the Black Mass and acknowledges his insufficiency; then, for the first and only time in the story, he calls on God for assistance.

In this story and in such other fictions as "The Minister's Black Veil," "Ethan Brand," and *The Scarlet Letter* (1850), Hawthorne depicts the inner conflict resulting from a guilt that is suppressed, felt to be unshareable and unforgivable. Regardless of whether it is justified, Brown's feeling of guilt is real, and to call his experience "only a dream" is to undervalue dreams, which, though read in vastly different ways over the centuries, have always been considered vitally significant by interpreters. Even if Brown is regarded as irrational, letting one night destroy his life, Hawthorne makes the reader feel such irrationality as a dreadful possibility.

*Style and Technique*

Hawthorne renders Brown's deterioration plausible by a blend of means, one of them being his surprising ability to adapt to his purposes a fictional mode seemingly much better suited to the purposes of medieval and Renaissance authors than those of nineteenth century novelists. Normally, allegory is sharp and clear as far as it goes, the limits of its applicability plain. Hawthorne's story portrays the traditional Christian conviction that when a good man forsakes his Faith, he is liable to Hell. When the Devil taxes Brown with being late for his appointment in the forest, his answer, "Faith kept me back a while," is as purely allegorical as it can be.

Hawthorne, however, goes on to complicate this idea. Not only are presumably pious people—guardians of the faith such as the minister and deacon—on the way to a satanic communion, but also the character who symbolizes faith. It may not be noticed at the beginning that Brown seems more protective of Faith than she of him. It may even pass unnoticed that Brown identifies Faith by her pink ribbon, a very fragile and decorative artifact for a character representing such a presumably powerful virtue. At the climax of the story, however, for the good man to counsel faith, rather than the opposite, is an incongruity that can hardly be missed. Then Hawthorne has them separated in a way that casts doubt on whether she, and indeed the whole diabolical crowd, were ever there. Brown was certainly there, but whether he has dreamed all or part of the night's events cannot be determined conclusively. Finally, he is reunited with her again for the duration of his life, but unhappily, his only alternative to full-scale evil is a life of gloom and misanthropy. However, the story offers nothing more effective than faith to combat moral debasement.

Unlike the authors of the medieval morality plays, Edmund Spenser, John Bunyan, and other moral allegorists, Hawthorne employed allegory not to demonstrate a moral proposition or the effects of accepting or rejecting the proposition but to establish a moral context in which good and evil deeds remain identifiable while their causes, effects, and interrelationships become mysterious and problematic. To abandon faith is still evil; to rejoin faith is not so obviously good. The sins remain the traditional ones: lust, murder, worshiping false gods. No one, however, seems to remember how to live cleanly and charitably.

Hawthorne accentuates the ambiguity of his allegory by frequent use of such expressions as "perhaps," "as if," "seemed," "as it were," "some affirm that," and "he could have well-nigh sworn." Thus hedged about, the full meaning of his story is as shadowy as his forest. In addition, he poses a number of unanswered and often unanswerable questions, such as whether Brown had somehow dreamed his lurid adventure.

Such techniques suggest that while Hawthorne delighted in posing moral questions and examining the moral content of human behavior, his main interest here, and in his fiction generally, was plumbing the psychology of the moral life. Looking back on the Calvinist heritage, he wrote of the pressures it exerted on the psyches of believers. He was no amateur theologian but rather an artist. He does not say what Young Goodman Brown should have done or indeed whether he could have done other than what he did; rather, the author portrays a condition that is felt to be intolerable and yet irremediable.

*Robert P. Ellis*

# YOU'RE UGLY TOO

*Author:* Lorrie Moore (1957-     )
*Type of plot:* Psychological
*Time of plot:* The 1980's
*Locale:* Paris, Illinois, and New York City
*First published:* 1989

> *Principal characters:*
> ZOË HENDRICKS, a single college instructor in the Midwest
> EVAN, her sister
> CHARLIE, Evan's fiancé
> EARL, a single man whom Zoë meets

## The Story

"You're Ugly Too" is told in the third person through the perspective of Zoë Hendricks, a single woman in academia seemingly doomed to a series of unrewarding relationships with the opposite sex. Her situation is a common one for professional women, and the story would be simply depressing if not for Zoë's wry sense of humor. When she visits her sister in New York City, she meets another single man, who turns out to be the epitome of men incapable of true intimacy.

Zoë lives in an Illinois town, incongruously named Paris, where she teaches history at a small liberal arts college with the equally incongruous name, Hilldale-Versailles. She has been hired primarily as a means of avoiding a sex-discrimination suit, and her male colleagues do not treat her seriously. Zoë's sense of ironic humor quickly degenerates into sarcasm, and her student evaluations are slipping. She finds her students good-natured enough, but inane, lacking even minimal intellectual curiosity about anything historical or geographic.

Zoë manages to plug along in her job, saving herself by frequent trips or vacations away from the Midwest, where every man expects her to be a physically mature version of Heidi, the charming Swiss orphan in the Johanna Spyri classic novel. She is writing a book on humor in the American presidency, but her progress is slowed by her meticulous, compulsive revisions. Zoë desperately awaits the arrival of the mail each day and watches television in her bedroom into the late hours of the night. She even buys a house but quickly loses any interest in personalizing it with her own decor. In fact, she is not quite sure that the woman she sees in the mirror each day is herself.

Zoë has had three unsuccessful relationships in her three years at this midwestern liberal arts college. The first relationship was with a parking ticket bureaucrat (his occupation suggests the paucity of available men). Their relationship ended with the suggestion that she buy new clothes. Zoë, who likes her clothes, casually flicked an ant off her sleeve, and the man got extremely upset because the ant landed in his car, a snazzy convertible (vainly inappropriate for midwestern weather). The second man was much sweeter and even appreciated the arts, but Zoë was frequently disconcerted by the odd things that he did and said. For example, he stole garnishes from her dinner plate and then acted enraged that she did not notice. A third man, Murray Peterson, was a political science professor who took Zoë on double dates with other professors and their wives. Murray would then proceed to flirt outrageously with these wives. The last of these dates ended when Zoë suggested that even a clever dog could do what the wife claimed to be her great mental feats.

Just before leaving to visit her sister in New York, Zoë discovers that she has a tumor in her abdomen. Rather than waiting to hear the diagnosis (possibly ovarian cancer), she boards the plane for New York. Once there, she learns that her sister, Evan, plans to marry Charlie, her long-term lover. Evan tells her this news immediately after complaining about the boredom and sexlessness of their relationship.

At a Halloween party held by her sister, Zoë meets Earl, a man disguised as a naked woman. He wears a body suit with large rubber breasts and strategically placed steel wool. The steel wool and rubber breasts shift throughout the evening, producing yet another comic effect. Zoë is dressed as a bonehead, but a reversal of their disguises might be more character appropriate. Zoë and Earl go out onto the balcony of this classy high-rise Manhattan apartment. The ensuing conversation serves to epitomize the impossibility of intimacy between many single men and women of the late twentieth century. Earl does not get any of Zoë's jokes, changes the subject whenever Zoë begins to talk, and never listens to her seriously even when she brings up the serious subject of her health. The story ends with Zoë's playful push against Earl, who is leaning on the railing of a twentieth floor balcony. Earl does not go over the railing, and Zoë claims that she was just kidding.

*Themes and Meanings*

The protagonists of Lorrie Moore's stories are typically women who feel isolated in the world in which they live. These women, whether married or single, are unable to find true intimacy with the men in their lives and also cannot find any real degree of satisfaction in their careers or lifestyles. All efforts at self-help fail. The only thing that does not fail is their sense of humor in viewing their situations.

Zoë Hendricks genuinely tries to find satisfaction in her career and lifestyle. She is interested in the subject that she teaches and in her research on humor in the American presidency. She begins her academic career with the utmost goodwill toward her students, singing songs to them and allowing them to call her at home. When the small midwestern town proves stifling, she seeks diversion in larger cities and more interesting places. Zoë even buys a house but finds it hard to live in this house or to make it her own by changing the decor. She dates single men when the opportunity arises.

In spite of all of her efforts, Zoë remains isolated from virtually everyone—the academic community, the men whom she dates, and even most women, who somehow seem to find satisfaction in their lives. Her sister, Evan, for example, is happy in her relatively trivial occupation as a part-time food designer, one who prepares food for photo shoots. Neither is her sister particularly bothered by the degeneration of intimacy between herself and her future husband. Most people seem to like Evan better than Zoë. Earl, the man disguised as a naked woman, perhaps sums it up best when he expresses a preference for women who work part time over professional women. Women with brains, it seems, are not usually well liked.

Zoë's saving grace, at least for the reader, is her ever-present, wry sense of humor. It is difficult to pinpoint any serious character flaws in Zoë that would lead her to such a state of isolation. She is perhaps a perfectionist who expects too much from both herself and others. The real flaw, however, seems to be the late twentieth century world, which allows women to assume professional roles but does not really appreciate independent, thinking women with an occasionally nasty twist in their sense of humor.

*Style and Technique*

The external plot of "You're Ugly Too" is obviously not very important for Moore's purposes. The plot is little more than a particular situation to highlight what is going on inside of Zoë's head. A brief sketch of her academic career and unsuccessful romances sets the scene for her trip to New York where she meets yet another romantic cripple.

Moore's use of a third-person narration, which closely follows the consciousness of Zoë Hendricks, allows the reader to see the woman from both the outside and the inside. The reader is thoroughly sympathetic with Zoë, particularly if the reader has experienced firsthand some of the pitfalls of academic teaching and a few unsuccessful relationships. However, one can also see that Zoë partly creates the distance between herself and others. Zoë remains appealing primarily because of her wry sense of humor when looking at both herself and her world.

Moore's stories have been compared to the stories of Raymond Carver, Bobbie Ann Mason, and Flannery O'Connor. The pervasive comic despair of Moore's stories may be similar to that of O'Connor's stories, but in theme she is much closer to Carver. Her characters rarely, if ever, achieve moments of epiphany; such a move might imply easy answers, and Moore clearly disdains easy answers to the complex angst suffered by her women characters. Moore's style is simple, reminiscent of both Mason and Carver. However, humor is Moore's pervading trademark. Occasionally, this humor threatens to usurp the sad, underlying truths of her stories, but in "You're Ugly Too," Moore maintains a fine balance.

*Nancy E. Sherrod*

# YOUTH

*Author:* Joseph Conrad (Jósef Teodor Konrad Nałęcz Korzeniowski, 1857-1924)
*Type of plot:* Adventure
*Time of plot:* 1880
*Locale:* Aboard an English freighter bound for the East
*First published:* 1902

> *Principal characters:*
> MARLOWE, the protagonist and second mate
> CAPTAIN JOHN BEARD, the skipper of the *Judea*
> MAHON, the first mate

*The Story*

At age forty-two, Marlowe sits drinking with four other Englishmen who began their working lives in the merchant service. Most have other work ashore now, but they share the bond of seafaring men. He tells them the story of his first trip to the East, when he was an adventurous young man of twenty and had hired on for the first time as an officer, second mate on an old freighter bound for Bangkok.

Engraved on the stern of the ship was "Judea, London. Do or Die," a grandiloquent motto that appealed to the youthful enthusiasm of her youngest officer. Her skipper, John Beard, was also on his first voyage as captain, but at sixty years of age, he was an old hand in the merchant service. The first mate Mahon was also an old man. Much of the underlying irony that pervades this adventure is the implied contrast between what such an experience meant to a high-spirited young man and what it must have meant to the old captain. The storyteller, now midway between the ignorant youth he once was and the sorrowful but dignified old man, appreciates both perspectives.

The ill-fated *Judea* had nothing but trouble from the very beginning. She had not even reached the port where she was to be loaded with coal, when her ballast shifted dangerously in a murderous North Sea storm. Everyone began shoveling sand ballast to right the listing ship. It took them sixteen days to get from London to the Tyne, where they were delayed for two months because they had lost their turn at loading. When at last all was ready, they were rammed by a steamer, requiring further repair and three weeks' delay.

The *Judea* actually made it out into the Atlantic when another storm brought on an even more desperate struggle with multiple leaks. The crew pumped water furiously from the leaky hold for days and nights as the ship began to break into pieces about them. Only with great difficulty did they flounder back to the English coast, where the ship was unloaded and put in dry dock for repair.

The crew departed in disgust at that point, and the frustrated officers had to bring in another crew from far away because everyone around had learned of the bad luck of the *Judea*. Even the rats deserted the ship at Falmouth, a development of ominous portent. Marlowe and Mahon joked of the obvious stupidity of rats, however, because they should have left before, when the ship was really unseaworthy. Now, it was well caulked and shipshape.

The freighter got clear to the Indian Ocean before further disaster assailed it. The coal in the hold started smoldering from spontaneous combustion. Whereas in the Atlantic they had pumped for dear life to prevent drowning, they now poured ocean water into the hold to prevent being burned alive, wishing for the old leaks, which would have flooded the coal more efficiently. At last the smoke stopped pouring from the pile, but only as a precursor to another calamity. As the men began to relax for the first time in many days, the hold exploded from trapped gases, resulting in serious damage to both the ship and its men.

The "Do or Die" *Judea* eventually fulfilled the second part of her motto, sinking in flames as the men watched from three small lifeboats. Marlowe eventually reached Java as the captain of a rowboat with two crew members.

*Themes and Meanings*

This is one of the most autobiographical of Joseph Conrad's sea stories, chronicling his own first voyage to the East and his first position as an officer. Conrad went to sea at the age of seventeen, but in 1881 he shipped in a freighter called the *Palestine*, for which the *Judea* is a pseudonym. The story probably reflects quite accurately the heartbreaking frustrations and failures, from the captain's standpoint, that often plagued such overaged seagoing vessels. It also expresses the rare power of the romantic young man's ability to convert an extremely painful, tedious, and dangerous experience into a glamorous test of his strength, courage, and ability. What must have been the most dismal failure to the old skipper on his first and probably only chance to be a captain was for the youthful mate a resounding success.

Even in the most dreadful and tedious circumstances, as when they are pumping frantically to stay afloat, the protagonist is enjoying even the misery of it all:

> And there was somewhere in me the thought: By Jove! this is the deuce of an adventure—something you read about; and it is my first voyage as second mate—and I am only twenty—and here I am lasting it out as well as any of these men, and keeping my chaps up to the mark. I was pleased. I would not have given up the experience for worlds. I had moments of exultation. Whenever the old dismantled craft pitched heavily with her counter high in the air, she seemed to me to throw up, like an appeal, like a defiance, like a cry to the clouds without mercy, the words written on her stern: "Judea, London. Do or Die."

If the story is a paean to the optimism and exhilaration of youth in the face of hardship, it is also a more muted tribute to the perseverance and honor of age when the daily battle with the sea is no longer a romantic game. The spry old skipper is treated with humor and respect, a considerate and valiant little man in the face of inevitable defeat. He insists on remaining on the burning ship until the last minute and conscientiously, though foolishly, tries to save as much as he can for his employers:

The old man warned us in his gentle and inflexible way that it was part of our duty to save for the underwriters as much as we could of the ship's gear. Accordingly we went to work aft, while she blazed forward to give us plenty of light. We lugged out a lot of rubbish. What didn't we save? An old barometer fixed with an absurd quantity of screws nearly cost me my life: a sudden rush of smoke came on me, and I just got away in time. There were various stores, bolts of canvas, coils of rope; the poop looked like a marine bazaar, and the boats were lumbered to the gunwales. One would have thought the old man wanted to take as much as he could of his first command with him. He was very, very quiet, but off his balance evidently. Would you believe it? He wanted to take a length of old stream-cable and a kedge-anchor with him in the long-boat. We said, "Ay, ay, sir," deferentially, and on the quiet let the things slip overboard.

"Youth," like other sea stories by Conrad, suggests that basic analogy between a voyage and the whole of human life. It may be perceived differently by the participants, but it induces in them, at least in times of danger, a rare comradeship emanating from a shared fate.

### Style and Technique

Conrad combined a genius for realistic detail with an ability to embellish experience with human emotion. Though in some stories, such as *Heart of Darkness* (1902), he produced an almost too-melodramatic overlay of suggestive implications, he never seriously misrepresented the scenes he described, which he knew from personal experience. "Youth" is quite free of "purple passages," without obscuring either the grim reality of the voyage or the absurdly romantic glow in which the young mate experienced it.

Conrad's sentence style itself suggests the exhausting, mind-deadening experience of undergoing a relentless storm and the continual, repetitive struggle to stay alive. The experience is evoked by a series of short phrases presented in parallel structure— "It blew day after day: it blew with spite, without interval, without mercy, without rest"—or by rhythms that mirror the endless, mindless tedium of pumping water from the leaking hull.

The framing of the story as a true sea yarn told to a group of drinking companions lends a convenient distance to the adventure, so that it carries a conscious irony inappropriate to the narrator's youthful self. In one sense, "Youth" is a kind of trial run for the framing technique, which became more important in *Heart of Darkness*, in which Marlowe sits cross-legged like a Buddha in a boat on the Thames with a similar group of former seamen. In "Youth," Marlowe has not yet attained that implication of inscrutable wisdom as the man initiated into the mysteries of evil at the heart of human beings. He speaks here not at all of the evils of humans, but of the hardness of their lot and the courage with which ordinary people may face the threat of death. More than that, he marvels at the fact that such a life can seem like fun.

*Katherine Snipes*

# THE ZULU AND THE ZEIDE

*Author:* Dan Jacobson (1929-    )
*Type of plot:* Domestic realism
*Time of plot:* 1956
*Locale:* A city in South Africa, probably Kimberley
*First published:* 1956

> *Principal characters:*
> HARRY GROSSMAN, a prosperous Jewish immigrant to South
>     Africa
> HIS FATHER, the "Zeide" (grandfather)
> JOHANNES and
> PAULUS, Zulu servants

*The Story*

Three characters in this story—Harry, his father, and Paulus—are physically large men, and this is reinforced by the name Dan Jacobson chooses for Harry and his father: Grossman (as gross means "large" in German). However, though Harry has inherited from his father a great strength, the old man is no longer strong and senility has destroyed much of his mental capacity. On the other hand, his "passion for freedom," which causes him constantly to run away from home, is his understandable desire to escape from a household in which he knows that he has no real place.

To Harry, the old man's senile flights are a nuisance, a social embarrassment, and a source of resentment and guilt. The resentment is against a father whose past failures were the reason for which Harry had to work so hard as a young man. When his father, setting off for South Africa, was somehow diverted to Argentina, his wife was forced to go into debt to help him come home. Harry had to work for years to pay off the debt, to finance their passage to South Africa, and, because the old man could not hold a job, to support them when they got there. Because he was forced at an early age to fill his father's economic role, he hates the old man, though he also cannot escape the sense that he owes his father filial affection. His guilt for his failings as a son is submerged in his bitterness about what he considers to have been his father's exploitation. To make matters worse, the old man in his senility demands, "What do you want in my house? . . . Out of my house!"

Harry's Zulu servant Johannes proposes using Paulus, a "raw boy" from the country, who, he claims, is his brother, as a caretaker for the old man. In fact, Paulus may only be his relative or someone from his own village. This close identification of the two Zulus with each other is important in the story because it contrasts with the mutual alienation that characterizes Harry's household. The Jews also were once a tribe, but Harry and his family are incapable of thinking even in family terms, let alone in the tribal terms of Johannes and Paulus. Harry is suspicious of Johannes's suggestion, but he consents because he thinks it would be a fine joke on his father and, because he considers Africans an inferior race, on Paulus as well.

Paulus solves the problem of the old man's constantly running away in the simplest way: He goes with him. The two men wander through the streets of the city together, often getting lost because neither can read street signs, but in a strange way they become friends. The old man calls Paulus Der Schwarzer and Paulus calls him Baas Zeide, using the Yiddish word for grandfather that he has heard Harry's children use. Paulus bathes and dresses the Zeide, trims his hair and beard, and even carries him to bed. Because Paulus clearly cares for the old man as Harry believes he himself should care for him, Harry feels a guilty irritation, yet he enjoys his joke: By reducing his father to the level of Paulus, he has reduced him to the lowest possible level in a racist society. When he makes his cruelty worse by saying that he plans to send Paulus away, he is frustrated by the response of the old man, who merely goes to Paulus's room to sit there with him "for security," as though realizing that Harry would never enter an African's room.

Because of the affection between the Zulu and the Zeide, Harry's rage is also directed at Paulus. Once, when he is accusing Paulus of tiring the old man needlessly by taking him too far—apparently forgetting that Paulus is the follower, not the leader, in the wanderings—he is enraged by Paulus's inability to understand English, accuses him of willfully misunderstanding him, and ridicules his lowly status in society: "You'll always be where you are, running to do what the white baas tells you to do. . . . Do you think I understood English when I came here?"

One day, Harry quarrels with his father when Paulus has the afternoon off. The old man calls for Der Schwarzer, and Harry tries to tell him that Paulus will return. Then he pleads with him to let him do for him what Paulus would do. "Please. . . . Why can't you ask it of me? You can ask me—haven't I done enough for you already?" By now the old man is weeping, as if in grief for the lost Paulus or perhaps in rage at Harry for sending him away at last. Finally Harry leaves him, and his father hysterically runs into the street and is hit and killed by a bicyclist. The argument that led to his father's death is a terrible secret with which Harry is left for the rest of his life.

At the funeral, Harry's wife and children and even Paulus weep for the old man. Harry, however, is unrepentant. He pays off Paulus and tells Johannes to tell him to leave; Johannes must remind the Baas that Paulus also wants his "savings" (wages withheld by the employer to keep a "boy" from wasting his earning on foolish things). When Harry asks contemptuously why Paulus would want to save money, Johannes says, "He is saving, baas . . . to bring his family to this town also." At this point, something cracks in Harry, and on the verge of tears he stares at the two Zulus and with "guilt and despair" cries, "What else could I have done? I did my best."

### Themes and Meanings

This story reveals the preoccupations that appear in much of Jacobson's writing: the conflict between fathers and sons, the experience of Jews in South Africa, and the conflict of the races. Much of its power derives from the reader's realization that, in spite of Harry's obvious cruelty and his family's insensitivity to the grandfather, no one is really to blame for what happens. Harry feels a great guilt for his part in his father's death, but he is himself the victim of the burdensome duty that he has borne all of his life as the head of the family. The Zeide has always been incompetent and foolish, and even as a boy Harry had to fill his father's role. In a sense, the Zeide has always been his child.

At the same time, Paulus, though he is called a "boy" in the racist society of South Africa, is more of a man than Harry and more of a son to the Zeide. Indeed, the Zulu and the Zeide, in spite of their lack of a common language, communicate with each other more than Harry is able to communicate with his father. Harry's household is, in fact, a microcosm of the larger society of South Africa. Harry himself was once a "raw boy" from the country (Europe, in his case) and an outsider; he came to South Africa to make his way and, as Paulus hopes to do, to bring his family after him. Paulus and the Zeide are both victims of the bigotry of Harry's household. Both are wanderers in the streets, scorned by the white men, who look away when they see them because they cannot bear to see the "degradation" of the old man, reduced at the end of his life to the care of a "Kaffir."

It is the realization that he himself is an advanced version of Paulus, a noble and heroic figure toward whom he has always felt only contempt, that breaks him down at the end of the story. Paulus, working mightily to bring his family to town, is a painful reminder to Harry of what he himself once was and an even more painful reminder of his own inability to love.

*Style and Technique*

Jacobson's methods, here as elsewhere in his work, are subtle. The style is quiet, and the language does not reveal, except by inference, the feelings of the author. Jacobson chooses to let scene support characterization, as when he shows the lack of true family bonds in Harry's life by saying that the doors in his house were "curiously masculine in appearance, like the house of a widower." The manner of his writing most resembles that of Anton Chekhov, one of Jacobson's masters. The story is told simply, without comment, and the reader is left to reach his own conclusions about the material.

These methods contribute to the power of the story. The terrible pathos is enhanced by the quiet unfolding of the story, and the three-part plot seems painfully inevitable. The problem of what to do with the old man is defined; the advent of Paulus solves the problem but makes matters worse for Harry; finally, the old man dies and Harry is forced to grieve, not because of the death but because of the realization that he once was what the pathetic Paulus is now. Not that Jacobson tells the reader what Harry realizes. He merely lets Paulus speak, and Harry's response tells the rest. Nothing has happened in a sense, but everything has happened.

*Robert L. Berner*

# GLOSSARY

*Allegory:* Literary mode in which characters in a narrative personify abstract ideas or qualities and so give a second level of meaning to the work, in addition to the surface narrative. Modern examples may be found in Nathaniel Hawthorne's "The Artist of the Beautiful" and the stories and novels of Franz Kafka.

*Allusion:* Reference to a person or event, either historical or from a literary work, which gives another literary work a wider frame of reference and adds depth to its meaning.

*Ambiguity:* Capacity of language to suggest two or more levels of meaning within a single expression, thus conveying a rich, concentrated effect. Ambiguity was defined by William Empson as "any verbal nuance, however, slight, which gives room for alternative reactions to the same piece of language." It has been suggested that because of the short story's highly compressed form, ambiguity may play a more important role in the form than it does in the novel.

*Anachronism:* Event, person, or thing placed outside—usually earlier than—its proper historical era.

*Anecdote:* Short narration of a single interesting incident or event. An anecdote differs from a short story in that it does not have a plot, relates a single episode, and does not range over different times and places.

*Antagonist:* Character in fiction who stands in opposition, or rivalry, to the protagonist.

*Anthology:* Collection of prose or poetry, usually by various writers. Often serves to introduce the work of little-known authors to a wider audience.

*Aphorism:* Short, concise statement that states an opinion, precept, or general truth, such as Alexander Pope's "Hope springs eternal in the human breast."

*Aporia:* Interpretative point in a story that basically cannot be decided, usually as the result of some gap or absence.

*Archetypal theme:* Recurring thematic patterns in literature.

*Archetype:* Term used by psychologist Carl Jung to describe what he called "primordial images," which exist in the "collective unconscious" of humankind and are manifested in myths, religion, literature, and dreams. Now used broadly in literary criticism to refer to character types, motifs, images, symbols, and plot patterns recurring in many different literary forms and works. The embodiment of archetypes in a work of literature can make a powerful impression on the reader.

*Atmosphere:* Mood or tone of a work; it is often associated with setting but can also be established by action or dialogue. The opening paragraphs of Edgar Allan Poe's "The Fall of the House of Usher" and James Joyce's "Araby" provide good examples of atmosphere created early in the works and pervading the remainder of the story.

*Black humor:* General term of modern origin that refers to a form of "sick humor" that is intended to produce laughter out of the morbid and the taboo. Examples are the works of Joseph Heller, Thomas Pynchon, Günter Grass, and Kurt Vonnegut.

*Burlesque:* Work that, by imitating attitudes, styles, institutions, and people, aims to amuse. Burlesque differs from satire in that it aims to ridicule simply for the sake of amusement rather than for political or social change.

*Canon:* Standard or authoritative list of literary works that are widely accepted as outstanding representatives of their period and genre. In recent literary criticism, however, the established canon has come under fierce assault for its alleged culture and gender bias.

*Canonize:* Act of adding a literary work to the list of works that form the primary tradition of a genre or literature in general. For example, a number of stories by female and African American writers previously excluded from the canon of the short story, such as Charlotte Perkins Gilman's "The Yellow Wallpaper" and Charles Waddell Chesnutt's "The Sheriff's Children," have recently been canonized.

*Caricature:* Form of writing that focuses on unique qualities of a person and then exaggerates and distorts those qualities in order to ridicule the person and what he or she represents. Contemporary writers, such as Flannery O'Connor, have used caricature for serious and satiric purposes in such stories as "Good Country People" and "A Good Man Is Hard to Find."

*Character type:* Term that may refer to the convention of using stock characters, such as the *miles gloriosus* (braggart soldier) of Renaissance and Roman comedy, the figure of vice in medieval morality plays, or the clever servant in Elizabethan comedy.

*Classic/Classicism:* Literary stance or value system consciously based on the example of classical Greek and Roman literature. While the term is applied to an enormous diversity of artists in many different periods and in many different national literatures, it generally denotes a cluster of values including formal discipline, restrained expression, reverence of tradition, and an objective rather than subjective orientation. Often contrasted to Romanticism.

*Climax:* Similar to crisis, the moment in a work of fiction at which the action reaches a turning point and the plot begins to be resolved. Unlike crisis, the term is also used to refer to the moment in which the reader's emotional involvement with the work reaches its point of highest intensity.

*Comic story:* Form encompassing a wide variety of modes and inflections, such as parody, burlesque, satire, irony, and humor. Frequently, the defining quality of comic characters is that they lack self-awareness; the reader tends not to identify with them but perceives them from a detached point of view, more as objects than persons.

*Conflict:* Struggle that develops as a result of the opposition between the protagonist and another person, the natural world, society, or some force within the self. In short fiction, the conflict is most often between the protagonist and some strong force either within the protagonist or within the given state of the human condition.

*Conte:* French for tale, a conte was originally a short adventure tale. In the nineteenth century, the term was used to describe a tightly constructed short story. In England, the term is used to describe a work longer than a short story and shorter than a novel.

*Crisis:* Turning point in the plot, at which the opposing forces reach the point that a resolution must take place.

*Criticism:* Study and evaluation of works of literature. Theoretical criticism sets out general principles for interpretation. Practical criticism offers interpretations of particular works or authors.

*Deconstruction:* Literary theory, primarily attributed to French critic Jacques Derrida, which has spawned a wide variety of practical applications, the most prominent being the critical tactic of laying bare a text's self-reflexivity, that is, showing how it continually refers to and subverts its own way of meaning.

*Defamiliarization:* Term coined by the Russian Formalists to indicate a process by which the writer makes the reader perceive the concrete uniqueness of an object, event, or idea that has been generalized by routine and habit.

*Dénouement:* Literally, "unknotting"; the conclusion of a work of drama or fiction, in which a plot is unraveled and a mystery resolved.

*Detective story:* The classic detective story (or mystery) is a highly formalized and logically structured mode of fiction in which the focus is on a crime solved by a detective through interpretation of evidence and clever reasoning. Many modern practitioners of the genre, however, such as Raymond Chandler, Patricia Highsmith, and Ross Macdonald, have placed less emphasis on the puzzlelike qualities of the detective story and have focused instead on characterization, theme, and other elements of mainstream fiction. The form was first developed in short fiction by Edgar Allan Poe; Jorge Luis Borges has also used the convention in short stories.

*Deus ex machina:* Latin, meaning "god out of the machine." In the Greek theater, it referred to the lowering of a god out of a mechanism onto the stage to untangle the plot or save the hero. It has come to signify any artificial device employed for the easy resolution of dramatic difficulties.

*Device:* Any technique used in literature in order to gain a specific effect. The poet uses the device of figurative language, for example, while the prose writer may use the devices of foreshadowing, flashback, and so on, in order to create a desired effect.

*Dialogics:* Theory that fiction is a dialogic genre in which many different voices are held in suspension without becoming merged into a single authoritative voice. Developed by Russian critic Mikhail Bakhtin.

*Didactic literature:* Literature that seeks to instruct, give guidance, or teach a lesson. Didactic literature normally has a moral, religious, or philosophical purpose, or it will expound a branch of knowledge. It is distinguished from imaginative works, in which the aesthetic product takes precedence over any moral intent.

*Diegesis:* Hypothetical world of a story, as if it actually existed in real space and time. It is the illusory universe of the story created by its linguistic structure.

*Doppelgänger:* Double or counterpart of a person, sometimes endowed with ghostly qualities. A fictional *Doppelgänger* often reflects a suppressed side of his or her personality, as in the short stories of E. T. A. Hoffmann. Isaac Bashevis Singer and Jorge Luis Borges, among other modern writers, have also employed the *Doppelgänger* with striking effect.

*Dream vision:* Allegorical form common in the Middle Ages, in which the narrator or a character falls asleep and dreams a dream that becomes the actual framed story. Subtle variations of the form have been used by Nathaniel Hawthorne in "Young Goodman Brown" and by Edgar Allan Poe in "The Pit and the Pendulum."

*Dualism:* Theory that the universe is explicable in terms of two basic, conflicting entities, such as good and evil, mind and matter, or the physical and the spiritual.

*Effect:* Total, unified impression, or impact, made upon the reader by a literary work. Every aspect of the work—plot, characterization, style, and so on—is seen to directly contribute to this overall effect.

*Epiphany:* Literary application of this religious term was popularized by James Joyce in his book *Stephen Hero* (1944): "By an epiphany he meant a sudden spiritual manifestation, whether in the vulgarity of speech or of gesture or in a memorable phase of the mind itself." Many short stories since Joyce's collection *Dubliners* (1914) have been analyzed as epiphanic stories in which a character or the reader experiences a sudden revelation of meaning.

*Epistolary fiction:* Work of fiction in which the narrative is carried forward by means of letters written by the characters.

*Euphony:* Language that creates a harmonious and pleasing effect; the opposite of cacophony, which is a combination of harsh and discordant sounds.

*Existentialism:* Philosophy and attitude of mind that gained wide currency in religious and artistic thought after the end of World War II. Typical concerns of existential writers are human beings' estrangement from society, their awareness that the world is meaningless, and their recognition that one must turn from external props to the self. The novels of Albert Camus and Franz Kafka provide examples of existentialist beliefs.

*Exposition:* Part or parts of a work of fiction that provide necessary background information. Exposition not only provides the time and place of the action but also introduces readers to the fictive world of the story, acquainting them with the ground rules of the work. In the short story, exposition is usually elliptical.

*Expressionism:* Beginning in German theater at the start of the twentieth century, expressionism became the dominant movement in the decade following World War I. It abandoned realism and relied on a conscious distortion of external reality in order to portray the world as it is "viewed emotionally." The movement spread to fiction and poetry.

*Fable:* One of the oldest narrative forms. Usually takes the form of an analogy in which animals or inanimate objects speak to illustrate a moral lesson. The most famous examples are the fables of Aesop, who used the form orally in 600 B.C.E.

*Fairy tale:* Form of folktale in which supernatural events or characters are prominent. Fairy tales usually depict a realm of reality beyond that of the natural world and in which the laws of the natural world are suspended.

*Figurative language:* Any use of language that departs from the usual or ordinary meaning to gain a poetic or otherwise special effect. Figurative language embodies various figures of speech, such as irony, metaphor, simile, and many others.

*Flashback:* Scene that depicts an earlier event; it can be presented as a reminiscence by a character in a story, or it can simply be inserted into the narrative.

*Flat characters:* Term coined by E. M. Forster for fictional characters who neither grow nor change during the course of a narrative and who thus may be easily classified as character types. Their opposite is rounded characters.

*Folktale:* Short prose narrative, usually handed down orally, found in all cultures of the world. The term is often used interchangeably with myth, fable, and fairy tale.

*Form:* Organizing principle in a work of literature, the manner in which its elements are put together in relation to its total effect. The term is sometimes used interchangeably with structure and is often contrasted with content: If form is the building, content is what is in the building and what the building is specifically designed to express.

*Frame story:* Story that provides a framework for another story (or stories) told within it. The form is ancient and was used by Geoffrey Chaucer in *The Canterbury Tales* (1387-1400).

*Framework:* When used in connection with a frame story, the framework is the narrative setting, within which other stories are told. The framework may also have a plot of its own. More generally, the framework is similar to structure, referring to the general outline of a work.

*Genre study:* Concept of studying literature by classification and definition of types or kinds, such as tragedy, comedy, epic, lyrical, and pastoral.

*Gothic genre:* Form of fiction developed in the late eighteenth century that focuses on horror and the supernatural. Examples include Matthew Gregory Lewis's *The Monk: A Romance*, 1796 (also published as *Ambrosio: Or, The Monk*), Mary Wollstonecraft Shelley's *Frankenstein* (1818), and the short fiction of Edgar Allan Poe. In modern literature, the gothic genre can be found in the fiction of Truman Capote.

*Grotesque:* Characterized by a breakup of the everyday world by mysterious forces, the form differs from fantasy in that the reader is not sure whether to react with humor or horror. Examples include the stories of E. T. A. Hoffmann and Franz Kafka.

*Hasidic tale:* Hasidism was a Jewish mystical sect formed in the eighteenth century. The term "Hasidic tale" is used to describe some American short fiction, much of it written in the 1960's, which reflected the spirit of Hasidism, particularly the belief in the immanence of God in all things. Among writers attracted to Hasidic tales are Saul Bellow, Philip Roth, Norman Mailer, and Shmuel Yosef Agnon.

*Hyperbole:* Greek term for "overshooting" that refers to the use of gross exaggeration for rhetorical effect, based on the assumption that the reader will not be persuaded of the literal truth of the overstatement. Can be used for serious or comic effect.

*Imagery:* Often defined as the verbal stimulation of sensory perception. Although the word betrays a visual bias, imagery, in fact, calls on all five senses. In its simplest form, imagery re-creates a physical sensation in a clear, literal manner; it becomes more complex when a poet employs metaphor and other figures of speech to re-create experience.

*In medias res:* Latin phrase used by Horace, meaning literally "into the midst of things." It refers to a literary technique of beginning the narrative when the action has already begun. The term is used particularly in connection with the epic, which traditionally begins *in medias res*.

*Initiation story:* Story in which protagonists, usually children or young persons, go through an experience, sometimes painful or disconcerting, that carries them from innocence to some new form of knowledge and maturity. William Faulkner's "The Bear," Nathaniel Hawthorne's "Young Goodman Brown," Alice Walker's "To Hell with Dying," and Robert Penn Warren's "Blackberry Winter" are examples of the form.

*Interior monologue:* Defined as the speech of a character designed to introduce the reader directly to that character's internal life, the form differs from other monologues in that it attempts to reproduce thought before any logical organization is imposed upon it.

*Interpretation:* Analysis of the meaning of a literary work. Interpretation will attempt to explicate the theme, structure, and other components of the work, often focusing on obscure or ambiguous passages.

*Irrealism:* Term often used to refer to modern or postmodern fiction that is presented self-consciously as a fiction or fabulation rather than a mimesis of external reality.

The best-known practitioners of irrealism are John Barth, Robert Coover, and Donald Barthelme.

*Legend:* Narrative that is handed down from generation to generation, usually associated with a particular place and a specific event. A legend may often have more historical truth than a myth, and the protagonist is usually a person rather than a supernatural being.

*Leitmotif:* From the German, meaning "leading motif." Any repetition—of a word, phrase, situation, or idea—that occurs within a single work or group of related works.

*Literary short story:* Term that was current in American criticism in the 1940's to distinguish the short fiction of Ernest Hemingway, Eudora Welty, Sherwood Anderson, and others from the popular pulp and slick fiction of the day.

*Local color:* Usually refers to a movement in literature, especially in the United States, in the latter part of the nineteenth century. The focus was on the environment, atmosphere, and milieu of a particular region. For example, Mark Twain wrote about the Mississippi region; Sarah Orne Jewett wrote about New England. The term can also be used to refer to any work that represents the characteristics of a particular region.

*Lyric short story:* Form in which the emphasis is on internal changes, moods, and feelings. The lyric story is usually open-ended and depends on the figurative language generally associated with poetry. Examples of lyric stories are the works of Ivan Turgenev, Anton Chekhov, Katherine Mansfield, Sherwood Anderson, Conrad Aiken, and John Updike.

*Malaprop/Malapropism:* Malapropism occurs when one word is confused with another because of a similarity in sound between them. The term is derived from the character Mistress Malaprop in Richard Brinsley Sheridan's *The Rivals* (1775), who, for example, uses the word "illiterate" when she really means "obliterate" and mistakes "progeny" for "prodigy."

*Marginalization:* Process by which an individual or a group is deemed secondary to a dominant group in power and thus denied access to the benefits enjoyed by the dominant group; for example, in the past women were marginalized by men and nonwhites were marginalized by whites.

*Medieval romance:* Medieval romances, which originated in twelfth century France, were tales of adventure in which a knight would embark on a perilous quest to win the hand of a lady, perform a service for his king, or seek the Holy Grail. He had to overcome many obstacles, including dragons and other monsters—magic spells and enchantments were prominent, and the romance embodied the chivalric ideals of courage, honor, refined manners, and courtly love.

*Metafiction:* Fiction that manifests a reflexive tendency, such as Vladimir Nabokov's *Pale Fire* (1962), and John Fowles's *The French Lieutenant's Woman* (1969). The emphasis is on the loosening of the work's illusion of reality to expose the reality of its illusion. Such terms as "irrealism," "postmodernist fiction," and "antifiction" are also used to refer to this type of fiction.

*Metaphor:* Figure of speech in which two dissimilar objects are imaginatively identified (rather than merely compared) on the assumption that they share one or more qualities: "She is the rose, the glory of the day" (Edmund Spenser). The term is often used in modern criticism in a wider sense to identify analogies of all kinds in literature, painting, and film.

*Metonymy:* Figure of speech in which an object that is closely related to a word comes to stand for the word itself, such as when one says "the White House" when meaning the "president."

*Minimalist movement:* School of fiction writing that developed in the late 1970's and early 1980's and that John Barthes has characterized as the "less is more school." Minimalism attempts to convey much by saying little, to render contemporary reality in precise, pared-down prose that suggests more than it directly states. Leading minimalist writers are Raymond Carver and Ann Beattie.

*Modern short story:* Short story form dating from the nineteenth century that is associated with the names of Edgar Allan Poe (who is often credited with inventing the form) and Nathaniel Hawthorne in the United States, Honoré de Balzac in France, and E. T. A. Hoffmann in Germany. In his influential critical writings, Poe defined the short story as being limited to "a certain unique or single effect," to which every detail in the story should contribute.

*Monologue:* Any speech or narrative presented by one person. It can sometimes be used to refer to any lengthy speech, in which one person monopolizes the conversation.

*Motif:* Incident or situation in a story that serves as the basis of its structure, creating by repetition and variation a patterned recurrence and consequently a general theme. Russian Formalist critics distinguish between bound motifs, which cannot be omitted without disturbing the thematic structure of the story, and unbound motifs, which serve merely to create the illusion of external reality. In this sense, motif is the same as leitmotif.

*Myth:* Anonymous traditional story, often involving supernatural beings or the interaction between gods and human beings and dealing with the basic questions of how the world and human society came to be as they are. Myth is an important term in contemporary literary criticism.

*Narrative:* Account in prose or verse of an event or series of events, whether real or imagined.

*Narrative persona:* "Persona" means literally "mask": It is the self created by the author and through whom the narrative is told. The persona is not to be identified with the author, even when the two may seem to resemble each other.

*Narratology:* Theoretical study of narrative structures and ways of meaning. Most all major literary theories have a branch of study known as narratology.

*Narrator:* Character who recounts the narrative. There are many different types of narrators: The first-person narrator is a character in the story and can be recognized by his or her use of "I"; third-person narrators may be limited or omniscient. In the former, the narrator is confined to knowledge of the minds and emotions of one or, at most, a few characters. In the latter, the narrator knows everything, seeing into the minds of all the characters. Rarely, second-person narration may be used.

*Novel:* Fictional prose form, longer than a short story or novelette. The term embraces a wide range of types, but the novel usually includes a more complicated plot and a wider cast of characters than the short story. The focus is often on the development of individual characterization and the presentation of a social world and a detailed environment.

*Novella, Novelette, Novelle, Nouvelle:* Terms for forms of fiction that are longer than a short story and shorter than a novel. *Novella,* the Italian term, is usually used to refer to American works in this genre, such as Joseph Conrad's *Heart of Darkness* (1902) and Henry James's *The Turn of the Screw* (1898). *Novelle* is the German term; *nouvelle,* the French; "novelette," the British. The term "novel" derived from these terms.

*Objective correlative:* Key concept in modern formalist criticism, coined by T. S. Eliot in *The Sacred Wood* (1920). An objective correlative is a situation, an event, or an object that, when presented or described in a literary work, expresses a particular emotion and serves as a precise formula by which the same emotion can be evoked in the reader.

*Oral tale:* Wide-ranging term that can include everything from gossip to myths, legends, folktales, and jokes. Among the terms used by folklorist Stith Thompson to classify oral tales (*The Folktale*, 1951) are *märchen*, fairy tale, household tale, *conte populaire*, novella, hero tale, local tradition, migratory legend, explanatory tale, humorous anecdote, and merry tale.

*Oral tradition:* Material that is transmitted by word of mouth, often through chants or songs, from generation to generation. Homer's epics, for example, were originally passed down orally and employ formulas to make memorization easier. Often, ballads, folklore, and proverbs are also passed down in this way.

*Other:* By a process of psychological or cultural projection, an individual or a dominant group accuses those of a different race or gender of all the negative qualities they themselves possess and then respond to them as if they were "other" than themselves.

*Oxymoron:* Closely related to paradox, an oxymoron occurs when two words of opposite meaning are placed in juxtaposition, such as "wise fool," "devilish angel," or "loving hate."

*Parable:* Short, simple, and usually allegorical story that teaches a moral lesson. In the West, the most famous parables are those told in the Gospels by Jesus Christ.

*Paradox:* Statement that initially seems to be illogical or self-contradictory yet eventually proves to embody a complex truth. In New Criticism, the term is used to embrace any complexity of language that sustains multiple meanings and deviates from the norms of ordinary language use.

*Parataxis:* Placing of clauses or phrases in a series without the use of coordinating or subordinating terms.

*Parody:* Literary work that imitates or burlesques another work or author for the purpose of ridicule. Twentieth century parodists include E. B. White and James Thurber.

*Periodical essay/sketch:* Informal in tone and style and applied to a wide range of topics, the periodical essay originated in the early eighteenth century. It is associated in particular with Joseph Addison and Richard Steele and their informal periodical, *The Spectator.*

*Personification:* Figure of speech that ascribes human qualities to abstractions or inanimate objects.

*Plot:* Manner in which authors arrange their material, not only to create the sequence of events in a play or story but also to suggest how those events are connected in a cause-and-effect relationship. There is a great variety of plot patterns, each of which is designed to create a particular effect.

*Point of view:* Perspective from which a story is presented to the reader. In simplest terms, it refers to whether narration is first person (directly addressed to the reader as if told by one involved in the narrative) or third person (usually a more objective, distanced perspective).

*Postcolonial:* Literary approach that focuses on English-language texts from countries and cultures formerly colonized or dominated by the United States or the British Empire, and other European countries. Postcolonialists focus on the literature of such countries as Australia, New Zealand, Africa, South America, and such cultural groups as African Americans and Native Americans.

*Postmodern:* Although this term is so broad it is interpreted differently by many different critics, it basically refers to a trend by which the literary work calls attention to itself as an artifice rather than a mirror held up to external reality.

*Prose.* Ordinary speech or writing that lacks the metrical form of verse and that characterizes most short stories.

*Protagonist:* Originally, in the Greek drama, the "first actor," who played the leading role. The term has come to signify the most important character in a drama or story. It is not unusual for a work to contain more than one protagonist.

*Pun:* A pun occurs when words that have similar pronunciations have entirely different meanings. The result may be a surprise recognition of an unusual or striking connection, or, more often, a humorously accidental connection.

*Realism:* Literary technique in which the primary convention is to render an illusion of fidelity to external reality. Realism is often identified as the primary method of the novel form; the realist movement in the late nineteenth century coincided with the full development of the novel form.

*Reminiscence:* Account, written or spoken, of remembered events.

*Rhetorical device:* Rhetoric is the art of using words clearly and effectively, in speech or writing, in order to influence or persuade. A rhetorical device is a figure of speech, or way of using language, employed to this end. It can include such elements as choice of words, rhythms, repetition, apostrophe, invocation, chiasmus, zeugma, antithesis, and the rhetorical question (a question to which no answer is expected).

*Romance:* Originally, any work written in Old French. In the Middle Ages, romances were about knights and their adventures. In modern times, the term has also been used to describe a type of prose fiction in which, unlike the novel, realism plays little part. Prose romances often give expression to the quest for transcendent truths.

*Romanticism:* Movement of the late eighteenth and nineteenth centuries that exalted individualism over collectivism, revolution over conservatism, innovation over tradition, imagination over reason, and spontaneity over restraint. Romanticism regarded art as self-expression; it strove to heal the cleavage between object and subject and expressed a longing for the infinite in all things. It stressed the innate goodness of human beings and the evils of the institutions that would stultify human creativity.

*Rounded characters:* Fully realized fictional characters who demonstrate complex and occasionally contradictory attributes, as well as a capacity to grow and change. The opposite of flat characters.

*Satire:* Form of literature that employs the comedic devices of wit, irony, and exaggeration to expose, ridicule, and condemn human folly, vice, and stupidity. Justifying satire, Alexander Pope wrote that "nothing moves strongly but satire, and those who are ashamed of nothing else are so of being ridiculous."

*Setting:* Circumstances and environment, both temporal and spatial, of a narrative. The term also applies to the physical elements of a theatrical production, such as scenery and properties. Setting is an important element in the creation of atmosphere.

*Short story:* Concise work of fiction, shorter than a novella, that is usually more concerned with mood, effect, or a single event than with plot or extensive characterization.

*Signifier/Signified:* Linguist Ferdinand de Saussure proposed that all words are signs made up of a "signifier," which is the written mark or the spoken sound of the word, and a "signified," which is the concept for which the mark or sound stands.

*Simile:* Type of metaphor in which two things are compared. It can usually be recognized by the use of the words "like," "as," "appears," or "seems": "Float like a butterfly, sting like a bee" (Muhammad Ali); "The holy time is quiet as a nun" (William Wordsworth).

*Skaz:* Term used in Russian criticism to describe a narrative technique that presents an oral narrative of a lowbrow speaker.

*Sketch:* Brief narrative form originating in the eighteenth century, derived from the artist's sketch. The focus of a sketch is on a single person, place, or incident; it lacks a developed plot, theme, or characterization.

*Story line:* Events that happen within a story. The story line of a work of fiction differs from the plot, which is the manner in which the events are arranged by the author to suggest a cause-and-effect relationship.

*Stream of consciousness:* Narrative technique used in modern fiction by which an author tries to embody the total range of consciousness of a character, without any authorial comment or explanation. Sensations, thoughts, memories, and associations pour out in an uninterrupted, prerational, and prelogical flow.

*Structuralism:* Structuralism is based on the idea of intrinsic, self-sufficient structures that do not require reference to external elements. A structure is a system of transformations that involves the interplay of laws inherent in the system itself. The structuralist literary critic attempts, by using models derived from modern linguistic theory, to define the structural principles that operate intertextually throughout the whole of literature as well as principles that operate in genres and in individual works.

*Style:* Style is the manner of expression, or how the writer tells the story. The most appropriate style is that which is perfectly suited to conveying whatever idea, emotion, or other effect that the author wishes to convey. Elements of style include diction, sentence structure, imagery, rhythm, and coherence.

*Subjective/Objective:* Terms used in critical theory. Subjective refers to works that express the ideas and emotions, the values and judgments of the authors. Objective works are those that appear to be free of the personal sentiments of authors, who take a detached view of the events they record.

*Symbolism:* Literary movement encompassing the work of a group of French writers in the latter half of the nineteenth century that included Charles Baudelaire, Stéphane Mallarmé, and Paul Verlaine. According to Symbolism, a mystical correspondence exists between the natural and spiritual worlds.

*Tale:* General term for a simple prose or verse narrative. In the context of the short story, a tale is a story in which the emphasis is on the course of the action rather than on the minds of the characters.

*Tall-tale:* Humorous tale popular in the American West; the story usually makes use of realistic detail and common speech, but it tells a tale of impossible events that most often focus on a single legendary, superhuman figure, such as Paul Bunyan or David Crockett.

*Technique:* Both the method of procedure in creating an artistic work and the degree of expertise shown in following the procedure.

*Theme:* Loosely defined as what a literary work means, theme is the underlying idea, the abstract concept, that the author is trying to convey: "the search for love," "the growth of wisdom," or some such formulation.

*Tone:* Strictly defined, tone is the authors' attitudes toward their subjects, their personas, themselves, their audiences, or their societies. The tone of a work may be serious, playful, formal, informal, morose, loving, ironic, and so on; it can be thought of as the dominant mood of a work, and it plays a large part in the total effect.

*Trope:* Literally "turn" or "conversion"; a figure of speech in which a word or phrase is used in a way that deviates from the normal or literal sense.

*Vehicle:* Used with the term "tenor" to understand the two elements of a metaphor. The tenor is the subject of the metaphor, and the vehicle is the image by which the subject is presented. The terms were coined by I. A. Richards.

*Verisimilitude:* Term used in literary criticism referring to the degree to which a literary work gives the appearance of being true or real, even though the events depicted may in fact be far removed from the actual.

*Vignette:* Sketch, essay, or brief narrative characterized by precision, economy, and grace. The term can also be applied to brief short stories, less than five hundred words long.

*Yarn:* Oral tale or a written transcription of what purports to be an oral tale. The yarn is usually a broadly comic tale, the classic example of which is Mark Twain's "Jim Baker's Bluejay Yarn." The yarn achieves its comic effect by juxtaposing realistic detail and incredible events; tellers of the tale protest that they are telling the truth; listeners know differently.

*Bryan Aubrey,*
*updated by Charles E. May*

# BIBLIOGRAPHY

## General Studies

Allen, Walter. *The Short Story in English*. Oxford, England: Clarendon Press, 1981. Historical study of the development of the form in England and the United States. Primarily a series of biographical discussions of authors and summary discussions of stories.

Allende, Isabel. "The Short Story." *Journal of Modern Literature* 20 (Summer, 1996): 21-28. This personal account of storytelling makes suggestions about differences between the novel and the short story, the story's demand for believability, the story's focus on change, the story's relationship to dream, and the story as events transformed by poetic truth.

Averill, Deborah. *The Irish Short Story from George Moore to Frank O'Connor*. Washington, D.C.: University Press of America, 1982. Introductory study of the Irish short story intended primarily for teachers and students.

Aycock, Wendell M., ed. *The Teller and the Tale: Aspects of the Short Story*. Lubbock: Texas Tech Press, 1982. Collection of papers presented at a scholarly conference focusing on various aspects of short fiction, including its oral roots, the use of silences in the text, and realism versus antirealism.

Barth, John. "It's a Short Story" In *Further Fridays: Essays, Lectures, and Other Nonfiction, 1984-1994*. New York: Little, Brown and Company, 1995. Personal account by a "congenital novelist" of his brief love affair with the short story during the writing of *Chimera* (1972) and the stories in *Lost in the Funhouse* (1968).

Bayley, John. *The Short Story: Henry James to Elizabeth Bowen*. New York: St. Martin's Press, 1988. Discussion of some of what Bayley calls the "special effects" of the short-story form, particularly its relationship to poetic techniques and devices. Much of the book consists of analyses of significant stories by Henry James, Ernest Hemingway, Rudyard Kipling, Anton Chekhov, D. H. Lawrence, James Joyce, and Elizabeth Bowen.

Beachcroft, T. O. *The Modest Art: A Survey of the Short Story in English*. London: Oxford University Press, 1968. Historical survey of the major figures of the English short story from Geoffrey Chaucer to Doris Lessing.

Blythe, Will, ed. *Why I Write: Thoughts on the Craft of Fiction*. Boston: Little, Brown, 1998. Essays by various writers about writing fiction including essays on short-story writing by Joy Williams, Thom Jones, and Mary Gaitskill.

Bone, Robert, *Down Home: A History of Afro-American Short Fiction from Its Beginnings to the End of the Harlem Renaissance*. New York: Capricorn Books, 1975. Provides a background for the African American folktale, the Brer Rabbit Tales, and the local-color writers; devotes a chapter each to Paul Laurence Dunbar, Charles Waddell Chesnutt, Jean Toomer, Langston Hughes, and Arna Bontemps.

Bonheim, Helmut. *The Narrative Modes: Techniques of the Short Story*. Cambridge, England: D. S. Brewer, 1982. Systematic and statistical study of the short-story form, focusing on basic short-story techniques, especially short-story beginnings and endings.

Burgess, Anthony. "Anthony Burgess on the Short Story." *Journal of the Short Story in English*, no. 2 (1984): 31-47. Burgess admits that he disdains the short story because he cannot write it. He says that the novel presents an epoch, while the short story presents a revelation. Discusses different types of stories, distinguishing between the literary short story, which is patterned, and the commercial form, which is anecdotal.

Cortázar, Julio. "Some Aspects of the Short Story." *Arizona Quarterly*, Spring, 1982, 5-17. A discussion of the invariable elements that give a good short story its particular atmosphere.

Curnutt, Kirk. *Wise Economies: Brevity and Storytelling in American Short Stories*. Moscow: University of Idaho Press, 1997. Historical analysis of the short story's development as the structuring of the tension between brevity and storytelling. Shows how stylistic brevity as an evolving aesthetic practice redefined the interpretive demands placed on readers.

Current-Garcia, Eugene. *The American Short Story, Before 1850*. Boston: Twayne, 1985. Focuses on the types of magazine fiction before 1820. Devotes individual chapters to Washington Irving, Nathaniel Hawthorne, and Edgar Allan Poe. Also includes a chapter on William Gilmore Simms and the frontier humorists, such as George Washington Harris.

Ferguson, Suzanne C. "Defining the Short Story: Impressionism and Form." *Modern Fiction Studies* 28 (Spring, 1982): 13-24. Argues that there is no single characteristic or cluster of characteristics that distinguishes the short story from the novel; suggests that what is called the modern short story is a manifestation of impressionism rather than a discrete genre.

Firchow, Peter E. "The Americaness of the American Short Story." *Journal of the Short Story in English* 10 (Spring, 1988): 45-66. Examines the common claim that the short story is a particularly American art form. Surveys and critiques a number of critics who have debated the issue; analyzes generic criteria for determining what is a short story, such as self-consciousness and length. Concludes that a short story is simply a story that is short and that the American short story is not unique to America but is merely a story that deals with American cultural contexts.

Flora, Joseph M., ed. *The English Short Story, 1880-1945*. Boston: Twayne, 1985. Collection of essays on a number of British short-story writers during the period, including Rudyard Kipling, D. H. Lawrence, Virginia Woolf, Saki, A. E. Coppard, P. G. Wodehouse, and V. S. Pritchett.

Fusco, Richard. *Maupassant and the American Short Story: The Influence of Form at the Turn of the Century*. University Park: Pennsylvania State University Press, 1994. Argues that Maupassant's influence on the twentieth century short story rivals that of Anton Chekhov.

Gerlach, John. *Toward the End: Closure and Structure in the American Short Story*. Tuscaloosa: University of Alabama Press, 1985. Detailed theoretical study of the

American short story, focusing particularly on the importance of closure, or the ending of the form; examines a number of stories in some detail in terms of the concept of closure.

Hallett, Cynthia J. "Minimalism and the Short Story." *Studies in Short Fiction* 33 (Fall, 1996): 487-495. A discussion of some of the characteristics of so-called minimalism based on analysis of stories by Raymond Carver, Mary Robison, and Amy Hempel.

Hanson, Clare. *Short Stories and Short Fictions, 1880-1980.* New York: St. Martin's Press, 1985. Argues that during the period covered, the authority of the teller, usually a first-person "framing" narrator who guaranteed the authenticity of the tale, was questioned by many modernist writers.

_____, ed. *Re-reading the Short Story.* New York: St. Martin's Press, 1989. Contributions to this collection include essays by Clare Hanson on the poetics of short fiction, Nicole Ward Jouve on the nature of short stories, and David Miall on "text and affect."

Head, Dominic. *The Modernist Short Story.* Cambridge: Cambridge University Press, 1992. Examination of the short story's formal characteristics from a theoretical framework derived from Louis Althusser and Bakhtin.

Iftekharuddin, Farhat, Mary Rohrberger, and Maurice Lee, eds. *Speaking of the Short Story: Interviews with Contemporary Writers.* Jackson: University Press of Mississippi, 1997. Collection of twenty-one interviews on the short story with short-story writers such as Isabel Allende, Rudolfo A. Anaya, Ellen Douglas, Richard Ford, Bharati Mukherjee, and Leslie Marmon Silko and short story critics such as Susan Lohafer, Charles May, and Mary Rohrberger.

Kaylor, Noel Harold, Jr., ed. *Creative and Critical Approaches to the Short Story.* Lewiston, N.Y.: Edwin Mellen Press, 1997. Collection including essays by Suzanne Hunter Brown on the "Chronotope of the Short Story," Suzanne C. Ferguson on local color and setting in English stories, Thomas M. Leitch on the so-called *New Yorker* school, Susan Lohafer on "preclosure" in "open" stories, Charles E. May on obsession, and Hilary Siebert on "outside history."

Kennedy, J. Gerald, ed. *Modern American Short Story Sequences: Composite Fictions and Fictive Communities.* Cambridge: Cambridge University Press, 1995. Anthology of essays by various critics on short-story sequence collections such as Jean Toomer's *Cane* (1923), Ernest Hemingway's *In Our Time* (1924, 1925), William Faulkner's *Go Down, Moses* (1942), John Updike's *Olinger Stories: A Selection* (1964), Sherwood Anderson's *Winesburg, Ohio* (1919), and several others.

Kilroy, James F., ed. *The Irish Short Story: A Critical History.* Boston: Twayne, 1984. Essays organized mostly around periods of Irish writing. Contributors include James F. Carens, Janet Egleson Dunleavy, Robert Hogan, and Gregory A. Schirmer. Kilroy's introduction offers an abbreviated survey of the Irish short story, beginning with Maria Edgeworth's *Castle Rackrent* (1800). The focus is on the relationship between historical and social events in Ireland and the development of fiction in Ireland.

Levy, Andrews. *The Culture and Commerce of the American Short Story.* Cambridge: Cambridge University Press, 1993. Historical survey showing how the short story became an image of American values through political movements, editorial policies, and changes in education.

"Literary Magazine Editors on the State of the Short Story." *Literary Review* 37 (Summer, 1994): 619-649. Editors of a number of literary magazines that publish short fiction discuss future short-story trends, the importance of innovation to the short story, and the relationship between author vision and a good story.

Lohafer, Susan. *Coming to Terms with the Short Story.* Baton Rouge: Louisiana State University Press, 1983. Highly suggestive theoretical study of the short story that focuses on the sentence unit of the form as a way of showing how it differs from the novel.

Lohafer, Susan, and Jo Ellyn Clarey, eds. *Short Story Theory at a Crossroads.* Baton Rouge: Louisiana State University Press, 1989. Broad collection of essays on discourse analysis, definitions, short-shorts, genres, narrative techniques, motivation, and many other subjects. Among the contributors are Helmut Bonheim, Suzanne C. Ferguson, Charles E. May, William O'Rourke, Mary Rohrberger, and Austin Wright.

Lounsberry, Barbara, et al., eds. *The Tales We Tell: Perspectives on the Short Story.* Westport, Conn.: Greenwood Press, 1998. Collection of essays on such subjects as minimalism, cognitive science, "hyperstories," and the origins of the short story by scholars and leading writers, including Ewing Campbell, Mary Rohrberger, Stephen Pett, R. C. Feddersen, Robert Coover, Susan Lohafer, Charles E. May, and Joyce Carol Oates.

May, Charles E. "Artifice and Artificiality in the Short Story." *Story* 1 (Spring, 1990): 72-82. Discusses the artificial and formalized nature of the endings of short stories, arguing that the short story is the most aesthetic narrative form; discusses the ending of several representative stories.

_____, ed. *Critical Survey of Short Fiction.* 2d Rev. ed., Pasadena, Calif.: Salem Press, 2001. Seven-volume reference work that contains detailed profiles of 480 writers, plus essays on the history and theory of short-fiction writing and short fiction in regions of the world. Special research tools include lists of major award-winning stories, a chronology, and an extensive bibliography.

_____. "Prolegomenon to a Generic Study of the Short Story." *Studies in Short Fiction* 33 (Fall, 1996): 461-474. Tries to lay the groundwork for a generic theory of the short story in terms of new theories of genre.

_____. "Reality in the Modern Short Story" *Style* 27 (Fall, 1993): 369-379. Argues that realism in the modern short story from Chekhov to Raymond Carver is not the simple mimesis of the realistic novel but rather the use of highly compressed selective detail configured to metaphorically objectify that which cannot be described directly.

Moser, Charles A., ed. *The Russian Short Story: A Critical History.* Boston: Twayne, 1986. Contributors to this collection including Julian Connolly on later nineteenth and early twentieth century writers, Eva Kagan-Kans on mid-nineteenth century writers, Rudolf Neuhauser on the mid- to late twentieth century, and Victor Terras on the early to mid-nineteenth century.

Orel, Harold. *The Victorian Short Story: Development and Triumph of a Literary Genre*. Cambridge, England: Cambridge University Press, 1986. Contains chapters on Joseph Sheridan Le Fanu, Charles Dickens, Anthony Trollope, Thomas Hardy, Robert Louis Stevenson, Rudyard Kipling, H. G. Wells, and Joseph Conrad. Focuses on the relevant biographical and sociocultural factors and says something about writers' relationships with editors and periodicals.

O'Toole, L. Michael. *Structure, Style, and Interpretation in the Russian Short Story*. New Haven, Conn.: Yale University Press, 1982. Analysis of a few major stories by Nikolai Leskov, Nikolai Gogol, Alexander Pushkin, Maxim Gorky, Ivan Turgenev, and Anton Chekhov, in terms of the Formalist theories of Viktor Shklovsky, Boris Eikhenbaum, Boris Tomashevsky, Mikhail Bakhtin, and Vladimir Propp, and the structuralist theories of Roland Barthes and Tzvetan Todorov.

Palakeel, Thomas. "Third World Short Story as National Allegory?" *Journal of Modern Literature* 20 (Summer, 1996): 97-102. Argues against Frederic Jameson's claim that third-world fictions are always national allegories. Points out that this claim is even more damaging to the short story than to the novel because the short story is the most energetic literary activity in the Third World; argues that Jameson's theory cripples any non-Western literature that tries to deal with the psychological or spiritual reality of the individual.

Pasco, Allan H. "The Short Story: The Short of It." *Style* 27 (Fall, 1993): 442-451. Suggests a list of qualities of the short story generated by its brevity, such as the assumptions of considerable background on the part of the reader and that readers will absorb and remember all elements of the work. Claims that the short story shuns amplification in favor of inference, that it is usually single rather than multivalent, that it tends toward the general, and that it remains foreign to loosely motivated detail.

Peden, Margaret Sayers, ed. *The Latin American Short Story: A Critical History*. Boston: Twayne, 1983. Essays organized around periods of writers by such contributors as John S. Brushwood, Naomi Lindstrom, and George R. McMurray,

Peden, William. *The American Short Story: Continuity and Change, 1940-1975*, 2d ed. Boston: Houghton Mifflin, 1975. Includes chapters on publishing and the short story since 1940; the stories of suburbia by John Cheever, John Updike, and others; stories of physical illness and abnormality by James Purdy, Tennessee Williams, Flannery O'Connor, Joyce Carol Oates; stories by Jewish writers such as Bernard Malamud, Saul Bellow, J. D. Salinger, Grace Paley, Philip Roth, and Isaac Bashevis Singer; stories by black writers such as Langston Hughes, Richard Wright, Ann Petry, and Toni Cade Bambera.

Price, Kenneth M., and Susan Belasco Smith, eds. *Periodical Literature in Nineteenth-Century America*. Charlottesville: University Press of Virginia, 1995. Collection of essays on how periodicals transformed the American literary marketplace between

1830 and 1890. Critics suggest how the development of the periodical as a market for short fiction had a powerful influence on the development of the form as a unique American genre.

Rhode, Robert D. *Setting in the American Short Story of Local Color: 1865-1900.* The Hague: Mouton, 1975. Study of the various functions that setting plays in the local-color story in the late nineteenth century, from setting as merely background to setting in relation to character and setting as personification.

Shaw, Valerie. *The Short Story: A Critical Introduction.* London: Longman, 1983. Desultory discussion of the form, without a theoretical approach and little sympathy for a unified approach to the form. The focus is on British story writers primarily, with one chapter on the transitional figure Robert Louis Stevenson. Other chapters deal with the patterned form to the artless tale form, with chapters on character, setting, and subject matter.

Siebert, Hilary. "Did We Both Read the Same Story? Interpreting Cultural Contexts from Oral Discourses with the American Short Story." *Short Story* n.s. 6 (Spring, 1998). The history of the short story is one of many different types of discourses, both oral and written, blending together. The result of this textual tension and diversity is that educated readers may not be familiar with the variety of discourse conventions and thus read the stories incorrectly.

Sodowsky, Roland. "The Minimalist Short Story: Its Definition, Writers, and (Small) Heyday." *Studies in Short Fiction* 33 (Fall, 1996): 529-540. Historical survey of minimalism's dominance of the short-story marketplace in the late 1970's and early 1980's in the United States. Based on an examination of short stories in such magazines as *The New Yorker, The Atlantic Monthly, Esquire,* and *Harper's* between 1975 and 1990, Sodowsky isolates and summarizes some of the basic characteristics of the minimalist short story.

Stevick, Philip, ed. *The American Short Story, 1900-1945.* Boston: Twayne, 1984. Collection of essays by various critics. Stevick's introduction, a historical overview of the development of the twentieth century short story, is a good introduction to many of the features of the modern short story and how they came about at the beginning of the century. Contributors include Ellen Kimbel on the first decades of the twentieth century, Thomas A. Gullason on the 1920's, James G. Watson on the 1930's and early 1940's, and Mary Rohrberger on regionalism.

Vanatta, Dennis, ed. *The English Short Story, 1945-1980.* Boston: Twayne, 1985. Essays by John J. Stinson on the late 1940's, Dean Baldwin on the 1950's, Jean Pickering on the 1960's, and Walter Evans on the 1970's.

Vischik, Reingard M., and Barbara Korte, eds. *Modes of Narrative.* Wurzburg: Konigshausen and Neumann, 1990. This eclectic collection includes useful essays by Walter Pache on modern English short stories and Franz K. Stanzel on "textual power."

Werlock, Abby H. P., ed. *The Facts on File Companion to the American Short Story.* New York: Facts on File, 2000. Alphabetically arranged entries cover aspects of the American short story from the early nineteenth century to the 1990's. They in-

4775

clude author biographies and bibliographies, plot synopses, character sketches, and major short-story analyses.

Wright, Austin. "The Writer Meets the Critic on the Great Novel/Short Story Divide." *Journal of Modern Literature* 20 (Summer, 1996): 13-19. A personal account by a short-story critic and novelist of some of the basic differences between the critical enterprise and the writing of fiction, as well as some of the generic differences between the short story and the novel.

## Studies of Individual Authors

The seventy-seven authors for whom bibliographies are provided below include every writer who is represented by five or more stories in *Masterplots II: Short Stories Series, Revised*. Also included are several other important writers for whom individual bibliographies were provided in the original *Masterplots II: Short Stories Series*. Additional information on every writer in this list can be found in *Critical Survey of Short Fiction* (2001), which contains articles with annotated bibliographies on 480 short-story writers.

*Conrad Aiken*

Butscher, Edward. *Conrad Aiken: Poet of White Horse Vale*. Athens: University of Georgia Press, 1988.

Hoffman, Frederick J. *Conrad Aiken*. New York: Twayne, 1962.

Seigal, Catharine. *The Fictive World of Conrad Aiken: A Celebration of Consciousness*. De Kalb: Northern Illinois University Press, 1993.

Spivey, Ted R. *Time's Stop in Savannah: Conrad Aiken's Inner Journey*. Macon, Ga.: Mercer University Press, 1997.

Spivey, Ted R., and Arthur Waterman, eds. *Conrad Aiken: A Priest of Consciousness*. New York: AMS Press, 1989.


*Sherwood Anderson*

Campbell, Hilbert H. "The 'Shadow People': Feodor Sologub and Sherwood Anderson's *Winesburg, Ohio*." *Studies in Short Fiction* 33 (Winter, 1996): 51-58.

Campbell, Hilbert H., and Charles E. Modlin, eds. *Sherwood Anderson: Centennial Studies*. Troy, N. Y.: Whitston, 1976.

Ellis, James. "Sherwood Anderson's Fear of Sexuality: Horses, Men, and Homosexuality." *Studies in Short Fiction* 30 (Fall, 1993): 595-601.

Hansen, Tom. "Who's a Fool? A Rereading of Sherwood Anderson's 'I'm a Fool.'" *The Midwest Quarterly* 38 (Summer, 1997): 372-379.

Papinchak, Robert Allen. *Sherwood Anderson: A Study of the Short Fiction*. New York: Twayne, 1992.


*Isaac Babel*

Ehre, Milton. "Babel's *Red Cavalry:* Epic and Pathos, History and Culture." *Slavic Review* 40 (1981): 228-240.

Falen, James E. *Isaac Babel, Russian Master of the Short Story.* Knoxville: University of Tennessee Press, 1974.

Luplow, Carol. *Isaac Babel's Red Cavalry.* Ann Arbor, Mich.: Ardis, 1982.

Mendelson, Danuta. *Metaphor in Babel's Short Stories.* Ann Arbor, Mich.: Ardis, 1982.

Shcheglov, Yuri K. "Some Themes and Archetypes in Babel's *Red Cavalry.*" *Slavic Review* 53 (Fall, 1994): 653-670.

Sicher, Efraim. *Style and Structure in the Prose of Isaak Babel.* Columbus, Ohio: Slavica, 1986.


*James Baldwin*

Leming, David. *James Baldwin: A Biography.* New York: Alfred A. Knopf, 1994.

Porter, Horace A. *Stealing the Fire: The Art and Protest of James Baldwin.* Middletown, Conn.: Wesleyan University Press, 1989.

Sanderson, Jim. "Grace in 'Sonny's Blues.'" *Short Story,* n.s. 6 (Fall, 1998): 85-95.

Sherard, Tracey. "Sonny's Bebop: Baldwin's 'Blues Text' as Intracultural Critique." *African American Review* 32 (Winter, 1998): 691-705.

Standley, Fred L., and Nancy V. Burt, eds. *Critical Essays on James Baldwin.* Boston: G. K. Hall, 1988.

Tsomondo, Thorell. "No Other Tale to Tell: 'Sonny's Blues' and 'Waiting for the Rain.'" *Critique* 36 (Spring, 1995): 195-209.


*John Barth*

Barth, John. "Interview." *Short Story,* n.s. 1 (Spring, 1993): 110-118.

Bowen, Zack. *A Reader's Guide to John Barth.* Westport, Conn.: Greenwood Press, 1994.

Fogel, Stan, and Gordon Slethaug. *Understanding John Barth.* Columbia: University of South Carolina Press, 1990.

Schulz, Max F. *The Muses of John Barth: Tradition and Metafiction from "Lost in the Funhouse" to "The Tidewater Tales."* Baltimore: Johns Hopkins University Press, 1990.

Waldmeir, Joseph J., ed. *Critical Essays on John Barth.* Boston: G. K. Hall, 1980.

Walkiewicz, E. P. *John Barth.* Boston: Twayne, 1986.


*Donald Barthelme*

Klinkowitz, Jerome. *Donald Barthelme: An Exhibition.* Durham, N.C.: Duke University Press, 1991.

Molesworth, Charles. *Donald Barthelme's Fiction: The Ironist Saved from Drowning.* Columbia: University of Missouri Press, 1982.

Olsen, Lance, ed. *Review of Contemporary Fiction* 11 (Summer, 1991).

Patteson, Richard, ed. *Critical Essays on Donald Barthelme.* New York: G. K. Hall, 1992.

Roe, Barbara L. *Donald Barthelme: A Study of the Short Fiction*. New York: Twayne, 1992.

Stengel, Wayne B. *The Shape of Art in the Stories of Donald Barthelme*. Baton Rouge: Louisiana State University Press, 1985.

*Ann Beattie*

Beattie, Ann. "An Interview with Ann Beattie." Interview by Steven R. Centola. *Contemporary Literature* 31 (Winter, 1990): 405-422.

Berman, Jaye, ed. *The Critical Response to Ann Beattie*. Westport, Conn.: Greenwood Press, 1993.

Hansen, Ron. "Just Sitting There Scared to Death." *The New York Times Book Review*, May 26, 1991, 3, 14.

Murphy, Christina. *Ann Beattie*. Boston: Twayne, 1986.

Opperman, Harry, and Christina Murphy. "Ann Beattie (1947-  )."

*Saul Bellow*

Bellow, Saul. "Moving Quickly: An Interview with Saul Bellow." *Salmagundi* (Spring/Summer, 1995): 32-53.

Boyers, Robert. "Captains of Intellect." *Salmagundi* (Spring/Summer, 1995): 100-108.

*The Georgia Review* 49 (Spring, 1995). Special issue on Bellow.

Miller, Ruth. *Saul Bellow: A Biography of the Imagination*. New York: St. Martin's Press, 1991.

Pifer, Ellen. *Saul Bellow Against the Grain*. Philadelphia: University of Pennsylvania Press, 1990.

*Ambrose Bierce*

Butterfield, Herbie. "'Our Bedfellow Death': The Short Stories of Ambrose Bierce." In *The Nineteenth Century American Short Story*, edited by A. Robert Lee. Totowa, N.J.: Barnes & Noble, 1985.

Davidson, Cathy N. *The Experimental Fictions of Ambrose Bierce: Structuring the Ineffable*. Lincoln: University of Nebraska Press, 1984.

Davidson, Cathy N., ed. *Critical Essays on Ambrose Bierce*. Boston: G. K. Hall, 1982.

Schaefer, Michael W. *Just What War Is: The Civil War Writings of De Forest and Bierce*. Knoxville: University of Tennesse Press, 1997.

Woodruff, Stuart C. *The Short Stories of Ambrose Bierce: A Study in Polarity*. Pittsburgh: University of Pittsburgh Press, 1964.

*Heinrich Böll*

Conard, Robert C. *Understanding Heinrich Böll*. Columbia: University of South Carolina Press, 1992.

Crampton, Patricia, trans. *Heinrich Böll, on His Death: Selected Obituaries and the Last Interview*. Bonn: Inter Nationes, 1985.

Macpherson, Enid. *A Student's Guide to Böll*. London: Heinemann Educational Books, 1972.

Reid, J. H. *Heinrich Böll: A German for His Time*. New York: Berg, 1988.

Zachau, Reinhard K. *The Narrative Fiction of Heinrich Böll*. Cambridge, England: Cambridge University Press, 1997.

## Jorge Luis Borges

Aizenberg, Edna, ed. *Borges and His Successors*. Columbia: University of Missouri Press, 1990.

Nunez-Faraco, Humberto. "In Search of *The Aleph*: Memory, Truth, and Falsehood in Borges's Poetics." *The Modern Language Review* 92 (July, 1997): 613-629.

Soud, Stephen E. "Borges the Golem-Maker: Intimations of 'Presence' in 'The Circular Ruins.'" *MLN* 110 (September, 1995): 739-754.

Stabb, Martin S. *Borges Revisited*. Boston: Twayne, 1991.

Yates, Donald A. *Jorge Luis Borges: Life, Work, and Criticism*. Fredericton, Canada: York Press, 1985.

Zubizarreta, Armando F. "'Borges and I,' a Narrative Sleight of Hand." *Studies in 20th Century Literature* 22 (Summer, 1998): 371-381.

## Elizabeth Bowen

Austin, Allan E. *Elizabeth Bowen*. Rev. ed. New York: Twayne, 1989.

Bloom, Harold, ed. *Elizabeth Bowen: Modern Critical Views*. New York: Chelsea House, 1987.

Craig, Patricia. *Elizabeth Bowen*. Harmondsworth, Middlesex, England: Penguin Books, 1986.

Jarrett, Mary. "Ambiguous Ghosts: The Short Stories of Elizabeth Bowen." *Journal of the Short Story in English*, no. 8 (Spring, 1987): 71-79.

Lassner, Phyllis. *Elizabeth Bowen: A Study of the Short Fiction*. New York: Twayne, 1991.

Lee, Hermione. *Elizabeth Bowen: An Estimation*. London: Vision Press, 1981.

## Morley Callaghan

Boire, Gary A. *Morley Callaghan: Literary Anarchist*. Toronto: ECW Press, 1994.

Hoar, Victor. *Morley Callaghan*. Toronto: Copp Clark, 1969.

Marin, Rick. "Morley Callaghan." *The American Spectator* 24 (February, 1991): 36-37.

Morley, Patricia. *Morley Callaghan*. Toronto: McClelland and Stewart, 1978.

Tracey, Grant. "One Great Way to Read Short Stories: Studying Character Deflection in Morley Callaghan's 'All the Years of Her Life.'" In *Short Stories in the Classroom*, edited by Carole L. Hamilton and Peter Kratzke. Urbana, Ill.: National Council of Teachers of English, 1999.

*Truman Capote*

Brinnin, John Malcolm. *Truman Capote: Dear Heart, Old Buddy.* Rev. ed. New York: Delacorte Press, 1986.

Clarke, Gerald. *Capote: A Biography.* New York: Simon & Schuster, 1988.

Garson, Helen S. *Truman Capote: A Study of the Short Fiction.* New York: Twayne, 1992.

Grobel, Lawrence. *Conversations with Capote.* New York: New American Library, 1985.

Inge, M. Thomas, ed. *Truman Capote: Conversations.* Jackson: University Press of Mississippi, 1987.


*Raymond Carver*

Bugeja, Michael. "Tarnish and Silver: An Analysis of Carver's Cathedral." *South Dakota Review* 24, no. 3 (1986): 73-87.

Campbell, Ewing. *Raymond Carver: A Study of the Short Fiction.* New York: Twayne, 1992.

Kesset, Kirk. *The Stories of Raymond Carver.* Athens: Ohio University Press, 1995.

Runyon, Randolph Paul. *Reading Raymond Carver.* Syracuse, N.Y.: Syracuse University Press, 1992.

Saltzman, Arthur M. *Understanding Raymond Carver.* Columbia: University of South Carolina Press, 1988.

Scofield, Martin. "Story and History in Raymond Carver." *Critique* 40 (Spring, 1999): 266-280.


*John Cheever*

Bosha, Francis J. *John Cheever: A Reference Guide.* Boston: G. K. Hall, 1981.

_____, ed. *The Critical Response to John Cheever.* Westport, Conn.: Greenwood Press, 1994.

Hipkiss, Robert. "'The Country Husband': A Model Cheever Achievement." *Studies in Short Fiction* 27 (Fall, 1990): 577-585.

Meanor, Patrick. *John Cheever Revisited.* New York: Twayne, 1995.

O'Hara, James E. *John Cheever: A Study of the Short Fiction.* Boston: Twayne, 1989.


*Anton Chekhov*

Johnson, Ronald J. *Anton Chekhov: A Study of the Short Fiction.* New York: Twayne, 1993.

Lantz, K. A. *Anton Chekhov: A Reference Guide to Literature.* Boston: G. K. Hall, 1985.

McMillin, Arnold. "Chekhov and the Soviet Village Prose Writers: Affinities of Fact and Fiction." *The Modern Language Review* 93 (July, 1998): 754-761.

Martin, David W. "Chekhov and the Modern Short Story in English." *Neophilologus* 71 (1987): 129-143.

Prose, Francine. "Learning from Chekhov." *Western Humanities Review* 41 (1987): 1-14.

Rayfield, Donald. *Anton Chekhov: A Life.* New York: Henry Holt, 1998.


*Kate Chopin*

Brown, Pearl L. "Awakened Men in Kate Chopin's Creole Stories." *ATQ*, n.s. 13, no. 1 (March, 1999).

Koloski, Bernard. *Kate Chopin: A Study of the Short Fiction.* New York: Twayne, 1996.

Seyersted, Per. *Kate Chopin: A Critical Biography.* Baton Rouge: Louisiana State University Press, 1980.

Skaggs, Peggy. *Kate Chopin.* Boston: Twayne, 1985.

Toth, Emily. *Kate Chopin.* New York: William Morrow, 1990.

_____. *Unveiling Kate Chopin.* Jackson: University Press of Mississippi, 1999.


*Joseph Conrad*

Billy, Ted. *A Wilderness of Words: Closure and Disclosure in Conrad's Short Fiction.* Lubbock: Texas Tech University Press, 1997.

DeKoven, Marianne. "Conrad's Unrest." *Journal of Modern Literature* 21 (Winter, 1997/1998): 241-249.

Graver, Lawrence. *Conrad's Short Fiction.* Berkeley: University of California Press, 1969.

Johnson, A. James M. "Victorian Anthropology, Racism, and *Heart of Darkness.*" *Ariel* 28 (October, 1997): 111-131.

Kingsbury, Celia M. "'Infinities of Absolution': Reason, Rumor, and Duty in Joseph Conrad's 'The Tale.'" *Modern Fiction Studies* 44 (Fall, 1998): 715-729.

Stape, J. H. *The Cambridge Companion to Joseph Conrad.* Cambridge, England: Cambridge University Press, 1996.


*A. E. Coppard*

Allen, Walter. *The Short Story in English.* New York: Oxford University Press, 1981.

Bates, H. E. "Katherine Mansfield and A. E. Coppard." In *The Modern Short Story: A Critical Survey.* London: Evensford Productions, 1972.

Beachcroft, T. O. *The Modest Art: A Survey of the Short Story in English.* New York: Oxford University Press, 1968.

Ginden, James. "A. E. Coppard and H. E. Bates." In *The English Short Story, 1880-1945: A Critical History,* edited by Joseph M. Flora. Boston: Twayne, 1985.

O'Connor, Frank. *The Lonely Voice: A Study of the Short Story.* New York: World Publishing, 1962.


*Julio Cortázar*

Alonso, Carlos J., ed. *Julio Cortázar: New Readings.* New York: Cambridge University Press, 1998.

Hernandez del Castillo, Ana. *Keats, Poe, and the Shaping of Cortázar's Mythopoesis.* Amsterdam: John Benjamins, 1981.

Peavler, Terry J. *Julio Cortázar.* Boston: Twayne, 1990.

Stavans, Ilan. *Julio Cortázar: A Study of the Short Fiction.* New York: Twayne, 1996.

Sugano, Marian Zwerling. "Beyond What Meets the Eye: The Photographic Analogy in Cortázar's Short Stories." *Style* 27 (Fall, 1993): 332-351.


*Stephen Crane*

Berryman, John. *Stephen Crane.* New York: William Sloane Associates, 1950.

Colvert, James B. *Stephen Crane.* New York: Harcourt Brace Jovanovich, 1984.

_____. "Stephen Crane and Postmodern Theory." *American Literary Realism* 28 (Fall, 1995): 4-22.

Davis, Linda H. *Badge of Courage: The Life of Stephen Crane.* Boston: Houghton Mifflin, 1998.

Metress, Christopher. "From Indifference to Anxiety: Knowledge and the Reader in 'The Open Boat.'" *Studies in Short Fiction* 28 (Winter, 1991): 47-53.

Wolford, Chester L. *Stephen Crane: A Study of the Short Fiction.* Boston: Twayne, 1989.


*Isak Dinesen*

Bassoff, Bruce. "Babette Can Cook: Life and Art in Three Stories by Isak Dinesen." *Studies in Short Fiction* 27 (Summer, 1990): 385-389.

Donelson, Linda. *Out of Isak Dinesen in Africa: The Untold Story.* Iowa City, Iowa: Coulsong List, 1995.

Migel, Parmenia. *Titania: The Biography of Isak Dinesen.* New York: Random House, 1967.

Mullins, Maire. "Home, Community, and the Gift That Gives in Isak Dinesen's 'Babette's Feast.'" *Women's Studies* 23 (1994): 217-228.

Rashkin, Esther. "A Recipe for Mourning: Isak Dinesen's 'Babette's Feast.'" *Style* 29 (Fall, 1995): 356-374.

Stambaugh, Sara. *The Witch and the Goddess in the Stories of Isak Dinesen: A Feminist Reading.* Ann Arbor: UMI Research Press, 1988.


*Fyodor Dostoevski*

Catteau, Jacques. *Dostoevsky and the Process of Literary Creation.* Translated by Audrey Littlewood. Cambridge, England: Cambridge University Press, 1989.

Frank, Joseph. *Dostoevsky: The Miraculous Years, 1865-1871.* Princeton, N.J.: Princeton University Press, 1995.

Jackson, Robert Louis, ed. *Dialogues with Dostoevsky: The Overwhelming Questions.* Stanford, Calif.: Stanford University Press, 1993.

Mochulsky, K. V. *Dostoevsky: His Life and Work.* Translated by Michael Minihan. Princeton, N.J.: Princeton University Press, 1967.

Straus, Nina Pelikan. *Dostoevsky and the Woman Question: Rereadings at the End of a Century.* New York: St. Martin's Press, 1994.


### Arthur Conan Doyle

Hodgson, John A., ed. *Sherlock Holmes: The Major Stories with Contemporary Critical Essays.* New York: St. Martin's Press, 1994.

Jaffee, Jacqueline A. *Arthur Conan Doyle.* Boston: Twayne, 1987.

Jann, Rosemary. *The Adventures of Sherlock Holmes: Detecting Social Order.* New York: Twayne, 1995.

Kestner, Joseph A. "Real Men: Construction of Masculinity in the Sherlock Holmes Narratives." *Studies in the Literary Imagination* 29 (Spring, 1996): 73-88.

Orel, Harold, ed. *Critical Essays on Sir Arthur Conan Doyle.* New York: G. K. Hall, 1992.

Stashower, Daniel. *Teller of Tales: The Life of Arthur Conan Doyle.* New York: Henry Holt, 1999.


### Andre Dubus

Feeney, Joseph J. "Poised for Fame: Andre Dubus at Fifty." *America* 155 (November 15, 1986): 296-299.

Kennedy, Thomas E. *Andre Dubus: A Study of the Short Fiction.* Boston: Twayne, 1988.

Miner, Madone. "Jumping from One Heart to Another: How Andre Dubus Writes About Women." *Critique* 39 (Fall, 1997): 18-31.

Rowe, Anne E. "Andre Dubus." In *Contemporary Fiction Writers of the South*, edited by Joseph M. Flora and Robert Bain. Westport, Conn.: Greenwood Press, 1993.

Todd, David Yandell. "An Interview with Andre Dubus." *Yale Review* 86 (July, 1998): 89-110.


### Louise Erdrich

Bruchac, Joseph. "Whatever Is Really Yours: An Interview with Louise Erdrich." In *Survival This Way: Interviews with American Indian Poets.* Tucson: University of Arizona Press, 1987.

Coltelli, Laura. *Winged Words: American Indian Writers Speak* Lincoln: University of Nebraska Press, 1990.

Erdrich, Louise. *Conversations with Louise Erdrich and Michael Dorris.* Edited by Allan Chavkin and Nancy Feyl Chavkin. Jackson: University Press of Mississippi, 1994.

Ferguson, Suzanne. "The Short Stories of Louise Erdrich's Novels." *Studies in Short Fiction* 33 (1996): 541-555.

Stone, Brad. "Scenes from a Marriage: Louise Erdrich's New Novel—and Her Life." *Newsweek* 131, no. 12 (March 23, 1998): 69.

*William Faulkner*

Carothers, James. *William Faulkner's Short Stories*. Ann Arbor, Mich.: UMI Research Press, 1985.

Fargnoli, A. Nicholas, and Michael Golay. *William Faulkner A to Z: The Essential Reference to His Life and Work*. New York: Facts on File, 2001.

Ferguson, James. *Faulkner's Short Fiction*. Knoxville: University of Tennessee Press, 1991.

Jones, Diane Brown. *A Reader's Guide to the Short Stories of William Faulkner*. New York: G. K. Hall, 1994.

*The Mississippi Quarterly* 50 (Summer, 1997). Special issue on Faulkner.

Singal, Daniel J. *William Faulkner: The Making of a Modernist*. Chapel Hill: University of North Carolina Press, 1997.


*F. Scott Fitzgerald*

Eble, Kenneth. *F. Scott Fitzgerald*. Rev. ed. Boston: Twayne, 1977.

Gale, Robert L. *An F. Scott Fitzgerald Encyclopedia*. Westport, Conn.: Greenwood Press, 1998.

Lee, A. Robert, ed. *Scott Fitzgerald: The Promises of Life*. New York: St. Martin's Press, 1989.

Mangum, Bryant. *A Fortune Yet: Money in the Art of F. Scott Fitzgerald's Short Stories*. New York: Garland, 1991.

Petry, Alice Hall. *Fitzgerald's Craft of Short Fiction*. Ann Arbor: UMI Research Press, 1989.

Tate, Mary Jo. *F. Scott Fitzgerald A to Z: The Essential Reference to His Life and Work*. New York: Facts on File, 1998.


*Mavis Gallant*

Besner, Neil. *The Light of Imagination: Mavis Gallant's Fiction*. Vancouver: University of British Columbia Press, 1988.

Jewison, Don. "Speaking of Mirrors: Imagery and Narration in Two Novellas by Mavis Gallant." *Studies in Canadian Literature* 10, nos. 1, 2 (1985): 94-109.

Keefer, Janice Kulyk. *Reading Mavis Gallant*. Toronto: Oxford University Press, 1989.

Merler, Grazia. *Mavis Gallant: Narrative Patterns and Devices*. Ottawa: Tecumseh Press, 1978.

Schaub, Danielle. *Mavis Gallant*. New York: Twayne, 1998.

Simmons, Diane. "Remittance Men: Exile and Identity in the Short Stories of Mavis Gallant." In *Canadian Women: Writing Fiction*, edited by Mickey Pearlman. Jackson: University Press of Mississippi, 1993.


*Nikolai Gogol*

Erlich, Victor. *Gogol*. New Haven, Conn.: Yale University Press, 1969.

Fanger, Donald L. *The Creation of Nikolai Gogol*. Cambridge, Mass.: The Belknap Press of Harvard University Press, 1979.

Gippius, V. V. *Gogol*. Translated by Robert Maguire. Ann Arbor, Mich.: Ardis, 1981.
Maguire, Robert A. *Exploring Gogol*. Stanford, Calif.: Stanford University Press, 1994.
Maguire, Robert A., ed. *Gogol from the Twentieth Century: Eleven Essays*. Princeton, N.J.: Princeton University Press, 1974.
Rancour-Laferriere, David. *Out from Under Gogol's "Overcoat": A Psychoanalytic Study*. Ann Arbor, Mich.: Ardis, 1982.

*Nadine Gordimer*

Bazin, Nancy Topping, and Marilyn Dallman Seymour, eds. *Conversations with Nadine Gordimer*. Jackson: University Press of Mississippi, 1990.
Ettin, Andre Vogel. *Betrayals of the Body Politic: The Literary Commitments of Nadine Gordimer*. Charlottesville: University Press of Virginia, 1995.
King, Bruce, ed. *The Later Fiction of Nadine Gordimer*. New York: St. Martin's Press, 1993.
Smith, Rowland, ed. *Critical Essays on Nadine Gordimer*. Boston: G. K. Hall, 1990.
Temple-Thurston, Barbara. *Nadine Gordimer Revisited*. New York: Twayne, 1999.

*Graham Greene*

Bayley, John. "Graham Greene: The Short Stories." In *Graham Greene: A Reevaluation*. New York: St. Martin's Press, 1990.
De Vitis, A. A. *Graham Greene*. Rev. ed. Boston: Twayne, 1986.
Evans, Robert O., ed. *Graham Greene: Some Critical Considerations*. Lexington: University Press of Kentucky, 1963.
Kelly, Richard. *Graham Greene: A Study of the Short Fiction*. New York: Twayne, 1992.
McEwan, Neil. *Graham Greene*. New York: St. Martin's Press, 1988.
O'Prey, Paul. *A Reader's Guide to Graham Greene*. London: Thames and Hudson, 1988.

*Nathaniel Hawthorne*

Bunge, Nancy. *Nathaniel Hawthorne: A Study of the Short Fiction*. New York: Twayne, 1993.
Mackenzie, Manfred. "Hawthorne's 'Roger Malvin's Burial': A Postcolonial Reading." *New Literary History* 27 (Summer, 1996): 459-472.
McKee, Kathryn B. "'A Small Heap of Glittering Fragments': Hawthorne's Discontent with the Short Story Form." *ATQ*, n.s. 8 (June, 1994): 137-147.
Newman, Lea Bertani Vozar. *A Reader's Guide to the Short Stories of Nathaniel Hawthorne*. Boston: G. K. Hall, 1979.
Swope, Richard. "Approaching the Threshold(s) in Postmodern Detective Fiction: Hawthorne's 'Wakefield' and Other Missing Persons." *Critique* 39 (Spring, 1998): 207-227.

*Ernest Hemingway*

Benson, Jackson J., ed. *New Critical Approaches to the Short Stories of Ernest Hemingway*. Durham, N.C.: Duke University Press, 1990.

Berman, Ron. "Vaudeville Philosophers: 'The Killers.'" *Twentieth Century Literature* 45 (Spring, 1999): 79-93.

Dubus, Andre. "A Hemingway Story." *The Kenyon Review*, n.s. 19 (Spring, 1997): 141-147.

Flora, Joseph M. *Ernest Hemingway: A Study of the Short Fiction*. Boston: Twayne, 1989.

Nolan, Charles J., Jr. "Hemingway's Complicated Enquiry in *Men Without Women*." *Studies in Short Fiction* 32 (Spring, 1995): 217-222.

Oliver, Charles. *Ernest Hemingway A to Z: The Essential Reference to His Life and Work*. New York: Facts on File, 1999.


*O. Henry*

Current-Garcia, Eugene. *O. Henry: A Study of the Short Fiction*. New York: Twayne, 1993.

Eichenbaum, Boris. *O. Henry and the Theory of the Short Story*. Translated by I. R. Titunik. Ann Arbor: University of Michigan, 1968.

Evans, Walter. "'A Municipal Report': O. Henry and Postmodernism." *Tennessee Studies in Literature* 26 (1981): 101-116.

Gallegly, Joseph. *From Alamo Plaza to Jack Harris's Saloon: O. Henry and the Southwest He Knew*. The Hague: Mouton, 1970.

Monteiro, George. "Hemingway, O. Henry, and the Surprise Ending." *Prairie Schooner* 47, no. 4 (1973-1974): 296-302.

Stuart, David. *O. Henry: A Biography of William Sydney Porter*. Chelsea, Mich.: Scarborough House, 1990.


*Henry James*

Bell, Millicent. "'The Pupil' and the Unmentionable Subject." *Raritan* 16 (Winter, 1997): 50-63.

Gage, Richard P. *Order and Design: Henry James Titled Story Sequences*. New York: Peter Lang, 1988.

Hocks, Richard A. *Henry James: A Study of the Short Fiction*. Boston: Twayne, 1990.

Horne, Philip. "Henry James and the Economy of the Short Story." In *Modernist Writers and the Marketplace*, edited by Ian Willison, Warwick Gould, and Warren Chernaik. London: Macmillan, 1996.

Martin, W. R., and Warren U. Ober. *Henry James's Apprenticeship: The Tales, 1864-1882*. Toronto: P. D. Meany Publishers, 1994.

Rawlings, Peter. "A Kodak Refraction of Henry James's 'The Real Thing.'" *Journal of American Studies* 32 (December, 1998): 447-462.

*James Joyce*

Benstock, Bernard. *Narrative Con/Texts in "Dubliners."* Urbana: University of Illinois Press, 1994.

Bosinelli, Rosa M. Bollettieri, and Harold F. Mosher, Jr., eds. *ReJoycing: New Readings of "Dubliners."* Lexington: University Press of Kentucky, 1998.

Brunsdale, Mitzi M. *James Joyce: A Study of the Short Fiction.* New York: Twayne, 1993.

Fargnoli, Nicholas, and Michael P. Gillespie. *James Joyce A to Z: The Essential Reference to the Life and Work.* New York: Oxford University Press, 1995.

Leonard, Garry M. *Reading "Dubliners" Again: A Lacanian Perspective.* Syracuse, N.Y.: Syracuse University Press, 1993.

Schwarz, Daniel R., ed. *"The Dead" by James Joyce.* New York: St. Martin's Press, 1994.


*Franz Kafka*

Bloom, Harold, ed. *Franz Kafka.* New York: Chelsea House, 1986.

Boa, Elizabeth. *Kafka: Gender, Class, and Race in the Letters and Fictions.* New York: Oxford University Press, 1996.

Corngold, Stanley. *Franz Kafka: The Necessity of Form.* Ithaca, N.Y.: Cornell University Press, 1988.

Flores, Angel, ed. *The Problem of "The Judgement": Eleven Approaches to Kafka's Story.* New York: Gordian Press, 1976.

Oz, Amos. "A Log in a Freshet: On the Beginning of Kafka's 'A Country Doctor.'" *Partisan Review* 66 (Spring, 1999): 211-217.

Speirs, Ronald, and Beatrice Sandberg. *Franz Kafka.* New York: St. Martin's Press, 1997.


*Rudyard Kipling*

Bauer, Helen Pike. *Rudyard Kipling: A Study of the Short Fiction.* New York: Twayne, 1994.

Hai, Ambreen. "On Truth and Lie in a Colonial Sense: Kipling's Tales of Tale-Telling." *ELH* 64 (Summer, 1997): 599-625.

Orel, Harold, ed. *Critical Essays on Rudyard Kipling.* Boston: G. K. Hall, 1990.

Pinney, Thomas. *In Praise of Kipling.* Austin: Harry Ransom Humanities Research Center, University of Texas at Austin, 1996.

Seymour-Smith, Martin. *Rudyard Kipling.* New York: St. Martin's Press, 1989.


*Mary Lavin*

Hawthorne, Mark D. "Words That Do Not Speak Themselves: Mary Lavin's 'Happiness.'" *Studies in Short Fiction* 31 (Fall, 1994): 683-688.

Kelly, A. A. *Mary Lavin: A Study.* New York: Barnes & Noble Books, 1980.

Neary, Michael. "Flora's Answer to the Irish Question: A Study of Mary Lavin's 'The Becker Wives.'" *Twentieth Century Literature* 42 (Winter, 1996): 516-525.

Peterson, Richard F. *Mary Lavin*. Boston: Twayne, 1980.

Shumaker, Jeanette Roberts. "Sacrificial Women in Short Stories by Mary Lavin and Edna O'Brien." *Studies in Short Fiction* 32 (Spring, 1995): 185-197.

Vertreace, Martha. "The Goddess Resurrected in Mary Lavin's Short Fiction." In *The Anna Book: Searching for Anna in Literary History*, edited by Mickey Perlman. Westport, Conn.: Greenwood Press, 1992.


*D. H. Lawrence*

Bell, Michael. *D. H. Lawrence: Language and Being*. Cambridge, England: Cambridge University Press, 1992.

Black, Michael. *D. H. Lawrence: The Early Fiction*. New York: Cambridge University Press, 1986.

Ellis, David. *D. H. Lawrence: Dying Game, 1922-1930*. New York: Cambridge University Press, 1997.

Harris, Janice Hubbard. *The Short Fiction of D. H. Lawrence*. New Brunswick, N.J.: Rutgers University Press, 1984.

Schneider, Daniel J. *The Consciousness of D. H. Lawrence: An Intellectual Biography*. Lawrence: University Press of Kansas, 1986.

Thornton, Weldon. *D. H. Lawrence: A Study of the Short Fiction*. New York: Twayne, 1993.


*Doris Lessing*

Butcher, Margaret. "'Two Forks of a Road': Divergence and Convergence in the Short Stories of Doris Lessing." *Modern Fiction Studies* 26 (1980): 55-61.

Halisky, Linda H. "Redeeming the Irrational: The Inexplicable Heroines of 'A Sorrowful Woman' and 'To Room Nineteen.'" *Studies in Short Fiction* 27 (Winter, 1990): 45-54.

Pickering, Jean. *Understanding Doris Lessing*. Columbia: University of South Carolina Press, 1990.

Tyler, Lisa. "Our Mothers' Gardens: Doris Lessing's 'Among the Roses.'" *Studies in Short Fiction* 31 (Spring, 1994): 163-173.

Whittaker, Ruth. *Doris Lessing*. New York: St. Martin's Press, 1988.


*Bernard Malamud*

Abramson, Edward A. *Bernard Malamud Revisited*. New York: Twayne, 1993.

Giroux, Robert. "On Bernard Malamud." *Partisan Review* 64 (Summer, 1997): 409-413.

Sío-Castiñeira, Begoña. *The Short Stories of Bernard Malamud: In Search of Jewish Post-Immigrant Identity*. New York: Peter Lang, 1998.

Sloan, Gary. "Malamud's Unmagic Barrel." *Studies in Short Fiction* 32 (Winter, 1995): 51-57.

Watts, Eileen H. "Jewish Self-Hatred in Malamud's 'The Jewbird.'" *MELUS* 21 (Summer, 1996): 157-163.

*Thomas Mann*

Berlin, Jeffrey B., ed. *Approaches to Teaching Mann's "Death in Venice" and Other Short Fiction*. New York: The Modern Language Association, 1992.

Cullander, Cecil C. H. "Why Thomas Mann Wrote." *The Virginia Quarterly Review* 75 (Winter, 1999): 31-48.

Heilbut, Anthony. *Thomas Mann: Eros and Literature*. New York: Knopf, 1996.

Mann, Thomas. *Death in Venice*. Edited by Naomi Ritter. Boston: Bedford Books, 1998.

Reed, T. J. *Thomas Mann: The Uses of Tradition*. New York: Oxford University Press, 1996.

Travers, Martin. *Thomas Mann*. New York: St. Martin's Press, 1992.


*Katherine Mansfield*

Daly, Saralyn R. *Katherine Mansfield*. Rev. ed. New York: Twayne, 1994.

Darrohn, Christine. "'Blown to Bits': Katherine Mansfield's 'The Garden-Party' and the Great War." *Modern Fiction Studies* 44 (Fall, 1998): 514-539.

Hankin, C. A. *Katherine Mansfield and Her Confessional Stories*. New York: St. Martin's Press, 1983.

Nathan, Rhoda B. *Critical Essays on Katherine Mansfield*. New York: G. K. Hall, 1993.

New, W. H. "Mansfield in the Act of Writing." *Journal of Modern Literature* 20 (Summer, 1996): 51-63.


*Guy de Maupassant*

Fusco, Richard. *Maupassant and the American Short Story: The Influence of Form at the Turn of the Century*. University Park: Pennsylvania State University Press, 1994.

Harris, Trevor A. Le V. *Maupassant in the Hall of Mirrors: Ironies and Repetition in the Work of Guy de Maupassant*. Houndmills, England: Macmillan, 1990.

Lloyd, Christopher, and Robert Lethbridge, eds. *Maupassant conteur et romancer.* Durham: University of Durham, 1994.

Sullivan, Edward. *Maupassant: The Short Stories*. Great Neck, N.Y.: Barron's, 1962.

Wallace, Albert H. *Guy de Maupassant*. New York: Twayne, 1973.


*Herman Melville*

Dillingham, William B. *Melville's Short Fiction, 1853-1856*. Athens: University of Georgia Press, 1977.

Levine, Robert S., ed. *The Cambridge Companion to Herman Melville*. Cambridge, England: Cambridge University Press, 1998.

McCall, Dan. *The Silence of Bartleby*. Ithaca, N.Y.: Cornell University Press, 1989.

Newman, Lea Bertani Vozar. *A Reader's Guide to the Short Stories of Herman Melville*. Boston: G. K. Hall, 1986.

Rollyson, Carl, and Lisa Paddock. *Herman Melville A to Z: The Essential Reference to His Life and Work.* New York: Facts on File, 2001.

Updike, John. "The Appetite for Truth: On Melville's Shorter Fiction." *The Yale Review* 85 (October, 1997): 24-47.

*Alice Munro*

Canitz, A. E. Christa, and Roger Seamon. "The Rhetoric of Fictional Realism in the Stories of Alice Munro." *Canadian Literature*, no. 150 (Autumn, 1996): 67-80.

Goldman, Marlene. "Penning in the Bodies: The Construction of Gendered Subjects in Alice Munro's 'Boys and Girls.'" *Studies in Canadian Literature* 15, no. 1 (1990): 62-75.

Mayberry, Katherine J. "'Every Last Thing . . . Everlasting': Alice Munro and the Limits of Narrative." *Studies in Short Fiction* 29 (Fall, 1992): 531-541.

Murphy, Georgeann. "The Art of Alice Munro: Memory, Identity, and the Aesthetics of Connection." In *Canadian Women: Writing Fiction*, edited by Mickey Pearlman. Jackson: University Press of Mississippi, 1993.

Rasporich, Beverly. *Dance of the Sexes: Art and Gender in the Fiction of Alice Munro.* Edmonton: University of Alberta Press, 1990.

*Vladimir Nabokov*

Nicol, Charles, and Gennady Barabtarlo. *A Small Alpine Form: Studies in Nabokov's Short Fiction.* New York: Garland, 1993.

Parker, Stephen Jan. *Understanding Vladimir Nabokov.* Columbia: University of South Carolina Press, 1987.

_____. "Vladimir Nabokov and the Short Story." *Russian Literature Triquarterly*, no. 24 (1991): 63-72.

Shrayer, Maxim D. "Mapping Narrative Space in Nabokov's Short Fiction." *The Slavonic and East European Review* 75 (October, 1997): 624-641.

_____. *The World of Nabokov's Stories.* Austin: University of Texas Press, 1999.

*R. K. Narayan*

Bery, Ashok. "'Changing the Script': R. K. Narayan and Hinduism." *Ariel* 28 (April, 1997): 7-20.

Kain, Geoffrey, ed. *R. K. Narayan: Contemporary Critical Essays.* East Lansing: Michigan State University Press, 1993.

Knippling, Alpana Sharma. "R. K. Narayan, Raja Rao, and Modern English Discourse in Colonial India." *Modern Fiction Studies* 39 (Spring, 1993): 169-186.

Naik, M. K. *The Ironic Vision: A Study of the Fiction of R. K. Narayan.* New Delhi: Sterling, 1983.

Urstad, Tone Sundt. "Symbolism in R. K. Narayan's 'Naga.'" *Studies in Short Fiction* 31 (Summer, 1994): 425-432.

*Joyce Carol Oates*

Bastian, Katherine. *Joyce Carol Oates's Short Stories: Between Tradition and Innovation.* Frankfurt: Verlag Peter Lang, 1983.

Johnson, Greg. "A Barbarous Eden: Joyce Carol Oates's First Collection." *Studies in Short Fiction* 30 (Winter, 1993): 1-14.

_____. *Invisible Writer: A Biography of Joyce Carol Oates.* New York: Penguin Putnam, 1998.

_____. *Joyce Carol Oates: A Study of the Short Fiction.* New York: Twayne, 1994.

Wesley, Marilyn. *Refusal and Transgression in Joyce Carol Oates's Fiction.* Westport, Conn.: Greenwood, 1993.


*Edna O'Brien*

Gillespie, Michael Patrick. "(S)he Was Too Scrupulous Always." In *The Comic Tradition in Irish Women Writers*, edited by Theresa O'Connor. Gainesville: University Press of Florida, 1996.

O'Brien, Edna. "Interview." *Paris Review* 26 (Summer, 1984): 22-50.

O'Brien, Peggy. "The Silly and the Serious: An Assessment of Edna O'Brien." *The Massachusetts Review* 28 (Autumn, 1987): 474-488.

O'Hara, Kiera. "Love Objects: Love and Obsession in the Stories of Edna O'Brien." *Studies in Short Fiction* 30 (Summer, 1993): 317-326.

Shumaker, Jeanette Roberts. "Sacrificial Women in Short Stories by Mary Lavin and Edna O'Brien." *Studies in Short Fiction* 32 (Spring, 1995): 185-197.


*Frank O'Connor*

Evans, Robert C., and Richard Harp, eds. *Frank O'Connor: New Perspectives.* West Cornwall, Conn.: Locust Hill Press, 1998.

McKeon, Jim. *Frank O'Connor: A Life.* Edinburgh: Mainstream Publishing, 1998.

Steinman, Michael. *Frank O'Connor at Work.* Basingstoke: Macmillan, 1990.

Tomory, William M. *Frank O'Connor.* Boston: Twayne, 1980.

Wohlgelernter, Maurice. *Frank O'Connor: An Introduction.* New York: Columbia University Press, 1977.


*Seán O'Faoláin*

Bonaccorso, Richard. *Seán O'Faoláin's Irish Vision.* Albany: State University of New York Press, 1987.

Butler, Pierce. *Seán O'Faoláin: A Study of the Short Fiction.* New York: Twayne, 1993.

Hanley, Katherine. "The Short Stories of Seán O'Faoláin: Theory and Practice." *Eire-Ireland* 6 (1971): 3-11.

Harmon, Maurice. *Seán O'Faoláin.* London: Constable, 1994.

Neary, Michael. "Whispered Presences in Seán O'Faoláin's Stories." *Studies in Short Fiction* 32 (Winter, 1995): 11-20.


*Cynthia Ozick*

Bloom, Harold, ed. *Cynthia Ozick: Modern Critical Views.* New York: Chelsea House, 1986.

Cohen, Sarah Blacher. *Cynthia Ozick's Comic Art: From Levity to Liturgy.* Bloomington: Indiana University Press, 1994.

Friedman, Lawrence S. *Understanding Cynthia Ozick.* Columbia: University of South Carolina Press, 1991.

Kauvar, Elaine M. *Cynthia Ozick's Fiction: Tradition and Invention.* Bloomington: Indiana University Press, 1993.

Pinsker, Sanford. *The Uncompromising Fiction of Cynthia Ozick.* Columbia: University of Missouri Press, 1987.

Strandberg, Victor. *Greek Mind, Jewish Soul: The Conflicted Art of Cynthia Ozick.* Madison: University of Wisconsin Press, 1994.

*Grace Paley*

Arcana, Judith. *Grace Paley's Life Stories: A Literary Biography.* Urbana: University of Illinois Press, 1993.

Bach, Gerhard, and Blaine Hall, eds. *Conversations with Grace Paley.* Jackson: University Press of Mississippi, 1997.

Isaacs, Neil D. *Grace Paley: A Study of the Short Fiction.* Boston: Twayne, 1990.

Meyer, Adam. "Faith and the 'Black Thing': Political Action and Self-Questioning in Grace Paley's Short Fiction." *Studies in Short Fiction* 31 (Winter, 1994): 79-89.

Taylor, Jacqueline. *Grace Paley: Illuminating the Dark Lives.* Austin: University of Texas, 1990.

*Edgar Allan Poe*

Burluck, Michael L. *Grim Phantasms: Fear in Poe's Short Fiction.* New York: Garland, 1993.

Martin, Terry J. *Rhetorical Deception in the Short Fiction of Hawthorne, Poe, and Melville.* Lewiston, N.Y.: Edwin Mellen Press, 1998.

May, Charles E. *Edgar Allan Poe: A Study of the Short Fiction.* Boston: Twayne, 1991.

Suva, Dawn B. *Edgar Allan Poe A to Z: The Essential Reference to His Life and Work.* New York: Facts on File, 2001.

Thoms, Peter. *Detection and Its Designs: Narrative and Power in Nineteenth-Century Detective Fiction.* Athens: Ohio University Press, 1998.

*Katherine Anne Porter*

Fornataro-Neil, M. K. "Constructed Narratives and Writing Identity in the Fiction of Katherine Anne Porter." *Twentieth Century Literature* 44 (Fall, 1998): 349-361.

Liberman, M. M. *Katherine Anne Porter's Fiction.* Detroit: Wayne State University Press, 1971.

Spencer, Virginia, ed. *"Flowering Judas": Katherine Anne Porter.* New Brunswick, N.J.: Rutgers University Press, 1993.

Stout, Janis. *Katherine Anne Porter: A Sense of the Times.* Charlottesville: University Press of Virginia, 1995.

Walsh, Thomas F. *Katherine Anne Porter and Mexico*. Austin: University of Texas Press, 1992.

### J. F. Powers

Evans, Fallon, ed. *J. F. Powers*. St. Louis: Herder, 1968.

Gussow, Mel. "J. F. Powers, Eighty-one, Dies." *The New York Times*, June 17, 1999, p. C23.

Hagopian, John V. *J. F. Powers*. New York: Twayne, 1968.

McCarthy, Colman. "The Craft of J. F. Powers." *Washington Post*, June 12, 1993, p. A21.

Powers, Katherine A. "Reflections of J. F. Powers: Author, Father, Clear-Eyed Observer." *Boston Globe*, July 18, 1999, p. K4.

### V. S. Pritchett

Angell, Roger. "Marching Life." *The New Yorker* 73 (December 22-29, 1997): 126-134.

Baldwin, Dean. *V. S. Pritchett*. Boston: Twayne, 1987.

Pritchett, V. S. "An Interview with V. S. Pritchett." Interview by Ben Forkner and Philippe Sejourne. *Journal of the Short Story in English* 6 (1986): 11-38.

Stinson, John J. *V. S. Pritchett: A Study of the Short Fiction*. New York: Twayne, 1992.

Theroux, Paul. "V. S. Pritchett." *The New York Times Book Review* 102 (May 25, 1997): 27.

### J. D. Salinger

Alexander, Paul. *Salinger: A Biography*. Los Angeles: Renaissance Books, 1999.

Bloom, Harold, ed. *J. D. Salinger: Modern Critical Views:* New York: Chelsea House, 1987.

French, Warren. *J. D. Salinger, Revisited*. Boston: Twayne, 1988.

Pinsker, Sanford. *"The Catcher in the Rye": Innocence Under Pressure*. New York: Twayne, 1993.

Purcell, William F. "Narrative Voice in J. D. Salinger's 'Both Parties Concerned' and 'I'm Crazy.'" *Studies in Short Fiction* 33 (Spring, 1996): 278-280.

### Isaac Bashevis Singer

Alexander, Edward. *Isaac Bashevis Singer: A Study of the Short Fiction*. Boston: Twayne, 1990.

Farrell, Grace, ed. *Critical Essays on Isaac Bashevis Singer*. New York: G. K. Hall, 1996.

_____, ed. *Isaac Bashevis Singer: Conversations*. Jackson: University Press of Mississippi, 1992.

Hadda, Janet. *Isaac Bashevis Singer: A Life*. New York: Oxford University Press, 1997.

Kresh, Paul. *Isaac Bashevis Singer: The Magician of West Eighty-sixth Street*. New York: Dial Press, 1979.

*Jean Stafford*
Goodman, Charlotte. *Jean Stafford: The Savage Heart*. Austin: University of Texas Press, 1990.
Hulbert, Ann. *The Interior Castle: The Art and Life of Jean Stafford*. New York: A. A. Knopf, 1992.
Roberts, David. *Jean Stafford: A Biography*. Boston: Little, Brown, 1988.
Walsh, Mary Ellen Williams. *Jean Stafford*. Boston: Twayne, 1985.
Wilson, Mary Ann. *Jean Stafford: A Study of the Short Fiction*. New York: Twayne, 1996.

*John Steinbeck*
French, Warren. *John Steinbeck's Fiction Revisited*. New York: Twayne, 1994.
Hayashi, Tetsumaro, ed. *Steinbeck's Short Stories in "The Long Valley": Essays in Criticism*. Muncie, Ind.: Steinbeck Research Institution, 1991.
Hughes, R. S. *John Steinbeck: A Study of the Short Fiction*. New York: Twayne, 1989.
Johnson, Claudia Durst, ed. *Understanding "Of Mice and Men," "The Red Pony," and "The Pearl": A Student Casebook to Issues, Sources, and Historical Documents*. Westport, Conn.: Greenwood Press, 1997.
Parini, Jay. *John Steinbeck: A Biography*. New York: Henry Holt, 1995.
Timmerman, John H. *The Dramatic Landscape of Steinbeck's Short Stories*. Norman: University of Oklahoma Press, 1990.

*Robert Louis Stevenson*
Bell, Ian. *Dreams of Exile: Robert Louis Stevenson: A Biography*. New York: Henry Holt, 1992.
Bevan, Bryan. "The Versatility of Robert Louis Stevenson." *Contemporary Review* 264 (June, 1994): 316-319.
Calder, Jenni. *Robert Louis Stevenson: A Life Study*. New York: Oxford University Press, 1980.
McLaughlin, Kevin. "The Financial Imp: Ethics and Finance in Nineteenth-Century Fiction." *Novel* 29 (Winter, 1996): 165-183.
McLynn, Frank. *Robert Louis Stevenson: A Biography*. New York: Random House, 1995.

*Peter Taylor*
Robinson, Clayton. "Peter Taylor." In *Literature of Tennessee*, edited by Ray Willbanks. Rome, Ga.: Mercer University Press, 1984.
Robison, James C. *Peter Taylor: A Study of the Short Fiction*. Boston: Twayne, 1987.
Samarco, C. Vincent. "Taylor's 'The Old Forest.'" *The Explicator* 57 (Fall, 1998): 51-53.

Stephens, C. Ralph, and Lynda B. Salamon, eds. *The Craft of Peter Taylor.* Tuscaloosa: University of Alabama Press, 1995.

Taylor, Peter. "Interview with Peter Taylor." Interview by J. H. E. Paine. *Journal of the Short Story in English* 9 (Fall, 1987): 14-35.

### Dylan Thomas

Ackerman, John. *Dylan Thomas: His Life and Work.* New York: St. Martin's Press, 1996.

Davies, James A. *A Reference Companion to Dylan Thomas.* Westport, Conn.: Greenwood Press, 1998.

FitzGibbon, Constantine. *The Life of Dylan Thomas.* London: J. M. Dent & Sons, 1965.

Kidder, Rushworth M. *Dylan Thomas: The Country of the Spirit.* Princeton, N.J.: Princeton University Press, 1973.

Tindall, William York. *A Reader's Guide to Dylan Thomas.* Syracuse, N.Y.: Syracuse University Press, 1996.

### Leo Tolstoy

Christian, R. F. *Tolstoy: A Critical Introduction.* Cambridge, England: Cambridge University Press, 1969.

Jahn, Gary R. *The Death of Ivan Ilich: An Interpretation.* New York: Twayne, 1993.

Orwin, Donna Tussig. *Tolstoy's Art and Thought, 1847-1880.* Princeton, N.J.: Princeton University Press, 1993.

Seifrid, Thomas. "Gazing on Life's Page: Perspectival Vision in Tolstoy." *PMLA* 113 (May, 1998): 436-448.

Steiner, George. *Tolstoy or Dostoevsky: An Essay in the Old Criticism.* 2d ed. New Haven, Conn.: Yale University Press, 1996.

### William Trevor

Bonaccorso, Richard. "William Trevor's Martyrs for Truth." *Studies in Short Fiction* 34 (Winter, 1997): 113-118.

Haughey, Jim. "Joyce and Trevor's Dubliners: The Legacy of Colonialism." *Studies in Short Fiction* 32 (Summer, 1995): 355-365.

MacKenna, Dolores. *William Trevor: The Writer and His Work.* Dublin: New Island, 1999.

Paulson, Suzanne Morrow. *William Trevor: A Study of the Short Fiction.* New York: Twayne, 1993.

Rhodes, Robert E. "William Trevor's Stories of the Troubles." In *Contemporary Irish Writing*, edited by James D. Brophy and Raymond D. Porter. Boston: Twayne, 1983.

### Ivan Turgenev

Allen, Elizabeth Cheresh. *Beyond Realism: Turgenev's Poetics of Secular Salvation.* Stanford, Calif.: Stanford University Press, 1992.

Brouwer, Sander. *Character in the Short Prose of Ivan Sergeevic Turgenev.* Atlanta: Rodopi, 1996.

Knowles, A. V. *Ivan Turgenev.* Boston: Twayne, 1988.

Seeley, Frank Friedeberg. *Turgenev: A Reading of His Fiction.* New York: Cambridge University Press, 1991.

Sheidley, William E. "'Born in Imitation of Someone Else': Reading Turgenev's 'Hamlet of the Shchigrovsky District' as a Version of Hamlet." *Studies in Short Fiction* 27 (Summer, 1990): 391-398.

*Mark Twain*

Camfield, Gregg. *The Oxford Reader's Companion to Mark Twain.* New York: Oxford University Press, 2002.

Messent, Peter B. *The Short Works of Mark Twain: A Critical Study.* Philadelphia: University of Pennsylvania Press, 2001.

Rasmussen, R. Kent. *Mark Twain A to Z: The Essential Reference to His Life and Writings.* 2d ed. New York: Facts on File, 2004.

Sloane, David E. E. *Student Companion to Mark Twain.* New York: Greenwood Press, 2001.

Wilson, James D. *A Reader's Guide to the Short Stories of Mark Twain.* Boston: G. K. Hall, 1987.

Wonham, Henry B. *Mark Twain and the Art of the Tall Tale.* New York: Oxford University Press, 1993.

*John Updike*

Hunt, George W. *John Updike and the Three Secret Things: Sex, Religion, and Art.* Grand Rapids, Mich.: Wm. B. Eerdmans, 1980.

Luscher, Robert M. *John Updike: A Study of the Short Fiction.* New York: Twayne, 1993.

Macnaughton, William R., ed. *Critical Essays on John Updike.* Boston: G. K. Hall, 1982.

Newman, Judie. *John Updike.* New York: St. Martin's Press, 1988.

Schiff, James A. *John Updike Revisited.* New York: Twayne, 1998.

*Alice Walker*

Bauer, Margaret D. "Alice Walker: Another Southern Writer Criticizing Codes Not Put to 'Everyday Use.'" *Studies in Short Fiction* 29 (Spring, 1992): 143-151.

Bloxham, Laura J. "Alice [Malsenior] Walker." In *Contemporary Fiction Writers of the South*, edited by Joseph M. Flora and Robert Bain. Westport, Conn.: Greenwood Press, 1993.

Gates, Henry Louis, Jr., and K. A. Appiah. *Alice Walker: Critical Perspectives Past and Present.* New York: Amistad, 1993.

Petry, Alice Hall. "Walker: The Achievement of the Short Fiction." In *Alice Walker:*

*Critical Perspectives Past and Present*, edited by Henry Louis Gates, Jr., and K. A. Appiah. New York: Amistad, 1993.

Wade-Gayles, Gloria. "Black, Southern, Womanist: The Genius of Alice Walker." In *Southern Women Writers: The New Generation*, edited by Tonette Bond Inge. Tuscaloosa: University of Alabama Press, 1990.

*Eudora Welty*

*Georgia Review* 53 (Spring, 1999). Special issue on Welty.

Kaplansky, Leslie A. "Cinematic Rhythms in the Short Fiction of Eudora Welty." *Studies in Short Fiction* 33 (Fall, 1996): 579-589.

*Mississippi Quarterly* 50 (Fall, 1997). Special issue on Welty.

Waldron, Ann. *Eudora Welty: A Writer's Life*. New York: Doubleday, 1998.

Weston, Ruth D. *Gothic Traditions and Narrative Techniques in the Fiction of Eudora Welty*. Baton Rouge: Louisiana State University Press, 1994.

*Tennessee Williams*

Leverich, Lyle. *The Unknown Tennessee Williams*. New York: Crown Publishers, 1995.

Martin, Robert A., ed. *Critical Essays on Tennessee Williams*. New York: G. K. Hall, 1997.

Roudané, Matthew C., ed. *The Cambridge Companion to Tennessee Williams*. Cambridge, England: Cambridge University Press, 1997.

Spoto, Gary. *The Kindness of Strangers: The Life of Tennessee Williams*. Boston: Little, Brown, 1985.

Vannatta, Dennis. *Tennessee Williams: A Study of the Short Fiction*. Boston: Twayne, 1988.

*Thomas Wolfe*

Bentz, Joseph. "The Influence of Modernist Structure in the Short Fiction of Thomas Wolfe." *Studies in Short Fiction* 31 (Spring, 1994): 149-162.

Bloom, Harold, ed. *Thomas Wolfe*. New York: Chelsea House, 1987.

Field, Leslie A., ed. *Thomas Wolfe: Three Decades of Criticism*. New York: New York University Press, 1968.

Idol, John Lane, Jr. *A Thomas Wolfe Companion*. New York: Greenwood Press, 1987.

Phillipson, John S., ed. *Critical Essays on Thomas Wolfe*. Boston: G. K. Hall, 1985.

*Charles E. May and the Editors*

# CHRONOLOGICAL LIST OF TITLES

The 1,490 stories covered in *Masterplots II: Short Stories Series, Revised Edition* are listed below in order of their first years of publication. Note that several stories were published for the first time well after their authors died. More complete information can be found in the articles, which are arranged alphabetically by story title.

**1706**

Defoe, Daniel. "A True Relation of the Apparition of One Mrs. Veal"

**1805**

Brown, Charles Brockden. "Somnambulism"

**1807**

Kleist, Heinrich von. "The Earthquake in Chile"

**1808**

Kleist, Heinrich von. "The Marquise of O——"

**1809**

Hoffmann, E. T. A. "Ritter Gluck"

**1810**

Kleist, Heinrich von. "The Beggarwoman of Locarno"

**1811**

Kleist, Heinrich von. "The Engagement in Santo Domingo"

**1815**

Hoffmann, E. T. A. "A New Year's Eve Adventure"

**1816**

Hoffmann, E. T. A. "The Sandman"

**1819**

Hoffmann, E. T. A. "The Story of Serapion"

Irving, Washington. "Rip Van Winkle"

**1820**

Irving, Washington. "The Legend of Sleepy Hollow"

**1824**

Austin, William. "Peter Rugg, the Missing Man"

Irving, Washington. "Adventure of the German Student"

_____. "The Devil and Tom Walker"

Scott, Sir Walter. "Wandering Willie's Tale"

**1827**

Scott, Sir Walter. "The Two Drovers"

**1829**

Mérimée, Prosper. "Mateo Falcone"

**1830**

Balzac, Honoré de. "Gobseck"

Carleton, William. "The Donagh"

_____. "Wildgoose Lodge"

**1831**

Balzac, Honoré de. "The Unknown Masterpiece"

Hawthorne, Nathaniel. "My Kinsman, Major Molineux"

Flaubert, Gustave. "Hérodias"
_____. "Legend of St. Julian,
Hospitaler, The"
_____. "A Simple Heart"
Stevenson, Robert Louis. "A Lodging
for the Night"
Woolson, Constance Fenimore.
"Rodman the Keeper"

## 1878

Stevenson, Robert Louis. "The Suicide
Club"

## 1879

Twain, Mark. "Jim Baker's Bluejay
Yarn"

## 1880

Harris, Joel Chandler. "The Sad Fate of
Mr. Fox"
_____. "The Wonderful Tar-Baby Story"
Maupassant, Guy de. "Boule de Suif"
Verga, Giovanni. "The She-Wolf"

## 1881

Leskov, Nikolai. "Lefty"
Machado de Assis, Joaquim Maria.
"The Psychiatrist"
Maupassant, Guy de. "A Family
Affair"
_____. "Madame Tellier's
Establishment"

## 1882

Maupassant, Guy de. "Mademoiselle
Fifi"
Stevenson, Robert Louis. "The Sire de
Malétroit's Door"
Stockton, Frank R. "The Lady or the
Tiger?"

## 1883

Hardy, Thomas. "The Three Strangers"

Maupassant, Guy de. "The Piece of
String"
Verga, Giovanni. "Consolation"
Villiers De L'Isle-Adam, Auguste.
"The Desire to Be a Man"

## 1884

Maupassant, Guy de. "The Necklace"

## 1885

Kipling, Rudyard. "The Strange Ride
of Morrowbie Jukes"
Maupassant, Guy de. "Two Little
Soldiers"

## 1886

Chekhov, Anton. "The Chemist's Wife"
_____. "Easter Eve"
_____. "Misery"
_____. "A Trifling Occurrence"
_____. "Vanka"
Jewett, Sarah Orne. "A White Heron"
Kipling, Rudyard. "Lispeth"
Maupassant, Guy de. "The Horla"
Tolstoy, Leo. "The Death of Ivan
Ilyich"
_____. "How Much Land Does a Man
Need?"
_____. "The Three Hermits"

## 1887

Chekhov, Anton. "Enemies"
_____. "The Kiss"
Jewett, Sarah Orne. "The Courting of
Sister Wisby"
Maupassant, Guy de. "Love"
Stevenson, Robert Louis. "Markheim"

## 1888

Chekhov, Anton. "The Bet"
_____. "The Steppe"
Chesnutt, Charles Waddell. "The
Goophered Grapevine"

## 1897

Conrad, Joseph. "An Outpost of
   Progress"
Mann, Thomas. "Little Herr
   Friedemann"

## 1898

Chekhov, Anton. "Gooseberries"
_____. "The Man in a Case"
Chesnutt, Charles Waddell. "The Wife
   of His Youth"
Conrad, Joseph. "The Lagoon"
Crane, Stephen. "The Blue Hotel"
_____. "The Bride Comes to Yellow
   Sky"
_____. "Death and the Child"
_____. "The Monster"
_____. "The Open Boat"
Hearn, Lafcadio. "The Boy Who Drew
   Cats"
James, Henry. "In the Cage"
Wells, H. G. "The Man Who Could
   Work Miracles"

## 1899

Chekhov, Anton. "The Darling"
_____. "The Lady with the Dog"
Chesnutt, Charles Waddell. "The
   Passing of Grandison"
_____. "The Sheriff's Children"
Crane, Stephen. "An Episode of War"
Gorky, Maxim. "Twenty-six Men and a
   Girl"
James, Henry. "Europe"
Twain, Mark. "The Man That
   Corrupted Hadleyburg"

## 1900

Crane, Stephen. "The Upturned Face"
Gissing, George. "The House of
   Cobwebs"
James, Henry. "The Great Good Place"
_____. "The Tree of Knowledge"

## 1902

Chekhov, Anton. "The Bishop"
Conrad, Joseph. "Typhoon"
_____. "Youth"
Jacobs, W. W. "The Monkey's Paw"
Kipling, Rudyard. "Wireless"
London, Jack. "To Build a Fire"
Mann, Thomas. "Gladius Dei"
Norris, Frank. "A Deal in Wheat"

## 1903

Conrad, Joseph. "Amy Foster"
Doyle, Arthur Conan. "The Adventure
   of the Dancing Men"
James, Henry. "The Beast in the
   Jungle"
Mann, Thomas. "The Infant Prodigy"
_____. "Tonio Kröger"
_____. "Tristan"
Moore, George. "Home Sickness"
_____. "Julia Cahill's Curse"
_____. "So On He Fares"

## 1904

Dunbar, Paul Laurence. "The
   Scapegoat"
Forster, E. M. "The Other Side of the
   Hedge"
_____. "The Road from Colonus"
France, Anatole. "Putois"
Henry, O. "The Furnished Room"
James, M. R. "'Oh, Whistle, and I'll
   Come to You, My Lad'"
Joyce, James. "Eveline"
_____. "The Sisters"
Kipling, Rudyard. "They"
Unamuno Y Jugo, Miguel De. "The
   Madness of Doctor Montarco"
Wells, H. G. "The Country of the
   Blind"
Wharton, Edith. "The Other Two"

**1905**

Cather, Willa. "Paul's Case"

_____. "The Sculptor's Funeral"

Futrelle, Jacques. "The Problem of Cell Thirteen"

Henry, O. "The Gift of the Magi"

Howells, William Dean. "Editha"

**1906**

Andreyev, Leonid. "Lazarus"

Henry, O. "Mammon and the Archer"

Kuprin, Aleksandr Ivanovich. "The Outrage"

**1907**

Blackwood, Algernon. "The Willows"

Henry, O. "The Ransom of Red Chief"

Walser, Robert. "Kleist in Thun"

**1908**

Conrad, Joseph. "Il Conde"

Dunsany, Lord. "The Ghosts"

James, Henry. "The Jolly Corner"

Lagerlöf, Selma. "The Silver Mine"

**1909**

Freeman, Mary E. Wilkins. "Old Woman Magoun"

Henry, O. "A Municipal Report"

Sui Sin Far. "In the Land of the Free"

**1910**

Dunsany, Lord. "Idle Days on the Yann"

Galsworthy, John. "The Japanese Quince"

**1911**

Chesterton, G. K. "The Blue Cross"

_____. "The Hammer of God"

_____. "The Invisible Man"

Forster, E. M. "The Celestial Omnibus"

Lawrence, D. H. "Odour of Chrysanthemums"

London, Jack. "A Piece of Steak"

Onions, Oliver. "The Beckoning Fair One"

Saki. "The Schartz-Metterklume Method"

_____. "Sredni Vashtar"

Tolstoy, Leo. "Alyosha the Pot"

**1912**

Beerbohm, Max. "The Mote in the Middle Distance, H*nry J*m*s"

Conrad, Joseph. "The Secret Sharer"

Mann, Thomas. "Death in Venice"

Mansfield, Katherine. "The Woman at the Store"

Saki. "Laura"

**1913**

Aleichem, Sholom. "On Account of a Hat"

Hesse, Hermann. "The Poet"

**1914**

Joyce, James. "Araby"

_____. "The Boarding House"

_____. "Clay"

_____. "Counterparts"

_____. "The Dead"

_____. "Grace"

_____. "Ivy Day in the Committee Room"

_____. "A Little Cloud"

_____. "A Painful Case"

_____. "Two Gallants"

Lawrence, D. H. "The Prussian Officer"

_____. "The White Stocking"

Saki. "The Open Window"

West, Rebecca. "Indissoluble Matrimony"

**1915**

Akutagawa, Ryūnosuke. "Rashōmon"

Benn, Gottfried. "Brains"

Bunin, Ivan. "The Gentleman from San Francisco"
Kafka, Franz. "The Metamorphosis"
Lardner, Ring. "Harmony"

**1916**
Cobb, Irvin S. "Dogged Underdog"
Dreiser, Theodore. "The Lost Phoebe"

**1917**
Conrad, Joseph. "The Tale"
Kafka, Franz. "Jackals and Arabs"
_____. "A Report to an Academy"
Mansfield, Katherine. "Prelude"
Walser, Robert. "The Walk"
Woolf, Virginia. "The Mark on the Wall"

**1918**
Ferber, Edna. "The Three of Them"
Mansfield, Katherine. "Bliss"

**1919**
Anderson, Sherwood. "Hands"
_____. "Sophistication"
Kafka, Franz. "A Country Doctor"
_____. "In the Penal Colony"
Lawrence, D. H. "Tickets, Please"
Pirandello, Luigi. "War"
Saki. "The Interlopers"
Yezierska, Anzia. "The Fat of the Land"

**1920**
Beerbohm, Max. "Enoch Soames"
Cather, Willa. "Coming, Aphrodite"
_____. "Neighbor Rosicky"
Fitzgerald, F. Scott. "May Day"
Hesse, Hermann. "Within and Without"
Mansfield, Katherine. "Miss Brill"
Quiroga, Horacio. "The Dead Man"
Sinclair, May. "The Bambino"
Steele, Wilbur Daniel. "Footfalls"

**1921**
Anderson, Sherwood. "The Egg"
_____. "I Want to Know Why"
Coppard, A. E. "Adam and Eve and Pinch Me"
_____. "Arabesque the Mouse"
Lardner, Ring. "Some Like Them Cold"
Mansfield, Katherine. "The Daughters of the Late Colonel"
_____. "Her First Ball"
Maugham, W. Somerset. "Rain"
Woolf, Virginia. "A Haunted House"

**1922**
Aiken, Conrad. "The Dark City"
Akutagawa, Ryūnosuke. "In a Grove"
Anderson, Sherwood. "I'm a Fool"
Fitzgerald, F. Scott. "The Diamond as Big as the Ritz"
Huxley, Aldous. "The Gioconda Smile"
Kafka, Franz. "A Hunger Artist"
Lardner, Ring. "The Golden Honeymoon"
Lawrence, D. H. "The Blind Man"
_____. "The Horse Dealer's Daughter"
Mansfield, Katherine. "At the Bay"
_____. "The Fly"
_____. "The Garden-Party"
_____. "Marriage à la Mode"
Pasternak, Boris. "The Childhood of Luvers"
Porter, Katherine Anne. "María Concepción"
Toomer, Jean. "Fern"

**1923**
Anderson, Sherwood. "The Man Who Became a Woman"
Babel, Isaac. "How It Was Done in Odessa"
De La Mare, Walter. "Seaton's Aunt"
Fisher, Rudolph. "Miss Cynthie"

Čapek, Karel. "The Last Judgment"
Lovecraft, H. P. "The Dunwich Horror"
Parker, Dorothy. "Big Blonde"
Porter, Katherine Anne. "Theft"

**1930**

Asturias, Miguel Ángel. "Tatuana's
    Tale"
Bowen, Elizabeth. "Her Table Spread"
Faulkner, William. "Red Leaves"
_____. "A Rose for Emily"
Mann, Thomas. "Mario and the
    Magician"
March, William. "The Little Wife"
Perelman, S. J. "The Love Decoy"
Porter, Katherine Anne. "Flowering
    Judas"
_____. "The Jilting of Granny
    Weatherall"

**1931**

Babel, Isaac. "In the Basement"
Faulkner, William. "Dry September"
_____. "Spotted Horses"
_____. "That Evening Sun"
Fitzgerald, F. Scott. "Babylon
    Revisited"
Gordon, Caroline. "The Ice House"
Kafka, Franz. "The Burrow"
_____. "The Great Wall of China"
_____. "The Hunter Gracchus"
Maugham, W. Somerset. "The Alien
    Corn"
O'Connor, Frank. "Guests of the
    Nation"

**1932**

Agnon, Shmuel Yosef. "The Kerchief"
_____. "Impulse"
_____. "Silent Snow, Secret Snow"
Babel, Isaac. "Guy de Maupassant"
Beckett, Samuel. "Dante and the
    Lobster"

Callaghan, Morley. "A Sick Call"
Dunsany, Lord. "The Two Bottles of
    Relish"
Fitzgerald, F. Scott. "Crazy Sunday"
Hemingway, Ernest. "After the Storm"
McKay, Claude. "Truant"
O'Faoláin, Seán. "Midsummer Night
    Madness"
Steele, Wilbur Daniel. "How Beautiful
    with Shoes"

**1933**

Agnon, Shmuel Yosef. "A Whole
    Loaf"
Bontemps, Arna. "A Summer
    Tragedy"
Gordon, Caroline. "Old Red"
Hemingway, Ernest. "A Clean, Well-
    Lighted Place"
Hurston, Zora Neale. "The Gilded Six-
    Bits"
Plomer, William. "The Child of Queen
    Victoria"
Steinbeck, John. "The Gift"
Wharton, Edith. "Roman Fever"

**1934**

Bates, H. E. "The Gleaner"
Dinesen, Isak. "The Deluge at
    Norderney"
_____. "The Monkey"
_____. "The Supper at Elsinore"
Faulkner, William. "Wash"
Hall, Radclyffe. "Miss Ogilvy Finds
    Herself"
Saroyan, William. "The Daring Young
    Man on the Flying Trapeze"
Schulz, Bruno. "Cinnamon Shops"
_____. "The Street of Crocodiles"
Thomas, Dylan. "After the Fair"
_____. "The Enemies"

O'Connor, Frank. "First Confession"
Shaw, Irwin. "The Girls in Their
    Summer Dresses"
_____. "Sailor Off the *Bremen*"
Stuart, Jesse. "Split Cherry Tree"
Thomas, Dylan. "The Fight"
Thurber, James. "The Secret Life of
    Walter Mitty"
Welty, Eudora. "Petrified Man"
White, E. B. "The Door"
Williams, Tennessee. "The Field of
    Blue Children"

**1940**
Borges, Jorge Luis. "The Circular
    Ruins"
_____. "Tlön, Uqbar, Orbis Tertius"
Clark, Walter Van Tilburg. "Hook"
Colette. "The Rainy Moon"
Collier, John. "Witch's Money"
Kawabata, Yasunari. "The Mole"
Moravia, Alberto. "The Fall"
Pritchett, V. S. "The Saint"
Saroyan, William. "The Summer of the
    Beautiful White Horse"
Schwartz, Delmore. "America!
    America!"
Taylor, Peter. "The Fancy Woman"
Welty, Eudora. "Keela, the Outcast
    Indian Maiden"
Wright, Richard. "The Man Who Was
    Almost a Man"

**1941**
Algren, Nelson. "A Bottle of Milk for
    Mother"
Asimov, Isaac. "Nightfall"
Borges, Jorge Luis. "The Garden of
    Forking Paths"
_____. "The Lottery in Babylon"
Bowen, Elizabeth. "The Demon Lover"
_____. "A Queer Heart"
_____. "Summer Night"

Clark, Walter Van Tilburg. "The
    Portable Phonograph"
Dazai, Osamu. "Eight Views of Tokyo"
McCullers, Carson. "Madame Zilensky
    and the King of Finland"
Nin, Anaïs. "Under a Glass Bell"
Porter, Katherine Anne. "The Leaning
    Tower"
Shaw, Irwin. "The Eighty-Yard Run"
Stegner, Wallace. "Butcher Bird"
Still, James. "The Moving"
Welty, Eudora. "Powerhouse"
_____. "A Visit of Charity"
_____. "Why I Live at the P.O."
_____. "A Worn Path"

**1942**
Borges, Jorge Luis. "The Library of
    Babel"
_____. "Pierre Menard, Author of the
    Quixote"
Colette. "The Sick Child"
Dinesen, Isak. "The Sailor-Boy's Tale"
_____. "Sorrow-Acre"
Faulkner, William. "Delta Autumn"
Horgan, Paul. "The Peach Stone"
McCullers, Carson. "A Tree. A Rock.
    A Cloud."
Stuart, Jesse. "Dawn of Remembered
    Spring"
_____. "Spring Victory"
Thurber, James. "The Catbird Seat"
Welty, Eudora. "The Wide Net"
Wright, Richard. "The Man Who Lived
    Underground"

**1943**
Bunin, Ivan. "Dark Avenues"
Capote, Truman. "A Tree of Night"
Colette. "The Kepi"
_____. "The Tender Shoot"
McCullers, Carson. "The Ballad of the
    Sad Café"

Nabokov, Vladimir. "That in Aleppo Once"

Powers, J. F. "Lions, Harts, Leaping Does"

Trilling, Lionel. "Of This Time, Of That Place"

Woolf, Virginia. "Together and Apart"

**1944**

Borges, Jorge Luis. "Funes, the Memorious"

_____. "The Secret Miracle"

_____. "The Shape of the Sword"

_____. "The South"

_____. "Theme of the Traitor and the Hero"

Bowen, Elizabeth. "The Happy Autumn Fields"

_____. "Mysterious Kôr"

Clark, Walter Van Tilburg. "The Wind and the Snow of Winter"

Ellison, Ralph. "Flying Home"

_____. "King of the Bingo Game"

Lavin, Mary. "The Nun's Mother"

_____. "A Wet Day"

_____. "The Will"

O'Faoláin, Seán. "The Man Who Invented Sin"

Porter, Katherine Anne. "The Downward Path to Wisdom"

Powers, J. F. "The Old Bird"

Singer, Isaac Bashevis. "The Spinoza of Market Street"

**1945**

Algren, Nelson. "How the Devil Came Down Division Street"

Borges, Jorge Luis. "The Aleph"

Bowen, Elizabeth. "Ivy Gripped the Steps"

Bowles, Paul. "The Scorpion"

Capote, Truman. "Miriam"

_____. "My Side of the Matter"

Gordon, Caroline. "Her Quaint Honor"

O'Connor, Frank. "A Story by Maupassant"

Pritchett, V. S. "It May Never Happen"

Singer, Isaac Bashevis. "Gimpel the Fool"

_____. "Short Friday"

Steinbeck, John. "The Pearl"

West, Jessamyn. "The Pacing Goose"

**1946**

Bates, H. E. "The Cruise of _The Breadwinner_"

Boyle, Kay. "Winter Night"

Capote, Truman. "The Headless Hawk"

O'Connor, Frank. "Christmas Morning"

_____. "Legal Aid"

O'Faoláin, Seán. "Innocence"

O'Flaherty, Liam. "Two Lovely Beasts"

Petry, Ann. "Like a Winding Sheet"

Powers, J. F. "Prince of Darkness"

Shaw, Irwin. "Act of Faith"

Warren, Robert Penn. "Blackberry Winter"

**1947**

Bowles, Paul. "A Distant Episode"

Bradbury, Ray. "I See You Never"

Cheever, John. "The Enormous Radio"

Dazai, Osamu. "Villon's Wife"

Ellison, Ralph. "Battle Royal"

Farrell, James T. "Saturday Night"

Gordimer, Nadine. "The Train from Rhodesia"

Greene, Graham. "A Drive in the Country"

Narayan, R. K. "An Astrologer's Day"

_____. "Under the Banyan Tree"

O'Connor, Frank. "Judas"

Perelman, S. J. "A Critical Introduction to _The Best of S. J. Perelman_ by Sidney Namlerep"

Petry, Ann. "In Darkness and
   Confusion"
_____. "Solo on the Drums"
Powers, J. F. "The Forks"
_____. "The Valiant Woman"
Sansom, William. "How Claeys Died"
_____. "The Vertical Ladder"
_____. "The Wall"
Stafford, Jean. "The Interior Castle"
Stegner, Wallace. "Beyond the Glass
   Mountain"
White, E. B. "The Second Tree from
   the Corner"

**1948**
Borowski, Tadeusz. "This Way for the
   Gas, Ladies and Gentleman"
_____. "The World of Stone"
Capote, Truman. "Children on Their
   Birthdays"
Jackson, Shirley. "Charles"
_____. "The Lottery"
Morris, Wright. "The Ram in the
   Thicket"
Nabokov, Vladimir. "Signs and
   Symbols"
O'Connor, Frank. "The Drunkard"
O'Faoláin, Seán. "The Fur Coat"
_____. "The Trout"
_____. "Up the Bare Stairs"
Salinger, J. D. "A Perfect Day for
   Bananafish"
_____. "Uncle Wiggily in Connecticut"
Welch, Denton. "When I Was Thirteen"
Welty, Eudora. "Shower of Gold"
West, Jessamyn. "Road to the Isles"

**1949**
Boyle, Kay. "Summer Evening"
Greene, Graham. "Across the Bridge"
_____. "The Hint of an Explanation"
Leong, Monfoon. "New Year for Fong
   Wing"

Yamamoto, Hisaye. "Seventeen
   Syllables"

**1950**
Böll, Heinrich. "Across the Bridge"
Bowles, Paul. "The Delicate Prey"
Bradbury, Ray. "There Will Come Soft
   Rains"
Calvino, Italo. "Big Fish, Little Fish"
Dinesen, Isak. "Babette's Feast"
Horgan, Paul. "National Honeymoon"
Malamud, Bernard. "The Prison"
O'Connor, Frank. "My Oedipus
   Complex"
Salinger, J. D. "For Esmé with Love
   and Squalor"
Saroyan, William. "The Parsley
   Garden"
Stafford, Jean. "A Country Love Story"
Téllez, Hernando. "Just Lather, That's
   All"
Vonnegut, Kurt. "EPICAC"
Williams, Tennessee. "The
   Resemblance Between a Violin Case
   and a Coffin"

**1951**
Bellow, Saul. "Looking for Mr. Green"
Bradbury, Ray. "The Veldt"
Calisher, Hortense. "In Greenwich
   There Are Many Gravelled Walks"
Cheever, John. "Goodbye, My
   Brother"
Clarke, Arthur C. "The Sentinel"
Collier, John. "The Chaser"
_____. "De Mortuis"
Gold, Herbert. "The Heart of the
   Artichoke"
Lavin, Mary. "The Widow's Son"
Lewis, Wyndham. "Time the Tiger"
Rooney, Frank. "The Cyclists' Raid"
Taylor, Peter. "What You Hear from
   'Em?"

_____. "Tomorrow and Tomorrow and
So Forth"

**1956**

Capote, Truman. "A Christmas
Memory"
Cortázar, Julio. "Axolotl"
_____. "End of the Game"
Gallant, Mavis. "Going Ashore"
Gordimer, Nadine. "The Smell of
Death and Flowers"
Jacobson, Dan. "The Zulu and the
Zeide"
Malamud, Bernard. "A Summer's
Reading"
_____. "Take Pity"
O'Connor, Flannery. "Greenleaf"
Olsen, Tillie. "I Stand Here Ironing"
Purdy, James. "Don't Call Me by My
Right Name"
Rosenfeld, Isaac. "King Solomon"

**1957**

Bates, H. E. "Death of a Huntsman"
Berriault, Gina. "The Stone Boy"
Bowles, Jane. "A Stick of Green
Candy"
Brodkey, Harold. "First Love and
Other Sorrows"
Camus, Albert. "The Adulterous
Woman"
_____. "The Guest"
Dinesen, Isak. "The Blank Page"
_____. "The Cardinal's First Tale"
Lessing, Doris. "The Day Stalin
Died"
Mrożek, Sławomir. "The Elephant"
O'Connor, Frank. "The Man of the
World"
O'Faoláin, Seán. "Childybawn"
Purdy, James. "Color of Darkness"
_____. "Why Can't They Tell You
Why?"

Singer, Isaac Bashevis. "The
Gentleman from Cracow"
Stafford, Jean. "A Reasonable
Facsimile"
Svevo, Italo. "This Indolence of
Mine"

**1958**

Baldwin, James. "Come Out the
Wilderness"
_____. "Sonny's Blues"
Bellow, Saul. "Leaving the Yellow
House"
Böll, Heinrich. "Murke's Collected
Silences"
Buzzati, Dino. "Seven Floors"
Carpentier, Alejo. "Journey Back to
the Source"
_____. "Like the Night"
Cortázar, Julio. "Blow-Up"
Elliott, George P. "Among the Dangs"
Hughes, Langston. "Thank You,
M'am"
Malamud, Bernard. "The Last
Mohican"
O'Connor, Flannery. "The Enduring
Chill"
Ōe, Kenzaburō. "Prize Stock"
Roth, Philip. "The Conversion of the
Jews"
Spark, Muriel. "The Portobello Road"
Taylor, Elizabeth. "The Blush"
Taylor, Peter. "Venus, Cupid, Folly,
and Time"

**1959**

Bates, H. E. "The House with the
Grape-vine"
Donoso, José. "The Walk"
Gallant, Mavis. "Jorinda and Jorindel"
Garrett, George. "An Evening
Performance"
Hall, Lawrence Sargent. "The Ledge"

**1963**

Brown, Frank London. "Singing
Dinah's Song"

Calvino, Italo. "The Watcher"

Cheever, John. "Metamorphoses"

Colter, Cyrus. "The Beach Umbrella"

Gaines, Ernest J. "Just Like a Tree"

_____. "The Sky Is Gray"

Gallant, Mavis. "The Ice Wagon Going
Down the Street"

Kelley, William Melvin. "The Only
Man on Liberty Street"

Kiely, Benedict. "The Heroes in the
Dark House"

Kundera, Milan. "The Golden Apple of
Eternal Desire"

Laurence, Margaret. "The Loons"

Lessing, Doris. "How I Finally Lost
My Heart"

_____. "Mrs. Fortescue"

_____. "To Room Nineteen"

_____. "A Woman on a Roof"

Malamud, Bernard. "Black Is My
Favorite Color"

_____. "The Jewbird"

Oates, Joyce Carol. "Upon the
Sweeping Flood"

Oz, Amos. "Where the Jackals Howl"

Parédes, Américo. "The Hammon and
the Beans"

Price, Reynolds. "A Chain of Love"

Rive, Richard. "The Bench"

Sillitoe, Alan. "The Ragman's
Daughter"

Solzhenitsyn, Aleksandr. "Matryona's
House"

Welty, Eudora. "Where Is the Voice
Coming From?"

**1964**

Aksyonov, Vassily. "Little Whale,
Varnisher of Reality"

Barthelme, Donald. "Margins"

Cheever, John. "The Angel of the
Bridge"

_____. "The Brigadier and the Golf
Widow"

_____. "The Swimmer"

_____. "The World of Apples"

Fuentes, Carlos. "The Doll Queen"

_____. "The Two Elenas"

Kelley, William Melvin. "A Visit to
Grandmother"

La Guma, Alex. "Blankets"

Montague, John. "An Occasion of
Sin"

Ngugi wa Thiong'o. "A Meeting in
the Dark"

O'Connor, Flannery. "Revelation"

Ōe, Kenzaburō. "Aghwee the Sky
Monster"

Oz, Amos. "Nomad and Viper"

Pynchon, Thomas. "The Secret
Integration"

Updike, John. "Leaves"

**1965**

Baldwin, James. "Going to Meet the
Man"

Beckett, Samuel. "Imagination Dead
Imagine"

Calvino, Italo. "The Distance of the
Moon"

Connell, Evan S., Jr. "Saint
Augustine's Pigeon"

Cowan, Peter. "The Tractor"

Elkin, Stanley. "A Poetics for Bullies"

Ellison, Harlan. "'Repent, Harlequin!'
Said the Ticktockman"

Hughes, Langston. "Gospel Singers"

Larner, Jeremy. "Oh, the Wonder!"

Maclaren-Ross, Julian. "A Bit of a
Smash in Madras"

Narayan, R. K. "A Horse and Two
Goats"

O'Connor, Flannery. "Parker's Back"

Maxwell, William. "The Gardens of Mont-Saint-Michel"

Michaels, Leonard. "City Boy"

Nhât, Tiên. "An Unsound Sleep"

Oates, Joyce Carol. "How I Contemplated the World from the Detroit House of Correction and Began My Life over Again"

_____. "Unmailed, Unwritten Letters"

Silko, Leslie Marmon. "The Man to Send Rain Clouds"

Twain, Mark. "The Chronicle of Young Satan"

Woiwode, Larry. "The Suitor"

**1970**

Barthelme, Donald. "The Glass Mountain"

_____. "Paraguay"

_____. "Views of My Father Weeping"

Borges, Jorge Luis. "The Gospel According to Mark"

Davenport, Guy. "The Aeroplanes at Brescia"

Kavan, Anna. "Julia and the Bazooka"

Madden, David. "No Trace"

Narayan, R. K. "Uncle"

Oates, Joyce Carol. "In the Region of Ice"

_____. "What Is the Connection Between Men and Women?"

Price, Reynolds. "Truth and Lies"

**1971**

Bambara, Toni Cade. "Gorilla, My Love"

_____. "Raymond's Run"

Buzzati, Dino. "The Count's Wife"

Carver, Raymond. "Neighbors"

Castellanos, Rosario. "Cooking Lesson"

Clarke, Austin. "Leaving This Island Place"

Dumas, Henry. "Ark of Bones"

Godwin, Gail. "Dream Children"

_____. "A Sorrowful Woman"

Gordimer, Nadine. "Livingstone's Companions"

Greenberg, Joanne. "The Supremacy of the Hunza"

Holst, Spencer. "The Language of Cats"

_____. "On Hope"

Matheson, Richard. "Duel"

Matthews, Jack. "On the Shore of Chad Creek"

Michaels, Leonard. "Murderers"

Paley, Grace. "A Conversation with My Father"

Petry, Ann. "The Witness"

Rivera, Tomás. ". . . and the earth did not part"

_____. "First Communion"

Sanchez, Sonia. "After Saturday Nite Comes Sunday"

Walker, Alice. "A Sudden Trip Home in the Spring"

Warner, Sylvia Townsend. "But at the Stroke of Midnight"

Wiebe, Rudy. "Where Is the Voice Coming From?"

Williams, Tennessee. "Happy August the Tenth"

**1972**

Angelou, Maya. "Steady Going Up"

Bambara, Toni Cade. "The Lesson"

_____. "My Man Bovanne"

Barthelme, Donald. "Critique de la Vie Quotidienne"

_____. "Wrack"

Fox, Robert. "A Fable"

García Márquez, Gabriel. "Blacamán the Good, Vendor of Miracles"

Greenberg, Joanne. "Hunting Season"

Oates, Joyce Carol. "The Lady with the Pet Dog"

**1977**

Allen, Woody. "The Kugelmass Episode"

Atwood, Margaret. "The Man from Mars"

_____. "The Sin-Eater"

Beattie, Ann. "Shifting"

Brodkey, Harold. "Verona"

Carver, Raymond. "So Much Water So Close to Home"

Cortázar, Julio. "Apocalypse at Solentiname"

Dubus, Andre. "The Fat Girl"

Gardner, John. "Redemption"

Head, Bessie. "The Collector of Treasures"

_____. "Looking for a Rain God"

Helprin, Mark. "The Schreuderspitze"

Jones, Gayl. "White Rat"

Martínez, Max. "Faustino"

Munro, Alice. "The Beggar Maid"

_____. "Royal Beatings"

Paley, Grace. "Dreamers in a Dead Language"

Pancake, Breece D'J. "Trilobites"

Robison, Mary. "Pretty Ice"

Santos, Bienvenido N. "Immigration Blues"

**1978**

Bellow, Saul. "A Silver Dish"

Desai, Anita. "Games at Twilight"

McEwan, Ian. "Psychopolis"

McGahern, John. "All Sorts of Impossible Things"

_____. "The Beginning of an Idea"

Munro, Alice. "Wild Swans"

O'Brien, Edna. "A Rose in the Heart of New York"

Phillips, Jayne Anne. "Home"

Shalamov, Varlam. "A Child's Drawings"

_____. "The Snake Charmer"

Swift, Graham. "Learning to Swim"

Trevor, William. "Death in Jerusalem"

Vaughn, Stephanie. "Able, Baker, Charlie, Dog

**1979**

Adams, Alice. "Snow"

Beattie, Ann. "The Burning House"

_____. "The Cinderella Waltz"

Bulosan, Carlos. "Silence"

Carey, Peter. "The Last Days of a Famous Mime"

Carter, Angela. "The Bloody Chamber"

Dennison, George. "The Smiles of Konarak"

Gallant, Mavis. "Speck's Idea"

Mori, Toshio. "Japanese Hamlet"

Phillips, Jayne Anne. "Black Tickets"

_____. "Lechery"

Strand, Mark. "Mr. and Mrs. Baby"

Targan, Barry. "Old Light"

_____. "The Rags of Time"

Taylor, Peter. "The Old Forest"

**1980**

Bourjaily, Vance. "The Amish Farmer"

Carter, Angela. "Black Venus"

Chappell, Fred. "Children of Strikers"

Connell, Evan S., Jr. "The Fisherman from Chihuahua"

Dubus, Andre. "Killings"

Gilchrist, Ellen. "Traveler"

Gordimer, Nadine. "A Soldier's Embrace"

_____. "Town and Country Lovers"

Kingston, Maxine Hong. "On Discovery"

Mason, Bobbie Ann. "Shiloh"

Ozick, Cynthia. "The Shawl"

Singer, Isaac Bashevis. "Moon and Madness"

Stern, Richard G. "Wissler Remembers"

Dubus, Andre. "A Father's Story"
Gallant, Mavis. "Lena"
Kincaid, Jamaica. "Girl"
_____. "My Mother"
Klass, Perri. "Not a Good Girl"
Morris, Wright. "Glimpse into Another Country"
Mukherjee, Bharati. "The World According to Hsü"
Oates, Joyce Carol. "Nairobi"
Ozick, Cynthia. "Rosa"
Robison, Mary. "An Amateur's Guide to the Night"
Valenzuela, Luisa. "Up Among the Eagles"

## 1984

Apple, Max. "Bridging"
Banks, Russell. "Sarah Cole"
Baxter, Charles. "The Cliff"
Beattie, Ann. "In the White Night"
Boyle, T. Coraghessan. "The Hector Quesadilla Story"
Canin, Ethan. "Emperor of the Air"
Cooper, J. California. "Color Me Real"
Davenport, Guy. "The Bowmen of Shu"
Erdrich, Louise. "Saint Marie"
Gilchrist, Ellen. "Victory over Japan"
Gordimer, Nadine. "Something Out There"
Hood, Mary. "A Country Girl"
Leavitt, David. "Counting Months"
L'Heureux, John. "The Comedian"
Mahfouz, Naguib. "The Norwegian Rat"
Minot, Susan. "Lust"
_____. "Thanksgiving Day"
Mistry, Rohinton. "Condolence Visit"
O'Brien, Edna. "Forgiveness"
Simpson, Mona. "Approximations"
Tyler, Anne. "Teenage Wasteland"
Wilson, Robley. "Fathers"

## 1985

Abbott, Lee K. "The Valley of Sin"
Bausch, Richard. "The Man Who Knew Belle Starr"
Baxter, Charles. "Gryphon"
Beattie, Ann. "Janus"
Burke, James Lee. "The Convict"
Cameron, Peter. "Excerpts from Swan Lake"
Chappell, Fred. "The Storytellers"
Conroy, Frank. "Midair"
Dove, Rita. "Aunt Carrie"
Dybek, Stuart. "Bijou"
_____. "Blight"
Erdrich, Louise. "The Beet Queen"
Faust, Irvin. "The Year of the Hot Jock"
Ford, Richard. "Communist"
Hempel, Amy. "Going"
_____. "In the Cemetery Where Al Jolson Is Buried"
_____. "Today Will Be a Quiet Day"
Johnson, Charles. "Moving Pictures"
Kaplan, David Michael. "Doe Season"
Kaufman, Bel. "Sunday in the Park"
Macleod, Alistair. "As Birds Bring Forth the Sun"
Madden, David. "Willis Carr at Bleak House"
Mason, Bobbie Ann. "Big Bertha Stories"
Mohr, Nicholasa. "Aunt Rosana's Rocker"
Narayan, R. K. "House Opposite"
Nugent, Beth. "City of Boys"
Painter, Pamela. "The Bridge"
Simpson, Mona. "Lawns"
Spencer, Elizabeth. "The Cousins"
Tabucchi, Antonio. "A Riddle"
Tallent, Elizabeth. "No One's a Mystery"
Viramontes, Helena María. "The Cariboo Café"

Kingsolver, Barbara. "Homeland"
_____. "Islands on the Moon"
McKnight, Reginald. "The Kind of
Light That Shines on Texas"
Millhauser, Steven. "Eisenheim the
Illusionist"
Momaday, N. Scott. "She Is Beautiful
in Her Whole Being"
Moore, Lorrie. "You're Ugly Too"
Oates, Joyce Carol. "Heat"
_____. "The Swimmers"
Prose, Francine. "Cimarron"
Romero, Danny. "Summer League"
Saro-Wiwa, Ken. "Africa Kills Her
Sun"
Tallent, Elizabeth. "Prowler"
Tan, Amy. "Two Kinds"
Tilghman, Christopher. "In a Father's
Place"
Wideman, John Edgar. "Fever"

## 1990

Ballard, J. G. "Dream Cargoes"
Barnes, Julian. "Dragons"
Bass, Rick. "The Wait"
Bell, Madison Smartt. "Dragon's Seed"
Braverman, Kate. "Tall Tales from the
Mekong Delta"
Brown, Larry. "Big Bad Love"
_____. "Sleep"
Doerr, Harriet. "Way Stations"
Erdrich, Louise. "The Leap"
Fernández, Roberta. "Amanda"
_____. "Esmeralda"
Harjo, Joy. "The Flood"
Houston, Pam. "How to Talk to a
Hunter"
Johnson, Denis. "Car Crash While
Hitchhiking"
Leavitt, David. "Gravity"
McMillan, Terry. "Ma'Dear"
O'Brien, Tim. "The Sweetheart of the
Song Tra Bong"

Offutt, Chris. "Aunt Granny Lith"
Ozick, Cynthia. "Puttermesser Paired"
Ponce, Mary Helen. "Enero"
Price, Reynolds. "His Final Mother"
Prose, Francine. "Dog Stories"
Sukenick, Ronald. "Ecco"
Updike, John. "A Sandstone
Farmhouse"
Villanueva, Alma. "People of the Dog"

## 1991

Allen, Paula Gunn. "Deer Woman"
Bloom, Amy. "Silver Water"
Cisneros, Sandra. "One Holy Night"
_____. "Woman Hollering Creek"
Gallant, Mavis. "Across the Bridge"
Gautreaux, Tim. "Same Place, Same
Things"
Harjo, Joy. "The Northern Lights"
Johnson, Denis. "Emergency"
Jones, Thom. "The Pugilist at Rest"
Landis, Geoffrey A. "A Walk in the
Sun"
Lopez, Barry. "Remembering Orchards"
Murakami, Haruki. "The Elephant
Vanishes"
Ríos, Alberto. "Waltz of the Fat Man"
Sarris, Greg. "Slaughterhouse"

## 1992

Anaya, Rudolfo A. "In Search of
Epifano"
_____. "The Man Who Found a Pistol"
Butler, Robert Olen. "A Good Scent
from a Strange Mountain"
Chávez, Denise. "Saints"
Dixon, Stephen. "Man, Woman and
Boy"
Gaitskill, Mary. "The Girl on the
Plane"
García, Guy. "Frazer Avenue"
García, Lionel G. "The Day They Took
My Uncle"

Hospital, Janette Turner. "Unperformed Experiments Have No Results"

Jones, Thom. "A White Horse"

Mars-Jones, Adam. "Bears in Mourning"

Ponce, Mary Helen. "The Marijuana Party"

Villarreal, José Antonio. "The Laughter of My Father"

### 1993

Alexie, Sherman. "This Is What It Means to Say Phoenix, Arizona"

Boyd, William. "The Dream Lover"

Byatt, A. S. "Medusa's Ankles"

Chang, Lan Samantha. "Pipa's Story"

Dark, Alice Elliott. "In the Gloaming"

Earley, Tony. "Charlotte"

_____. "The Prophet from Jupiter"

Gallant, Mavis. "Dédé"

López, Jack. "Easy Time"

Martínez, Víctor. "The Baseball Glove"

Offutt, Chris. "Melungeons"

Ortiz Cofer, Judith. "American History"

Powell, Padgett. "Trick or Treat"

Vizenor, Gerald. "Moccasin Game"

Woiwode, Larry. "Silent Passengers"

Yoshimoto, Mahoko. "Helix"

### 1994

Barrett, Andrea. "The Behavior of the Hawkweeds"

Byers, Michael. "Settled on the Cranberry Coast"

Chandra, Vikram. "Dharma"

Eisenberg, Deborah. "The Girl Who Left Her Sock on the Floor"

Gilchrist, Ellen. "The Stucco House"

King, Stephen. "The Man in the Black Suit"

Lombreglia, Ralph. "Somebody Up There Likes Me"

### 1995

Butler, Robert Olen. "Jealous Husband Returns in Form of Parrot"

Chang, Lan Samantha. "The Eve of the Spirit Festival"

Chaon, Dan. "Fitting Ends"

Danticat, Edwidge. "Night Women"

Davies, Peter Ho. "The Ugliest House in the World"

Gordon, Mary. "Intertextuality"

Jen, Gish. "Birthmates"

Perabo, Susan. "Some Say the World"

Thompson, Jean. "All Shall Love Me and Despair"

Thon, Melanie Rae. "First, Body"

### 1996

Amis, Martin. "State of England"

Billman, Jon. "When We Were Wolves"

Díaz, Junot. "Fiesta, 1980"

Dubus, Andre. "Dancing After Hours"

Gordon, Mary. "City Life"

Ha Jin. "Saboteur"

Moody, Rick. "Demonology"

Munro, Alice. "The Love of a Good Woman"

Saunders, George. "The Falls"

Shields, Carol. "Mirrors"

### 1997

Chamoiseau, Patrick. "The Old Man Slave and the Mastiff"

Davis, Lydia. "The House Behind"

Dobyns, Stephen. "Eating Naked"

Evenson, Brian. "Two Brothers"

Gautreaux, Tim. "Welding with Children"

Millhauser, Steven. "The Knife Thrower"

Moore, Lorrie. "People Like That Are the Only People Here"

Proulx, E. Annie. "Brokeback
　　Mountain"
_____. "The Half-Skinned Steer"

## 1998

Bass, Rick. "The Hermit's Story"
Bender, Aimee. "The Girl in the
　　Flammable Skirt"
Benedict, Pinckney. "Miracle Boy"
Budnitz, Judy. "Dog Days"
Chabon, Michael. "Son of the
　　Wolfman"
Englander, Nathan. "The Tumblers"
Fromm, Pete. "Night Swimming"
Lahiri, Jhumpa. "Interpreter of
　　Maladies"
Moore, Lorrie. "Terrific Mother"
Munro, Alice. "Save the Reaper"

## 1999

Alexie, Sherman. "The Toughest Indian
　　in the World"
Brockmeier, Kevin. "These Hands"
Carlson, Ron. "The Ordinary Son"
Englander, Nathan. "The Gilgul of Park
　　Avenue"
_____. "The Twenty-seventh Man"
Foley, Sylvia. "Life in the Air Ocean"
Gurganus, Allan. "He's at the Office"
Ha Jin. "The Bridegroom"

Lahiri, Jhumpa. "The Third and Final
　　Continent"
Lordan, Beth. "The Man with the
　　Lapdog"
McCann, Colum. "Everything in This
　　Country Must"
Mosley, Walter. "Pet Fly"
Proulx, E. Annie. "The Bunchgrass
　　Edge of the World"

## 2000

Banks, Russell. "The Moor"
Barrett, Andrea. "Servants of the Map"
Beattie, Ann. "The Big-Breasted
　　Pilgrim"
Carlson, Ron. "At the Jim Bridger"
Chaon, Dan. "Big Me"
Gay, William. "The Paperhanger"
Klam, Matthew. "Sam the Cat"
Lopez, Barry. "Light Action in the
　　Caribbean"
Malouf, David. "Dream Stuff"
Means, David. "Assorted Fire Events"
Munro, Alice. "Floating Bridge"
Saunders, George. "Pastoralia"
Schickler, David. "The Smoker"

## 2001

Nelson, Antonya. "Female Trouble"

# MASTERPLOTS II

## SHORT STORY SERIES
### REVISED EDITION

# TITLE INDEX

# AUTHOR INDEX

# AUTHOR INDEX

# GEOGRAPHICAL INDEX

# GEOGRAPHICAL INDEX

GEOGRAPHICAL INDEX

# GEOGRAPHICAL INDEX

GEOGRAPHICAL INDEX

# TYPE OF PLOT INDEX

## CATEGORIES

# TYPE OF PLOT INDEX

# TYPE OF PLOT INDEX

REGIONAL